D0212164

EX LIBRIS
SOUTH ORANGE
PUBLIC LIBRARY

AIR WARFARE

An International Encyclopedia

AIR WARFARE

An International Encyclopedia

VOLUME ONE, A–L

EDITED BY

Walter J. Boyne

ASSOCIATE EDITORS

Michael Fopp

Fred Johnsen

Stéphane Nicolaou

George M. Watson Jr.

FOREWORD BY

Michael J. Dugan

A B C — C L I O

Santa Barbara, California   Denver, Colorado   Oxford, England

Library of Congress Cataloging-in-Publication Data
Air warfare: an international encyclopedia / edited by Walter J. Boyne ;
foreword by Michael J. Dugan.
p. cm.
Includes bibliographical references and index.
ISBN 1-57607-345-9 (hardcover : alk. paper) ISBN 1-57607-729-2 (e-book)
1. Aeronautics, Military—Encyclopedias. I. Boyne, Walter J., 1929–
UG628.A73 2002
358.4'003—dc21
2002002251

07 06 05 04 03 02 10 9 8 7 6 5 4 3 2 1

This book is also available on the World Wide Web as an e-book. Visit abc-clio.com for details.

ABC-CLIO, Inc.
130 Cremona Drive, P.O. Box 1911
Santa Barbara, California 93116-1911

This book is printed on acid-free paper.
Manufactured in the United States of America

CONTENTS

Alphabetical List of Entries, vii

Foreword, xix

Preface, xxvii

List of Maps, xxix

List of Terms, Acronyms, and Abbreviations, xxxi

VOLUME 1: Entries A-L

VOLUME 2: Entries M–Z

Selected Bibliography, 727

List of Contributors, 733

Index, 737

ALPHABETICAL LIST OF ENTRIES

Aces
Acosta, Bertrand B. (1895–1954)
Ader, Clement (1841–1925)
Aerial Radio Navigation
Aerial Refueling
Aerial Torpedoes
Aeritalia
Aermacchi
Aeroflot
Aeronautica Nazionale Repubblicana (ANR)
Aeronautical Research Establishments
Afghanistan War (1978–1992)
Agusta
Aichi Aircraft
Air America
Air Commandos
Air (Aerospace) Defense Command (ADC)
Air Interdiction (AI)
Air National Guard (ANG)
Air Rescue
Air Superiority
Air Technical Intelligence
Airborne Battlefield Command and Control Center (ABCCC)
Airborne Early Warning (AEW)
Airborne Laser
Aircraft Armament
Aircraft Carriers, Development of
AirLand Battle
Airlift Operations, U.S.
Airlines, Service in Wartime by
Airships
Alam el Halfa, Battle of (1942)
Albatros Aircraft
Alenia
Aleutian Islands Air War
Algeria
Alksnis, Yakov I. (1897–1940)
ALLIED FORCE (1999)
American Volunteer Group
Amet-Khan, Sultan (1916–1971)
An Loc, Battle of (1972)
Anderson, Orvil "Arson" (1895–1965)
Andrews, Frank Maxwell (1884–1943)
Ansaldo
Antimissile Defense
Antisatellite Capability
Antisubmarine Warfare (ASW)
Antonov Aircraft
ANVIL (1944)
Anzio, Battle of (1944)
Apollo Space Program
Arado Ar 234 Blitz
ARC LIGHT
Argentine Aircraft Industry
ARGUMENT (BIG WEEK, 1944)
Armstrong, Neil A. (1930–)
Armstrong Whitworth Aircraft
Arnold, Henry H. "Hap" (1886–1950)
Artillery Spotting
Atlantic, Battle of the (1940–1945)
Atomic Bomb
Austria-Hungary
Automobile Industry, Wartime Mobilization of
Aviation and the Arts
Aviation Medicine
Avro 504
Avro Aircraft
Avro Canada Aircraft (A. V. Roe Canada)
Avro Lancaster

Avro Vulcan
AWPD/1 and AWPD/42

BABYLIFT (1975)
Bachem BP-20 (Ba 349) Natter
Bader, Douglas R. S. (1910–1982)
Baer, Heinz (1913–1957)
Baikonur Cosmodrome
Balbo, Italo (1896–1940)
Baldwin, Stanley (1867–1947)
Balikpapan
The Balkans, Air Operations in (1941)
The Balkans and Early Air Combat (1912–1913)
Ballistic Missile Early Warning System (BMEWS)
Balloons
Bapaume, Battle of (1918)
Baracca, Francesco (1888–1918)
BARBAROSSA
Barker, William George (1894–1930)
Barkhorn, Gerhard (1919–1983)
BAT 21
Bay of Pigs Invasion
Beaverbrook, Lord (1879–1964)
Béchereau, Louis (1880–1970)
Beech Aircraft
Bell AH-1 Cobra
Bell Aircraft
Bell OH-13 Sioux
Bell P-39 Airacobra and P-63 Kingcobra
Bell P-59A Airacomet
Bell Tilt-Rotors
Bell UH-1 Iroquois ("Huey")
Bell X-1
Beriev Aircraft
Berlin Air Battles (1940–1945)
Berlin Airlift
Bien Hoa Air Base
Bikini Atoll Tests
Birkigt, Marc (1878–1953)
Bishop, William (1894–1956)
Bismarck, Air Operations Against the
Bismarck Sea, Air Battle of (1943)
Bissel, Clayton L. (1896–1973)
Blackburn Aircraft
Blériot Aircraft
Blimps, Military Use of
Blitzkrieg
Blohm and Voss Aircraft
Bock's Car
Boeing (McDonnell Douglas/Hughes) AH-64 Apache
Boeing (North American Rockwell) B1-B Lancer
Boeing B-17 Flying Fortress
Boeing B-29 Superfortress
Boeing B-47 Stratojet
Boeing B-52 Stratofortress
Boeing (McDonnell Douglas) C-17 Globemaster III
Boeing Aircraft
Boeing (McDonnell Douglas) F-15 Eagle
Boeing (McDonnell Douglas) F/A-18 Hornet
Boeing (McDonnell Douglas) KC-10 Extender
Boeing KC-135 Stratotanker
Boeing-Vertol CH-47 Chinook
Boelcke, Oswald (1891–1916)
Bolling Mission
BOLO (1967)
Bong, Richard I. (1920–1945)
Boulton Paul Aircraft
Boyd, Albert (1906–1976)
Boyington, Gregory "Pappy" (1912–1988)
Braun, Wernher von (1912–1977)
Brazil, Air Operations in World War II
Brazilian Aircraft Industry
Breda Aircraft
Breguet Aircraft
Bristol Aircraft (Early Years, World War I)
Bristol Aircraft (Post–World War I)
Bristol Beaufighter
Bristol, Delbert L. (1918–1980)
Britain, Battle of (1940)
British Aerospace
British Aerospace Harrier
British Commonwealth Air Training Plan (BCATP)
British Pacific Fleet
Bulge, Battle of the (1944–1945)
Bureau of Aircraft Production (BAP)
Bureau of Naval Aeronautics (BNA)
Burma
Busemann, Adolf (1901–1986)
Bush, George Herbert Walker (1924–)

Cactus Air Force
Cambodia Bombings
Camm, Sydney (1893–1966)
Canadian Air Force (Royal Canadian Air Force)
Cant Aircraft
Cape Canaveral
Cape Engano, Battle of (1944)
Caproni Aircraft (Early Years)
Caproni Aircraft (Post–World War I)
CASA Aircraft
Casablanca Conference
Cassino, Battle of (November 1943–June 1944)

Caudron Aircraft (Early Years)
Caudron Aircraft (Post–World War I)
Cessna Aircraft
Chadwick, Roy (1893–1947)
Chamberlain, Neville (1869–1940)
Channel Dash
Chateau Thierry, Battle of (1918)
Chennault, Claire L. (1890–1958)
Cheshire, Geoffrey Leonard (1917–1992)
Chinese Air Force and U.S. Aid
Chinese-American Composite Wing
Chinese Communist Air Force (People's Liberation Army Air Force [PLAAF])
Chkalov, Valeri Pavlovich (1904–1938)
Churchill, Winston S. (1874–1965)
Civil Air Patrol (CAP, in World War II)
Civil Aviation: Impact of Military Advances
Civil Aviation: Impact on the Military
Civil War (U.S.) and Use of Balloons
Civil Wars
Clark, Joseph J. "Jocko" (1893–1971)
Clark, Mark W. (1896–1984)
Clark, Wesley K. (1944–)
Clay, Lucius D. (1897–1978)
Close Air Support
Cold War
Cold War and Commercial Aviation
College Eye Task Force (CETF)
Colonial Wars
Combat Cargo Command
Combat Search and Rescue (CSAR)
Combined Bomber Offensive
Command of the Air (Giulio Douhet, 1921)
COMMANDO HUNT (1968–1972)
Commonwealth of Independent States (CIS)
Coningham, Arthur "Mary" (1895–1948)
Consolidated Aircraft Corporation (CONVAIR, Convair)
Consolidated B-24 Liberator
Consolidated B-36 Peacemaker
Consolidated PBY Catalina
Continental Air Command (CONAC)
Convair B-58 Hustler
Convair F-102 Delta Dagger and F-106 Delta Dart
Coppens, Baron Willy (1892–1986)
Coral Sea, Battle of the (1942)
CORONA Spy Satellites (Discover)
Counterinsurgency Operations
Coventry Air Raids
Crete, Battle of (1941)
CROSSROADS (1946)
CRUSADER (1941)
Cuban Missile Crisis
Cunningham, Randall "Duke" (1941–)
Curtiss Aircraft
Curtiss Biplane Fighters
Curtiss, Glenn Hammond (1878–1930)
Curtiss JN-4 "Jenny"
Curtiss P-40 Warhawk
Curtiss-Wright Corporation

Dargue, Herbert A. (1886–1941)
Dassault, Marcel (1892–1986)
Dassault Mirage III
Dassault Mystère IVA
Davis, Benjamin Oliver Jr. (1912–)
De Havilland Aircraft (Early Years and World War I)
De Havilland Aircraft (Post–World War I)
De Havilland D.H. 98 Mosquito
De Havilland Tiger Moth
Defense Advanced Research Projects Agency (DARPA)
Defense Support Program (DSP) and Missile Detection
Defense Suppression
DELIBERATE FORCE (1995)
Deptula, David A. (1952–)
DESERT FOX (1998)
DESERT SHIELD (1990)
DESERT STORM (1991)
Dewoitine Aircraft
Dien Bien Phu, Battle of (1954)
Dieppe, Battle of (1942)
Distant Early Warning (DEW)
Doolittle, James H. (1896–1993)
Dornier Aircraft
Dornier Do 217
Douglas, William Sholto (1893–1970)
Douglas A-4 Skyhawk
Douglas A-20 Havoc
Douglas A/B-26 Invader
Douglas Aircraft
Douglas C-47 Transport
Douglas D-558
Douglas SBD Dauntless
Douglas World Cruiser
Dowding, Hugh C.T. (1882–1970)
Dresden, Bombing of (1945)
Dunkirk

Eagle Squadrons
Eaker, Ira C. (1896–1987)
Eastern Solomons, Battle of the (1942)
Ebro 33: Rescue Efforts
Egyptian Air Force

Ejection Seats
El Alamein, Air Battles of (1942)
EL DORADO CANYON (1986)
Electronic Warfare (EW)
Ellyson, Theodore Gordon (1885–1928)
Ely, Eugene (1886–1911)
ENDURING FREEDOM
Energy Maneuverability
Engine Technology
English Electric Aircraft
English Electric Canberra
English Electric Lightning
Enlisted Pilots in U.S. Military Services
Enola Gay
Ethiopian War
Eurofighter Typhoon

Fairchild A-10 Thunderbolt II
Fairchild Aircraft
Fairchild C-82 Packet and C-119 Flying Boxcar
Fairchild, Muir Stephen (1894–1950)
Fairey Aircraft
Fairey Swordfish
Falaise-Argentan Pocket
Falkland Islands War
Far East Air Forces (FEAF)
Farman Aircraft
Farman Pushers
Ferrets
Fiat
Field Manual 100-20 (U.S. Army)
Fieseler Fi 156 Storch
Fighter Air Corps, 64th (Soviet Air Force)
Finletter Commission
Finnish Air Force (Early Years)
Finnish Air Force (in Russo-Finnish Wars)
Finnish Air Force (Recent History)
First Aero Squadron
First Marine Air Wing
Fleet Air Arm
Fletcher, Frank Jack (1885–1973)
Flight Refuelling Ltd.
Flying Boats
Focke-Wulf Aircraft
Focke-Wulf Fw 190
Focke-Wulf Fw 200 Condor
Fokker Aircraft (Early Years, World War I)
Fokker Aircraft (Post–World War I)
Folland, Henry Phillip (1889–1954)
Fonck, René Paul (1894–1953)
Football War
Ford Motor Company
Ford, William Wallace (1898–1986)
Foss, Joseph J. (1915–)
Foulois, Benjamin D. (1879–1967)
France, Battle for (1940)
Franco, Francisco (1892–1975)
FRANTIC (1944)
Franz, Anselm (1900–1994)
French Air Doctrine
French Air Force
French Aircraft Development and Production (World War I–Early World War II)
French Aircraft Development and Production (World War II–Present)
French Army Light Air Force
French Missile Production and Development
French Naval Air Force (Aéronavale)
FREQUENT WIND (1975)
Frontal Aviation
Fuchida, Mitsuo (1903–1973)

Gabreski, Francis S. (1919–2002)
Gagarin, Yuri (1934–1968)
Gallai, Mark (1914–1998)
Galland, Adolf (1912–1996)
Garros, Roland (1888–1918)
Gasoline
Gavin, James Maurice (1907–1990)
Geisler, Hans-Ferdinand (1891–1966)
Gemini Space Program
Genda, A. Minoru (1904–1989)
General Dynamics
General Dynamics F-111 Aardvark
George, Harold Lee (1893–1986)
German Air Force (Luftwaffe, World War II)
German Air Service (Luftstreitkräfte, World War I)
German Aircraft Development and Production, Post–World War II
German Imperial Naval Air Service (World War I)
German Naval Airship Division
German Rocket Development
Germany and World War II Air Battles (1940–1945)
Gibson, Guy P. (1918–1944)
Gilbert Islands
Global Navigation Satellite Systems (GNSS)
Gloster Aircraft
Gloster E.28/39 (G.40) Pioneer
Gloster Meteor
Gnôme/Gnôme-Rhône Rotary Engines
Goddard, Robert H. (1882–1945)
Goering, Hermann (1893–1946)

Golovanov, Aleksandr (1904–1975)
GOMORRAH (1943)
Gotha Bombers
Great Britain, Missile Development and Production in
Greece
Greek Air Force
Greim, Robert Ritter von (1892–1945)
Grizodubova, Valentina Stepanova (1910–1993)
Groves, Leslie Richard (1896–1970)
Grumman A-6E Intruder
Grumman Aircraft
Grumman Biplane Fighters
Grumman EA-6B Prowler
Grumman F-14 Tomcat
Grumman F4F Wildcat
Grumman F6F Hellcat
Grumman F9F Panther/Cougar
Grumman TBF/TBM Avenger
Guadalcanal
Guam, Battles of (1944)
Guernica
Guideline (SA-2) Surface-to-Air Missile
Gulf of Tonkin Resolution
Gulf War (1991)
Gun Sights
Gunships
Gurevich, Mikhail I. (1892–1976)
Guynemer, Georges (1894–1917)

Haiphong Air Attacks
Halberstädt Aircraft
Halsey, William Frederick (1882–1959)
Hamburg Bombing Campaign
Handley Page Aircraft (Early Years/World War I)
Handley Page Aircraft (Post–World War I)
Handley Page Halifax
Handley Page Victor
Hannover Aircraft
Hanoi Air Attacks
Hansell, Haywood S., Jr. (1903–1988)
Hanson, Robert M. (1920–1944)
Harris, Arthur T. (1892–1984))
Hartmann, Erich (1922–1993)
Hawker Aircraft
Hawker Hunter
Hawker Hurricane
Hawker-Siddeley Aircraft
Hawker Typhoon and Tempest
Heinemann, Edward H. (1908–1991)
Heinkel Aircraft
Heinkel He 111 (1934–1945)
Helicopter Operations in the U.S. Army
Helicopters
Henschel Aircraft
HERCULES (1942)
Herrman, Hajo (1913–)
Hess, Rudolph (1894–1987)
Hiroshima
Ho Chi Minh Trail
Holloway, Bruce K. (1912–1999)
Horikoshi, Jiro (1903–1982)
Horner, Charles A. (1936–)
Horten Flying Wings
Howard, James Howell (1913–1995)
Howze, Hamilton Hawkins (1908–1998)
Hump Airlift
Hunsaker, Jerome Clarke (1886–1984)
HUSKY (1943)
Hutton, Carl Irven (1907–1966)

Ia Drang Valley, Battle of (1965)
Ilya Muromets
Ilyushin Aircraft
Ilyushin Il-2 Shturmovik
Imperial Russian Air Service
Independent Bombing Force (World War I)
Indian and Pakistani Airpower
Indochina
Inoue, Shigeyoshi (1889–1975)
INSTANT THUNDER (1990)
Iran Hostages Rescue Operation
Iraqi Air Force
Israel Aircraft Industries (IAI)
Israeli Air Force
Israeli-Arab Conflicts
Italian Air Force (Post–World War II)
Italian Aircraft Development
Italian Campaign (1943–1945)
Italo-Turkish War (1911–1912)
Iwamoto, Tetsuzo (1916–1955)
Iwo Jima

Jabara, James (1923–1966)
James, Daniel "Chappie" (1920–1978)
Japan, Air Operations Against (1942–1945)
Japanese Air Self-Defense Force (JASDF)
Japanese Army Air Force, Imperial (JAAF)
Japanese Naval Air Force, Imperial (JNAF)
Jeschonnek, Hans (1899–1943)
Johnson, Clarence L. "Kelly" (1910–1990)
Johnson, Robert S. (1920–1998)
Joint Strike Fighter (JSF)

Jointness
Jones, David C. (1921–)
Junkers Aircraft
Junkers Ju 52/3m, Ju 87 Stuka, and Ju 88

Kaman Aircraft
Kamikaze Attacks
Kammhuber, Josef (1896–1986)
Kamov Helicopters
Kármán, Theodore von (1881–1963)
Kartveli, Alexander (1896–1974)
Kawanishi Aircraft
Kawasaki Aircraft
Kearby, Neel (1911–1944)
Kenney, George (1889–1997)
Kesselring, Albert (1885–1960)
Khalkin Gol Air Battles (1939)
Khe Sanh
Khomyakova, Valeriya (1914–1942)
Khryukin, Timofei T. (1910–1953)
Kindelberger, James H. "Dutch" (1895–1962)
King, Ernest Joseph (1878–1956)
Kites
Kittinger, Joseph W., Jr.(1928–)
Koldunov, Aleksandr (1923–1992)
Koller, Karl (1898–1951)
Korean War
Korolyov, Sergei (1907–1966)
Korten, Guenther (1898–1944)
KOSMOS
Kozakov, Aleksandr (1889–1919)
Kozhedub, Ivan (1920–1991)
Kreipe, Werner (1905–1967)
Kuban Air Battles
Kursk, Battle of (1943)
Kutakhov, Pavel (1914–1984)

Lafayette Escadrille/Flying Corps
Langley, USS
Laos
Lavochkin Aircraft
Leahy, William D. (1875–1959)
Leigh-Mallory, Trafford (1892–1944)
LeMay, Curtis Emerson (1906–1990)
Lend-Lease Aircraft
Lewandowska (Dowbór-Musnicka), Janina (1908–1940)
Leyte Gulf, Battle of (1944)
Liberty Engine
Liberty, USS
LINEBACKER (1972)
LINEBACKER II (1972)
Link Trainer
Lippisch, Alexander Martin (1894–1976)
Litvyak, Lidya (1921–1943)
Locarno Conference
Lockheed Aircraft
Lockheed F-104 Starfighter
Lockheed Hudson
Lockheed Martin Aircraft
Lockheed Martin C-130 Hercules
Lockheed Martin C-5 Galaxy
Lockheed Martin F-117 Nighthawk
Lockheed Martin F-16 Fighting Falcon
Lockheed Martin F-22 Raptor
Lockheed P-38 Lightning
Lockheed P/F-80 Shooting Star
Lockheed SR-71 Blackbird
Lockheed T-33
Lockheed U-2 Dragon Lady
Loehr, Alexander (1885–1947)
Logistics
London Naval Agreement (1930)
LOOKING GLASS
Lovett, Robert A. (1895–1986)
Ludendorff, Erich (1865–1937)
Luetzow, Guenther (1912–1945)
Lufbery, Gervais Raoul (1885–1918)
Luke, Frank Jr. (1897–1918)

MacArthur, Douglas (1880–1964)
Macchi Aircraft (Aermacchi)
MacDonald, Charles H. (1915–)
Mach, Ernst (1838–1916)
Magic
Magnetic Anomaly Detection
Malaya, Battles of (1941–1942)
Malta, Siege of
Manned Orbiting Laboratory (MOL)
Mannock, Edward (1887–1918)
Mao Tse-tung (1893–1976)
Mareth Line, Battles of the (1943)
Marinelli, Jack L. (1917–1982)
MARKET-GARDEN (1944)
Marseille, Hans-Joachim (1919–1942)
Marshall Islands (1943–1944)
Martin Aircraft
Martin B-10/B-12 Bomber
Martin B-26 Marauder
Martin-Baker Aircraft
Martini, Wolfgang (1891–1963)
Massive Retaliation
Mayaguez Incident

McCain, John S. (1884–1945)
McCampbell, David S. (1910–1996)
McConnell, Joseph C. (1922–1954)
McDonnell Aircraft
McDonnell Douglas Aircraft
McDonnell F-4 Phantom II
McGuire, Thomas B., Jr. (1920–1945)
Mediterranean Theater of Operations (World War II)
Menoher, Charles Thomas (1862–1930)
Mercedes Engines
Mercury Space Program
Messerschmitt, Willy (1898–1978)
Messerschmitt Bf 109
Messerschmitt Me 163 Komet
Messerschmitt Me 262
Meyer, John C. (1919–1975)
Midway, Battle of (1942)
MiG Alley
Mikoyan, Artem I. (1905–1970)
Mikoyan-Gurevich (MiG) Aircraft
Mikoyan-Gurevich MiG-17
Mikoyan-Gurevich MiG-21
Mikoyan-Gurevich MiG-29
Mil Aircraft
Milch, Erhard (1892–1972)
Miles Aircraft
Missiles, Air-to-Air and Surface-to-Surface
Missiles, Intercontinental Ballistic (ICBMs)
Missiles, Intermediate-Range Ballistic (IRBMs)
Missiles, Surface-to-Air (SAMs)
Mitchell, Reginald J. (1895–1937)
Mitchell, William “Billy” (1879–1936)
Mitscher, Marc Andrew (1887–1947)
Mitsubishi A6M Reisen (“Zero”)
Mitsubishi Aircraft
Mitsubishi G4M (“Betty”)
Moelders, Werner (1913–1941)
Moffett, William Adger (1869–1933)
Morane-Saulnier 406
Morane-Saulnier Aircraft
Mu Gia Pass
Muencheberg, Joachim (1918–1943)
Multiple Independently Targetable Reentry Vehicle (MIRV)
Mussolini, Benito (1883–1945)
Mutual Assured Destruction

Nagasaki
Nagumo, Chuichi (1886–1944)
Nakajima Aircraft
National Advisory Committee for Aeronautics (NACA)
National Aeronautics and Space Administration (NASA)
National Emergency Airborne Command Post (NEACP)
National Security Act of 1947
National Security Council (NSC)
Naval Aircraft Factory (NAF)
NAVSTAR Global Positioning System
Nesterov, Pyotr (1887–1914)
Netherlands East Indies (1942)
Neuve Chapelle, Battle of (1915)
Nguyen Cao Ky (1930–)
NICKEL GRASS (1973)
Nieuport Aircraft
Nieuport-Delage NiD-29
Night Witches (46th Guards Night Bomber Regiment)
Nimitz, Chester William (1885–1966)
Nishizawa, Hiroyoshi (1920–1944)
Nonlethal Weapons
Normandie-Niemen Squadron
Normandy, Task Force
Norstad, Lauris (1907–1988)
North African Campaign
North American Aerospace Defense Command (NORAD)
North American Aviation
North American B-25 Mitchell
North American B-45 Tornado
North American B-70 Valkyrie
North American F-86 Sabre
North American OV-10 Bronco
North American P-51 Mustang
North American T-6 Texan
North American X-15
North Atlantic Treaty Organization (NATO)
Northrop Aircraft
Northrop Flying Wings
Northrop Grumman B-2 Spirit
Northrop T-38 Talon, F-5 Freedom Fighter, and Tiger II
Norwegian Air Campaign (1940)
Novikov, Aleksandr Aleksandrovich (1900–1976)
Nowotny, Walter (1920–1944)

O’Grady, Scott
Ohain, Hans Joachim Pabst von (1911–1998)
O’Hare, Edward H. (1914–1943)
Okinawa
Olympic Arena/Guardian Challenge
Onishi, Takijiro (1891–1945)
Osirak Nuclear Reactor
Ozawa, Jisaburo (1886–1966)

Pacific Air Forces
Pakistan Air Force
Palau, Battle of (1944)
Palomares Nuclear Incident
Panama Invasion (1989)
Panavia Tornado
Panay, USS
Pantelleria
Pape, Robert A. (1960–)
Parachutes
Paris Air Agreement
Park, Keith Rodney (1892–1975)
Patrick, Mason Mathews (1863–1942)
Patterson, Robert Porter (1891–1952)
Pattle, Marmaduke Thomas St. John (1914–1941)
Pave Nail
Pearl Harbor
PEDESTAL (1942)
Peenemünde
Peltz, Dietrich (1914–)
Pepelyaev, Evgenii Georgievich (1918–)
Pershing, John Joseph (1860–1948)
Peru-Ecuador Boundary Conflict
Petersen, Frank E. (1932–)
Petlyakov Aircraft
Pfalz Aircraft
Philippines (1941, 1944)
Piaggio Aircraft
Piasecki Helicopters
Pilatus
Piper Aircraft
Platz, Reinhold (1886–1996)
Ploesti Oil Refineries
POINTBLANK (1942–1945)
Pokryshkin, Aleksandr (1913–1985)
Poland, Aircraft Development and Production
Polikarpov, Nikolai N. (1892–1944)
Polish Air Force
Polish Auxiliary Women's Air Force Service (1943–1945) and [British] Air Transport Auxiliary (1941–1945)
Portal, Charles (1893–1971)
Porte, John C. (1884–1919)
Potez 25
Potez 63
Potez Aircraft
Powers, Francis Gary (1929–1977)
Precision-Guided Munitions
Preddy, George E., Jr. (1919–1944)
Presidential Aircraft
Pressurized Cabins and Cockpits
Prisoners of War
Propellers
Pueblo, USS
PZL Aircraft (Panstwowe Zaklady Lotnicze)

Quesada, Elwood R. (1904–1993)
Question Mark

Rabaul
Radar and How It Works
Radar, and the Battle of Britain
Rall, Guenther (1918–)
Raskova (Malinina), Marina Mikhaylovna (1912–1943)
Ravens (1966–1974)
Read, Albert C.(1887–1967)
Reber, Samuel (1864–1933)
Reeves, Joseph M. (1872–1948)
Regia Aeronautica (Pre–World War II)
Regia Aeronautica (World War II)
Reitsch, Hanna (1912–1979)
Republic Aircraft
Republic F-105 Thunderchief
Republic F-84 Thunderjet, Thunderstreak, and Thunderflash
Republic P-47 Thunderbolt
Request for Data R-40C: The XP-54, XP-55, and XP-56 Fighter Programs
Research Aircraft
Richthofen, Manfred von (1892–1918)
Richthofen, Wolfram Freiherr von (1895–1945)
Rickenbacker, Edward Vernon (1890–1973)
Ridgway, Matthew Bunker (1895–1993)
Risner, Robinson (1925–)
Ritchie, Richard S. "Steve" (1942–)
Rocket Research in Germany (World War II)
Rockwell International
ROLLING THUNDER (1965–1968)
Rosendahl, Charles E. (1892–1977)
Royal Aircraft Factory
Royal Australian Air Force (RAAF)
Royal Bulgarian Air Force
Royal Flying Corps (RFC)/Royal Naval Air Service (RNAS)/ Royal Air Force (RAF)
Royal Norwegian Air Force (RNAF)
Royal Thai Air Force (RTAF)
Royal Yugoslav Air Force (RYAF)
Rudel, Hans-Ulrich (1916–1982)
Rudenko, S. I. (1904–1990)
Ruhr Bombing Campaign
Rumpler Aircraft
Russian Air Force (Post-Soviet)
Ryan Aircraft

Saab Aircraft
Saab J-29 Tunnan
Saab J-35 Draken
Saab J-37 Viggen
Saab JAS-39 Gripen
Safonov, Boris (1915–1942)
SAGE (Semiautomated Ground Environment) Defense System
Saint Mihiel, Battle of (1918)
Saint-Exupéry, Antoine de (1900–1944)
Sakai, Saburo (1916–2000)
Salerno, Battle of (1943)
Salmond, John M. (1881–1968)
Salmson Aircraft
Salyut
Samson, Charles R. (1883–1931)
Santa Cruz, Battle of (1942)
Saro Aircraft
Satellite Command and Control
Satellites
Schmid, Josef (1901–1956)
Schnaufer, Heinz-Wolfgang (1922–1950)
Schriever, Bernard A. "Bennie" (1910–)
Schütte, Johann (1873–1940)
Schwarzkopf, H. Norman (1934–)
Schweinfurt-Regensburg Raids
SENTRY (Samos) Reconnaissance System
Seversky, Alexander P. de (1894–1974)
Seversky Aircraft
Shenyang J-6 and J-8
Short Aircraft (Early Years and World War I)
Short Aircraft (Post–World War I)
Short Stirling
Short Sunderland
Short, Michael C. (1944–)
SIAI Marchetti
Signals Intelligence (SIGINT)
Sikorsky, Igor I. (1889–1972)
Sikorsky S-55/H-19 Chickasaw
Sikorsky S-61R/CH-3/HH-3 ("Jolly Green Giant")
Sikorsky S-64 Skycrane/CH-54 Tarhe
Sikorsky S-65/CH-53 Sea Stallion
Sikorsky S-70
Sikorsky UH-60 Black Hawk
Single Integrated Operation Plan (SIOP)
Six Day War
Slessor, John C. (1897–)
Smushkevich, Yakov "General Douglas" (1902–1941)
SNCASO 4050 Vautour
Sokolovsky, Vasily Danilovich (1897–1968)
Somalia
Somerville, James F. (1882–1949)
Somme, Battle of the (1916)
Sopwith Aircraft
Sopwith, Thomas O. M. (1888–1989)
Sosnowska-Karpik, Irena (1922–1990)
South Atlantic/Trans-Africa Air Route
Southeast Asia Air War (1965–1972)
Soviet Air Force
Soviet Aircraft Development and Production
Soviet Volunteer Pilots
Soviet Women Pilots
Soviet Women's Combat Wings (1942–1945)
Soyuz Space Vehicle
Spaatz, Carl Andrew (1891–1974)
Space Shuttle, and Military Use
Space Stations
SPAD Aircraft
Spanish Air Force
Spanish Civil War
Special Operations
Speer, Albert (1905–1981)
Sperrle, Hugo (1885–1953)
Spruance, Raymond A. (1886–1969)
Sputnik
Squier, George Owen (1865–1934)
Stalingrad, Battle of (1942–1943)
Stapp, John Paul (1910–1999)
Stearman Aircraft
STEEL TIGER (1965–1968)
Steinhoff, Johannes (1913–1994)
STRANGLE (1951)
Strategic Air Command
Strategic Arms Limitation Treaty (SALT)
Strategic Arms Reduction Talks (START)
Strategic Bombing
Strategic Defense Initiative (SDI, "Star Wars")
Strategic Triad Concept
Student, Kurt (1890–1978)
Stumpff, Hans-Juergen (1889–1968)
SUD Aviation
Sueter, Murray (1872–1960)
Suez Crisis
Sugita, Shoichi (1924–1945)
Sukhoi Aircraft
Sukhoi Su-24
Sukhoi Su-27
Supermarine Aircraft
Supermarine Spitfire
Suprun, Stepan (1907–1941)
Sutyagin, Nikolai (1923–1986)
Swedish Air Force

Swiss Air Force
Swiss Aircraft Industry
Syrian Air Force
Systems Management

TACAMO
Tactical Air Command (TAC)
Tactical Air Warfare
Tank, Kurt (1898–1983)
Taran (Ramming)
Taranto Air Attack (1940)
Tarawa, Battle of (1943)
Task Force 38/58
Task Force 77
Taylor, Maxwell Davenport (1901–1987)
Tedder, Arthur W. (1890–1967)
Tereshkova, Valentina (1937–)
Terror-Bombing
Terrorism
Thomsen, Hermann von der Lieth (1867–1942)
Tibbets, Paul W. (1915–)
Tokugawa, Yoshitoshi (1882–1963)
Tokyo Air Raids
Top Gun
TORCH (1942)
Towers, John H. (1885–1955)
Trenchard, Hugh (1873–1956)
Truman, Harry S.
TsAGI
Tsiolkovsky, Konstantin Eduardovich (1857–1935)
Tunner, William H. (1906–1983)
Tupolev Aircraft
Tuskegee Airmen
Twining, Nathan F. (1897–1983)

Udet, Ernst (1896–1941)
Ugaki, Matome (1890–1945)
Ultra
United Aircraft
United States Air Force: Organizational History
United States Air Forces in Europe (USAFE)
United States Army Air Corps (USAAC)
United States Army Air Forces
United States Army Air Service
United States Army Signal Corps
United States Navy
Unmanned Aerial Vehicles
U.S. Air Corps Tactical School (ACTS)
U.S. Air Force Academy
U.S. Air Force Doctrine
U.S. Aircraft Development and Production (World War I)
U.S. Army Aviation: Operations
U.S. Army Aviation: Origins
U.S. Coast Guard Aviation
U.S. Marine Corps Aviation
U.S. Navy, Chief of Naval Operations (CNO)
U.S. Navy, Office of the Secretary
U.S. Postal Air Mail Service
U.S. Strategic Bombing Survey (SBS)

V-1 Missile and V-2 Rocket
Valencia, Eugene A. (1921–)
Vandenberg, Hoyt S. (1899–1954)
Vang Pao (1929–)
VARSITY (1945)
V-Bombers
Verdun, Battle of (1916)
Versailles Treaty
Vertol (Piasecki) H-21
Verville, Alfred (1890–1970)
Vian, Philip L. (1894–1968)
Vichy French Air Force
Vickers Aircraft
Vickers Valiant
Vietnam War
Vietnamese Air Force (North)
Vietnamese Air Force (South)
Vimy Ridge, Battle of (1917)
Vo Nguyen Giap (1912–)
Voisin Aircraft
Voskhod
Voss, Werner (1897–1917)
Vostok
Vought A-7 Corsair II
Vought Aircraft
Vought F4U Corsair
Vought F-8 Crusader
Vought VE-7

Wake Island, Battles of (1941–1945)
Warden, John A. III (1943–)
Warning Systems
Warsaw Pact Aviation
Washington Naval Conference
Weapons System
Welch, Larry D. (1934–)
Wells, Edward C. (1910–1986)
Wells, Herbert George (1866–1946)
Westland Lynx

Westland Lysander
Wever, Walter (1887–1936)
Weyland, Otto P. "Opie"
White, Thomas Dresser (1901–1965)
Whittle, Frank (1907–1996)
Wild Weasel
Williams, Robert R. (1918–)
Wind Tunnels
Winter War (1939–1940)
Women Airforce Service Pilots
Women in Air Combat
Women in the Air Force (WAF)
Women in the Aircraft Industry (World War II)
Women's Auxiliary Air Force
Women's Auxiliary Ferrying Squadron
Worden, Hector (1885–1916)
World War I Aviation
World War II Aviation
World War II Conferences
Wright, Orville (1871–1948)
Wright, Wilbur (1867–1912)
Wright-Patterson Air Force Base
Yakovlev, Aleksandr S. (1906–1989)
Yamaguchi, Tamon (1892–1942)
Yamamoto, Isoroku (1884–1943)
Yeager, Charles E. (1923–)
Yom Kippur War (October War)
Y-Service

Zeppelin, Ferdinand Von (1838–1917)
Zero-Length Launcher
Zuckert, Eugene M. (1911–2000)

FOREWORD

A first in the field of military studies, *Air Warfare: An International Encyclopedia* is a wealth of information—a comprehensive source of names and places, planes and aces, designers and builders. But more than anything it is a record of ideas, developed and brought to fruition over the past century, relating to the conduct of warfare in the third dimension. The men and women, the thinkers and visionaries, the planners and executers of air warfare had new and different ideas about the use of the air—and space—for the prosecution of war and the preservation of peace.

This foreword is meant to unify the sweeping and diverging elements that follow. Most of the writings about air warfare focus on its very visible characteristics—air vehicles and propulsion systems, the victories achieved, the losses suffered, the tons delivered, the damage inflicted—intended and unintended.

Vehicles for air warfare command a wide-ranging mix of such "visibles": materials, design, controls, power plants. And though there has been great diffusion of engineering knowledge across national boundaries, these elements were, and are, largely pursued independently by nations that had the resources to do so. Few nations have successfully fielded effective air forces, yet there is a significant display of visibles that nations throughout history have fielded. The two volumes that make up this ground-breaking publication capture in great detail those visible characteristics and the men and women who dreamed, developed, and deployed them.

Beyond this visible content—and arguably more important to the development of air warfare—are the largely invisible elements that provided the conceptual and analytical basis for designing, funding, producing, deploying, and employing air forces and the logistical framework so necessary for effective use.

Air warfare is fundamentally about new ideas and the resulting new weapons and concepts for their employment; it is not, primarily, about airplanes and pilots; it is not about the platforms from which new weapons are employed. Those elements are the visibles that are the easy to observe and to write about. The unseen and the unreported are much more central to the essence of air warfare and its achievements. The ideas that stimulated and supported war in the third dimension envisioned, and still envision, a changing conflict environment in which air forces would take the fight directly to the political source of an enemy's strength, avoiding the deadly contest at the front. For centuries nations have fought their enemies at the front—from the periphery to the rear—toward some high-priority physical objective, the destruction or threatened destruction of which would cause the enemy to sue for peace.

Airmen had a different idea; they sought to take mortal combat directly to the high-priority objectives—so-called centers of gravity—bypassing the time-honored sacrifice of young men, sometimes by the thousands, at the front. This new notion of war, this new thinking, has received mixed reviews. From questions about its morality—as if killing 50,000 friendly ground forces at the front on separate occasions within a 25-year period did not raise questions of morality for the USA—to questions about its effectiveness, air warfare has generated almost as many detractors as it has supporters. The ensuing intellectual and political debate generated widely divergent views on both sides. The debate has sharpened the critical analysis of air operations far beyond the review and analysis of other areas of warfare, and from that crucible of debate has sprung more pertinent ideas, more compelling concepts, more useful weapons. The introduction of the intercontinental ballistic missile, the ubiquitous employment of space-based capabilities supporting surface and air warfare, the migration and diffusion of reconnaissance from horseback to airplane to spacecraft and, now, to unmanned aerial vehicles demonstrate the capacity of an idea-based movement to adapt to new circumstances—not just new technology, not just piloted vehicles, but to the ideas that drive innovation.

The new ideas associated with air warfare are either revolutionary or conventional depending on one's viewpoint of war as an instrument of national policy. A viewpoint suggesting more revolutionary ideas holds that air warfare changes everything but policy: New means of warfare require new military doctrines and new relationships among the armed forces of a nation; new air warfare capabilities require different planning efforts to maximize the political utility and military power of the evolving force, including air, land, and sea elements; new capabilities afford new concepts of operations and, potentially, less predictable approaches to dealing with enemy forces; incrementalism does not suffice. A viewpoint suggesting that ideas relating to air warfare are more conventional holds that little changes: Human nature has not changed over the millennia; therefore, the causes of, and the events in, war will be familiar; the functions of the armed forces do not change; relationships among combatants may evolve for lots of reasons, but not as the result of any passing technological phenomenon in the third dimension; change in military affairs is continuous, slow, and incremental.

The 1970 pamphlet "Men, Machines, and Modern Times," written by the distinguished naval historian Samuel Eliot Morison, captures the difficulty in acknowledging value and effecting change in traditional military societies (and in the traditional steel and rail industries as well) some 150 years ago. Accepting the advent of the unknowns of steam over the knowns of wind and sail; accepting rifling in the field and deck pieces for armies and navies; accepting breach loaders—each dastardly, revolutionary ideas that were fought hard and for all the wrong reasons. The introduction of breach-loading weapons merits some elaboration: President Lincoln, attempting to recruit and deploy sufficient forces for the Civil War, was effectively opposed, even neutralized, by the insistence of the Union Army's Colonel of Ordnance that federal troops be equipped with muzzle loaders designed a half-century earlier. There are various estimates of the cost of the delay in adapting to the changed circumstances; the patented Colt could, and eventually did, multiply the effectiveness of each soldier so equipped by a factor of two or three. Lincoln's recruiting efforts and the eventual cost of the war were extended by the rejection of change. Adapting to change is a painful exercise for military forces. The burden of history and tradition—and especially of success—is one of the major reasons.

In some 5,000 years of recorded history it appears that man has fought in organized formations on the ground virtually every year (and the same at sea for almost 3,500 years). In the long view of history, air warfare is but a footnote to the vast compendia of battles and heroes of war on land and at sea. Yet the vector of accomplishment demonstrated by air forces in the past 100 years has commanded broad attention and high expectations. In particular, those on the receiving end—on land and at sea—of aerial attack have expressed their respect for the power and impact—physical and psychological—of this still new element of warfare.

Such respect is not universal. There is great tension among the leadership of various service elements in virtually every country over the attention and the approbation paid by the public to the illusion, the promise, and the results of air warfare. This attention is reflected in national debates, policy decisions, and their consequent impact on force structures and operations. The tension manifests itself in many ways and applies well beyond the competition for resources among those who fight in the air, on the ground, and at sea.

Most air forces are subordinate organizational elements of their nations' armies, and the leadership of the army determines, in large measure, the political, doctrinal, and operational environment in which the its force exists. For example, in China the People's Liberation Army Air Force (PLAAF) is an integral arm of the Peoples' Liberation Army. It is not in any way a separate air force, and neither is it an equal player when decisions are made about force development, force structure, and force employment. The purpose of an air force in such an environment is to maximize the contributions of ground combat operations toward achieving the nation's military objectives. The organizational, deployment, and employment concepts of the PLAAF are much more closely aligned with ideas of Alexander, Caesar, and Napoleon than with those of Douhet, Trenchard, and Doolittle. Consequently, the research and development, the training, the standards, the norms, and the operations of the PLAAF are derived from the warfighting needs of the ground forces. Such historical development and the continuing imperatives of traditional ground warfare have limited, in many regards, the potential of air forces to fully exploit the different capabilities inherent in air operations.

These limits are not solely military. In most nations military tradition is embodied in its army. In those few nations with a civil and military seafaring history, the navy may get equal opportunity; nevertheless, for purposes of military involvement in international affairs, for internal security considerations, and in many cases for various internal police powers, the army is the political force of choice when the head of government is seeking a new chief of defense staff (or, in the United States, a new Chairman of the Joint Chiefs of Staff). This selection further limits the breadth of military advice that governments can bring to bear on defense and military issues.

An additional limiting factor has to do with the insight and advice that political leaders can, and do, get from defense intellectuals. Political scientists and classically trained historians understand from their research that war is fought on the ground and on the sea; libraries are full of volumes by men—made famous by their own military exploits and by the work of scholars—who have written in great detail of the formations and the armaments, of the marches and the maneuvers, of the decisions that created victories and defeats. The history of ground and naval warfare is recorded in handsome drawings, outlining the progress of friendly and opposing forces in painstaking detail, including precise time lines, none of which reflect the chaos of real battle. Carefully drawn maps and charts with red lines and blue lines, depicting the positions and the timing that the various forces executed an envelopment or "crossed the T," capture for eternity the tactical analysis and the strategic decisionmaking of the victorious generals and admirals and the triumphs of their forces. Detailed analysis of war from the loser's perspective is rare, and war from an airman's perspective is rarer yet. Airmen typically do not write, and firsthand reports of battles fought from the air are almost nonexistent and becoming more so.

The "first draft of history" is the label that news reporters, particularly in time of war, like to assign to the results of their daily work; they pride themselves in firsthand observation and carefully crafted reports thereof. Churchill made an early name for himself reporting on the Boer War. Today's journalists do the same tasks with somewhat faster transmission of their stories. Even Churchill, careful observer that he was, would have great difficulty covering today's aerial operations—few combatants, small cockpits, no space for observers, hundreds of miles deep in enemy territory, closing speeds of 500–1,500–15,000 miles per hour, unseen electronic combat, stealthy participants on both sides—and submitting gripping copy.

All of this captures how aerial warfare is differentiated by outside observers from warfare on the ground and at sea: Only the effects of air operations are observable, measurable, and reportable. For ground and sea operations, reporters can see, touch, and feel; the activity is the story—the forced march, the thunder of shelling, the smell of cordite, the after-action interview, the personal sense of fear and camaraderie with the engaged troops. For air operations reporters, in large measure, can report only on results. There are more reports by far of the preparation of the aircraft and weapons, the launching and the recovery of missions from aircraft carriers, than of the conduct of combat operations by naval aviators and their formations. For the news industry the story is about "how the game is played." Who won is of some interest, but the preferred story is one that follows the ball play-by-play, that fills airtime and column inches, that captures the feelings of the wounded sergeant, that permits the reporter to do the "standup shot" in front of the burning hulk. The preferred story covers individual bravery and unit actions with evident risk-taking and on-scene heroes. How the game is played by modern air forces is unseen, untold, and unreported, and consequently history books will continue to accumulate a disproportionate amount of data and analysis on ground warfare. Some are very good; other works, for example, *Certain Victory: The U.S. Army in the Gulf War,* by (Major General) Robert H. Scales Jr., will unfortunately fill libraries and scholars with seriously flawed data. Certain Victory is a pompous, self-congratulatory dream about the Gulf War of 1990–1991; it is a press-agent approach to scholarly writing about war, and unfortunately policy analysts will continue to cite it.

For several reasons the person on the street is interested in results; he has sons and daughters, nieces and nephews; he is interested in peace and prosperity, not glory and laurels. If unseen and unreported air operations can secure his interests, he is not confused by the perspective of intellectuals in the media and elsewhere. In the United States the most widely attended outdoor attractions are air shows; Americans are captivated by airplanes, aviation, and aviators. It is probably not an accident that the first man to fly was an American; the first to cross the Atlantic solo was an American; the first to fly supersonic was an American; the first to walk on the moon was an American. Americans have been, and are, fascinated by air and space accomplishments and reflect this fascination in their political and financial support of advancing air and space developments.

A consequence of this fascination is high expectations of air operations, air forces, and air commanders. The political and public fallout of an air incident are far more widely reported, investigated, and acted on than a similar event in any other medium. These considerations apply to military forces. For example, the terrorist attack on the USS Cole in the port of Aden, Yemen, in 1998 resulted in the deaths of 18 sailors, a naval court of inquiry into the performance of the ship's captain, and a determination of no formal administrative or judicial action; a terrorist attack on Khobar Towers in Dhahran, Saudi Arabia, in June 1996 resulted in the deaths of 18 airmen, an investigation by a politically appointed outsider, and public humiliation for the air commander; an ill-conceived operation in Somalia, a U.S. initiative, resulted in the deaths of 19 soldiers and has yet to be investigated. Expectations are higher; the standards are different for airmen.

Higher expectations are also reflected in the treatment of results, intended and unintended. Air operations are no doubt a blunt instrument of national policy; they deal with weapons in tons; they have a history, brief as it is, of scattering those tons approximately 1,000 feet, more or less, around (World War II–era) aiming points. Even today, with much more precise technology and techniques, it is not unusual to hear of unintended or "collateral" damage from air-delivered weapons. It is highly unusual, however, to hear of collateral damage from friendly sea and ground operations. Villages, towns, and cities overrun by mechanized infantry or armored divisions seldom generate complaints of collateral damage; weeks, months, or years later, when the displaced persons finally return to their homes, they are more interested in rebuilding—and news reporters have found fresher stories. The prevalence of TV cameras, the depth of air operations in enemy territory, and the utility for enemy information warfare (propaganda) purposes make collateral damage stories the preferred option for depicting air warfare.

Selected physical damage, vivid images of "innocent civilians," and anguished interviews by survivors make air warfare appear dysfunctional to the political solution of the problem at hand. Ground and surface naval forces are highly unlikely to damage or destroy the embassy of a great power; air warfare bears a special burden. The reality is, in all areas of warfare, death, dismemberment, damage, and destruction—intended and unintended—are the essence of combat operations; the more successful a nation is in limiting unintended results, the more egregious the remaining examples will seem. As for intended results, because there are no moving lines on the ground and there are no easily observed and measured symbols of "advance," air operations may appear ineffective until a political collapse occurs, until the enemy forgoes military (for diplomatic) action. The few examples where air forces were permitted to take a leading role—the Berlin Airlift, the LINEBACKER operations, the Falklands campaign, the Gulf War, Kosovo—have resulted in prompt and effective operations with a minimum cost in blood and treasure.

Four fundamental assumptions were held by the early visionaries of air warfare and are held by today's day-to-day operational air commanders in every theater of operations. Air forces will be able to: identify, find, hit, and destroy high-priority objectives. These assumptions were, and are, sometimes valid.

Not until the last twenty years of the twentieth century did the technical tools and the operational techniques start to become widely available to give high confidence that virtually all delivery vehicles would routinely solve the navigation problem and find the assigned objective. The introduction of inertial navigation equipment and the Global Positioning System gives those nations that have the means to install and train with this equipment virtual assurance that missions will arrive in the assigned objective area. The next issue—hitting the assigned target or target area, using the correct coordinates, and placing the aiming device on the correct physical entity—is not trivial. Although there have been great technical advancements in precision-guided weapon development, there are natural and enemy-created impediments. Weather affects all military and naval operations, and even the latest weapons and guidance systems are not immune from these effects. Enemy-created effects are broader: active and passive defenses, concealment, deception, camouflage, movement—all serve to complicate the end-game difficulty of dealing with an assigned objective. Nevertheless, the probability of hitting, photographing, or resupplying the assigned objective is a high-probability event today for appropriately prepared forces.

The issue of sufficient damage or destruction, given that the objective is struck, is an enduring challenge. Matching the most appropriate weapon to the characteristics of the target is an art; doing so while minimizing collateral damage is a fine art. Hardening fixed facilities and replicating the critical components of high-value potential targets will make damage and destruction continuing issues; a bigger hammer is not necessarily the answer; the answer in many cases is a vulnerability analysis and selection of the key node. This is part of the enduring intellectual problem of warfare, to which we turn next.

To identify the most appropriate objective, or the most appropriate element embedded within a target area, is the major continuing challenge of air warfare. Choosing the most appropriate objectives, prioritizing across a broad area of operations, and identifying the most critical enemy function or functions that can, individually or in conjunction with a coherent campaign plan, best achieve the nations war aims in the quickest and most economical manner are the problem for air-war planning. The difficulty of allocating scarce resources against the most appropriate military objective in an active enemy system is the most demanding intellectual problem faced by war planners. All of the competitive issues seen in modern business and athletic competition are brought to bear—with the added complexity of the sure knowledge that the opponent, at best, is doing everything in its power to kill each friendly competitor and, at worst, to destroy the armed forces and the social fabric of the friendly nation or nations.

This burden of identifying the most appropriate objective falls, of course, on all military and naval commanders; however, for air commanders it is arguably a more complex problem because ranges, payloads, and potential military and political impacts have greater scope. Furthermore, the most appropriate objectives are likely to be critical components of organic systems—the communications, the transportation, the electrical power, the petrochemical, the other industrial, the agricultural, and the military and political infrastructures—that underpin the enemy's power base. In World War II air forces contented themselves with striking facilities—enemy headquarters, air bases, rail yards; today the standard is to cripple the military and political functions that the facilities support. Today the standard is to achieve specific operational effects within the enemy's political and military system; this, in turn, demands serious insight into the enemy's organization well beyond order-of-battle analysis. Such functional understanding of enemy doctrine and procedures is in itself a powerful weapon, but it is not free of costs.

A consequence of the imperative to identify the most appropriate operational effects and the related objectives for air operations is a requirement to maintain an intelligence function fine-tuned to the new standards. The easy answer for most nations is the amorphous central and defense intelligence agencies that produce products pitched to the needs of the policy establishments. These nations have structured their collection and reporting assets so that the military commanders—except for actions such as prisoner interrogations and documents collected on the battlefield—are the last to have access to important strategic and operational intelligence. The more technology has advanced, the greater the investments in strategic and national intelligence systems and the greater the gap between the capability of military forces and their capacity for operational assessment and decisionmaking—effective operational intelligence. For the United States this gap is abundantly apparent in recent events in Aden, Somalia, Serbia, and elsewhere.

Another area for which "one size fits all" is the wrong answer is logistical support of combat forces. Ground, naval, and air forces have major real differences in operating environments that shape service doctrine and philosophy and that, in turn, drive design, size, shape, firepower, mobility, maintainability, and reliability of service equipments. The notion—prompted largely by financially savvy policymakers with little or no interest and experience in military and naval affairs—that service equipments ought to be commoditized—conceived, acquired, and maintained by a civilian entity that could enforce commonality—is a creeping disease endemic in virtually all democratic nations. Virtually every senator or member of parliament in every nation around the world understands air operations; they fly home almost every weekend; they assess takeoffs, landings, and on-time arrivals. They would not dream of advising a submarine captain on operations, but airmen are fair game.

For air warfare this notion of commoditization—commonality at all costs—is particularly painful; the development of new ideas has been fostered in various nations by the willingness of airmen and astronauts to experiment beyond the edges of conventional thinking, to engage a broad cross-section of scientists and strategists to explore unconventional methods to achieve engineering, tactical, and operational results. In the United States the demise of Air Force Systems Command was a seminal event, limiting what had been a hugely successful enterprise devoted to assembling the best thinkers available, military and civilian, to bring the possibilities of science and engineering to bear on emerging military problems. The elimination of this organization portends the decline of U.S. military air and space leadership.

Similarly, the structure of the maintenance, supply, distribution, and data systems that support military forces needs to adjust to the operating patterns and performance of the supported force. Air forces operate from long distances, often from sanctuaries well outside the area of operations; the ability to connect regularly and efficiently to a centralized logistical system on virtually an hourly basis changes the materials and the skills required at each location for the conduct of operations. Armies and navies, in contrast, are typically not so well connected to global air transportation nets and thus require different and more extensive sets of on-hand machinery, materials, and skills to manufacture and repair critical parts.

Global air transportation is the least heralded element in air warfare. Unrecognized by the early air warfare thinkers—who wrote extensively about bomber, pursuit, and observation tasks—military airlift evolved from an appreciation for the growing utility of civil aviation fleets; civilian aircraft were embraced to do similar tasks in a military situation. From the World War II regional experience of flying the Hump, to the Berlin Airlift, to Operation NICKEL GRASS (the strategic resupply of Israeli forces in 1973), to the deployment and redeployment of warfighting and peacekeeping forces around the world, air transportation fleets have become the sine qua non of conflict management. The Berlin Airlift is, arguably, the twentieth century's premier example of military art at its highest level of accomplishment—no "combat" casualties, yet the allied powers achieved their strategic goals, preserved the political status of, and access to, Berlin, and set the tone for the next fifty years of European political and military history. Many nations have found the political and economic tools to integrate military and civilian air transportation into global strategic lift capability.

Since the beginning of the Cold War the United States has deployed, supported, and redeployed, by air, significant military forces for operations in Korea, Western Europe, Southeast Asia, and Southwest Asia plus smaller forces to Panama, Somalia, Bosnia, Kosovo, and Afghanistan. This view of global transportation includes the aerial "transportation and delivery" fuel to extend the range and duty time of other forces, including other lift, surveillance, bomber, fighter, and space vehicles. There is no historical precedent for the global scope of major operations conducted by U.S. forces during this period. The combination of inflight refueling, intercontinental strategic airlift, and the more local tactical airlift is the crucial determinant of force deployment and, in many cases, force sustainment. Strategic mobility is a very operational capability. Whereas heavy materiel typically moves by commercial sealift, personnel, high-value supplies, and casualty evacuation are important airlift tasks. Moreover, the U.S. fleet of T-tailed aircraft is the transportation mode of choice for every peacekeeping and humanitarian mission conducted by blue-helmeted troops and others worldwide.

The term "independent air force" has, for better or for worse, confused and complicated the debate about the development and employment of air capabilities. Air forces clearly cannot exist "independent" of the structures and the operational activities of the rest of a nation's military establishment. Air forces need to be and must be integrated into the totality of the nation's forces. The potential contributions of an independent air force need to be viewed, however, through eyes untainted by the burden of traditional military history. Training, logistics, and intelligence, among other functions, that suffice, or even excel, at the pace a rhythm of ground or sea operations have little in common with the needs of air and space warfare. The most appropriate objectives for tactical and operational planning are different depending on the vision and experience of the commander in chief. Those who argue for independent air operations ask that their forces be valued for their independent contributions to the war effort and not solely for their contributions to maximizing the combat power of some other element. This is not an argument for anarchy or autonomous air action. Some overall political and military authority, with the best interests of the nation in mind and a sophisticated view of operational possibilities, must orchestrate all of the military tools available to force an early end to hostilities on favorable terms.

Navies seem to have found a way to balance the new with the old. For those nations with a substantial naval component, the fleet has reoriented itself to fully exploit modern offensive and defensive capabilities. Submarines, occasionally, and aircraft carriers are the visibles of modern navies; both are accommodated in integrated operations. Fleets are built around carriers; fleet operations are built around carrier operations, which, in turn, are built around air operations.

Even in those circumstances where there is an independent air force, the history and the politics of each nation have typically hobbled the application of air capabilities to the views, history, and operational experience of the nation's senior service. Thus, the elegant Australian War Memorial in Canberra, with its columns and columns of war dead, listed battalion after battalion, overwhelmingly from the doomed battle at Gallipoli, has defined for years, and will define for many decades, if not centuries, the historical image of Australian war experience, the willingness to serve, the sacrifice made. This image has colored, and will continue to color, the military leadership that Australian politicians choose and thus the nature of the advice they will receive from the senior military leadership, regardless of the nature of the extant political-military circumstances.

I do not argue that air forces and air force leaders have better advice to give than do competent military professionals from other backgrounds. I do argue that airmen are not wedded to thousands of years of history and tradition and therefore have less intellectual and institutional baggage in giving sound military advice.

Two observations by senior commanders will suffice to bookend the traditional views of many ground-force officers concerning contributions of air operations to the conduct of warfare. The first is a quote from Douglas Haig, prior to becoming commander in chief of the British Expeditionary Force during World war I, in a 1914 address to the British Army Staff College: "I hope none of you gentleman are so foolish as to think that aeroplanes will be usefully employed for reconnaissance from the air. There is only one way for a commander to get information by reconnaissance and that is by the use of cavalry."

The second comes thanks to Wesley K. Clark, the retired U.S. Army general who was the senior U.S. military commander in Europe and senior commander for the North Atlantic Treaty Organization during the 1999 war in Kosovo. In his memoirs he took no cognizance of the contributions of air operations to the NATO effort (except for two chapters on Task Force Hawk, the 5,000-man, 24-helicopter U.S. Army unit that did not participate in combat operations). The B-2 bomber—the stealth platform that penetrated Serbian air defenses with impunity and served as the workhorse of General Clark's engaged forces—is not mentioned.

Notwithstanding the views of traditionalists, air warfare has proven itself a valuable addition to the tools of statecraft. At the publication of *Air Warfare: An International Encyclopedia,* the centennial anniversary of the first successful flight of a heavier-than-air machine has yet to come to pass, and humanity's initial ventures into space are barely 40 years old. Yet the pace of new ideas, the introduction of new concepts, and their translation into valued instruments of national power is breathtaking. Nations that can find the considerable resources required to field effective air forces can enhance the value of their traditional forces and can use this rapidly evolving instrument of military power to better preserve, protect, and defend their interests, wherever they may be.

—*Mike Dugan*
General, USAF (Ret.)

PREFACE

In planning this encyclopedia with my colleagues, many goals were set forth, but there were three that we considered most important. The first was to include entries that provided information on the most significant individuals, events, weapons, industries, strategies, and tactics of the roughly 200-year history of international airpower. The second was to make an initial assessment of the importance of each entry. The third was to reach out to the entire aviation community for contributions and to preserve, insofar as possible, the original flavor of those contributions. There were many aspects to this process. Some authors were distinguished scholars, long accustomed to writing encyclopedia entries, and integrating their work was straightforward. Some authors were experts in their fields but not academics, and so their entries were sometimes less formal. Other authors were so technically expert that their entries had to be simplified to be understood by the average reader, yet their exact meaning had to be preserved. In yet other instances, some entries reflected the fact that English was not the scholar's native tongue. Because we tried to keep all the entries as original as possible, entries written by foreign scholars were revised only for the sake of clarity.

The methods we employed were direct. We made an appeal to the academic community as well as to the legion of aviation historians that specialized in various areas of airpower history. In attempting to provide a broad coverage, we understood that some elements of airpower history had already been well described in the past and were easily accessible to the reader. Still, some elements had been virtually ignored. Based on this understanding, we decided to sometimes limit the coverage of well-known subjects while giving greater coverage to those less well known.

There were some obvious trade-offs that had to be considered. Given that there was a limit on the size of the encyclopedia, a decision had to be made as to the number of entries to be included. If fewer topics were selected, more words could be devoted to each. If more topics were included, each would contain fewer words. Our initial list ran to roughly 1,300 entries, but it soon became evident that this was too many. We were also presented with many new ideas from the contributors, often reflecting their specialized interests, and this caused a continuous evaluation of which entries to retain and which to sacrifice.

As a result of these deliberations, we settled on some 990 entries running nearly 500,000 words. The length of a given entry can vary, from as few as 100 words to as many as 7,500 words. Our saving grace was often the cross-references provided at the end of most entries. These guide the reader to additional information on the subject and, of course, lead to still more sources of scholarship.

In making these difficult decisions, an iterative process was established with the editors and the contributors. An initial list was reduced and circulated, and the contributors who elected to participate responded with observations and suggestions that ultimately resulted in encyclopedia you now see. I should also mention that this work owes a great debt to the Internet and its related technology, which made the entire process possible and was an invaluable way to reach new contributors, many in foreign countries.

A note on the use of specialized terminology, acronyms, and abbreviations: Given the complexity of the subject matter, we have tried to be as consistent and clear as possible. Common acronyms appear in the entry's headword; other acronyms are typically defined at first instance within an entry. Widely recognized acronyms, such as USAF and RAF, are not formally defined in the text. To help the reader keep track of the many acronyms and abbreviations, we provide a complete list of terms, acronyms, and abbreviations. We encourage readers to rely on this comprehensive list of airpower-related terminology.

I would like to express my gratitude to my associate editors—all distinguished in their fields—who made so many insightful suggestions and contributions. In alphabetical order, they are Michael Fopp, director of the Royal Air Force Museum; Fred Johnsen, a noted author and historian; Stéphane Nicolaou, curator at the marvelous Musée de l'Air et de l'Espace at Le Bourget Field, near Paris, and a well-known author; and the indefatigable George M. Watson Jr., a U.S. Air Force historian whose many suggestions and quick responses to my calls made the task easier. My admiration for Spencer C. Tucker is unbounded, for I now know the effort he has put forth in editing other encyclopedias. Spence was good enough to ask me to participate, and I thank him for the experience. It is a delight to work with the people at ABC-CLIO, especially Alicia Merritt and Liz Kincaid. Wally Meeks, as usual, was helpful with his good ideas.

My most appreciative and humble thanks go to the contributors, whose entries were fascinating to read and whose patience with my nagging was remarkable. Not only did they work willingly and punctually; they were also the source of most of the photographs you will find in the two volumes. I also want to express my appreciation to a few would-be contributors who signed on but could not deliver; I know that circumstances must have prevented your participation, and want you all to know that the editors and contributors understand.

Finally, I cannot put into words the gratitude I feel to my family, who cheerfully put up with my submersion at the computer as I worked to bring this project to fruition.

—*Walter J. Boyne*
Ashburn, Virginia

MAPS

War in the Balkans, 65

Barbarossa, 69

The Results of the Blitzkrieg: France, 22 June 1940, 88

The Battle of Britain, 107

Persian Gulf War, 282

Japan, 334

Korean War, 355

The Mediterranean, 407

War in Southeast Asia, 677

The Western Front as Stabilized in 1915, 703

TERMS, ACRONYMS, AND ABBREVIATIONS

AA	antiaircraft
AAA	antiaircraft artillery
AAF	Argentine Air Force
AAMs	air-to-air missiles
AB	Agusta-Bell
ABCCC	Airborne Battlefield Command and Control Center
ABDA	American, British, Dutch, Australian
ABL	airborne laser
ABM	antiballistic missile
ACCS	Air Command and Control System; also: Airborne Command and Control Squadron
ACFC	Air Corps Ferrying Command
ACG	Air Commando Group
ACTS	Air Corps Tactical School
ACWP	Automotive Council of War Production
AD	Air Division
ADC	Air (Aerospace) Defense Command
ADRC	Air Documents Research Center
ADVON	Advanced Echelon
AEA	Aeronautical Experiment Association
AEF	Aerospace Expeditionary Force
AEW	airborne early warning
AF	Air Force
AFB	Air Force Base
AFC	Armed Forces Council
AFDD	Air Force Doctrine Document
AFM	Air Force Manual
AFMC	Air Force Material Command
AI	air interdiction
AIRCENT	Allied Air Forces Central Europe
ALAT	Army Light Air Force
ALCS	airborne launch-control system
ALERT	Attack and Launch Early Reporting to Theater
AMC	Air Mobility Command
AME	Aeronautica Militar Espanola
ANG	Air National Guard
ANR	Aeronautica Nazionale (National) Repubblicana
AOC	air officer commanding
ARM	antiradiation missile
ARPA	Advanced Research Projects Agency
ARRS	Aerospace Rescue and Recovery Service
ARVN	Army of the Republic of Vietnam
ASAT	antisatellite
ASC	Air Support Command
ASM	air-to-surface missile
ASTS	Air Service Tactical School
ASW	antisubmarine warfare
ATC	Air Transport Command
ATF	Advanced Tactical Fighter
ATGM	antitank guided missle
ATI	air technical intelligence
AVG	American Volunteer Group (Flying Tigers)
AWACS	Airborne Warning and Control System
AWPD	Air War Plans Division
BAe	British Aerospace
BAP	Bureau of Aircraft Production
BCATP	British Commonwealth Air Training Plan
BFW	Bayerische Flugzeugwerke
bhp	brake horsepower
BIS	British Interplanetary Society
BMEWS	Ballistic Missile Early Warning System
BNA	Bureau of Naval Aeronautics
BPF	British Pacific Fleet
BPR	bypass ration
CAB	Caproni Aeronautica Bergamasca
CACW	Chinese-American Composite Wing
CAF	Chinese Air Force
CAP	Civil Air Patrol; Combat Air Patrol
CAS	close air support
CAT	Civil Air Transport

CATF	China Air Task Force
CBI	China-Burma-India
CBO	Combined Bomber Offensive
CCP	Chinese Communist Party
CENTAF	United States Central Air Forces
CEO	chief executive officer
CETF	College Eye Task Force
CGS	Continental Ground Station
CIA	Central Intelligence Agency
CINC	commander in chief
CINCPAC	Commander in Chief, Pacific Fleet
CIS	Commonwealth of Independent States
CNAC	China National Aviation Corporation
CNO	Chief of Naval Operations
CNT	Cantiere Navale Triestino
COMINCH	commander in chief of the U.S. Fleet
COMUSMACV	U.S. Military Assistance Command, Vietnam
CONAC	Continental Air Command
CONAD	Continental Air Defense Command
CPTP	Civilian Pilot Training Program
CRAF	Civil Reserve Air Fleet
CRDA	Cantieri Riuniti Dell'Adriatico
CRT	cathode-ray-tube
CSAR	Combat Search and Rescue
CSAS	Comando Servizi Aerei Speciali (Special Air Services Command)
CTA	Centro Tecnico Aerospacial
CVE	escort carrier
DARPA	Defense Advanced Research Projects Agency
DASC	Direct Air Support Center
DATF	Desert Air Task Force
DCNO (Air)	Deputy Chief of Naval Operations for Air
DFC	Distinguished Flying Cross
DMSP	Defense Meteorological Satellite Program
DMZ	demilitarized zone
DNSS	Defense Navigation Satellite System
DOD	Department of Defense (U.S.)
DOS	Department of State (U.S.)
DRA	Democratic Republic of Afghanistan
DRV	Democratic Republic of Vietnam
DSC	Distinguished Service Cross
DSP	Defense Support Program
DVS	Commercial Pilot Training School
EAP	Experimental Aircraft Program
ECCM	electronic counter-countermeasures
ECM	electronic countermeasures
EDA	Ejército del Aire
EGNOS	European Global Navigation Overlay System
ELINT	electronic intelligence
EOP	Executive Office of the President
ER/ELINT	electronic reconnaissance/intelligence
ESM	Electronic support measures
ETO	European Theater of Operations
EVA	extravehicular activity
EW	Electronic warfare
FAA	Fleet Air Arm
FAC	forward air control/controllers
FAH	Fuerza Aerea Hondureña
FBW	fly-by-wire
FEAF	Far East Air Forces
FECOM	Far East Command
Fliegerkorps	Luftwaffe air corps
FM	Field Manual
FMA	Fabrica Militar de Aviones (Military Aircraft Factory)
FSTA	Future Strategic Tanker Aircraft
GCI	ground-controlled interceptor
GEO	geostationary orbit
GGS	Gyro Gun Sights
GHQ	General Headquarters
GHQ AF	General Headquarters Air Force (U.S.)
GIAP	Gvardeiskii Istrebitelnyi Aviatsionnyi Polk (Guards Fighter Air Regiment, Soviet Union)
GLONASS	Global Navigation Satellite System
GNBAP	Gvardeiskii Nochnoi Bombardirovochnyi Aviatsionnyi Polk (Guards Night Bomber Air Regiment, Soviet Union)
GNSS	Global Navigation Satellite System
GPS	Global Positioning System
GSDF	Ground Self-Defense Force
GvNBAP	Guards Night Bomber Aviation Regiment (Soviet Union)
Himmelbett	German radar system for night fighters
hp	horsepower
HQ	headquarters
HSA	Hawker-Siddeley Aircraft
HSD	Hawker-Siddeley Dynamics
HSU	Hero of the Soviet Union
HUD	head-up display
IADS	integrated air defense systems
IAF	Israeli Defense Force/Air Force
IAI	Israel Aircraft Industries
IAK	Istrebitelnyi Aviatsionnyi Korpus (Fighter Air Corps, Soviet Union)
IAP	Istrebitelnyi Aviatsionnyi Polk (Fighter Air Regiment, Soviet Union)
ICBM	intercontinental ballistic missile
IDSCS	Initial Defense Satellite Communications System
IFR	Instrument Flight Rules
IJN	Imperial Japanese Navy
IMAM	Industrie Meccaniche e Aeronautiche Meridionali
IOC	Initial Operational Capability
IQAF	Iraqi Air Force
IR	infrared

IRBM	intermediate-range ballistic missile
ItAF	Italian Air Force
JAAF	Japanese Army Air Force, Imperial
Jagdgeschwader	Luftwaffe fighter wing
Jagdstaffel (Jasta)	Luftwaffe fighter squadron
Jagdverband	Luftwaffe fighter unit
JASDF	Japanese Air Self-Defense Force
JATO	jet-assisted takeoff
JCS	Joint Chiefs of Staff
JNAF	Japanese Naval Air Force, Imperial
JPO	Joint Program Office
JSDF	Japanese Self-Defense Forces
JSF	Joint Strike Fighter
JSOTF	Joint Special Operations Task Force
Kampfgeschwader	Luftwaffe bomber wing
kph	kilometers per hour
Kriegsmarine	German Navy
LAMPS	Light Airborne Multipurpose System
Lichtenstein	type of German airborne radar
LORAN	long-range electronic navigation
LPS	Large Processing Station
LRP	Long-Range Penetration
Luftfahrtruppe	German aviation troops
Luftflotte	Luftwaffe air fleet
Luftstreitkräfte	German Air Service (World War I)
Luftwaffe	German Air Force (World War II)
MAAF	Mediterranean Allied Air Forces
MAAG	Military Assistance Advisory Group Vietnam
MAC	Military Airlift Command
MACV	Military Assistance Command Vietnam
MAD	magnetic airborne detection; mutual assured destruction
MAL	mat-landing
MANPADS	man-portable air defense system
MATS	Military Air Transport Service
MCM	mine countermeasures
MCT	Mobile Communication Terminal
MEO	middle-earth orbit
MGS	Mobile Ground System
MGT	Mobile Ground Terminal
MHz	megahertz
MIDAS	Missile Defense Alarm System
MIRACL	Mid-Infrared Advanced Chemical Laser
MIRV	Multiple Independently Targetable Reentry Vehicle
MIT	Massachusetts Institute of Technology
mm	millimeter
mph	miles per hour
MRBM	medium-range ballistic missiles
MRC	Military Revolutionary Council
MSDF	Maritime Self-Defense Force
MTU	Moteren und Turbine Union
NACA	National Advisory Committee for Aeronautics
NAF	Naval Aircraft Factory
NAP	naval aviation pilot
NASA	National Aeronautics and Space Administration
NASAF	Northwest African Strategic Air Forces
NATO	North Atlantic Treaty Organization
NATS	Naval Air Transport Service
NAVAIDS	aids to navigation.
NAVFE	Naval Forces Far East
NAVSTAR	Navigation Satellite Time and Ranging
NBAP	Night Bomber Aviation Regiment (Soviet Union)
NBS	National Bureau of Standards
NCO	noncommissioned officer
NEACP	National Emergency Airborne Command Post
NIAP	Nochnoi Istrebitel'nyi Aviatsionnyi Polk (Night Fighter Air Regiment, Soviet Union)
NLC	National Leadership Committee
NORAD	North American Air Defense Command
NPT	Nuclear Non-Proliferation Treaty
NRO	National Reconnaissance Office
NSA	National Security Act of 1947; also: National Security Advisor
NSC	National Security Council
NVA	North Vietnamese Army
NVAF	North Vietnamese Air Force
OGS	Overseas Ground Station
ONR	Office of Naval Research
OPEC	Organization of Petroleum Exporting Countries
OSS	Office of Strategic Services
PACAF	Pacific Air Forces
PACOM	Pacific Command
PAF	Pakistan Air Force
PAVN	People's Army of Vietnam (North Vietnamese Army)
PGMs	precision-guided munitions
PLAAF	People's Liberation Army Air Force (Chinese Communist Air Force)
PLSK	Pomonicza Lotnicza S-UBA Kobiet (Auxiliary Women's Air Force Service, Poland)
POL	petroleum, oil, lubricants
POW	prisoner of war
PPI	plan position indicator
PVO	Voiska Protivovozdushnoi Oborony (Antiaircraft Defense Forces, Soviet Union)
PWS	Podlaska Wytwornia Samolotow
PZL	Panstwowe Zaklady Lotnicze (National Aviation Establishments, Poland)
RA	Regia Aeronautica
RAE	Royal Aircraft Establishment
RAF	Royal Air Force
RAND	Research and development think tank
RCAF	Royal Canadian Air Force

REAF Royal Egyptian Air Force
Reichsluftverteidigung Air Defense of Germany
RFC Royal Flying Corps
RGS Relay Ground Station
Riesenflugzeug giant aircraft
RLA Royal Laotian Army
RLM Reich Air Ministry
RN Royal Navy
RNAF Royal Norwegian Air Force
RNAS Royal Naval Air Service
ROC Republic of China
ROE Rules of Engagement
ROTC Reserve Officer Training Corps
rpm revolutions per minute
RTAF Royal Thai Air Force
RVN Republic of Vietnam
RVNAF Republic of Vietnam Air Force
RYAF Royal Yugoslav Air Force
SA selective availability
SAAC Swiss American Aircraft Corporation
SAC Strategic Air Commansd
SAGE Semi-Automatic Ground Environment
SAR search and rescue
SARH semiactive radar-homing
SARTAF Search and Rescue Task Force
SBIRS Space-Based Infrared System
SBS United States Strategic Bombing Survey
Schlachtstaffel Luftwaffe battle flight
Schräge Musik German upward-firing armament
SEAD suppression of enemy air defenses
Seeluftstreitkräfte German naval air force
Seenotdienst Luftwaffe air rescue service
SEP specific excess power
shp shaft horsepower
SIAI Società Idrovolanti Alta Italia
SIGINT signals intelligence
SIOP Single Integrated Operation Plan
SL Schütte-Lanz airship factory
SLBM submarine-launched ballistic missile
SNCA Société Nationale de Constructions Aéronautiques (National Aircraft Building Company)
SOCONY Standard Oil of New York
SOF Special Operations Forces
SPS Simplified Processing Station
SRBM short-range ballistic missile
Staffeln Luftwaffe squadrons
STC Satellite Test Center
STOL short takeoff and landing
SVAF South Vietnamese Air Force
TAC Tactical Air Command
TACAN Tactical Air Navigation
TACC Tactical Air Control Center
TBMs tactical ballistic missiles
TEREC tactical electronic reconnaissance sensor
TFA Task Force Alpha
TOA time-of-arrival
TOW tube-launched, optically tracked, wired-guided missile
TsAGI Tsentral'nyi Aero-Gidrodinamicheskii Institut (Central Aerodynamics and Hydrodynamics Institute, Soviet Union)
UAC United Aircraft Corporation
UATC United Aircraft and Transport Corporation
UAV uninhabited aerial vehicle
UCAV uninhabited combat aerial vehicle
UN United Nations
USA United States Army
USAAC United States Army Air Corps
USAAF United States Army Air Forces
USAF United States Air Force
USAFE United States Air Forces in Europe
USAFFE United States Army Forces Far East
USMA United States Military Academy
USN United States Navy
USSR Union of Soviet Socialist Republics
USTRANSCOM United States Transportation Command
VC Vietcong
VIP very important person
VLF very-low-frequency
VOR Very High Frequency Omnidirectional Radio Station
VORTAC a combination of VOR and TACAN
VSTOL very short takeoff and landing
V/STOL vertical/short takeoff and landing
VTOL vertical takeoff and landing
VVS Vozdushno-voennye Sily (Air Forces, Soviet Union)
WAAF Women's Auxiliary Air Force
WAF Women in the Air Force
WAFS Women's Auxiliary Ferrying Squadron
WASP Women Airforce Service Pilots
WDD Western Development Division
WFTD Woman's Flying Training Detachment
WPB War Production Board
WRAF Women's Royal Air Force
ZAT territorial air zone
ZEL zero-length launcher

AIR WARFARE

An International Encyclopedia

Aces

According to the traditional definition, an "ace" is a fighter pilot who has attained five confirmed kills of enemy aircraft. Though not technically an ace by this standard, World War I French pilot Roland Garros began the tradition of aerial combat with a clever ploy. He devised a means to shield his wooden propeller with metal so a machine gun could shoot through the arc (bullets that hit the blades would ricochet off). In a mere 18 days in early 1915, he shot down three German aircraft and claimed two others. Press reports of his exploits were the first to use the French slang "ace" to mean at least five enemy aircraft downed—although the term soon came to require five or more *confirmed* aircraft shot down. The German word was *kanone,* indicating a star turn; 10 victories were required for that designation.

The French definition of five confirmed became accepted during World War I and reappeared in later wars. The idea of achieving ace status quickly became popular among fliers and the general public. As World War I degenerated into static trench warfare with horrific losses and virtually no glory, the contests among pilots to raise scores achieved considerable public following. The pilots became the heroes whom people needed in a protracted and bitter war. And they were heroes in later wars as well.

The following table lists the highest-ranking aces from several conflicts since 1914. An excellent study by Al Bowers and David Lednicer indicates that there may have been as many as 10,000 aces in at least 27 countries, and some women also became aces.

World War I (1914–1918)

These totals of kills include balloons and aircraft; both were fighter targets. This listing is selective but includes the top aces of the major powers.

Manfred von Richthofen, Germany, 80
Rene Fonck, France, 75
E. C. Mannock, Britain, 73
W. A. Bishop, Britain, 72
Ernst Udet, Germany, 62
R. Collishaw, Canada, 60
J. T. B. McCudden, 57
Georges Guynemer, France, 54
A. W. Beauchamp-Proctor, South Africa, 54
D. R. MacLauren, Canada, 54
Charles Nungesser, France, 45
Godwin Brumowski, Austria-Hungary, 40
Oswald Boelcke, Germany, 40
Willy Coppens, Belgium, 37
Francesco Baracca, Italy, 34
Edward Rickenbacker, U.S., 26

Spanish Civil War (1936–1939)

Many of these pilots later attained even higher scores while fighting World War II; the list below includes the top aces on either side of the civil conflict.

Joaquin García Morato y Castaño, Nationalist, 40
Andres García Lacalle, Republican, 11+

China-Japan-Manchuria (1937–1945)

This theater became part of World War II but was fought over a longer period. The American Volunteer Group (the Flying Tigers) were in action on behalf of China in 1941–1942, totaling 286 confirmed kills. Only the top scorers are listed:

Hiromichi Shinohara, Japan, 58
Mitsuyoshi Tarui, Japan, 28

Kenji Shimada, Japan, 27
Robert Neale, AVG, 16
David Lee Hill, AVG, 12
Liu Chi-Sun, China, 11

Russo-Finnish Wars (1940–1944)

In this sidebar to World War II, Finnish pilots used a mixed bag of aircraft from other nations including obsolete U.S. models with which they did well against the Russians (there is no data for the Russian side of this conflict). No less than 87 Finnish pilots were credited with at least five kills. The top three:

Eino Juutilainen, Finland, 94
Hans Wind, Finland, 78
Eino Luukkanen, Finland, 54

World War II (1939–1945)

Pilots from nations rapidly overrun often were able to join the Allies and thus fight for the war's duration—and run up higher scores. The French allowed pilots to include probable kills, unlike other nations. Russia provided the only female fighter aces—and by the end of the war more than 150 Russian pilots claimed scores of at least 20 (50 had 30 or more). Germany enjoyed more than 100 aces who gained more than 100 victories each (most from the Eastern Front)—and 35 had more than 200 each for the highest counts of aces in any war. Werner Mölders (Germany) was the first ace from any country to exceed 100 kills. Heinz Bär (Germany) became the first jet ace with 16 confirmed victories. Of Japanese pilots, nearly 140 claimed 10 or more victories. Only the top-tier aces from each country are included here.

Erich Hartmann, Germany, 352
Gerhard Barkhorn, Germany, 301
Gunther Rail, Germany, 275
Otto Kittel, Germany, 267
Walter Nowotny, Germany, 258
Hiroyoshi Nishizawa, Japan, 87
Tetsuzo Iwamoto, Japan, 80
Shoichi Sugita, Japan, 70
Saburo Sakai, Japan, 64
Ivan Kozhedub, Russia, 62
Aleksandr Pokryshkin, Russia, 59
Grigori Retchkalov, Russia, 58
Nikolai Gulaev, Russia, 57
Arsenii Vorozheikin, Russia, 52
Marmaduke Pattle, South Africa, 51
Richard Bong, U.S., 40
Thomas McGuire, U.S., 38
John E. Johnson, Britain, 38
David McCampbell, U.S., 34
Brendan Finucane, Ireland, 32
A. G. Malan, South Africa, 32
Franco Lucchini, Italy, 26
Adriano Visconti, Italy, 26
Marcel Albert, France, 23
Jean Demozay, France, 21
Stanislav Skalski, Poland, 21
Witold Urbanowicz, Poland, 20
Sven Heglund, Norway, 16

Korean War (1950–1953)

The Korean War included the first jet-versus-jet combat missions. By the end of the war, nearly 40 pilots flying the F-86 Sabre had become aces. Newly revealed records indicate that the Soviet Union claimed at least 44 aces.

Joseph McConnell Jr., U.S., 16
James Jabara, U.S., 15
Manuel Fernandez, U.S., 14
George A. Davis Jr., U.S., 14
Royal N. Baker, U.S., 13
Nikolay Sutigan, Soviet Union, 21
Evgenii Pepelyaev, Soviet Union, 20
Alexander Smorchkov, Soviet Union, 15
Lev Schukin, Soviet Union, 14
Dmitry Oskin, Soviet Union,15
Nikolay Dokashenko, Soviet Union, 14
Sergey Kramarenko, Soviet Union, 13

Vietnam War (1965–1973)

During the Vietnam War, several aces shot down their enemies using air-to-air missiles rather than gunfire, as in previous wars. The North Vietnamese claimed 17 aces.

Colonel Toon (Tomb), North Vietnam, 13+ (most probably a fictional character)
Nguyen Van Coc, 9
Mai Van Cuong, 8
Phan Thanh Ngan, 8
Nguyen Van Bay, North Vietnam, 7+
Charles DeBellevue, U.S., 6
Richard Ritchie, U.S., 5
Jeffrey Feinstein, U.S., 5
Randy Cunningham, U.S., 5
William Driscoll, U.S., 5
Robin Olds, U.S., 5, plus 12 in World War II (there has been no official confirmation on Olds's fifth victory)

Middle Eastern Wars

Israel has been very secretive about the men who became aces, but recent lists indicate at least 34, with Giorora Avan

(Epstein) leading the list with 17 victories. Egypt claims six aces, Syria five.

Indo-Pakistani Wars

In the Indo-Pakistani conflicts, Pakistan claims two aces, with Mohammad M. Alam having nine victories.

All over the world, scholars are busy reviewing claims, all of which are subject to argument over time. For the most part, the claims were made in good faith, most were confirmed, but in the confusion of battle mistakes were no doubt made.

Christopher H. Sterling

References

Cunningham, Robert. *Aces High.* St. Louis: General Dynamics, 1977.

Harris, John Norman. *Knights of the Air, Canadian Aces of World War I.* Toronto: Macmillan, 1963.

Hess, W. N. *The Allied Aces of World War II.* New York: Arco, 1966.

______. *The American Aces of World War II and Korea.* New York: Arco, 1968.

Robertson, Bruce, ed. *Air Aces of the 1914–1918 War.* London: Harleyford, 1959.

Shores, Christopher. *Fighter Aces.* London: Hamlyn, 1975.

______. *Air Aces.* Novato, CA: Presidio Press, 1983.

Tolliver, Raymond, and Trevor Constable. *Fighter Aces.* New York: Macmillan, 1965.

Acosta, Bertrand B. (1895–1954)

Aviation pioneer. Born in San Diego, California, on 15 January 1895, Bertrand Blanchard "Bert" Acosta taught himself to fly and is thought to have built and flown his first airplane in 1910. He joined the Curtiss School of Aviation at San Diego's North Island as a mechanic in 1914 and became part of the instructional staff in 1915. Acosta spent much of the next two years at the Curtiss school in Ontario, Canada, training pilots for the Royal Flying Corps and the Royal Naval Air Service. After America declared war on Germany in April 1917, Acosta returned to the United States to teach Army pilot candidates at Mineola Field, on Long Island.

Following the war, Acosta helped establish the first airmail routes, took a Junkers transport airplane on a 60-city tour of the United States, and was both speed racer and endurance flier during the golden age of aviation. His contemporaries considered him one of the great natural fliers, and it was said that "he could put wings on a barn door and make it fly." In 1921, Acosta won the Pulitzer Trophy race flying at an average speed of 176.7 mph. According to the 1928 edition of *Who's Who in American Aeronautics,* he was the first American pilot to fly 200 mph.

In April 1927, he established an endurance record with copilot Clarence D. Chamberlin by remaining in the air without refueling for 51 hours. Between 12 and 14 April, Chamberlin and Acosta covered an estimated 4,100 miles, more than 500 miles farther than the distance from New York to Paris. Shortly thereafter, Acosta flew the Atlantic as part of a four-man crew led by the world-famous explorer, Richard E. Byrd. The crew may have reached Paris, but instrument problems and poor weather forced them to double back and ditch the plane in the ocean near the village of Ver-sur-Mer on 1 July 1927. Despite the inglorious finish and losing the transatlantic race to Charles Lindbergh by nearly two months, the crew received great international acclaim.

In November 1937, Acosta went to Spain to fly for the Loyalist cause. Flying obsolete bombers against targets protected by advanced German fighters proved a challenge, and the Acosta fliers did not receive the recognition and reward for their accomplishments they thought they deserved. Disillusioned, Acosta left Spain early in 1938. Poor health seems to have kept him grounded during World War II.

Acosta worked as a carpenter in a Catholic monastery in Garrison, New York, for a time in the early 1950s, and Admiral Byrd paid for Acosta, who was suffering from tuberculosis, to spend the last two years of his life at the Jewish Consumptives' Relief Sanatorium in Denver. Acosta died on 1 September 1954. His obituary in the *New York Times* noted that the veteran flier had been married twice and "was beset with troubles of various kinds throughout most of his adult life." Acosta's memory is perpetuated at the Portal of the Folded Wings, a shrine to early aviators in Los Angeles.

Bruce A. Ashcroft

See also

Curtiss, Glenn Hammond; Junkers Aircraft

References

"Bert Acosta, 59, a Veteran Flier." *New York Times,* 2 September 1954.

"Bertram Blanchard Acosta." In *Who's Who in American Aeronautics.* New York: Aviation, 1928.

Vecsey, George, and George C. Dade. *Getting Off the Ground: The Pioneers of Aviation Speak for Themselves.* New York: E. P. Dutton, 1979.

Ader, Clement (1841–1925)

French aviation pioneer born in Muret who carried out flight experiments in the late nineteenth century. Ader performed a brief, uncontrolled takeoff in one of his machines in 1890. Although ultimately unsuccessful in controlled flight (he claimed to have flown in 1897, but evidence is scarce), he remained interested in military aviation and wrote four books on its potential. The most important of those works was *L'aviation militaire* (1909), intended to teach officers about possible structures for an air force, multiple aircraft functions, and even the potential of an "aircraft carrier boat." (A year later, Eugene Ely performed the first takeoff from a ship.) Lacking the benefit of warfare experience at the turn of the century, few military thinkers initially paid close attention to Ader's published work, although it remains a classic in the development of air war thinking.

Guillaume de Syon

References

Carlier, Claude. *L'affaire Clément Ader.* Paris: Perrin, 1990.

Gibbs Smith, Charles. *Clément Ader.* London: HMSO, 1967.

Lissarague, Pierre. *Clément Ader inventeur d'avions.* Paris: Privat, 1990.

Aerial Radio Navigation

Originated from Guglielmo Marconi's techniques of wireless telegraphy. Initially termed "wireless direction finding," aerial navigation has evolved from simple electronic devices and lighted airways to a sophisticated satellite system capable of determining the position of an aircraft to within a few feet. Navigational aids today are known by the generic acronym NAVAIDS.

The first attempts at ground-based aerial electronic navigation were German navy Zeppelins using a Telefunken compass. These terrestrially based navigation aids, or "rotating beacons," were used to guide the Zeppelins on their bombing raids to England. The Zeppelin's radio operator could determine the craft's position by triangulating between two or more ground stations. Although this technique worked well with the slow-moving Zeppelins, it proved impractical for faster, smaller aircraft.

In 1908, the U.S. National Bureau of Standards (NBS) began collaborating with both the U.S. Navy and U.S. Army on radio research, and by the beginning of World War I the NBS had become the focal point for studying communications and navigation technologies.

In July 1918, the U.S. Post Office approached the NBS for assistance in developing an electronic aeronautical navigation device for use in the newly formed Air Mail Service. But in 1921, the Post Office was forced to abandon its research because of budget cuts and renewed pressure to begin a transcontinental airmail service. Second Assistant Postmaster Otto Praeger now turned to the U.S. Army, which had earlier experimented with a system of towered, rotating lights for guiding pilots. This was the genesis of the lighted airway, and through the efforts of the Post Office it soon became the foundation for the first commercial airways.

The lighted airways worked well—but only in good weather. Although the Post Office focused its resources in the lighted airway system, it again began limited research in electronic NAVAIDS in 1925. The limited federal budget of 1925 continued to hinder the efforts of not only the Post Office but also the Army and the NBS as well. If air transport operations were limited to lighted airways that could be used only when the weather was good, then precise navigation required to support all-weather high-altitude flight would be impossible.

With Congress's passage of the Air Commerce Act of 1926, responsibility for the promotion of aviation, as well as the construction of an infrastructure to support all-weather flights, fell to the newly formed Bureau of Air Commerce within the Department of Commerce. The new law also charged the NBS with responsibility for the research and development of NAVAIDS. The earlier efforts of the Post Office, army, and NBS thus had laid the groundwork for the Low Frequency Radio Range, marker beacon, nondirectional beacon, and instrument landing system. A now properly funded NBS soon moved these NAVAIDS from the laboratory to a system of four-course, Low Frequency Radio Ranges that supported instrument flight.

The NBS continued to improve the Low Frequency Radio Ranges and through research overcame inherent problems such as night effect (the tendency for the signal to "wander" during night operations), as well as interference from other stations.

Continued research and development perfected the instrument landing system. Begun in the early 1930s, this system was in wide use after World War II. Problems associated with low-frequency navigation aids were soon overcome by developing NAVAIDS that broadcast on higher frequencies. The NBS was able to develop and begin fielding the Very High Frequency Omnidirectional Range Station (VOR) during the late 1940s. The VOR was a marked improvement over the Low Frequency Radio Ranges because it enabled pilots to select specific courses to or from navigation stations while overcoming problems associated with the Low Frequency Radio Ranges. The VOR and its military version (known as TACAN, for Tactical Air Navigation), as well as the hybrid system known as VORTAC have become the mainstay of aerial navigation in the United States and the world.

Randy Johnson

References

Johnson, Randy. "Herbert Hoover and the Aeronautical Telecommunications System: His Influence on Its Development and Deployment, as Secretary of Commerce." Ph.D. diss., Ohio University, 1999.

Keen, R. *Wireless Direction Finding,* 3rd ed. London: Iliffe and Sons Limited, 1938.

Komons, Nick A. *Bonfires to Beacons: Federal Civil Aviation Policy under the Air Commerce Act, 1926–1938.* Washington, DC: U.S. Government Printing Office, 1978.

Leary, William M. *Aerial Pioneers: The U.S. Air Mail Service, 1918–1927.* Washington, DC: Smithsonian Institution Press, 1985.
Snyder, Wilbert F., and Bragaw, Charles L. *Achievement in Radio: Seventy Years of Radio Science, Technology, Standards, and Measurement at the National Bureau of Standards.* Washington, DC: U.S. Government Printing Office, 1986.

Aerial Refueling

A tactic employed to extend the range, endurance, and payload of aircraft. Various stunts were performed in the United States in the 1920s to demonstrate aerial refueling's potential, and experiments by the RAF in the 1930s proved its feasibility. Aerial refueling was studied in World War II, but aircraft capabilities met wartime requirements. The Cold War prodded this technique into reality. U.S. bombers needed aerial refueling to reach targets around the world. Frequent demonstrations of this capability took place as the Strategic Air Command stood alert against Soviet forces.

The first aerial refueling system, developed in Britain by Sir Alan Cobham, utilized a hose and grapnel. The tanker and receiver aircraft rendezvoused with lines extended. Using the grapnels to hook the line and reel it in, the receiver could accept fuel. However, this required the receiver crew to retrieve the line and make the connections.

Single-seat aircraft became refuelable with the development of the probe-and-drogue system in 1949. The tanker would trail a hose while flying ahead of the receiver. The receiver, with a probe mounted on a wing or on the aircraft nose, would fly close enough to the tanker's hose to make contact. The connection was facilitated by a drogue—a basket to catch the probe—funneling it into the nozzle. This system remains the most popular worldwide, used by the U.S. Navy, Marines, NATO, and most air forces.

The U.S. Air Force uses the Boeing flying boom. This telescoping tube, affixed to the tanker's aft body, is used to mate the tanker and receiver. It transfers fuel much faster than the probe-and-drogue setup. General Curtis LeMay deemed this essential for refueling large aircraft, such as the B-52 bomber. Thus, the KC-135, with its flying boom, was selected in 1955 as the USAF's primary tanker. It remains in service today. Virtually all USAF strategic airlifters are air-refuelable. This global-reach capability enhances U.S. ability to project power worldwide.

The first combat air refueling took place on 6 July 1951, when a USAF KB-29 linked up with a flight of RF-80s over Korea. Refueling greatly extended the range of Japan-based fighters and reconnaissance aircraft in both Korea and Vietnam. Perhaps the most dramatic uses of aerial refueling have occurred in long-range strike missions. During the Vietnam War, aerial refueling enabled bombers based on Guam to hit targets in Vietnam. In the Falklands War, Vulcan tankers refueled bombers on transatlantic missions. U.S. bombing raids against Libya, Iraq, and Serbia launched from Britain and the United States would have been impossible without multiple aerial refuelings.

Aerial refueling is a force extender and a force multiplier. The U.S. deployment for the Gulf War, as well as later peacekeeping and contingency operations, were accelerated by the ability to move fighters and cargo aircraft rapidly using aerial refueling. Whether expediting humanitarian aid, providing loiter time to combat air patrols, or supporting strike missions halfway across the globe, aerial refueling has proven an invaluable resource.

Thirteen nations have this capability: Canada, China, France, Israel, Italy, Netherlands, Russia, Saudi Arabia, Singapore, Spain, Turkey, United Kingdom, and United States.

James M. Pfaff

References

Byrd, Vernon B. *Passing Gas: The History of Inflight Refueling.* Chico, CA: Byrd, 1994.
Hopkins, Robert S. III. *Boeing KC-135 Stratotanker.* Leicester, UK: Midland Counties, 1997.
Lloyd, Alwyn T. *KC-135 Stratotanker.* Waukesha, WI: Kalmbach, 1994.

Aerial Torpedoes

The world's first precision-guided munitions. As early as April 1915, Elmer Sperry began developing unmanned flying bombs by combining his company's research on sea torpedoes and automatic flight control systems. Following the U.S. entry into World War I in 1917, Sperry received navy funding to accelerate development of his aerial torpedo—a remote-controlled aircraft for use against submarines. Employing gyroscopes for directional control, the world's first cruise missile flew approximately one-half mile without a human pilot on 6 March 1918. However, the early aerial torpedoes were crude and unreliable, resulting in cancellation of the Sperry project in January 1919. Thereafter, the navy's interest in aerial torpedoes shifted to torpedo-bombers.

During the interwar years, the U.S. Army contracted with Elmer's son Lawrence Sperry to continue its own wartime aerial torpedo project, the "Kettering Bug." By the early 1920s, an improved torpedo was making successful flights, but continuing problems with directional control forced Sperry to incorporate radio control for increased accuracy. In March 1922, a torpedo flew 63 miles and scored a direct hit on its target, but this success required 18 radio corrections from a chase aircraft.

General William "Billy" Mitchell was among the first Army Air Service officers to enthusiastically support the development of aerial torpedoes. In 1927, he foresaw the potential threat such weapons posed to England, and his 1930 book *Skyways* argued that offensive airpower would continue its advantage over ground and air defenses, as future bombers might launch aerial torpedoes from 100 miles away. However, insufficient funds led General Henry "Hap" Arnold to cancel the project in 1932 in favor of precision bombsight development and the emerging doctrine of daylight precision strategic bombing.

Paul G. Gillespie

See also

Precision-Guided Munitions

References

McFarland, Stephen F. *America's Pursuit of Precision Bombing, 1910–1945.* Washington, DC: Smithsonian Institution Press, 1995.

Aeritalia

Italian aerospace industry formed in November 1969 by merging the private Fiat airframe business with the government-owned Aerfer (descended from Industrie Meccaniche e Aeronautiche Meridionali, or IMAM) and Salmoiraghi (a Milan instruments manufacturer); in 1976, Fiat sold its 50 percent share to IRI-Finmeccanica, which became sole owner. Because for decades Aeritalia had been the cable address of Fiat's Aeronautica d'Italia, the name had a significant history, but it also reflected the mandate to become the national industry leader. The company pursued a policy of international collaboration, as well as investment in the underdeveloped area of southern Italy.

In addition to building the F-104S fighter and G.91Y ground attack aircraft, the Turin combat aircraft division participated in the design and production of the Panavia Tornado and the early stages of Eurofighter development. Transport aircraft activity was concentrated in Naples, adding manufacture of the G.222 tactical airlifter (1970) to that of Douglas airliner structures inherited from Aerfer. Aeritalia joined the Boeing 767 program at inception, and in 1980 it formed (with Aérospatiale) a consortium to design and build the ATR turboprop commuter. The year 1981 proved crucial, bringing the first profits, acquisitions (conversion specialist Aeronavali, light aircraft manufacturer Partenavia, shareholdings in Aermacchi and RPV specialist Meteor), and the launch of the AMX attack aircraft, an Italian-Brazilian project that also involved Aermacchi and Embraer. In 1985, Aeritalia acquired aero-engine manufacturer Alfa Romeo Avio and, later, a 40 percent share in Piaggio.

A turning point in the gradual development of the Aeritalia space business was the European Space Agency's Spacelab, flown on STS-9 *Columbia* in November 1983. This led to work on other modules, including the U.S. Spacelab and European *Columbus.* In the launcher field, Aeritalia built the structures of the Alfa rocket for the Italian Ministry of Defense and then the liquid propellant tanks for Europe's Ariane missile. The company also built numerous satellites.

In December 1990, IRI-Finmeccanica merged Aeritalia with its radar and missile industry, Selenia, forming Alenia.

Gregory Alegi

See also

Aermacchi; Alenia; Breda; Eurofighter Typhoon; Fiat; Lockheed F-104 "Starfighter"; Panavia Tornado

References

Catalanotto, Baldassare, and Cesare Falessi. *1969–1989: Twenty Years of Aeritalia.* Milan: Scheiwiller, 1989.
Gianvanni, Paolo. *AMX.* Florence, Italy: EDAI, 1999.

Aermacchi

Oldest Italian aircraft manufacturer in continuous existence. The company was founded as Nieuport-Macchi on 1 May 1913, after Giulio Macchi (1866–1935) and his French partners had already built their first aircraft for an Italian army competition.

In World War I, Nieuport-Macchi supplied one-fifth of all aircraft built in Italy, including the vast majority of fighters; indeed, it was an Ni.11 that on 7 April 1916 scored the first Italian air-to-air victory. After building the Ni.17, the company switched to the Hanriot HD.1, the standard Italian fighter at the time of the Armistice. In May 1915, Nieuport-Macchi was asked to copy a captured Lohner flying boat. This led to the establishment of a seaplane department, which quickly acquired autonomous design capabilities, immediately identified as "Macchi" types and epitomized by the M.5 (1916), the most widely produced flying-boat fighter of all time and the first that could best landplane fighters. Its successor, the M.7 (1918), would serve for 20 years.

Reflecting its maturity, the company in April 1924 became Aeronautica Macchi. By then, Mario Castoldi (1888–1968) had joined as chief designer. In the lean postwar years, Macchi employed around 200 people and lived on license production and small batches of its M.18 and M.24 military seaplanes. Invited to design the Italian competitor for the 1926 Schneider Trophy race, Macchi and Castoldi produced the winning M.39. Its M.52 (1927) and M.67

(1929) descendants were unsuccessful, but the C.72 (1931) broke the world speed record in 1934.

Macchi built some SIAI S.81 and S.79 bombers under license, in part at its new AUSA subsidiary, but the racing experience and the chairmanship of Paolo Foresio (1900–1980) had transformed it, as the 1936 fighter competition proved. The Fiat G.50 was already in production, but the C.200 (1937) was so superior that the Regia Aeronautica (the Italian air force) was forced to order it. Together with the C.202 (1940) and C.205 (1942) variants with German inline engines, and including those built under license by Breda and SAI Ambrosini, production ran to 2,600 aircraft, or one-fourth of the entire Italian World War II output.

In 1945, Castoldi was succeeded by Ermanno Bazzocchi (b. 1914). After some difficult years, Macchi settled upon a mix of license production (D.H. 100 Vampire jets, Fokker S.11 trainers, Lockheed CL-401s), overhauls (T-33s), and original designs. These included the MB.308 sportplane (1947) and especially the MB.326 jet trainer (1957), which would become the all-time Italian aviation export success and the first jet built in South Africa and Brazil, in addition to Australia. Its MB.339 derivative (1976) was adopted by the Italian air force, equipping (among other units) the Frecce Tricolori display team. It was sold in seven countries but lost the U.S. J-PATS competition it had entered in association with Lockheed.

In 1980, Aeronautica Macchi became the parent company of the new Aermacchi manufacturing subsidiary, a share in which was acquired by Aeritalia, then a partner in the Italian-Brazilian AMX attack aircraft program, which proved disappointing. To diversify, Aermacchi joined the Dornier Do.328 commuter program. In 1996, Aermacchi obtained from Agusta the SIAI Marchetti SF.260 and S.211 single-engine trainers, completing its range with the M-290 RediGO acquired from Valmet of Finland. Production was moved to Venegono airfield and the original Varese factory was sold. Aermacchi teamed with Yakovlev of Russia on a joint advanced trainer program but, after the experimental phase, decided to develop its own M-346.

In fall 2000, the Foresio family was negotiating the sale of its 75 percent share to Finmeccanica, the parent company of Alenia Aerospazio, with the stated purpose of making Aermacchi the training aircraft division of EADS, or the European Aeronautical Defense Systems. By 2002, these plans were on hold.

Gregory Alegi

See also

Aeritalia; Agusta; Alenia; Italian Air Force; Italian Aircraft Development; Regia Aeronautica (Pre–World War II); Regia Aeronautica (World War II); SIAI Marchetti

References

Alegi, Gregory. *Macchi M.5.* Berkhamsted, UK: Albatros, 2001.
Apostolo, Giorgio. *Aermacchi: From Nieuports to AMX.* Milan, Italy: GAE, 1991.

Aeroflot

Created by the Soviet Union as an instrument of national policy to provide affordable public transport for people and materials throughout the vast expanses of the Soviet empire; in this objective, it succeeded. In the course of steady expansion, after the teething troubles of the early years had been overcome, it became the largest airline in the world. Its domestic route network stretched across no less than 11 time zones—almost halfway round the globe.

Even before World War I (1914–1918), Russian aeronautical science was well advanced. With the Treaty of Rapallo, signed on 16 April 1922, the Soviets were able to take advantage of German technology. Junkers aircraft were assembled in Moscow, and a semblance of an air network took root.

On 1 May 1922, a joint Soviet-German airline, Deruluft, began services directly from Berlin to Moscow, using Fokker-Grulich F.III monoplanes. From 1 August to 25 September, flights were made between Moscow and Nizhne Novgorod by some Junkers F.13s on the occasion of the annual fair in the latter city.

On 9 February 1923, a national airline was organized when, by decree, the Red Air Force's Glavvozdykhoflot was charged with the establishment of an airline. The responsibility was soon transferred to Dobrolet (the All-Russian Volunteer Air Fleet), the direct ancestor of Aeroflot. The first scheduled services were on intercity routes in the soon-to-be-established Soviet socialist republics in Central Asia.

Dobrolet began to build a national network of air routes. In 1929, it had started air mail service from Moscow to Irkutsk, in central Siberia, a distance of almost 3,000 miles, followed by full passenger service in 1931. In 1930, Dobrolet took over the southern lines from Moscow to the Black Sea and the Caspian from Ukrvozdukhput, the Ukrainian airline based in Kharkov, which had started service in 1923. In the same year, it opened another isolated route in the Far East, as a branch from Khabarovsk, on the Trans-Siberian Railway, to Aleksandrovsk, on the island of Sakhalin. A link with Central Asia had been forged with a route from Moscow to Tashkent. Standard equipment at this time was the eight-seat Kalinin K-5, which had a marked resemblance to the Dornier Merkur.

By the early 1930s, the Soviet aircraft industry was beginning to establish itself. In July 1929, Mikhail Gromov (as revered in Russia as Lindbergh was in the United States) made his second goodwill tour of Europe with the ANT-9 Krylya Sovyetov (Wings of the Soviets).

In 1932, the Soviet Union consolidated its airline industry. Dobrolet became Aeroflot, which completed the trans-Siberian route in 1933, following the line of the famous railway but making the Moscow-Pacific journey in about three days instead of two weeks. By 1934, the airline had dispensed with foreign aircraft as Andrei Tupolev, preeminent among Russian designers, began to create workmanlike machines that did not break records but were adequate for the challenging task of coping with the Siberian climate. The four-engine ANT-6 was put into service with Aviaarktika, founded in 1930 specifically to develop aviation in the Arctic.

In June 1937, the single-engine Tupolev ANT-25 was used by Valery Chkalov and his crew, who flew nonstop over the North Pole from Moscow to Vancouver, Washington; a month later, not to be outdone, Gromov flew nonstop from Moscow to San Jacinto, California.

By 1940, the year the Soviet Union entered World War II, Aeroflot's route map was impressive, with many routes radiating from Moscow to link all Soviet major cities and industrial areas and venturing to a few points in eastern Europe. It had also taken over Deruluft, the jointly owned German-Soviet airline that since 1922 (following the signing of the Treaty of Rapallo) had linked Berlin with Moscow and St. Petersburg; ANT-9s were serving neutral Stockholm.

The wartime years saw the introduction of the ubiquitous Douglas DC-3, more than 6,000 of which were built under license as the Lisunov Li-2 in Tashkent.

The early postwar years saw a gradual recovery to peacetime conditions. Aeroflot did its best using indigenous designs and, rather like the British, had to start almost from scratch, as the war effort had demanded full concentration on military types. Two fine aircraft designers joined Andrei Tupolev in the commercial field. Sergei Ilyushin saw his Convair 240–like, 18-seat Ilyushin Il-12 go into service in 1946, with the improved 32-seat Il-14 following in 1954.

Another unheralded success was the Polikarpov U-2, a versatile performer, beloved among Soviet airmen as a trainer (rather like the U.S. Piper Cub or the British Tiger Moth) and used selectively by Aeroflot. One of the most versatile Aeroflot aircraft was the Antonov An-2, which made its first flight on 31 August 1947. This 12-seat biplane was at home on wheels, floats, or skis, could land and take off in about 100 meters, and was used by the thousands all over the Soviet Union, serving hundreds of communities from the Baltic Sea to the Bering Strait. Total production exceeded 20,000.

Aeroflot struggled along with the Il-14 as its flagship until the Soviet aircraft industry took the world by surprise on 22 March 1956, when a government delegation flew into London in a 50-seat Tupolev Tu-104 jet airliner. It entered service with Aeroflot on 15 September of that year, on the Moscow-Omsk-Irkutsk route, cutting the time from 18 hours to seven, and took its place in history as the first sustained airline jet service in the world.

The Soviet aircraft manufacturing industry shifted into high gear in 1957. The Ilyushin Il-18, the giant Tupolev Tu-114, and the Antonov An-10, all four-engined turboprops, entered service in that year. Aeroflot deployed them everywhere, and quite a few were exported. The An-10 became the standard equipment for the Arctic regions and started a Great Circle route from Moscow to Khabarovsk, via northern Siberia, in August 1960. In a similar way, Andrei Tupolev's Tu-114 was remarkable, being for several years the largest and longest-range airliner in the world. It was also the first Soviet-built airliner to be operated by a noncommunist airline, when Japan Air Lines used it for its Tokyo-Moscow service.

The Soviet solution to the long-range airliner was the Ilyushin Il-62, which was modeled on the British Vickers VC-10 and entered domestic service on 10 March 1967 and international service (to Canada) on 15 September. The direct Moscow–New York route, via Shannon and Gander, opened on 15 July 1968, and Aeroflot began to reach across the globe. Measured by passenger-kilometers flown, it was now, by a considerable margin, the largest airline in the world.

During the latter decades of the twentieth century, Aeroflot took its place among the flag-carrier airlines of the world and acquitted itself well. Its reputation for elegant service was not up to the standards of Western airlines, but Aeroflot's safety record, based on statistics rather than perception, was no worse than those of many Western airlines. The pilots and aircrews were proud and competent. They had to be: The airfields in Siberia were often potholed, and navigational aids across the endless taiga and tundra were few and far between.

Under the communist system, Aeroflot had no competition within the Soviet Union. It was the state airline, and so it enjoyed a monopoly as the transportation service of the entire country, and its aircraft provided all kinds of aerial work: crop-spraying, forestry and fishing patrols, ambulance and emergency services, and support in building oil pipelines, power lines, and railroads. Additionally, it was the air transport service for the Soviet armed forces, its role ranging from special flights for top brass to the transport of political prisoners to the labor camps of the Gulag.

By 1990, its route network was enormous. Almost 2,000 small communities in the Soviet Union were served by the ubiquitous An-2, backed up by the Czech Let L410 19-seat turboprop and the 32-seat Yakovlev Yak-40 trijet feederliner. Antonov An-24 twin turboprops were to be seen everywhere. On the main routes, Il-14s and Tu-104s had been replaced by 700 Tupolev Tu-134 twinjets and more than 1,000 Tu-154 trijets, the Soviet equivalents of the Douglas DC-9 and the Boeing 727, respectively. Aeroflot helicopters, ranging from the eight-seat Mil Mi-4 to the huge Mil Mi-26, with a payload of 20 tons, performed work of all kinds, from airlifts of electricity transmission towers to passenger service into remote Arctic villages where no airfields existed. Its freighter aircraft included the massive Antonov An-124, whose immense fuselage could swallow a Lockheed C-5A. Its wide-bodied 350-seat Ilyushin Il-86 passenger flagship had the unique convenience of a lower-level baggage compartment, enabling passengers to board and disembark far more quickly than on other jumbo jets. By 1991, when the transition from Soviet Union to the Commonwealth of Independent States took place, Aeroflot had almost 11,000 aircraft, including 3,000 An-2s and 3,400 helicopters. Staff numbers exceeded 600,000.

With the dissolution of the Soviet Union in 1991, the all-embracing Aeroflot was dismantled. Its assets in aircraft, installations, and staff were distributed among 32 local regions, and new, independent airlines were created in its place. Its fleet now reduced to 103 airliners, the aging giant was reduced to a shadow, retaining responsibility only for overseas and foreign routes. Relieved of the obligation to use Soviet-built (now Russian or Ukrainian) aircraft, Aeroflot turned to the West for more efficient equipment. On 24 January 1990, it confirmed an order for Airbus A310s. Service standards have visibly improved, and its safety record is no longer questioned. As it enters the twenty-first century, Aeroflot is now the aerial standard-bearer of the new Russia, a respected member of the worldwide fraternity of airlines.

R.E.G. Davies

See also

Tupolev Aircraft

References

Davies, R.E.G. *A History of the World's Airlines.* London: Oxford University Press, 1964.

Aeronautica Nazionale Repubblicana (ANR)

Italian air service during World War II. After the Italian armistice in World War II, Germany formed the Repubblica Sociale Italiana (RSI; the Italian Social Republic) in territory still under Nazi control and reinstalled Mussolini as leader. The respected Colonel Ernesto Botto was appointed undersecretary for aeronautics of the unified Ministry of National Defense (later changed to Ministry of Armed Forces) and set out to form the Aeronautica Repubblicana (AR; the Republican Air Force). Many rallied to Botto's radio appeals to defend Italian skies, and manpower eventually rose to 15,000, including nonfliers who often joined solely to support their families or escape deportation to Germany. Eventually, the Germans allowed Botto to form, for each specialty, a group consisting of three operational squadrons and one training squadron, a communications regiment, an antiaircraft artillery organization, and a parachute regiment. In reality, the AR formed two fighter groups (which went into action against Allied bombers in January and April 1944), a torpedo-bomber group (March 1944), and a transport group (April 1944, which operated solely in Finland). Paratroopers fought as infantry on the Anzio front, but other flying units never became operational.

The AR operated gallantly under Luftflotte 2 (Second Air Force) control, albeit its effectiveness was limited by resources and the Nazis' grip on Italian industry, facilities, and manpower. Further problems arose from fascist attempts to politicize the AR, which caused Botto to resign in March 1944. He was replaced by General Arrigo Tessari, who obtained some Messerschmitt Bf 109 fighters from the Germans but was unable to change the Nazis' hostility. June 1944 saw the AR strike Gibraltar from southern France and change its name to the Aeronautica Nazionale (National) Repubblicana, but in August 1944 Luftflotte 2 attempted to incorporate it forcibly. When the Italians refused to swear oaths to Hitler and wear German uniforms, Mussolini interceded with Hitler, and Operation PHÖNIX was canceled.

Tessari was sacked with those who had assisted the Germans, and his place was taken by General Ruggero Bonomi. Unfortunately, the ANR had been gutted, and it was only in November 1944 that the 2d Fighter Group returned to combat, followed by the 1st Fighter Group in February 1945. Despite heavy losses, the two units fought until mid-April. The ANR disbanded or surrendered to the Allies in an orderly fashion, but on 29 April the 1st Fighter Group's beloved commander, Major Adriano Visconti, was summarily executed by communist partisans and instantly became a hero-martyr. All other ANR personnel were expelled from the Italian armed forces; some were readmitted during the Cold War.

Gregory Alegi

References

Alegi, Gregory. "La Legione che non fu mai." *Storia Contemporanea* 33, 6 (December 1992).

Beale, N., F. D'Amico, and G. Valentini. *Air War Italy.* Shrewsbury, UK: Airlife, 1996.

Brookes, Andrew. *Air War over Italy.* Shepperton, UK: Ian Allan, 2000.

D'Amico, Ferdinando, and Gabriele Valentini. *Regia Aeronautica.* Vol. 2. Carrolton, TX: Squadron/Signal, 1986.

Aeronautical Research Establishments

As politicians, military officials, and industrialists came to recognize the potential utility of airpower, aeronautical research establishments rose to advance aviation research and development. Large, well-financed research facilities were launched in most European nations and the United States as the military, industry, and academy converged to promote inquiry on the problems of flight.

France and Germany were early proponents of airpower. France centered aeronautical research first at the Aviation Science Institute, Athena Coustenis Observatorie, Meudon, and later at a special laboratory beneath the Eiffel Tower. In 1912, the German government and industry organized the German Aviation Fund to raise money for military aircraft. This fund supplied partial funding for the German Research Institute for Aviation, a civilian agency created as a central conduit for aeronautical investigation. This institute performed technical inquiries for the military and industry—though its civilian emphasis eroded as World War I approached. In 1916, the German War Ministry drew up plans for an extensive aeronautical research facility at Rechlin on Muritz Lake. In 1918, Rechlin became the chief aeronautical experiment station and testing site for the German Army. The Treaty of Versailles forbade Germany an air force, but testing and research continued at Rechlin under the auspices of the Rapallo Treaty. When Hitler created the Luftwaffe in 1935, Rechlin became the chief experimental facility for the Reich Air Ministry. Rechlin continued in this capacity throughout the 1930s and World War II, contributing much to the development of the Luftwaffe. Badly bombed in the final days of the war, Rechlin's once extensive facilities were virtually wiped out at war's end. Today an aeronautical museum sits on the site.

The United States and Great Britain followed their French and German counterparts in building aeronautical research establishments. Aviation inquiry in the United States received impetus in 1915 when Congress established the National Advisory Committee for Aeronautics (NACA) to correct America's deficiencies in aviation. NACA's enabling legislation offered the possibility of an aeronautical research laboratory, and in 1916 Congress appropriated $85,000 for that purpose. In 1920, Langley Memorial Aeronautical Laboratory, NACA's first research facility, was formally dedicated. Langley allowed NACA to abandon its previous policymaking role and concentrate on research. NACA expanded Langley's facilities and subsequently opened two additional laboratories: the Ames Aeronautical Laboratory and the Flight Propulsion Research Laboratory.

Britain's interest in airpower began as early as 1892, when the War Office created a balloon factory to design and build dirigibles. As interest in dirigibles waned, the factory changed its emphasis and, after moving to Farnborough in 1912, became the Royal Aircraft Factory. In 1916, the British government decided to transfer design and manufacture of aircraft to industry, confining Farnborough to research. In 1918, the War Ministry renamed it the Royal Aircraft Establishment (RAE) to avoid confusion with RAF, the acronym for the Royal Air Force. The RAE would remain Britain's chief aeronautical research facility for the reminder of the century.

In the space age, research establishments have continued to explore new frontiers in flight. France has centered its research at the Office National d'Etudes et de Recherches Aerospatiales, a public institution responsible to the French Ministry of Defense. In reunified Germany, the German Aerospace Center has sustained a long tradition of aviation research and development. The U.S. National Aeronautics and Space Administration (NASA), NACA's successor, has expanded research at Langley, Ames, and other research facilities around the country. The establishment at Farnborough has undergone various name changes in response to developments and changing research agendas. In 1988, it became the Royal Aerospace Establishment; in 1991, the Defense Research Agency; and in 1995, the Defense Evaluation and Research Agency. Farnborough retained its military emphasis throughout the years, but in the wake of declining military research in the late 1990s the Labor Government decided to divest itself of the facility and shift it to civilian purposes—a move that drew the ire of the Conservative Party and press. The Ministry of Defense selected TAG Aviation to operate the facility when it shifted from military to civilian operations in 2001.

Daniel E. Worthington

See also

Balloons; British Aerospace; German Air Force (Luftwaffe); National Advisory Committee for Aeronautics; National Aeronautics and Space Administration; Wind Tunnels; World War I Aviation; World War II Aviation

References

Gray, George W. *Frontiers of Flight: The Story of NACA Research.* New York: Knopf, 1948.

Morrow, John H. Jr. *Building German Airpower, 1909–1914.* Knoxville: University of Tennessee Press, 1976.

———. *Great War in the Air: Military Aviation from 1909 to 1921.* Washington, DC: Smithsonian Institution Press, 1993.

Schultz, James. *Winds of Change: Expanding the Frontiers of Flight: Langley Research Center's 75 Years of Accomplishment, 1917–1992.* Washington, DC: National Aeronautics and Space Administration, 1992.

Afghanistan War (1978–1992)

The 1978–1992 war started after Afghan communists took power in April 1978 and established the Democratic Republic of Afghanistan (DRA). The air force—organized and equipped along Soviet lines since the 1950s—failed to defeat widespread Islamic guerrillas supported by Pakistan and, eventually, the United States.

In 1979, the Soviets sent advisers and helicopters to help the DRA. In December 1979, the Soviets invaded Afghanistan, making extensive use of transport aircraft to airlift forces, replacing failed communist leaders with a pro-Moscow leader. Strong Soviet ground and air forces were then involved in a bitter guerrilla war from 1979 to 1989.

Soviet and DRA helicopters proved vital for air assaults, tactical mobility, and firepower. Much use was made of fighter-bombers, creating immense refugee flows, plus high-altitude bombing by strategic bombers and converted transports. Transport aircraft provided resupply from the Soviet Union.

The Afghan resistance had minimal air defenses until extensive aid arrived from the United States (and other friendly countries). One stronghold, the Panjshir Valley, was defended by only 13 heavy machine guns in 1982 but more than 200 by 1984. The resistance had no aircraft. The only air combat occurred during Soviet and DRA air strikes on proresistance Pakistani forces during 1984–1987. Twelve aircraft were shot down by Pakistan. One Pakistani F-16 was lost to friendly fire. The resistance had a few Soviet-designed SA-7 man-portable SAMs until 1986. Then, U.S.-designed Stinger SAMs were supplied. Although high Stinger claims were not borne out postwar, its dozens of kills still had a tremendous impact.

Political change in the Soviet Union led to withdrawal of combat forces in 1989. Soviet combat losses for 1979–1989 were 118 airplanes and 333 helicopters, the DRA 111 airplanes and 160 helicopters. In 1989, the Afghan air force that the Soviets had built up helped repulse resistance attacks, especially at Jalalabad. They were supported by a large-scale Soviet resupply airlift, which continued until the end of 1991. The pro-Moscow regime fell in April 1992.

David C. Isby

See also

Counterinsurgency Operations; Mil Aircraft

References

Isby, David C. *War in a Distant Country.* London: Arms and Armour, 1989.

Urban, Mark. *War in Afghanistan,* 2nd ed. London: Macmillan, 1990.

Youssaf, Mohammed, and Mark Adkin. *The Bear Trap.* London: Leo Cooper, 1992.

Agusta

Italian helicopter manufacturer. Giovanni Agusta (1879–1927) flew a biplane glider in Capua in 1910. A foreman and inspector with Caproni during World War I, after the Armistice Agusta established in Libya an aircraft overhaul business (although the firm was incorporated only in May 1953). Returning to Italy, in 1924 Agusta built a hangar at Cascina Costa (near Varese) on land leased from the Regia Aeronautica (the Italian air force). Activity focused on maintenance and the manufacture of spares, but several motorglider prototypes were built. The first series production was an order for Romano Ro.41 biplanes under license, the company's first series production. In World War II Agusta continued to overhaul aircraft and build Ro.41 and Avia FL.3 trainers.

In 1952, Agusta agreed to build the Bell 47 helicopter under license. The first Agusta-Bell (AB) 47 flew in May 1954 and was followed by more than 1,000 production models. Large quantities of the entire Bell range were built, including the AB.204, .205, .206, .212, and .412. Augusta production included the Sikorsky H-3/S-61 family and the Boeing CH-47.

To cope with demand, the firm subcontracted airframe work to neighboring SIAI Marchetti, which Agusta bought in 1973. Agusta gradually established its design capability, and after some experimental types, the advanced A.109 (1971) was put into production, some 700 being built by 2001. At its 1985 peak, Agusta employed about 10,000 people in three divisions—helicopters (accounting for 76 percent of sales), airplanes (21 percent), and aerospace systems (2 percent).

Agusta was acquired in 2001 by IRI-Finmeccanica, cutting its workforce to 6,000. Agusta launched the BA.609 tiltrotor and AB.139 tactical helicopter with Bell. A merger with Westland was announced in summer 2000 and received antitrust approval in November.

Gregory Alegi

See also

Bell Aircraft; Boeing-Vertol CH-47 "Chinook"; Breda; Caproni Aircraft; Helicopters, Military Use; SIAI Marchetti

References

Donald, David, and Jon Lake, eds. *Encyclopedia of World Military Aircraft.* London: Aerospace, 1996.

Aichi Aircraft

Aichi Tokei Denki K.K. (Aichi Clock and Electric Company Ltd.), the fourth largest aircraft manufacturer in Japan during World War II. Aichi entered into the industry in 1920 when it began making airframes and expanded in 1927 when Aichi began building engines.

Aichi had four primary aircraft that it produced. The D3A, which carried the Allied code name "Val," was a fixed-gear dive-bomber that sank more Allied fighting ships than any other Axis aircraft. The Val was most famous for its devastating role at Pearl Harbor. Although the plane's technology was outdated by war's end, it was still in service with many units and as a kamikaze weapon.

The D4Y Suisei (Allied code name "Judy") was designed by Yokosuka Aircraft but was mass-produced by Aichi. Its original role was to replace the Val in its dive-bombing duties, but it evolved into the role of reconnaissance and night interception. The Judy first saw combat in February 1944 at Truk Island. Late in the war the Judy was also used as a kamikaze weapon.

Aichi's E16A Zuiun floatplane (Allied code name "Paul") was originally designed as a reconnaissance aircraft but evolved into a dive-bomber.

The B7A Ryusei (Allied code name "Grace") was Aichi's torpedo-bomber. The aircraft was unique for the Japanese Imperial Navy, for it sported a gull-wing design. Production of the Grace was devastated in May 1945 when an earthquake hit the Tokai district in Japan. At war's end only about 100 B7As had been produced.

David A. Pluth

References

Francillon, Rene J. *Japanese Aircraft of the Pacific War.* London: Putnam Aeronautical Books, 1970.

Air America

Airline secretly owned by the U.S. Central Intelligence Agency (CIA). The airline's roots date to 1950, when the CIA purchased the assets of Civil Air Transport (CAT), an airline that had been started in China after World War II by General Claire L. Chennault. CAT continued to fly commercial routes throughout Asia, acting as a privately owned commercial airline. At the same time, under the corporate guise of CAT Inc., it provided airplanes and crews for secret intelligence operations. By the summer of 1970, the airline had almost 50 twin-engine transports, short takeoff and landing aircraft, and 30 helicopters dedicated to operations in Laos.

Air America crews transported tens of thousands of troops and refugees. They flew nighttime airdrop missions over the Ho Chi Minh Trail and engaged in numerous clandestine operations. Without Air America's presence, the CIA's effort in Laos could not have been sustained. In January 1961, Air America delivered weapons to the first 300 trainees.

With authorization to arm and train 1,000 Hmoung tribesmen as a test of the concept, CIA station chief James W. "Bill" Lair visited Vang Pao and arranged for an arms drop at Pa Dong, the famous mountaintop base south of the Plain of Jars. During the war in Laos, Air America was called upon to perform paramilitary tasks at great risk to the aircrews involved. Some Air America pilots flew in Laos for more than a decade, braving enemy fire and surmounting challenging operational conditions with rare skill and determination. As pointed out by a senior agency official during the dedication of a plaque to Air America personnel at CIA Headquarters in May 1988: "The aircrew, maintenance, and other professional aviation skills they applied on our behalf were extraordinary. But, above all, they brought a dedication to our mission and the highest standards of personal courage in the conduct of that mission."

In April 1972, CIA Director Richard Helms ended a lengthy debate within the CIA over the continued need for a covert airlift capability, and he ordered the agency to divest itself of ownership and control of Air America and related companies. Air America would be retained only until the end of the war in Southeast Asia.

Henry M. Holden

References

Robbins, Christopher. *Air America.* New York: Putnam, 1979.
Love, Terry. *Wings of Air America.* Atglen, PA: Schiffer, 1998.

Air Commandos

The 1st Air Commando Group (ACG) achieved several military "firsts" in the jungles of Asia while more glamorous campaigns in Europe captured headlines during World War II. Japan invaded Burma on 23 December 1941 to cut off Allied supplies between India and China, to use Burma as a wedge to strike into China and India, and as a buffer to protect Japan's conquests of Thailand, French Indochina, and China.

Burma's rail and road development was minimal; rivers were the major means of transport. The region's mountains, rivers, jungles, insects, and drenching monsoons posed a problem for invaders and British forces in Burma were minimal, trusting in topography and climate to aid their defense. Burma command was placed under General Archibald Wavell, commander of British forces in India, on 12 December 1941. When Chiang Kai-shek offered Chinese armies, a dubious Wavell accepted, because with the help came Claire L. Chennault's American Volunteer Group, the famous Flying Tigers.

Singapore fell on 15 February 1942, giving Japan access to the Malay Peninsula. General Sir Harold Alexander abandoned Rangoon on 8 March 1942, cutting off support for Allied defenders in Burma. British Major General William J. Slim left more than half of his army, not trained for jungle warfare, in Burma and escaped with 12,000 men, reaching India on 16 May 1942. U.S. Lieutenant General Joseph W. Stilwell, seeking to defend the Mandalay railway, led a Chinese army into Burma that broke in the face of the enemy. Without rail or road, Stilwell trekked into Imphal, India, three days later.

In March 1942, British Colonel Orde C. Wingate noted that Japan had light concentrations of lesser-trained troops in Burma's interior. He proposed Long-Range Penetration (LRP)—a commando force placed behind Japanese lines. LRP would create confusion in enemy areas, cutting off supplies and communications to weaken coordination of enemy campaigns. At the Quebec Conference in 1943, U.S. President Franklin D. Roosevelt and British Prime Minister Winston Churchill endorsed Wingate's strategy and urged U.S. Army Air Forces General Henry H. "Hap" Arnold to develop a plan. Arnold wrote: "We visualized an air commando force, the first in military history. Large numbers of Allied ground troops would be conveyed by aircraft deep into Burma, and once there they would be supplied wholly by air. General Wingate believed that, while the Japanese were excellent jungle fighters, well-trained Allied troops could defeat them at their own game, provided they were mobile, in sufficient force, and exploited the military value of surprise."

On 26 August 1943, British Admiral Lord Louis Mountbatten and Arnold proposed an experiment in aerial warfare: a highly mobile LRP force, complete with its own transportation and services. It was code-named Project Nine, and Arnold found resourceful leaders in Lieutenant Colonel Phillip G. Cochran, who had distinguished himself leading a P-40 squadron in North Africa, and Lieutenant Colonel John R. Alison, well experienced in the P-40 in China with Chennault.

In December 1943, Project Nine, renamed the 5318th Provisional Unit, equipped with Sikorsky YR4 helicopters, L-5 and L-1 light planes, B-25s, P-51s, Noorduyn C-64s, Waco CG4A gliders, and C-47s, began training with Wingate's Special Force. On 5 March 1944, Operation THURSDAY was launched. C-47s towed gliders from India, more than 200 miles over 7,000-foot mountains, to land 539 men, three pack mules, and almost 33 tons of equipment, including a bulldozer, at "Broadway," 165 miles inside Japanese lines. Only 37 of the 52 gliders made it; the force lost 31 killed and 40 wounded to crashes. Without enemy resistance, a runway was graded and used by C-47s and P-51s to attack Japanese airfields, provide supplies and close air support for Wingate's forces, and disrupt enemy transport and communications.

On 24 March Wingate was killed in an air crash; five days later the unit was officially named the 1st Air Commando Group. By May 1944, monsoons made aerial supply impossible, the 1st ACG and the Special Forces troops were fatigued, and the unit was withdrawn and reorganized. The bomber section was eliminated, troop carrier squadrons were added to transport Chinese troops and supply China, and new P-47s allowed operations to resume. Success led to a 2d and 3d ACG composed of fighter squadrons, aircraft maintenance, personnel support facilities, medical detachments, and troop carrier squadrons of C-47s and gliders. The 2d ACG arrived in India in December 1944. The 3d ACG went to the Philippines in late 1944 and flew missions to Formosa and the China coast before moving to Japan in October 1945. All ACGs were disbanded by 1948.

Richard C. DeAngelis

References

Arnold, Gen. H. H. "The Aerial Invasion of Burma." *National Geographic Magazine* 86, 2 (1944): 129–148.

Sciutti, Capt. W. J., USAF. "The First Air Commando Group, August 1943–May 1944." *Journal of the American Aviation Historical Society* 13, 3(1968): 178–185.

Van Wagner, R. D. *Any Place, Any Time, Any Where: The 1st Air Commandos in WW II.* Atglen, PA: Schiffer Military History, 1998.

Air (Aerospace) Defense Command (ADC)

Major U.S. Air Force command responsible for the air defense of the United States. The first command with this name was established as a small planning headquarters on 26 February 1940, but it was disbanded in June 1941. ADC was revived on 21 March 1946 as one of the three central USAF combat commands of the Cold War, along with Strategic Air Command (SAC) and Tactical Air Command (TAC). ADC and TAC were soon overshadowed by SAC and sorely lacked for funding; as a result, in November 1948 both were folded into the newly created Continental Air Command (CONAC). ADC continued only as a planning command within CONAC and was abolished altogether in July 1950. In January 1951, however, in the wake of the first Soviet atomic test and massive increases in U.S. defense spending, ADC was reestablished as a major command. Cooperation with the Canadian armed forces, already close since the establishment of the Permanent Joint Board on Defense in August 1940, grew even closer in 1951 with the appointment of Royal Canadian Air Force liaison officers to ADC headquarters.

During its heyday in the 1950s and early 1960s, ADC rapidly expanded in resources and influence as it attempted to keep pace with the growth of the Soviet strategic nuclear threat. At its height in the late 1950s, ADC's budget rivaled that of SAC, with ADC's 250,000 personnel exercising control over air defenses that included more than 2,000 fighter-interceptors and several different series of radar installations that sprawled from Alaska to Greenland. To coordinate the air defense activities of the other services, in September 1954 ADC was subordinated to the newly created joint Continental Air Defense Command (CONAD). This closer interservice cooperation was soon followed by closer international cooperation with the creation in September 1957 of North American Air Defense Command (NORAD) and its system of joint command of U.S. and Canadian air defenses.

After the first Soviet ICBM tests of 1957, fears of a "bomber gap" were soon replaced by fears of a "missile gap," which threatened to make many of ADC's weapons systems obsolete just as they were coming on line. As the major component force of both CONAD and NORAD, ADC gradually shifted its emphasis from antiaircraft defense to antimissile warning and defense, a change recognized in 1968 by its designation as the Aerospace Defense Command. Throughout the 1970s, most of its air defense missions were transferred to units of the Air Force Reserve and the Air National Guard, and in March 1980 ADC was disbanded, its remaining units divided among TAC and SAC.

David Rezelman

See also

Antimissile Defense; Ballistic Missile Early Warning System; Cold War; Continental Air Command; Distant Early Warning; North American Air Defense Command; SAGE Defense System; Sputnik; Strategic Air Command; Tactical Air Command

References

Bruce-Briggs, B. *The Shield of Faith: A Chronicle of Strategic Defense from Zeppelins to Star Wars.* New York: Simon and Schuster, 1988.

Schaffel, Kenneth. *The Emerging Shield: The Air Force and the Evolution of Continental Air Defense, 1945–1960.* Washington, DC: Office of Air Force History, United States Air Force, 1991.

Air Interdiction (AI)

The delay, disruption, or destruction of enemy forces or supplies en route to the battle area. A distinction is often made between strategic and tactical interdiction. The former refers to operations whose effects are broad and long-term; tactical operations are designed to affect events rapidly and in a localized area.

AI is a core airpower mission that has been conducted since World War I by virtually all air forces. In that war, the goal was to isolate the battlefield by strafing and bombing enemy supply lines. Favorite targets were railroad lines, bridges, and truck convoys. Due to the primitive state of aircraft and weapons technology, as well as the undeveloped nature of air doctrine and tactics, AI missions in World War I were of limited utility.

The potential of AI was clearly recognized, however, and during World War II it once again became a major mission of air forces. Although AI operations were conducted in all theaters, the most extensive and thoroughly analyzed were those of the United States and United Kingdom against the Axis. Specifically, the Allies launched major AI efforts in the North African, Italian, and Normandy campaigns. The venues for these three campaigns were markedly different in terms of weather, terrain, the enemy's supply and transportation infrastructure, and the availability of intelligence regarding the enemy. As a consequence of these differences, the results of AI also varied. The greatest success was in the desert terrain of North Africa, where Axis forces also relied heavily on vulnerable and visible sea convoys across the Mediterranean Sea. The Italian campaign, by contrast, was characterized by mountainous terrain, poor weather conditions, and shortened German supply lines. The diverse results of these two campaigns taught air planners differing lessons.

AI has continued to play a major role in conflicts since World War II. It was used extensively in U.S. conflicts in Korea, Vietnam, Iraq, and Serbia, as well as in wars between Israel and the Arab states in the Middle East. Once again, differing local conditions and political restraints have had an enormous effect on how AI was conducted and the degree to which it was successful. In Vietnam, for example, the strategic interdiction campaign known as ROLLING THUNDER (1965–1968) was largely unsuccessful. The dense jungle terrain, poor intelligence on enemy movements, and political restrictions on targets struck made U.S. AI efforts largely futile. The flow of supplies and reinforcements from North Vietnam to their units in South Vietnam was not seriously affected. In contrast, Coalition AI efforts in the Gulf War (1991) were extremely successful in isolating front-line Iraqi units from their bases in the rear. Intelligence, much of it derived from space and airborne sensors, gave an unusually clear picture of enemy locations, and the open desert terrain similarly facilitated AI operations.

When assessing AI efforts over the past century, it is possible to identify several factors that will have an impact on success. First, air superiority is essential for AI because it permits a more thorough identification and attack of enemy forces and supplies while also exposing the attacking aircraft to less risk. Second, intelligence regarding enemy dispositions, movements, stockpiles, and intentions is crucial. In the North African campaign, for example, "Ultra" intelligence sources gave the Allies a clear picture of Axis shipping in the Mediterranean. In contrast, in Vietnam the United States had a very poor understanding of Vietcong and North Vietnamese activities. Third, weather and terrain will have a major impact on AI's success or failure. One factor included

The Lockheed Martin F-16s of the Air National Guard have taken on a prominence in American skies since the terrorist strike of 11 September 2001. This Fighting Falcon of the 174th Tactical Fighter Wing is truly a part of the "Total Force" of U.S. air power. (U.S. Air Force)

here is the ability to conduct AI at night or in marginal weather—conditions that assist the clandestine movement of forces and supplies. Fourth, AI operations must be persistent. If an enemy is allowed a respite, it will resupply and stockpile, making the AI effort ineffective. Fifth, air planners must have realistic objectives. It is virtually impossible to totally isolate the battle area—something will always get through, and that amount may be enough to sustain the enemy. For example, even if 95 percent of all supplies to Axis forces in Italy during World War II had been stopped—an impressive feat—there would still have been enough matériel getting through for Axis forces to conduct effective defensive operations. The sixth factor is related and is perhaps the most important: There is a symbiotic relationship between air and surface forces in a successful AI campaign. An enemy that is quiescent and stationary consumes few resources while also presenting few targets. If, by contrast, enemy forces are attacked and flushed from their defensive positions by friendly surface forces, they will consume far more resources, especially fuel and ammunition, while also exposing themselves to air attack.

AI will continue to be an important mission in future conflicts, and it will continue to evolve in character. Enemy forces can be expected to become increasingly adept at camouflage, deception, hardening, air defense, and the use of decoys. Air forces, however, have new air- and space-based sensors, as well as increasingly effective munitions, which make it easier to locate and destroy enemy forces and supplies.

Phillip S. Meilinger

See also

Missiles, Air-to-Air; ROLLING THUNDER; STRANGLE; Tactical Air Warfare

References

Mark, Eduard. *Aerial Interdiction: Air Power and the Land Battle in Three American Wars.* Washington, DC: Center for Air Force History, 1994.

Prados, John. *The Blood Road: The Ho Chi Minh Trail and the Vietnam War.* New York: John Wiley and Sons, 1999.

Sallager, F.M. *Operation "Strangle": A Case Study of Tactical Air Interdiction.* Santa Monica, CA: RAND, 1972.

Staaveren, Jacob Van. *The United States Air Force in Southeast Asia: Interdiction in Southern Laos, 1960–1968.* Washington, DC: Center for Air Force History, 1993.

Air National Guard (ANG)

U.S. service arm that claims a heritage dating to the states' flying squadrons between the world wars, but its official existence dates to defense reorganization in 1947. Under the National Guard Bureau, it is a state organization with a federal mission and U.S. Air Force funding, training, organization, and equipment. In peacetime, it provides humanitarian and disaster assistance under state control; its units are subject to activation in national emergency.

Air Force leaders accepted the ANG due to the political influence of its backers, then left it marginally competent, poorly trained, and poorly equipped, the playground of the "weekend warrior." Mobilization for the Korean War in 1950 was a fiasco, forcing the Air Force to upgrade the ANG's quality in the 1950s. Under President Dwight Eisenhower's New Look, the guard gradually became a competent if limited force. The Berlin crisis of 1961 demonstrated that the ANG was still inferior to the regular Air Force, unready for combat.

In the 1960s the Air Force attempted to desegregate its ANG elements, and it controlled the ANG only when it activated. There was no way of forcing the state units to integrate against their will. Only after the Civil Rights Act of 1964 did the first halting steps begin. In the 1970s the ANG integrated.

The turning point came in 1968. To placate the South Koreans, who feared an invasion after the *Pueblo* crisis, President Lyndon Johnson sent 350 Air Force planes and mobilized 14,000 reservists. After the Tet Offensive, the politically cautious Johnson mobilized 22,000 more for service in Vietnam. The ANG units were combat-ready or became deployable within a month of activation and from June 1968 through April 1969 flew 24,124 sorties and 38,614 combat hours at a cost of seven pilots, one intelligence officer, and 14 planes. The ANG demonstrated competence equal to the regulars.

The guard performance in 1968–1969 allowed a switch to Melvin R. Laird's total force policy in 1970. The ANG enjoyed modern equipment, training, and near equality with the regulars. Over the next two decades, the ANG slowly assumed primary missions once dominated by regulars. DESERT STORM and other Air Force operations depended on the ANG.

John Barnhill

References

Gropman, Alan L. *The Air Force Integrates, 1945–1964.* 2d ed. Washington, DC: Smithsonian Institution Press, 1998.

Gross, Dr. Charles J. "A Different Breed of Cats: The Air National Guard and the 1968 Reserve Mobilizations." *Air University Review* 34, 2 (January-February 1983).

Air Rescue

Air rescue, specifically combat air rescue, dates back to before World War II when the German Luftwaffe established the Seenotdienst, its equivalent of an air rescue service. The Germans converted a small number of Heinkel 59 (He 59) biplane floatplanes and incorporated rescue boats for service in the Seenotdienst. During World War II, both England and the United States established dedicated air-sea rescue units, but it was the Germans who first pioneered what would become known as combat search and rescue (SAR) to include using dedicated rescue aircraft and boats as well as incorporating fighter planes as escorts.

Before the Battle of Britain, rescue aircraft were treated as sanitary vehicles, or "flying ambulances." But in 1940, British Prime Minister Winston Churchill ordered Seenotdienst aircraft shot down when it was discovered the Germans were using them for reconnaissance as well as aircrew recovery. Since then, combat aircrew recovery vehicles have been fair game.

Although Germany led the way in developing air rescue, the U.S. Army Air Forces soon caught up. Rescue versions of the B-17 and B-29, designated the SB-17 and SB-29, were used to drop life rafts and even laminated mahogany boats to downed crews. Before the war's end, 0A-10 Catalina flying boats and Sikorsky R-4 and R-6 helicopters were used, the latter being credited with saving 43 airmen from the jungles of Indochina and Burma.

During the Korean War, the U.S. Air Force added Sikorsky H-5s and, later, much more capable H-19s to the inventory of the Air Rescue Service. These aircraft, escorted by North American F-51 Mustangs and working in conjunction with SA-16 twin-engine amphibians, picked up 170 U.S. Air Force, Navy, and Marine aviators along with 84 Allied airmen. Among those rescued was Captain Joseph C. McConnell Jr., who would go on to become the leading ace of the Vietnam War.

It was during the Vietnam War that the Search and Rescue Task Force (SARTAF) came of age. Helicopters, a rescue control aircraft, dedicated fighter escorts, and forward air control aircraft all worked as part of a team with specially assigned tasks and tactics developed to cover a variety of situations.

During the Vietnam War, the introduction of air-refuelable Sikorsky HH-3Es in 1965, as well as the longer-range, more capable HH-53 in 1967, revolutionized aircrew recovery. SARTAF evolved from using Douglas HC-54s to Lockheed HC-130s capable of performing both the command and control and air refueling tasks. Throughout the war, the most reliable rescue escort fighter was the venerable Douglas A-1 Skyraider (operating under the call sign "Spad"). Although the composition of SARTAF changed as the war dragged on, with A-1s being replaced by Vought A-7s toward the end of the conflict, the basic elements and mission remained the same. By the time the war ended in April 1975, the Aerospace Rescue and Recovery Service (ARRS) was credited with saving 3,888 lives, of which 2,870 were U.S. military personnel. Combat aircrew recovery missions ranged all over the theater, even to the suburbs of the enemy capital; in October 1970, ARRS crews ferried Special Forces teams in a failed attempt to rescue POWs confined in the infamous Son Tay prison some 26 miles north of downtown Hanoi.

Today, combat SAR capabilities are resident in the Special Operations Command and the Air Force's reserve components. Their duties range from plucking hapless crews from sinking vessels, to darting deep into Bosnia and Serbia to rescue downed airmen, to flying combat rescue air patrol for ongoing operations in the Middle East. As the U.S. Air Force enters the twenty-first century, the men and women of the Aerospace Rescue and Recovery Service continue in their heroic tradition "that others may live."

Earl H. Tilford Jr.

References

Berger, Carl, ed. *The United States Air Force in Southeast Asia: An Illustrated Account.* Washington, DC: Office of Air Force History, 1984.

Craven, Wesley Fran, and James Lea Cate, eds. *Army Air Forces in World War II, Volume 7: Services Around the World.* Chicago: University of Chicago Press, 1958.

Tilford, Earl H. Jr. *The United States Air Force Search and Rescue in Southeast Asia, 1967–1975.* Washington, DC: Office of Air Force History, 1980.

Air Superiority

Generally defined as the degree of air dominance that gives one force the ability to conduct air operations over the forces and territory of another while denying that same ability to the enemy.

It was realized early on during World War I that air superiority increasingly was a necessity for successful military operations on land, at sea, and in the air. In fact, the first military air mission was observation—the reconnaissance of enemy territory. In order to mask operations and maintain secrecy, however, it was necessary to prevent enemy reconnaissance. This led quickly to air-to-air combat and the quest for air superiority.

The battle for air superiority became a long and costly process during World War II but, to a great extent, determined the outcome of battles, campaigns, and even the war. Clearly, the Battle of Britain saved the British from German invasion. When the Germans and Japanese eventually lost control of their own skies, they suffered tremendous disadvantages and casualties as a result. Air superiority has been a factor in all conflicts since World War II, although it is also apparent that air superiority is of less utility in an unconventional or guerrilla war.

It is important to remember the two components of air superiority: to deny the enemy air operations while also conducting them yourself. In order for air forces to be truly effective, both conditions are necessary. This dual nature means that a potential adversary need not build a modern air force to contest the sky; it merely needs to build a capable ground-based air defense system to prevent airpower being used against him. Because the West, and especially the United States, relies heavily on airpower to achieve its objectives, this is a significant concern.

Another issue often discussed is whether air superiority is required at the theater level or simply at the local level where other military operations are occurring. These two concepts would require significantly different forces and doctrines for their implementation. The United States especially has generally opted for the former and attempted to gain air superiority over an entire theater. Indeed, U.S. military leaders believe that having the initiative is crucial and that the air superiority battle is best fought over the enemy's territory rather than over one's own. Similarly, the geographical situation can play a determining role in how and where the air battle will be fought. For example, the United States—protected by two oceans—has never had to contend for air superiority over its own territory; by contrast, Germany—with hostile powers on its borders—had a far more immediate problem in controlling its skies during both world wars.

The method used to gain air superiority is variable and to a great extent depends on the targets chosen. Typical candidates for attack are the aircraft themselves—either in the air or on the ground—air bases, aircrew members, command and control facilities, radar networks, aircraft/engine factories, and fuel supplies.

Air superiority is likely to remain a key requirement for twenty-first-century military operations. The extension of military operations into space will require enhanced technology and employment concepts to ensure space superiority as well.

Phillip S. Meilinger

See also

Air Defense Command; Airborne Early Warning; Britain, Battle of; Defense Suppression; MiG Alley; Missiles, Air-to-Air

References

Cooling, Benjamin F., ed. *Case Studies in the Achievement of Air Superiority.* Washington, DC: Center for Air Force History, 1994.

McFarland, Stephen L., and Wesley Newton. *To Command the Sky: The Battle for Air Superiority Over Germany, 1942–1944.* Washington, DC: Smithsonian Institution Press, 1991.

Spick, Mike. *Fighter Pilot Tactics: The Techniques of Daylight Air Combat.* New York: Stein and Day, 1983.

Walker, J. R. *Air Superiority.* London: Brassey's, 1989.

Air Technical Intelligence

As Europe marched toward war early in the twentieth century, the industrial nations raced to develop advanced aircraft. American aviation, isolated from the war geographically and politically, lagged behind technologically, industrially, and militarily. Major General George O. Squier, head of the Aviation Section of the U.S. Army Signal Corps, forerunner to today's U.S. Air Force, invited engineers from England, France, and Italy to visit the United States. In turn, more than 100 American engineers and military planners under the direction of Colonel Raynal C. Bolling traveled to Europe in June 1917 to investigate European technology.

In July of that year, the first foreign aircraft, a British de Havilland D.H. 4, arrived in New York for study. In October, the Army Signal Corps selected a site north of Dayton, Ohio, at which to build an aviation engineering and testing center—McCook Field. The D.H. 4 also moved to Dayton, where it was used as a pattern for the manufacture of the aircraft, outfitted with American-made machine guns, instruments, and a Liberty engine. When produced in the United States, it was designated the DH-4.

The field's missions included the evaluation of foreign scientific and technical programs related to aircraft—the bedrock of air technical intelligence (ATI). Early work focused on copying or modifying foreign aircraft for American industry; in time, the Foreign Data Section acted as a clearinghouse for information internally to the U.S. Army's Airplane Engineering Department and externally to American business, education, and military organizations. The unit also translated foreign documents into English. Following the war, the Armistice with Germany brought 347 aircraft to the United States for study and as war relics. In addition, the technical intelligence agency acquired British, French, and Italian airplanes and a collection of engines, machine guns and aerial cannons, navigation equipment, parachutes, and aircraft manufacturing machinery. In 1927, the missions at McCook Field moved across town to Wright Field.

During the 1930s, European and Japanese aircraft industries surpassed U.S. industries. With the commencement of World War II, the ATI function at Wright Field grew from fewer than 100 people in July 1941 to nearly 750 by December 1945. Front-line troops sent back captured enemy equipment to Wright Field for assessment. The first German and Japanese aircraft arrived in 1943, and captured equipment soon filled six buildings, a large outdoor storage area, and part of a flight line hangar. One early ATI program involved the collection of factory markings and nameplates, which resulted in the intensive bombing efforts against German ball-bearing plants in 1943. Data collected from the nameplates from some 1,000 Japanese aircraft provided one of the best sources of target data for manufacturing plants on the home islands of Japan.

The most famous World War II ATI missions in Europe were Project Lusty and Operation PAPERCLIP. Project Lusty brought fame to Colonel Harold E. Watson, twice commander of the Air Force's Air Technical Intelligence Center. Watson and a group of handpicked pilots (known as "Watson's Whizzers") gathered German aircraft from the battlefield and sent them back to Wright Field for study. The best known of these aircraft was the Messerschmitt Me 262 jet fighter.

Colonel Donald L. Putt—who would go on to attain the rank of lieutenant general, command the Air Research and Development Command in 1953, and serve as the military director of the Air Force Scientific Advisory Board—provided overall guidance for Project Lusty and the collection of aircraft, equipment, and German technical documents in the European theater of operations. Eventually, the German aircraft gathered in Europe, plus V-1 and V-2 missiles, migrated to Freeman Field, Indiana, for evaluation. ATI experts and aviation engineers tested captured Japanese equipment at the Middletown Air Depot south of Dayton. Foreign aircraft also went to Muroc Field (later renamed Edwards AFB), California, for flight-testing, and the U.S. Navy had a test and evaluation center at Patuxent River, Maryland.

Operation PAPERCLIP brought more than 200 German scientists and technicians to Wright Field for collaboration with their American counterparts. Initially assigned to the intelligence branch, most of the scientists eventually went to work in the various Wright Field labs. Colonel Howard M. McCoy organized and headed the Air Documents Research Center (ADRC) in London, England, which translated, cataloged, indexed, and microfilmed captured German documents. In 1946, the center moved to Wright Field and became the Air Documents Division within the intelligence organization. Three hundred people processed more than 1,500 tons of documents, adding 100,000 new technical terms to the English language. The technical knowledge gained from these documents revolutionized American industry. In addition to the aviation-related advances, new designs for vacuum tubes used in communications, the development of magnetic tapes used in tape recordings and computers, night-vision devices, improvements in liquid and solid fuels, and advances in textiles, drugs, and food preservation were made available to American manufacturers. The original ADRC function moved to Washington, D.C., becoming today's Defense Technical Information Center. Other PAPERCLIP scientists, the most famous of whom was Wernher von Braun, helped America develop its space and missile programs.

In the Pacific theater of war, General Douglas MacArthur authorized intelligence personnel to take charge of crashed and captured Japanese aircraft and personnel. Captain Frank T. McCoy and Technical Sergeant Francis Williams helped organize a materiel section for air technical intelligence operations in Melbourne, Australia, in 1942. In addition to providing information on aircraft and weapons performance, Captain McCoy and Sergeant Williams assigned code names to Japanese aircraft—feminine names for bombers and masculine names for fighters. It may not be surprising that "Frank" and "Frances" became the names of two Japanese aircraft. In October 1944, now Lieutenant Colonel McCoy became officer-in-charge of the newly formed Technical Air Intelligence Unit attached to the Far East Air Forces.

The experiences of World War II shaped the future of the U.S. Air Force's scientific and technical intelligence mission. A July 1947 study articulated a threefold mission for ATI:

1. Ensure the prevention of strategic, tactical, or technological surprise from any source.
2. Provide intelligence required for command decisions and counsel upon air preparedness and air operations.
3. Ensure appropriate counterintelligence measures.

Between 1945 and 1950, the mission focus changed. Although the U.S. Air Force's ATI mission had established an office to track Soviet weapons as early as 1943, it remained small; German and Japanese projects were the top priority. ATI efforts turned increasingly toward the emerging technological threat posed by the Russians in the late 1940s.

Bruce A. Ashcroft

See also

Air Technical Intelligence; Japan, Air Operations Against; World War I Aviation; World War II Aviation; Wright-Patterson Air Force Base

References

Ashcroft, Bruce A. *The Beginnings of Air Technical Intelligence, 1912–1941.* Wright-Patterson AFB, OH: National Air Intelligence Center, 1994.

Jones, R. V. *The Wizard War: British Scientific Intelligence, 1939–1945.* New York: Coward, McCann and Geoghegan, 1978.

Lasby, Clarence G. *Project Paperclip.* New York: Atheneum, 1975.

Airborne Battlefield Command and Control Center (ABCCC)

Airborne command and control system for executing air-to-ground and special forces operations. Consists of a mission capsule inside a specially configured EC-130 aircraft.

The mission capsule is a 47-foot, 19,000-pound unit containing 15 consoles. A standard crew consists of 12 positions: Director, Airborne Battlestaff, Battlestaff Operations Officer, four weapons controllers, close air support coordinator, an intelligence officer and technician, two communications systems operators, and a maintenance technician, although the crew can be tailored differently for specialized missions. The crew works at computer workstations that graphically depict areas of interests. The capsule, possessing no onboard sensors, builds a situational representation of the theater through data inputs from other sensor platforms, pilot reports, and coordination with ground combat elements.

The operations officer and controllers provide updated targeting information, process postattack assessments, and coordinate air-to-ground strike requests with other agencies to ensure prompt, efficient targeting. The intelligence section provides and receives threat updates to inbound and outbound strike aircraft, as well as maintaining ground order of battle status. The communications operators provide secure radio and satellite communications capability for the crew. The maintenance technician performs any inflight repair to the ABCCC capsule systems.

The aircraft is an inflight-refuelable EC-130 modified version of the C-130 Hercules transport aircraft. It carries a flight crew of four: pilot, copilot, navigator, and flight engineer.

Braxton Eisel

References

U.S. Department of Defense, United States Air Force. *42d Airborne Command and Control Squadron.* Davis-Monthan Air Force Base, AZ: USAF, 1999.

Airborne Early Warning (AEW)

AEW involves using sensors carried onboard aircraft to detect, track, report, identify, and respond to adversary air or surface (land or sea) vehicular movement.

First realistically conceived as a U.S. Navy requirement to extend the early detection of enemy aircraft to a carrier fleet in 1942, the first production AEW aircraft, a TBM-3W modified from the Avenger torpedo-bomber, flew in 1945. This early version of a dedicated AEW aircraft, as well as succeeding versions of other modified navel aircraft, all used variants of the APS-20 airborne search radar.

The U.S. Air Force and Navy operated larger AEW platforms starting in the early 1950s. Both used versions of the Lockheed Constellation airliner. This system carried both a search radar in a radome underneath the fuselage and a height-finder radar mounted above the fuselage. Used extensively in orbits designed to detect Soviet bombers attacking the United States, the USAF EC- and RC-121s and the USN WV-2 Warning Star saw service in Southeast Asia, providing radar coverage over North Vietnam.

The U.S. Navy gained its first purpose-built AEW plat-

A sentinel in the sky, the Boeing AWACS is a force multiplier, able to detect enemy aircraft and electronics and control the actions of friendly aircraft. (U.S. Air Force)

form in the E-2 series of aircraft. Carrying a crew of five (two pilots, three mission crew), the E-2 merged the long range of shore-based aircraft with the compactness needed for carrier operations. Numerous countries operate the E-2 both shore-based and afloat.

The U.S. Air Force received its first true AEW aircraft in 1976 with the arrival of the Airborne Warning and Control System (AWACS) based on the Boeing 707 airframe. Carrying a large mission crew and capable of inflight refueling, the E-3 Sentry became the standard for land-based AEW aircraft. It is operated by air forces of the United States, Britain, France, Saudi Arabia, and the North Atlantic Treaty Organization. Japan operates the AWACS system, but on a modified Boeing 767.

Other countries have developed different options for AEW. Some are large, complex systems like Chile's Condor or Russia's Mainstay, but others have opted for smaller, less expensive systems like Sweden's Argus airborne system or the British Royal Navy's helicopter-borne AEW.

The newest entry in the AEW field is that of ground surveillance. Platforms such as the USAF's E-8 Joint STARS system employ a radar optimized for ground reconnaissance. It can detect very small or very slow moving vehicles from long ranges.

Braxton Eisel

References

Armistead, Edwin Leigh LCDR, USN. *Grease Pencils and Fluorescent Bananas: The History of Airborne Early Warning Aircraft.* Virginia Beach, VA.: E. L. Armistead, 1996.

Hirst, Mike. *Airborne Early Warning: Design, Development, and Operations.* London. Osprey, 1983.

Price, Alfred. *Instruments of Darkness: The History of Electronic Warfare.* New York: Charles Scribner's Sons, 1978.

Airborne Laser

The airborne laser (ABL) fires a laser beam that can destroy a short-range ballistic missile (SRBM) hundreds of miles away as it lifts off its launching pad, before it starts its deadly trajectory toward a target. The laser generates heat that forms a stress fracture, and the rocket's internal pressure causes it to burst open. Though a revolutionary weapon, its

The great hope for the future is that an airborne laser can destroy enemy ballistic missiles with a blast of concentrated energy. (Boeing)

technology is off the shelf. Operators on a Boeing 747-400 focus a basketball-sized beam from the laser onto the missile. There are three smaller lasers on the aircraft. One "lights up" a target; a second tracks it; the third is a beacon laser that controls the laser. The ABL uses beam control to find and track a target and adjust the laser as it travels through the atmosphere. The airborne laser's mirror is an adaptive optic. Minute electric actuators, like tiny pistons, distort the mirror to keep pace with atmospheric changes. The ABL is the first truly new weapon of the future battlefield. It will clearly move the U.S. Air Force into a new era. When it enters active duty in the early 2000s, it will be a flying missile defense system. It is mobile and can be in theater in hours, protecting troops on the ground.

David C. Arnold

Aircraft Armament

At the start of World War I, most aircraft were used in purely scouting roles. It was not long, however, before the belligerents experimented with crude offensive devices such as bricks, heavy weights, and metal darts. Rifles and pistols were routinely used as late as 1916, some pilots having success with Martini or Winchester carbines strapped to the struts of a single-seat scout aircraft.

Machine guns were carried on two-seat aircraft from around 1915, typically a .303-inch Lewis or 7.92mm MG-08/15 (Spandau), usually operated by the observer. Initially, guns were mounted on pin and socket mounts on each side of the cockpit, requiring the gun to be manhandled to another socket if an attack developed from an unexpected direction. In 1915, F. W. Scarff of the Admiralty Air Department developed a 360-degree ring mounting that soon became standard equipment on both sides.

The real breakthrough in aerial combat came in April 1915, when Roland Garros mounted a machine gun on his Morane scout and fitted deflector plates to the propeller to deflect the bullets that struck the blades. Garros was eventually shot down and captured, and Anthony Fokker developed the idea into an interrupter mechanism that prevented the gun from firing when obstructed by the propeller. The Fokker E.I Eindecker gave German pilots a significant advantage over the Allies, causing mild panic and hastening the introduction of synchronized forward-firing machine guns on Allied aircraft. The standard fighter armament during the later years of the war and for a number of years afterward was two rifle-caliber machine guns firing through the propeller.

Aircraft Armament (1916–1956)

Year	*Weapon*	*Caliber*	*Rate of Fire*	*Weight*	*Muzzle Velocity*	*Projectile Weight*
1916	Vickers Mk I	0.303 in	850 rpm	24.5 lbs	2,499 ft/sec	0.4 oz
1929	Browning M2	0.30 in	1,150 rpm	21.8 lbs	2,660 ft/sec	0.4 oz
1933	Browning M2	0.50 in	750 rpm	64 lbs	2,750 ft/sec	1.17 oz
1941	Hispano Suiza Mk II	20mm	650 rpm	109 lbs	2,880 ft/sec	4.4 oz
1944	Mauser MG 213 C	20mm	1,400 rpm	165.4 lbs	3,445 ft/sec	4.4 oz (est.)
1956	ADEN	30mm	1,200–1,400 rpm	192 lbs	2,625 ft/sec	8.0 oz
1956	General Electric M61A1	20mm	6,000 rpm	265 lbs	3,380 ft/sec	4.6 oz

As bombers flew higher and faster, low temperatures and the force of the slipstream made it increasingly difficult to aim weapons. An initial solution was to put a protective screen or cupola over the Scarff ring, followed by the introduction of a fully powered turret on the Boulton and Paul "Overstrand" in 1935. All new British bomber designs were modified to include powered turrets where appropriate, usually using twin or quad .303-inch guns. The later U.S. turrets were more effective, with heavier .5-inch weapons and more armor.

In the mid-1930s, it became clear that the increasing use of armor on aircraft would require a heavier-caliber weapon. The Hispano-Suiza 20mm cannon was probably the best weapon available at the start of World War II. In service use it was considered to be reliable and was capable of downing an aircraft with very few hits (about three hits for a fighter-sized target, perhaps 20 for a large bomber).

As World War II approached, fighters were carrying four, six, or eight guns, usually in the wings, and the issue of harmonization (aiming the guns to converge at a point in front of the aircraft) began to assume greater importance. Fighters in the Royal Air Force were initially harmonized at much too long a range in the mistaken belief that a few hits were better than none at all; this was corrected following operational experience during the Battle of Britain.

In 1942, a German requirement for a high-performance cannon led in 1944 to the Mauser MG 213 family of weapons. The 20mm version of this remarkable weapon could fire 1,400 shells per minute with a muzzle velocity of 3445 feet per second, and used a five-chamber revolving cylinder to increase the rate of fire. This gun was the starting point for almost every new gun developed outside the Soviet Union since 1945, including the U.S. M39, the French DEFA, and the British ADEN.

Probably the most important weapon in the West is the GE M61 Vulcan cannon, first used in the Lockheed F-104A in 1954. Its bulk and mass are substantial, requiring an installation tailored individually for each aircraft, yet the performance of the weapon is such that only one is needed. Podded versions of the M61 were used (initially without air-to-air gun sights) on U.S. Air Force F-4 Phantoms in the Vietnam War and were almost immediately successful.

Andy Blackburn

See also

Garros, Roland

References

Clarke, R. Wallace. *British Aircraft Armament.* 2 vols. London: PSL/Haynes, 1993–1994.

Gunston, Bill. *The Illustrated Encyclopedia of Aircraft Armament.* London: Salamander, 1987.

Aircraft Carriers, Development of

Carriers are warships with a flight deck on which airplanes can be launched and landed. Prior to World War I, several of the world's navies commissioned vessels as parent ships for seaplanes. These carriers, all adapted from existing merchant vessels or obsolete warships, featured enhanced handling gear and, often, primitive deck hangars.

When war began, Britain, France, Germany, and Japan all added similar mercantile conversions to their fleets. By 1915, British seaplane carriers incorporated inclined foredeck runways from which seaplanes using wheeled trolleys could take off. Landplanes, offering superior performance, soon supplemented and later supplanted seaplanes, although their crews had to either ditch or attempt to reach land at the end of each mission.

After successful 1917 experiments in landing small aircraft on existing runways, the Royal Navy refitted the converted large cruiser *Furious* with an aft landing deck, retain-

The USS Bunker Hill *was an Essex class carrier and took two kamikaze hits on 11 May 1945. It survived and was ready for action by July of that year but saw no further combat. (U.S. Navy)*

ing the original central superstructure. *Furious* operated successfully throughout 1918, although turbulence made landings hazardous; the arrival of the carrier *Argus* in September demonstrated the superiority of the flush-deck configuration.

At war's end, Britain had commissioned a further cruiser conversion, *Vindictive,* configured like *Furious;* was converting an incomplete former Chilean battleship into a flush-deck carrier with an offset island as *Eagle;* and had laid down *Hermes,* its first vessel constructed as a carrier from the keel up, also flush-decked with an island. Japan laid down *Hosho,* a similar carrier, in 1919, and the United States began conversion of the oiler *Jupiter* into the flush-deck carrier *Langley* in 1920.

Provisions of the 1921 Washington Treaty freed large U.S., British, French, and Japanese hulls for conversion into carriers. The United States and France converted two battlecruisers and a battleship respectively into the flush-deck carriers *Lexington, Saratoga,* and *Béarn.* British and Japanese concepts emphasizing rapid aircraft launching led both navies to develop designs incorporating multiple flight-deck levels to permit launching of several aircraft simultaneously. Britain rebuilt *Furious* with a three-quarter-length flush deck and a forward launching deck at a lower level and similarly converted two near-sister ships, *Courageous* and *Glorious.* Japan took this idea farther and configured a battleship and a battlecruiser, *Kaga* and *Akagi,* as carriers with two forward launching decks beneath the main deck. Both navies learned through experience that efficient deck-handling procedures were more effective in increasing launch rates, and Japan subsequently rebuilt its two carriers with conventional flush decks.

During the 1930s, Japan and the United States added new carriers to their fleets. Although constrained by Washington Treaty provisions, both navies evolved effective designs that became the basis for later construction. The *Soryu* and *Yorktown* classes combined large flight decks, substantial air groups, strong defensive armament (for the period), high speed, and long range in vessels suitable for extended oceanic operations. Britain, however, was a latecomer to new carrier construction in the 1930s. *Ark Royal,* commissioned in 1939, incorporated internal hangars, an enclosed bow, and a flight deck that was also the vessel's principal strength deck—all features that characterized subsequent British carrier designs.

The carriers that Britain, Japan, and the United States commissioned during World War II derived from their earlier 1930s designs. Japan commissioned the *Shokaku* class in 1941, followed by *Taiho,* a variant incorporating an armored flight deck, and laid down the six-ship *Unryu* class (derived directly from *Soryu*) in 1942–1943, although only two vessels entered service. The United States standardized the *Essex* class, an expansion of *Yorktown.* No less than 32 units were ordered, of which 24 were completed to serve as the backbone of U.S. carrier forces from 1943. They combined powerful offensive and defensive features in hulls whose size conferred great adaptability to changing operational requirements. British wartime carriers introduced armor protection for flight decks and hangar sides. Incorporating this feature into the basic *Ark Royal* design produced vessels that proved very effective in the confined waters of the Mediterranean and in the face of kamikaze attacks, but it also carried severe penalties. Capacity was slashed, hangars were cramped, and it proved difficult and expensive to upgrade these ships after the war.

All three navies commissioned other carriers to meet wartime exigencies. Escort carriers, either simple conversions from mercantile hulls or equivalent new construction vessels, spearheaded antisubmarine operations, provided air cover for convoys and invasion forces, supported amphibious forces ashore, replenished the fast carrier air groups, and trained new aircrews. To circumvent Washington Treaty quantitative limitations, Japan designed fast naval auxiliaries and passenger liners for quick conversion into carriers. From 1940 on, conversions from five auxiliaries and three liners joined the Combined Fleet as frontline light fleet carriers. In addition, Japan converted one *Yamato*-class battleship hull, *Shinano,* into a huge carrier that never entered operational service, and commenced conversion of an incomplete cruiser as a light fleet carrier. The United States also deployed converted warships—the nine *Independence*-class light fleet carriers based on *Cleveland*-class cruiser hulls formed an integral part of the fast carrier force from early 1943.

Britain also appreciated the need for smaller, less-sophisticated carriers that could enter service more quickly but chose to construct new vessels rather than convert existing hulls. Four *Colossus*-class light fleet carriers served with British Pacific Fleet in late 1945 and joined six sisters to form the core of British carrier power into the later 1950s, operating throughout the Korean War and at Suez in 1956. Many of them, as well as the five semisisters of the *Magnificent* class, later went to other navies, serving with Argentina, Australia, Brazil, Canada, France, India, and the Netherlands. Four larger updated carriers of similar design entered the Royal Navy after World War II, serving as fleet carriers and later as amphibious assault ships. The last, *Hermes,* saw action in the Falklands in 1982 and was sold to India in 1986.

Jet aircraft operation affected carrier design. Long takeoff and landing runs, heavier aircraft, higher approach speeds, and slow throttle response marginalized safe operation from existing carriers. Three British inventions—steam catapults, angled flight decks, and optical landing aids—made routine jet operation practical but forced changes in ship design. Navies reconstructed their existing larger, more modern carriers and modified the designs of vessels still under construction. The U.S. Navy, whose axial-decked *Midway*-class carriers had already set a new benchmark for size, led the way in adopting these innovations in new construction. The four *Forrestal*-class supercarriers and their improved *Kittyhawk*-class half-sisters became the prototypes for all subsequent U.S. fleet carriers, whose current design crystallized when nuclear power was adopted for *Enterprise,* commissioned in 1961. These carriers are marked by their huge size (angled flights decks run more than 1,000 feet and are 250 feet wide), four long, powerful steam catapults, and sophisticated landing aids—all essential to operate air groups of some 80 jet aircraft. Other navies have not been able to afford carriers of this size, but their smaller conventional vessels have been much less capable.

Since the 1970s, V/STOL aircraft have added a new dimension to carrier design. Britain, the Soviet Union, and Spain commissioned smaller carriers specifically configured to operate a mix of V/STOL jet attack or fighter aircraft and large antisubmarine helicopters, epitomized by the British *Invincible* and Soviet *Kiev* classes. These types, however, trade smaller size and less demanding equipment (they do not need catapults and arresting gear) for a less capable air group, particularly in range and the ability to incorporate long-range early warning and antisubmarine search aircraft.

Paul E. Fontenoy

See also

Airborne Early Warning; anti-submarine warfare; Atlantic, Battle of the; Bismarck, Air Operations Against; British Pacific Fleet; Canadian Air Force; Cape Engano, Battle of; Coral Sea, Battle of the; DESERT SHIELD; DESERT STORM; Eastern Solomons, Battle of;

Falkland Islands War; Fleet Air Arm; French Naval Air Force; Iwo Jima; Japanese Naval Air Force, Imperial; Kamikaze Attacks; Korean War; Leyte Gulf, Battle of; London Naval Agreement; Marshall Islands; Mediterranean Theater of Operations; Midway, Battle of; Norwegian Air Campaign; Okinawa; Santa Cruz, Battle of; Suez Crisis; Taranto Air Attack; Task Force 38/58; Task Force 77; United States Navy, and Aviation; USS Langley; Washington Naval Conference

References

Chesnau, Roger. *Aircraft Carriers of the World, 1914 to the Present: An Illustrated Encyclopedia.* 2nd ed. London: Arms and Armour Press, 1992.

Friedman, Norman. *U.S. Aircraft Carriers: An Illustrated Design History.* Annapolis, MD: Naval Institute Press, 1983.

______. *British Carrier Aviation: The Evolution of the Ships and Their Aircraft.* Annapolis, MD: Naval Institute Press, 1988.

Jentschura, Hansgeorg, Dieter Jung, and Peter Mickel. *Warships of the Imperial Japanese Navy, 1869–1945.* London: Arms and Armour Press, 1977.

AirLand Battle

The official U.S. Army warfighting doctrine during the Gulf War. First announced in 1982, it was formulated at the Army's Training and Doctrine Command at Fort Monroe, Virginia, and at the Army Command and General Staff College at Fort Leavenworth, Kansas, in coordination with the Air Force's Tactical Air Command. Revised in 1986, AirLand Battle doctrine reintroduced the concept of operational art, the intermediate level of war between military strategy and tactics, that was to define the modern battlefield.

Under this doctrinal concept, combat included not only fighting along the line of contact—now called close operations—but also deep operations "directed against enemy forces not in contact [to] create the conditions for future victory," as well as rear operations to assure freedom of maneuver and protection of critical logistical resources. It envisioned Army–Air Force cooperation and mutual support and called for simultaneous battles on the forward line and deep in the enemy's rear echelon in close concert with airpower.

AirLand Battle marked a definite turning away from atomic theorists, who maintained that conventional war was obsolete in the nuclear age. Emphasizing campaign planning, maneuver, and fluidity of action, AirLand Battle was validated in the Gulf War.

James H. Willbanks

See also

Close Air Support; Tactical Air Command

References

Field Manual 100–5: Operations. Washington, DC: U.S. Government Printing Office, 1982.

Romjue, John L. *From Active Defense to AirLand Battle: The Development of Army Doctrine, 1973–1982.* Fort Monroe, VA: U.S. Army Training and Doctrine Command, 1984.

Summers, Colonel Harry G. Jr. *On Strategy II: A Critical Analysis of the Gulf War.* New York: Dell, 1991.

Airlift Operations, U.S.

The first U.S. airlift operations began during World War I using four British-designed de Havilland DH-4 biplanes to drop supplies to the beleaguered Lost Battalion in the Argonne Forest. One aircraft was successful, and the crew, consisting of Lieutenants Harold Goettler and Erwin Bleckley, were posthumously awarded of Medals of Honor for their actions on 6 October 1918.

Airlift operations within the U.S. military began in the mid-1920s. The aircraft primarily supported operations of combat and headquarters units. The first transport aircraft for the U.S. Army Air Service, built in 1919, was the Martin T-1, based on the MB-1 bomber. Its fuselage was redesigned to enclose the cockpit and provide accommodations for up to 10 passengers.

For the brief period 15 May-29 August 1919, the Army flew mail for the U.S. Postal Service. First in this long series of aircraft was the Douglas C-1, an enlarged version of the famed World Cruisers that made the first round-the-world flight in 1924. Transport aircraft were procured in small quantities of one to 10 from the C-1 through the C-31, indicating the low priority of such aircraft to the service (the General Aircraft [American Fokker] C-14 was the exception, with 20 being procured). It was not until the advent of the Douglas C-32 (the military version of the commercial DC-2) that airlift became a serious issue with the military.

In fiscal year 1942, the Army procured 24 C-32s as troop transports, 18 C-33s for freighters, and a pair of C-34s as VIP transports. That year was also the start of orders for 3,144 Curtiss C-46 Commandos, capable of carrying 50 troops. A total of 9,583 Douglas C-47 Skytrains (the military version of the commercial DC-3) were also produced for the Army as well as the Navy and Allied nations. Both the C-46 and C-47 saw service during World War II and Korea. The C-47 soldiered on through the Vietnam War.

Management of such a large transport force was a major undertaking. First, the operations were divided between strategic and tactical airlift. Strategic operations initially began with ferrying Lend-Lease aircraft to England. This mission was performed by the Air Corps Ferrying Command, established on 29 May 1941. By 7 December 1941, the command had delivered some 1,300 aircraft to the Allied forces around the world. Ferrying Command was redesignated Air

Transport Command (ATC) on 20 June 1942, and although it continued its role in ferrying aircraft, it was primarily tasked with providing all strategic airlift for the War Department, delivering personnel and materiel critical to the war effort throughout the world. At its peak, ATC had more than 3,700 aircraft supported by more than 300,000 personnel.

The first ATC was activated on 1 May 1942. The command was designated the I Troop Carrier Command in July 1942. This organization was a major command that reported directly to Headquarters Army Air Forces and was responsible for training troop carrier units and personnel within the United States for parachute troops, airborne infantry, and glider units. The I Troop Carrier Command was disbanded on 5 November 1945. Theater operations were conducted by the IX Troop Carrier Command, activated in England on 16 October 1943.

With the end of World War II, a major postwar demobilization occurred on 31 March 1946. Headquartered at Greenville Army Air Base, South Carolina, the Third Air Force (Troop Carrier) served as the sole troop carrier organization within the Army Air Forces between 21 March and 1 November 1946, until absorbed into the Ninth Air Force and losing all mission identity. It was not until 20 March 1951 that the Eighteenth Air Force was established within Tactical Air Command (TAC) with the specific mission of troop carrier operations in support of the Army.

Units of the Eighteenth Air Force were transferred to the Far East Air Forces Combat Cargo Command during the Korean War. Initially, the Combat Cargo Command was a provisional unit. On 5 January 1951, the unit was designated the 315th Air Division (Combat Cargo). Throughout the war, elements of this unit provided all major airlift utilizing C-46, C--47, Fairchild C-119, and Douglas C-124 "Globemaster IIs." The Eighteenth Air Force continued troop carrier operations within the United States until 1 January 1958, when the mission was transferred to the Twelfth Air Force.

The Air Force Reserve provided troop carrier units to augment the active-duty forces. Nineteen Reserve groups were activated for the Korean War. In 1957, the Reserves dropped their fighter role and almost exclusively performed troop carrier operations with 45 squadrons. An excellent showing of the Reserve troop carrier units during an exercise in August 1960 proved their capabilities, resulting in TAC and the Army regularly asking for their services. For 19 years, the Reserve troop carrier units employed the C-119 as their principal aircraft.

The Naval Air Transport Service (NATS) was formed on 12 December 1941. Though much smaller than the Army's ATC, NATS was equipped with 429 aircraft supported by 26,000 personnel. Its mission was to provide a global air transportation network between naval establishments and naval areas of operation.

The postwar reorganization of the military inevitably led to a new air transportation command that would serve most airlift needs of all services and the Department of Defense. On 1 June 1948, both ATC and NATS were discontinued, inactivated, and replaced by a new joint command: the Military Air Transport Service (MATS). The new organization was commanded by USAF Major General Laurence S. Kuter, with USN Rear Admiral John P. Whitney as vice commander. MATS reported directly to the USAF Chief of Staff. Upon its establishment, MATS had 766 USAF and 58 USN aircraft and was manned by 54,164 personnel from the Air Force, Navy, and Civil Service. MATS operated three divisions: Atlantic, Continental, and Pacific—each providing service within its own geographic areas.

In addition to airlift, MATS also controlled the Airways and Air Communications Service; Air Photographic and Charting Service; Air Weather Service; Air Rescue Service; and Flight Service (the latter providing operational control of all military aircraft operating within the United States).

Operation VITTLES—the Berlin Airlift—became the first test of MATS when the Soviets blockaded the city of Berlin on 25 June 1948. The airlift succeeded admirably. In it airpower in the form of compassionate relief became a major diplomatic weapon.

On 7 December 1956, the Department of Defense designated MATS as the single manager of all airlift service; however, other commands had smaller integral airlift capabilities. The command began with gaining a pair of C-124–equipped heavy troop carrier wings from TAC.

MATS was designated Military Airlift Command (MAC) on 1 January 1966. In addition to its strategic airlift mission, it gained the traditional base flight operations for all other commands within the USAF. MAC designated the former MATS Eastern Transport Division the Twenty-first Air Force; the Western Transport Division the Twenty-second Air Force; and the Air Rescue Service became the Aerospace Rescue and Recovery Service under the Twenty-third Air Force. MAC also designated the Air Photographic and Charting Service the Aerospace Audio-Visual Service. The Air Weather Service essentially remained the same. Because of its joint service mission, MAC was designated a specified command on 1 February 1977, thereby coming under the direction of the Joint Chiefs of Staff. MAC was designated Air Mobility Command (MAC) on 1 June 1992, essentially retaining all of its missions.

As the military did not have sufficient airlift capability for a major international emergency, the Civil Reserve Air Fleet (CRAF) was instituted in 1952. Commercial airlines identified certain aircraft and crews that could be called up (much like the Air National Guard and Reserve forces) to supplement the USAF's airlift requirements. Participating airlines dedicated 300 C-54–equivalent four-engine aircraft to CRAF. Although civilian airlines routinely supported USAF requirements, it was not until the Gulf War in 1990 that CRAF was activated.

In July 1960, after hostilities erupted in the Congo when Belgium gave that nation its independence, MATS dedicated a large portion of its airlift capability for support until January 1964, when peace was established. During this period, MATS flew 2,128 missions, transporting 63,798 personnel and 18,593 tons of cargo. This was known as Operation NEW TAPE. Lessons learned showed that MATS would be required to take on a combat role in the form of airdrop and paratroop operations. By the mid-1960s, these combat missions were transferred from TAC to MATS.

MAC evolved from an all–piston-powered organization to one equipped with all-turbine aircraft during the 1960s. In addition, air refueling was added to their mission—transport crews were trained to receive fuel from Strategic Air Command (SAC) tankers.

Between 1964 and 1973, MAC provided the bulk of the strategic airlift for the Vietnam War. MAC also flew tactical airlift operations within the theater. MAC personnel flew air-rescue missions, provided air weather service, and audiovisual services in the theater. When North Vietnamese units encircled U.S. Marines at Khe Sanh, South Vietnam, in mid-December 1967, it was tactical airlift that kept the ground forces supplied.

On 12 May 1968, a U.S. Special Forces camp at Kham Duc was overrun by communist forces. In the course of the day, it was learned that a three-man tactical control team had been left behind at the base. Lieutenant Colonel Joe M. Jackson landed his Fairchild C-123 on the field and successfully evacuated the team. For his actions that day Colonel Jackson became the only airlifter to be awarded the Medal of Honor.

In October 1973, the MAC airlift supplying arms and supplies to Israel was considered by many to be the decisive event in the eventual victory of Israeli forces over those of Egypt and Syria. The airlift also validated the Lockheed C-5A as an indispensable airlift aircraft.

During the Gulf War, MAC aircraft were the air bridge required to provide most all of the initial requirements for the Coalition forces. The sealift required three weeks to sail to the Gulf region. Afterward, MAC provided a continual aerial supply line for critical cargo and the bulk of the U.S. personnel movement between 1990 and 1991.

With the change from MAC to Air Mobility Command (AMC) on 1 June 1992 came the transfer of SAC's KC-135 and KC-10 tanker fleet.

The United States Transportation Command (USTRANSCOM), a joint-services organization reporting to the Joint Chiefs of Staff, was organized on 1 April 1987 and activated on 1 October 1988. USTRANSCOM headquarters is colocated at Scott AFB, Illinois, with the AMC, and commanded by the commander in chief of AMC. The new command oversees all air, sea, and land transportation requirements for the Pentagon.

The mission flexibility of America's airlift forces permit it to not only perform its military function but also serve humanity. Between 1947 and 1994, USAF transport and rescue aircraft flew 568 humanitarian missions around the world, not counting the thousands of times combat aircraft had flown vitally needed vaccines and human organs. The United States is the only nation that has the capability to deliver such aid anywhere in the world on a moment's notice.

Alwyn T. Lloyd

See also

Berlin Airlift; Boeing KC-10 Extender; Boeing KC-135 Stratotanker; Fairchild C-82 Packet and Fairchild C-119 Flying Boxcar; Strategic Air Command; Tactical Air Command

References

Anything, Anywhere, Anytime: An Illustrated History of Military Airlift Command 1941-1991. Scott AFB, IL: Military Airlift Command History Office, May 1991.

Bowers, Ray L. *The United States Air Force in Southeast Asia—Tactical Airlift.* Washington, DC: Office of Air Force History, 1983.

Mauer, Mauer. *Air Force Combat Units of World War II.* Washington, DC: Office of Air Force History, 1983.

Ravenstein, Charles A. *The Organization and Lineage of the United States Air Force.* USAF Warrior Studies. Washington, DC: Office of Air Force History, 1986.

Airlines, Service in Wartime by

As the United States entered World War II in late 1941, the military was woefully short of air transport capacity. Although hundreds of transports (chiefly C-46s and C-47s) were on order, few had been delivered. Given the pressing need to build up strength, the only place to obtain needed air transport was from the nation's airlines. Air carriers had focused on passenger and mail traffic rather than cargo (commercial freight amounted to but 2–3 percent of airline gross revenues before Pearl Harbor), yet they could provide trained pilots as well as aircraft to fly. The airlines quickly grew to reflect wartime needs as carriers radically changed how they operated, though at no time were the airlines wholly taken over by the military. The changes began with airliners themselves.

In a series of War Department decisions in December 1941 and early 1942, the Air Corps Ferry Command (Air Transport Command [ATC] in June 1942) requisitioned 193 out of the total U.S. airline fleet of 359 airplanes. Most were twin-engine DC-3s with a handful of four-engine Boeing 307s and 314s. Often the trained crews went with the aircraft, placing the civilian fliers under military orders. New four-engine DC-4s and Constellations under order for the airlines when the war began were diverted to military needs and became C-54s (heavily used in all theaters) and C-69s (only a few by 1945).

Airline aircraft and crews accomplished 88 percent of ATC transport work in 1942, but as the military built up its own air transport capacity, the role of airlines declined—to 68 percent in 1943, only a third by 1944, and about 20 percent in 1945. ATC operated 1,000 of its own aircraft by end of 1943 and 3,700 by end of the war less than two years later. Thus, by early 1944 many of the requisitioned airliners began to be returned to their original owners, easing some of the limitations on civilian flying.

Under the press of government and military need, airliner usage and load factors sharply increased. With more than half its fleet out of the picture, an airline system of priority use was put into place immediately; government-priority mandates came into force in early 1942. Under these, military and other government needs came first; civilians flew only if space was available (rare during the first two years of war). Slowly, a massive program of airfield building and improvements made it easier. During the war, airports went from small grass fields in many cases to massive cement runways, allowing larger aircraft, longer takeoffs, and heavier take-off and landing weights. Although most of these were military at first, many became civil airfields after the war.

Most airlines greatly expanded their routes as military needs dictated. This new service would lay the groundwork for arguments over postwar airline operations. This was especially true of transoceanic services, where Pan American's prewar monopoly was broken under the pressing need for more capacity. TWA, for example, became a transatlantic service, ferrying high-priority personnel and cargo to and from Britain. Northwest and United expanded operations to Alaska and Hawaii, respectively. American Export Airlines, though created by the shipping company American Export in 1937, began flying its three VS-42 four-engine flying boats across the Atlantic in mid-1942. Pan Am expanded on its own overseas service. In a series of agreements with the U.S. and British governments in mid-1941, Pan Am created three subsidiaries to undertake special missions. Pan American Air Ferries was established to deliver American aircraft to Khartoum from Miami. Pan American Airways Co. was created to operate an air service from the United States to West Africa. And Pan American Airways-Africa, Ltd., focused on developing the airfields, and then air service, across Africa. This service was extended to Cairo and Tehran after the United States entered the war.

Airlines provided key personnel to the military. At the top, for example, American Airlines President Cyrus R. Smith became the deputy to assist Gen. Harold George in building up the ATC. Smith's operational experience was vital in the rapid development of the military's own cargo and passenger capacity. But thousands of others—especially pilots and mechanics—followed, either working on military projects under contract or going directly into the military. This infusion of talent was vital to the relatively short time it took to create a high-capacity military air transport operation.

Among the Allied powers, airline operations all but stopped save for direct military support roles. Britain's Imperial Airways (which became BOAC in mid-1940) ceased civil operation and came under military command. Headquarters were relocated west to Bristol; landplane and seaplane bases moved farther west as well. Imperial maintained civilian service between London and Paris until the German occupation of the latter in June 1940. Flying-boat services to Africa and the Horseshoe Route around the Indian Ocean to Australia and New Zealand began in mid-1940 and operated until Japanese advances in early 1942. Then Australia's QANTAS flew Catalina seaplanes from Ceylon to Perth, a distance of 3,500 miles; these "double sunrise" flights made up the longest nonstop air route of the war and took 27–30 hours with a 1,200-pound payload. To the extent their equipment escaped loss through battle or occupation, KLM, Sabena, Air France, and QANTAS (among others) used their surviving airliners or were forced to use "interim types" (converted bombers) as further development of promising airliners had to be cancelled for the duration. In the Far East, China's CNAC conducted refugee flights as well as food and cargo deliveries. Facing extreme problems of airliner and airport maintenance, especially in the celebrated flights over the Himalayan Hump, CNAC made a big contribution in the war against Japan.

Airlines of the Axis nations saw their fortunes more directly impacted by the battlefield. Germany's Lufthansa, about to launch service to South America, across the North Atlantic, and even to Asia when the war began in 1939, saw these plans quashed (not to be realized for two decades) and operated routes only in occupied Europe and to Spain. Its final service in May 1945 was from the northern German coast into Norway (Lufthansa was banned from resuming service until 1955). Italy's Ala Littoria served Germany and Italian colonies in North Africa. Japanese airlines came under direct military control, with extensive army and navy routes to Southeast Asia and out to Pacific islands (Japanese airline service was banned from 1945 to 1952).

The Korean War (1950–1953) again forced the military to turn to airlines for help, though on a far smaller scale. Trans-Ocean, United, Pan American, and Northwest, all with Pacific experience, flew for the Military Air Transport Service, carrying troops and priority cargo into staging airfields in

Japan (the military flew into Korea itself). Drawing on the Korean experience, in 1952 the Air Transport Association (the airlines' trade organization) and the Department of Defense cooperated to create the Civil Reserve Air Fleet (CRAF). This established the specific airliners the military could automatically requisition. CRAF included government financing to enhance the cargo-carrying capacity of airliners, especially of wide-body jets after 1970.

The several Middle East wars from the 1950s into the 1970s proved the value of a national airline when El Al was the only carrier to connect Israel with the outside world. El Al stripped interiors to carry freight and to evacuate tourists and then had to deal with the sharp drop-off in tourism traffic after each conflict. In the 1990–1991 Gulf War, 11 scheduled and 13 supplemental carriers took part under CRAF in 5,300 missions carrying 64 percent of troops and 27 percent of war cargo.

CRAF did not play a part in the Vietnam War because the U.S. military buildup, beginning in 1961, was so gradual. World and other supplemental carriers as well as major airlines provided regular charter service, carrying military personnel into the battle area and out for recreation in East Asian and Hawaii. Some "airline" operations, such as Air America, were really camouflage for covert operations by the CIA. And several carriers were on hand for the final evacuations as the war ended. CRAF was used with good results in the Gulf War.

Christopher H. Sterling

See also

Air America; Berlin Airlift

References

Craven, Wesley F., and James L. Cate, eds. *The Army Air Forces in World War II, Volume 7: Services Around the World.* Chicago: University of Chicago Press, 1958 (reprinted by Government Printing Office, 1983), "Air Transport."

Culbert, Tom, and Andy Dawson. *PanAfrica: Across the Sahara in 1941 with Pan Am.* McLean, VA: Paladwr Press, 1998.

Davies, R.E.G. *A History of the World's Airlines.* London: Oxford University Press, 1964, chap. 15, "Air Transport at War," pp. 225–240.

Serling, Robert J. *When the Airlines Went to War.* New York: Kensington Books, 1998.

Airships

Prior to World War I, Germany had pioneered the development of the rigid airship. This was principally the work of one man, Count Ferdinand von Zeppelin, who had become intrigued with the thought of lighter-than-air flight after observing the use of balloons during the American Civil War. In November 1909, Zeppelin airships equipped DELAG, the world's first commercial airline operation. Development work continued in the years prior to the war, funded largely by public subscription and government investment. The giant airships became a source of national pride, and despite the fact that other manufacturers entered the field, the name "Zeppelin" was so closely associated with their construction that it has become synonymous with the word "airship."

The rigidity in a rigid airship came from a welded duralumin framework that formed the body of the cigar-shaped craft. Inside this skeleton were a number of gas cells containing the highly flammable hydrogen that made the ship lighter than air. The inside of the body was accessible during flight for maintenance and repair purposes, entry being gained by ladder from the gondolas suspended beneath its underside, lateral movement running over a catwalk that spanned the length of the ship. Engines housed in the gondolas provided forward movement. Later models had a machine gun station on the top of the envelope for defense against aerial attack.

The German army and navy both operated airships, but it was the Naval Airship Division, under the zealous direction of Fregattenkapitän (Frigate Captain) Peter Strasser, that really made the giant craft famous.

The German Zeppelins became a matter of national concern for the British. In the early days of World War I, the British imagined they might be attacked at any moment, but the Zeppelins did not attack until the night of 19–20 January 1915.

Early in the war, British response to the attacks was weak. Searchlights would seek out the Zeppelins, and ground fire would be aimed in their direction, but defending aircraft were too slow in climb rate and lacked adequate performance to reach the altitudes where Zeppelins operated. It was 2 September 1916 before an airship (the Schütte-Lanz SL11) was downed on British soil. The victor was Second Lieutenant William Leefe Robinson, who received the Victoria Cross for his feat.

Improvements came on both sides, but fighter performance eventually matched and then overtook progress in airship design, leading to a decrease in the frequency of Zeppelin attacks and, in time, their suspension in favor of a bombing program built around Gothas and *Riesenflugzeug* (giant aircraft).

The biggest airship disaster of the war came on the night of 19–20 October 1917 in the so-called Silent Raid, so named because the airships reached such great heights over England (three of the Zeppelins making it past 21,000 feet, the L55 reaching 24,000 feet) that their engines could not be heard; the Silent Raid resulted in the loss of five of the 11 ships that left Germany for London. It was a victory for

Mother Nature, however, not the British defense, as the airships fell victim to gale-force winds that had not been predicted prior to their departure. The raid marked the beginning of the end for the airship as a military weapon.

Over the course of the war, the Naval Airship Division mounted 306 raids, which succeeded in getting 177 ships over England and producing £1,527,544 in property damage in Great Britain, against the loss of 53 airships. The last to be lost, the L70, went down before the guns of Major Egbert Cadbury and Captain Robert Leckie during the last airship raid of the war, on the evening of 5–6 August 1918. On board, in personal command of the raid, was the Leader of Airships himself, Peter Strasser.

Although less glamorous and accorded far less attention than the raids on England, reconnaissance airships arguably performed more valuable work for naval operations in the North Sea and the Baltic. Over the North Sea, they had made 971 scouting flights, more than three times the number of flights devoted to raiding England. These flights took place over the 399 days that weather made it possible (out of the 1,559 total days of the war) for an impressive 25.6 percent ratio.

The bulk of British achievement came in nonrigid form. Nonrigid airships, generically known as blimps, lacked the complex internal structure of their rigid counterparts and, like balloons, relied on the pressure of the lifting to maintain the ship's shape. British nonrigids also had less complex provision for the crew. Many times, in fact, the British gondola simply consisted of an airplane fuselage stripped of its wings and tail assembly and hung from the underside of the gas envelope. The nonrigid was also much smaller than the typical Zeppelin, with the crew generally numbering no more than two or three. Used for scouting purposes, some of the British airships carried a small bombload for use against enemy ships that might be encountered. Their chief value was in their ability to spot the enemy and then place a wireless call to nearby surface craft, which were better suited to handle the problem.

At the beginning of the war, airships were generally limited to patrols of 2–4 hours. By the war's end, duration had increased to an impressive 12 hours (an improvement that certainly was hard on the crew), but airspeed was still as little as 5–10 mph if adverse winds were encountered.

Like their heavier-than-air counterparts, airships, whether rigid or nonrigid, contributed more to World War I by what they could see than what they could hit. By the time hostilities renewed in 1939, aviation technology had progressed to the point that airships' low performance was no longer acceptable, and they had long since passed from the military scene.

James Streckfuss

See also

Balloons; German Naval Airship Division; World War I Aviation

References

Mowthorpe, Ces. *Battlebags: British Airships of the First World War.* Phoenix Mill, Gloucheştershire, UK: Sutton, 1995.

Robinson, Dr. Douglas. *The Zeppelin in Combat.* London: G. T. Foulis, 1962.

Alam el Halfa, Battle of (1942)

Marked the defeat of the Afrika Korps's last attempt to reach Alexandria. Within 17 days of assuming his Egyptian command, General Bernard L. Montgomery led his first major action against the Afrika Korps's final effort to break through the Eighth Army's defenses and gain the Suez Canal. The successful British repulse of Axis forces at Alam el Halfa (31 August–6 September 1942) enjoyed massive assistance from the RAF and USAAF flying combined in the Western Desert Air Force.

German Field Marshal Erwin Rommel noted after the battle that Allied airpower rendered all of his tactical plans useless. He bitterly likened his troops to nineteenth-century "savages" in the face of sustained, heavy aerial attacks.

These attacks actually began on 21 August and wrecked Rommel's motorized and armored formations, broke up his infantry concentrations, and struck his supply dumps. Allied pilots also played havoc with Axis lines of communication and reinforcement. In addition to units of the RAF and South African Air Force, the USAAF's 57th Fighter Group (equipped with Curtiss P-40s) and the 12th Medium Bomb Group (operating North American B-25s) participated in the action.

After Alam el Halfa, the Eighth Army never again lost air superiority to Rommel's forces.

D. R. Dorondo

See also

El Alamein, Air Battles of; North African Campaign; Regia Aeronautica (World War II)

References

Boyne, Walter J. *Clash of Wings: World War II in the Air.* New York: Simon and Schuster, 1994.

Gilbert, Adrian, ed. *The Imperial War Museum Book of the Desert War.* London: Motorbooks International, 1995.

Heckmann, Wolf. *Rommel's War in Africa.* Trans. Stephen Seago. Garden City, NY: Doubleday, 1981.

Albatros Aircraft

Next to Fokker, Albatros designs are probably the best-known German aerial products of World War I. Unlike

Fokker, however, the activities of the Albatros factory were not confined primarily to the design and production of fighters. Throughout the war, it turned out aircraft aimed at fulfilling practically every air service function, including unarmed trainers (B types), armed two-seaters (C types), seaplanes (W types), armored ground attack aircraft (J types), bombers (G types), and, of course, the famous Albatros D line of single-seat fighters. The *Riesenflugzeug,* or giant aircraft, was the notable exception.

Thousands of Albatros aircraft were built, and they served on every front on which the German army and navy fought. It is perhaps ironic that only two original Albatrosses survive today, both of them D.Va single-seat fighters: one in the National Air and Space Museum in Washington, D.C., the other in the Australian War Memorial in Canberra.

Despite their varying functions, Albatros designs had a strong family resemblance. All had a plywood-covered, semimonocoque fuselage, which provided strength beyond the normal wood-framed, wire-braced structure of the day. Use of Mercedes, Benz, or Argus inline engines of various horsepower ratings was also common to Albatros designs.

Armament on the two-seaters consisted of a Parabellum machine gun for the observer, fitted to a rotating ringmount and, after the invention of the interrupter gear, a single Spandau gun mounted on the engine hood that fired through the propeller. On the single-seat D fighters, twin Spandau guns were carried.

The best known of the Albatros stable was the D.III, the single-seater that devastated the Royal Flying Corps (RFC) during the spring of 1917. The fuselage of the D.III and its successors, the D.V and D.Va, was vintage Albatros, but the sesquiplane wing layout was inspired by the success of the Nieuport. The bracing that connected the upper wing to the lower gave rise to the nickname "V-strutter" in RFC combat reports. It also led to occasional wing failures when thrown about in combat, a problem that contributed to its eventual replacement by the Fokker D.VII. A D.III variant used by Austria-Hungary was preferred over its own designs and had better performance than its Western Front counterpart.

Like other German aircraft manufacturers, Albatros became a victim of the aviation ban imposed on Germany by the Versailles Treaty and disappeared following World War I.

James Streckfuss

See also

Fokker Aircraft (Early Years)

References

Gray, Peter, and Owen Thetford. *German Aircraft of the First World War.* London: Putnam, 1962.

Lamberton, William, and E. F. Cheesman. *Fighter Aircraft of the 1914–1918 War.* London: Harleyford, 1960.

______. *Reconnaissance and Bomber Aircraft of the 1914–1918 War.* London: Harleyford, 1962.

Alenia

The leading Italian aerospace company. Alenia was formed on 20 December 1990 following the decision by the IRI-Finmeccanica state conglomerate to merge its subsidiaries Aeritalia and Selenia into a single high-technology company with improved international competitiveness. The liquidation of state conglomerate EFIM also brought Agusta into IRI-Finmeccanica, whose restructuring thus came to coincide with the painful rationalization of the Italian aerospace industry. Alenia completed the key Aeritalia programs, including Tornado and AMX, but sold or discontinued marginal businesses like Partenavia. To facilitate international alliances, in 1997 Alfa Avio was sold to Fiat Avio; Alenia then split into Alenia Aerospazio and Alenia Difesa, the latter comprising the radar, missile, and OTO Melara activities. In 1998, Alenia Difesa joined Marconi to form Alenia Marconi Systems.

In April 2000, the Alenia military product line comprised the Eurofighter Typhoon, C-27J airlifter (with Lockheed Martin), ATR42 maritime patrol versions, and the Airbus A400M airlifter project; commercial aircraft included the ATR commuter (more than 600 built) and major structural components for several Airbus, Boeing, and Dassault types, plus overhauls and conversions. Space activities included satellites as well as various inhabited and structural elements of the International Space Station.

Gregory Alegi

References

Donald, David, and Jon Lake, eds. *Encyclopedia of World Military Aircraft.* London: Aerospace, 1996.

Aleutian Islands Air War

U.S.-Japanese conflicts in U.S. territory during World War II. The prospect of an enemy conquest of Alaska was very real when a Japanese task force moved against the Aleutian Islands in 1942. Japan sought to establish bases from which to strike the U.S. West Coast. Although strategically positioned, the extreme climate of the region rendered it a difficult area for aviation. Nearly continuous fog, high winds, extreme cold, williwaws (blizzards), and mountainous islands make the Aleutians a risky place to fly even today with the most modern equipment. In the 1940s, it was extremely hazardous.

The Japanese established bases at Attu, on the west end of the Aleutians, and nearer to Alaska, at Kiska. Allied forces fought off an attack on Dutch Harbor (3–4 June 1942). U.S. bases at Cold Bay and Umnak were supplemented farther out the island chain on Adak and Amchitka. Airplanes were often overturned in their parking spots by the ferocious williwaws. Supply problems added to the burden.

The Japanese also suffered from the weather, and the U.S. Navy's blockade made resupply nearly impossible. U.S. bombers repeatedly struck the Japanese garrisons.

Finally, in May 1943 the United States seized Attu. U.S. fighters and bombers supported the three-week operation. In the only air-to-air battle of the campaign, five Lockheed P-38s drove off 16 Mitsubishi G4M "Betty" bombers, dispatched from the Kurile Islands north of Hokkaido. Only seven Japanese aircraft returned home. No further support was forthcoming for the Japanese on Attu. The Americans were victorious, but nearly 4,000 G.I.s were casualties, many due to cold and frostbite. Only 28 of the 3,000 defenders were taken alive. Kiska was evacuated by the Japanese navy, in great secrecy, under the cover of the dreadful weather, much to the relief of invading U.S. and Canadian soldiers.

Attu and nearby Shemya Island served as bases for a campaign against the Kuriles. During the last two years of the war, 1,500 sorties were flown against the northern reaches of Japan, hitting naval and air bases. These operations by a few dozen bombers tied up 500 enemy airplanes (more than 10 percent of the Japanese air force at war's end) and more than 40,000 troops by threatening invasion from the north, the same worry that had haunted U.S. planners in 1942. The Aleutian campaigns cost the United States 56 airplanes in combat and 209 to weather. Japanese losses also reflected the harsh climate: 69 combat losses against 200 weather losses.

Aleutian bases established during World War II went on to play a prominent role throughout the long Cold War struggle.

James M. Pfaff

References

Cloe, John Haile. *The Aleutian Warriors.* Missoula, MT: Pictorial Histories, 1993.

Cohen, Stan. *The Forgotten War.* Missoula, MT: Pictorial Histories, 1993.

Garfield, Brian. *The Thousand-Mile War.* Fairbanks: University of Alaska Press, 1996.

Jablonski, Edward. *Airwar.* Garden City, NY: Doubleday, 1971.

Algeria

From 1954 to 1962, France sought to maintain control of its colony in Algeria using a mix of ground, naval, and air forces to fight Algerian rebels. Initially, air operations remained limited due to the commitment of aircraft and personnel to the Indochina front.

By 1959, however, some 40 percent of French airpower was on Algerian territory, and another 20 percent based in France supported the effort. The hardware eventually amounted to some 600 airplanes and 600 helicopters from the three services. The air interdiction practices allowed the French to seal off the Algerian border, preventing rebel support from neighboring Morocco and Tunisia. In addition, heavy helicopter use to ferry commandos helped defeat organized rebel forces. However, such efforts failed to remove the psychological impact of war and ongoing terrorism, to the point where negotiations between the two sides led to Algerian independence in 1962.

Guillaume de Syon

References

Guerilla Warfare and Airpower in Algeria, 1954–1960. Maxwell AFB, AL: Air University, 1965.

Heger, Michel. *Djebel Amour Djebel Amer: Hélicos Marine en Algérie 1956–1962* Paris: Presses de la Cité, 1998.

Shrader, Charles R. *The First Helicopter War: Logistics and Mobility in Algeria 1954–1962.* Westport, CT: Praeger, 1999.

Alksnis, Yakov I. (1897–1940)

Commander of the Red Air Force during the 1930s. Yakov Ivanovich Alksnis was born in 1897 in Latvia. He joined the Bolshevik Party in 1916 and participated in the Russian Revolution and civil war. Remaining in the Red Army, he became an aviator during the 1920s, and in June 1931 he was appointed commander of the Red Air Force. He was closely associated with Mikhail Tukhachevsky, a former Chief of Staff and later marshal of the Soviet Union, and under his command the Red Air Force saw rapid expansion and modernization. Notable was the large-scale introduction of the TB-3, the world's first four-motor monoplane bomber, though these bombers were not intended as an independent strike force. He also oversaw the dispatch of pilots to fight in Spain. In December 1937, during the purge of the Soviet high command, Alksnis was arrested on false charges of treason. He was executed in 1940.

George M. Mellinger

See also

Polikarpov, Nikolai N.; Soviet Volunteer Pilots; Tupolev Aircraft

References

Andersson, Lennart. *Soviet Aircraft and Aviation 1917–1941.* London: Putnam 1994.

Erickson, John, *The Soviet High Command.* London: Macmillan, 1962.

Rapoport, Vitaly, and Yuri Alexeev. *High Treason Essays on the History of the Red Army, 1918–1938.* Durham, NC: Duke University Press,1985.

ALLIED FORCE (1999)

NATO code name for peacemaking air campaign designed to protect ethnic Albanians in the Yugoslav province of Kosovo from Serb aggression and to force Yugoslav authorities to agree to a peace settlement. Operation ALLIED FORCE is often hailed as the first time in military history that airpower has achieved victory in a conflict on its own. Indeed, Operation ALLIED FORCE played a prominent role in ending ethnic cleansing in Kosovo, returning more than 840,000 refugees to their homes and restoring a semblance of peace to the troubled province.

Operation ALLIED FORCE rose from the ashes of the failed Rambouillet peace negotiations in January-February 1999, when a Serb delegation refused to accept a NATO peace plan for Kosovo. As negotiations collapsed on 19 March, Yugoslav President Slobodan Milosevic initiated Operation HORSESHOE, an operation designed to cleanse Kosovo of its ethnic Albanian population by force before NATO forces could be brought to bear. In the face of Yugoslav intransigence and escalating violence in Kosovo, NATO decided to proceed with Operation ALLIED FORCE on 24 March.

Initially, ALLIED FORCE was intended to be a short conflict with limited objectives. NATO would demonstrate its resolve to Milosevic, who would accept a negotiated settlement in the face of a limited NATO bombardment. ALLIED FORCE would then achieve its objectives of stopping the killing in Kosovo, returning refugees to their homes and creating the conditions for a political settlement. For the first nine days of the operation, NATO aircraft focused on so-called Phase I targets: the Yugoslav Integrated Air Defense System, command and control, and heavy weapons in Kosovo. NATO had 214 combat aircraft at its disposal as the conflict began, arrayed against a Yugoslav air defense system equipped with 16 MiG-29 Fulcrum fighters. Regardless, NATO aircraft achieved air superiority on the first night of the war. To avoid aircraft losses, Lieutenant General Michael Short restricted NATO fliers to a minimum altitude of 15,000 feet.

When Milosevic did not give in, NATO moved on to Phase II targets on 3 April and began targeting Yugoslav military forces south of the 44th Parallel. As the conflict continued to drag on and the refugee crisis worsened, ALLIED FORCE began to focus on the morale of the Serb public rather than Milosevic himself. On 1 May, NATO expanded its target set to include lines of communications, refineries, and electric power grids in Serbia. Despite a major setback following the accidental bombing of the Chinese Embassy on 7 May, NATO aircraft kept up a steady effort of about 250 combat sorties per day until Yugoslav military authorities agreed to NATO demands on 9 June.

Although historian John Keegan lauded ALLIED FORCE as proving a war can be won by airpower alone, Milosevic's capitulation coincided with other key events of the conflict. In the last days of May, NATO leaders began publicly discussing options for a NATO ground offensive against Yugoslavia before the end of 1999. In addition, rebels of the Kosovo Liberation Army began a major offensive against Yugoslav forces in Kosovo on 26 May. Although the offensive failed, Yugoslav forces were forced to deploy to meet the rebel threat, which exposed their fielded forces to NATO air attack. Regardless, NATO airpower was the catalyst in ending ethnic cleansing in Kosovo in 1999.

Mark D. Witzel

References

Carpenter, Ten Galen, ed. *NATO's Empty Victory,* Washington, DC: CATO Institute, 2000.

Daalder, Ivo H., Michael E. and O'Hanlon. *Winning Ugly: NATO's War to Save Kosovo.* Washington, DC: Brookings Institute Press, 2000.

American Volunteer Group

World War II organization of volunteer fliers in China. The American Volunteer Group (AVG), popularly known as the Flying Tigers, grew out of Chinese President Chiang Kaishek's desire for U.S. airplanes and pilots to protect the Burma Road, China's only access route to the outside world. By the fall of 1940, Japanese forces had blockaded the Chinese coast, leaving an unimproved mountainous route from Rangoon, Burma, to Kunming, China, as the beleaguered nation's logistical lifeline. Claire L. Chennault, Chiang's air adviser, prepared a plan for a special volunteer American air unit to guard the road. Supported strongly by Secretary of the Treasury Henry Morgenthau, Chennault's scheme won President Franklin D. Roosevelt's approval in the winter of 1940–1941.

Allocated 100 Curtiss P-40s, Chennault received permission to recruit personnel from the U.S. military services. Officially constituted for service with the Chinese Air Force on 1 August 1941, the AVG began training at Tongoo, Burma, close to Rangoon, in the fall of 1941. By early December, the organization had 82 pilots and 79 aircraft that were formed into three squadrons.

Following the Japanese attack on Pearl Harbor on 7 December 1941, Chennault sent two squadrons to Kunming to protect the Burma Road while one squadron remained in Rangoon to fight alongside the Royal Air Force. The AVG saw its first action on 20 December 1941, when Chennault's fliers shot down six of 10 Japanese bombers over Kunming.

During the early months of 1942, when the news of U.S. losses in the Pacific seemed a litany of despair, the AVG provided the only positive news from Asia. The young airmen, in their shark-nosed P-40s—painting the nose with this fearsome image was an idea borrowed from the RAF in Africa—soon became national heroes in both China and the United States. Thanks in large part to the tactical training provided by Chennault and to an efficient early warning network of ground spotters, AVG pilots scored impressive victories over the Japanese at a time when Imperial forces seemed unstoppable elsewhere.

On 4 July 1942, the AVG was officially demobilized. Recalled to U.S. military service, Chennault became commander of the China Air Task Force. Few of his AVG pilots, however, accepted induction into the U.S. Army Air Forces.

The AVG left behind an impressive record, claiming 296 enemy aircraft shot down (a figure questioned by later authors) and losing only 14 P-40s in aerial combat (with another 72 P-40s lost in accidents or abandoned). Twenty-two Americans were killed or captured; another three individuals died in training accidents.

Romanticized by the media at the time and later, the AVG nonetheless performed superbly under extraordinarily difficult circumstances. But perhaps even more important than any military contribution was their public relations value in the United States during the darkest days of World War II.

William M. Leary

See also

Chennault, Claire L.

References

Byrd, Martha. *Chennault: Giving Wings to the Tiger.* Tuscaloosa: University of Alabama Press, 1987.

Chennault, Claire Lee. *Way of a Fighter.* New York: Putnam's, 1949.

Ford, Daniel. *Flying Tigers: Claire Chennault and the American Volunteer Group.* Washington, DC: Smithsonian Institution Press, 1991.

Amet-Khan, Sultan (1916–1971)

Soviet fighter ace and twice Hero of the Soviet Union. Sultan Amet-Khan was born on 25 October 1916 in Crimea in a Tatar family. He completed flight school in 1940. Initially unsuccessful, not until 31 May 1942 would he tally a score, ramming a Ju 88 with his Hurricane fighter. Many successes followed thereafter. In October 1942, he was transferred to the 9 GIAP (Guards Fighter Air Regiment), composed of handpicked pilots and equipped first with the Yak-1, later the P-39L, and finally the La-7. On 24 August 1943 Amet-Khan was named a Hero of the Soviet Union for 19 individual and 11 group victories. During the war, Major Amet-Khan completed 603 sorties and scored 30 individual and 19 group victories in 150 air combats. He was accorded the honor a second time on 29 June 1945. After the war he became a military test pilot. He was killed testing a Tu-16LL on 2 February 1971.

George M. Mellinger

References

Bodrikhin, Nikolai, *Sovetskie Asy, ocherki o Sovetskikh letchikakh.* Moscow: TAMP Moscow, 1998.

Seidl, Hans D. *Stalin's Eagles: An Illustrated Study of the Soviet Aces of World War II and Korea.* Atglen, PA: Schiffer, 1998.

An Loc, Battle of (1972)

Major battle during the 1972 North Vietnamese Nguyen Hue (Easter) Offensive in which U.S. airpower proved the decisive factor. The Battle of An Loc, the capital of Binh Long Province in the III Corps Tactical Zone and only 65 miles from Saigon, was the southernmost prong of the Nguyen Hue Offensive, which was a large-scale, three-pronged conventional attack launched on 30 March 1972 (the other main communist attacks were aimed at Quang Tri and Kontum). On 5 April, North Vietnamese forces crossed the Cambodian border into the III Corps area of operations. After a feint at Tay Ninh City, the main attack was launched against Lôc Ninh, which was quickly overwhelmed, opening up a direct route down Highway QL-13 to Saigon through An Loc and Lai Khe. After the fall of Lôc Ninh, the North Vietnamese forces, consisting of the Fifth, Seventh, and Ninth Vietcong/North Vietnamese Army Divisions, surrounded An Loc, effectively cutting it off from outside ground reinforcement and resupply. On 3 April, after heavily shelling the city for hours, the North Vietnamese launched a massive infantry attack supported by T-54 and PT-76 tanks from several directions. The North Vietnamese attackers were almost successful in hand-to-hand and house-to-house fighting, but fires from AH-1G Cobra helicopters and continuous tactical air support from U.S. Air Force, Navy, and Marine fighter-bombers and Air Force AC-130 Spectre gunships enabled the defenders to hold out against the initial assault, but not before they were pushed into an area less than a mile square. Another critical factor in the ability of South Vietnamese forces to hold out in this and subsequent attacks was the impact of the B-52 ARC LIGHT missions that ringed the city and precluded the North Vietnamese forces from massing and completely overrunning the besieged defenders. The South Vietnamese suffered repeated ground attacks and round-the-clock heavy shelling, but, aided by U.S. Army advisers and U.S. airpower, they continued to hold ground against overwhelming odds, though sustaining heavy casualties. During the course of the battle, 252 B-52 missions were flown and 9,023 tactical air strikes were carried out. During the siege, which was finally lifted in June, the three attacking North Vietnamese divisions sustained an estimated 10,000 casualties and lost most of their tanks and heavy artillery. South Vietnamese losses were 5,400 casualties, including 2,300 dead or missing. Although An Loc was in ruins, U.S. airpower had proved decisive, and the defenders had blocked a direct assault on Saigon and effectively blunted the North Vietnamese Easter Offensive in the South.

James H. Willbanks

See also

ARC LIGHT; Boeing B-52 Stratofortress; Gunships; Helicopters, Military Use; McDonnell F-4 Phantom II; Vo Nguyen Giap

References

Pimlott, John. *Vietnam: The Decisive Battles.* New York: Macmillan, 1990.

Willbanks, James H. *Thiet Giap! The Battle of An Loc, April 1972.* Fort Leavenworth, KS: The Combat Studies Institute, 1993.

Anderson, Orville "Arson" (1895–1965)

U.S. Air Force general and airpower theorist. Orville "Arson" Anderson was born in Springville, Utah, on 2 May 1895. After leaving Brigham Young University before earning his degree, he enlisted in the U.S. Army Signal Corps Aviation Section in August 1917. Commissioned a second lieutenant a year later after completing balloon observer training, Anderson gained renown for participating in the airship flights of *Explorer I* (1934) and *Explorer II* (1935), the latter flight setting an altitude record of 72,395 feet. Anderson graduated from the Air Corps Tactical School (1937) and the Command and General Staff School (1938).

Anderson's initiation in studying and formulating philosophies of airpower began in 1938 when he became the executive secretary to the Air Corps Board at Maxwell Field. Successive assignments during World War II included Chief of Plans Division at Army Air Forces Headquarters (1941–1943), chairman of the Combined Operational Planning Committee, European Theater of Operations (1943–1944), and senior military adviser, U.S. Strategic Bombing Survey (1945–1946). Anderson also served as deputy commander for operations, Eighth Air Force (1944–1945). Promotions merited by Anderson to general-officer grade included brigadier general (1942) and major general (1944).

During World War II, Anderson authored "A Study to Determine the Minimum Air Power the United States Should Have at the Conclusion of the War in Europe" (1943), which promoted a postwar plan dictating that the USAAF be strengthened so as to ensure world peace and stability under U.S. leadership and act as a countermeasure to the superior number of Soviet ground forces. Believing that U.S. ability to win future wars depended mainly on the development of superior technology and superior strategy, Anderson eagerly accepted the assignment of commandant of the Air War College, Maxwell AFB (1946–1950). As commandant, Anderson accentuated the necessity for the continuous integrated development of technology, strategy, and efficient use of military manpower in creating an effective airpower theory. Anderson's tenure as commandant of the Air War College ended abruptly in September 1950, when his comments to a civilian reporter concerning use of atomic weapons against the Soviet Union caused General Hoyt S. Vandenberg, Air Force Chief of Staff, to relieve him. General Anderson retired from military service in December 1950 and died at Maxwell AFB, Alabama, on 23 August 1965.

Mark R. Grandstaff

References

Anderson, Orvil A. *The Reminiscences of General Orvil A. Anderson.*

Futrell, Robert, and Eldon W. Downs. "In Appreciation: Major General Orvil Anderson." *Aerospace Historian* 12, 4 (1965): 103–105.

Andrews, Frank Maxwell (1884–1943)

U.S. Army lieutenant general and early advocate of offensive airpower. A West Point graduate (1906), Andrews joined the U.S. cavalry as a second lieutenant. He served in the cavalry for 11 years. When the United States entered World War I, Andrews received a transfer to the Aviation Section of the U.S. Army Signal Corps. He received his wings in 1918 and served in various stateside positions, including commander of U.S. flying fields.

In the 1930s, cost-conscious Army leaders advocated purchase of less expensive light and medium bombers such as the B-18 Bolo. Andrews wanted Boeing's four-engine

Model 299 heavy bomber, better known as the B-17 Flying Fortress. To Andrews, GHQ AF was the offensive arm of Army aviation, and he became a vocal proponent of strategic bombardment theories and the acquisition of heavy bombers.

On 30 October 1935, at Wright Field, Ohio, the prototype YB-17 crashed in flames during takeoff. Despite the setback, Andrews persisted, and his vision and determination saved the B-17. He convinced the Army to buy 13 B-17s for experimental purposes. Many called the B-17s "Andrews's Folly," but events of World War II soon proved his wisdom.

Following the January 1943 Casablanca Conference, General Dwight D. Eisenhower made Lieutenant General Andrews commander of the European theater of operations for the Air Corps. Andrews performed his duties with dedication and verve. On the afternoon of 3 May 1943, during an inspection tour, General Andrews's B-24D Liberator, fighting foggy conditions, crashed into a hillside while attempting to land at the Royal Air Force Base at Kaldadarnes, Iceland. Andrews and 13 others were killed. Only the tailgunner survived.

Andrews was buried at Arlington National Cemetery. On 31 March 1949, Andrews Air Force Base, Maryland, was named in his honor. During his career, he received the Distinguished Service Medal, Distinguished Flying Cross, and Air Medal, along with many other decorations and honors.

William Head

References

Copp, DeWitt S. "Frank M. Andrews: Marshall's Airman." In John L. Frisbee, ed., *Makers of the United States Air Force.* Washington, DC: Office of Air Force History, 1987.

Head, William P. *Every Inch a Soldier: Augustine Warner Robins and the Building of U.S. Airpower.* College Station: Texas A&M University Press, 1995.

Ansaldo

Italian leader in heavy engineering. The Ansaldo firm was created in 1852 in Genova to grant the Kingdom of Sardinia independence from foreign industry. Named after its general manager, Giovanni Ansaldo (1819–1859), it soon became a shipbuilding and armaments conglomerate and entered the aviation field in 1916. The first contract was for Sopwith Baby floatplanes under license, but the arrival of Giuseppe Brezzi (1878–1958), just released from the army, led to Ansaldo being chosen to build a new fighter type. Designed by army engineers Savoja and Verduzio, and easily recognized by the triangular rear fuselage and "W" arrangement of its wing struts, it was designated the SVA and flew in March 1917. Rejected as a fighter, with its speed and range it made many notable flights, including the 1918 Vienna raid led by Gabriele d'Annunzio (1863–1938) and the 1920 Rome-to-Tokyo flight. It is estimated that about 2,000 single- and two-seat variants were built until 1926.

Ansaldo expanded, building new plants and acquiring the Pomilio firm in Turin. Disagreements over royalties owed to Savoja and Verduzio led Brezzi to introduce new Ansaldo types, starting with the A.1 Balilla fighter that saw little combat in World War I but was used successfully in Poland against the Soviets in 1921–1922.

After World War I, Ansaldo sought markets abroad and in 1920 accounted for two-thirds of all Italian aircraft exports. It also introduced the A.300, a general-purpose biplane used extensively for army cooperation and training. But Ansaldo had overextended itself and was in a difficult financial position. The airframe activities were first concentrated in Turin, then formed into a separate company, Aeronautica Ansaldo, which obtained a license for the all-metal Dewoitine D.1 fighter, building it in the AC.2 and AC.3 variants. In 1925, Aeronautica Ansaldo was sold to Fiat, becoming its aircraft division under the name Aeronautica d'Italia.

Gregory Alegi

See also

Fiat; Italian Aircraft Development

References

Alegi, Gregory. *Ansaldo SVA 5.* Berkhamsted, UK: Albatros, 1993.

_______. *Ansaldo A.1 Balilla.* Berkhamsted, UK: Albatros, 2001.

_______. *Ansaldo (Sopwith) Baby.* Berkhamsted, UK: Albatros, 2001.

Castronovo, Valerio, ed. *L'Ansaldo e la grande guerra, 1915–1918.* Bari, Italy: Laterza, 1997.

Antimissile Defense

The use of defensive missiles and other means to destroy incoming missiles. Attempts at antiballistic missile (ABM) defense are almost as old as ballistic missiles themselves, but the daunting prospect of trying to "hit a bullet with a bullet" prevented most attempts from getting beyond the planning stages until the stakes were raised by the advent of nuclear-tipped intercontinental ballistic missiles (ICBMs) in the late 1950s.

In the United States, ABM development continued throughout the late 1950s and 1960s but was slowed due to the daunting technical challenge as well as growing concern, in government and the public, that even if an ABM system could be made to work it would only accelerate the arms race. In 1969, the Sentinel program, with its ambitious goal of city defense, was transformed while still in development into the more limited Safeguard program, aimed now only at protecting a limited number of ICBM fields.

In the Soviet Union, tests associated with its ABM program began as early as 1961, and by 1970 or 1971 the massive Galosh ABM system, built around Moscow, was probably fully operational. In May 1972, the United States and the Soviet Union signed the ABM Treaty, limiting research to the laboratory and allowing each side only two ABM sites of no more than 100 launchers each (reduced to one site in 1974). The U.S. site at Grand Forks, North Dakota, finally became operational in 1975, only to be canceled by Congress that same year; the Soviet system around Moscow continued in operation well into the 1980s.

ABM research continued in both superpowers, however, refueled by Ronald Reagan's dramatic March 1983 announcement of the new Strategic Defense Initiative. Although the so-called Star Wars system has never been deployed, its specter played an important role in the arms race during the last years of the Cold War. In the 1990s, with the advent of precision-guided munitions, the prospect of interceptor missiles that did not have to use nuclear warheads of their own became a realistic possibility for the first time. A very public demonstration of this was the use of U.S. Patriot missiles to intercept Iraqi Scud missiles over Saudi Arabia and Israel. Though later analysis concluded that far fewer of the Scuds may have been destroyed than was initially believed, the Scuds were more of a political and public relations problem than they were a military threat anyway, so in a sense the Patriot missiles accomplished their mission as soon as the media reported that they had. At the turn of the twenty-first century, the ABM controversy showed no signs of abating, as U.S. programs for both theater and national missile defense continued.

David Rezelman

See also

Air Defense Command; Antisatellite Capability; Ballistic Missile Early Warning System; Defense Advanced Research Projects Agency; Distant Early Warning; Missiles, Intercontinental Ballistic; Missiles, Surface-to-Air; North American Air Defense Command; Precision-Guided Munitions; SAGE Defense System; Strategic Arms Limitation Talks; Strategic Defense Initiative

References

Baucom, Donald R. *The Origins of SDI, 1944–1983.* Lawrence: University Press of Kansas, 1992.

Carter, Ashton B., and David N. Schwartz, eds. *Ballistic Missile Defense.* Washington, DC: Brookings Institution, 1984.

Antisatellite Capability

The United States first started work on antisatellite (ASAT) systems during the late 1950s. But the threat that these systems were intended to counter—Soviet nuclear weapons orbiting in space—failed to materialize. Because of the limitations of early guidance systems, antisatellite weapons had to use a nuclear warhead, but as the detonation of nuclear warheads would damage U.S. satellites as well, the capability was of questionable military value.

The U.S. Army's Nike-Zeus missile was originally developed as part of an antiballistic missile (ABM) system, but exoatmospheric missiles by definition provided a limited ASAT capability. A limited test series launched eight Nike-Zeus missiles from Kwajalein Island, and the first successful U.S. antisatellite intercept took place on 23 May 1963.

During 1964 the U.S. Air Force deployed several nuclear-tipped Thor launch vehicles that were modified for the antisatellite mission on Johnston Island in the Pacific, and the so-called Program 437 system was tested at least 16 times until its retirement in 1976. Following this the U.S. emphasis shifted to nonnuclear kinetic kill mechanisms.

The ASM-135A antisatellite missile was the primary U.S. ASAT effort during the early 1980s. Launched from a McDonnell-Douglas F-15 Eagle, this two-stage rocket carried a miniature kinetic kill vehicle that used an infrared sensor to home in on the target. A single operational test took place on 13 September 1985 against the Solwind P78-1 satellite, which was destroyed. Political and funding concerns cancelled the program in 1988.

The existing Mid-Infrared Advanced Chemical Laser (MIRACL) located at White Sands Missile Range, New Mexico, is in the process of adapting the laser for use against satellites. In addition to MIRACL, the Pentagon is working on two other ground-based ASATs based on excimer and free-electron lasers. Both technologies could be operational by 2010. The directed energy systems would have the ability to destroy large numbers of satellites in a very short period of time, compared to the kinetic energy ASAT.

Dennis R. Jenkins

References

Jenkins, Dennis R. *McDonnell Douglas F-15 Eagle: Supreme Heavy-Weight Fighter.* Leicester, UK: Aerofax/Midland Counties, 1998.

Antisubmarine Warfare (ASW)

ASW seeks to neutralize the fighting capacities of submarines. Strategically, ASW forces accomplish their mission by containing, destroying, or limiting the effectiveness of submarine fleets. Tactically, ASW operations include four components: surveillance and reconnaissance; detection; tracking; and attack and destruction.

Stealth and invisibility are the submarine's greatest allies; it can approach and attack its target without detection. Prenuclear submarines, however, were forced to surface periodically, leaving them vulnerable to discovery and attack.

Military tacticians conceived the idea of using airplanes against submarines before World War I. In 1911, the British Admiralty, acknowledging the potential destructiveness of submarines, appointed a committee to study means for defending against the menace. Lieutenant Hugh Williamson, captain of the British submarine B-3, was one of the officers solicited for ideas. A pilot as well as a submariner, Williamson advocated, in his paper "The Aeroplane in Use Against the Submarine," utilizing flying machines to neutralize hostile submarines.

By Christmas 1914, balloons, airships, and other vehicles were reconnoitering submarines and tracking their movements. Kite balloons and dirigibles proved adept at locating submarines, consequently making their operations more hazardous and less productive. Within a few months, aircraft armed with small bombs were attacking submarines and inflicting damage. It was not until September 1916 that an airplane succeeded in sinking a submarine operating in open sea. Nonetheless, airplanes received substantial ASW duty, and by 1917 patrol aircraft were a fixture in Allied convoys traveling the Atlantic and Mediterranean.

Military strategists drew three lessons from World War I airborne ASW. First, they discovered that any air presence, irrespective of its size, was better than none at all. As Williamson predicted, aircraft exerted the greatest pressure on submarines by forcing them to submerge, denying them the tactical advantage and thereby neutralizing them. The second lesson was that aircraft needed a dependable detection device if they hoped to fully participate in ASW. Finally, military officials concluded that antisubmarine aircraft needed technological advances in aerodynamics, weaponry, and telegraphy.

The outbreak of World War II saw the Royal Air Force, the U.S. Naval Aviation Corps, and other agencies responsible for aerial ASW ill-equipped for their missions. Budgetary constraints left admirals and generals little money to test and equip their airplanes with radar, sonar, and other antisubmarine innovations. Few planes were equipped with ship-search radar, sonar, or hydrophones. Most planes continued to use bombs, bombsights, and bomb-release gear that were substandard or obsolete.

During World War II, airborne ASW evolved into a substantial threat as a result of advances in tactics, aircraft, submarine detection, and weaponry. Better coordination between patrol aircraft and convoy vessels increased the efficiency of both, and new long-range machines and aircraft carriers allowed for longer and wider surveillance and reconnaissance. Strategic bombing wreaked havoc on submarine pens, yards, and installations. Radar, sonar, and magnetic airborne detection (MAD) enabled airplanes to locate and track submarines. Air-dropped depth charges and homing torpedoes permitted air units to more easily destroy their prey.

Yet by war's end, submarines had evolved sufficiently to thwart their airborne antagonists. Fast snorkel boats like the German Type XXI were practically impervious to airborne radar and MAD gear, again leaving aircraft without effective means to detect submarines. Technically, if not militarily, submarines emerged from the war victorious.

Even today there is no single detection device capable of leading an aircraft to a submerged submarine. Modern ASW aircraft rely on a combination of radar, sonar, and magnetic, exhaust-trail, and infrared detectors to pinpoint the location of vessels. Onboard computers enable pilots to process data drawn from these various sensors. Once they have found their prey, aircraft employ acoustic homing torpedoes, guided missiles, and rockets to deliver the mortal blow.

With silent, nonmagnetic submarines on the horizon, the future of aerial ASW poses significant challenges. Detection sensors and ordnance currently available seems powerless against vessels operating several miles beneath the surface. Yet despite these limitations, aircraft retain the speed, flexibility, and elusiveness that have traditionally made them dangerous to submarines. Aircraft will continue to operate as a destructive platform and, perhaps more important, as a constraining force whose mere presence restricts submarines to innocuous movements near the ocean floor.

Daniel E. Worthington

See also

Aerial Torpedoes; Balloons; Flying Boats; Helicopters, Military Use; Magnetic Airborne Detection; Radar; Sikorsky, Igor I.; World War I Aviation; World War II Aviation

References

Price, Alfred. *Aircraft Versus Submarine: The Evolution of the Anti-Submarine Aircraft, 1912–1980.* London: Jane's Information Group, 1980.

Terraine, John. *The U-Boat Wars, 1916–1945.* New York: G. P. Putnam's Sons, 1989.

Antonov Aircraft

Soviet aircraft design bureau specializing in military transport aircraft. Oleg Konstantinovich Antonov was born in Moscow in 1906, and from 1923 through the 1930s he specialized in the design and construction of gliders. During World War II, he was assigned to the Yakovlev bureau. He established his own Antonov design bureau in Siberia in 1946, relocating almost immediately to Kiev. The Antonov An 2 appeared in 1947. Although it was ridiculed in the West for its seemingly outdated biplane configuration, it proved well-adapted for its role as a civilian and military light transport capable of operating from undeveloped fields, carrying a dozen passengers.

When production ended in 1992, a total of 17,400 An 2s had been built in the Soviet Union and Poland, plus another 1,500 in China. A more modern design, the An 8, appeared in 1958, a twin-engine, high-tail, shoulder-wing transport similar in concept to the Lockheed Hercules. After a short production run, two larger four-motor derivatives, the An 10 civilian airliner and the military An 12, appeared. The An 12, was even more like the C-130 and was capable of carrying light armored vehicles or 100 paratroops. Notable was the presence of a gun turret in the tail, present even on most civilian examples. With 1,265 examples produced, it became the Soviet Union's main transport and was widely exported.

During the period 1962–1992, Antonov also produced the An 24, An 26, An 30, and An 32 twin-motor, high-wing transports, all bearing more than a family resemblance, each optimized for slightly different functions, from feeder airliner to light cargo aircraft to aerial survey. Although the An 30 and An 32 were produced in small series, some 1,400 examples each of the An 24 and An 26 each were produced, and both were widely exported. Only 66 of the huge An 22s, with four contrarotating turboprops, were produced from 1965 to 1975; this aircraft was capable of transporting Scud missile launchers or two T-55 tanks and remains in limited service. Its successor is the An 124, a four-turbofan transport in the class of the C-5A and capable of lifting 150 tons.

A stretched variant of the An 124, with six fan-jet engines and a twin tail, is the An 225, the largest (except for the Hughes Hercules flying boat) and most powerful aircraft ever built. This aircraft was designed specifically for piggyback transport of the Buran space shuttle. With the termination of the Russian shuttle program, the single An 225 has been grounded. The new generation of Antonov transports is the An 72 and An 74 family, with twin jets mounted over the shoulder-high wings. These transports have been in limited production from the late 1980s for both Russia and Ukraine.

George M. Mellinger

References

Gunston, Bill. *The Encyclopedia of Russian Aircraft, 1975–1995.* Osceola, WI: Motorbooks International, 1995.

ANVIL (1944)

Allied code name for invasion of southern France on 15 August 1944. Other commitments limited air support until 5 August, when the Mediterranean Allied Air Forces (MAAF) began hitting Luftwaffe bases, lines of communications, and coastal defenses. To hide the location of the landings, MAAF struck four potential beaches. The limited supply of ammunition for the naval guns made airpower even more important in the preassault bombardment. MAAF effectively interdicted German movements, but clouds hampered the final prelanding bombardment.

Grant Weller

See also

Mediterranean Theater of Operations

References

Clarke, Jeffrey J., and Robert Ross Smith. *Riviera to the Rhine.* Washington, DC: Center of Military History, 1993.

Anzio, Battle of (1944)

The Allies' attempted end run, launched on 22 January 1944, to outflank the Germans' Gustav Line in Italy. The Wehrmacht's fierce resistance at Cassino occasioned the Allied decision to execute an amphibious landing farther up Italy's Tyrrhenian coast. As early as 13 January the XII Bomber Command and XII Air Support Command (XII ASC; later redesignated XII Tactical Air Command, or XII TAC) began preparatory attacks ranging from central Italy to the coasts of France. Units of the Fifteenth Air Force (Fifteenth AF) also participated. Employing every type of aircraft from Curtiss P-40 and North American A-36 fighter-bombers to Boeing B-17 and Consolidated B-24 heavy bombers, USAAF fliers pounded Axis airfields, railroads, road junctions, bridges, and targets of opportunity. Simultaneously they engaged Axis aircraft (almost entirely German) over Anzio's environs in a largely successful battle for aerial superiority.

At the assault's beginning on 22 January 1944, "nearly the entire Twelfth Air Force [was] dedicated to supporting the invasion." In addition, the Fifteenth AF dealt the Luftwaffe a severe blow by heavily bombing its airfields and repair facilities in the Po Valley on 30 January. Nevertheless, Allied forces failed to break out immediately. Taking advantage, German forces savagely counterattacked the beaches on 16 February. In response, XII ASC and Fifteenth AF flew more than 250 fighter and fighter-bomber sorties to help stem the German advance.

More than 800 Fifteenth AF bomber sorties (North American B-25s, in addition to B-17s and B-24s) followed the next day, not counting continuing attacks by single-engine aircraft even as the Luftwaffe's Messerschmitt Bf 109s and Focke-Wulf Fw 190s flew approximately 80 combat sorties of their own in close support of the German assaults.

The Allies' furious pace sustained itself to the end of the critical phase of the German attacks on 20 February.

Then three months of sustained positional warfare followed, as the beachhead remained contained by the German Fourteenth Army. Throughout the period, Allied airpower harassed German forces and attempted to keep the pressure off the beleaguered U.S. VI Corps. When the breakout finally did occur in May, Allied airpower played a key part. Strikes by XII TAC aircraft hit German lines of communication southeast of Rome, long-range artillery positions, and supply dumps. The railroad running northwest from the key local objective of Cisterna was repeatedly bombed and strafed, as were German gun positions around VI Corps's perimeter. Heavy bombers of 15th AF were tasked to hit Velletri and Sezze while a forward air controller attached to VI Corps HQ directed fighter-bombers to targets of opportunity. Despite overcast conditions on D-Day (23 May), XII TAC fighter-bombers flew 722 sorties on that day alone. Overall, Mediterranean Allied air force aircraft executed more than 73,000 effective sorties and dropped some 51,500 tons of bombs during Operation DIADEM, the simultaneous attacks on the Gustav Line and the breakout at Anzio. Twelfth Air Force alone was credited with destroying more than 6,500 motorized vehicles, tracked and wheeled, during the period.

D. R. Dorondo

References

Craven, Wesley F., and James L. Cate, eds. *The Army Air Forces in World War II, Volume 3: Europe: ARGUMENT to V-E Day, January 1944 to May 1945*, Washington, DC: Office of Air Force History, 1983.

Fisher, Ernest F. *Cassino to the Alps: United States Army in WWII: The Mediterranean Theater of Operations.* Washington, DC: Center of Military History, 1993.

Hammel, Eric. *Air War Europa: America's Air War Against Germany in Europe and North Africa. Chronology, 1942–1945.* Pacifica, CA: Pacifica Press, 1994.

Apollo Space Program

In 1961, President John F. Kennedy issued a public challenge that called for the United States to land a man on the moon before the end of 1969. Thus began a crash course designed in part to respond to repeated Soviet successes in space. Although the manned aspect of the challenge first involved the Mercury and Gemini programs, it also called for the investigation of lunar conditions and the construction of a rocket capable of reaching the moon. Thus, the existing Project Lunar Orbiter was modified to serve the needs of Apollo by measuring radiation and photographing the moon closely. Five such missions were launched by 1967; in parallel, seven Surveyor missions were sent to land on the moon (two failed), thereby providing critical information to Apollo planners.

In the meantime, a lunar vehicle had to be designed from scratch. Several formulas existed on paper for a lunar landing, each with advantages and shortcomings that depended on the number of passengers, the weight requirements, and what kind of vehicle would land on the moon. Eventually, the National Aeronautics and Space Administration (NASA) approved a new rocket, the massive Saturn V, with a three-man command module, which was developed and built by North American Aviation (later Rockwell). The command module was attached to a service module that contained all fuel, maneuvering rockets, and oxygen supplies. Above the capsule, an escape tower was installed for use during the launch phase of the flight. Although tested multiple times from 1964 onward, the capsule required modifications following a tragic accident during a ground test on 27 January 1967, when the crew of Apollo-Saturn 204 (a training mission later renamed Apollo 1) died on the launchpad at Cape Canaveral during a simulated flight.

Eighteen months later, in October 1968, Apollo 7, the first manned mission, went into earth orbit. By then engineers at the Grumman Corporation were feverishly solving last-minute problems on the Lunar Module (LM), which was to serve as the landing vehicle. The strange shape of the contraption belied its extreme complexity, which involved the use of two engines in nonatmospheric conditions, guidance thrusters, and a landing gear that was light yet sturdy. When the details were finally settled, the LM was to take two of the three astronauts to the lunar surface.

In December 1968, Apollo 8 orbited the moon for the first time. Three missions later, Apollo 11 successfully landed Neil Armstrong and Edwin Aldrin on the moon on 21 July 1969 (Michael Collins piloted the Apollo command module). Another six missions were launched, five of which were successful (Apollo 13 almost ended in disaster, but its crew returned safely to earth). The technical achievement of the Apollo program was stupendous and represented the culmination of technical efforts that dated back to the German rocket program in World War II. However, the splendid achievement happened amid turmoil over the ongoing Vietnam War, rising social problems, and a declining economy, all of which prompted President Richard Nixon to scale back the program. Consequently, Apollo 17 became the last mission to the moon.

Apollo command modules were used, however, in the linking with the Skylab space station in 1973 and with a Soyuz capsule in 1975. Two completed Saturn V rockets remained unused, however, and have since become exhibits at NASA's Johnson and Kennedy Space Centers. The Apollo program did demonstrate a mastery of technocratic planning, but it failed to establish a clear legacy on which NASA could effectively build future programs. Consequently, such projects as the Space Shuttle faced considerable delays and troubles due to lack of direction from the White House and Congress.

Guillaume de Syon

See also
Gemini Project; Mercury Space Program

References
Compton, W. David. *Where No Man Has Gone Before: A History of Apollo Lunar Exploration Missions.* Washington, DC: NASA, 1989.
Logsdon, John M. *The Decision to Go to the Moon: Project Apollo and the National Interest.* Cambridge, MA: MIT Press, 1970.
McCurdy, Howard. *Space and the American Imagination.* Washington, DC: Smithsonian Institution Press, 1997.

Arado Ar 234 Blitz

The world's first jet bomber. The Blitz (or Lightning) entered Luftwaffe service early in 1945, having already served in a reconnaissance role. More than 200 of the twin-jet aircraft were manufactured, but because of fuel shortages and transportation problems, perhaps half actually reached combat units. Development began in late 1940, with the first prototype completed by 1943. The Junkers Jumo turbojets had developmental problems that, in turn, delayed the Ar 234's maiden flight until 15 June 1943. Because of its narrow fuselage, with inadequate room for retractable landing gear, early versions took off on a trolley that was jettisoned as the plane lifted off. Later the wheels themselves were jettisoned. Additional prototypes flew later in 1943 with larger BMW engines. The B models of 1944 had traditional landing gear and first flew on 10 March 1944. Initial reconnaissance missions took place in the summer of 1944. The C models in production at the end of the war used four engines (in paired nacelles) rather than two. In all, more than 30 experimental models were built, but operations came too late to have any effect on the war. The only surviving example, a B model, is in the National Air and Space Museum in Washington, D.C.

Christopher H. Sterling

References
Kober, Franz. *The World's First Jet Bombers—Arado 234, Ju 287.* West Chester, PA: Schiffer, 1990.
Myhra, David. *Arado 234C.* Atglen, PA: Schiffer, 2000.
Smith, Richard K., and Eddie J. Creek. *Arado 234 Blitz.* Sturbridge, MA: Monogram Aviation, 1992.

ARC LIGHT

Code name and general term for the use of B-52 Stratofortress bombing missions to support ground tactical opera-

The world's first operational jet bomber was the slender, fast Arado Ar 234. Highly effective, it was built in small numbers and too late to affect the outcome of the war. (Walter J. Boyne)

tions, to interdict enemy supply lines in Vietnam, Cambodia, and Laos, and later to strike targets in North Vietnam. In 1964, the U.S. Air Force began to train strategic bomber crews in the delivery of conventional munitions. Under Project Big Belly, all B-52Ds were modified so that they could carry nearly 30 tons of conventional bombs. B-52s were deployed to air force bases in Guam and Thailand. ARC LIGHT operations were most often close air support bombing raids of enemy base camps, troops concentrations, and/or supply lines.

They were used for the first time in support of troops in contact during the Battle of the Ia Drang Valley in November 1965. Releasing their bombs from 30,000 feet, the B-52s could neither be seen nor heard from the ground as they inflicted awesome damage. B-52s were instrumental in breaking up enemy concentrations besieging Khe Sanh in 1968 and Pleiku and An Loc in 1972.

The two most famous B-52 operations were LINEBACKER and LINEBACKER II. President Richard Nixon ordered LINEBACKER to stem the tide of the North Vietnamese Army's 1972 Easter Offensive. In December 1972, Nixon ordered LINEBACKER II, the so-called Christmas bombings. During this operation, B-52s bombed Hanoi and Haiphong to force North Vietnamese negotiators back to the table at the Paris peace talks.

Between June 1965 and August 1973, 126,615 B-52 sorties were flown over Southeast Asia. During those operations, the U.S. Air Force lost 31 B-52s: 18 from hostile fire over North Vietnam and 13 from operational causes.

James H. Willbanks

See also

An Loc, Battle of; Boeing B-52 Stratofortress; Cambodia Bombings; Khe Sanh; LINEBACKER I; LINEBACKER II

References

Berger, Carl, ed. *The United States Air Force in Southeast Asia.* Washington, DC: U.S. Government Printing Office, 1977.

Morrocco, John. *The Vietnam Experience: Thunder from Above—The Air War, 1941–1968.* Boston: Boston Publishing Company, 1984.

_______. *The Vietnam Experience: Rain of Fire.* Boston: Boston Publishing Company, 1985.

Argentine Aircraft Industry

Recent decades have been difficult for Argentina, formerly a prosperous and modernizing nation now struggling to preserve its industrial base. Lockheed Martin seems to have assured a continuing aeronautical tradition by acquiring, from Argentina's privatizing government, Latin America's oldest aircraft factory (dating from 1927) in the industrial city of Cordoba.

From Argentina's earliest powered flights in 1910, the simple airplanes of the era were constructed locally. European advances were closely linked to Buenos Aires via ample steamship connection and plentiful immigration from Italy and elsewhere. World War I was a disruption, but a new stream of aircraft and airmen began arriving in 1919.

Growth in population and wealth reached a peak in the 1920s, and the Fabrica Militar de Aviones (FMA; Military Aircraft Factory) was inaugurated by the government in 1927. License production of engines and aircraft commenced, with the British-designed Avro 504-J and Bristol F.2B and the French Dewoitine D.21 fighter being the initial products. Many indigenous designs followed.

A great variety of military and civil aircraft would be built over the years. A spectacular era occurred after World War II, as European talent once again refreshed Argentine airpower. Kurt Tank, designer of the Luftwaffe's formidable Focke-Wulf Fw 190 fighter, built five examples of his swept-wing jet design, as the IA-33 Pulqui II. The IA-27 Pulqui I had been a basic straight-wing jet prototype. Examples of these and other national designs are preserved in Argentine museums.

Many British military aircraft were imported after World War II and, later, U.S. aircraft, after diplomatic relations improved (Argentina was pro-Nazi until 1945). The FMA in Cordoba constructed transports, trainers, and light aircraft; foreign as well as domestic designs were assembled. But the old factory lost some of its earlier prominence as the nation's economic problems limited its business. Restricted funding came with political change after Argentina lost the 1982 Falklands War with Great Britain.

Plans to link up with the expanding Brazilian light airliner business failed to mature. Development of the Condor 500-mile-range missile also ended. Lockheed Martin, which in 1995 negotiated a 25-year lease on the Cordoba facilities, with further extension foreseen, was a welcome newcomer. Meanwhile, Argentina had supported the U.N. Coalition during the 1991 Gulf War. With Argentina's foreign policy aligning with NATO, a desperately needed upgrade to the nation's air force came in the form of the Douglas A-4AR "Fighting Hawk." Argentina had flown similar A-4 Skyhawks in the 1982 Falklands War, but the aircraft of 15 years later are remanufactured with modern controls and systems by Lockheed Martin in Cordoba.

Meanwhile, several FMA products that had languished have found new life. The IA-63 Pampa jet trainer, begun in 1979 in collaboration with Germany's Dornier, is again on the market, now supported by a reinvigorated plant. The IA-58 Pucara, used during the Falklands conflict, may again be built in small numbers. The AMX light fighter-bomber, a joint project with Aermacchi, may also see more production due to the type's success in the Balkans with the Italian air force.

Many developing nations are attempting to initiate aviation industries to supply local needs and to boost technological levels. Argentina is a different case, with a substantial tradition of aircraft manufacture. It appears that Cordoba will continue to be one of the more important centers of airpower in the Southern Hemisphere for years into the future.

Gary Kuhn

ARGUMENT (BIG WEEK, 1944)

BIG WEEK, formally known as Operation ARGUMENT, was the Allied code name for a coordinated assault in February 1944 upon German fighter factories and ball-bearing works located in Germany, Austria, and occupied Poland. These attacks were mounted by the U.S. Eighth Air Force flying from England and the U.S. Fifteenth Air Force flying from Italy. Daylight raids by U.S. bombers were supplemented by Royal Air Force area-bombing by night. Operation ARGUMENT sought to disrupt fighter production, compelling German fighters into the air where they could be destroyed. Only thus could German airpower be defeated and the success of the forthcoming Allied invasion of the continent be assured. Air superiority, the key goal of this offensive, could not have been achieved without the long-range North American P-51 Mustang fighter that escorted U.S. bombers to their targets.

For this attack, U.S. Strategic Air Forces in Europe massed 1,180 operational B-17 and B-24 bombers, as well as 676 operational P-47, P-38, and P-51 fighters. The German defensive force comprised 350 Fw 190 and Bf 109 fighters, 100 twin-engine Me 110, 210, and 410 machines, and 50 night-fighters. Armed with 210mm rockets, the twin-engine fighters were the worst threat to U.S. bombers.

Hammer blows fell upon Messerschmitt plants at Regensburg, Leipzig, Augsburg, and Gotha. Focke Wulf factories were hit at Kreising, Tutow, and Posen. Ball-bearing works at Schweinfurt, Stuttgart, and Steyr were pounded. Bad weather brought BIG WEEK to an end after 25 February.

The Americans lost 227 bombers (5.9 percent), and the RAF lost 157 (6.7 percent); 42 U.S. fighters were also lost.

The Germans lost an estimated 700 fighters in production, and 232 aircraft awaiting delivery were destroyed. Luftwaffe Quartermaster's documents conceded that 282 fighters were shot down. The twin-engine force was decimated. Although increased German efforts could produce more fighters, the 100 veteran pilots and combat leaders killed during BIG WEEK were irreplaceable.

The task begun during Operation ARGUMENT would be completed with attacks on Berlin in March and strafing of German airfields in April and May, ensuring Allied air superiority for the Normandy invasion on 6 June 1944.

Sherwood S. Cordier

See also

German Air Force (Luftwaffe); North American P-51 Mustang; Spaatz, Carl Andrew; Strategic Bombing

References

Goodson, James A. *Tumult in the Clouds.* New York: St. Martin's, 1983.
Knoke, Heinz. *I Flew for the Führer.* London: Evans Brothers, 1953.

Armstrong, Neil A. (1930–)

U.S. test pilot and astronaut. Armstrong was born in Wapakoneta, Ohio, on 5 August 1930. Upon receiving a scholarship from the U.S. Navy, he enrolled at Purdue University and began studies in aeronautical engineering. In 1949, the Navy called him to active duty. During the Korean War, he served as an aviator and flew 78 combat missions while assigned to the aircraft carrier USS *Essex.* By 1955, Armstrong completed his bachelor of science degree at Purdue and became a research pilot for the National Advisory Committee for Aeronautics (NACA) and then its successor, the National Aeronautics and Space Administration (NASA). In 1962, he piloted the X-15 rocket plane to an altitude of 207,500 feet and to a speed of 3,765 mph.

Later in 1962, he was selected with the second group of astronauts. His first space flight occurred in March 1966 aboard Gemini 8. He and fellow crewmate David Scott reached earth orbit and achieved the first successful docking with another spacecraft. Shortly after docking with the Agena target vehicle, both spacecraft began to tumble wildly. Though he was successful in disengaging from the Agena, a stuck thruster on the Gemini vehicle forced Armstrong to make an emergency landing in the Pacific Ocean. In January 1969, he was chosen as crew commander of Apollo 11. On 16 July 1969, Armstrong, along with Buzz Aldrin and Michael Collins, rode a Saturn 5 rocket to the moon. He and Aldrin descended to the moon's surface in the Lunar Module *Eagle.* Hours later, Armstrong became the first human to step onto the lunar surface.

After returning to earth, Armstrong held the position of NASA deputy associate administrator for aeronautics (1970–1971) and a professorship at the University of Cincinnati (1971–1979). Currently, he is chairman of AIL Technologies, Inc., and sits on many other corporate boards.

Mark E. Kahn

A great test pilot and the first man to walk on the moon, Neil Armstrong pats the X-15 with respect, knowing it was the most advanced test aircraft in the world. (NASA)

See also

Apollo Space Program; Gemini Project; National Aeronautics and Space Administration; North American X-15

References

Chaikin, Andrew. *A Man on the Moon: The Voyages of the Apollo Astronauts.* New York: Penguin Books, 1994.

Compton, William, David. *Where No Man Has Gone Before: A History of Apollo Lunar Exploration Missions.* Washington, DC: U.S. Government Printing Office, NASA SP-4214, 1989.

Armstrong Whitworth Aircraft

British aircraft manufacturer. Like several aircraft firms in Great Britain and in Germany, Armstrong Whitworth descended from local shipbuilding firms. It entered aviation initially with the manufacture of aircraft engines and propellers. It launched into aircraft design and manufacture in 1913, its efforts enhanced by the acquisition of Frederick Koolhoven as a designer.

During World War I, the principal contribution by Armstrong Whitworth to the war effort was the FK.8 (the "Big Ack"), of which 1,652 were built by 1918. A reconnaissance aircraft, the FK.8 (the letter designation deriving from the initials of the designer) proved to be a major improvement over the earlier Royal Aircraft Factory BE.2c observation planes in which so many Royal Flying Corps crews were sacrificed. The FK.8 proved to be versatile, performing well in the ground attack and bombing roles as well as the usual tasks of an observation plane.

After the war, the firm was reorganized into two firms, Armstrong Siddeley Motors and Sir W. G. Armstrong Whitworth Aircraft. It was able not only to survive but also to prosper during the interwar years with the introduction of two biplanes powered by radial engines. The first of these was the Siskin, a delightfully aerobatic aircraft that was the star of the Hendon Displays. Aesthetically displeasing, the Siskin in its later models offered a 156 mph top speed and superb maneuverability. The Royal Air Force purchased 485 of them at a time when most manufacturers were fighting for orders.

Its sibling was the equally plain-looking Atlas, an army cooperation aircraft that replaced the aging Bristol fighters that many RAF units still flew. Like the Siskin, the Atlas was of metal construction with fabric covering and retained the fixed-pitch propeller attached to an uncowled radial engine, fixed landing gear, and open cockpits. The Atlas remained in production until 1933, with 446 being purchased. Armstrong Whitworth was thus well positioned to compete for the new orders that were on the horizon because of the threat of war.

The firm made a complete departure from past practice with its next aircraft, the famed Whitley. It was of all-metal, stressed-skin construction and had well-cowled engines, an enclosed cockpit, and retractable landing gear.

The Whitley did well early in World War II as a bomber but was soon relegated to other duties when the four-engine bombers came on the scene and Armstrong Whitworth was tasked to build Avro Lancasters. It continued to build other manufacturer's designs after the war, including the Hawker Sea Hawk and Gloster Meteor. The only company products to reach production were the Argosy freighters, of which 72 were built. After a series of mergers, the name disappeared when it became part of Hawker-Siddeley Aviation in 1965.

Walter J. Boyne

References

Bruce, J. M. *British Aeroplanes, 1914–1918.* New York: Funk and Wagnalls, 1957.

Gunston, Bill. *World Encyclopedia of Aircraft Manufacturers.* Sparkford, UK: Patrick Stephens, 1993.

Arnold, Henry H. "Hap" (1886–1950)

Pioneer U.S. military aviator and later the general who had primary responsibility for building the most powerful air force of any combatant nation during World War II.

Henry H. Arnold was born on June 25, 1886, into a family that had a long tradition of military service. Following graduation from West Point in 1907, he spent two years in the Philippines until returning to Governors Island, New York, were he observed flights by the Wright brothers, Glenn H. Curtiss, and other early pilots. Arnold soon volunteered for flight training, which he successfully completed in 1911.

Over the next few years he served as a stunt flier in several movies, and on June 1, 1912, at College Park, Maryland, he established an altitude record of 6,500 feet in a Model B Wright biplane, a feat that earned him the first MacKay Trophy, presented annually thereafter for the most meritorious accomplishment in military aviation.

At the outbreak of World War I, Arnold was recalled from the Panama Canal Zone, where he had organized the 7th Aero Squadron, to Washington to head the information office of the Aviation Section of the U.S. Army Signal Corps. Rising swiftly in rank, he became the youngest full colonel in the U.S. Army. He asked for and received a combat assignment but never realized it because of illness.

During the immediate post–World War I years, Colonel Arnold served in a variety of supervisory positions in California, culminating as commanding officer of Rockwell Field, San Diego. Because of his continuing support of Brigadier General Billy Mitchell, who had angered the War Department with his constant badgering to gain public support for a separate air force, Major General Mason Partrick, chief of the Air Service, "exiled" Arnold to Fort Riley, Kansas, in February 1926.

Back in favor in the redesignated U.S. Army Air Corps and after graduating from the Command and General Staff College at Fort Leavenworth, Kansas, in 1929, Arnold completed a two-year tour at Wright Field, Ohio. Then he received one of his most important career assignments: as commanding officer of March Field, California, where he experimented with squadron fighter tactics, cargo airlift operations, and long-range bombing missions that helped estab-

The first—and to date only—General of the Air Force, Henry H. "Hap" Arnold. He literally worked himself to death in the service of his country. (George M. Watson, Jr.).

lish operational procedures used by the U.S. Army Air Forces during World War II.

During the early 1930s, Colonel Arnold sought every opportunity to publicize the Army Air Corps and the role of airpower in war. He addressed civic gatherings and luncheons, attended fairs and rodeos, and developed a close rapport with many Hollywood producers and movie stars. He also made lasting friendships with members of the scientific community at the California Institute of Technology, including Dr. Theodore von Kármán, the renowned aerodynamicist.

In 1934, Arnold was called to Washington to lead a flight of 10 B-10 bombers from Washington to Alaska and back, a round-trip of 7,630 miles. The successful flight won Arnold an invitation to the White House from President Franklin D. Roosevelt, a second MacKay Trophy, as well as his first star and a new assignment as commander of the 1st Wing, General Headquarters Air Force, located at March Field. He was back in Washington in less than a year as assistant chief of the Air Corps, a position he held until September 1938, when he became chief, succeeding Major General Oscar Westover, who was killed in a plane crash.

As the Nazi onslaught dismembered Europe, General Arnold recognized that existing and proposed air bases would not be able to handle the pilot training load, so he turned to civilian flying schools to provide primary instruction. By December 1941, some 40 schools were managing the Army Air Forces' entire primary flight training program, freeing military installations to concentrate on advanced flight instruction.

General Arnold also devised a plan to establish airfields and weather stations in Greenland (April 1941) and Iceland (July 1941). The significance of these bases, whose construction was originally criticized because they were thought to be vulnerable to enemy attack, was best expressed by General Dwight D. Eisenhower. Arnold's plan, he said, "enabled us to send thousands of fighter planes to Europe under their own power, thus saving enormous sums of money that would have had to be put into shipping to transport them."

Several months after Germany launched World War II, on September 1, 1939, Arnold formally requested permission to contract for studies to build a very-long-range bomber. This aircraft, later designated the B-29 Superfortress, would perform spectacularly in the war against Japan.

Throughout World War II, General Arnold and General George Marshall, Army Chief of Staff, worked closely on matters affecting the USAAF. Arnold's unrivaled knowledge of the USAAF, and his long personal friendship with Marshall, helped both men. As the war proceeded, both agreed that establishing an independent air force ought to await the end of the conflict.

Arnold was known for driving his subordinates hard, but he also drove himself hard. During the war he suffered two heart attacks; the first in May 1943 prevented him from attending the third Washington Conference. His second heart attack struck him down in March 1945 and prevented him from attending the Malta Conference between British and U.S. officials and the Yalta Conference, which also included the Russians. He was on his feet in less than a month when he flew to Europe to visit his commanders and General Eisenhower.

In May 1945, Arnold turned his attention to the war in the Pacific and visited the Marianas, observing the B-29 squadrons and reviewing the strategic air campaign against Japan. After a B-29 dropped the first atomic bomb on Hiroshima, Japan's capitulation soon followed. Arnold retired on March 1, 1946, and left Washington for his ranch at Sonoma, California, where he worked on his memoirs, *Global Mission.*

Honors followed Arnold's retirement. Congress promoted him to the permanent five-star grade of General of the Army in 1946, and in May 1949 President Harry Truman awarded him the permanent five-star rank of General of the Air Force. His greatest reward came in 1947 with the passage of the National Security Act, which established the U.S. Air Force as an independent service arm—a goal Arnold and his commanders had long sought. He suffered three more heart attacks; the last one, on January 15, 1950, was fatal. Robert A. Lovett, the wartime assistant secretary of war for air, eulogized Arnold at the burial ceremony at Arlington National Cemetery, stating that he was as much a casualty of the war as if he had been severely injured in the line of duty.

George M. Watson Jr.

References

Arnold, Henry H. *Global Mission.* New York: Harper and Bros., 1949.

Copp, Dewitt S. *A Few Great Captains: The Men and Events that Shaped the Development of U.S. Air Power.* Garden City, NY: Doubleday, 1980.

______. *Forged in Fire: Strategy and Decision in the Air War over Europe, 1940–1945.* Garden City, NY: Doubleday, 1982.

Watson, George M. Jr. "A 5-Star Leader," *Airman* 30, 6 (June 1986): 29–32.

Artillery Spotting

One of the primary missions in the early history of air warfare. Aviation's most important use during World War I was reconnaissance, and on the Western Front, reconnaissance's biggest subdivision was artillery regulation.

Spotting was still done the old-fashioned way, by climbing a hill and looking through binoculars, but to this tried-and-true method balloons and airplanes were added. Both corrected fire by telling batteries whether shots were falling long or short, left or right of the target, using a sectioned circle aligned with local maps to further pinpoint the references.

Balloons kept in touch by telephone, but airplanes employed less exact means. Visual techniques were used, the airplane signaling by light flashes or flares, the battery "talking" back via large, white cloth letters laid on the ground. One-way wireless was also employed, the aircraft being able to tap out Morse messages to a receiver on the ground but being unable to receive itself. As transmitters required a weighted wire antenna that had to be reeled in if attacked (or in any case before landing), this method had a downside. Improvements in aviation and in radio technology changed things dramatically by World War II, eliminating these primitive methods, but the basic idea of the "spotter" as the artilleryman's eye in the sky remained important.

James Streckfuss

See also

Balloons; World War I Aviation

References

Imrie, Alex. *Pictorial History of the German Army Air Service, 1914–1918.* Chigago: Henry Regnery, 1971.

Watkins, Nicholas C. *The Western Front from the Air.* Phoenix Mill, Glouchstershire, UK: Sutton, 1999.

Atlantic, Battle of the (1940–1945)

The critical campaign to secure the transoceanic link between Europe and the Western Hemisphere. Winning the Battle of the Atlantic ensured the Allies' ability to project their greater strategic power onto and over the continent of Europe and the Mediterranean. Only thus could the European Axis powers be defeated; but airpower over the Atlantic was not unique to World War II. As early as 1918, fully 685 aircraft and 103 airships of the Western Powers had patrolled the Western Approaches and the Narrow Seas. By 1939, airpower's role in an Atlantic war had only grown. Adolf Hitler's Kriegsmarine (Navy) constituted a genuine threat to the Allies' survival.

The Kriegsmarine exhibited dash, aggressiveness, and technical proficiency, particularly regarding naval gunnery and in the U-boat service. By contrast, the Seeluftstreitkräfte (Naval Air Force) remained a miniscule, largely land-bound stepchild subordinated to the Luftwaffe. Nevertheless, 13.4 percent of all Allied vessels sunk in the Atlantic fell prey to German airpower. The X Fliegerkorps (Air Corps) in Norway and Kampfgeschwader 40 (40th Bomber Wing) on the Atlantic Coast of France demonstrated particular proficiency in attacks on shipping. The latter unit employed, among other types, the Focke-Wulf Fw 200 Condor, a long-range reconnaissance bomber famously called the "scourge of the Atlantic" by Winston Churchill for its deadly efficiency between 1940 and 1942. The X Fliegerkorps operated aircraft such as the Junkers Ju 87 Stuka dive-bomber and Ju 88 and Heinkel He 111 torpedo-bombers. Heinkel also supplied the rugged and versatile He 115 twin-engine torpedo-bomber/floatplane.

Before U.S. entry into the war, Great Britain responded to Germany's Atlantic threat with vigor. Eventually four groups of RAF Coastal Command were activated under the British Admiralty's operational control. Coastal Command patrolled inshore waters flying standard RAF types such as Bristol Beaufort and Beaufighter torpedo-bombers. Besides early models of the Boeing B-17 Flying Fortress and the remarkable Consolidated B-24 Liberator (also flown by the Royal Canadian Air Force), Coastal Command employed the Short Sunderland flying boat, whose 20-hour endurance and heavy defensive armament earned it the German nickname "Flying Porcupine."

Complementing Coastal Command, the Royal Navy's far-ranging carriers embarked Fairey Swordfish, Albacore, and Barracuda torpedo-bombers. British combat air patrol pilots manned Gloster Sea Gladiator biplanes, and, later, Fairey Fulmars, Hawker Sea Hurricanes, and Supermarine Seafires. Supplementing these fighter aircraft were Grumman F4F Wildcats ("Martlets" in British service) and F6F Hellcats. Chance-Vought F4U Corsairs entered the Royal Navy's inventory later. As events demonstrated, the Royal Navy's organic airpower, though limited in strength compared to the U.S. Navy's, proved crucial not only in helping drive the Kriegsmarine's surface raiders from the North Atlantic—especially apparent in the sinking of the battleship *Bismarck*—but also in defeating the submarine menace during the period 1943–1945. In addition, the U.S. Navy, though officially neutral, became increasingly active in the war in, and over, the Atlantic. The USS *Long Island,* the U.S. Navy's first escort carrier (eventually designated CVEs), was commissioned on 2 June 1941 with the potential aim of providing air cover for the so-called midocean gap lying beyond the effective range of shore-based antisubmarine patrols. Later the USS *Wasp* ferried 30 Curtiss P-40 Warhawks to Iceland on 25 July to protect that vital North Atlantic way station. After December 1941, U.S. coastal antisubmarine sweeps flown by Consolidated PBY Catalina patrol-bombers and, occasionally, blimps proved of limited effectiveness. Nevertheless, the U.S. Navy increased the pressure against the U-boats even while fighting a two-ocean war. Only the CVEs in U.S. and British service, however, would truly succeed in bringing airpower effectively to bear against the sub-

While bombers could be flown across the Atlantic routinely, it was more expeditious to deliver fighters by ship, and carriers were sometimes pressed into service to do so. Here Lockheed P-38s and Curtiss P-40s get a helping hand across the sea. (U.S. Navy)

marines. Embarking between six and 30 aircraft, these "baby flattops" formed the core of hunter-killer groups beginning in mid-1942. Using "Huff Duff" high-frequency direction-finding, Leigh lights, homing torpedoes, and fin-stabilized depth charges as well as machine guns and cannons, the group's pilots attacked the U-boats with increasing effectiveness. The fliers' principal aircraft were Grumman TBF/TBM Avenger torpedo-bombers supported by Wildcats. During 1944 the U.S. Navy's hunter-killer groups claimed 16 U-boats destroyed, another 17 being credited to aviators of the Royal Navy. By war's end, some 63 German submarines had been sunk by U.S. Navy aircraft.

In the Mid-Atlantic and South Atlantic, too, airpower proved crucial to Allied success. For Operation TORCH, the U.S. Navy supplied one fleet and several escort carriers embarking Wildcats and Avengers to support the landings of early November 1942. In addition, the escort carrier USS *Chenango* ferried the Warhawks of the USAAF's 33rd Fighter Group to Morocco for operations ashore. Farther south a midocean barrier centered on Ascension Island. There U.S. Navy Consolidated PB4Y-1 Privateers helped prevent marauding German surface raiders and submarines from causing havoc in the southern shipping lanes, including the ferry route for aircraft from eastern Brazil to Takoradi on the Ghanaian coast.

D. R. Dorondo

See also

Fleet Air Arm; United States Navy, and Aviation

References

Macintyre, Donald. *Aircraft Carrier: The Majestic Weapon.* Ballantine's Illustrated History of World War II, ed. Barrie Pitt, NY: Ballantine Books, 1971.

Polmar, Norman. *Aggressors: Carrier Power versus Fighting Ship.* Charlottesville, VA: Howell Press, 1990.

Wood, Tony, and Bill Gunston. *Hitler's Luftwaffe.* London: Salamander Military Press, 1990.

Atomic Bomb

Weapon developed by the United States to end World War II. In August 1939, prominent American scientists headed by Albert Einstein wrote to warn President Franklin D. Roosevelt that scientists in Nazi Germany were conducting experiments to purify uranium-235 (U-235), an essential ingredient for building an atomic bomb. The president authorized a committee to determine whether nuclear fission was possible, for at that time no ordinary chemical extraction method could separate U-235 from the more common—and nonfissionable—Uranium-238 (U-238).

When émigré German scientists working in Britain deemed such a process feasible, the British government in 1941 sent the United States a report discussing the realities of nuclear fusion. American scientists, anxious that the Germans had a two-year lead, encouraged Roosevelt to initiate a crash program to build an atomic bomb.

The U.S. Office of Scientific Research and Development took the organizational lead on the project, but the War Department assumed control in the autumn of 1942. The latter gave the project its code name, the Manhattan Engineer District, which was shortened to the Manhattan Project. Soon a huge enrichment laboratory and plant was built at Oak Ridge, Tennessee. Harold C. Urey and his colleagues at Columbia University devised an extraction system that was based on the principle of gaseous diffusion, and Ernest O. Lawrence at the University of California–Berkeley implemented a magnetic process to separate the two isotopes U-235 and U-238. A gas centrifuge was then used to separate the lighter U-235 from the heavier, nonfissionable U-238. Following this, only one final test remained: to "split the atom."

More than $2 billion was spent and some of the most renowned minds of the time worked on the Manhattan Project. One of those scientists was J. Robert Oppenheimer, who oversaw the project from conception to completion. Brigadier General Leslie R. Groves, who had served as deputy chief of the Army Corps of Engineers Construction Division and who oversaw the building of the Pentagon, would serve as the military authority over the project. His military colleagues considered him an "able, aggressive, and industrious officer who repeatedly demonstrated superior engineering, administrative, and organizational abilities."

With the bomb becoming a reality, it was now viewed as more than a must-have defensive weapon against the Germans and Japanese. Now it was perceived as the offensive

The Boeing B-29 Bock's Car, which dropped the atomic bomb on Nagasaki, can be found at the magnificent Air Force Museum at Wright Patterson Air Force Base, Ohio. (U.S. Air Force)

trump card that could not only terminate the war but also be used by the victors in their efforts to police the world after the war.

With the establishment of the Los Alamos facility on 1 April 1943, where the world's first atomic bomb would eventually be constructed, the army's basic structure of organization to administer the program was in place. In the spring of 1944, Chief of Army Air Forces General Henry "Hap" Arnold and Brigadier General Groves agreed on the broad division of responsibilities in preparing to actually deliver the atomic bomb to a target. The USAAF would organize and train the requisite tactical bomb unit and exercise control over delivery of the bomb. The Manhattan Project (i.e., Groves) would receive from the USAAF whatever assistance it needed in ballistic testing of bombs and air transportation of materials and equipment. The USAAF unit subsequently designated to deliver the bombs on Hiroshima and Nagasaki was the 509th Composite Group, formally activated on 17 December 1944. The bomb was successfully tested on 16 July 1945 at Alamogordo, New Mexico, and less than a month later the Japanese surrendered. The atomic bomb ushered in a new postwar atomic reality: It would be used as a military and diplomatic deterrent by the Western powers against Soviet aggression. The means to carry and deliver the atomic message would be the world's strongest force: the United States Air Force.

George M. Watson Jr.

See also

Arnold, Henry H. "Hap"; Hiroshima

References

Dear, I.C.B., gen, ed. and M.R.D. Foot, cons. ed. *The Oxford Companion to World War II.* Oxford: Oxford University Press, 1995.

Feis, Herbert. *Japan Subdued: The Atomic Bomb and the End of the War in the Pacific.* Princeton: Princeton University Press, 1961.

Groves, Leslie R. *Now It Can Be Told: The Story of the Manhattan Project.* New York: Harper and Row, 1962.

Jones, Vincent C. *Manhattan: The Army and the Atomic Bomb.* United States Army in World War II. Washington, DC: Center of Military History, Department of the Army, 1985.

Austria-Hungary

A major power in the early use of air warfare. Aviation roots ran deep in the Austro-Hungarian Empire, which undertook the world's first aerial attack in 1849: two unmanned balloons, laden with explosives, launched and aimed at the Italian arsenal in Venice.

Following this promising beginning, however, progress slowed, and by the time World War I erupted the Dual Monarchy could only lay claim to a single aircraft builder, Lohner. Lacking the industrial capacity of Germany, Austro-Hungary's aviation did not develop as rapidly prior to, or during, the war. A good comparison can be seen in the prewar investment of the two powers: Austria-Hungary spent the equivalent of $318,307 on military aviation in 1914, whereas German investment that same year was $14,836,726. Despite the inauspicious start, however, Austro-Hungarian achievements were impressive.

During the war, the aircraft industry expanded to the point that, at the Armistice, another nine companies had joined Lohner in the aircraft field. It should be pointed out, however, that many of these firms, such as the Ostdeutsch Albatros Werke (East German Albatros Work), were branches of German aviation companies set up in the Habsburg Empire to assure that the wartime military needs of Germany's ally were met, as well as to exploit the possibilities of the Austro-Hungarian market. The number of workers engaged in aviation production had grown steadily as well, from 1,400 in 1914 to 12,000 in October 1918. Those 12,000 workers had managed to produce a respectable 4,768 aircraft for the army and another 413 for the navy, as well as 4,900 engines. The design departments were also busy, cranking out some 125 different prototypes, as well as two tethered helicopter designs intended to replace observation balloons.

Many names with bright futures came out of the Austro-Hungarian design offices of World War I, including Ernest Mach, Ferdinand Porsche, and Igo Etrich, among others.

Wartime command of the Austro-Hungarian Luftfahrtruppe (Aviation Troops) fell to the very capable Oberst (Colonel) Emil Uzelac, a post held by generals in the other European air forces. Uzelac was highly regarded by his superiors as well as the troops under his command and was noted for regularly seeking out the advice and opinions of the lower ranks when inspecting aviation fields. Both a pilot and an engineer, as well as being organizationally gifted, Uzelac was able to mold the Luftfahrtruppe into a highly effective fighting force that soldiered on right up to the end of the empire.

Austria-Hungary, like its German ally, was forced to fight on two fronts: Russia to the north and Italy to the south. Its position was complicated even further by the diverse and stratified society that populated the Dual Monarchy, where 14 different languages were spoken. Although the language of command was uniformly understood, its vocabulary was limited to approximately 200 words. This forced the burden of day-to-day management onto local noncommissioned officers (NCOs) who were able to communicate with the troops. Yet despite the heavy reliance placed on its NCO force, the stiffly structured social tradition of the Austro-Hungarian military denied these men promotion to the officer corps. In Germany, a talented and successful NCO pilot might expect a promotion to the commissioned ranks, but this never happened in the Austro-Hungarian military. Of the 49 Luftfahrtruppe pilots who achieved ace status during the war, 19 were NCOs. Only one of those 19, Josef Kiss, whose 19 victories placed him fifth on the aces' list, was promoted to *Leutnant* (second lieutenant), and that honor was achieved only posthumously.

Aircraft and airmen operating in Austria-Hungary had to be rugged to withstand the rigors of the mountainous terrain over which the aerial battles were fought. Oftentimes, a forced landing was deadlier than an opposing airman. Naval operations were equally hazardous, with regular trips in frail-looking Lohner flying boats from the naval air station at Pola across the Adriatic and back to and from that favorite target, Venice.

In the end it all came to nothing. Like its German counterpart, the Luftfahrtruppe did not survive the Armistice. With the collapse of the Habsburg Empire and the end of the war, Austria-Hungary was obliged to dismantle its air force. Under the supervision of the Inter-Allied Control Commission, the remnants of the Austro-Hungarian aviation accomplishment were reduced to cinders.

James Streckfuss

See also

Caproni Aircraft; World War I Aviation

References

Grosz, Peter M., George Haddow, and Peter Schiemer. *Austro-Hungarian Army Aircraft of World War One.* Mountain View, CA: Flying Machines Press, 1993.

O'Connor, Dr. Martin. *Air Aces of the Austro-Hungarian Empire, 1914–1918.* Mesa, AZ: Champlin Fighter Museum Press, 1986.

Automobile Industry, Wartime Mobilization of

The American automobile industry responded slowly to agitation for industrial mobilization before World Wars I and II. When conflict erupted in August 1914, automakers decidedly endorsed President Woodrow Wilson's proclamation of neutrality. Automotive executives opposed schemes to divert raw materials, capital, and labor to defense production. Henry Ford, a strident pacifist, forbade Ford Motor Company from producing for sale to any belligerent.

Attitudes changed after the sinking of the *Lusitania.* Convinced that war was imminent, conservative automakers began clamoring for preparedness. Howard Coffin, vice president of the Hudson Motor Car Company and president of the Society of Automobile Engineers, became the spokesperson for this group, but he was ineffective in mobilizing their efforts.

Once the United States entered the war, patriotism prompted automakers to embrace industrial mobilization. Ford abandoned his neutral stance and pledged his factories to war production without concern for profit. Hudson, Packard, and other manufacturers inventoried their facilities and converted their plants to arms production.

Though committed to all phases of the war effort, automakers were interested chiefly in aviation. Public confidence was so high that in July 1917 Congress appropriated $640 million for army aviation. Coffin convinced Congress to establish the Aircraft Production Board to administer the appropriation and facilitate the design and manufacture of airplanes. Automobile executives dominated the board, and they labored tirelessly to convert their factories to aircraft production. Work began immediately on a standardized airplane engine; within weeks, designs for the Liberty engine were finalized and production under way.

Grandiose plans for American aviation were unrealized; automakers proved unable to produce aircraft in appreciable numbers. Rapid changes in technology and design made aircraft unsuitable for assembly-line manufacturing. Aircraft manufacturers, moreover, resisted the automakers' forays into airplane design and manufacturing. The greatest success of the automobile manufacturers was in the mass-production of the Liberty.

By September 1939, automakers again faced the prospect of converting their factories to defense production. In May 1940, William Knudson, president of General Motors, arrived in Washington as head of production for the National Defense Advisory Committee. In that capacity he worked to persuade automakers that the country must prepare for war and that the auto industry was obligated to participate. Aware of the importance of airpower, Knudsen decided to recruit the automobile industry to produce aircraft for the United States and Britain. Automakers agreed to produce airplane parts for Wright-Martin, Boeing, and other aircraft companies. The Automotive Committee for Air Defense was formed to administer this program and facilitate cooperation between automotive and aircraft manufacturers.

In January 1942, the War Production Board (WPB) terminated civilian auto production, and automobile factories shifted to defense manufacturing. The WPB further facilitated conversion by relaxing New Deal antitrust and regulatory policies. In January, automobile leaders established the Automotive Council of War Production (ACWP) to serve as a clearinghouse of information, equipment, blueprints, and designs to expedite war production. The ACWP assumed the activities of the Automotive Committee for Air Defense, working feverishly to reduce mutual distrust and suspicion between aircraft and automobile manufacturers.

Daniel E. Worthington

When the United States mobilized its industry for World War II, it had not yet recovered from the depression, and companies understood that providing a good cafeteria was an important part of their responsibility. (U.S. Air Force)

See also
World War I Aviation; World War II Aviation

References

Cardozier, V. R. *The Mobilization of the United States in World War II: How the Government, Military, and Industry Prepared for War.* Jefferson, NC: McFarland, 1995.

Cuff, Robert D. *The War Industries Board: Business-Government Relations During World War I.* Baltimore: Johns Hopkins University Press, 1973.

Morrow, John H. Jr. *The Great War in the Air: Military Aviation from 1909 to 1921.* Washington, DC: Smithsonian Institution Press, 1993.

Nelson, Donald M. *Arsenal of Democracy: The Story of American War Production.* New York: DaCapo Press, 1973.

Aviation and the Arts

Film has long been and remains today a popular medium for the treatment of aviation topics in four major genres: entertainment, recruiting, morale-building, and antiwar protest. Indeed, the history of aviation is closely mirrored in the history of film. The first Academy Award ever given for Best Picture went to the 1927 film *Wings.* With the onset of the Great Depression, films were largely escapist and lighthearted and tended to exclude aviation-related subjects. World War II changed this as film became a powerful source for recruitment and morale-building in the military and on the home front. John Wayne in *Flying Tigers* (1942) and Robert Preston in *Wake Island* (1942) garnered strong support for U.S. involvement in the war. *Memphis Belle* (1943) highlighted the determinism of the first U.S. B-17 crew to finish its mandatory 25 combat missions, as did the fictionalized *Air Force* (1943). The air war called for more than just pilots, and *Bombardiers* (1943) proved hugely successful as a recruiting tool.

The Cold War spawned a new generation of films dependent on aviation, not all of which portrayed airpower in a positive light. *Twelve O'Clock High* (1949) showed the personal strain of combat and leadership in a B-17 wing. Jimmy Stewart, a distinguished pilot, starred in *Strategic Air Command* (1955), which called on reservists once again to don a uniform. That same year, *Bridges at Toko-Ri,* adapted from James Michener's novel, served as a powerful antiwar statement, whereas the peril of Soviet espionage was the central theme in *Jet Pilot* (1957). Films during the 1960s grappled with the price of nuclear holocaust in the taut drama *Failsafe* (1964), the farce *Dr. Strangelove* (1964), and the final film in the Strategic Air Command trilogy, *A Gathering of Eagles* (1963). Robert Duvall's masterful portrayal in *The Great Santini* (1980) addressed issues such as the peacetime military, racism, and coming of age, topics previously thought beyond the bounds of traditional aviation cinema. Few films had the popular impact of *Top Gun* (1986), which became the ultimate naval aviation recruiting tool.

As with film, aviation literature has grown with the evolution of aerospace. Charles Lindbergh's *We* (1927) inspired American boys with the urge to fly, providing a ready source of pilots for World War II. Other memoirs such as Robert L. Scott's *God Is My Co-pilot* (1943) and Ted Lawson's *Thirty Seconds Over Tokyo* (1943) added to this patriotic fervor.

General Curtis E. LeMay was not a man given to small talk, but his admiration for a great combat pilot, Jimmy Stewart, was enhanced by Stewart's excellent performance in the film Strategic Air Command. *(U.S. Air Force)*

Throughout the Cold War, aviation literature touted the strengths (or weaknesses) of strategic airpower, then the cornerstone of U.S. national security policy. Tom Wolfe's *The Right Stuff* (1979) offered a captivating view of the early years of the U.S. space race. Through the turn of the century, aviation literature has focused largely on descriptive or technical studies, often based on newly declassified material such as Chris Pocock's *The U-2 Spyplane* (2000) or former Soviet sources like Piotr Butowski and Jay Miller's *OKB MiG: A History of the Design Bureau and Its Aircraft* (1991). Life stories have proven a ready source for aviation literature, with Amelia Earhart's unfinished *Last Flight* (1937), Antoine de Saint-Exupery's *Airman's Odyssey* (1939), Ernest K. Gann's *Fate Is the Hunter* (1961), and Jack Broughton's *Thud Ridge* (1969) among the most significant. Fiction continues to be a popular source for aviation literature, with Craig Thomas's *Firefox* (1977) and Dale Brown's *Flight of the Old Dog* (1987) reaching "superthriller" status in mass-market sales.

Early aviation art tended toward the dramatic, forsaking detail for emotion. Security concerns also blurred the precision in art, especially during World War II and the Cold War. Painters such as Robert Taylor, Keith Ferris, and Mike Machat were crucial in reversing this trend. Taylor, for example, not only painted highly detailed aircraft in authentic markings but also placed them in historical situations. His *Most Memorable Day* depicts Luftwaffe ace General Adolf Galland during a 1941 mission and is countersigned by the artist, Galland, and other Luftwaffe pilots.

Much, if not all, of the work of Taylor and others is bound in multiple-edition color volumes prized by collectors. Ferris showed that life imitates art, as military camouflage schemes derive from artist conceptions, most notably the false canopy. Photography earned its place in aviation art as flight crews and combat camera crews photographed their many missions in both peacetime and war. Strategic Air Command crewmember Clifford Goodie's *Strategic Air Command: A Portrait* (1965) is a definitive black-and-white photo compendium. The work of Hiroshi Seo, Katsuhiko Tokunaga, George Hall, and Jim Benson defined popular aviation photography and appears regularly in books, articles, corporate publications, and official publications around the world.

Robert S. Hopkins

See also

Saint-Exupery, Antoine de

References

Handleman, Philip, and Walter J. Boyne. *Aviation: A History Through Art.* Charlottesville, VA: Howell Press, 1992.

Aviation Medicine

The science of aviation medicine originated during World War I, when it was recognized that aviators required unique mental and physical attributes and needed special medical care. Early aviators had to endure a myriad of physical challenges never before encountered. Extreme forces of acceleration and deceleration, rapid pressure changes, inadequate oxygen at high altitudes, intense cold, violent winds, blinding glare, prolonged exposure to noise and sickening engine fumes, and dizzying disturbances of the equilibrium—all made specialized screening and care of fliers mandatory. By 1918, all the major powers had medical services dedicated to aviation.

The concept of the flight surgeon was an innovation of senior U.S. medical officers in 1918. After observing the Western Allies' aviation units in action, they became convinced of the need for a specially trained "doctor for the pilot" assigned to a flying unit and dedicated exclusively to treating flying personnel. Although aviation has changed dramatically over the decades, the flight surgeon has survived the test of time. Today, flight surgeons are routinely assigned to U.S. military flying units.

In the years following World War I, advances in flight medicine became even more vital to aviation, as aircraft performance continued to increase at a phenomenal rate. Much greater speeds and forces, higher altitudes, greater extremes in pressure and temperature, and—perhaps more important—the increased complexity and potential destructive capabilities of modern aircraft dictated more stringent medical screening and care of fliers.

These changes also stimulated an increased emphasis on research in the realm of flight physiology. High altitude oxygen systems, pressurized cabins, g-suits, ejection seats and thousands of other life safety developments, can be traced to early research in flight physiology. It is likely that neither combat flying in World War II nor the operation of modern jet aircraft would have been possible without the vital research performed by flight medicine pioneers. The increased comprehension of flight physiology, and the development of aviation life safety equipment that resulted from this research, greatly increased flight safety and paved the way for future space travel.

Steven A. Ruffin

References

Armstrong, Harry. *Principles and Practice of Aviation Medicine,* Baltimore: Williams and Wilkins, 1939.

Benford, Robert. *The Heritage of Aviation Medicine: An Annotated Directory of Early Artifacts.* Washington, DC: Aerospace Medical Association, 1979.

Robinson, Douglas. *The Dangerous Sky: A History of Aviation Medicine.* Seattle: University of Washington Press, 1973.

Avro 504

Early British aircraft that had one of the longest production runs in the history of aviation; brainchild of Alliott Verdon Roe (A. V. Roe). Designed in 1913, it continued in production until 1931. To make it appear the company had many previous designs, A. V. Roe christened it the Type 504 instead of Avro 4, although it was only his fourth design. The plane used an 80-hp Gnome engine with a maximum speed of 82 mph (132 kph). Its wingspan was 36 feet (11 meters) with an overall length of 29.5 feet (9 meters). Flying controls incorporated a joystick and a foot-operated rudder bar. One unique feature on early 504 models was a skid that kept tall grass away from the undercarriage wheels and served as a shock absorber upon landing.

Prior to and during World War I, Allied powers initially chose this aircraft because of its endurance, but its potential as a fighter was quickly recognized. The 504 was the first British airplane to attack a flying Zeppelin, but as a war machine it had limited use. The secret to its longevity as a type rested in its inherent stability, reliability, and ease of control, features that made it an ideal trainer. It was the primary trainer used in British military training schools during World War I. The fact that Prince George, and later King George V, learned to fly in an Avro 504 is evidence of the relative safety of the design.

A. V. Roe's pioneering design capabilities were often disparaged. During his early experiments, because of a superstitious misunderstanding of the science of flight, he was often jailed for endangering the public and himself. And even when his genius was fully displayed with the 504 design, military officials still meddled with his designs, frustrating Roe immeasurably. During the post–World War I period, Roe modified the Avro 504 to include an enclosed cockpit, an all-metal design, and eventually the ability to carry passengers. But by 1928 Roe gave up the fight for control of his designs and sold the company. The Avro 504 remained in production until 1931, having trained an entire generation of military pilots both at home and abroad.

Wendy Coble

References

Lanchberry, Edward. *A. V. Roe: A Biography of Sir Alliott Verdon Roe, O.B.E.* London: Bodley Head, 1956.

Avro Aircraft

Firm founded by Alliott Verdon Roe, who made his first short hops in an aircraft in 1907. Educated as an engineer and a draftsman, Roe's first successful aircraft was a 9-hp triplane that flew in 1909. He adopted the triplane mode for a number of years and was successful both in flying and selling them.

He founded A. V. Roe and Company in 1910 and built the world's first cabin monoplane and cabin biplane during 1912. In 1913, he created the Avro 504, a classic aircraft that was improved over time and saw service in combat and as a trainer. An Avro 504 was the first British aircraft to be brought down by enemy gunfire, on 22 August 1914. Avro 504s also conducted one of the first strategic bombing operations in history when they attacked the Zeppelin sheds at Friedrichshafen on 21 November 1914. The Avro 504N remained the standard RAF trainer until the early 1930s, and a few Avro 504s were actually in service during World War II.

A. V. Roe sold his company in 1928, leaving to form Saunders-Roe. Avro continued production, principally prototypes and a number of excellent biplane trainers, including the Tutor. It then commenced manufacture of the Avro Anson, a twin-engine aircraft built in many variations; more than 11,000 were produced.

The principal Avro contribution to World War II was the Lancaster, which would lead to the York, Lancastrian, Lincoln, Tudor, and Shackleton aircraft, which were built in relatively small numbers compared to the Lancaster. Research in a jet-powered version of the Tudor provided a basis for a revolutionary aircraft, the Avro Vulcan.

In the general consolidation of British aircraft manufacturers, Avro became a part of Hawker-Siddeley in 1960, a firm that A. V. Roe had helped found in 1935. The name Avro was retained as a part of the Avro Whitworth group until 1963.

Avro Canada was formed by Hawker-Siddeley in 1945 and produced a number of prominent aircraft including, the CF-100 all-weather interceptor and one of the most advanced aircraft of the era, the CF-105 "Arrow." Avro Canada was subsequently acquired by Bombardier.

Walter J. Boyne

See also

Avro Lancaster; Avro Vulcan

References

Gunston, Bill. *World Encyclopedia of Aircraft Manufacturers.* Sparkford, UK: Patrick Stephens, 1993.

Penrose, Harald. *British Aviation: The Pioneer Years.* London: Putnam, 1967

Avro Canada Aircraft (A. V. Roe Canada)

A.V. Roe Canada Limited was established in 1945 by Sir Roy Dobson as a wholly owned subsidiary of the UK-based Hawker-Siddeley Group and was based in Malton, Ontario. In its brief history, from 1945 to 1962, Avro Canada became a world leader in the design of commercial as well as military aircraft.

Following the end of World War II, Avro Canada began work on a passenger jet for Trans Canada Airlines (now Air Canada). In 1946, the Gas Turbine Division (later Orenda Engines) was created to develop jet engines for future Avro aircraft.

The Avro Canada C-102 Jetliner was conceived, designed, and built in Canada. In 1949, the C-102, the world's first commercial passenger jet aircraft, made its debut with four Rolls-Royce Derwent engines, a distinction it shares with the British de Havilland Comet.

Unfortunately, the Canadian government withdrew funding for the program when the Korean War broke out in 1950. In 1956, the C-102 program was officially canceled and the aircraft was broken up. This decision effectively killed Canada's commercial aviation industry.

The Avro CF-100 Canuck was Canada's only operational aircraft designed and built in Canada. It was powered by two Orenda jet engines and was a long-range all-weather interceptor that first flew in January 1950. It entered operational service in 1953 and saw service in the home-defence role (NORAD) as well as overseas as part of Canada's NATO commitment. Approximately 700 of the CF-100 and its variants were built, and it remained in operational service with the Royal Canadian Air Force (RCAF) until 1981. Of these, some 53 were built and sold to Belgium. The CF-100 was NATO's first all-weather fighter, and it performed admirably in the skies over Europe during the Cold War.

Even before the CF-100 was first unveiled, work had begun on its replacement—the truly revolutionary Avro CF-105 Arrow. The CF-105 was a twin-engine delta-wing all-weather supersonic interceptor designed and developed for the RCAF to counter long-range Soviet bombers. No prototypes were ever built; instead, the Arrow was designed to go straight from the drawing board into preproduction. A total of five CF-105 Mk.1s were built. The Arrow was the first aircraft to incorporate fly-by-wire technology that allowed the aircraft to take off and land automatically. It was equipped with the Hughes MX-1179 armament system. By 1956, three years after design work began, some 450 engineers, technicians, and draftsmen were working on the design and development of this sophisticated aircraft and its various systems.

Development problems forced Avro Canada to equip the first five aircraft (Mk.1s) with Pratt and Whitney J75 turbojet engines. Subsequent CF-105s were to be fitted with the more powerful Iroquois engines, capable of producing 26,000 pounds/thrust each. The CF-105 first rolled out of its

The Canadian designed and built Avro CF-100 proved to be a marvelous interceptor, giving excellent service for many years. (Shawn Cafferky)

hangar in Malton on 4 October 1957, the same day the Soviets launched Sputnik, the world's first satellite.

In 1958, the CF-105 began flight-testing, and the aircraft exceeded all expectations. The aircraft reached Mach 1.98 and was capable of carrying four to six Sparrow missiles and up to 12 Falcon missiles in an internal missile bay. It had a range of 2,000 miles. The Canadian government canceled the CF-105 program on 20 February 1959, citing escalating costs, failure to sell the CF-105 and Iroquois engines to allies, and the advent of the missile age. Canada decided instead to purchase the Bomarc missile system and 60 Voodoo F-101B interceptors from the United States.

The cancellation of the CF-105 program spelled the end for Avro Canada, and some 14,000 employees were let go (as were 25,000 others employed by subcontractors across the country). After the cancellation of the CF-105 program, production tooling and blueprints were destroyed. The CF-105s were also destroyed—sold for scrap and then cut to pieces. No record was left of this truly revolutionary aircraft. The little that remains—a single nose cone, for example—rests in the National Aviation Museum in Ottawa.

Shawn Cafferky

See also

Avro Aircraft

References

Floyd, James C. *The Avro Canada C-102 Jetliner.* Erin, Ontario: Boston Mills Press, 1986.

Milberry, Larry. *The Avro CF-100.* Toronto: CANAV Books, 1981.

Peden, Murray. *The Fall of an Arrow.* Toronto: Stoddart, 1987.

Stewart, Greig. *Shutting Down the National Dream: A. V. Roe and the Tragedy of the Avro Arrow.* Toronto: McGraw-Hill Ryerson, 1988.

Avro Lancaster

Great Britain's world-famous bomber. The Lancaster was a product of A. V. Roe Ltd., whose design team was led by Roy Chadwick. It had been developed from the earlier Manches-

The finest British heavy bomber of World War II was undoubtedly the Avro Lancaster, a favorite of "Bomber" Harris for his famous Bomber Command. (Big Bird Aviation)

ter, the engines of which had given great cause for concern since its service introduction and led to early withdrawal from the ranks of the RAF.

The redesign included an extension of the wingspan to the allowable maximum of 102 feet plus the installation of four Rolls-Royce Merlins instead of the previous Vultures. The first prototype made its maiden flight, complete with triple fins, on 9 January 1941. After initial flight-testing, some alterations were made to the airframe, the greatest of which were the twin tailfins plus the installation of ventral and dorsal gun turrets.

Service deliveries began to RAF No. 44 Squadron, which undertook its first mission in March 1942. Other units within Bomber Command were reequipped with the Lancaster until 60 squadrons were operating the type. The most famous of these was No. 617 Squadron, which carried out the Dam Busters Raid on 17 May 1943. This unit was also responsible for the deployment of the Tallboy and Grand Slam special bombs.

The Lancaster was also subject to modifications. Some were fairly minor, such as the Lancaster II, with Bristol Hercules engines and a bulged bomb bay; others saw the creation of a completely new type. The Avro York featured a new fuselage, the remainder being pure Lancaster.

After the cessation of hostilities, Bomber Command reduced its strength to a handful of squadrons, although some aircraft were reallocated to Coastal Command as well as units in the Far East and Middle East. Other surplus aircraft were delivered to the air forces of Australia, Canada, Egypt, and France, among others. The final development of the Lancaster resulted in the appearance of the Lincoln bomber, which in turn evolved into the Shackleton antisubmarine patrol aircraft.

Kev Darling

References

Darling, Kev. *Avro Lancaster.* Ramsbury, UK: Crowood Press, 1999.

Avro Vulcan

The first delta-wing bomber to enter military service. A product of a 1947 Air Staff requirement, the British Vulcan used the delta planform, which in theory reduced wing loading and drag and increased space for fuel and weapons. However, it took a revision of the leading edge for these benefits to be fully achieved.

The first flight of the prototype, the VX770, took place on 30 August 1952. Service deliveries to the RAF began on 22 February 1957 to No. 230 Operational Conversion Unit at Waddington, the first operational squadron to equip being No. 83. Total production of the first variant, the Vulcan B.1, reached 45 aircraft.

Extension of the Vulcan's capabilities saw the addition of

The last and longest-lived of Great Britain's "V-bomber" force, the Avro Vulcan, was fast and maneuverable. (Kev Darling)

electronic countermeasures equipment in a modified rear fuselage, a cranked and drooped leading edge, and an in-flight refueling system. This new type was redesignated the Vulcan B.1A and was capable of rapid deployment in support of British interests overseas.

Following the success of the first Vulcan variant, the Avro design team developed the concept to produce the far more capable B.2. Changes included a refined wing that featured elevons on the wings' trailing edge in place of the earlier ailerons and elevators. The span of the wing was increased to 111 feet, which allowed extra fuel to be carried and thereby increased the range.

On 1 July 1960, the Vulcan B.2 entered RAF service, where it initially supplemented the earlier Vulcans. The final Vulcan B.2 was delivered in January 1965. Eventually, Vulcan B.2s saw service with nine UK-based squadrons plus two in Cyprus.

The Vulcan's moment of fame came during the Falklands War in 1982, when it flew long-range bombing missions from the Wideawake airfield on Ascension Island to targets surrounding Port Stanley and the Stanley airfield. The last bomber retired in 1985.

Two other versions of the Vulcan were produced by conversion. These were the B.2MRR for strategic reconnaissance and the K.2 tanker, the last variant in service.

Kev Darling

References

Darling, Kev. *RAF Avro Vulcan.* North Branch, MN: Specialty Press, 1999.

Brookes, Andrew. *V Force.* London: Jane's Information Group, 1982.

AWPD/1 and AWPD/42

In July 1941, President Franklin D. Roosevelt asked the secretaries of war and the navy to review their needs to achieve an effective war footing. Henry "Hap" Arnold, commanding the U.S. Army Air Forces, which was reorganized in June 1941, persuaded the Army War Plans Division head to allow the USAAF to prepare its own report, freeing the War Plans Division to concentrate on the needs of land forces. Arnold formed the Air War Plans Division (AWPD) under Colonel Harold L. George. Joined with Colonel George were Major Laurence S. Kuter, Major Haywood S. Hansell Jr., and Lieutenant Colonel Kenneth Walker. They believed that precision daylight bombing was feasible to pinpoint attacks on specific high value targets.

Colonel George and his team formulated a policy that came to be known as AWPD/1; it called for air operations in defense of the Western Hemisphere, relentless air attacks against Germany, and strategic defense in the Pacific theater. The planning team listed 154 targets for its strategic bombing: airframe assembly plants and associated metal production, some 50 electrical generating stations, 47 key points in the transportation network, mostly railroads, and all of the 27 synthetic petroleum plants in Germany.

AWPD/1 declared that the USAAF could launch a campaign in less than a year—half the time the army needed to prepare for war in Europe. It proposed that six months of strategic bombing of enemy targets, together with neutralization of the Luftwaffe, submarine, and naval facilities, would render a land campaign unnecessary. To achieve these objectives, using precision bombing, AWPD/1 calculated the need for 13,000 medium, heavy, and very heavy bombers worldwide. The plan called for a total of 63,500 operational aircraft, including trainers, reconnaissance, light bombers, dive-bombers, cargo planes, and others, not counting replacements. Laurence Kuter calculated the manpower requirements at 2,160,000 men, more than Pershing's entire American Expeditionary force in World War I. Projections of monthly losses of aircraft of 20 percent and personnel losses of 15 percent required that the original force would have to be entirely replaced within the six-month period. Fortunately, though the aircraft and personnel requirements were very accurate, the loss projections were not. The plan was approved in September 1941. AWPD/1 projections formed the basis for production schedules for new aircraft and for training schedules for the USAAF, and the strategic bomber offensive against Germany became accepted as both USAAF and U.S. government policy.

AWPD/1 expectations that German industry could be destroyed by daylight precision bombing because, at least in theory, 90 percent of the bombs dropped on a clear day would explode within one-quarter mile of the target, were born of optimism. In fact, the enemy's electrical power grid proved to be more difficult to bomb accurately than expected; hydroelectric dams required bombs too large to fit inside the bomb bays of the bombers and would have to be released from precariously low altitudes. Petroleum supplies were the Achilles' heel in the enemy's infrastructure, but attacks on oil and the enemy's transportation system would not begin until later in the war.

On 25 August 1942 President Roosevelt called upon General Arnold for a reassessment of future airpower needs. The team that drafted the original AWPD/1 had been reassigned, but Hansell returned from the United Kingdom to direct preparation of a new USAAF plan. The experience of six months of war mandated some changes. Allied shipping losses in the Atlantic redirected bombing priorities to the German U-boat pens. The B-17s and B-24s had proven they could manage round-trip missions to German targets, therefore AWPD/42 recommended that all B-29s to be produced be used against Japan without revealing the number of B-29s to be put it into operation or the date of deployment. As presented, AWPD/42 resembled AWPD/1 in its optimistic assumptions.

The combined Chiefs of Staff denied top priority requested for the USAAF and wanted clarification of Royal Air Force and USAAF bomber roles in Europe. It was decided that the RAF would continue night bombing and the USAAF would do daylight precision bombing. With a few minor modifications, the plan was approved on 9 September 1942 and became the foundation for U.S. strategic airpower. After the war ended, Hansell assessed the effectiveness of AWPD/1 and AWPD/42. He noted that the estimated number of combat groups called for was within 2 percent and the total number of officers and men was within 5.5 percent. He wrote that Japan's ecosystem was shattered by July 1945.

Richard C. DeAngelis

References

Arnold, Henry H. *Global Mission.* New York: Harper and Bros., 1949.

Bowman, Martin W. *USAAF Handbook, 1939–1945.* Mechanicsburg, PA: Stackpole Books, 1997.

Coffey, Thomas M. *Hap: The Story of the U.S. Air Force and the Man Who Built It.* New York: Viking Press, 1982.

Pogue, Forrest C. *George C. Marshall: Ordeal and Hope, 1939–1942.* 3 vols. New York: Viking Press, 1966.

B

BABYLIFT (1975)

U.S. code name for airlift of orphans during the Vietnam War. Two years after the United States signed a cease-fire agreement with Vietnam, South Vietnam was crumbling under assault from North Vietnamese troops. By mid-April 1975, Saigon was falling and the situation was deteriorating rapidly. Humanitarian groups working with orphans in Vietnam requested that the U.S. government undertake an emergency evacuation. With South Vietnam's reluctant agreement, U.S. President Gerald Ford announced on 3 April 1975 that Operation BABYLIFT would fly some of the estimated 70,000 orphans out of Vietnam. Throughout the month, 30 flights—a combination of private, chartered, and military transport planes—were planned to evacuate babies and children.

Tragically, one of the first official government flights of Operation BABYLIFT was struck by disaster. A USAF C-5A Galaxy cargo plane departed with more than 300 children and accompanying adults. Forty miles out of Saigon and 23,000 feet up in the air, an explosion blew off the rear doors of the aircraft. In a remarkable demonstration of flying skills, the pilots were able to turn the plane back toward Saigon. The damaged plane crash-landed 2 miles from the Tan Son Nhut airport. Sadly, more than half of the children and adults aboard the aircraft died. Many of the 170 survivors were injured. On that same day, a Pan American Airways Boeing 747 chartered by Holt International carried 409 children and 60 escorts, the largest planeload of BABYLIFT.

During the time of Operation BABYLIFT, military and private planes flew out more than 2,000 babies and children to be adopted by families in the United States; approximately 1,300 children were flown to Canada, Europe, and Australia.

Albert Atkins

References

Martin, Allison. "The Legacy of Operation Baby Lift." *Adoption Today* 2, 4 (March 2000): 550.

Bachem BP-20 (Ba 349) Natter

Conceived as an expendable rocket–powered manned interceptor to be launched from a vertical ramp, the Natter (Adder) was semirecoverable (pilot bails out; engine separates from structure and is parachuted for recovery). This approach by Dipl.-Ing. (Graduate Engineer) Erich Bachem was possibly inspired by the July 1939 proposal from Wernher von Braun to the RLM (the Reich Air Ministry) that did not receive a receptive audience until Bachem's August 1944 proposal. The craft's structure was entirely of wood, to be fabricated in cabinet shops. It was powered by one Walter HWK509A-2 bifuel rocket engine of 3,750 pounds/thrust, and boosted by two or four Schmidding 2,650 pounds/thrust solid-fuel rockets that were separated after takeoff. The Natter had a monocoque fuselage and spar-rib wing construction, both with plywood covering. Armament was initially 24 R4M spin-stabilized rockets, later revised to 48 Rohr-batterie rockets.

Fifty prototypes were contracted for and 34 were built. An enlarged version with more fuel and more wing area was also contracted for as the Ba 349B, and three service-test examples were built. The first flight (towed) of the Ba 349A was behind an He 111 on 14 December 1944. The first manned flight, but without power, was on 14 February 1945. The first powered flight (unmanned) was on 25 February 1945. A manned, powered vertical takeoff was attempted on 1 March 1945 but was not successful for unknown reasons. It is not known if the Ba 349B flew. Development of a further refined Ba 349C continued until the war ended. Construction was sponsored jointly by the SS (*Schutzstaffeln,* or protection squads) and the RLM.

The tiny Bachem had a gross weight of 3,900 pounds, a maximum speed of 620 mph, and a range of approximately 50 miles.

Douglas G. Culy

References
Dressel, Joachim. *Natter—Bachem Ba 349.* Atglen, PA: Schiffer, 1994.
Green, William, and Gordon Swanborough. *The Complete Book of Fighters.* London: Salamander, 1994.

Bader, Douglas R. S. (1910–1982)

Battle of Britain fighter pilot, squadron leader, and tactician; developed and championed the controversial "Big Wing" theory of defense.

Born on 10 February 1910 in London, Bader attended the Royal Air Force college at Cranwell. Graduating in 1930, he was posted to his first fighter squadron. He crashed in 1931 while performing low-level aerobatics, subsequently losing both legs. Invalided out of the service in 1933, Bader worked for the Shell Petroleum Company until 1939.

Following the start of World War II, Bader gained readmittance to the RAF. He passed his flying examinations and again became a fighter pilot, flying Hawker Hurricanes in England. In early 1940, he transferred as a flight commander to a Spitfire squadron. In June he was given command of No. 242 Squadron, again flying Hurricanes. This squadron, based at Coltishall in the English Midlands, was part of RAF Fighter Command's No. 12 Group.

Dissatisfied with the standard RAF tactics at the time—that is, tight formations and "line-astern" attacks—Bader experimented with looser formations and simultaneous attacks by all available aircraft. During the height of the Battle of Britain, Bader was similarly frustrated by the more southerly based No. 11 Group's strategy of attacking large Luftwaffe formations with a relatively small number of British fighters, often no more than a squadron.

Bader was convinced that attacking simultaneously with three of more squadrons—the so-called Big Wing—was the answer to inflicting more damage on the attacking bombers. Even though a junior officer, Bader appealed directly to No. 12 Group's commander, Air Vice-Marshall Sir Trafford Leigh-Mallory, for support of his idea. As a result of that meeting, Bader's No. 242 Squadron, along with Nos. 19 and 310, were posted to Duxford to implement the concept.

The controversy over the Big Wing continues to this day due to the trade-off in time needed to assemble and position such a large formation of fighters and the necessity to intercept the German attackers before they could drop their bombs. When it worked, the Big Wing concentrated a mass of force against the Luftwaffe and scored numerous successes. Just as often, however, the Big Wing missed taking part in the raid because the intruding aircraft had struck and departed before the massing defenders could get into position.

On 9 August 1941, Bader was shot down over France. He spent the rest of the war as a German prisoner of war, attempting numerous escapes. At the conclusion of the war, Bader was released from captivity and led the Battle of Britain flypast in the postwar victory parade. He left the RAF in February 1946 with 22.5 confirmed victories, the Distinguished Flying Cross, and the Distinguished Service Order with bar.

Douglas Bader was knighted in 1976. He died of a heart attack on 5 September 1982 in London.

Braxton Eisel

References
Brickhill, Paul. *Reach for the Sky.* New York: W. W. Norton, 1954.
Terraine, John. *A Time for Courage: The Royal Air Force in the European War, 1939–1945.* New York: Macmillan, 1985.

Baer, Heinz (1913–1957)

One of the dominant personalities of the Luftwaffe fighter force and one of the very few pilots to fly in combat for all of World War II. Heinz "Pritzl" Baer scored his first victory on 25 September 1939, as an *Unteroffizier* (corporal), and his 221st and last on 29 April 1945 while serving as a lieutenant colonel in command of Jagdverband 44 (JV 44; 44th Fighter Unit). Baer was the highest-scoring German jet ace, with 16 victories, and the second-highest day scorer against the Western Allies. In February 1942, he became the seventh member of the Wehrmacht to be awarded the Oak Leaves with Swords to the Knight's Cross of the Iron Cross, but a disagreement with Reichsmarschall Hermann Goering kept him from any higher decorations, and his outspoken refusal to obey orders that he considered reckless brought him a demotion in 1943. However, his combat record prevented his court-martial, and in mid-1944 he was given command of, first, Jagdgeschwader 1 (JG 1; 1st Fighter Wing), and later JG 3, two of the most successful units in the Reichsluftverteidigung (Air Defense of Germany). Baer was killed in the crash of a light airplane in 1957.

Donald Caldwell

See also
German Air Force (Luftwaffe)

References
Obermeier, E. *Die Ritterkreuztraeger der Luftwaffe, 1939–1945, Band I: Jagdflieger* [Recipients of the Knight's Cross]. Mainz, Germany: Verlag Dieter Hoffmann, 1989.

Baikonur Cosmodrome

Soviet/Russian space launch site. All Soviet and Russian manned space flights to date have been launched from Baikonur. Other noteworthy launches include the Salyut space stations, the components of the Mir space station, the unsuccessful test-launches of the N-1 moon rocket, and the single unmanned flight of the Buran shuttle.

Baikonur Cosmodrome is located near Tyura-Tam in eastern Kazakhstan, approximately 1,200 miles southeast of Moscow. The original town of Baikonur lies 230 miles to the northwest; its name was used (unsuccessfully) to conceal the actual location from Western intelligence. Known successively as Tashkent-90, Zarya (Dawn), Zvezdograd (Startown), and Leninsk, the staff settlement near the cosmodrome officially became Baikonur only in 1995.

Construction began in early 1955, after it became clear that the Soviet Union's existing test range at Kapustin Yar was too small for the missiles and launch vehicles to come. The original Baikonur facility, built to test the R-7 intercontinental ballistic missile, was completed in December 1956. The mission soon expanded to include space launch activities, and Sputnik, the world's first artificial satellite, was launched from Baikonur on 4 October 1957.

With the construction of additional launch sites, the cosmodrome now covers approximately 600 square miles. Today, in addition to manned Soyuz flights, Baikonur launches unmanned Proton, Molnia, Zenit, and Tsiklon boosters carrying a variety of scientific and military payloads.

Mark E. Wise

See also

Gagarin, Yuri; Missiles, Intercontinental Ballistic; Salyut; Soyuz Space Vehicle; Voskhod; Vostok

References

Bilhartz, Terry D. "Space Centers and Launch Sites in the Soviet Union." In Frank N. Magill, ed., *Magill's Survey of Science, Space Exploration Series.* Vol. 4. Pasadena, CA: Salem Press, 1989, pp. 1592–1598.

Balbo, Italo (1896–1940)

Italian politician and airpower advocate. Born in Quartesana (Ferrara) on 5 June 1896, Italo Balbo served as lieutenant in the mountain troops in World War I. After the Armistice he obtained a degree in political science and joined the fascist movement. A born leader, he made a vital contribution to fascism's seizure of power by securing the support of the Po Valley landowners and directing the March on Rome of 28 October 1922.

Perhaps the most charismatic figure of Fascist Italy, Italo Balbo led great armadas of seaplanes from his country to the United States. (Gregory Alegi)

After a brief period as undersecretary for national economy, Balbo became undersecretary for aeronautics on 6 November 1926. He ran the Ministry for Aeronautics for seven years, succeeding Benito Mussolini as minister in September 1929. Balbo obtained a military pilot's license in June 1927 and in 1934 was declared "qualified on all aircraft in service." In August 1928, Balbo transferred from the fascist militia to the Regia Aeronautica (the Italian air force), his rank being equivalent to three-star general.

During his tenure, Balbo defined the mission and spirit of the Regia Aeronautica, earning recognition as the father of Italian aviation. Balbo's work concentrated on creating a solid organization, but his image is forever linked to the four formation flights of 1928–1933 that culminated in the spectacular Italy–United States–Italy flight made by 24 SIAI Marchetti S.55X flying boats. Shortly after being promoted to Air Marshal by Mussolini in August 1933, Balbo was relieved from his post and appointed governor of Libya, a position that also made him commander in chief of forces in the colony.

An admirer of the United States, Balbo was an outspoken opponent of Mussolini's alliance with Germany, anti-Semitic laws, and the June 1940 declaration of war. Because of this, his death on 28 June 1940 in an SIAI S.79 shot down by Italian antiaircraft fire over Tobruk was rumored to have been orchestrated by Mussolini to eliminate a rival. Modern scholarship has completely disproved the notion.

Gregory Alegi

See also

Regia Aeronautica (Pre–World War II); Regia Aeronautica (World War II); SIAI Marchetti

References

Alegi, Gregory. "28 giugno 1940. La morte di Italo Balbo." *Storia Contemporanea* 24, 5 (October 1993).

Santoro, Carlo M., ed. *Italo Balbo: Aviazione e potere aereo.* Rome: Aeronautica Militare, 1998.

Segrè, Claudio G. *Italo Balbo: A Fascist Life.* Berkeley: University of California Press, 1987.

Baldwin, Stanley (1867–1947)

A Conservative member of Parliament from 1908 until his retirement in 1937. Stanley Baldwin served as British prime minister from 1923 to 1929 and again from 1935 to 1937. He was Britain's leader during the 1926 General Strike and the abdication crisis a decade later. Baldwin is perceived today as a key participant in Britain's reluctance in the 1930s to play any role in the Spanish civil war or to face the growing German menace by rearming. He argued that domestic public opinion would not support such a move. Only toward the end of his leadership did he support a rearmament program, though reflecting little outward concern about the growing European crisis. With Neville Chamberlain, he successfully kept Winston Churchill out of high government office throughout the 1930s.

Christopher H. Sterling

See also

"Ten-Year Rule"; Chamberlain, Neville; Churchill, Winston; Royal Flying Corps/Royal Naval Air Service/Royal Air Force; Trenchard, Hugh

References

Baldwin-Young, Kenneth. *Stanley Baldwin.* London: Weidenfeld and Nicolson, 1976.

Young, G. M. *Stanley Baldwin.* London: Rupert Hart-Davis, 1952.

Balikpapan

The location of heavy bomber attacks against Japanese oil installations. Balikpapan, on the island of Borneo in the Netherlands East Indies, was the site of the second largest oil and refinery complex owned by the Japanese. The site produced more than 5 million barrels of oil annually, second only to the Palembang complex on Sumatra. The Allies constructed a strategic air base at Darwin, Australia, in the hopes of using B-29s against the oil facilities, but these aircraft did not become available. However, the Allied advances in New Guinea brought Borneo just into range of the B-24s of the Fifth and Thirteenth Air Forces. The long range to the target required stripping the B-24s of much of their armor and ammunition.

The first raid was launched on September 30, but heavy cloud cover over the target rendered it ineffective. An elite naval fighter unit intercepted and shot down four bombers.

Four squadrons of raiders returned on 3 October and were intercepted by more than 40 fighters, the bombers losing seven of their number. In spite of this opposition, a number of hits were scored on the modern Pandasari refinery.

Such heavy losses could not be continually sustained, but arrangements were made for adding special drop tanks to P-47s and P-38s that could thereby provide a few minutes of fighter cover over the target. Escorted raids attacked Balikpapan three times from 8 October to 10 October. The fighter escort gave the attackers a decisive advantage, and much damage was done. A last attack on 18 October was ineffective because of weather.

Total U.S. losses were 22 bombers and nine fighters; 433 tons of bombs were delivered to the target. The refineries were rebuilt and shortly operating again, but the continuing Allied advance soon interdicted the shipping routes from the East Indies, and the flow of oil to Japan ceased.

Balikpapan provides a good example of the usefulness of modifying aircraft—both bombers and fighters—for specific missions, but it also shows the difficulty of causing sustained damage to industrial targets with small conventional bomb tonnages.

Frank E. Watson

References

Craven, Wesley F., and James L. Cate, eds. *The Army Air Forces in World War II, Volume 5: Pacific: Matterhorn to Nagasaki, June 1944–August 1945.* Chicago: University of Chicago Press, 1953.

The Balkans, Air Operations in (1941)

German campaigns in the Balkans resulted from Benito Mussolini's botched invasion of Greece in October 1940 and from the overthrow of the Yugoslav government in March 1941. The Luftwaffe buildup began in November 1940, and by March 1941 490 aircraft were based in Romania and Bulgaria. In early April, 600 additional aircraft were rushed to the Balkans. VIII Fliegerkorps executed air operations under the command of General der Flieger Wolfram von Richthofen.

The attack began on 6 April, with an air strike on Belgrade (Operation PUNISHMENT). The target was the city center; industrial and transportation targets were excluded so the Germans could exploit the economy after conquering Yugoslavia. The Luftwaffe attacked in the morning primarily with high explosives and in the afternoon primarily with incendiaries, starting fires that guided the subsequent night attack. The Yugoslav air force was quickly destroyed, and the Germans lost only two fighters. The attack killed some 17,000 people and cut nearly all communications between the Yugoslav high command and the armed forces. The Yugoslav army was paralyzed and easily crushed by the Wehrmacht.

VIII Fliegerkorps then focused on reconnaissance, airfield attacks, interdiction, and close air support. The Luftwaffe supported a three-pronged armored thrust that reached Belgrade on 12 April. The Luftwaffe cleared the path for a diversionary attack on Zagreb and for the pursuit operations that seized Sarajevo on 15 April. Yugoslavia surrendered on 17 April, after negligible German losses.

German air operations in Greece, like those in Yugoslavia, focused primarily on reconnaissance, interdiction, close air support, and airfield attacks. Tactical aircraft played a key role in breaking the Metaxas Line and the positions (Platamon, Pinios Gorge, Thermopylae) the British established to delay the German advance down the peninsula. Airborne forces conducted the most notable German air operations in the campaign. On 26 April, 400 Ju 52s dropped two reinforced parachute battalions on Corinth but failed to prevent large numbers of British troops from escaping the mainland. The British suffered heavy casualties, however, as air attacks sank 26 ships. Airdrops were used to seize some Aegean islands. A major airborne operation (MERKUR) was launched against Crete on 20 May, with German forces consisting of elements of two airborne divisions and two mountain divisions, 700 transports and gliders, and 750 fighters and bombers. Planning and intelligence were poor—German forces were dispersed over a wide area and suffered heavy casualties when they landed among Commonwealth forces. Thus, the Germans nearly lost—the Royal Navy repelled a German seaborne convoy, and Commonwealth troops fought fiercely. Eventually, the Germans captured the Maleme airfield and could fly in mountain troops as reinforcements. Crete fell on 1 June, costing the Germans 5,000 casualties and 350 aircraft, inflicting perhaps 15,000 Commonwealth casualties plus painful naval losses.

Airpower played a decisive role in enabling Germany to conquer Yugoslavia and Greece quickly and with minimal casualties. Even token aerial opposition would have greatly slowed German movements through mountainous Balkan terrain and from inflicting punishing losses on the Royal Navy during operations in Greece and Crete.

James D. Perry

References

Murray, Williamson. *Luftwaffe.* Baltimore: Nautical and Aviation, 1985.

U.S. Army Center of Military History. *The German Campaign in the Balkans (Spring 1941).* Washington, DC: U.S. Government Printing Office, 1984.

The Balkans and Early Air Combat (1912–1913)

The First Balkan War (1912–1913) pitted the Balkan League of Bulgaria, Greece, and Serbia against Turkey. It marked a significant point in the history of military aviation, the first international war during which all combatants deployed aircraft operationally.

Serbia was the earliest to form an air arm. Reacting to the 1909 Bosnia-Herzegovina crisis with Austria, Serbia purchased two German observation balloons. In 1912, as war with Turkey loomed, Serbia sent six pilot-candidates to France for training and purchased 11 French aircraft. Its aviators completed training just in time, and on 24 December 1912 the Serbia Aviation Command formed at Nis. Serbian aircraft conducted reconnaissance flights from March 1913. Sergeant Mihajlo Petrovic, killed in action over Skadar in March, was the second combat casualty in military aviation history.

Greece established an air service in late 1911, sending six officers to France for training and purchasing French equipment. Its Aviation Company formed at Larissa in late September 1912 while the navy established its own air service in mid-November. Greek reconnaissance operations commenced on 21 October 1912 (5 October, according to the Julian calendar then in use in Greece) in Thessalia. On 5 February (24 January) 1913, a Greek naval Farman pusher, flown by army Lieutenant Michael Moutousis with Ensign Aristidis Moraitinis as his observer, flew over Turkish naval units off Nara (Nagara Point) in the Dardanelles and dropped four bombs over the dockyard, inflicting no damage and drawing return rifle fire that also missed. Greek aviation activity continued up to the end of the war on 30 May 1913.

Turkey established a balloon unit in 1911 and sent officers to France for flight training the following year. Turkey reacted to events in its war with Italy by expanding its air arm, purchasing close to two dozen aircraft from France, Germany, and Britain. Turkish aircraft undertook frequent reconnaissance missions throughout the First Balkan War.

Bulgaria's air arm was more extemporized. About 12 aircraft, mainly French, were purchased and manned mostly by foreign pilots. These Bulgarian aircraft also undertook reconnaissance missions and one pilot, Topradzijev, achieved the dubious distinction of becoming the first aviation casualty of the war when his Blériot crashed while returning from an operation in December 1912.

Despite their small scale, aircraft operations during the First Balkan War accurately prefigured early events in World War I and validated the importance of aviation in warfare.

Paul E. Fontenoy

See also

Italo-Turkish War

References

Lawson, Eric, and Jane Lawson. *The First Air Campaign.* Conshohocken, UK: Combined Books, 1996.

Layman, R. D. *Naval Aviation in the First World War: Its Impact and Influence.* Annapolis, MD: Naval Institute Press, 1996.

Morrow, John H. Jr. *The Great War in the Air: Military Aviation from 1909 to 1921.* Washington, DC: Smithsonian Institution Press, 1993.

Ballistic Missile Early Warning System (BMEWS)

Network of three radars designed to give early warning of ballistic missile attack on North America or Western Europe. Though the U.S. Air Force doubted that a successful defense against incoming ballistic missiles was feasible, warning of such an attack was a priority. As early as 1955 the Air Force had recommended the creation of a system of three radars designed specifically to detect incoming missiles, but it was not until the Soviet ICBM test of August 1957, and its highly publicized successor Sputnik two months later, that a similar recommendation received high priority within the U.S. Department of Defense.

Construction commenced in the summer of 1958, and the first site (at Thule, Greenland) gradually became operational throughout late 1960. The last two sites, at Clear, Alaska, and Fylingdales Moor, England, became operational in June 1961 and September 1963, respectively. Upon detection of a missile launched against the United States (or Western Europe as well, in the case of the British site), warning would be transmitted instantaneously to air defense command posts within the United States and Britain. Though the warning provided would only be approximately 15–20 minutes in the case of a Soviet ICBM launched via a polar route against a target within the continental United States, even this amount of time would allow some bombers of the Strategic Air Command to be scrambled into the air and other air defense procedures to be initiated.

Even before it was deployed, however, there were serious

questions about the vulnerability of the BMEWS system to a variety of countermeasures. The three radar sites would presumably be among the very first targets struck in a nuclear war and were also thought to be highly vulnerable to the electromagnetic pulse produced by the high-altitude detonation of a large nuclear warhead. Further, attacks not coming in from the north (such as a missile launched from Cuba) could not be detected by the BMEWS sites. Early warning satellites did provide some redundant warning capability beginning in the early 1960s, and as these satellites grew in sophistication they gradually replaced BMEWS as the primary means of detecting incoming ballistic missiles. The multiple redundancies in U.S. missile warning systems proved invaluable in minimizing the danger from the many false alarms associated with the BMEWS system, such as the famous 1960 incident where the Greenland site reported a Soviet missile attack after detecting what turned out to be the moon rising over the horizon. BMEWS remained in service throughout the Cold War, and in the 1980s and 1990s its three sites were upgraded with phased-array radars.

David Rezelman

See also

Air Defense Command; Antimissile Defense; Cold War; Distant Early Warning; Missiles, Intercontinental Ballistic; North American Air Defense Command; Radar; Satellites; Sputnik; Strategic Air Command; Strategic Defense Initiative

References

Baucom, Donald R. *The Origins of SDI, 1944–1983.* Lawrence: University Press of Kansas, 1992.

Carter, Ashton B., and David N. Schwartz, eds. *Ballistic Missile Defense.* Washington, DC: Brookings Institution, 1984.

Ray, Thomas W. *History of BMEWS, 1957–1964. Air Defense Command Historical Study* 32 (1965).

Sagan, Scott D. *The Limits of Safety: Organizations, Accidents, and Nuclear Weapons.* Princeton: Princeton University Press, 1993.

Balloons

The first military use of a man-carrying balloon occurred on 26 June 1794, when Captain Jean-Marie Joseph Coutelle ascended for observation at the Battle of Fleurus. Lighter-than-air craft again saw action in other conflicts, including the American Civil War, when aeronauts used tethered balloons to spy for both armies. But it was during World War I that balloons reached their military zenith.

Reconnaissance was aviation's chief product during World War I, but aviation was not the primary method of getting visual information on the enemy. Climbing to high ground and observing through binoculars was still the favored approach. But as possession of the high ground was often with the enemy, hovering or flying overhead was often

This sketch from the Civil War shows how both sides used balloons to spy on the enemy. (Library of Congress)

the only solution. In that chain, the tethered balloon occupied the middle ground between the man on the hill and the man in the airplane.

Balloons and airplanes each had advantages. Balloons could stay aloft for hours and remain in constant telephone contact with one or more artillery batteries, regulating their fire by telling the commander whether his shots were falling long or short or left or right of his target. Balloons were not used exclusively by the artillery, though, because the range or angle of the target in relation to the observer often dictated the closer look possible from the airplane.

The down side was that the balloon was always visible to the enemy and in constant danger of attack. Troops often complained about the presence of a balloon because it drew artillery fire. Enemy pilots considered them formidable targets. Hydrogen-filled, they burned beautifully, but attacking aircraft had to get in close due to the relative ineffectiveness of incendiary ammunition at that time. Because of this, balloons were heavily defended, both by antiaircraft (unusually effective in this case, because, unlike trying to locate aircraft at unknown altitudes, the altitude of balloons—and, therefore, their attackers—was always known) and friendly fighters, which were only a phone call away. Given these factors, pilots who specialized in attacking balloons were highly respected, though considered suicidal.

World War I was unusually suited to the use of observation balloons because of the trenches. By the time fighting in Europe renewed in 1939, technological advances in aviation and the nature of the fighting forced the tethered balloon into a new role: protection. During World War II, balloons proved valuable in forming a barrage around London and other places, holding long steel cables that threatened enemy bombers. Advances in aviation since have eliminated balloons from war and elevated them to the peaceful uses we see them in today.

James Streckfuss

References

Hodges, Goderic. *Memoirs of an Old Balloonatic.* London: William Kimber, 1972.

Ovitt, Spalding West, ed. *The Balloon Section of the American Expeditionary Force.* New Haven, CT: Turtle, Morehouse, 1919.

Bapaume, Battle of (1918)

World War I battle that heralded the rise of air support. By August 1918, the value of aerial operations was no longer debated. At the Battle of Bapaume, a truly coordinated effort with the ground fighting can be seen. The battle opened with rain that interfered to some degree, but RAF No. 73 Squadron was still able to perform ground attack duties, as well as watching out for enemy tanks. As the weather cleared, Handley Pages performed the heavy work of bombing bridges, and the night-flying Sopwith Camels of 151 Squadron flew offensive patrols in search of German ground attack aircraft. On the evening of 24/25 August, they engaged two from Schlachtstaffel 16 (No. 16 Battle Flight) and claimed both as victories. The day of round-the-clock air support had arrived.

James Streckfuss

See also

Royal Flying Corps/Royal Naval Air Service/Royal Air Force; World War I Aviation

References

Raleigh, Sir Walter, and H. A. Jones. *The War in the Air: Being the Story of the Part Played in the Great War by the Royal Air Force.* 6 vols. Oxford: Clarendon Press, 1922–1937.

Baracca, Francesco (1888–1918)

Italy's "ace of aces," achieving the rank of major. A prewar pilot as well as a member of the regular army, Baracca was already in military aviation when World War I began. In 1915, he was sent to Paris to train on Nieuports, later returning to the No. 1a Squadriglia (Squadron). By the end of 1917, Baracca had run his score to 30 but then hit a dry spell, not scoring again until the following May. On 15 June, he brought down a double, bringing his victory list to its final number—34. Four days later he was killed under uncertain circumstances. The No. 91a Squadriglia, which he commanded, was renamed in his honor.

In April 1917, he had adopted a black rampant horse as his personal insignia and had it applied to all his subsequent aircraft. The insignia was given to Enzo Ferrari after the war and can be seen today on Ferrari sports cars.

James Streckfuss

References

Franks, Norman, Russell Guest, and Gregory Alegi. *Above the War Fronts.* London: Grub Street, 1997.

BARBAROSSA

Nazi invasion of the Soviet Union during World War II. Airpower had been important in what became known as Operation BARBAROSSA long before the Germans attacked the Soviet Union on 22 June 1941. German reconnaissance flights, under Colonel Theo Rowehl, had overflown Soviet territory for months, mapping the principal targets.

When the war began, the Luftwaffe was inferior in num-

bers to the Red Air Force, with only 2,770 aircraft deployed for the invasion against some 4,000 aircraft stationed in the West. The equipment and training of the Luftwaffe was far superior, however, and the Red Air Force was handicapped by the loss of many of its best leaders to Stalin's infamous purges. The initial results of the Luftwaffe attack were dazzling, and by 5 October the Red Air Force had lost more than 5,000 aircraft. Many of these were obsolete types, such as the Polikarpov I-16, and they would be replaced by much more advanced aircraft as a result of both Lend-Lease and the miraculous transfer of the Soviet aviation industry eastward from European Russia to the Ural Mountains. The Luftwaffe's failure to develop a long-range bombing force had handicapped it in the Battle of Britain. The same failure would prove to be fatal in BARBAROSSA.

The rapid advance of German forces placed great strains on the Luftwaffe, which suffered losses to Soviet fighters as well as to the intense ground fire encountered in close air-support activity. These strains were increased during the harsh Russian winter, which the Luftwaffe was ill-equipped to endure. The intense cold halted trucks bringing fuel and supplies, made field maintenance a torture, and often prevented German aircraft from flying.

Despite the difficulties, the Luftwaffe managed to maintain air superiority over selected areas of the Eastern Front for the next two years. It was of invaluable assistance to the German army, for German airpower was able to compensate in part for the increasing Soviet superiority in manpower and armor. Field Marshall Wolfram von Richthofen, a cousin of Manfred von Richthofen and an eight-victory ace in World War I, became a master of close air support and the aerial resupply of cut-off forces, but even he was unable to reverse the Luftwaffe's trend toward defeat.

Soviet strength grew steadily, and by Stalingrad's surrender on 31 January 1943, Germany could establish air superiority only locally and on a temporary basis. Both air forces concentrated their efforts on close air support, and in this the Red Air Force became immensely more successful, operating its Ilyushin Il-2 Shturmoviks in great numbers and with great success.

The production battle had also tilted in favor of the Soviet Union. In 1942, Germany was able to produce 15,409 aircraft for use on three fronts, while the Soviet Union produced 25,240 aircraft solely for use against Germany. These were supplemented by reinforcements from Great Britain and the United States. The disparity in strength would grow with each succeeding year.

By mid-1943, the Luftwaffe was so diminished in numbers that it had to be used as a fire brigade, rushing from point to point to stave off the most dangerous Soviet advances. The experience, bravery, and skill of the Luftwaffe pilots enabled some of them to run up unprecedented victory totals, with Erich Hartmann achieving the top score of 352. But such aces were rare, and most of the Luftwaffe pilots were simply ground down in the unending series of sorties that they were called upon to fly.

By the time the Red Army began its final offensive to Berlin in the early months of 1945, it possessed no less than 7,500 fighters, many of which were equal to the best the Germans could offer. The Luftwaffe had less than 400 fighters to oppose them. The Soviet Union had defeated Germany's air force in the air—and on the production line.

Walter J. Boyne

See also

German Air Force (Luftwaffe); Ilyushin Il-2 Shturmovik; Lend-Lease Aircraft; Soviet Air Force; World War II Aviation

References

Boyne, Walter J. *Clash of Wings: World War II in the Air.* New York: Simon and Schuster, 1994.

Barker, William George (1894–1930)

Early flier, sadly overshadowed in popular history by other fliers. Major William George Barker was one of the great airmen of World War I, having achieved 50 victories and been awarded the Victoria Cross, the Distinguished Service Order with bar, the Military Cross with two bars, the Croix-de-Guerre, and many other decorations. His wartime achievements were crowned with what many historians believe to be one of the most heroic and one-sided dogfights of the war, in which Barker engaged 15 Fokker D.VII aircraft and, though severely wounded, managed to shoot down four of the enemy aircraft.

Barker was of pioneer stock, having been born in a log cabin in Dauphin, Manitoba, Canada. In December 1914, he joined the 1st Canadian Mounted Rifles, spending his first winter in France as a machine-gunner in the trenches. In March 1916, he became an observer in the Royal Flying Corps and was commissioned as a member of No. 9 Squadron. After entering claims for two victories as a gunner, he entered pilot training in November 1916. (Neither of the two victories were credited to him, but he was decorated with the Military Cross.)

While flying the notorious Royal Aircraft Factory RE 8 (the "Harry Tate") he forced an enemy aircraft down and was awarded a bar to his Military Cross. He was wounded, then transferred to become an instructor pilot, a fact that probably saved his life, for it gave him experience and seasoning that would serve him well when he joined the famous RAF No. 56 squadron in October 1917. He immediately began his scoring and in the next year achieved 50 victories, including nine balloons. Forty-seven of his victories were achieved on the Italian front, most of them, amazingly enough, in one aircraft, his Sopwith Camel B6313. He became a true master of the tricky Camel and was, in addition, an excellent shot.

After his highly successful tour in Italy, he returned to Great Britain and, after checking out in a Sopwith Snipe, obtained permission to take it to France for familiarization. It was there, on 27 October 1918, when he had his epic battle with enemy Fokkers, for which he was awarded the Victoria Cross.

His wounds took him out of World War I combat, and upon his return to Canada he had a mixed career in business and in the service. Sadly, he was killed in a flying accident on 12 March 1930 at Rockcliffe Aerodrome, Ontario.

Walter J. Boyne

See also

Sopwith Aircraft

References

Ralph, Wayne. *Barker V.C.* London: Grub Street, 1997.

Shores, Christopher, Norman Franks, and Russel Guest. *Above the Trenches.* London: Grub Street, 1990.

Barkhorn, Gerhard (1919–1983)

The second highest-scoring fighter pilot of all time; major general in Germany's post–World War II air force. A Luftwaffe officer cadet from 1937, Barkhorn joined Jagdgeschwader 52 (JG 52; 52d Fighter Wing) during the Battle of Britain and spent most of World War II on the Eastern Front with that famous fighter unit. He flew 120 combat missions before claiming his first air victory, in July 1941, but from May 1942 his score increased rapidly. In January 1944, he became the first German fighter pilot to complete 1,000 combat sorties, on a mission during which he downed his 238th Soviet aircraft. Shortly thereafter he was awarded the Oak Leaves with Swords to the Knight's Cross of the Iron Cross. He left JG 52 in January 1945, after scoring his 301st victory, and briefly commanded JG 6 as a major before joining Adolf Galland's Jagdverband 44 (JV 44—the "Jet Unit of the Aces"; 44th Fighter Unit). A flying accident in April 1945 took him out of the war.

Barkhorn joined the postwar Bundesluftwaffe (the West German Air Force) and rose to the rank of major general before retiring in 1975. In 1983, Barkhorn and his wife were killed in an automobile accident while touring.

Donald Caldwell

See also

German Air Force (Luftwaffe)

References

Obermeier, E. *Die Ritterkreuztraeger der Luftwaffe, 1939–1945, Band I: Jagdflieger* [Recipients of the Knight's Cross]. Mainz, Germany: Verlag Dieter Hoffmann, 1989.

Battle of Britain (1940)

See Britain, Battle of

BAT 21

The rescue operation for BAT 21 Bravo, 2–18 April 1972, South Vietnam. This rescue was the largest rescue operation of the conflict in Southeast Asia. BAT 21 was an EB-66 electronic jamming and reconnaissance aircraft. On 2 April, it was hit and destroyed by a North Vietnamese surface-to-air missile as it and another EB-66, BAT 22, escorted three B-52s dispatched to bomb invading North Vietnamese units at the beginning of what has come to be known as the Easter Offensive.

Only one crewmember, Lieutenant Colonel Iceal "Gene" Hambleton, was able to eject from his stricken aircraft. His personal call sign for the rescue operation was BAT 21 Bravo. Immediately, U.S. Army helicopters tried to rescue Lieutenant Colonel Hambleton. But the North Vietnamese guns drove them off and downed one—a UH1 Huey, call sign Blueghost 39. Three of its crewmembers were killed and one was captured.

The next day, Sikorsky Jolly Green Giant helicopters from the 37th Aerospace Rescue and Recovery Squadron made two attempts to pick up BAT 21 Bravo. Both times, they were driven off with heavy damage to their aircraft. Additionally, an OV-10, call sign Nail 38, was hit and downed by an enemy missile. Its pilot, Captain Bill Henderson, was captured. Its navigator, 1st Lieutenant Mark Clark, call sign Nail 38 Bravo, was able to hide and await rescue like Lieutenant Colonel Hambleton.

For two more days, rescue forces fought the weather and enemy forces to try to rescue the two airmen. They could not get in. Instead, hundreds of air strikes were put in to beat down the enemy gunners. But 6 April dawned bright and clear. So, after 42 more air strikes were put in, a rescue force of four HH-53s and six escorting A-1 "Sandy" aircraft launched to make another attempt to recover the two evading Americans. They were assisted by several forward air controllers in O-2s and OV-10s and numerous other support aircraft.

The lead HH-53, Jolly Green 67, was designated to make the rescue attempt. But as it came to a hover over BAT 21 Bravo, it was raked by heavy enemy fire. The escorting A-1s tried to engage the enemy guns, but they could not get them all.

The A-1 pilots could see what the ground fire was doing to the helicopter, and several screamed for the crew to abort the rescue. The crew of Jolly Green 67 complied and tried to maneuver their stricken aircraft to safety. But the enemy fire continued and so damaged the craft that it crashed in a huge fireball a few kilometers south of the survivors. The fire was intense and lasted several days. There were never any indications of survivors.

The A-1 pilots were shocked by the turn of events. The other helicopters were ready to move into the area and make another attempt. But Sandy 01, the leader of the task force, was not willing to risk another aircraft. He terminated the mission; it was just too dangerous.

The next day, another OV-10 supporting the rescue, call sign Covey 282, was shot down in the same area. The pilot, 1st Lieutenant Bruce Walker, call sign Covey 282 Alpha, was on the ground and evading like the two earlier airmen. His crewman, U.S. Marine 1st Lieutenant Larry Potts, was never heard from. With this news, General Creighton Abrams, the overall U.S. commander in Saigon, directed that there would be no more helicopter rescue efforts for the three downed fliers.

Instead, a ground team was formed to attempt to infiltrate through enemy lines and pick them up. It was planned and directed by U.S. Marine Lieutenant Colonel Andy Anderson and led by U.S. Navy SEAL Lieutenant Tom Norris. From 10 through 12 April, the team operated through enemy lines and rescued Clark and Hambleton. They also intended to rescue Walker, but on 18 April he was discovered by Vietcong troops and killed. The rescues were over. Later, Norris would get the Medal of Honor for the mission; his assistant, South Vietnamese commando Nguyen Van Kiet, would receive the U.S. Navy Cross.

This was the largest sustained rescue operation of the Vietnam War. More than 800 air strikes, including B-52s, were expended in direct support. Numerous helicopters, A-1s, and forward air controller aircraft were shot down or damaged. A total of 11 men were killed.

Darrel Whitcomb

References

Whitcomb, Darrel. *The Rescue of Bat 21.* Annapolis, MD: Naval Institute Press, 1998

Bay of Pigs Invasion

The 1961 U.S.-backed invasion of Cuba by expatriates. During the 1960 presidential campaign, Democratic candidate John F. Kennedy called Cuban dictator Fidel Castro "a source of maximum danger." He criticized Republican President Dwight D. Eisenhower and Vice President Richard M. Nixon for allowing the "communist satellite" (i.e., Cuba) to spring up on "our very doorstep" and called for "a serious offensive" against the island nation. In turn, Nixon described Kennedy as "dangerously irresponsible" for supporting Cuban refugees trying to overthrow Castro. At that very moment, with presidential approval, covert CIA plans were under way to invade Cuba.

At the time, the CIA enjoyed a special place in government, with a budget reputedly around $1 billion. Later dubbed the "Cuban Invasion Authority," they had built their anticommunist reputation by organizing the 1954 overthrow of the communist-tainted government in Guatemala. In 1960, many CIA leaders privately bragged that their 1,500 Cuban trainees would soon "Guatemalize" Cuba.

The training for the invasion had begun in March 1960, ironically, at sites located in Guatemala. Although the training was modern, the weapons were surplus World War II and Korean War items that included obsolete aircraft.

When Kennedy came to the White House, he found the Cuban-invasion issue on his front doorstep. The CIA assured him of success and of the support of the Cuban people. Kennedy, at first reluctant, felt pressure to go forward, especially since public opinion favored some sort of intervention and Kennedy, during the campaign, had promised to do something about Castro and Cuba. He also feared that the exiles might embarrass him publicly if he failed to act. Even so, on 12 April 1961 Kennedy publicly declared that under no circumstances would the U.S. military become directly involved in Cuban affairs.

Still, he approved the operation, and on 17 April the refugee army landed in force at Bahía de Cochinos (Bay of Pigs) on the southern coast of Cuba. After initial success, things began to unravel. With Castro in direct control of his forces, the Cuban air force soon won control of the skies, and his ground forces surrounded the invaders on the beaches. When Kennedy, under great pressure, refused to send apparently promised U.S. air support, the refugees had little choice but to surrender. With 250,000 Cuban militiamen on alert and almost no popular support, the invasion quickly and completely collapsed.

The entire fiasco was a blow to U.S. prestige. In turn, Castro used the affair to "confirm" his accusations of "Yankee aggression." In fact, the United States had violated its own neutrality policies and laws as well as the spirit, if not the letter, of the United Nations Charter. Worst of all, Kennedy had kept his own UN Ambassador, Adlai Stevenson, in the dark. This caused Stevenson to lie unwittingly when he had declared on 17 April that America had "no complicity in the invasion."

In retrospect, the CIA botched the operation. No such operation could have succeeded without the large-scale internal support of anti-Castro Cubans. These potential supporters were offended by the CIA's inclusion in the exile leadership of henchmen from the regime of hated former dictator Fulgencio Batista. The CIA never alerted the Cuban underground. Instead Castro, ever vigilant to U.S. activities, had rounded up thousands of suspects just prior to the invasion.

The CIA operated as a virtual law unto itself, often ignoring the State Department and other agencies, particularly with regard to Cuban popular support and the viability of the landing site.

In spite of Republican and foreign criticism, Kennedy

shunned the opportunity to publicly search for scapegoats. He assumed "full responsibility" for what some Europeans called "a Hungary in reverse." Privately, he blamed the CIA and Joint Chiefs of Staff for poor intelligence and planning. As one historian later noted, even though there was plenty of blame to go around, no one ever seemed to question the policy of attempting to overthrow a sovereign government. Neither did they seem to realize that such an action would push Castro, already seeking a strong anti-U.S. ally, into the waiting arms of the Soviet Union.

Castro emerged stronger than ever. Concurrently, the Soviet Union mistakenly concluded that Kennedy lacked the iron nerve for brinkmanship. By 1962, this would lead to a buildup of Soviet missiles in Cuba and what became known as the Cuban Missile Crisis.

Other byproducts included a seemingly endless economic blockade of Cuba as well as protracted U.S. refusal to recognize the Castro government. The United States made sure Cuba was ousted from the Organization of American States, supported the U.S. Information Agency's anti-Castro program, continued aid to anti-Castro forces, and sponsored assassination plots against the dictator.

Throughout the aftermath, the 1,200 men languishing in Cuban jails weighed heavily on Kennedy's and the public's conscience. In December 1962, the United States violated its own Cuban embargo laws, designed to topple Castro, and opted to allow "private" negotiations and funding to pay Castro $53 million in badly needed food and medical supplies to effect the release of the refugees. Kennedy was roundly criticized for caving in to Castro's demands. Arizona Senator and 1964 Republican presidential candidate Barry Goldwater declared that Kennedy had succumbed to international "blackmail."

William Head

References

Brugioni, Dino A. *Eyeball to Eyeball: The Inside Story of The Cuban Missile Crisis.* New York: Random House, 1991.

Higgins, Trumbull. *The Perfect Failure: Kennedy, Eisenhower, and the CIA at the Bay of Pigs.* New York: Norton, 1987.

Larson, David L. *The Cuban Crisis of 1962.* 2nd ed. New York: Harper and Row, 1986.

Walton, Richard J. *Cold War and Counterrevolution: The Foreign Policy of John F. Kennedy.* Baltimore: Penguin, 1973.

Wyden, Peter. *Bay of Pigs: The Untold Story.* New York: Simon and Schuster, 1980 [1979].

Beaverbrook, Lord (1879–1964)

William Maxwell Aitken earned a fortune as a Canadian stockbroker, moving to Britain before World War I. He entered Parliament in 1910. He was in charge of British propaganda efforts from 1916 to 1918 and was granted the title of Lord Beaverbrook in 1918. Between the wars he became an important British newspaper publisher of the leading *Daily Express* and (in 1929) the *Evening Standard,* both of which published articles by Winston Churchill. During World War II, Churchill, a close friend, appointed Beaverbrook minister for aircraft production (1940–1941), minister of supply (1941–1942), minister of war production (1942), and Lord Privy Seal (1943–1945). Beaverbrook played a central role in focusing Britain's successful production of thousands of fighters and bombers for the Royal Air Force.

Christopher H. Sterling

See also

Churchill, Winston

References

Chisholm, Anne, and Michael Davie. *Lord Beaverbrook: A Life.* New York: Knopf, 1993.

Béchereau, Louis (1880–1970)

Born in 1880 at Plou, France; worked first with the Ader team on cars. In 1909, Deperdussin asked Béchereau to built a canard monoplane, starting a fruitful association. He conceived the first Deperdussin "Monocoque" in 1910. Its racing development won the Gordon Bennett Trophy at Chicago in 1912. The following year, a very-short-span version powered by a 160-hp Gnôme engine, won the trophy, exceeding 203 kph.

After Deperdussin's bankruptcy, the factory was bought by Blériot and retained the acronym SPAD. Béchereau worked on the SPAD VII, a high-performance biplane powered by a Hispano-Suiza 180-hp engine. Reaching squadrons in 1916, the SPAD VII and the later SPAD XIII were the Western allies' most successful fighters, possessing speed, agility, and structural integrity; 7,500 were built.

In 1919 Béchereau joined Bernard, then Salmson, and associated with Kellner in 1932, but his creative work was over. After World War II he worked for Morane-Saulnier before retiring. He died in 1970.

Stephane Nicolaou

Beech Aircraft

The Beech Aircraft Company was founded in 1932 by aviation pioneer Walter H. Beech. Beech began his aircraft manufacturing career in 1924, when he joined forces with fellow

The Beech C-45 served as a utility plane for many years; it was pleasant to fly but tricky to land. (Walter J. Boyne)

aviation pioneers Clyde Cessna and Lloyd Stearman to found the Travel Air Manufacturing Company. The company flourished and by 1929 had become the world's largest producer of commercial aircraft. When the 1929 stock market crash sent aircraft sales into a tailspin, Travel Air merged with the larger Curtiss-Wright Corporation, where Walter Beech accepted an executive position.

In 1932, Walter Beech left Curtiss-Wright to form the Beech Aircraft Company. The first design to emerge from his Wichita factory was the Model 17R Staggerwing. This fast and luxurious single-engine biplane performed better than most military aircraft of the era and gained lasting fame by winning the 1936 Bendix race.

In 1937, the company—now incorporated—introduced its second design, the Beech Model 18 twin-engine monoplane. The versatile Twin Beech proved particularly successful as a military trainer and transport. During World War II, 90 percent of U.S. bombardiers and navigators trained in the Twin Beech.

During the war, Beech produced more than 7,400 military aircraft of various types, plus thousands more subcontracted from other companies. Accordingly, the company was awarded five Army-Navy E awards for production efficiency, an accomplishment only one out of 20 war contracting firms achieved.

After the war, Beech quickly transitioned to the manufacture of moderately priced high-performance commercial aircraft. The company soon replaced the aging Staggerwing with the lighter and more affordable Beech Model 35 Bonanza. This outstanding aircraft was destined to enjoy an unprecedented 35-year production run, and its design served as the basis for the Beechcraft T-34 Mentor, which replaced the T-6 Texan in 1953–1954 as the standard U.S. Air Force and Navy basic trainer.

When Walter Beech died in 1950, the company continued to thrive under the able leadership of his widow and business partner, Olive Beech. It expanded and diversified, subcontracting with major aerospace manufacturers, in addition to continuing to produce successful aircraft. Beech Aircraft Corporation merged with the Raytheon Company in 1980 and has continued to hold its place as a leader in business aviation. Both Walter and Olive Beech are inductees of the National Aviation Hall of Fame.

Steven A. Ruffin

References

McDaniel, William H. *The History of Beech.* Wichita KS: McCormick-Armstrong, 1971.

Phillips, Edward H. *Beechcraft—Pursuit of Perfection: A History of Beechcraft Airplanes.* Eagan, MN: Flying Books, 1992.

Bell AH-1 Cobra

During the Vietnam War, the Bell UH-1 Iroquois helicopter proved too slow to escort the new Boeing-Vertol CH-47 Chinooks that were being used to ferry troops into combat. Bell Helicopter won the competition for an interim, fast, armed escort helicopter while the Army was developing the AH-56A Cheyenne gunship, which was ultimately canceled in 1972. The AH-1 Cobra (Bell Model 209) used the transmission, rotor system, and engine from the UH-1C and a two-man crew in a streamlined fuselage that was only 38 inches wide—a much smaller target than the 100-inch-wide UH-1.

The Cobra quickly proved its worth in Vietnam and was ordered by the U.S. Marine Corps and a number of foreign governments in both single- and twin-engine derivatives. Standard armament includes a nose-mounted 7.62mm minigun or 20mm chain gun, plus a variety of missiles, rockets, or other weapons under its stub wings. The Marine Corps version is even capable of carrying AIM-9 Sidewinder air-to-air missiles.

The U.S. Army began to retire the last of the AH-1s in 2000 in favor of additional Boeing AH-64 Apaches. But the U.S. Marine Corps has elected to put its AH-1s through an extensive remanufacturing program to keep them viable until the year 2025 or later. Many other countries are also considering upgrades to their AH-1s, and in fact the helicopter is still in limited production.

Dennis R. Jenkins

See also

Bell UH-1 Iroquois; Boeing AH-64 Apache

References

Allen, Patrick. *The Helicopter: An Illustrated History of Rotary-Winged Aircraft.* Shrewsbury, UK: Airlife, 1996.

Brown, David A. *The Bell Helicopter Textron Story: Changing the Way the World Flies.* Arlington, TX: Aerofax, 1995.

Bell Aircraft

U.S. aircraft and helicopter manufacturer. Innovation characterized Bell designs from its 1935 beginnings. Unorthodox thinking produced the World War II P-39 Airacobra and P-63 Kingcobra that found limited advocacy in the U.S. Army Air Forces, as well as the revolutionary X-1, the first aircraft to exceed the speed of sound.

Founder Lawrence D. Bell gained experience working for Martin and Consolidated in the 1920s and 1930s. When Reuben Fleet decided to relocate Consolidated Aircraft Corporation from Buffalo, New York, to San Diego, California, in 1935, Larry Bell chose to remain behind and create his own aircraft company, initially using the same buildings Consolidated had occupied. From the outset, the Bell team showed a willingness to innovate. The company's first aircraft, the Airacuda heavy fighter, used twin pusher engines to enable the front of each nacelle to house a gunner and large-bore weapons to defeat interceptors of bomber formations. Though the Airacuda did not enter full production, it set the tone for the company's free-thinking designs.

The P-39 Airacobra of 1938, and the follow-on P-63 Kingcobra, netted Bell quantity production orders for more than 9,500 and 3,300 units respectively. Tricycle landing gear, a midmounted engine, and 37mm nose armament in these designs manifested Bell's continuing innovation. The company also built America's first jet aircraft, the P-59 Airacomet, which flew in October 1942. The Airacomet was a learning tool for industry and the Army Air Forces. Though not competitive for World War II combat, the P-59 showcased Bell's ability to pioneer aeronautical designs.

Bell constructed the XS-1 (later X-1) rocket research aircraft to meet an AAF-inspired probe into transonic and supersonic flight. On 14 October 1947, Captain Charles E. Yeager became the first human to fly faster than sound, in an X-1. Bell's swept-wing X-2 was the first aircraft to attain Mach 3 on 27 September 1956, although the aircraft crashed during that mission.

While the upstate New York operations of Bell Aircraft were diminishing after wartime fighter production subsided, helicopters gave impetus to Bell after World War II. The successful Bell Model 47 helicopter was built in the northern United States until Bell helicopter production moved to Fort Worth, Texas, in 1951. Bell ended fixed-wing aircraft programs in 1956, the same year Lawrence Bell died following a heart attack.

In 1960, Textron bought Bell's helicopter enterprises. The expanding helicopter line included the UH-1 for the U.S. Army, the commercial JetRanger, and the AH-1 Cobra gunship. Textron's Bell Aerospace Corporation continued non-helicopter activities in Buffalo, including reaction controls for the X-15 and delivery of NASA Lunar Landing Research Vehicles. Bell Helicopter Textron established a plant in Montreal, Canada, in 1985, adding to capacity already established in Fort Worth and Amarillo, Texas.

Frederick A. Johnsen

See also

Bell P-39 Airacobra and P-63 Kingcobra; Bell UH-1 Iroquois; Bell X-1

References

Johnsen, Frederick A. *Bell P-39/P-63 Airacobra and Kingcobra.* Warbird Tech Series Volume 17. North Branch, MN: Specialty Press, 1998.

Bell OH-13 Sioux

The Bell Model 47 (U.S. military designation H-13 Sioux) was awarded Helicopter Type Certificate No. 1 on 8 May 1946 and became one of the most popular light utility helicopters ever built. The Model 47 was produced continuously in several countries for more than 30 years, and military versions have been used by at least 40 different countries. The U.S. Army Air Forces procured its first YR-13 (later redesignated H-13) in December 1946.

The Sioux was powered by a single Lycoming piston engine driving a two-blade main rotor and a two-blade tailrotor. Later models of the H-13 had a top speed of 106 mph and a cruising speed of 80 mph. The H-13 was used for observation, reconnaissance, training, and medical evacuation. In the first extensive application of a helicopter in the medevac role, a cocoonlike stretcher pod could be mounted on each landing skid, a sight made familiar by the television show *M*A*S*H.* The OH-13 earned the nickname "Angel of Mercy" for evacuating some 18,000 United Nations casualties during the war. The OH-13 also saw service during the early days of the Vietnam War before the fielding of the OH-6A Cayuse in early 1968.

Dennis R. Jenkins

References

Allen, Patrick. *The Helicopter: An Illustrated History of Rotary-Winged Aircraft.* Shrewsbury, UK: Airlife, 1996.

Brown, David A. *The Bell Helicopter Textron Story: Changing the Way the World Flies.* Arlington, TX: Aerofax, 1995.

Bell P-39 Airacobra and P-63 Kingcobra

Design of the Bell XP-39, a U.S. fighter, was initiated in June 1936, and its development contract was dated 7 October 1937. The Bell Airacobra was conceived as the smallest fighter aircraft (length: 28'8"; span: 35'10"; wing area 200 sq.ft.) that could be built around the 1,150-shp Allison V-1710 engine with a single-stage supercharger, a turbocharger under the engine, with two .30-caliber plus two .50-caliber machine guns and a 37mm cannon in the nose. Two guns were moved to the wings in the P-39C version.

Two unusual features were the engine location behind the pilot, both being over the wing, and tricycle landing gear. It was of riveted aluminum construction but featured two longitudinal fuselage center-section spars and three wing spars, making a very rigid structure. Automotive fabrication techniques were used to facilitate mass production more so than for most other airplanes of World War II. The prototype first flew on 6 April 1939, demonstrating nearly 390 mph at a gross weight of 5,550 pounds, less armor and armament, at 20,000-feet altitude within five minutes from takeoff. Thirteen YP-39 service-test aircraft were produced, without the turbocharger, and delivered from September through December 1940. The production version (P-39C) weighed 7,075 pounds fueled (100 gallons) and armed, in spite of the turbocharger being removed, because of the addition of cockpit armor plate and four machine guns in the wings. The wingspan (34'0") and overall length (30'2"; area being 213 sq.ft.) were also increased. Initial operational capability was February 1941. Weight increased to 7,650 pounds for the definitive P-39D version (compared with 9,000 pounds for the P-51A), which was first delivered in April 1941. Maximum speed of the P-39C was 375 mph at 15,000 feet, that for the P-39D was 360 mph.

The P-39 design, like the P-38 Lightning's, was based on a turbocharged engine. Turbocharger production problems, as well as a greater need for the turbos for bombers and the P-38, led to the U.S. Army decision to remove the turbocharger, which relegated the P-39 to low-altitude missions. Its small amount of fuel tankage forestalled use in escort missions. Attempts to use it at higher altitudes caused it to be wrongly condemned as a bad-performing aircraft. Objective evaluations ranked the P-39 slightly above the P-40 (which itself has been wrongly maligned for the same reason as the P-39) as an all-around fighter aircraft. The Army ordered an initial batch of 80 P-39s, but the first major production contract was for France; its capitulation led to Britain's receiving the aircraft, which they did not appreciate. The P-39 was eventually assigned to 24 U.S. Army fighter and reconnaissance groups. Five thousand P-39s were enthusiastically accepted by Russia and were applied to low-level interception and ground attack missions. A grand total of approximately 10,000 P-39s were built, with little change from the YP-39 configuration. Laminar-flow wings and a two-stage supercharged V-1710 were experimentally fitted to the P-39, but the successor P-63 Kingcobra was designed to accept these improvements while maintaining the central engine installation and other features of the P-39.

The P-63, despite its similarity to the P-39, was an all-new design to take advantage of the longer Allison two-stage supercharged engine and of new aerodynamic lessons learned from the evaluation of P-39 performance problems. Length was 32'8", wing span was 38'4", and wing area was 248 sq.ft.; maximum weight was 8,350 pounds. The new laminar-flow wing and the addition of a supercharger stage, even without more fuel-tank volume, gave the P-63 much greater range and altitude performance. The longer supercharger placed the engine and cockpit farther forward, the cockpit being in front of the wing. The P-63 development contract was dated 27 June 1941; it first flew on 7 December 1942, and the first production units were delivered in October 1943. More than 3,300 P-63s were built, with more than 2,400 going to Russia.

There will always be a PR man, and the Bell Aircraft Company made good use of one in this photo of their products. From the top, the XP-77, P-39, P-63, and P-59. (U.S. Air Force)

The P-63 was used in the United States for operational training and as a gunnery target, a highly armored version produced for this purpose. The armed version carried the same 37mm cannon and two .50-caliber guns in the nose, in addition to one .50-caliber gun mounted in a pod under each wing. It could also carry three 500-pound bombs or three auxiliary fuel tanks under the fuselage and wings. The Russians used the P-63 as they did the P-39. The French received about 200 P-63s, and they and the Russians flew their P-63s in action into the early 1950s.

Douglas G. Culy

References

Wagner, Ray. *American Combat Planes.* 3rd ed. Garden City, NY: Doubleday, 1982.

Bell P-59A Airacomet

On 15 May 1941, the British Gloster E28/39 made its first flight. General Henry H. "Hap" Arnold had seen the aircraft during a visit to Britain the previous month, and when he returned home he asked General Electric to manufacture copies of the Whittle engine under the I-A designation. Because of its close proximity to the General Electric plant, Bell Aircraft was ordered to build an airframe to accommodate two of the new jet engines. These were designated XP-59A as an attempt to disguise them as a version of the now-cancelled XP-59 (no "A") pusher-propeller fighter. The first XP-59A was secretly shipped by train from Buffalo to the West Coast.

The official first flight of the XP-59A was on 2 October 1942 at Muroc Army Air Field in California (now Edwards Air Force Base). America's first jet fighter was a single-seat midwing monoplane powered by two I-A engines of 1,400 pounds/thrust each. A top speed of 404 mph at 25,000 feet was demonstrated, disappointing given that later P-47s and P-51s could easily best it by 20–30 mph. Nevertheless, 13 service-test and 100 production models were ordered, with the third going to Britain in exchange for a Gloster Meteor prototype, and two YP-59As going to the U.S. Navy for evaluation. On 30 October 1943, the production order was cut in half—eventually 20 P-59As were delivered with J31-GE-3 engines, and 30 P-59Bs used slightly more powerful J31-GE-5 engines and had an extra 66 gallons of fuel. All were delivered by the end of May 1945.

Surprisingly, given the pioneering nature of its power plant, none of the service-test models were lost. The P-59 was not fast enough to be suitable as a weapon, but it proved useful in training pilots destined for the Lockheed P-80 "Shooting Star." The shortcomings of the P-59 became even more obvious after the Air Force had a chance to examine the German Me 262 jet fighter toward the end of the war in Europe.

Dennis R. Jenkins

See also

Gloster Meteor; Messerschmitt Me 262

References

Wagner, Ray. *American Combat Planes.* 3rd ed. Garden City, NY: Doubleday, 1982.

Bell Tilt-Rotors

The Bell V-22 Osprey tilt-rotor is just beginning to enter military service. It is the first tilt-rotor to see operational service. Bell is already at work on a civilian version (Bell Boeing Model 609) and has recently shown conceptual designs of a much larger four-rotor version (called the V-44 by the industry press) capable of replacing the Lockheed C-130 Hercules.

But the tilt-rotor is not new. Henry Berliner built a tilt-rotor biplane during the 1920s and actually demonstrated forward speeds over 40 mph. George Lehberger patented a single-shaft tilt-rotor "flying machine" in September 1930, and the Focke-Achgelis FA 269 was a pusher tilt-rotor designed in 1942. The Platt LePage firm proposed a large tilt-rotor passenger aircraft during the late 1940s, and although the aircraft was never built, Haviland Platt received a patent on it in 1955.

The Transcendental Aircraft Corporation of New Castle, Delaware, went one better—actually building a small Model 1-G single-seat experimental aircraft. Unfortunately, after more than 100 successful flights that had almost demonstrated the full range of motion required, the aircraft crashed. A subsequent Model 2 version was not extensively tested due to lack of funds.

A common voice through many early concepts was that of Robert L. Lichten. He had worked for Platt and Transcendental before heading for Bell Aircraft. There he was given the chance to develop the Bell Model 200 in response to an October 1953 military order for two full-scale "tilting-thrust-vector convertiplanes." The first of the XV-3 tilt-rotors made its maiden flight on 11 August 1955, and the XV-3s proved to be valuable research tools for the next 13 years.

Bell began flying the definitive XV-15 demonstrator on 3 May 1977, the first turbine-powered tilt-rotor. As with many aircraft types, turbine power revolutionized the concept. The XV-15, although a relatively small aircraft, successfully demonstrated many of the operational aspects of an operational tilt-rotor. The U.S. military, particularly the Marine Corps, was impressed. In June 1986, a Bell-Boeing team was selected for the development of the V-22 Osprey.

Dennis R. Jenkins

References

Maisel, Martin D., Demo J. Giulianetti, and Daniel C. Dugan. *The History of the XV-15 Tilt Rotor Research Aircraft.* SP-2000–4517. Washington, DC: NASA, 2000.

Bell UH-1 Iroquois ("Huey")

In 1955, the Bell Model 204 won a U.S. Army competition for a utility helicopter suitable for front-line casualty evacuation, general utility, and training duties, and it would become the first turbine-powered helicopter to equip U.S. Army units. The aircraft was originally designated HU-1, giving rise to the nickname "Huey-copter" or "Huey," a name that survived the redesignation to UH-1 in 1962. The Huey is the most universal military aircraft of the modern era, serving in all four branches of the American uniformed services and in the armed forces of at least 48 other nations. Eventually, more than 9,000 Hueys (Models 204/205/212) were built—4,890 UH-1H models alone.

The Huey soon found itself in the jungles of Southeast Asia. The first arrived in 1962, and by the end of the war 1,213 UH-1s were lost to hostile action and a further 1,380 to other operational causes. Hueys armed with only two M60D door guns, called "Slicks" because of their uncluttered external appearance, were the backbone of all air-mobile combat operations in Vietnam. Unarmed medevac versions were called "Dust Offs," because of the clouds of dust kicked up when landing. Until the arrival of the AH-1 Cobra, armed UH-1C and UH-1Ms protected the Slicks on their missions.

The U.S. Army began to retire the last of the UH-1s in 2000 in favor of additional Sikorsky UH-60 Black Hawks. But the U.S. Marine Corps has elected to put its UH-1s through an extensive remanufacturing program to keep them viable until the year 2025 or later. Many other countries are also considering upgrades to their UH-1s.

Dennis R. Jenkins

See also
Bell AH-1 Cobra; Sikorsky UH-60 Black Hawk

References
Allen, Patrick. *The Helicopter: An Illustrated History of Rotary-Winged Aircraft.* Shrewsbury, UK: Airlife, 1996.
Brown, David A. *The Bell Helicopter Textron Story: Changing the Way the World Flies.* Arlington, TX: Aerofax, 1995.

Bell X-1

U.S. research aircraft. The Bell X-1 was significant in the history of airpower because it proved there was no sound barrier and also provided design data and technology for future transonic and supersonic aircraft, including the movable horizontal stabilizer that made the later models of the F-86 so superior to MiG-15s in the Korean War. The first of the rocket-powered research aircraft, the X-1 (originally designated the XS-1), was a bullet-shaped airplane that was designed and built by the Bell Aircraft Company for the Army Air Forces and the National Advisory Committee for Aeronautics (NACA), which provided many of the design specifications. The mission of the X-1 was to investigate the transonic speed range (speeds from just below to just above the speed of sound) and, if possible, to break the so-called sound barrier.

The first of the three X-1s was glide-tested at Pinecastle Army Air Field, Florida, in early 1946. The first powered flight of the X-1 was made on 9 December 1946 at Edwards Air Force Base with Chalmers "Slick" Goodlin, a Bell test pilot, at the controls.

On 14 October 1947, with Air Force Captain Charles "Chuck" Yeager as pilot, the aircraft flew faster than the speed of sound for the first time. Yeager ignited the four-chambered XLR-11 rocket engines after a B-29 Superfortress air-launched it from under the bomb bay at 20,000 feet. The 6,000-pound/thrust ethyl alcohol/liquid oxygen–burning rockets, built by Reaction Motors, pushed the aircraft to a speed of 700 mph in level flight.

Yeager was also the pilot when the X-1 reached its maximum speed: 957 mph. Another USAF pilot, Lieutenant Colonel Frank Everest Jr., was credited with taking the X-1 to its maximum altitude of 71,902 feet. The number-three plane was destroyed in a fire before making powered flight.

More advanced versions of the X-1 (the X-1A, X-1B, and X-1E) flew faster. All of them gathered valuable data for future aircraft designs.

J. D. Hunley

See also
Research Aircraft; Yeager, Charles E.

References
Hallion, Richard P. *Supersonic Flight—Breaking the Sound Barrier and Beyond: The Story of the Bell X-1 and the Douglas D-558.* Rev. ed. London: Brassey's, 1997.
Rotundo, Louis. *Into the Unknown: The X-1 Story.* Washington, DC: Smithsonian Institution Press, 1994.
Young, James O. *Meeting the Challenge of Supersonic Flight.* Edwards AFB, CA: Air Force Flight Test Center History Office, 1997.

Beriev Aircraft

Chief designer and manufacturer of maritime aircraft in the Soviet Union. Georgii Mikhailovich Beriev was born in Georgia in 1902 and trained as an engineer in Leningrad after the Bolshevik Revolution. In 1928, he joined a design bureau for naval aircraft. His first task was to make improvements on the Savoia S.62, which had been bought from Italy for license production. In 1932, he launched his own design bureau based at Taganrog, on the Sea of Azov. His first design was the MBR-2 flying boat, which first flew in October 1932. Entering production in 1934, 1,365 were produced by the time Taganrog was overrun by the Germans. Though outdated, with its single pylon-mounted motor, it served as the main Soviet naval reconnaissance and antisubmarine aircraft throughout World War II, helping protect Lend-Lease convoys and even served as a nighttime bomber. It was retired from service in the late 1950s.

Beriev also was responsible for production of the GST, the Soviet-licensed version of the Consolidated PBY "Catalina"; only 27 examples were produced before the factories were overrun in 1942. Other prewar aircraft designed by Beriev were never allocated any priority, never advanced beyond prototype stage, or were produced in minuscule quantities.

From 1950 to 1957, Beriev produced for the Soviet Navy 123 examples of the Be-6, a large, twin-motor flying boat in the general class and format of the Martin Mariner. Beriev next designed the Be-10, a twin-jet swept-wing flying boat intended for antisubmarine patrol. Though it entered naval service, design problems were never completely eliminated, the concept was dated, and production ceased in 1961 after only 27 examples were produced.

Much more successful was the Be-12 amphibian flying boat, known to NATO as "Mail." This antisubmarine aircraft had a gull wing, twin tails, and two turboprop engines and was produced from 1964 to 1973; some of the 132 examples remained in service at the turn of the century. Others have been rebuilt as firefighting water bombers.

Beriev died in 1979, but his bureau continues. It has been

involved in the experiments with the Ekranoplane "wing-in-ground-effects" aircraft, as well as the new Be-42/A-40 Mermaid amphibious flying boat currently under development.

George M. Mellinger

References

Andersson, Lennart. *Soviet Aircraft and Aviation 1917–1941.* Annapolis, MD: Naval Institute Press, 1994.

Gunston, Bill. *The Encyclopedia of Russian Aircraft, 1875–1995.* Osceola, WI: Motorbooks International, 1995.

Berlin Air Battles (1940–1945)

The attempts to carry the aerial war to the capital of the Third Reich and draw out the Luftwaffe in its defense. Before August 1940, Berlin remained unscathed by Royal Air Force bombers. In that month, however, RAF Bomber Command launched two attacks in retaliation for the Luftwaffe's bombing of London. Executed by Vickers Wellington, Armstrong Whitworth Whitley, and Handley Page Hampden twin-engine bombers flying at the extremity of their ranges, the raids did very little damage and killed few people. They nonetheless marked the beginning a years-long campaign to take the war to Hitler's center of power. In what became the RAF's largely nighttime "city-busting" campaign, the objective was to sap German morale and cripple their industry by "dehousing" workers. If factories and administrative centers were hit as well, then so much the better. Such tactics rested principally upon early RAF bombers' ineffective defensive armament in daylight and a lack of accurate bombsights. Even the RAF's introduction of the four-engine Short Stirling and Handley Page Halifax bombers in 1941 and the superb Avro Lancaster in early 1942 did not significantly alter this operational doctrine.

Nevertheless, the weight of Bomber Command's assault on Berlin and other cities grew accordingly, and the Eighth Air Force of the U.S. Army Air Forces soon joined the fray. In late 1943, the RAF launched a sustained effort to pulverize the Reich capital. Building on the successful 1,000-bomber raids of 1942, Air Marshal Arthur "Bomber" Harris believed that Berlin's destruction would cost Germany the war. On 18 November, Harris ordered 444 heavy bombers to Berlin. Of that number only nine were lost. Harris, encouraged, kept up the effort. Bomber Command sent in 15 more major attacks by the end of March 1944. From the 9,111 sorties, 492 bombers failed to return. Another 95 crashed at their bases, and 859 others suffered battle damage. These raids did not include yet another 16 smaller harassing attacks during the same period. Altogether more than 1,000 RAF bombers of all types were lost during the efforts against Berlin.

Up to this time, the Eighth Air Force had not participated in the raids on Berlin. It was still recovering from severe losses suffered in the second half of 1943, during the raids on Schweinfurt and Regensburg. Its efforts were also affected by diversions to the newly established Fifteenth Air Force in Italy. The Eighth's effort against Berlin took shape, however, under the Combined Bomber Offensive (CBO) directive of 13 February 1944. The directive specified targeting Berlin whenever possible. Planners reasoned, in part, that the Luftwaffe would fight for the city, as it would fight for no other; and the consequent destruction of the Luftwaffe's planes, pilots, and infrastructure by the Allies' aerial forces remained the CBO's primary objective.

As over targets such as Hamburg in 1943, the RAF bombed at night, the Eighth Air Force during daylight. The dramatic difference in early 1944 was the presence of long-range escorts, principally North American P-51 Mustangs, that were able to accompany the bombers all the way to the target (indeed, beyond it) and back. The replacement of any German pilots killed became increasingly difficult due to the Luftwaffe's simultaneously constricted resources on the ground. That weakening of German airpower, in turn, would make an Allied invasion of northwestern Europe that much more likely to succeed. On 4 March 1944, the Eighth Air Force carried out its first daylight raid on the German capital. Three additional attacks followed before month's end. They comprised some 1,700 sorties by Boeing B-17 Flying Fortresses and Consolidated B-24 Liberators escorted by hordes of fighters. Specific targets included the VKF Erkner ball-bearing facility, the Bosch electrical works at Klein Machow, and the Daimler Benz engine factory at Genshagen.

The Luftwaffe reacted fiercely throughout. For example, 69 of the Eighth Air Force's big bombers fell on 6 March alone, losses as high as over Schweinfurt and Regensburg in 1943. In exchange, 81 German fighter aircraft were shot down on that same day. Still, the Eighth continued its effort throughout the rest of 1944 and into 1945 though the regularity of attacks on Berlin decreased. In addition, Fifteenth AF bombers executed their first large raid on the city on 24 March 1945, a mission exceeding 1,500 miles in total distance. The consequence, as Harris put it, was "the wrecking of Berlin from end to end," though Germany did not lose the war as a result.

Heavy and effective Luftwaffe flak served as Berlin's ground-based defense. As late as the Eighth Air Force's raid of 3 February 1945, these guns clawed fully 25 heavy bombers from the skies. In addition, radar-directed day- and night-fighters rose to defend the city. They included late-model Messerschmitt Bf 109s and Focke-Wulf Fw 190s carrying heavy machine guns, cannons of up to 30mm, and,

The United States responded to a military crisis, the Berlin Blockade, with a magnificent compassionate gesture, the Berlin Airlift. Douglas C-54s were soon bringing in more supplies by air than had previously been brought in by rail, road, and canal. (U.S. Air Force)

occasionally, air-to-air rockets. Also attacking the bombers were radar-equipped twin-engine Bf 110s armed (at night) with the dreaded Schräge Musik (Jazz Music) twin 30mm cannon designed to fire diagonally into the bombers' ventral surfaces. One twin-engine fighter, the follow-on Me 410 Hornisse (Hornet), even mounted a massive 50mm cannon—a true bomber-killer. Most fortunately for Allied airmen over Berlin, the potential of the elegant but deadly Me 262 Schwalbe (Swallow) cannon-armed jet fighter never materialized. Neither did that of the extraordinary Me 163 Komet (Comet) rocket-propelled interceptor.

D. R. Dorondo

See also

Avro Aircraft; German Air Force (Luftwaffe); Germany, and World War II Air Battles; Harris, Arthur T.; Messerschmitt, Willy; Royal Flying Corps/Royal Naval Air Service/Royal Air Force; Short Aircraft (Post–World War I); U.S. Army Air Forces

References

Craven, Wesley F., and James L. Cate, eds. *The Army Air Forces in World War II, Volume 3: Europe: ARGUMENT to V-E Day, January 1944 to May 1945,* Washington, DC: Office of Air Force History, 1983.

Frankland, Noble. "Bomber Offensive: The Devastation of Europe." In Barrie Pitt, ed., *Ballantine's Illustrated History of World War II.* New York: Ballantine Books, 1971.

Hammel, Eric. *Air War Europa: America's Air War Against Germany in Europe and North Africa. Chronology, 1942–1945.* Pacifica, CA: Pacifica Press, 1994.

Berlin Airlift

From June 1948 until September 1949, the early period of the Cold War, Western powers supplied the city of Berlin solely by means of air transport when Soviet forces cut off rail, river barge, and road traffic in a political power play to squeeze Britain, France, and the United States out of Berlin. Using a variety of aircraft, the Berlin Airlift continued until September, despite the fact that ground restrictions were lifted in mid-May 1949, as it took months to build up the city's stocks of vital supplies to a safe level.

When the airlift began on 24 June 1948, the Western powers were woefully outnumbered in troops, equipment, and aircraft by the Soviets occupying East Germany and half of Berlin. The notion of supplying a city of almost 3 million people only by air originated with a Royal Air Force official faced with the city's pre-airlift daily need of 15,000 imported tons of supplies, with 4,000 being the absolute minimum to survive. At the beginning, the U.S. Air Force could supply but 700 tons using the 25 available C-47 aircraft. The British pressed 40 Dakotas, 35 Avro Yorks, 26 Handley Page Hastings, and a few Sunderland flying boats into service on what the Americans soon dubbed Operation VITTLES (Operation LITTLE VITTLES was the dropping of candy by airlift pilots to Berlin children). Some British charter airlines also participated using Avro Tudors, Handley Page Halifaxes, and Consolidated Liberators. By August 1948, U.S. C-54s took the bulk of the airlift, more than 300 of them eventually participating, some loaned by U.S. nonscheduled airlines. Pilots flew up to 70 hours within any 30-day period.

The airlift soon established three air corridors, each 20 miles wide, across the Soviet zone of occupation to reach the Berlin airfields of Tegel, Gatow, and Tempelhof, plus one water base at Havelsee. Pavements were built or extended, often by Berliners working only with hand tools. Very careful flight paths were arranged due to the heavy traffic—with dozens of aircraft movements per hour. The average aircraft turnaround time in Berlin was less than 50 minutes, so intense was the pressure. Indeed, the full airlift scheme reached as far as the U.S. West Coast, whence came some of the supplies and to which some aircraft had to return for maintenance.

All told, the U.S. Air Force brought some 1.4 million tons of coal, nearly 300,000 tons of food, and 65,000 tons of other material into Berlin. This allowed a typical Berliner to receive, under a tight system of rations, 15 ounces each of bread and potatoes, 1.5 ounces of sugar, 1.75 ounces of prepared foods, 1.5 ounces of meat, and about an ounce of fats and a twentieth of an ounce of cheese. For the winter season, however, less than 30 pounds of heating fuel (be it coal or wood) were available per person. To help stretch supplies, some 15,000 children were flown out of Berlin during the airlift. Amazingly, only 22 accidents occurred, with 30 crew deaths. The airlift cost slightly more than $137 million in monetary values of the time. No airlift operation since has carried as much to so many in such a brief period of time.

Christopher H. Sterling

See also

Airlines, Service During Wartime

References

Barker, Dudley. *Berlin Air Lift: An Account of the British Contribution.* London: HMSO, 1949.

Collier, Richard. *Bridge Across the Sky: The Berlin Blockade and Airlift, 1948–1949.* New York: McGraw-Hill, 1978.

Pearcey, Arthur. *Berlin Airlift.* Shrewbury, UK: Airlife, 1997.

Bien Hoa Air Base

Base located 25 kilometers northeast of Saigon in South Vietnam. During the period 1961–1964, Bien Hoa, along with Da Nang and Tan Son Nhut, were the chief operating locations of U.S. Air Force advisers.

On the morning of 1 November 1964, Vietnamese communist troops attacked Bien Hoa. Positioning six 81mm mortars about 400 meters north of the base, the enemy gunners fired 60–80 rounds onto parked aircraft and troop billets. The Vietcong (VC) then withdrew undetected and unmolested, leaving behind damage completely disproportionate to the effort expended. The barrage killed four U.S. military personnel and wounded 30. Of 20 B-57 jet bombers hit, five were destroyed, eight were severely damaged, and seven were slightly damaged. Increasingly thereafter, U.S. air bases in the Republic of Vietnam (RVN) became routine targets for enemy ground attacks as well as standoff attacks.

On 16 May 1965 at Bien Hoa, an accidental explosion aboard a parked B-57 triggered a series of blasts that killed 28 and injured 77 people. The aircraft toll reached 10 B-57s, two A-2Hs, one A-1E, and one F-8U destroyed, plus 30 A-1Hs and one H-43 damaged. Also demolished were 12 pieces of aerospace ground equipment, 10 vehicles, and the JP-4 fuel dump. This one incident was more destructive than any single VC/NVA attack on any air base during the entire Vietnam War. The incident resulted in a U.S. Air Force–directed emergency program for revetment construction.

Bien Hoa Air Base, a major USAF/South Vietnamese air base that harbored all types of aircraft, was a consistent target for VC standoff harassment fire. While attempting to hit parked aircraft hidden under the ever-tightening rows of concrete revetments, VC rocket attacks often reaped secondary rewards by hitting ammo dumps and troop areas.

George M. Watson Jr.

References

Fox, Roger P. *Air Base Air Defense in the Republic of Vietnam, 1961–1973.* Washington, DC: Office of Air Force History, 1979.

Schlight, John. *The War in South Vietnam: The Years of the offensive 1965–1968.* United States Air Force in Southeast Asia Series. Washington, DC: Office of Air Force History, 1988.

Bikini Atoll Tests

Pacific Ocean site of early U.S. nuclear tests. At Bikini Atoll, 23 atmospheric nuclear and thermonuclear tests were conducted between 1946 and 1958. Bikini is one of 29 atolls and five islands that compose the Marshall Islands. It comprises a total of 2 square miles consisting of 36 islets on a reef 25 miles long. It was chosen as a test site because of its remoteness from regular air and sea routes. The original inhabitants were moved to other islands after Bikini became part of the Pacific nuclear proving ground of the United States.

The first post–World War II nuclear weapons test was conducted at Bikini in July of 1946. Operation CROSSROADS was designed to determine the effects of these bombs on naval vessels. In preparation, a fleet of more than 90 target ships with a support fleet of more than 150 vessels was assembled in the Bikini lagoon. The 42,000 participants witnessed a series that consisted of an airdropped bomb detonated at a height of 520 feet (ABLE) and an underwater shot conducted at a depth of 90 feet (BAKER). The tests produced mixed results. Only a few ships were sunk by the first bomb. The second detonation produced substantial fallout and contaminated part of the support fleet.

In the spring of 1954, Bikini Atoll became the site of Operation CASTLE. This testing series was the culmination in the development of the hydrogen bomb; between March and May six tests were conducted at Bikini and neighboring Enewetak. The most prominent of those tests was BRAVO. Despite unfavorable weather conditions and faulty pretest yield calculations, the test was executed on 1 March and produced a yield of 15 megatons and created a worldwide fallout scare.

After the blast had created a large crater in the reef, fallout spread and not only threatened the onsite service personal but contaminated Japanese fishermen and Marshall Islanders. The Japanese tuna trawler *Lucky Dragon,* with a crew of 23, was severely contaminated. Marshall Islanders on Rongelap (about 100 miles east of Bikini) were also severely contaminated, and many had to be treated for symptoms of beta and gamma radiation. A worldwide wave of protest followed, with international calls for an end to nuclear testing.

Despite the protests, testing continued. On Bikini, the last series was conducted in 1958. The Pacific phase of Operation HARDTACK consisted 34 nuclear detonations, all but two on Bikini and Enewetak.

Since 1960, the U.S. government and the original residents of the Bikini Atoll have been debating return provisions, rehabilitation plans, and compensation. The Nuclear Claims Council decided in March to award the people of Bikini $563 million in compensation for loss of value, restoration costs, and suffering and hardship.

Frank Schumacher

References

Niedenthal, Jack. *For the Good of Mankind: A History of the People of Bikini and Their Islands* Majuro: Bikini Atoll Local Government, 2001.

______. *The People of Bikini: From Exodus to Resettlement.* Majuro: Bikini Atoll Local Government, 1996.

Weisgall, Jonathan M. *Operation Crossroads: The Atomic Tests at Bikini Atoll.* Annapolis, MD: Naval Institute Press, 1994.

Birkigt, Marc (1878–1953)

Born in Geneva in 1878; studied there at the Ecole des Arts et Métiers. In 1899, he started working in Barcelona, where he launched the Hispano-Suiza firm in 1904, which quickly became an important car maker. In 1913, another one was built at Bois-Colombes in France, but its workers had to join the front in August 1914. Back in Spain, Birkigt designed a 150-hp aviation engine in October 1914. This revolutionary V-8 engine was accepted by a French committee in July 1915. Nearly 50,000 derivatives were ordered by Allied countries in three basic versions: 180-hp, 220-hp, and the Cannon engine. From 1923, Birkigt designed many aircraft engines giving 350 hp to 1,000 hp at the start of World War II. In 1936, he had to stop producing his legendary cars to concentrate on cannons and the 12Y engine that was used in great number. This mechanical genius died in Switzerland in 1953.

Stéphane Nicolaou

Bishop, William (1894–1956)

Canada's "Ace of Aces" during World War I; achieved the rank of Air Marshal in the British service. William "Billy" Bishop was studying at Canada's Royal Military College when he went to war in 1914. Dissatisfied with ground fighting, he transferred to flying the next year. Wounded as an observer, he retrained as a pilot and was assigned to Royal Flying Corps No. 60 Squadron in April 1917, where he ran his score to 47 before going back to England that summer. This tour is best remembered for his claimed solo raid on a German airfield on 2 June 1917. That action won him the Victoria Cross, but the lack of supporting evidence in German records for this and many other Bishop exploits has caused the accuracy of his record to be hotly contested. During this brief tour, his score climbed to 72, the highest number of claims by any pilot in British service.

James Streckfuss

See also

Royal Aircraft Factory; Royal Flying Corps/Royal Naval Air Service/Royal Air Force

References

Bishop, William Avery. *Winged Warfare.* London: Hodder and Stoughton, 1918.

Shores, Christopher, Norman Franks, and Russell Guest. *Above the Trenches.* London: Grub Street, 1990.

Bismarck, Air Operations Against the

Destruction of Germany's greatest warship. Although the German battleship *Bismarck* was eventually sunk by gunfire and torpedoes from British surface ships, it was aircraft reconnaissance and attacks that doomed the formidable ship. In May 1941, the *Bismarck* and the cruiser *Prinz Eugen* slipped into the Atlantic to raid British commerce. British capital ships intercepted them but were driven off with the loss of HMS *Hood,* but not before causing minor damage to the *Bismarck.* This damage prompted *Bismarck* to alter plans and attempt to return to France for repairs. Later, Swordfish torpedo-bombers from the *Victorious* hit the *Bismarck,* causing the first German fatality but no appreciable damage. *Bismarck* broke contact after covering *Prinz Eugen's* escape but was spotted by a British Catalina. Swordfish from HMS *Ark Royal* torpedoed and disabled *Bismarck's* rudder, allowing surface ships to close in and finish the battleship. The destruction of the *Bismarck* illustrated the vulnerability of surface ships to air attack, even from obsolescent aircraft.

Grant Weller

See also

Aircraft Carriers, Development of; Atlantic, Battle of the; Consolidated PBY Catalina; Fairey Aircraft

References

Maclean, Anne, and Suzanne Poole. *Fighting Ships of World Wars One and Two.* London: Peerage Books, 1986.

Bismarck Sea, Air Battle of (1943)

Destruction of Japanese convoy off New Guinea. On 1 March 1943, a Japanese convoy of eight transports and eight escorts left Rabaul, New Britain, bound for Lae, New Guinea, with troops and supplies. Allied intelligence analysis had accurately predicted the operation and Allied reconnaissance aircraft soon spotted and tracked the convoy. The ships came under attack from U.S. B-17s, B-25s, and P-38s, along with Beauforts, Beaufighters, and Bostons of the Royal Australian Air Force, all flying from Port Moresby and other bases in the Southwest Pacific. For weeks the Allies had practiced such missions and had modified many of their aircraft to increase their effectiveness against surface naval targets.

The Japanese were unable to effectively contest control of the air over the convoy, and Allied aircraft continued to launch devastating attacks over several days until all eight transports and five escorts were sunk. Only a few survivors from the transports reached the convoy's destination in New Guinea. The Japanese ceased to attempt regular supply convoys to eastern New Guinea, sealing the fate of the Imperial army in that area.

The battle again illustrated the difficulties of conducting naval operations in the face of enemy air superiority and the beneficial effects of intense mission-specific training and rehearsal.

Frank E. Watson

References

Craven, Wesley F., and James L. Cate, eds. *The Army Air Forces in World War II, Volume 4: The Pacific: Guadalcanal to Saipan, August 1942–July 1944.* Chicago: University of Chicago Press, 1950.

Bissell, Clayton L. (1896–1973)

Major general in the U.S. military. Born in Kane, Pennsylvania, Clayton Lawrence Bissell was among America's earliest military aviators. After earning a law degree in 1917 from Valparaiso University, Indiana, he enlisted and was commissioned (January 1918) in the Aviation Section of the U.S. Army Signal Corps Reserve. After initial training at Mohawk, Canada, he was assigned to Taliaferro Field, Texas, in November 1917. Sent to England, he trained with the 22d Aero Squadron and served in the Overseas Ferry Service before joining the 148th Aero Squadron in July 1918. Bissell destroyed five enemy planes, becoming an ace. Commanding the 638th American Fighter Squadron, he was promoted to captain in March 1919.

Captain Bissell returned to the United States and was assigned to Kelly Field, Texas, to command the 27th Aero Squadron and the Air Service Group. In June 1920, he went to Washington, D.C., as chief of the Tactical Operations Section in the Office of Air Service, and in December he was enrolled in the Air Service Field Officers' School at Langley Field, Virginia. Upon completion in June 1921 he served as flight commander of the 14th Squadron at Langley, and later instructed in the Air Service Field Officers' School.

Assigned to Washington, D.C., in November, Bissell served as assistant to Brigadier General William Mitchell for four years. Following a one-year posting with a round-the-world flight to British Columbia, Alaska, the Aleutians, Greenland, Labrador, Newfoundland, and the Maritime Provinces, he returned to Langley Field in December 1924 to serve as secretary of the Air Service Board. After instructing at the Air Corps Tactical School at Langley Field (September 1926–August 1931), Bissell studied at the Command and General Staff School at Fort Leavenworth, Kansas, followed by study at the Army War College and then the Chemical Warfare School at Edgewood Arsenal, Maryland, completing his studies in July 1934. Captain Bissell completed a tour with the 18th Pursuit Group at Schofield Barracks, Hawaii, as intelligence and operations officer, and then as commanding officer. He was promoted to major and returned to the mainland in July 1938 to attend the Naval War College at Newport, Rhode Island. In July 1939, he joined the War Department General Staff as a member of the War Plans Division.

In January 1942, Colonel Bissell joined Major General

Joseph W. Stilwell's staff in China and commanded all U.S. air forces in India, Burma, and China. As a brigadier general (21 April 1942), Bissell commanded the Tenth Air Force in India and Burma after the Fourteenth Air Force in China was activated under Claire L. Chennault. Bissell returned to the United States as a major general in August 1943 and became assistant Chief of Air Staff for intelligence at Air Force HQ in Washington. He later served the Office of the Assistant Chief of Staff for Intelligence on the War Department General Staff and was active in the Joint Security Control, the Joint Intelligence Committee, the Combined Intelligence Committee, and the psychological warfare program; he headed the War Department's historical program.

Bissell became military attaché to Great Britain in May 1946 and returned to the United States in October 1948. Posted to Headquarters U.S. Air Forces in Europe, at Wiesbaden, Germany, he returned to Washington in April 1950. General Bissell was awarded the Distinguished Service Cross, Distinguished Service Medal with two Oak Leaf Clusters, Silver Star, Distinguished Flying Cross and Air Medal, the British Distinguished Flying Cross, and several other foreign decorations. General Bissell retired from the USAF on 30 October 1950 and died on 1 January 1973.

Richard C. DeAngelis

References

Bowman, Martin W. *USAAF Handbook, 1939–1945.* Mechanicsburg, PA: Stackpole Books, 1997.

Chennault, Claire L. *Way of a Fighter.* Rpt. Tucson, AZ: Thorvardson Press, 1991.

Pogue, Forrest C. *George C. Marshall: Ordeal and Hope, 1939–1942.* 3 vols. New York: Viking Press, 1966.

Blackburn Aircraft

The Blackburn Aeroplane and Motor Co. Ltd. was formed in June 1914 to build the Royal Aircraft Factory B.E.2c that was adopted as standard equipment for the fledgling Royal Flying Corps and Royal Naval Air Service. During World War I, the company built a total of 111 of B.E.2s, developed the Sopwith Cuckoo torpedo-bomber (132 built) and built the Sopwith Baby seaplane in quantity (186) for the British Admiralty.

During the lean interwar years, Blackburn designed and built a variety of naval and civil aircraft, and specialized in torpedo-bombers such as the Dart, Ripon, and Shark. The Skua was a two-seat naval fighter/dive-bomber built to Air Ministry specification 0.27/34. The prototype first flew in February 1937, but the need for a carrier-borne dive-bomber was so urgent that 190 aircraft were ordered six months before the prototype flew. The Skua was rather underpowered for a fighter but enjoyed some success in the first months of the war, including the successful dive-bombing of the German cruiser *Königsberg* in Bergen Harbor on 10 April 1940. The Skua (190 built) was withdrawn from front-line service in August 1941 and was relegated to training and target-towing duties.

The Botha was a twin-engine land-based reconnaissance and torpedo-bomber developed to the same specification as the Bristol Beaufort. The specification was amended to include four crew members (rather than three), and it became clear that more power was required. Unfortunately, no Bristol Taurus radials were available for the program, so the aircraft went into production with the Bristol Perseus motor. A total of 580 were built. The Botha served with RAF Coastal Command during the first year of World War II and was relegated to training duties from the end of 1940.

During the war, Blackburn Aircraft built 1,700 Fairey Swordfish, 635 Fairey Barracuda Mk IIs, and 250 Short Sunderland aircraft under license.

The Firebrand first flew in February 1942. A total of 220 of all marks were built. The Firebrand was originally designed as a single-seat naval fighter, but following the adoption of the Supermarine Seafire as the standard Fleet Air Arm (FAA) fighter, it was redesigned as a high-performance torpedo-bomber after the first dozen fighters were built. Many early marks were used for trial purposes, and the Firebrand was in operational service from September 1945 to August 1953.

Blackburn was amalgamated with General Aircraft Ltd. on 1 January 1949 as Blackburn and General Aircraft Ltd. The Blackburn Beverley (47 built) was a General Aircraft design under an Air Ministry specification for a medium-range tactical transport. A total of 47 served with RAF Transport Command from 1956 to 1967, when they were replaced by the Lockheed C-130K "Hercules."

The Buccaneer was a two-seat low-level naval strike aircraft and first flew in July 1958. It was built to withstand the rigors of high-speed low-level flight and incorporated a number of structural and aerodynamic advances. It was capable of delivering nuclear or conventional weapons and was the first operational aircraft to be fitted with a head-up display. The first operational squadron, No. 801, embarked on HMS *Ark Royal* in February 1963.

The Buccaneer was pressed into RAF service as a replacement for the canceled General Dynamics F-111K, and the first unit (No. 12 Squadron) formed at RAF Honington in October 1969. With the run-down of the FAA's conventional carrier force, all surviving Buccaneers were transferred to the RAF during 1978.

The Buccaneer received numerous upgrades and modifications to its electronic systems and weapons fit throughout its service life, include laser-guided bomb delivery and designation using the Pave Spike system. During the 1991 Gulf War, Buccaneers were used to provide target designation services for Tornados following the RAF's abandonment of JP233 airfield attacks. A total of 189 production Buccaneers were built.

Blackburn Aircraft became a member company of the Hawker-Siddeley Group in May 1963.

Andy Blackburn

See also

Fairey Aircraft; Fleet Air Arm; General Dynamics F-111 Aardvark; Gulf War; Gun Sights; Short Sunderland; Supermarine Spitfire

References

Jackson, A. J. *Blackburn Aircraft Since 1909.* London: Putnam, 1968.

Blériot Aircraft

French aircraft manufacturer. Dealing himself into the growing company of early aviators in 1908 with an unsuccessful ornithopter design, Louis Blériot continued working until he finally achieved aerial immortality by being the first to fly across the English Channel. The flight was made in the Blériot 11, a delicate-looking monoplane with a partially open fuselage, powered by an Anzani engine of 25 hp. For the next few years and into the war, the fortunes of Blériot Aéronautique were built on the Type 11, which served in French, British, and Russian units performing reconnaissance and light bombing duties.

As the war progressed, the Type 11 was surpassed technologically by more modern designs, but it continued to serve in the French training schools both as a flying machine and in a not-quite-flyable role as a clipped-wing Penguin. Using Penguins, French student-pilots would conduct high-speed taxi runs to learn the feel of the aircraft's controls.

In 1913, Blériot acquired Armand Deperdussin's firm (Société Provisoire des Aéroplanes Deperdussin), which had produced SPAD aircraft. He retained the chief engineer, Louis Bécherau, and changed the firm's name to Société Anonyme pour l'Aviation et ses Dérives to retain the SPAD name. The SPAD fighters became France's main combat aircraft and served with other countries as well. His original Blériot firm continued production with a series of very large, very complex designs that were not adopted for general use.

James Streckfuss

See also

SPAD Aircraft

References

Davilla, Dr. James J., and Arthur M. Soltan. *French Aircraft of the First World War.* Mountain View, CA: Flying Machines Press, 1997.

Lamberton, William M., and E. F. Cheesman. *Reconnaissance and Bomber Aircraft of the 1914–1918 War.* London: Harleyford, 1962.

Blimps, Military Use of

Nonrigid airships for observation and gathering intelligence. The development of both the internal combustion engine and the dirigible balloon, or rigid airship, dates from the late 1800s and opened up even more military possibilities for their use. Large rigid and nonrigid airships were deployed offensively and defensively during World War I.

Count Ferdinand von Zeppelin, a pioneer in airship construction, developed large rigid airships prior to World War I that were used by the German army and navy. Nonrigid airships were also used during World War I by the Allies as a response to the German U-boat threat.

The nonrigid airship, or blimp, as it came to be called, soon proved its worth during the conflict patrolling the English Channel, Irish Sea, and the North Sea against submarines and scouting for mines. In all, the British built 374 blimps for service during the war. The primary advantage of the blimp compared to a heavier-than-air craft was its range. The British type C (Coastal), for example, carried a crew of five, mounted a machine gun, and had a speed of 50 mph; its endurance was more than 24 hours, which allowed a substantially wider radius of action than conventional aircraft. The United States Navy, aware of British successes with blimps, purchased more than 16 nonrigid airships from Goodyear between 1917 and 1918; they flew a total of 13,600 hours on antisubmarine patrols over the North Atlantic and bombed two German U-boats.

Following the war, Goodyear saw a role for blimps in the advertisement field. But blimps also continued to play a role in the military. Using helium as a substitute for flammable hydrogen ensured the survival of blimps for the foreseeable future. The United States was the only natural source of helium, and it became a world leader in the design and construction of nonrigid airships.

Blimps continued to increase in size, speed, and capacity by the outbreak of World War II. The Goodyear K class, the mainstay of the USN airship fleet, carried an eight-man crew and had a maximum speed of 77 mph with a range of 2,000 miles. The K class could carry four bombs, and later models were equipped with airborne radar for antisubmarine warfare operations. Goodyear built 135 K-class blimps for the USN before the end of the war.

USN blimps carried out a number of tasks during the war, including long-range air patrols, convoy protection, performing search-and-destroy missions, and directing surface ships in their searches for German submarines.

During World War II, the USN employed some 200 blimps in trade-protection duties primarily off the East Coast of the United States; some blimps saw service in the West Indies, Brazil, and in the Mediterranean. Following the end of World War II, the USN slashed the number of blimps in its inventory.

In the late 1950s, however, USN blimps, of the ZPG class, took on a new role when they became part of the North American Air Defense system's early warning chain. Equipped with airborne early warning radar (AEW), USN blimps patrolled off the U.S. East Coast for up to two weeks at a time, thereby extending the range of land-based radar. The completion of the distant early warning radar chain and the introduction of long-range fixed-wing patrol craft in the 1960s spelled the end of USN blimps. In 1962, the last were withdrawn from service; they were reverted to a commercial role.

Shawn Cafferky

References

Collier, Basil. *The Airship: A History.* New York: G. P. Putnam's Sons, 1974.

Hayward, Keith. *The Military Utility of Airships.* London: Royal United Services Institute for Defence Studies, 1998.

Vaeth, J.G. *Blimps and U-Boats: US Navy Airships in the Battle of the North Atlantic.* Annapolis, MD: U.S. Naval Institute, 1992.

Blitzkrieg

Concentrated application of Luftwaffe close air support and interdiction for rapidly advancing field columns. In World War I, the German army had gained valuable, though limited, expertise with the concept of aerial support of ground forces. The U.S. Marine Corps's post-1918 experiences in Nicaragua and the U.S. Navy's and Royal Air Force's dive-bombing trials also indirectly influenced German aviators' thinking in the 1920s.

Secret facilities at Lipetsk in the Soviet Union further allowed the German army to test aircraft types and operational doctrine banned by the Treaty of Versailles. By the time of the Nazis' rearmament program and the first major statement of German aerial doctrine—*The Conduct of Aerial War* (1935)—the Luftwaffe had as one of its missions the direct support of the army and navy. That particular role influenced the types of aircraft procured.

When war broke out in 1939, the Luftwaffe was primarily tasked to gain battlefield aerial supremacy, act as "flying artillery," deliver airborne forces, and interdict the enemy's movement in the hinterland. For the first mission, the Luftwaffe employed Messerschmitt Bf 109s. The flying artillery was provided principally by the ungainly but justly famous Junkers Ju 87 "Stuka," whose name became a synonym for German dive-bombers. Less famous, but nonetheless valuable, the Henschel Hs 123 biplane served in the ground attack role. Rugged and regarded fondly by its pilots, the Hs 123 would soldier on into 1944.

Paratroops flew in the similarly venerable Junkers Ju 52, affectionately known as "Auntie Ju." For aerial interdiction the Luftwaffe fielded large numbers of twin-engine types. These included the extremely versatile Heinkel He 111 and the Dornier Do 17 "Flying Pencil."

In Poland, Germany deployed some 1,600 aircraft, including nearly all 335 available Ju 87s. Quickly gaining aerial supremacy, the Luftwaffe devastated pockets of Polish resistance, most notably that of the Poznan Army in the Bzura River Cauldron.

Later, in May 1940, the Luftwaffe had more than 4,000 aircraft available for the campaign in the West, among them 380 dive-bombers and 475 troop transports. Again it gave another extraordinary demonstration of airpower in blitzkrieg. On 10 May 1940, German paratroops dropped onto the roof of Eben Emael, a crucial Belgian fortress, to seize it for advancing columns. Several days later, on 13–14 May, scores of Ju 87s blasted French defenders along the Meuse River near Sedan, allowing Panzer grenadiers to effect a major crossing of that strategic obstacle. In addition, German fighters annihilated British bombers sent to attack the bridgehead. At month's end, Luftwaffe level and dive-bombers harassed the Royal Army and Royal Navy unmercifully as they executed their desperate evacuation from Dunkirk. These and other victories established the Luftwaffe's fearsome reputation as the aerial arm of lightning war.

Although defeated in the Battle of Britain, the Luftwaffe went on to enjoy smaller-scale successes in the Balkans in early 1941. Staggering victories over an initially inept Red Air Force followed. Regardless of the defeats to come, the early blitzkrieg triumphs in Poland and France conveyed the sense of overwhelming might.

D. R. Dorondo

See also

Balkans, Air Operations; Britain, Battle of; German Air Force (Luftwaffe); Heinkel Aircraft; Junkers Aircraft; Messerschmitt, Willy

References

Corum, James S., and Richard R. Muller. *The Luftwaffe's Way of War: German Air Force Doctrine, 1911–1945.* Baltimore: Nautical and Aviation, 1998.

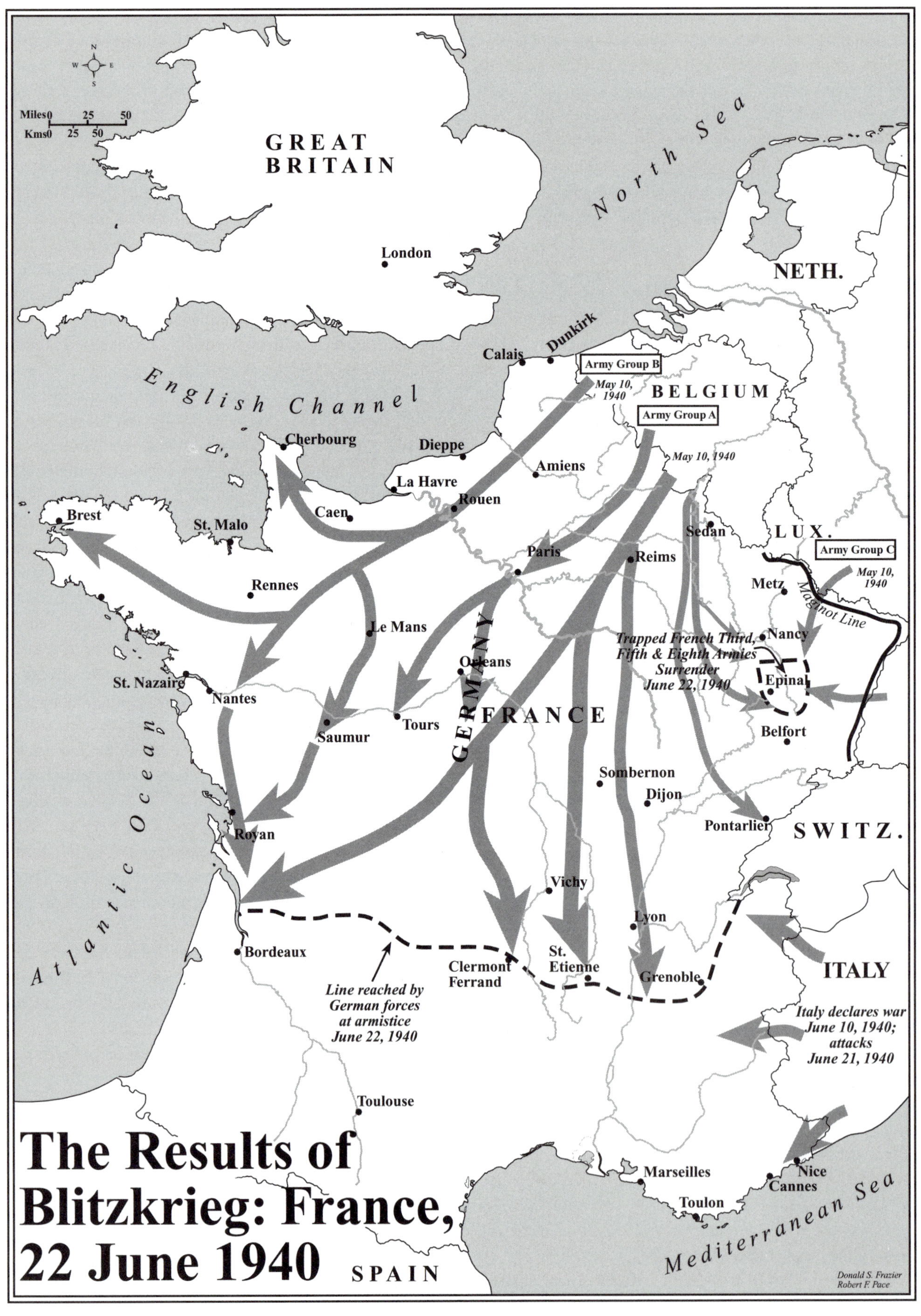

The Results of Blitzkrieg: France, 22 June 1940

Deichmann, Paul. *Spearhead for Blitzkrieg: Luftwaffe Operations in Support of the Army, 1939–1945.* London: Greenhill Books, 1996.
Weal, John. "Junkers Ju 87 Stukageschwader, 1937–1941." In Tony Holmes, ed., *Combat Aircraft.* London: Osprey, 1998.

Blohm and Voss Aircraft

Created in 1933 as a subsidiary of a shipbuilding firm established in 1877. The Hamburger Flugzeugbau GmbH (Hamburg Construction Company) was established to develop and manufacture aircraft. Richard Vogt was lured from Kawasaki to become chief designer.

The first aircraft, a biplane trainer, was rolled out in mid-1934. Manufacture of subassemblies and of other companies' aircraft under license proceeded apace, and a new factory and airfield were opened in September 1935. The Bv 138 three-engine flying boat, often dubbed the "Flying Shoe" for the shape of its fuselage, first flew in 1937 and, with 276 manufactured, was the only company design to achieve mass production. It was widely used for reconnaissance and minesweeping duties during the war. Three Ha 139 four-engine floatplanes followed for Lufthansa Airline transatlantic mail runs and wartime reconnaissance work. Nine Bv 141 asymmetric aircraft were used for observation duties on all fronts.

The first of two huge flying boats initiated by Lufthansa was the Bv 222 Wiking (Viking) with six engines. First flown in 1940, it was the largest operational flying boat of the war when it entered service in 1942. The Bv 222 aircraft were used for troop-carrying and freight and at least one long-distance mission to Japan. The even larger Bv 238 (which first flew in early 1944 with six engines on nearly 200-foot wings) was the heaviest aircraft in the world at the time. Only one model was completed, and it was destroyed in an Allied air attack just days before the war ended; two others were never completed.

Christopher H. Sterling

References

Nowarra, Heinz J. *Blohm and Voss Bv 138.* Atglen, PA: Schiffer, 1997.
______. *Blohm and Voss Bv 222 "Wiking" Bv 238.* Atglen, PA: Schiffer, 1997.

Bock's Car

Bomber that dropped the atomic bomb on Nagasaki. On 9 August 1945, Major Charles Sweeney, pilot of the Boeing B-29 named *Bock's Car,* dropped the second atomic weapon (code-named "Fat Man") on the city of Nagasaki, Japan. The order explicitly stated that while radar could be used as an aid, the "crew was to bring the bomb back to base" if the target could not be dropped visually.

After the first atomic bomb was dropped on Hiroshima on 6 August, U.S. commanders wanted a second bomb dropped as soon as possible to convince the Japanese that the United States had a huge arsenal of such weapons. Kokura was the primary target, but bad weather dictated going to the backup target, Nagasaki. Soon after the detonation of the second weapon, the Japanese government surrendered, eliminating the need for an Allied invasion and saving hundreds of thousands of American and possibly millions of Japanese lives.

Henry M. Holden

References

Rhodes, Richard, *The Making of the Atomic Bomb.* New York: Touchstone Books, 1995.

Boeing (McDonnell Douglas/Hughes) AH-64 Apache

Developed as a replacement for the cancelled AH-56 Cheyenne, the Hughes Model 77 was selected over the competing Bell AH-63. The first prototype made its maiden flight on 30 September 1975, and production deliveries began in January 1984. McDonnell Douglas purchased Hughes Helicopter on 6 January 1984 and subsequently merged with Boeing in 1998. More than 1,000 Apaches have been delivered, and production continues. The Apache is in service with the U.S. Army, Egypt, Greece, Israel, Netherlands, Saudi Arabia, United Arab Emirates, and the United Kingdom.

The AH-64 fleet consists of two models, the AH-64A and the newer AH-64D Longbow Apache. The Longbow fire-control radar provides the ability to detect, classify, and prioritize stationary and moving targets both on the ground and in the air. The AH-64 is powered by two 1,890-shp General Electric T700 gas-turbine engines; it has a top speed of 182 mph and a range of 300 miles.

Dennis R. Jenkins

See also

Bell AH-1 Cobra

References

Allen, Patrick. *The Helicopter: An Illustrated History of Rotary-Winged Aircraft.* Shrewsbury, UK: Airlife, 1996.

Boeing (North American Rockwell) B-1B Lancer

A four-engine long-range multirole heavy bomber capable

The Boeing B-1B had a long period of development but has proved its efficiency in the war on terrorism, where the bomber has become the primary weapon. (U.S. Air Force)

of supersonic flight and capable of carrying nuclear bombs. The B-1B holds 61 world records for speed, payload, and distance. Originally manufactured by North American Rockwell, it holds the world record for the fastest round-the-world flight (36 hours, 13 minutes).

The B-1B is similar in shape to the four B-1A prototypes built in the 1970s. The first operational B-1B was delivered to the U.S. Air Force at Dyess Air Force Base, Texas, in June 1985. The final B-1B was delivered on May 2, 1988. Its armament includes eight AGM-86B cruise missiles mounted internally plus four externally, 24 AGM-69 SRAM internally plus 14 externally, and 24 B61 or B83 special weapons.

B-1B Lancers flew 74 combat missions in Kosovo and dropped more than 5,000 conventional bombs.

Henry M. Holden

References

Goodall, James C. *America's Stealth Fighters and Bombers: B-2, F-117, YF-22, and YF-23.* Osceola, WI: MBI, 1992.

Boeing B-17 Flying Fortress

Legendary U.S. bomber that served in every theater of World War II. In May 1934, the U.S. Army Air Corps announced a competition for a new multiengine bomber. Each entrant was to be funded by the manufacturer and flown to Wright Field near Dayton, Ohio, for evaluation in late 1935. Douglas Aircraft decided to adapt its DC-2 transport into a stubby, deep-fuselage aircraft called the DB-1 (for Douglas Bomber One). Boeing, with the concurrence of the Air Corps, opted for a brand-new four-engined airplane, identified as the Model 299. It was based on the structural design of the Model 247 airliner along with the military features and engine arrangement of the XBLR-1, or future XB-15.

On 26 September 1934, Boeing's board of directors appropriated a sum of $275,000—nearly half the company's cash assets—for the project. The company would expend 153,080 engineering man-hours on the preliminary design of the Model 299. Eventually, the design costs would rise to $660,000. The airplane rolled out of Boeing's Plant 2 factory in Seattle, Washington, on 17 July and made its first flight on 28 July 1935.

During the flyoff the Boeing entry crashed as a result of the elevator control lock not being removed. The Army contract was awarded to Douglas for the production of 75 aircraft designated the B-18 Bolo. The crash of the Model 299 also resulted in the development of the flight-crew checklist—a feature found on almost every subsequent airplane. Continuing Air Corps interest in the Boeing entry led to the production of 12,726 B-17s, most by Boeing but also by Lockheed-Vega and Douglas.

The B-17 was powered by four Wright R-1820 engines. It had an 8,000-pound bombload, a service ceiling of 35,600 feet, and a range of 2,000 miles. Manned by a crew of 10, the aircraft mounted 13 .50-caliber machine guns for defensive armament.

Alwyn T. Lloyd

The demands of air combat caused many modifications to be made to Boeing's B-17, and among the most important of these was defensive firepower. This B-17G packed a powerful forward-firing turret to offset German frontal attacks. (U.S. Air Force)

References

Bowers, Peter M. *Boeing Aircraft Since 1916.* Annapolis, MD: Naval Institute Press, 1989.

Boeing B-29 Superfortress

U.S. strategic bomber during World War II; dropped the first atomic bombs. When Boeing designers began developing the B-29, the basic problem confronting them was how to propel a mass that was twice as heavy as the B-17 twice as fast. To meet this challenge, extremely powerful engines would be required. The B-29s were powered by Wright R-3350 Cyclone engines capable of developing 2,200 horsepower. The R-3350, however, was not fully developed and caused many problems for the B-29.

Boeing worked to reduce airplane drag in 13 critical areas, providing a combination of good landing and flight characteristics. A streamlined fuselage with enclosed defensive armament positions and a high-aspect ratio wing enabled high performance. The B-29 was also the first pressurized bomber.

The aircraft were based in China and later the Mariana Islands, where they brought the war to the Japanese homeland. Two of these aircraft dropped the atomic bombs on Japan, bringing World War II to a close.

Four factories built 3,965 B-29s. They served again during the Korean War and in a variety of post–World War II roles.

Alwyn T. Lloyd

See also

Boeing B-17 Flying Fortress

References

Bowers, Peter M. *Boeing Aircraft Since 1916.* Annapolis, MD: Naval Institute Press, 1989.

Lloyd, Alwyn T. *B-29 Superfortress in Detail and Scale.* Blue Ridge Summit, PA: Tab Books, 1983 (*Part 1 Production Versions*) and 1987 (*Part 2 Derivatives*).

Boeing B-47 Stratojet

Early U.S. jet bomber; predecessor of the B-52. When the U.S. Army Air Forces issued a requirement for a jet bomber in 1944, four manufacturers presented proposals. Boeing's design for the B-47 won for a number of reasons but especially because it was capable of carrying the outsized nuclear weapons of the day. It took five years of intensive testing to get the airplane ready for service. The range of the B-47 was a limiting factor from the outset. To overcome this deficiency, external fuel tanks and an inflight refueling system were added.

The B-47 became the cornerstone of the U.S. nuclear deterrent force until the B-52 came into the inventory. At the peak of its career, 1,365 B-47s were in Strategic Air Command's (SAC) inventory of 1,650 bombers. These aircraft never dropped a bomb in anger.

SAC initially deployed entire B-47 wings around the world to bases that were closer to the Soviet Union. Later, SAC deployed several B-47s from various wings to the forward operating areas in an effort to reduce the strain on the crews and their families.

Some authorities believe the B-47 to be the most important multijet engine aircraft in history because it sired the Boeing line of aircraft that included not only the KC-135 tanker and B-52 bomber but also the 707, 727, 737, 747, 757, 767, and 777 transports.

Alwyn T. Lloyd

References

Bowers, Peter M. *Boeing Aircraft Since 1916.* Annapolis, MD: Naval Institute Press, 1989.

Lloyd, Alwyn T. *B-47 Stratojet in Detail and Scale.* Blue Ridge Summit, PA: Tab Books, 1986.

Boeing B-52 Stratofortress

U.S. strategic bomber in service for a half-century. Boeing won a preliminary design contract over Convair in 1946 to design a new intercontinental strategic bomber. The B-52 first flew on 15 April 1952 and entered an extensive flight-test and service-evaluation program. Although 744 B-52s were built, the maximum number in service was 639 in 1962.

The aircraft served in Strategic Air Command as the mainstay of the nuclear deterrent force for more than 30

This photo, taken from the boom operator's position of a Boeing KC-135, represents a routine event that nonetheless takes tremendous skill: the refueling of a Boeing B-52 bomber. (U.S. Air Force)

The most important multijet aircraft in history, the Boeing B-47 enabled Boeing to become a dominant factor in both military and commercial aircraft production. (Walter J. Boyne)

Refueling a six-jet Boeing B-47 from a six-engine (four-piston, two-jet) Boeing KC-97 was no easy task, for the tanker had to fly at top speed, sometimes in a descent. As you can tell from the nose-up attitude of the B-47, it is flying as slow as it can and still not stalling. (U.S. Air Force)

years and continues to be a major asset in the strategic arena. During more than a decade of war in Vietnam, B-52s traded their nuclear mission for a conventional role. B-52Ds were modified under the Big Belly program and were able to carry up to 108 750-pound bombs. During the Christmas bombings over North Vietnam in 1972, B-52s were credited with finally bringing the enemy to the peace table. Of the 33 B-52s lost in Southeast Asia, 15 went down during Operation LINEBACKER II. B-52s dropped the greatest tonnage of iron bombs during the Gulf War; the war opened with seven B-52Gs flying a 35-hour round-trip mission to launch conventional cruise missiles.

Originally designed as a high-altitude bomber, the B-52 gradually became a low-level penetrator to avoid enemy radar. At first the B-52s flew at 500 feet, then with improved avionics were capable of flying at 400 knots 200 feet above ground level. Given that the airplane had a 185-foot wingspan, such flight was extremely challenging.

The B-52 has the distinction of having served three generations of aircrews. Now down to less than 100 B-52Hs, Air Combat Command expects to operate the aircraft until at least 2020.

Alwyn T. Lloyd

References

Boyne, Walter J. *Boeing B-52: A Documentary History.* Atglen, PA: Schiffer Military/Aviation History, 1994.

Lloyd, Alwyn T. *A Cold War Legacy: A Tribute to Strategic Air Command, 1946–1992.* Missoula, MT: Pictorial Histories, 2000.

Boeing (McDonnell Douglas) C-17 Globemaster III

The Boeing (formerly McDonnell Douglas) C-17 "Globemaster III" is the newest U.S. Air Force cargo airplane. It is 174 feet long and has a 170-foot span. It is a fly-by-wire aircraft that can carry payloads of 172,000 pounds at 41,000 feet and an airspeed of 575 mph. There are three crewmembers: pilot, copilot, and loadmaster. The cost-effective flight crew is made possible through the use of an advanced digital avionics system using four cathode-ray tube displays, two full-capability head-up displays, and advanced cargo systems.

The C-17 can take off and land on runways as short as 3,000 feet (914 meters) and as narrow as 90 feet (27.4 meters). Even on such narrow runways, the C-17 can turn around using a three-point star turn and its backing capability.

During normal testing, C-17s set 22 world records, including payload to altitude time-to-climb, as well as the short takeoff and landing mark in which the C-17 took off in less than 1,400 feet, carried a payload of 44,000 pounds to altitude, and landed in less than 1,400 feet.

In 1998, eight C-17s completed the longest airdrop mission in history, flying more than 8,000 miles from the United States to Central Asia, dropping troops and equipment after more than 19 hours in the air.

Henry M. Holden

References

Veronico, Nicholas A., and Jim Dunn. *Giant Cargo Planes.* Osceola, WI: MBI, 1999.

Boeing Aircraft

Major U.S. aircraft manufacturer founded by two friends: William E. Boeing, a prominent Seattle lumberman, landowner, and yachtsman; and Commander Conrad Westervelt, who headed the U.S. Navy shipyard in Seattle. They formed an informal partnership in 1914, and within two years their idea grew into the Pacific Aero Products Company. They decided to get into the aircraft business and purchased a Martin seaplane. Trials and tribulations with the Martin airplane gave them insight into how to do things better. Westervelt had given Boeing flying lessons. Between them they designed the company's first product—the Boeing and Westervelt seaplane. Boeing embarked on building several other seaplanes and started an air mail service between Vancouver, Washington, and Vancouver, British Columbia.

Boeing received a post–World War I contract to refurbish de Havilland DH-4 biplanes for the U.S. Army. Subsequent government contracts brought a series of pursuit airplanes for both the Navy and the Army. Several Boeing-designed airmail airplanes were also produced. In 1928 came the Model 80, a 12- or 18-place enclosed trimotor biplane that was employed on the Chicago–San Francisco route.

Boeing experimental aircraft led to the Model 247, the first twin-engine all-metal transport. This transport dominated the market until the advent of the Douglas DC-1 and DC-2.

During this period Boeing was part of a business empire known as United Aircraft and Transport Corporation, joining Boeing, the airframe designer/manufacturer; Pratt and Whitney, the engine builder; Hamilton Standard, producer of propellers; and a host of airlines, including Boeing Air Transport and United Airlines. This synergistic organization was disbanded as part of the Air Mail Act of 1934, under which the design and manufacturing operations were separated from the airline operations.

In a company-funded effort, Boeing entered the U.S. Army Air Corps 1934 multiengine bomber competition with

When the Boeing (McDonnell Douglas) F-15 was being developed, the cry was "Not a pound [of weight] for air to ground" but the F-15 E gained a few pounds and became a stellar ground-assault aircraft. (U.S. Air Force)

a four-engine airplane—the Model 299, forerunner of the famous B-17 Flying Fortress. This heavy bomber set the stage for the company's reputation in building sturdy, reliable airplanes with performance to match. Later models included the B-29, B-50, B-47, and B-52 bombers and the KC-135 tanker. In addition, Boeing led the way with jet airliners, beginning with the 707 and continuing until today.

Boeing's prowess in space programs and its program management skills were singularly recognized when the company was placed in charge of the overall technical management of NASA's manned space programs after the fateful oxygen fire aboard one of the Apollo spacecraft in 1967.

In a series of mergers during the mid-1990s, Boeing acquired Rockwell Aviation in 1996 and the McDonnell Douglas Corporation in 1997. Incorporated in the state of Delaware, the company has undergone several name changes: Pacific Aero Products Company, Boeing Airplane Company, Boeing Aircraft Company, Boeing Airplane Company, and now the Boeing Company.

Alwyn T. Lloyd

References

Bowers, Peter M., *Boeing Aircraft Since 1916*, London: Putnam; and Annapolis, MD: Naval Institute Press, 1989.

Boeing (McDonnell Douglas) F-15 Eagle

The F-15 was designed as a no-expenses-spared air-superiority fighter, and the first aircraft made its maiden flight on 27 July 1972. The F-15 quickly demonstrated it was far superior to existing fighters, although that capability was expensive to achieve. Israel ordered F-15A/Bs in addition to receiving some early test models. Slightly improved F-15C/Ds included a small amount of additional fuel and improved electronics. In addition to the United States, Israel and Saudi Arabia ordered the aircraft, and Japan set up its own production line for the substantially similar F-15J/DJ.

The F-15 proved to have a substantial air-to-ground capability, and the U.S. Air Force ordered the two-seat F-15E Strike Eagle into production as a replacement for the General Dynamics F-111 Aardvark. The first production F-15E made its maiden flight on 11 December 1986, and Israel and Saudi Arabia have ordered versions designated F-15I and F-15S.

The F-15 has seen a great deal of combat for a modern fighter, participating in several skirmishes at the hands of the Israeli Air Force and in Operation DESERT STORM with the air forces of the United States and Saudi Arabia. As of early 2000, the F-15 had scored more than 100 air-to-air kills against no air-to-air losses.

Dennis R. Jenkins

References

Jenkins, Dennis R. *McDonnell Douglas F-15 Eagle*. WarbirdTech Series Volume 9. North Branch, MN: Specialty Press, 1997.

_______. *McDonnell Douglas F-15 Eagle: Supreme Heavy-Weight Fighter.* Leicester, UK: Aerofax/Midland Counties, 1998.

There is no more demanding work than naval aviation, where the teamwork of air crew and deck crew is absolutely essential. Here Boeing F/A 18 Hornets prepare for a catapult takeoff. (U.S. Navy)

Boeing (McDonnell Douglas) F/A-18 Hornet

The Hornet is unique in that the basic design began as the U.S. Air Force Northrop YF-17 lightweight fighter prototype. After losing the competition to the General Dynamics F-16 Fighting Falcon, Northrop and teammate McDonnell Douglas won a U.S. Navy contract to develop a multirole fighter to supplement the Grumman F-14 Tomcat. The marriage was not always a happy one, and the teammates at one point sued one another over intellectual property rights concerning the marketing of the new aircraft.

The F/A-18 (the odd designation stands for fighter/attack) is equally adept at air-to-air missions or air-to-ground missions and proved it could perform both roles during the same mission during Operation DESERT STORM when a Navy Hornet shot down an Iraqi MiG while going on a strike mission.

The initial single-seat F/A-18As and two-seat F/A-18Bs were followed by improved F/A-18C/Ds that had greatly improved electronics. Australia, Canada, Finland, Kuwait, Malaysia, Spain, and Switzerland have all ordered versions of the Hornet. A total of 1,480 were manufactured.

In 1992, the U.S. Navy ordered an improved version—the F/A-18E/F. Although superficially similar, this is a much larger aircraft using a completely new airframe and engines. However, at least initially, the avionics are largely carried over from late-model F/A-18C/Ds. The Super Hornet also incorporates stealth technology to reduce its radar cross-section. The F/A-18E/F is expected to remain in production for the foreseeable future and will form the backbone of the U.S. Navy's air arm as the F-14 and earlier versions of the F/A-18 are retired.

Dennis R. Jenkins

The Boeing KC-10 tanker is employed for many specialized refueling jobs, including taking care of the Northrop B-2A. (U.S. Air Force)

See also

DESERT STORM

References

Jenkins, Dennis R. *F/A-18 Hornet: A Navy Success Story.* New York: McGraw-Hill, 2000.

Boeing (McDonnell Douglas) KC-10 Extender

U.S.-manufactured cargo and aerial-refueling aircraft. The KC-10 was the winner of the 1967 Advanced Cargo Tanker Aircraft competition against the McDonnell Douglas DC-10–30CF and the Boeing 747F. A new airplane was needed because the Lockheed C-5 Galaxy and L-1011 TriStar were out of production. On 19 December 1967, the contract was awarded to McDonnell Douglas.

The aircraft incorporated a new air-refueling boom that had a higher offload capability than the KC-135. The boom operator was seated on a bench in the rear of the aircraft. In addition, a hose drum unit can reel out a drogue for probe-and-drogue refueling.

The capacious cabin allows the aircraft to carry up to 27 standard cargo pallets. Several KC-10s are capable of carrying the War Reserve Spares Kits for an entire fighter wing; the KC-10 can then provide air refueling for the initial leg of a fighter-wing deployment. Coupled with KC-135s to provide en-route refueling for the KC-10s, an entire fighter wing can be deployed to anywhere in the world within 24 hours.

A total of 60 KC-10s were delivered to Strategic Air Command between 1981 and 1988.

Alwyn T. Lloyd

References

Lloyd, Alwyn T. *A Cold War Legacy: A Tribute to Strategic Air Command, 1946–1992.* Missoula, MT: Pictorial Histories, 2000.
Swanbrough, Gordon, and Peter M. Bowers. *United States Military Aircraft Since 1909.* Various eds. London: Putnam, 1963, 1981, and 1989.

Boeing KC-135 Stratotanker

U.S.-manufactured aerial-refueling tanker that entered service in the late 1950s. In conjunction with the U.S. Air

The most unsung and yet the most indispensable aircraft in the U.S. Air Force is the Boeing KC-135. This is an R model, with uprated engines. (U.S. Air Force)

Force, Boeing began the air-refueling business in earnest with the hose system, installing Air Refuelling Limited's equipment on B-29s. The system was retrofitted into 92 Superfortresses that were redesignated KB-29Ms; another 74 of the bombers were converted to be receivers and redesignated KB-29MRs. Marginal operational success was achieved.

Next, 116 Superfortresses were retrofitted with a Boeing-designed boom system and redesignated KB-29Ps, affording greater success. Strategic Air Command eagerly supported the boom-type refueling system because it allowed greater offload capability. The next-generation Boeing tanker was the Boeing KC-97 Stratofreighter, utilizing an improved flying boom. Of the 888 C-97s produced, 811 were delivered as KC-97E/F/G tankers. The larger aircraft carried an even greater fuel load than the KB-29s.

A direct outgrowth of the Model 367 Stratofreighter was the Model 367–80 prototype, which became the KC-135 Stratotanker. The Boeing identification for this next series of airplanes was Model 717, which was shorter and had a smaller fuselage diameter that the commercial 707 (the KC-135 flew a year earlier than the 707). The KC-135 incorporated further improvements to the boom. Of the 820 C/KC-135s produced by Boeing, 732 were tankers. Boeing build seven series of 135s, but subsequent modifications to the versatile airframe resulted in more than 40 series that can be identified by prefix and suffix.

Originally intended as a means to extend the range of bombers, the KC-135 became equally important to fighters and transports over the years. Beginning with the Vietnam War, no major USAF operation was possible without the extensive use of tankers. Like the B-52, the long-lived KC-135 will be in service for many years to come.

Alwyn T. Lloyd

See also
Boeing B-29 Superfortress

References

Hopkins, Robert S. III. *Boeing KC-135 Stratotanker—More Than Just a Tanker:* Leicester, UK: Aerofax/Midland Counties, 1997.

Boeing-Vertol CH-47 Chinook

U.S. transport helicopter. Development of the CH-47 (Boeing Model 114/414) began in 1956 to meet a U.S. Army requirement for an all-weather medium transport helicopter. The first of five YCH-47As made its initial hovering flight on 21 September 1961, and more than 1,100 Chinooks have been manufactured in the United States, Japan, and Italy. They serve in the U.S. Army, as well as the armed forces of Argentina, Australia, Canada, Egypt, Greece, Iran, Italy, Japan, Libya, Morocco, Netherlands, Singapore, South Korea, Spain, Thailand, and the United Kingdom.

The Chinook can be configured to carry up to 33 combat troops or, alternately, for medical evacuation, 24 litters. In 1982, the original CH-47A, B, and C model Chinooks reached their 20-year service life and were remanufactured into CH-47D models. Now, as the D model approaches its 20-year service-life limit, plans are under way to again remanufacture the aircraft and insert a variety of new technology sensors and avionics.

Like most all Boeing-Vertol designs, the Chinook uses two counterrotating main rotors instead of the more conventional single main rotor and antitorque tailrotor. Power comes from two 3,750-shp Allied Signal T55-L-712s located above the aft fuselage on each side of the aft pylon. The CH-47D can fly at airspeeds up to 170 knots at a gross weight up to 50,000 pounds, including payloads of up to 26,000 pounds.

Dennis R. Jenkins

References

Allen, Patrick. *The Helicopter: An Illustrated History of Rotary-Winged Aircraft.* Shrewsbury, UK: Airlife, 1996.

Bolling Mission

Shortly after the U.S. declaration of war in World War I, in April 1917, a group under Major Raynal Bolling was dispatched to Europe to study and recommend what types of aircraft should be manufactured in the United States. Bolling was selected to head the mission due to his negotiating skills as a lawyer and his interest in aviation.

Visiting Britain, France, and Italy, the group recommended several types for production, but rapid technological advances in Europe and production delays in the United States combined to ensure that most aircraft used by the United States during the war would be purchased abroad. The major exception was the British de Havilland D.H.4, which was manufactured in the United States as the de Havilland DH-4 and which reached the front in August 1918 in time for combat.

James Streckfuss

References

Gorrell, Edgar S. "What—No Airplanes?" *Journal of Air Law and Commerce* 12 (January 1941).

Streckfuss, James. "Bolling Mission." In Anne Cipriano Venzon, ed., *The United States in World War I: An Encyclopedia.* New York: Garland, 1995.

Boelcke, Oswald (1891–1916)

The father of fighter aviation, Oswald Boelcke started as regular army. Already a pilot when World War I began, Boelcke flew two-seaters until 1915, when he received one of the first Fokker "Eindeckers." Scoring early, he regularly competed for the leading spot with colleague Max Immelmann. Together they became the first airmen to win the Blue Max, but Immelmann's death in June 1916 prompted Boelcke's grounding. He returned to the front later that summer to mentor the pilots of Jasta 2. Running his score to 40, the first pilot to reach that number, Boelcke was killed on 28 October in a collision with one of his pupils, Erwin Boehme, when both swerved to avoid hitting Manfred von Richthofen. Boelcke is remembered as an outstanding teacher and considered by many to be the greatest fighter pilot of all time. His unit was renamed in his honor.

James Streckfuss

References

Boelcke, Oswald. *An Aviator's Field Book.* New York: National Military, 1917.

Franks, Norman L.R., Frank W. Bailey, and Russell Guest. *Above the Lines: The Aces and Fighter Units of the German Air Service, Naval Air Service, and Flanders Marine Corps, 1914–1918.* London: Grub Street, 1993.

BOLO (1967)

USAF code name for operation to lure North Vietnamese MiG fighters into combat. By December 1966, with Operation ROLLING THUNDER in full swing, Democratic Republic of Vietnam (DRV, i.e., North Vietnam) fighter-interceptors were becoming a major threat. Their tactics had become more aggressive and better coordinated with the introduction of a new ground-controlled interceptor (GCI) system and newer-model MiG-21s armed with Atoll infrared missiles.

Even so, President Lyndon B. Johnson would not allow (until April 1967) U.S. aircraft to attack enemy airfields near the Chinese border or in the suburbs of Hanoi for fear of killing civilians or Chinese advisers. The MiGs attacked in a fashion that forced U.S. aircraft to jettison their ordnance to meet the MiGs before reaching their targets. When U.S. planes attempted to engage the enemy, the DRV MiGs would retreat to their airfield sanctuaries.

To deal with this situation, Seventh Air Force officials devised a deceptive fighter sweep designated Operation BOLO. Designed to lure the MiGs into combat, the plan focused on the GCI's inherent inability to fully distinguish which aircraft the U.S. was deploying. The standard Air Force strike package included low-altitude Republic F-105 Thunderchiefs carrying bombs protected by high-altitude McDonnell F-4 Phantoms. In BOLO, F-4s assumed the identity of F-105s, including their electronic countermeasure emissions, attack patterns, and communications patterns. Republic F-105 Wild Weasels also provided suppression of enemy air defense as part of the operation.

The 2 January 1967 mission was led by Colonel Robin Olds of the 8th Tactical Fighter Wing (8th TFW). Plans called for simultaneous sweeps to enter the Hanoi target area from the east and west. The 8th TFW, based at Udon Air Base, Thailand, was to come in from Laos, while the 366th TFW, based at Da Nang, would attack from the Gulf of Tonkin.

Marginal morning weather delayed the operation until the afternoon, when three flights of F-4s from the 8th TFW reached the target. The first was led by Olds, the second by Lieutenant Colonel Daniel "Chappie" James, and the third by Captain John Stone.

After two passes over the Phuc Yen airfield, the MiG-21s attacked, expecting slow F-105s. An intense air battle lasted for 15 minutes, the largest aerial dogfight of the Vietnam War. The 12 F-4s shot down seven MiGs and had two probables. Olds was credited with two kills. The Americans suffered no losses.

Although limited in scope by the bad weather, BOLO was the greatest Allied aerial victory of the war. It destroyed nearly half of all the MiG-21s then in the DRV inventory, forcing their leaders to halt MiG operations just as the Americans had hoped. BOLO is generally acknowledged as one of the Air Force's greatest successes in Vietnam.

William Head

References

Bell, Kenneth. *100 Missions North.* Washington, DC: Brassey's, 1993.

Berger, Carl, ed. *The United States Air Force in Southeast Asia, 1961–1973: An Illustrated Account.* Washington, DC: Office of Air Force History, 1984.

Boyne, Walter J. "MiG Sweep." *Air Force Magazine* 81, 11 (November 1998).

Bong, Richard I. (1920–1945)

America's all-time leading fighter ace with 40 aerial victories over the Southwest Pacific during World War II; achieved the rank of major. A Poplar, Wisconsin, native born in 1920, Bong proved an unlikely hero. Once described as a "baby-faced cherub," he enlisted as an aviation cadet in 1941 and graduated in January 1942. After assignments as an instructor pilot at Luke Field, Arizona, and Hamilton Field, California, where Bong faced court-martial for "looping the loop" around the center span of San Francisco's Golden Gate Bridge, General George C. Kenney selected him as one of the first Lockheed P-38 pilots in the Fifth Air Force. On 27 December 1942, Bong scored his first two kills. By 8 January 1943, he was an ace.

After Bong topped Eddie Rickenbacker's legendary total of 26 victories, Kenney pulled the "innocent Norwegian boy" from combat and sent him to gunnery school. In October 1944, Bong resumed Fifth Air Force duty as a noncombatant gunnery instructor. Despite Kenney's mock orders to fire only in self-defense, Bong downed 12 more Japanese aircraft. Kenney recommended his favorite pilot for the Congressional Medal of Honor in December 1944. Worried about combat fatigue, Kenney ordered Bong back to the United States for a hero's welcome. Upon his return, Bong served as a test pilot for Lockheed's new P-80 jet aircraft. In this capacity, Bong died on 6 August 1945 in a crash, just hours after the dropping of the first atomic bomb. General Kenney's appreciation for Bong's skill, tenacity, and public relations value was shown by the Fifth Air Force commander's memoirs, *General Kenney Reports,* and Kenney's book *Dick Bong: Ace of Aces.* Many regarded Dick Bong as a link to the famed fighter aces of World War I, restoring a heroic human dimension to increasingly industrialized mass war.

John Farquahar

References

DuPre, Flint O. *U.S. Air Force Biographical Dictionary.* New York: Franklin Watts, 1965.

Gurney, Gene, and Mark P. Friedlander Jr., eds. *Five Down and Glory: A History of the American Air Ace.* New York: Arno Press, 1972.

Kenney, George C. *General Kenney Reports: A Personal History of the Pacific War.* Reprint. Washington, DC: Office of Air Force History, 1987.

Boulton Paul Aircraft

British aircraft manufacturer. Originally Boulton *and* Paul, the Norwich, England–based company had long specialized in structural engineering in both wood and steel, getting into aviation as a subcontractor during World War I.

Reorganized in 1934, the company moved to Wolverhampton to build the P.82 Defiant turret-equipped fighter that first flew in 1937. A low-wing, all-metal aircraft, its performance was severely limited by the size and weight of the power-turret machine gun installation. Still, more than 1,000 were built, with deliveries to active squadrons beginning in late 1939. Initially successful against Luftwaffe fighters, the plane soon lost its value when attacked from the front or beneath, where it was largely defenseless. The Defiant turned to the night-fighter role with some success, then finally to the air-sea rescue and target tug roles.

The P.108 Balliol advanced trainer flew in 1947 as the world's first single-engine turboprop aircraft. Subsequent models were equipped with Merlin piston engines; about 160 were built. The P.111 (1950) and P.120 (1952) were both delta-wing experimental jets. The company later specialized in powered flight controls for large military and civil aircraft, including fly-by-wire systems. Boulton Paul was acquired by Dowty in 1969.

Christopher H. Sterling

References

Boulton Paul Aircraft. Charleston, SC: Arcadia, 1999.

Swanborough, F. G. "Forty Years of Boulton Paul." *The Aeroplane* (8 July 1955): 54–62.

Boyd, Albert (1906–1976)

As USAF major general, considered the father of modern USAF flight-testing; dramatically expanded the role of USAF test pilots.

Albert Boyd was born in Rankin, Tennessee, in 1906. For six years beginning in 1929, he was an Army flight instructor. Schooling in aircraft maintenance and engineering prompted assignments at Chanute Field, Illinois, in 1935 and the Hawaii Air Depot during World War II until his promotion to full colonel, and reassignment to Patterson Field, Ohio, in February 1943.

Boyd became deputy commander for the Eighth Air Force Service Command in Europe in July 1944. With Allied victory, he became chief of the Army Air Forces Flight Test Division at Wright Field, Ohio, in October 1945. Boyd understood that postwar flight-testing must exploit enhanced equipment and top-notch pilots to properly evaluate new aircraft that pushed aeronautical frontiers at an increasing tempo.

He interjected Air Force test pilots more squarely into the flight-test process than they previously had been. Up to that time, Air Force pilots were used to validate the findings of company test pilots and the research pilots of the National Advisory Committee for Aeronautics. In the postwar 1940s, Colonel Boyd placed handpicked Air Force test pilots in the cockpits of major projects, including the supersonic Bell X-1.

On 19 June 1947, Boyd set an absolute speed record of 623.608 mph in a modified Lockheed P-80R jet over Muroc (later Edwards) Air Force Base. By February 1952, after commanding Edwards, Boyd was appointed vice commander, and later commander, of the Wright Aeronautical Development Center. In July 1955, Boyd's final Air Force assignment was deputy commander for weapons systems at Headquarters, Air Research and Development Command. When he retired in 1957, General Boyd had logged more than 23,000 hours in 723 aircraft variants. He died in St. Augustine, Florida, in 1976.

Frederick A. Johnsen

Boyington, Gregory "Pappy" (1912–1988)

U.S. Marine Corps colonel; World War II fighter ace. Born in Coeur d'Alene, Idaho, on 4 December 1912, Gregory "Pappy" Boyington is perhaps the most famous U.S. aviator of World War II. In 1930, Boyington entered the University of Washington, where he earned a degree in aeronautical engineering. After a brief stint as a draftsman at Boeing in 1935, he joined the Marine Corps to fly military aircraft. By 1941, he had built a reputation as a highly skilled, if somewhat undisciplined, fighter pilot and was serving as a Marine flight instructor in Florida.

Only months before the Japanese raid on Pearl Harbor, Boyington resigned his commission to join the newly formed American Volunteer Group (the Flying Tigers), a small provisional air force organized to defend China from Japan. Boyington shot down several Japanese aircraft before quitting the group in 1942. Soon after, he rejoined the Marine Corps but did not see combat until later in 1943 when he assembled the makeshift Fighter Squadron 214. Known to history as the Black Sheep Squadron, it proved to be one of the most effective air combat units in the South Pacific, with Boyington alone destroying 22 Japanese planes. However, in January 1944 he was himself shot down and forced to endure 20 harrowing months in Japanese prison camps. Upon his release, he received the Medal of Honor and the Navy Cross; he retired from active duty in 1947 with the rank of colonel.

"Turbulent" is the word that best describes Boyington's life after his military service. He married and divorced twice, moved from job to job, and battled debt and alcohol problems. A significant high point arrived in 1958 when he published his memoir, *Baa Baa Black Sheep.* An instant bestseller, the autobiography is still in print after more than four decades. Moreover, in the 1970s Boyington sold the book's movie rights and became a technical adviser to the short-lived, and much embellished, television series about his experience with the Black Sheep Squadron. Boyington died in California on 11 January 1988 and was buried in Arlington National Cemetery.

Jeffrey J. Matthews

See also

American Volunteer Group; Chennault, Claire L.; U.S. Marine Corps Aviation

References

Boyington, Gregory. *Baa Baa Black Sheep.* New York: Bantam Books, 1990 [1958].

Ford, Daniel. *Flying Tigers: Claire Chennault and the American Volunteer Group.* Washington, DC: Smithsonian Institution Press, 1991.

Braun, Wernher von (1912–1977)

A powerful influence on the fledgling U.S. space program. Wernher von Braun was inspired by Hermann Oberth's writings, which attracted him to one of Germany's many amateur rocket clubs. Impressed by von Braun's enthusiastic knowledge, Walter Dornberger, an artillery officer, asked the young engineer to help establish a national rocket program.

In 1937, von Braun's team moved to Peenemünde on the Baltic Sea, where it created the first modern rocket, the A-4 (V-2). Two years after its first launch on 3 October 1942, the V-2 began attacks on Europe. In 1945, the Gestapo arrested von Braun for talking about future spacecraft but released him. Following his release and realizing that the war was lost, von Braun gathered 127 scientists and departed Peenemünde to search for the U.S. Army.

The Americans captured von Braun and sent him and his team under Operation PAPERCLIP to launch captured V-2s for the new U.S. rocket program in White Sands, New Mexico. In 1950, von Braun's group moved to Huntsville, Alabama, to work in the U.S. Army's Redstone missile plant and designed the medium-range missiles Redstone, Jupiter, and Jupiter-C. After a U.S. satellite launch attempt failed, von Braun's team used a Jupiter-C to launch America's first satellite, *Explorer 1,* on 31 January 1958.

In 1960, the National Aeronautics and Space Administration (NASA) took over the Redstone plant and von Braun's group that subsequently led the Apollo program. To support Apollo the von Braun team designed, tested, and flew the Saturn I, Saturn I-B, and the largest spacecraft ever built, the 364-foot Saturn V. The Saturn V launched 27 men to the moon and allowed 12 Americans to walk on its surface. After Apollo, von Braun worked for NASA HQ and then transferred to Fairchild Industries until his untimely death from cancer in 1977.

John F. Graham

References

Ordway, Frederick I. III, and Ernst Stuhlinger. *Wernher von Braun—Crusader for Space: A Biographical Memoirs.* Malabar, FL: Krieger, 1994.

Brazil, Air Operations in World War II

In 1941, as airpower's importance was displayed in the European war, Brazil's army and navy air units were combined into the Brazilian Air Force. Meanwhile, the government steadily aligned itself with the Allies, despite large German, Italian, and Japanese immigrant populations. This led to hundreds of aircraft being provided by the United States via Lend-Lease. Initially, Fairchild PT-19 and Vultee BT-15 trainers were of the most importance. But later, fighters and other combat aircraft were provided.

Brazil's geographical position gave it a special importance. The so-called Brazilian Bulge—the northeast region of the country—faced West Africa across the South Atlantic. This was a crucial supply route to the Middle East and the Soviet Union. Money from Washington constructed land bases in northern Brazil, where mostly seaplanes had flown previously.

Submarine warfare became intense in 1942. Torpedoed ships pushed Brazil to declare war on Germany and Italy in August, after months of increasing conflict. U.S. antisubmarine patrols from Brazil were increasingly supplemented and finally replaced by the Brazilian Air Force. U-199 was sunk by a Brazilian Consolidated PBY flying boat in July 1943, after initial damage by a U.S. Martin PBM Mariner. Brazilian Lockheed Venturas patrolled by mid-1944.

Meanwhile, the Brazilian Air Force was training in the United States on Curtiss P-40s before switching to Republic P-47 Thunderbolts. The 1st Fighter Unit was trained in bomber escort, but duties in Italy from 31 October 1944 focused on attacking ground targets with 500-pound bombs. On 22 April 1945, the peak day, it flew 11 missions involving 44 flights (with 22 pilots). The unit destroyed 97 motorized and 35 animal-drawn vehicles, 14 buildings, several bridges, three artillery positions, and more. Brazil participated in World War II more than any other Latin American nation. Its strategic location produced early involvement. Ultimately, the Brazilian Expeditionary Force provided ground troops in Italy (1944–1945), supported by Brazilian Piper Cub L-4 spotter aircraft. The Brazilian Air Force achieved impressive statistics in destroying German army targets.

Brazilian airpower developed greatly during the war years. Five pilots were killed by antiaircraft fire and three more in accidents during just over six months of operations. Despite the losses, Brazilian airpower was much enhanced by the war-time experience. Even though governments after 1945 were less focused on aviation than was President Getulio Vargas (in power from 1930 to 1945), Brazil had an improved infrastructure and an experienced group of airmen. This experience paved the way for the growth of aviation in Brazil, which today has a thriving indigenous aircraft industry.

Gary Kuhn

Brazilian Aircraft Industry

The Brazilian firm Embraer (Empresa Brasileira de Aeronautica) has become a significant aircraft manufacturer internationally. It is a leading exporter of regional jetliners (earlier turboprop), and its rivalry with Canada's Bombardier firm parallels the Airbus-versus-Boeing struggle to sell larger airliners. Meanwhile, Embraer continues to produce military aircraft suited to national needs, also with some export success. It is a successful culmination of efforts by Brazilian governments to establish an indigenous aviation industry.

In the 1920s, Rio de Janeiro shipbuilder Henrique Lage and army officer A. G. Muniz began efforts to design and build aircraft. Subsequently, a few HL and Muniz light aircraft were produced. After 1930, the government of President Getulio Vargas was particularly interested in aviation, given Brazil's size, limited infrastructure, and need for development. The naval factory at Galeao, in Rio de Janeiro, became the government's factory.

Airpower came into sharper focus as World War II approached. Galeao constructed 40 Focke-Wulf Fw 44 trainers, 26 twin-engine Focke-Wulf Fw 58s, and 220 Fairchild PT-19 trainers.

As foreign sources of aircraft shifted to war production, Brazilian factories tried to fill the void. A plan to produce the North American T-6 Texan, the most complex aircraft yet attempted, suffered many delays, although 81 were ultimately built locally.

The industrial state of São Paulo began to eclipse Rio as the government launched the National Campaign of Aviation, which would provide planes to aero clubs. The great success of the 1940s was the CAP-4 Paulistinha (the name indicating its São Paulo origin). This Piper Cub look-alike reached one-a-day production by 1943, with nearly 800 built during the decade. A few years later, another 300 updated Neiva P.56 Paulistinhas would be constructed. These aircraft flew for many years in Brazil.

São Jose dos Campos, in São Paulo state, emerged in the 1960s as Brazil's center for airpower. The air force–funded Centro Tecnico Aerospacial (CTA) conducted research. Two factories constructed all-metal military trainers.

These plants would become Embraer and its Neiva subsidiary (for light civil aircraft production). The breakthrough airplane, begun at CTA and built at Embraer, was the EMB-110 Bandeirante, a twin-engine turboprop airliner for regional airline use. Meanwhile, the celebrated Ozires Silva began his managerial career as the company began to expand.

In addition to many air force and national feeder-liner Bandeirantes, export sales were good. Also in the small airliner niche was the subsequent EMB-120 Brasilia. Eventually, the regional jets EMB-145 and EMB-135 would be developed. Military types of moderate sophistication also succeeded. The Tucano turboprop trainer/light attack creation of the 1980s was adopted locally and abroad. Collaboration with Aermacchi led to the MB-326 (AT-26 in Brazil) fighter-bomber in the 1970s. The AMX's further development in the 1990s saw Italian versions employed with success in the Balkans.

Brazil's aircraft industry was shaped by the government to focus on national needs. A variety of touring and agricultural aircraft is produced for the domestic market; airliner exports improve the trade balance; and the majority of military aircraft are nationally produced. The latest projection of Brazilian airpower is Embraer's manufacture of airplanes dedicated to electronic detection and combat patrol of the vast Amazon region.

Gary Kuhn

Breda Aircraft

Founded in 1886 in Italy by Ernesto Breda (1852–1918) as a locomotive factory. The firm formed a dedicated aircraft unit (Section 5) in 1917 upon receiving an order for 600 Caproni Ca.5 bombers. Breda completed only two aircraft before the Armistice but thereafter remained involved in aviation, starting a flying school on the airfield adjacent to its Sesto San Giovanni works. For the next 15 years, Breda concentrated on touring monoplanes and biplane trainers (including the Ba.19 used by the first Italian acrobatic teams and the Ba.25 standard trainer), occasionally experimenting with multiengine bombers like the CC.20 and Ba.32.

In 1935, Breda acquired Officine Ferroviarie Meridionali and Industrie Aeronautiche Romeo, both located in Naples, and merged them into Industrie Meccaniche e Aeronautiche Meridionali (IMAM, later IMM). Its main products were the Ro.37 army cooperation two-seater (1934), Ro.43 observation floatplane (1936), and Ro.41 advanced trainer (1934).

Turning to all-metal technology, Breda introduced the Ba.64 and Ba.65 attack monoplanes (1935) and the Ba.88 twin-engine heavy fighter (1936). None met expectations, forcing Breda to build Macchi C.200 and C.202 fighters under license. To overcome this crisis, in 1942 Breda engaged

Filippo Zappata (1894–1994) and prepared to produce the Cant Z.1018 twin-engine bomber and its BZ.301–304 derivatives, but on 30 April 1944 the factory was virtually wiped out by U.S. bombers.

The postwar BZ.308 four-engine airliner (1948) and the BP.471 general-purpose twin (1950) were technically successful, but the lack of orders forced Breda to close Section 5. Already in a deep financial crisis, in 1952 Breda sold IMM to the state (it became known as Aerfer and would eventually merge into Aeritalia) but was itself taken over by the state conglomerate EFIM in 1962. It briefly returned to aviation in 1971, producing Hughes Model 500 helicopters through the BredaNardi joint venture, soon absorbed by Agusta.

Gregory Alegi

See also

Aermacchi; Cant Aircraft; Italian Aircraft Development

References

Castronovo, Valerio, ed. *La Breda 1886–1986: dalla Società Italiana Ernesto Breda alla Finanziaria Ernesto Breda.* Milan, Italy: Pizzi, 1986.

Garello, Giancarlo. *Breda Ba. 65.* Turin, Italy: La Bancarella Aeronautica, 1999.

Breguet Aircraft

Louis and Jacques Breguet, scions of the famous clock- and watch-making family, were interested in aviation at an early age. On 19 September 1907, they, in cooperation with Professor Charles Richet, created the first helicopter capable of lifting a man. A second model, the Breguet-Richet II, followed, but stability problems proved to be intractable and further development was abandoned.

Always innovative, the first Breguet aircraft flew in 1909 and featured the use of structural steel tubing. The Société des Avions Louis Breguet was formed in 1911 and continued to operate until 1971.

The Breguet 14 was one of the most successful aircraft of World War I and became the foundation for many later Breguet aircraft. The Breguet 14 was operated as both reconnaissance plane and bomber, and some 5,300 were built during the war. They were used in several theaters and, after the conflict, were widely exported to a dozen air forces around the world. Powered by a 300-hp Renault engine, the Model 14 had a top speed of 114 mph and could carry 88 pounds of bombs.

The next great Breguet success was the Model 19, which was also extensively exported and became engaged in many minor conflicts around the globe, with 3,280 being built. Specially modified versions were used to set many long-distance records.

Between the two world wars Breguet blossomed, building airliners, bombers, and flying boats, most of which were strikingly unattractive aesthetically. Breguet adopted a more modern, streamlined formula in its most successful series of aircraft, which began with the Bre.690 and entered production as the Bre.693. The Bre.693 served France during the German invasion in May and June 1940, suffering heavy losses.

Breguet was impressed by the Germans to build aircraft for the Luftwaffe during the occupation of France. After the war it built the large and rather rotund Breguet 761 in small numbers. Its principal postwar success came with the Breguet 1050 "Alize," a turboprop attack plane that served with the French navy for many years, and the Atlantic patrol aircraft.

The French government passed control of the company to Dassault in 1971, forming Avions Marcel Dassault/Breguet Aviation. Corporate identity was finally lost in 1990, when the name was changed to Dassault Aviation.

Walter J. Boyne

See also

Dassault, Marcel

References

Donald, David, gen. ed. *The Complete Encyclopedia of World Aircraft.* New York: Barnes and Noble, 1997.

Gunston, Bill. *World Encyclopedia of Aircraft Manufacturers.* Sparkford, UK: Patrick Stephens, 1993.

Bristol Aircraft (Early Years, World War I)

British and Colonial Aircraft Company Ltd. was well established prior to World War I, having produced a series of monoplanes and biplanes for sporting purposes. The most notable was the Boxkite and a sleek little biplane just appearing on the scene in the summer of 1914, the Scout.

In the next year, the Bristol Scout became one of the aircraft that had to deal with the Fokker monoplane. The problem was how to mount a machine gun given the lack of a British interrupter gear, which permitted firing through the propeller arc. One innovative solution mounted a Lewis gun at a 45-degree angle, the butt end being at the cockpit so the ammunition drum could be changed, the muzzle just clearing the spinning propeller. Effective use of a gun affixed in this manner required the greatest skill. One such gifted pilot was Captain Lanoe George Hawker, the first British ace of the war. In the course of a single patrol in a Bristol Scout with an oblique-mounted Lewis, Hawker brought down three German aircraft, the first triple victory of the war. For this singular feat he received the highest British decoration, the Victoria Cross.

Bristol also produced an outstanding monoplane fighter, the M.1, which fell victim to a ban on monoplanes imposed following a few structural failures prior to the war.

But it was the F.2, the famous Bristol Fighter, that etched the name of the company in historical stone. The Bristol Fighter ("Biff" or "Brisfit") was originally conceived as a two-seat general reconnaissance aircraft intended to replace the aging Royal Aircraft Factory BE.2 observer. By the time it appeared, however, it was realized that its compact size (from a distance it had the appearance of a large single-seater), good turn of speed and handling characteristics, and respectable firepower would be better utilized in fighter duties. Crews had some initial difficulties adjusting their thinking to this changed role and continued, for a time, to fly the Bristol as a conventional two-seater.

Appearing at the front in April 1917 in No. 48 Squadron, the Bristol initially garnered unfavorable reviews. This stemmed from a disastrous encounter between No. 48 Squadron and Jasta 11. The inexperienced British crew, led by William Leefe Robinson, who had received the Victoria Cross for shooting down the airship SL11 the previous year, did not appreciate the Bristol's ability as a fighter. Instead of attacking with the front gun, they adopted the traditional tactic of trying to position the rear gunner for a shot. The crack pilots of Jasta 11, led by Manfred von Richthofen, punished them, bringing down four of the six.

Despite this failure, the Bristol went on to great success, developing a reputation as the best British two-seater of the war. It continued in RAF service, though in sometimes highly altered form, well into the 1930s.

James Streckfuss

References

Bruce, J. M. *British Aeroplanes, 1914–1918.* London: Putnam, 1957.

Bristol Aircraft (Post–World War I)

The British firm Bristol developed a strong line of aircraft engines after World War I that were used as the preferred type in its aircraft designs. Blessed by good management and such excellent leaders as Roy Fedden, Frank Barnwell, and Stanley Uwins, Bristol built a series of aircraft during the interwar years, the most important of which were the Bulldog fighter and the Blenheim bomber. The Bulldog was a fixed-gear, open-cockpit biplane typical of the period, and the Blenheim was a modern twin-engine aircraft with retractable landing gear and enclosed cockpit. Although not terribly successful as a bomber, the Blenheim served ably as a night-fighter and antisubmarine warfare (ASW) aircraft.

Two developments of the Blenheim line, the Beaufort and the Beaufighter, were far more successful. The Beaufighter was adapted to many roles, including close air support, night-fighting, and antishipping strikes.

After World War II, Bristol built the huge Brabazon, a 230-foot-wingspan giant that was perhaps ahead of its time; only two were built. This was followed by the prosaic Freighter, a twin-engine, fixed-gear passenger/cargo plane. About 214 were built, and they served ably around the world for many years.

Bristol's final success was the beautiful four-engine Britannia, which served well as an airliner in several countries. Modified, it was successful both as a swing-tail freighter and as an ASW aircraft.

Bristol also developed a helicopter business, using Raoul Hafner's designs initially, but these were built in relatively small numbers. Bristol was absorbed into the British Aircraft Corporation in February 1960; Bristol Aero-Engines became first part of Bristol-Siddeley Engines and then was absorbed by Rolls-Royce.

Walter J. Boyne

References

Barnes, C. H. *Bristol Aircraft Since 1910.* London: Putnam, 1964.

Bristol Beaufighter

Because of a lack of night-fighting capability of the British Royal Air Force in 1938, a private venture of the Bristol Aeroplane Company developed and delivered the world's first true night-fighter to combine all the equipment necessary—radio, radar, armament, and performance—in only eight months, the Beaufighter.

The "Beau" was developed from the Beaufort general reconnaissance and torpedo-bomber, using its major components, including wings, tail assembly, and undercarriage. Only the main fuselage and the engine mountings were entirely new components. The first prototype with the normal crew size of two, a pilot and gunner, flew on 17 July 1939. A pair of Hercules 1,500-hp radial engines powered the aircraft, which was armed with a battery of four 20mm Hispano cannons in the fuselage nose, six 0.303-inch machine guns in the wings, and one 0.303-inch Vickers K or Browning gun in the dorsal position. In later versions, one 18-inch torpedo, mounted externally under the fuselage, or eight rocket projectiles could be carried as alternative to wing guns. By 21 September 1945, a total of 5,562 aircraft had been produced in the United Kingdom, having been flown by the air forces of Great Britain, Australia, New Zealand, and the United States.

From Europe to the Middle East and the Far East, all Beaufighters served with distinction, earning the title

"Whispering Death" from Japanese pilots, a remark referring to the speed at which one could suddenly appear with little or no warning.

Guy T. Noffsinger Jr.

References

Bingham, Victor. *Bristol Beaufighter.* Shrewsbury, UK: Airlife, 1995.

References

Bergerson, Frederic A. *The Army Gets an Air Force: Tactics of Insurgent Bureaucratic Politics.* Baltimore: Johns Hopkins University Press, 1980.

Raines, Edgar F. Jr. *Eyes of Artillery: The Origins of Modern U.S. Army Aviation in World War II.* Army Historical Series. Washington, DC: Center of Military History, Department of the Army, 2000.

Bristol, Delbert L. (1918–1980)

Colonel in the U.S. service. Born in Kansas City, Missouri, Bristol enlisted as a private in the Missouri National Guard in 1936. In 1939, he received a direct commission as a second lieutenant in the Field Artillery Reserve. Called to active duty early in 1941, he served at Fort Sill, Oklahoma, where 1st Lieutenant Robert R. Williams convinced him to obtain his civilian pilot's license. When Lieutenant Colonel William W. Ford organized a detachment to test the concept of organic air in the Field Artillery, he chose Bristol to be his adjutant.

Following the creation of the Field Artillery aviation program, Bristol accompanied the first serial of pilots and mechanics dispatched to the United Kingdom. When they were diverted to Northern Ireland as infantry replacements, Bristol talked his way into II Corps HQ in London and convinced the corps staff to rectify this error. He subsequently became the artillery air officer on the staff of the chief of artillery II Corps in North Africa and revitalized the program when it faced early termination. Subsequently appointed artillery air officer of the U.S. First Army, he developed plans to move liaison aircraft to the continent during the Normandy invasion and, during the Battle of the Bulge, personally vectored U.S. Army Air Forces fighter-bombers onto German armored columns.

In the 1940s and 1950s, he operated effectively behind the scenes to enlarge the scope and mission of U.S. Army aviation. He held assignments of increasing importance, culminating as acting director of Army Aviation in 1966. He publicly opposed the Johnson-McConnell Agreement, which transferred the Army's largest fixed-wing air transports to the Air Force and as a result was banished to Aviation Systems Command in St. Louis, Missouri. He retired in 1971.

Bristol was perhaps the key officer in keeping the Field Artillery aviation program viable during its initial shakedown in combat during World War II. He continued to be very influential after the conflict. Always a strong advocate of fixed-wing aircraft, he effectively precluded any chance of his further promotion by standing on principal.

Edgar F. Raines Jr.

Britain, Battle of (1940)

In June 1940, Adolf Hitler stood at a pinnacle of success. France lay vanquished and the British had been driven from the continent. Leading a war machine organized and equipped for swift victories in short conflicts, Hitler hoped Great Britain would quickly come to terms. When the British, inspired by Prime Minister Winston Churchill, refused to yield, Nazi Germany was compelled to improvise an invasion effort across the English Channel. The success of such a venture demanded control of the air over southeastern England. Thus the stage was set for a decisive air battle between the Luftwaffe and the Royal Air Force.

The Luftwaffe was a tactical air force dedicated to attacking enemy rail centers, roadways, and air bases, clearing the path for Germany's fast-moving armored forces. The crews of the Junkers Ju 87B "Stuka" single-engine dive-bomber were the elite of the Luftwaffe. Although an accurate bomber, the Stuka proved easy prey for enemy fighters. The Heinkel 111H, Dornier 17Z, and Junkers 88A twin-engine bombers were rugged but slow and also deficient in defensive armament.

In the Messerschmitt Bf 109E the Luftwaffe fielded an excellent single-engine fighter. It was well-armed, fast, and could outclimb and outdive its English adversaries. But visibility from the cockpit was poor, and its operating range was limited.

The Germans possessed a long-range fighter, the twin-engine Messerschmitt Bf 110C. It was fast, heavily armed, and handled well but could not match the acceleration and maneuverability of its RAF opponents.

Despite German shortcomings, the head of the Luftwaffe, Hermann Goering, was determined to win a decisive victory through bombing alone. Goering shared the widely held belief at that time that the bomber would always get through, that is, bomber forces would penetrate the enemy's defenses. In serviceable aircraft the Germans amassed 998 twin-engine bombers, 248 Stukas, 805 Bf 109 fighters, and 224 Bf 110 machines.

However, Britain in the late 1930s had developed the first defensive system against air attack incorporating the new

The Battle of Britain
RAF
Towns Bombed
Group Boundary
Group Headquarters
Luftwaffe
Fighter Base
Bomber Base
Stuka Base
Luftflotte Boundary
SCOTLAND
IRELAND
ENGLAND
Glasgow
Belfast
Fighter Command 13 Group (Saul)
Luftflotte 5 (Stumpff)
From Norway & Demark
Newcastle
Sunderland
Middlesbrough
Cover of High-level radar(15,000ft.)
Liverpool
Manchester
Hull
Sheffield
Cover of Low-level radar (500ft.)
North Sea
Fighter Command 12 Group (Leigh-Mallory)
Nottingham
Swansea
Birmingham
Coventry
Norwich
Cardiff
Luftflotte 2 (Kesselring)
Bristol
Bath
London
Ipswich
Thames Estuary
Fighter Command 10 Group (Brand)
Fighter Command 11 Group (Park)
Canterbury
Rotterdam
Exeter
Plymouth
Southampton
Portsmouth
Antwerp
Calais
Lille
English Channel
BELGIUM
Luftflotte 3 (Seperrle)
Cherbourg
Amiens
Le Havre
FRANCE
Paris
Rennes
N
W
E
S
Miles 0 25 50
Kms 0 25 50
Donald S. Frazier
Robert F. Pace

radio direction and ranging detection system (radar). Contrary to dominant thinking, Thomas Inskip, minister for the coordination of British defense, in 1937 argued that radar and fast monoplane fighters offered effective defense against bombers. Noting that Germany clearly wanted quick triumphs, Inskip asserted that the British did not need to decisively defeat Germany but rather resist German attack and survive. Britain could thus force Germany into a long war for which the Nazi regime was not prepared.

Air Marshal Hugh Dowding, as the Air Council member for Research and Development, worked closely with the scientist Robert Watson Watt in the practical application of radar for defensive purposes. Beginning in 1936 Dowding, as commander of RAF Fighter Command, developed the integrated air defense system vital to England's survival.

When approaching enemy aircraft were detected by the radar towers along the coast, their flight path over land was tracked by the Ground Observer Corps, a force of indispensable volunteers. These reports were phoned to Fighter Command headquarters and evaluated. Information so assessed was sent on to the Sector Operations centers threatened. The sector controller ordered squadrons into the air and guided them into action by radio. At all levels, the plotting tables showing the positions of warplanes were operated by the Women's Auxiliary Air Force.

On 9 August 1940, fighters available for combat in Fighter Command included 568 Hawker Hurricanes and 328 Supermarine Spitfires. Although the Hurricane 1 could not match the performance of the Bf 109E, it was easy to fly, could absorb much damage, and was quick to repair. The Spitfire was based upon an advanced elliptical wing design by Reginald Mitchell that featured maximum area, low wing loading, great strength, and as thin an airfoil as possible. The Spitfire proved a good match against the Bf 109E. Visibility in the Spitfire was excellent. Both fighters were armed with eight .303-caliber machine guns and featured armor protection for the pilot and a bulletproof windscreen.

Both British fighters benefited from 100-octane fuel. German aircraft used synthetic gasoline of 87–89 octane. Use of 100-octane fuel in the English Merlin engines raised horsepower from 1,030 to 1,310 (the Daimler Benz engine in the Bf 109E was rated at 1,175 hp). Consequently, the Hurricane was able to hold its own and the Spitfire gained an edge.

Tactically, the English began with a tight vee of three fighters, an unwieldy and obsolete formation. As the battle progressed, the British emulated the flexible German formation of two fighters—leader and wing man—developed in the course of the Spanish civil war.

Southeastern England, including London, was the main arena of the Battle of Britain. This was the area closest to the continent and within the 90-minute endurance of the 109E. Fighter Command's No. 11 Group bore the brunt of the fighting, aided by No. 12 Group adjacent to the north.

From 10 July to 11 August, Britons suffered German attacks on Channel convoys and fighter sweeps over southeastern England. Dowding limited the RAF response to such provocations. In August, the Germans unleashed an all-out assault on radar installations and air bases. Such raids began 12 August and were accompanied by nighttime bomber attacks on 13 August, utilizing electronic guidance beams, and falling upon Liverpool, Birmingham, Aberdeen, and Belfast. On 15 August, daylight blows fell upon England from occupied Norway and Denmark, but these German bombers and their Bf 110 escorts were intercepted by No. 13 Group, which inflicted nearly 20 percent losses on the attackers. "Black Thursday," as the Germans termed it, proved that daylight bombing could only be undertaken with Bf 109E fighter escort.

On August 19, Goering withdrew the Stuka dive-bombers from the battle. Some Bf 110 units were disbanded, and in less than three weeks 40 percent of their strength had been lost. However, German attacks on air bases intensified from 29 August through 6 September. Airbases in No. 11 Group were repeatedly hit. From past campaigns, German bomber crews were experienced in low-level operations against airfields.

Dowding did not dare withdraw from southeastern England. Such a move would open the door to invasion. Flying from English airstrips would be a great advantage for 109Es.

A high level of fighter production ensured warplane replacements for Fighter Command. But Dowding lost 25 percent of his pilots in a two-week period. Some new replacements had only 10 hours' flight time in a fighter. By early September, six out of seven sector airbases and stations were severely damaged. But time was running out for the Germans as well. The date for invading the British mainland had been repeatedly postponed. Now the storms of autumn loomed.

Convinced that Fighter Command had been largely destroyed, the Germans sought to bring the remaining English fighters to battle and eliminate them quickly. An attack on London would surely bring those fighters into action. On 7 September, 900 warplanes set forth to bomb London. The Germans were elated when mass raids by day and night churned London into a sea of flames. With London as the target, however, Fighter Command could rebuild its airbases, and pilots gained much-needed relief from constant pressure. Replacements could be given essential training.

During another massive daylight attack on 15 September, Dowding committed 300 British fighters into battle. The Germans had been repeatedly assured that only 50 English fighters remained. German elation now turned to bitter disillusionment. On 17 September Hitler postponed invasion plans indefinitely. A long ordeal, nighttime bombing, and later V-1 and V-2 attacks lay ahead for London and other English cities. But the threat of Nazi invasion never materialized again.

The myth of German invincibility had been shattered. Germany would be compelled to wage a long war. Britain would become the base where immense Allied forces would be amassed, the springboard from which Europe would be liberated and Nazi Germany defeated.

Sherwood S. Cordier

See also

Beaverbrook, Lord; Dowding, Hugh C.T.; Goering, Hermann; Radar; Royal Flying Corps/Royal Naval Air Service/Royal Air Force

References

Bickers, Richard Townshend, et al. *The Battle of Britain.* New York: Prentice-Hall, 1990.

Deighton, Len. *Fighter.* New York: Alfred A. Knopf, 1977.

Wood, Derek, with Derek Dempster. Rev. ed. *The Narrow Margin.* London: Arrow Books, 1969.

British Aerospace

The culmination of a series of aviation-industry mergers after the Aircraft and Shipbuilding Industries Act was passed in 1977 by the British government. Thus, on 29 April 1977 the British Aircraft Corporation, Hawker-Siddeley Aviation, Hawker-Siddeley Dynamics, and Scottish Aviation combined under one banner: British Aerospace (now BAe Systems).

The new organization inherited factories and installations at Brough, Chester, Filton, Kingston, Hatfield, Preston, Warton, Weybridge, and Woodford. Partial privatization of the conglomerate saw the final disappearance of the individual company identities; thereafter all products were identified by their new owner's name. Complete privatization followed in May 1985.

One of the consequences of this was a rationalization of the company's facilities; the Weybridge, Kingston, and Hatfield factories were closed and their products transferred elsewhere. Aircraft produced or supported by British Aerospace include the Harrier, Hawk, Nimrod (now being rebuilt to the MRA.4 standard), Tornado, and the Eurofighter Tornado.

Kev Darling

British Aerospace Harrier

The only vertical/short takeoff and landing aircraft to enter regular squadron service in any numbers. The Harrier began life as a development of the earlier P.1127 and Kestrel experimental and development aircraft.

Developed by the original parent company, Hawker-Siddeley, the Kestrel evolved into the Harrier, which was intended for use in the strike, attack, and reconnaissance role close to the front line of battle. To enable the aircraft to function effectively, full use is made of its V/STOL capability, which allows battlefield commanders almost instant access to air support.

It was on this premise that the first Harrier GR.1 aircraft were delivered to RAF No. 1 Squadron in December 1967, the first production version having made its maiden flight the previous August. A total of 131 Harriers were finally delivered, including 90 GR.1/As plus 17 trainer versions; 24 advanced GR.3s incorporated a laser-ranging and marked-target seeker in the nose, among other improvements. The surviving Harrier GR.1s were also converted to this standard.

It was this adaptability that first brought the Harrier in its earlier GR.1 form to the attention of the United States Marine Corps. Designated the AV-8A, the USMC aircraft underwent very few changes to suit it for Marine service.

Another version of the first-generation Harrier was built: the Sea Harrier developed for the Royal Navy. To enable the aircraft to perform its duties more efficiently, the nose was redesigned to accommodate the pilot in a higher seating position. This allowed fitting of a nose radar suited for the role of fleet defense.

Both British versions of the Harriers took part in the Falkland Islands War. The former attacked ground targets prior to and after the landings while the navy jets shot down Argentine aircraft in defense of the fleet.

Both early variants of the Harrier have now left the service of the RAF and the Fleet Air Arm, although the latter version has been rebuilt into the far more capable FRS.2. A similar fate befell the aircraft of the USMC, although not before some had been upgraded to AV-8C standard. Redundant aircraft from the USMC were later passed on to the navies of Spain and Thailand.

The second phase of Harrier development involved a joint venture between British Aerospace and McDonnell Douglas (later Boeing MDD). Essentially a total redesign, the new aircraft featured composite construction throughout. One of the major components is an enlarged wing capable of an increased weapons load on extra pylons. The fuselage also underwent some changes, especially in the nose area. As with the Sea Harrier, increased cockpit height allowed an array of sensors to be mounted in the nose; a revamped canopy increased the pilots vision area.

This new variant has been delivered to the USMC, the RAF, and the Italian navy. In common with the earlier-generation aircraft, batches of trainers were delivered to the operators of the single-seaters. Of the three aircraft types dedicated to V/STOL development worldwide, only the Harrier has became a success.

Kev Darling

References

Jenkins, Dennis R. *Boeing/BAE Harrier.* North Branch, MN: Specialty Press, 1998.

British Commonwealth Air Training Plan (BCATP)

A major contributor to the Allies' victory in the air war against the Axis powers during World War II.

The BCATP originated in the prewar strategic requirements of the Royal Air Force and in the long-time military, political, and cultural ties between Canada and Great Britain. During World War I, Canada served as a training centre for the Royal Flying Corps and RAF, and the RAF believed—mistakenly, as it turned out—that it could renew that arrangement during World War II. For William Lyon Mackenzie King, then Canadian prime minister, the issue was one of sovereignty: He refused outright to permit any of the training conducted in Canada to come under British control. On 17 December 1939, after protracted negotiations, the BCATP between Canada, Great Britain, Australia, and New Zealand was finally signed.

The BCATP was also dictated by geography and industrial mobilization as well as by demography. The plan's large-scale training commitments required numerous airfields and clear skies free from the threat of enemy air activity. Equally important, training had to take place close to the most important operational theater, Western Europe. Moreover, these training centers had to be located near an industrial base with potential expansion for airframes and engines for training aircraft. Canada was ideally suited in this regard. Finally, Canada, unlike the other dominions, had a larger population from which to recruit the aircrews.

The BCATP was part of the wider Empire Air Training Scheme designed to produce large numbers of trained aircrews. Canada, initially the largest contributor outside of Britain, adopted the BCATP designation. The British and the other partners, however, usually employed the imperial terminology until the summer of 1942. According to BCATP Article 15, the so-called Ottawa Agreement, dominion aircrews were to be identified with their country of origin by the creation within the RAF of distinctive dominion components. That way, dominion personnel would not be broken up into RAF squadrons, thereby maintaining effective control of national forces. The plan was to run until 31 March 1943 and was supposed to train some 90,000 personnel by the end of the three-year program. The BCATP exceeded all expectations.

The Royal Canadian Air Force (RCAF) controlled the program with assistance from the RAF; by 1943, the BCATP training centers were manned by 104,000 ground personnel operating approximately 10,000 aircraft.

More than 50 air-training schools were created in Canada alone between April 1940 and December 1941; by 1943 97 schools and 184 auxiliary establishments had been put in place. Nearly 40,000 trainees—more than half as many again as originally planned—passed through these schools during the same period; Canada contributed more than 80 percent of all students until May 1942. Some 33 training establishments were created in Australia, training approximately 9,600 personnel before they headed to Canada for advanced training; some 7,000 New Zealanders graduated from the training schools. Another 15,000 Australians received all of their flying training in Canada before being dispatched to Britain.

By war's end, the BCATP had produced 131,553 aircrewmen, of which 72,835 (51 percent overall) were Canadians. Moreover, of all the Commonwealth men trained during the war, fully 45 percent received some or all of their training in Canada. The costs of the program had risen significantly as well. Over the course of the program (1939–1945), the BCATP cost approximately $2 billion; Canada paid 72 percent. Canada was indeed, as U.S. President Franklin Roosevelt proclaimed, the "aerodrome of democracy."

Shawn Cafferky

See also

Canadian Air Force; Royal Australian Air Force; Royal Flying Corps/Royal Naval Air Service/Royal Air Force

References

Douglas, W.A.B. *The Creation of a National Air Force: The Official History of the Royal Canadian Air Force.* Vol. 2. Toronto: University of Toronto Press, 1986.

Dunmore, Spencer. *Wings for Victory: The Remarkable Story of the British Commonwealth Air Training Plan in Canada.* Toronto: McClelland and Stewart, 1994.

British Pacific Fleet

The British Pacific Fleet (BPF) formed on 22 November 1944 around four fleet carriers: *Indomitable, Victorious, Indefatigable,* and *Illustrious* (replaced 14 April 1945 by *Formidable*). After initially operating under the aegis of the East Indies Fleet, it left Trincomalee (Sri Lanka) on 16 January 1945 to join the U.S. Pacific Fleet at Okinawa.

En route, BPF launched two strikes against Sumatran oil refineries in the Palembang area. For the loss of 23 aircraft from all causes, BPF cut Japanese aviation gasoline output by 65 percent. This strike series was arguably BPF's greatest single contribution to the eventual victory over Japan.

BPF's mission assignment at Okinawa was to keep the six airfields in the Sakishima Gunto out of action in order to suppress Japanese air defenses against the invasion force and prevent aerial reinforcement of Okinawa itself. The carriers, between 26 March and 25 May, established a routine of two- to three-day strike serials followed by similar replenishment periods. Since the Japanese used crushed coral, in limitless supply, to construct these runways, bomb damage usually was repaired overnight. Although its unremitting efforts appeared fruitless, when less-capable U.S. escort carriers replaced BPF while it replenished, greater air activity against the invasion fleet demonstrated the British carriers' efficacy.

While BPF operated off Sakishima, kamikazes hit all the carriers (and *Formidable* and *Victorious* twice). Their armored flight decks resoundingly demonstrated their value—all were fully operational within a few hours, and only 44 ships' crewmen lost their lives.

Implacable replaced *Indomitable* as BPF rejoined the U.S. Pacific Fleet on 17 July for final attacks on Japan's home islands. Integrated into Third Fleet as Task Force 37, its aircraft launched a relentless attack on Japan's military and mercantile shipping, land transportation systems, industry, and remaining air assets. Operations continued until 15 August, although most of BPF had withdrawn by then to replenish, leaving only *Indefatigable* on the line.

Fleet Air Arm aviators earned their second Victoria Cross of the war, posthumously awarded on 9 August to Lieutenant Robert Hampton Gray for his courageous leadership during an attack that sank the escort *Amakusa*.

BPF carriers proved their toughness and efficiency during the Okinawa and home islands campaigns, sustaining high-intensity strike missions against airfields, shipping, and rail and road systems while maintaining effective fleet defense and surviving attacks that crippled their contemporaries in other navies.

Paul E. Fontenoy

See also

Fleet Air Arm; Okinawa; Task Force 38/58; Vian, Philip L.

References

Brown, J. David. *Carrier Operations in World War II: The Royal Navy.* London: Ian Allan, 1968.

______, ed. *The British Pacific and East Indies Fleets.* Liverpool, UK: Brodie, 1995.

Friedman, Norman. *British Carrier Aviation: The Evolution of the Ships and their Aircraft.* Annapolis, MD: Naval Institute Press, 1988.

Bulge, Battle of the (1944–1945)

World War II German surprise attack and Allied defense and counterattack in the Ardennes region of southwestern Belgium and northern Luxembourg from 16 December 1944 to 16 January 1945. The battle caused many problems for Allied commanders. The German planners scheduled the attack to take place during poor weather, which would limit the effects of Allied tactical airpower. Additionally, the German Luftwaffe concentrated significant air resources in an attempt to provide direct support to the offensive and to counter Allied air capabilities.

Although fog and snow limited air operations during much of the fighting, Allied airpower made significant contributions to the outcome of the battle. Even during bad weather, Allied pilots strove to provide reconnaissance support and to attack German targets through breaks in the weather.

When relatively clear conditions occurred, such as between 23 and 28 December and on 1, 2, and 5 January, the Allied air forces conducted extensive attacks on German forces and supply lines. The USAAF Ninth Air Force and the RAF Second Tactical Air Force provided direct support to Allied ground forces, conducted armed reconnaissance missions, waged an aggressive interdiction campaign, and defended against Luftwaffe operations. Senior Allied commanders also shifted elements of RAF Bomber Command and USAAF Eighth Air Force heavy bomber forces from the strategic bombing offensive against Germany to interdiction targets and airfield attacks. Both sides conducted airdrops—Luftwaffe air transport units supported the initial offensive with an airborne assault and with limited resupply drops, and USAAF air transport units provided support to the isolated American forces at Bastogne.

On 1 January 1945, the Luftwaffe conducted its last significant offensive operation of the war with a counter–air strike against 17 Allied airfields in Belgium, Holland, and France. Although Operation BODDENPLATTE (BASE PLATE) inflicted significant damage on some airfields, the Luftwaffe suffered heavy losses of aircraft and pilots that it could not afford at this point in the war. Although the Battle of the Bulge is normally remembered as exclusively a ground operation, airpower made important contributions to the ultimate success of the Allied forces.

Jerome V. Martin

See also

German Air Force (Luftwaffe); World War II Aviation

References

Craven, Wesley F. and James L. Cate, eds. *The Army Air Forces in World War II.* 7 vols. Chicago: University of Chicago Press, 1948–1957 (reissued, Washington, DC: U.S. Government Printing Office, 1983); see esp. vol 3.: *Europe: Argument to V-E Day, January 1944 to May 1945.*

Franks, Norman L. *The Battle of the Airfields, 1st January 1945.* London: William Kimber, 1982; 2nd ed. London: Grub Street, 1994.

Parker, Danny S. *To Win the Winter Sky: The Air War Over the Ardennes, 1944–1945.* Conshohoken, PA: Combined Books, 1994.

Bureau of Aircraft Production (BAP)

Immediately upon entering World War I, some optimists in the United States began talking about huge production programs that would "darken the skies of Europe with American aircraft." A year later the promised fleet had not arrived, though not for lack of effort. It was simply that no one in the United States, when the boast was made, had a real understanding of how difficult a task lay ahead.

In May 1918, in an attempt to solve the problem, two new agencies were created: the Division of Military Aeronautics (DMA), which dealt with personnel, and the Bureau of Aircraft Production, which handled equipment. John Ryan, the former president of Ananconda Copper and then chair of the Aircraft Board, a civilian agency, was appointed to head up the BAP. Both the BAP and the DMA became part of the Air Service. Despite this common assignment, a problem developed due to a lack of coordination between the two agencies. This was solved later in the summer with the promotion of Ryan to the post of director of the Air Service at a second assistant secretary of war level. The BAP had responsibility for deciding which aircraft the United States would build.

James Streckfuss

See also

U.S. Aircraft Development and Production (World War I)

References

Casari, Robert B. *Encyclopedia of U.S. Military Aircraft: The World War I Production Program.* 3 vols. Chillicothe, OH: Self-published, 1972–1975.

Hudson, John J. *Hostile Skies: A Combat History of the American Air Service in World War I.* Syracuse, NY: Syracuse University Press, 1968.

Bureau of Naval Aeronautics (BNA)

Created by the U.S. Congress in 1921 to advise the Secretary of the Navy, the Department of the Navy, and the Chief of Naval Operations on naval aviation. The BNA consolidated and centralized all administrative, logistical, and technological functions pertaining to aircraft under one administrative jurisdiction.

Prior to World War I, the Bureaus of Construction and Repair, Steam Engineering, and Navigation shared responsibility for naval aeronautics. In 1913, Secretary of the Navy Josephus Daniels appointed a board of officers led by Captain Washington I. Chambers, the officer in charge of aviation, to draw up a comprehensive plan for a naval aeronautics service. The subsequent Chambers Report recommended, among other things, the formation of a central aviation office to oversee naval aviation. In response, Secretary Daniels created the Office of Naval Aeronautics within the Division of Operations. This early effort at coordination proved disappointing; authority over aeronautics remained dispersed among the bureaus, with the Bureau of Construction and Repair leading the way.

Following the war, General William "Billy" Mitchell and other proponents of airpower urged Congress to create a central bureau to alleviate this administrative confusion and promote naval aviation. Congress consequently established the Bureau of Naval Aeronautics, responsible for matters pertaining to designing, building, and repairing Navy and Marine Corps aircraft.

Under Bureau Chief Admiral William A. Moffett, the BNA promoted use of airpower, working to incorporate aircraft into fleet operations and strategic planning. Determined to bring order and structure to naval aviation, Moffett and the BNA developed procedures for procuring and testing aircraft components, identifying and painting airships, and maintaining, repairing, and salvaging aircraft. The BNA also promoted pilot safety and improved shore stations and installations. A proponent of innovation, Moffett authorized pioneering research in aerology, aviation medicine, and radiotelegraphy. He defended naval aviation against congressional and naval opposition, battling successfully to prevent deficiencies in personnel, supplies, and appropriations.

During and after World War II, the BNA expanded the scope of its activities. During the war, it inaugurated a comprehensive pilot recruitment and training program—which laid the foundation for the wartime expansion of the Naval Aviation Corps. Following Moffett's legacy, the BNA continued to sponsor research and managed the introduction of radar, jet propulsion, satellites, helicopters, titanium alloys, and other innovations. It also worked closely with the aerospace industry on research, design, and production. The BNA continued oversight of naval aviation until 1959, when the new Bureau of Naval Weapons absorbed its functions.

Daniel E. Worthington

See also

Moffett, William Adger; U.S. Marine Corps Aviation; United States Navy, and Aviation

References

Grossnick, Roy A. *United States Naval Aviation, 1910–1955.*

Washington, DC: Naval Historical Center, Department of the Navy, 1997.

Turnbull, Archibald Douglas, and Clifford Lee Lord. *History of United States Naval Aviation.* New Haven: Yale University Press, 1949.

Burma

Protracted air campaign in support of ground operations during World War II. At the outbreak of war, Allied air defenses in Burma consisted of a single squadron of Brewster Buffaloes and the Curtiss P-40s of the American Volunteer Group (the famed Flying Tigers). They faced large numbers of Japanese aircraft based in Thailand and Indonesia. The air campaign opened in late December with Japanese attacks on the city of Rangoon that caused almost 30,000 civilian casualties.

In mid-January 1942, Japanese ground forces advanced into Burma supported by the Third Army Air Division. Although outnumbered, the Allied air forces in general fought well, but Japanese attacks on bases took their toll, and by late spring the campaign was over with the Japanese in possession of most of Burma. This cut the Burma Road, the only viable overland communication route to China, forcing supplies for China to be transported by air over the "Hump" of the Himalayas.

The Allies launched several offensive operations in late 1942 and 1943 with only limited success. Of particular interest was the operation of jungle-trained Chindit forces under Brigadier General Orde Wingate, who penetrated deep behind Japanese lines and were supplied entirely by air for extended periods. Operations by the British XV Corps in the Second Arakan Offensive in January 1944 were also supplied by air.

In early 1944, the Japanese Fifteenth Army attacked from western Burma into India but was stopped by British and Indian troops at Imphal and Kohima. Both defensive positions were surrounded for long periods of time, again supplied by the large number of Allied transport aircraft in the area until eventually relieved by forces advancing from India. Chindit operations continued, including the construction and operation of the Broadway air base behind Japanese lines. Broadway overstepped Allied capabilities, however, and Japanese air attack destroyed the aircraft based there.

By July 1944, Allied air strength had increased to 64 RAF and 26 U.S. squadrons, and a major Allied offensive was imminent. The most prevalent Allied aircraft were Hurricanes, but Spitfire, Beaufighter, P-40, and P-47 types contributed significantly, along with a variety of bomber aircraft. Unlike many of the well-known air battles in the Central and Southwest Pacific, Japanese air units were army units flying such aircraft as the Kawasaki Ki 43 and Ki 44.

The Japanese effectiveness had been spent in the Imphal and Kohima battles; the Allied advance, primarily by British, Indian, and Chinese forces, was hard-fought but steady, interrupted only by the monsoon season. It was supported by overwhelming airpower. Rangoon finally fell on 2 May 1945, and the campaign in Burma came to a close. Planned Allied operations in the theater against Malaya and Singapore had not begun when the war ended.

Frank E. Watson

See also

American Volunteer Group; Hump Airlift

References

Probert, Air Commodore Henry. *Forgotten Air Force: History of the RAF in the War Against Japan.* London: Brassey's, 1995.

Scott, Robert L. *God Is My Co-Pilot.* New York: Ballantine Books, 1956.

Busemann, Adolf (1901–1986)

German engineer; born in Lübeck, Germany, in 1901. After earning his Ph.D. in 1924, Busemann worked at the Max Planck Institute from 1925 to 1931 with Ludwig Prandtl. From 1931 to 1935, he taught at the University of Dresden and was involved in aerodynamic testing at the Göttingen wind tunnel laboratory. While there, he discovered that thin aerofoils delay and reduce drag as an aircraft approaches Mach 1. He later pointed out that swept-back wings might provide a solution to the vibration problem.

From 1936 to 1945, Busemann worked at the Hermann Goering Aeronautical Research Center in Völkenrode. In 1947, he came to the United States through Operation PAPERCLIP and later worked for the National Advisory Committee for Aeronautics (NACA) as chief scientist at Langley Field, Virginia. The successful application of his expertise was demonstrated in the design and production of the F-86 Sabre. Busemann remained with NACA/NASA until 1964. He then taught aeronautical engineering at the University of Colorado until 1971, when he retired. He died in 1986.

Guillaume de Syon

See also

Lippisch, Alexander Martin; Mach, Ernst

References

Hansen, James R. *Spaceflight Revolution.* Washington, DC: NASA, 1995.

Muenger, Elisabeth. *Searching the Horizon.* Washington, DC: NASA, 1985.

Bush, George Herbert Walker (1924–)

Lieutenant junior grade, U.S. Naval Reserve, later U.S. president. He flew 58 combat missions in the Pacific during World War II. Holder of Distinguished Flying Cross, Air Medal with two Gold Stars, and Presidential Unit Citation awarded to USS *San Jacinto.* Later became forty-first president of the United States (1989–1993). Father of George W. Bush, forty-third U.S. president (2001–).

George Bush was born 12 June 1924 in Milton, Massachusetts. Enlisting in the Navy on his eighteenth birthday, he was not yet 19 when he earned his wings to become the youngest naval aviator of his time.

Assigned as a photographic officer to Torpedo Squadron 51 (VT-51) aboard the light aircraft carrier USS *San Jacinto* (CVL-30), he flew the Grumman Avenger. His ship was part of Task Force 58 and took part in seven major operations ranging from the Marianas to Okinawa. VT-51's executive officer, Legare Hole, described Bush as "an exceptionally good pilot" who was also a "smart fellow." Additionally, Bush was well liked by the squadron's officers and enlisted men.

The mission of 2 September 1944 against a Japanese radio station on ChiChi Jima in the Bonin Islands is a fine example of Lieutenant Bush's war. As described in his Distinguished Flying Cross citation, his actions were courageous and disciplined. The antiaircraft fire was especially intense as he and his two crewmen attacked the facility. Their Avenger was hit at the start of his dive, but Bush elected to continue the attack despite the aircraft's being on fire. Their bombs caused damaging hits to the Japanese facility. One crewman was killed in the crash, and the other's parachute failed to properly open; Bush was the only survivor. After landing in the water, he was protected by circling aircraft until being rescued by the submarine USS *Finback* (SS-230). He would go on to a distinguished career in public service, holding America's highest elected office.

Scott R. DiMarco

References

Christmann, Timothy J. "Vice President Bush Calls World War II Experience 'Sobering.'" *Naval Aviation News* 67 (March–April 1985): 12–15.

C

Cactus Air Force

Allied aircraft on Guadalcanal (August 1942–February 1943). U.S. Marines landed on Guadalcanal on 7 August 1942. The Allied code name for the island of Guadalcanal was CACTUS, and the air units based on that island at newly won Henderson Field soon unofficially assumed the name Cactus Air Force. Operating on a logistical shoestring, Cactus succeeded in maintaining a land-based air presence over Guadalcanal in the most crucial days of that campaign. It achieved an effect out of all proportion to its numbers. On several occasions the operations of the entire Japanese Combined Fleet centered on eliminating Cactus Air Force and its base at Henderson Field.

Frank E. Watson

See also

Guadalcanal

Cambodia Bombings

Secret U.S. bombing of North Vietnamese sanctuaries in Cambodia. By the mid-1960s, North Vietnamese and Vietcong units had established base areas in eastern Cambodia from which to launch attacks into South Vietnam. In March 1969, President Richard Nixon, with the tacit approval of Cambodia's Prince Norodom Sihanouk, ordered bombing of these base areas to take pressure off the ongoing U.S. troop withdrawal from South Vietnam and to put pressure on the North Vietnamese to enter serious negotiations. Code-named Operation MENU, bombing would continue until Congress cut off funds for Cambodian operations in August 1973. By the time the MENU bombings ended, B-52 bombers had flown 16,527 sorties and dropped 383,851 tons of bombs on Cambodia.

Although elaborate measures were taken to keep the bombings secret lest their revelation fuel antiwar protests, the *New York Times* published a story about the bombings in May 1970, sparking heated debate about the legality and morality of the raids. The news infuriated Nixon, and the administration became obsessed with plugging information leaks to the press. The telephones of several journalists and government officials were wire-tapped, beginning the legal activities and coverup that would ultimately lead to the Watergate scandal, Congress's demand for Nixon's impeachment, and Nixon's unprecedented resignation.

The bombing of the Cambodian base areas and Cambodian attempts to constrain North Vietnamese expansion led to unrest within Cambodia, and on 18 March 1970 Prince Sihanouk, who was not in Cambodia at the time, was deposed by General Lon Nol.

James H. Willbanks

See also

ARC LIGHT; Ho Chi Minh Trail

References

Berger, Carl, ed. *The United States Air Force in Southeast Asia, 1961–1973: An Illustrated Account.* Washington, DC: Office of Air Force History, 1984.

Shawcross, William. *Sideshow: Kissinger, Nixon, and the Destruction of Cambodia.* New York: Simon and Schuster, 1979.

Camm, Sydney (1893–1966)

British aircraft designer. Born on 5 August 1893 in Windsor, Camm was apprenticed in woodworking, though he was also heavily involved in early aeronautics. In 1914, he joined the Martinsyde Aeroplane Company, eventually undertaking major design tasks there.

Camm joined the Hawker Engineering Company in 1923 as a senior draftsman, becoming chief designer only two years later. Camm's biplane designs were notable for their integrated elegance, imaginative conception, and structural strength allied to simplicity and stringent weight control. His Hart family of two-seaters, and related single-seat Fury types, broke new ground in performance and user-friendliness.

By 1933, Camm realized that biplane fighters had reached the limit of their useful development and began design of a monoplane that became the Hurricane. Even as this descendant of his earlier types entered production in 1938, Camm was working on its all-metal monocoque successor, the Typhoon, which he further developed into the Tempest and Sea Fury, the fastest and most robust British piston-engined fighters.

Although Camm quickly appreciated the jet engine's potential, his service designs actually formed the second and third generations of jet fighters. The Royal Navy's straight-wing Sea Hawk was followed by the very successful Hunter, which many hold to be the most elegant jet fighter of all time.

Government decisions frustrated Camm's desire to produce supersonic jets. Instead, in 1958 he initiated the revolutionary design, combining fast jet performance with VTOL operating characteristics, which became the Harrier, and witnessed its success before his death in Richmond, Surrey, on 12 March 1966.

Paul E. Fontenoy

See also

British Aerospace Harrier; Hawker Aircraft; Hawker Fury; Hawker Hunter; Hawker Hurricane; Hawker Typhoon and Tempest; Sopwith, Thomas O.M.

References

Mason, Francis K. *Hawker Aircraft Since 1920.* London: Putnam, 1991.

______. *The Hawker Hurricane.* London: Macdonald, 1962.

______. *Harrier.* Wellingborough, UK: Patrick Stephens, 1986.

Canadian Air Force (Royal Canadian Air Force)

The air component of the unified Canadian Forces. The Canadian Air Force supports a variety of domestic and international operations by providing an operationally ready, multipurpose, and combat-capable force. Its roles include surveillance and control of Canadian airspace; worldwide airlift; support to land and sea operations; and humanitarian operations. A special task of the Canadian Air Force is search and rescue throughout the expanses of Canada.

The Canadian Aviation Corps was formed in 1914 and was sent overseas early during World War I. Flight training began in Canada in 1915. In 1920, the Royal Canadian Air Force (RCAF) was established. With Canada's declaration of war against Germany in 1939, the RCAF hosted the British Commonwealth Air Training Plan. Canada trained 131,533 aircrewmen. Canadian airmen fought throughout the Battle of Britain and in all air campaigns in Europe. By D-Day, 33 bomber, fighter, and coastal squadrons participated in the aerial campaign to retake Europe.

The RCAF received its first jets, de Havilland Vampires, in 1948. In 1950 it joined the UN forces fighting in Korea, flying airlift missions and logging more than 34,000 flying hours. As the Cold War threatened North America, a U.S.-Canadian air defense agreement was signed in Washington, D.C., on 12 May 1958. This established the North American Air Defense Command.

In 1968, the RCAF was merged into the Canadian Forces. Canada has participated heavily in international peacekeeping efforts throughout the world. The Canadian Air Task Group flew against Iraq from Qatar during Operation DESERT STORM. During the Kosovo operation, Canadian CF-18s flew from Aviano Air Base, Italy. Equipped with precision-guided munitions, Canadian fighters led multinational packages against Serbian forces. At the same time, Canadian Forces members stationed in Geilenkirchen, Germany, with NATO AWACS supported the campaign.

The annual operating budget for the Canadian Air Force is approximately $2 billion. There are 14,500 members in the regular forces, with a small reserve. The Canadian Forces possess 122 CF-18 Hornets, 21 CP-140 patrol aircraft, 27 CT-133 trainers, 59 transports, and 140 helicopters. Thirteen wings are located across Canada, and a Canadian element is located in Geilenkirchen supporting NATO AWACS.

James M. Pfaff

See also

British Commonwealth Air Training Plan

Cant Aircraft

In 1921, the Cosulich family of Trieste decided to enter the aviation business. Already active in shipping and shipbuilding, they followed the same pattern by establishing first an air taxi service (SISA, 1921) and then a seaplane workshop at Monfalcone (within the existing Cantiere Navale Triestino, or CNT; 1923). SISA trained pilots for the Regia Aeronautica (the Italian air force) using CNT.7 and Cant.18 biplanes; from 1926 it added airline services, using the Cant.10 and Cant.22 cabin seaplanes. The workshops survived on license production and prototypes.

In 1930, CNT merged with other shipyards to form the Cantieri Riuniti Dell'Adriatico (CRDA), but aircraft continued to use the Cant designation. In 1933, CRDA was acquired by state conglomerate IRI, and Italo Balbo persuaded Filippo Zappata (1894–1994), then working with Blériot, to become chief designer. In the following nine years, CRDA flew 18 new types that garnered 40 world records; it also added a landplane factory, test department, and airfield as the workforce grew from 350 to 5,000. The Cant Z.501 (1934) and Z.506 (1935) seaplanes and Z.1007 landplane bomber (1937) became the standard Italian types in their categories. Zappata saw wooden airplanes as a temporary necessity, and his new designs were conceived with all-metal construction, including the Z.1018 bomber twin, Z.511 four-engine floatplane airliner, and Z.515 twin floatplane.

Around 1939 Zappata became disillusioned with CRDA and started negotiating with Breda, which he joined in 1942; in addition, military requirements fluctuated. The Z.1018 started in wood as "flying mockup," developed as a very different wooden preseries, and metamorphosed into metal for production—but with bomber, torpedo-bomber, and night-fighter variants. Not surprising, none of these types became operational before the Italian armistice in 1943. The ensuing German occupation and USAAF raids in March-April 1944 stopped all production, and only the shipyard was rebuilt after the war.

Gregory Alegi

See also

Balbo, Italo; Blériot Aircraft; Breda; Italian Aircraft Development; Regia Aeronautica (Pre–World War II); Regia Aeronautica (World War II)

References

Marcon, Tullio. *Cant Z.506.* Turin, Italy: La Bancarella Aeronautica, 1996.

Staccioli, Valerio, ed. *In cantiere. Tecnica, arte, lavoro: ottant'anni di attività dello stabilimento di Monfalcone.* Monfalcone, Italy: Edizioni della Laguna, 1988.

Zappata, Giuseppe, and Giorgio Evangelisti. *Le navi aeree di Filippo Zappata.* Florence, Italy: Editoriale Olimpia, 1996.

Cape Canaveral

Home of the Kennedy Space Center, on the Florida coast, and center stage for U.S. space launches since the late 1950s. It hosted the early—and unsuccessful—satellite launches by the U.S. Army, as well as the Apollo lunar launches. Today, "the Cape" is the site for many U.S. satellite and space shuttle launches. Its massive runways allow the space shuttle to end its journey where it begins, for optimal turnaround.

Cape Canaveral is also home to the Vehicle Assembly Building of the National Aeronautics and Space Administration (NASA). The structure, more than 30 stories high, is where the Apollo rockets were assembled and the Space Shuttle and other NASA projects are prepared for launch.

President John F. Kennedy was one of NASA's biggest advocates, and in the days following Kennedy's assassination President Lyndon Johnson made the controversial decision to rename the site Cape Kennedy in honor of the fallen president. The name stuck until 1973, when the U.S. Board of Geographic Names responded to a campaign by the Florida legislature to restore the original name.

Erich Streckfuss

References

Spaceline, Inc. (covering Cape Canaveral). http://www.spaceline.org.

Cape Engano, Battle of (1944)

Carrier engagement on 25 October 1944 northeast of Luzon, Philippines, during the Battle of Leyte Gulf.

As part of the Japanese operations that resulted in the massive Battle of Leyte Gulf, Admiral Jisaburo Ozawa's carrier force sailed south from Japan's Inland Sea on October 20 primarily as a decoy force. When reconnaissance aircraft located the Japanese carriers, most of Admiral William Halsey's U.S. Third Fleet moved northward to intercept. The battle was lopsided, with 787 U.S. naval aircraft opposed by only 29 Japanese. Although the U.S. bombing performance was below standard given the number of attacking aircraft, massive strikes sank the *Zuikaku, Chiyoda, Chitose,* and *Zuiho.* The remainder of the Japanese fleet, including the two hybrid battleship-carriers *Ise* and *Hyuga,* escaped during the night.

Even though he scored successes against Ozawa, Halsey has been roundly criticized for taking the bait of the empty Japanese carriers and allowing the Japanese surface fleet an opportunity for an advantageous engagement farther south at Leyte Gulf near the island of Samar. The Cape Engano action was followed closely by Admiral Chester Nimitz's famous message to Halsey: "Where is Task Force 34, the world wonders." Halsey's attention to the decoy carrier force while more or less ignoring the Japanese battleships to the south shows the extent to which naval thought revolved around airpower by 1944.

Frank E. Watson

See also

Leyte Gulf, Battle of

References

Morison, Samuel Eliot. *The Two Ocean War.* Boston: Little, Brown, 1963.

The Caproni Ca.3 had a fine performance for 1917 and was used by U.S. flyers as well as the Italian air force. (Gregory Alegi)

Caproni Aircraft (Early Years)

Gianni Caproni followed the 1908 European tidal wave of interest in aviation by building a glider with his friend, Henri Coanda. His interest continued, and by 1910 he had entered the aircraft business. Prior to World War I, Caproni designed a series of slow open-fuselage aircraft and, like many Europeans, built Blériot and other aircraft design copies on which the firm survived. In 1914, he patented the world's first monoplane fighter, a shoulder-wing design that mounted a flexible machine gun on a high pylon, allowing fire over the propeller or vertically above the aircraft. It was flown as the Ca.20 in 1916 and is now displayed at the Museum of Flight in Seattle. But it was the series of large bombers produced by the firm during World War I that won the company lasting fame.

A variety of Caproni biplane and triplane bombers were designed to deliver a large bombload on Austro-Hungarian forces across the Alps. In each case, the three engines (usually 150-hp Isotta Fraschini V4Bs) were housed in individual nacelles. The aircraft had a crew of two pilots, a nose gunner, and usually a rear gunner. The wings spanned more than 60 feet, and the typical Caproni was 30–40 feet long. The Caproni bombers had a speed of about 100 mph and service ceilings in the range of 12,000 feet. On occasion, however, it could perform impressively, as on 23 February 1918, when Italian instructor Federico Semprini looped a Caproni to demonstrate its capabilities to the group of American students under Fiorello LaGuardia at Foggia.

In addition to operating with Italian *squadriglia* (squadrons), Capronis were sold to the British and served with the Royal Naval Air Service at Taranto. The French built the Ca.3 under license, and the U.S. Northern Bombing Group used the Ca.5. The Caproni was also recommended for production in the United States by the Bolling Mission. The Ca.5s built by Fisher Body in Detroit were powered by the Liberty engine.

Caproni continued to figure prominently in Italian aviation following World War I through to the jet age.

James Streckfuss

See also

Bolling Mission

References

Abate, Rosario, Alegi Gregory, and Apostolo Giorgio. *Aeroplani Caproni: Gianni Caproni and His Aircraft, 1910–1983.* Trento, Italy: Museo Caproni, 1992.

Alegi, Gregory. *Caproni Ca.3.* Berkhamsted, UK: Albatros, 1999.

_______. "Douhet, Caproni, and the Origins of Strategic Bombing." London: Cross and Cockade International, 1995.

Caproni Aircraft (Post–World War I)

When armistice scuttled the plan for 4,000 Ca.5 bombers, Gianni Caproni (1886–1957) sought to replace military orders with airline sales and offered the ill-fated Ca.60 transatlantic flying boat (1920). Caproni concentrated production

It was not pretty, and it did not fly very fast, but the Caproni-Campini was Italy's first jet aircraft. (Walter J. Boyne)

at the Taliedo factory in Milan, and the wartime Vizzola factory became a flying school. Soon Caproni returned to bombers with the Ca.73 twin-engined inverted sesquiplane (1925), which finally ousted the wartime Ca.3 from Italian bomber units. Its layout was repeated on the Ca.79 and Ca.90 heavy bomber prototypes, designed to Guilio Douhet's "aerial battleship" concept.

The group reorganized in 1929 and began to acquire smaller firms. Moving from aircraft design to management, Caproni sought independence in the production process and bought engine and instrument makers, mining companies, wood industries, and weapons factories. A great believer in innovation, he sponsored many experimental types, including the Campini prototype (1940) that, although flawed by the lack of a gas turbine, was the world's second jet to fly.

Taliedo produced the Ca.100 basic trainer (1928) and the larger Ca.113 (1931), both also built under license in Bulgaria. In 1934–1939, the Ca.113 and its derivatives vied for the world altitude record, the Ca.161bis reaching 17,083 meters. From 1928, Taliedo also built a family of rugged high-wing monoplanes, including the Ca.101 (1929), Ca.111 (1932), and Ca.133 (1934), used with great success during the Ethiopian War.

Caproni Aeronautica Bergamasca (CAB), bought in 1929, produced designs by Cesare Pallavicino, including the Ca.309 colonial aircraft (1937) and Ca.313 light attack/advanced trainer (1939). Their success eventually led Pallavicino also to become technical director for Taliedo and Vizzola. In 1937, Caproni gained control of Reggiane, which introduced stressed-skin fighters with both Piaggio radials (RE.2000, 1939; RE 2002, 1940) and Daimler Benz inline engines (RE.2001, 1940; RE.2005, 1942).

By 1939, the Caproni group accounted for 28 percent of the Italian airframe workforce. In recognition of his contributions to aviation, Gianni Caproni was named count of Taliedo in 1940. Wartime production consisted mainly of various CAB types, in part exported to Germany, but considerations of industrial policy and engine availability prevented Reggiane and Vizzola from breaking into the fighter market. Among the many Caproni products were the CB midget submarines, used with some success in the Black Sea.

The postwar years were very bitter. Various executives were murdered by communists, and the Caproni brothers were forced into hiding; unions vetoed workforce cuts, destroying company finances. Unsupported by the government, Caproni diversified and before collapsing was able to complete the Ca.193 (1949) and F-5 jet trainer (1952). Caproni Vizzola, the last active branch, reentered the aviation field in 1962 with T-33 overhauls and progressed to build subassemblies for Aermacchi and Agusta. In 1968, it acquired Aviamilano and built its line of high-performance gliders that ultimately evolved into the C-22J light jet trainer (1980), the final Caproni aircraft to fly. The program was terminated by Agusta following its 1983 acquisition of Caproni Vizzola. Vigorously promoted by Maria Fede Caproni and her brother Giovanni, the company heritage is enshrined in the Caproni Museum, opened in Trento in 1992.

Gregory Alegi

See also

Caproni Aircraft (Early Years); Ethiopian War; Italian Aircraft Development; Regia Aeronautica (Pre–World War II); Regia Aeronautica (World War II)

References

Abate, Rosario, Gregory Alegi, and Giorgio Apostolo. *Aeroplani Caproni: Gianni Caproni and His Aircraft, 1910–1983.* Trento, Italy: Museo Caproni, 1992.

Alegi, Gregory. *Campini Caproni.* Turin, Italy: La Bancarella Aeronautica, 2000.

CASA Aircraft

One of the oldest aircraft manufacturers in the world, CASA was founded in 1932 by José Ortez Echague. The principal customer initially was the Spanish air force, and the major production runs were of license-built foreign designs. These included the Breguet 19, of which more than 400 were built, the ubiquitous Dornier Wal flying boat, and the Vickers Vildebeeste.

Aircraft of German design were licensed after the Spanish civil war, and, along with many trainers, the CASA factory turned out Junkers Ju 52/3s, Messerschmitt Bf 109 fighters, and Heinkel He 111 bombers, all under CASA designations. (Many of the Messerschmitts and Heinkels were used in the film *Battle of Britain,* and some of these subsequently became warbirds.)

CASA continued to build aircraft under license, including the Northrop F-5A/B, but also had notable success with aircraft of its own design, including a series of twin-engine transports that began with the CASA.201 Alcotan. Other successful indigenous designs included the C-101 Aviojet trainer, the C-212 Aviocar twin-turboprop transport, and the larger CASA CN.235 tactical transport.

Walter J. Boyne

References

Donald, David, gen. ed. *The Complete Encyclopedia of World Aircraft.* New York: Barnes and Noble, 1997.

Gunston, Bill. *World Encyclopedia of Aircraft Manufacturers.* Sparkford, UK: Patrick Stephens, 1993.

Casablanca Conference

January 1943 meeting of Allied leaders in Casablanca, Morocco, to discuss war strategy, plans, and resource allocation. They reaffirmed the Germany-first policy, which meant that U.S. heavy bombers would be concentrated in Europe rather than the Pacific. The Casablanca Conference also decided on an invasion of Sicily instead of a cross-channel attack in 1943; thus, U.S. air bases could be located on Germany's southern flank. More important, the Casablanca Conference saw Major General Ira C. Eaker, commander of the Eighth Air Force based in Britain, give a spirited defense of U.S. air doctrine that dictated daylight precision bombing operations. British Prime Minister Winston Churchill, initially skeptical and desirous of the U.S. bombers joining RAF Bomber Command in nighttime area attacks, relented after hearing Eaker's formulation of round-the-clock bombing of the German heartland.

On 21 January, the Combined Chiefs of Staff issued the Casablanca Directive. It stated that the ultimate objective of the Allied bomber offensive was "the progressive destruction and dislocation of the German military, industrial and economic system, and the undermining of the morale of the German people to a point where their capacity for armed resistance is fatally weakened." The targets to be struck, in order of priority, were specified as German submarine construction yards, aircraft industry, transportation, oil plants, and other industrial facilities.

Phillip S. Meilinger

See also

Eaker, Ira C.; POINTBLANK; Strategic Bombing

References

Craven, Frank Wesley, and James Lea Cate. *The Army Air Forces in World War II.* 7 vols. Chicago: University of Chicago Press, 1948–1958.

Foreign Relations of the United States: The Conferences at Washington, 1941–1942, and Casablanca, 1943. Washington, DC: U.S. Government Printing Office, 1968.

Webster, Charles, and Noble Frankland. *The Strategic Air Offensive Against Germany, 1939–1945.* 4 vols. London: HMSO, 1961.

Cassino, Battle of (November 1943–June 1944)

Between November 1943 and June 1944, Allied air operations supported ground operations in Italy and raised moral questions regarding culturally significant targets in northern Italy. As Allies forces advanced northward in Italy, they found their way blocked by Rapido River and the massif of Monte Cassino, topped by the famous Benedictine monastery of the same name. Several Allied attacks were repulsed with heavy casualties. The dominating position afforded by the monastery atop the mountain and its excellent position for observation for artillery fire prompted Allied commanders to ask that the monastery itself be bombed. After much argument and anguish, the decision was made, and on 15 February 1944 135 American heavy bombers and 87 medium bombers destroyed the 1,000-year-old monastery. The subsequent ground attack failed. Postwar investigation seems to indicate that the Germans were not using the monastery itself, although it was impossible for the Allies to know this at the time.

Even heavier attacks on Cassino town, by 16 Allied air groups, destroyed that village in March, but again the ground attack failed. Cassino eventually fell to the Polish II Corps in May only after a Free French attack had outflanked it to the southwest.

The decision to bomb Cassino provides the classic example of the air planners' quandary: judging the value of the destruction of a target versus the possible cultural (or in other cases economic) value of the target to society.

Frank E. Watson

See also
Italian Campaign

References

Hapgood, David, and D. Richardson. *Monte Cassino.* New York: Congdon and Weed, 1984

Caudron Aircraft (Early Years)

Founded by René and Gaston Caudron, one of the many pairs of brothers who seem to have gone into the aviation business in its early years. The Caudrons began their involvement in 1908 with a glider. They soon moved on and up to powered flight with a 25-hp tractor design.

Specializing in two-seater and multiseat types during World War I, the Caudrons equipped several of the early *escadrilles* (squadrons). The G 3 (G for "Gaston," the brother responsible for the design, later R models standing, of course, for "Rene") was a single-engine pusher powered by an Anzani radial. Its wings had the scalloped trailing edges common to the period. Directional control was achieved by a pair of rudders. The G 3 performed reconnaissance missions and dropped the occasional load of flechettes—light antipersonnel darts that looked like metal pencils with fins.

It was a G 3 equipped with floats that performed the first shipboard takeoff in French aviation history. The feat was accomplished from the deck of the *Foudre* on 8 May 1914 with René Caudron at the controls. The G 3 served until the end of the war as a trainer in French and U.S. flight schools.

The G 4 was a twin rotary-engine model that otherwise resembled its predecessor, the addition of the second power plant allowing a machine gun to be carried. The type was intended as an army reconnaissance aircraft and for artillery spotting duties but was also used on bombing missions and as a long-range fighter escort.

The most unusual Caudron, however, was the R 11. The R 11 was designed as a long-range escort for the Breguet 14 B2 bomber. It carried a crew of three and was powered by two Hispano Suiza or Renault engines. A total of 370 were built.

James Streckfuss

References

Davilla, James, and Arthur M. Soltan. *French Aircraft of the First World War.* Mountain View, CA: Flying Machines Press, 1997.

Caudron Aircraft (Post–World War I)

Caudron produced excellent trainers and sportplanes to the designs of Paul Deville after World War I. The Caudron C.270 "Luciole" was produced in large numbers, and many were requisitioned for use as liaison aircraft when World War II broke out.

Deville's Caudron C. 280 Phalene (Moth) corresponded in name and appearance to its contemporary, the de Havilland Puss Moth. A four-seat touring aircraft, it could achieve a top speed of 115 mph on its 145-hp Renault four-cylinder Bengali engine. About 240 Phalenes were built, a sizeable number for an aircraft of its type for the period.

Under the direction of a new designer, Marcel Riffard, Caudron created the C.440 Goeland, a twin-engine trainer/transport that could carry eight persons at 186 mph with its twin Renault engines. More than 1,700 of the aircraft were built, for it continued in production during the German occupation and was operated by the Luftwaffe.

The most exciting of the Caudron designs were the elegant racers that won the Coupe Deutsch de la Meurthe contests in the mid-1930s. These in turn led to a series of lightweight fighters by which France hoped to overcome the handicap of not having engines comparable to the German Daimler Benz series.

Primarily of wood construction, these sleek, low-wing fighters were powered by Renault engines of only 450 hp but could achieve a top speed of 300 mph. Only about 60 were built. Some of them went to Finland, and others were used to equip a Polish squadron fighting in France. After France's collapse, a few were used by the Vichy French air force, and 20 were seized by the Luftwaffe.

The Caudron firm continued to operate through 1946.

Walter J. Boyne

See also
Caudron Aircraft (Early Years)

References

Donald, David, gen. ed. *The Complete Encyclopedia of World Aircraft.* New York: Barnes and Noble, 1997.

Gunston, Bill. *World Encyclopedia of Aircraft Manufacturers.* Sparkford, UK: Patrick Stephens, 1993.

Cessna Aircraft

American aircraft manufacturing company. The Cessna Aircraft Company was formed in 1927 by pioneer aviator and aircraft designer Clyde V. Cessna, who taught himself to fly in 1911. In 1924, after several years of exhibition flying and some successful early aircraft designs, he teamed up with fellow pioneer designers and manufacturers Lloyd Stearman and Walter Beech to form the Travel Air Manufacturing Company.

In 1927, Cessna left Travel Air to form his own company. After he achieved several commercially successful designs, the effects of the Great Depression caused sales to decline and forced Cessna to close down his company. Soon afterward, when a close friend was killed flying a custom-built air racer Cessna had designed and built, Clyde Cessna seemed to lose his enthusiasm for aviation and decided to retire permanently from the aircraft manufacturing business.

In 1934, Cessna's nephews, Dwane and Dwight Wallace, joined fellow engineer Jerry Gerteis in an attempt to revive the company. Their highly successful C-34, a clean, cantilever-wing single-engine monoplane, quickly breathed new life into the struggling aircraft company. Before long, Cessna Aircraft gained even greater success with the manufacture of the twin-engine T-50. More than 5,000 of these aircraft were sold during World War II to the U.S. and Canadian governments as advanced bomber-trainers.

After the war, Cessna Aircraft engineers wisely concentrated on the design and manufacture of small, inexpensive aircraft intended for civilian use. Numerous successful tail-wheel designs, featuring side-by-side seating, rolled out of Cessna's Wichita factory, including such classics as the Models 120, 140, and 170 and radial-engine 190 and 195. In 1954, the twin-engine 310 with tricycle gear was introduced, soon followed by the single-engine four-place tricycle-geared 172, which became one of the best-selling commercial aircraft of all time. Another outstanding aircraft developed during this period was the extremely popular Cessna 150, undoubtedly the most widely used trainer of the 1960s and 1970s.

Cessna also somehow managed to capitalize on the considerably diminished post–World War II military market. Among its most successful military aircraft were the L-19/O1E Bird Dog, the T-37 Tweety Bird (Cessna's first jet aircraft), the A-37 Dragonfly, and the O-2A/B military version of the Cessna Skymaster.

By the mid-1980s, Cessna's sales and profits began to decline, attributed in large part to the general increase in liability lawsuits. This raised insurance premiums to a point where small aircraft could no longer be manufactured and sold at affordable rates. Consequently, Cessna stopped production of piston-engine aircraft in 1986 and, that same year, announced its acquisition by General Dynamics. Meanwhile, Cessna's manufacture of larger utility turboprop and jet aircraft, particularly the Citation business jet, continued to keep the company alive and well. In 1992, General Dynamics sold Cessna to Textron, Inc., under whose auspices Cessna continues to operate as a separate entity.

After more than 70 years, Cessna Aircraft has built more aircraft than any other company in the world. As it progresses into the twenty-first century, Cessna—a name that has become synonymous with general aviation—continues as an industry leader.

Steven A. Ruffin

References

Phillips, Edward H. *Cessna: A Master's Expression.* Eagan, MN: Flying Books, 1985.

Rodengen, Jeffrey L. *The Legend of Cessna.* Fort Lauderdale, FL: Write Stuff Enterprises, 1998.

Chadwick, Roy (1893–1947)

British aeronautical engineer. Born on 30 April 1893 in Farnworth, Lancashire, Chadwick studied engineering at Manchester College of Technology before joining Alliott Verdon Roe as designer for A. V. Roe and Company in 1911. He worked closely with Roe on the firm's early aircraft, culminating in the very successful Avro 504, which after front-line service as a bomber became Great Britain's standard basic trainer from 1916 until 1932.

After World War I, Chadwick, as Avro's chief designer, developed light aircraft, including the record-breaking Avian; military types, most notably the Tutor basic trainer; and a series of successful airliners, initially based upon Fokker tri-motors, that led to the Avro 652 and its military derivative, the Anson.

In 1937, Chadwick, who had experimented with structures for large all-metal aircraft for some years, designed the Manchester. This large, fast, heavily armed aircraft, capable of transporting a very substantial bombload over long ranges, entered production in 1939 and went into service the following year. It was not entirely successful because of deficiencies in its two Rolls-Royce Vulture engines. Chadwick proposed replacing these with four Merlins on a slightly extended wing. The result was the Lancaster, the most important and successful British heavy bomber of World War II; its final derivative, the maritime reconnaissance Shackleton, remained in front-line service into the 1980s.

Chadwick's final design was the Tudor, an interim pressurized transatlantic airliner. He died in the crash of a Tudor on a test flight on 23 August 1947.

Paul E. Fontenoy

See also
Avro 504; Avro Aircraft; Avro Lancaster

References
Jackson, A. J. *Avro Aircraft Since 1908.* London: Putnam, 1965.

Chamberlain, Neville (1869–1940)

Son of nineteenth-century British politician Joseph Chamberlain. Neville became mayor of Birmingham in 1915 and went on to serve as a member of Parliament (1918–1940), chancellor of the exchequer (1931–1937), and prime minister (1937–1940). He was the chief architect of Britain's policy of appeasement toward Germany's Nazi government and signed the notorious Munich Agreement in 1938, calling it "peace in our time."

Throughout the 1930s he resisted rearming on both financial and philosophical grounds and became bitter enemies with Winston Churchill, who urged support for the Royal Air Force. Only after Hitler took over the rest of Czechoslovakia did Chamberlain reluctantly drop his appeasement policy and actively support rearmament.

He was forced into declaring war when Hitler invaded Poland in September 1939 and had to call Churchill back into the government as First Lord of the Admiralty. After military debacles in Norway, Chamberlain resigned in May 1940 after failing to gain all-party support for a national government, paving the way for Churchill to take over.

Christopher H. Sterling

See also
Baldwin, Stanley; Churchill, Winston; Ten-Year Rule

References
Dilks, David. *Neville Chamberlain.* 2 vols. Cambridge, UK: Cambridge University Press, 1984.
Fuchser, Larry William. *Neville Chamberlain and Appeasement: A Study in the Politics of History.* New York: Norton, 1982.
Ruggiero, John. *Neville Chamberlain and British Rearmament: Pride, Prejudice, and Politics.* Westport, CT: Greenwood Press, 1999.

Channel Dash

The successful transit of the English Channel by the German capital ships *Scharnhorst, Gneisenau,* and *Prinz Eugen* from Brest, France, to Germany in February 1942. The operation was code-named CERBERUS by the Germans and was personally ordered by Adolf Hitler, who believed the ships were needed to protect Norway. Though they had long anticipated such a move, the British were caught by surprise and made only disjointed and unsuccessful air and naval efforts to stop the transit, hampered by German jamming and their own command failures. The British were embarrassed by their failure, but actually they were the winners. There was no planned invasion of Norway, and none of the German ships would again threaten British commerce in the Atlantic.

Grant Weller

See also
Atlantic, Battle of the; Fairey Aircraft; Royal Flying Corps/Royal Naval Air Service/Royal Air Force

References
Taylor, Theodore. *Battle in the English Channel.* New York: Avon, 1983.

Chateau Thierry, Battle of (1918)

Marked the real debut of the U.S. Air Service. Although the first American aircraft squadrons had operated in the relatively quiet Toul Sector since April 1918, and the 2d Company of the Balloon Section had been continually at the front since February, it was at Chateau Thierry that the 1st Pursuit Group and the I Corps Observation Group encountered heavy German opposition. It was also in this battle that units began to operate in a coordinated fashion rather than as independent units under close Allied supervision. For the first time also the squadrons were under an American commander, Colonel William Mitchell, who had tactical command of the observation units and administrative command of the pursuit group.

German forces at the battle included the famous Richthofen Flying Circus (Jagdgeschwader I). Although still formidable and more than capable of giving the neophyte Americans a hard time, the Flying Circus had suffered since Baron Manfred von Richthofen's loss in April and was by this time clearly past its prime. Lothar von Richthofen (the Baron's younger brother) observed during this period that he and Erich Lowenhardt were the about the only experienced pilots still remaining.

The American units acquitted themselves well and went on to greater achievements at Saint Mihiel and the Meuse Argonne.

James Streckfuss

References
Richthofen, Lothar von, and Janice Hayzlett, trans. "My First Time at the Front." *Over The Front* 14, 3 (1999): 231–241.
Thayer, Lucien M. *America's First Eagles: The Official History of the*

U.S. Air Service, A.E.F. (1917–1918). Mesa, AZ: Champlin Fighter Museum Press, 1983.

Chennault, Claire L. (1890–1958)

Major general in the U.S. military and leader of the famed Flying Tigers; he was a controversial Allied air commander in China during World War II. Chennault was born on 6 September 1890 in Commerce, Texas. He became a pilot in 1919 and specialized in fighter tactics. He retired from the U.S. Army in 1937 because of increasing deafness.

Following the 1937 Japanese invasion of China, Colonel Chennault became air adviser to General Chiang Kai-shek, accepting an offer to train fighter pilots for the Chinese air force. He returned to the United States in early 1941 to recruit American pilots to fly for the Chinese (which was done with the U.S. government's permission). Chennault formed the American Volunteer Group (Flying Tigers), which began flying against the Japanese on 20 December 1941 when their P-40B Tomahawks inflicted heavy damage on Japanese bombers attempting to attack Kunming. The Flying Tigers flew supplies, provided air cover for the Burma Road, succeeded in protecting the Chinese capital of Chunking, and fought the Japanese in the skies over southwestern China. Using surprise, mobility, precision flying, and unorthodox tactics, Chennault's pilots downed an estimated 286 Japanese aircraft while losing eight American pilots killed in action. Four other pilots were listed as missing, and three men were killed on the ground.

In April 1942, Chennault was recalled to active U.S. service, promoted to brigadier general, and given command of U.S. Army Air Forces units in China. These were consolidated as the Fourteenth Air Force in March 1943 under Chennault's command.

Major General Chennault resigned his command on 6 July 1945. He died in New Orleans on 27 July 1958.

James H. Willbanks

See also

American Volunteer Group; Curtiss P-40 "Warhawk"

References

Chennault, Claire L. *Way of a Fighter.* New York: G. P. Putnam's Sons, 1993.

O'Diear, James. *Touching the Clouds: The General Claire Chennault Story.* New York: Alexander Books, 1995.

Claire Chennault will never be forgotten for his role as the founder of the American Volunteer Group, the famous Flying Tigers of World War II. (U.S. Air Force)

Cheshire, Geoffrey Leonard (1917–1992)

One of the most decorated British bomber pilots during World War II; one of only seven Victoria Cross winners to survive that conflict. After the war he founded what is now one of the world's largest providers of charity homes for the elderly.

Cheshire was a poor student at Oxford University before the war—far more interested in parties and pranks than studying. He took RAF flight training and flew the first of his 101 wartime missions just six days after the Dunkirk evacuation in June 1940. He was the first junior officer to win the Distinguished Service Order after continuing a bombing attack on the Cologne railyards despite damage to his Whitley of No. 102 Squadron. He became the youngest group captain in RAF history at age 24 and moved on to fly Halifax bombers with No. 35 Squadron, authoring a well-received book in 1943. He was a pathfinder pilot with the 617th Squadron (the famed Dam Busters) after 1943. After his one-hundredth mission, he was awarded the Victoria Cross. His next and last mission was as one of two British observers at Nagasaki, where he witnessed the dropping of the second atomic bomb in August 1945.

His postwar career took a very different turn when he

was unable to find a suitable home for a dying older friend in 1948 and thus took the man into his own home. Others soon followed, and in 1948 Cheshire founded what became the Leonard Cheshire chain of charity homes for the ill and dying. There are now more than 250 of these in some 50 countries (the first outside of Britain was founded in 1955 in India).

Christopher H. Sterling

References

Braddon, Russell. *New Wings For a Warrior: The Story of Group Captain Leonard Cheshire.* New York: Rinehart, 1954.

Cheshire, Leonard. *Bomber Pilot: A Squadron Leader's Chronicle of Bombing Offensives 1939–1942.* London: Hutchinson, 1943.

Chinese Air Force and U.S. Aid

The Chinese Revolution of 1911 failed to establish a democratic republic, and China fragmented into warlord cliques that competed to control the Peking (Beijing) government and to maintain their independent satrapies during the early 1920s. Peking's use of airplanes to bomb targets during the Bailing Rebellion in July 1914 prompted several warlords to acquire aircraft and trained pilots. The greatest of these was Marshal Chang Tso-lin (Zhang Zuolin), the warlord of Dongbei (Manchuria). Clashes between the northern and central warlord factions in 1923–1924 involved as many as 70 planes. By 1925, the air force command of Marshal Chang consisted of five squadrons, staffed with foreign instructors and technicians, and 100 airplanes by Handley Page, Vickers, Curtiss, Vought, Ford, Junker, and Breguet.

In south China, Dr. Sun Yat-sen founded his second revolutionary government in Canton, Kwangtung Province, in 1917. In 1922, Yang Sen-yi, accompanied by two Americans, returned to Canton from the United States with hundreds of cases of aviation equipment and four Curtiss JN-series aircraft. An airplane shop was established, and a trainer designed by an American was manufactured with an American engine built at that shop—the first plane built in China. The Aviation Bureau was established in 1922, and in 1924 the Aviation School began. Under Sun's United Front, Soviet aviators taught Chinese cadets and flew alongside Chinese pilots during the Northern Expedition, led by Chiang Kai-shek in 1926 to defeat the warlords and unify China. Nationalist aircraft reconnoitered enemy defenses and supported attacking infantry troops. By the end of the 1920s, Chinese military leaders realized the importance of airpower.

During World War I, the powers sold arms to the Peking government. After 1917, fighting warlord factions resulted in such vast amounts of arms flowing into China that America urged the Western powers to halt arms sales to reduce the conflict. The powers could not agree on what constituted "military aircraft and accessories." The French thought commercial aircraft should be exempt; the U.S. Department of State sought to ban all planes, but in September 1920 the department allowed airplanes that were built strictly for commercial use. In January 1922, the U.S. Congress and President Warren G. Harding prohibited the exportation of arms and munitions of war to China, and in May the DOS again proclaimed that all airplanes were within the prohibition of embargo.

The Curtiss Company's sale of 12 planes to the Great China Airway Company created an outcry from the United Kingdom and Japan, which had forbid aircraft sales. The powers agreed that only commercial aircraft could be sold to China under the embargo. Despite the ban, arms and munitions, including airplanes, flowed into China because profits were enormous, thereby thwarting Nanking's attempts to unify the country.

In the 1920s, France and Great Britain sold aircraft to China, prompting U.S. manufacturers to complain. When the United States extended diplomatic recognition in 1928 to Chiang Kai-shek's Republic of China (ROC) government at Nanking, American manufacturers began to seek aircraft sales. The first modern American plane delivered to China since 1922, a Ryan "Brougham," similar to Charles Lindbergh's plane, was delivered in October 1928 to General Chang Wei-chiang (Zhang Weiqiang), director of the Canton Aviation Bureau, who took it on a flying tour that stirred great interest in American aircraft.

In 1929, a consortium of Americans created the Aviation Exploration Corporation, which signed an air-mail contract. Shortly afterward, the China Aircraft Company, representing Curtiss-Wright interests, joined other vendors to sell commercial aircraft in China. In April the consul at Canton reported that recently purchased planes had been fitted with machine guns, and other officials argued that if the United States did not sell the planes the Chinese would obtain them from other countries.

In March 1929, Nanking created the National Aviation Administration and in April adopted the designation Chinese Air Force (CAF). A national aviation conference in 1931 resolved to expand the air force and establish aviation schools and factories, and China turned to the United States for assistance. In August 1929, a reorganized CAF announced its intent to purchase 62 airplanes worth $1.25 million. The State Department approved 12 Chance-Vought Corsairs armed with machine guns and bomb racks, but it would not authorize armament. China threatened to buy British aircraft, and President Herbert Hoover intervened to ship the Chance-Vought aircraft, valued at almost $1 million. In April 1930, China purchased another 20 Corsairs with armament, bringing the total to 32 Chance-Vought planes in six months.

A number of Americans aided Chinese aviation development. Robert M. Short washed out of flight school and, after learning to fly by taking private lessons, became a second lieutenant in the Air Corps Reserve. He went to Shanghai in 1931 as a Boeing aircraft salesman. Short was hired as an instructor to oversee Chinese flight training and helped create a pursuit squadron. On several occasions he engaged Japanese planes and on 22 February was attacked by Japanese planes and became the first foreign pilot to die for China in Sino-Japanese hostilities.

Nanking bought German Junkers planes, but Chinese pilots feared them and preferred American planes for their quality and ruggedness. In February 1931, Chiang sent four air officers to the United States to tour aircraft factories and investigate aircraft purchases. That June, Nanking ordered 20 more Douglas observation planes, bringing the total to 43 U.S. military planes for the year. The 1931 CAF inventory showed eight squadrons of serviceable aircraft: 30 Douglas, 32 Corsairs, five Junkers, and 15 other types. Between 1931 and 1935, the Nationalist air force helped to crush the Chinese Communist Party (CCP). Following the Japanese takeover of Manchuria, the CAF avoided combat for fear that the Japanese would bomb Nanking. In February 1932, the Nanking government, reinforced with 30 planes from Canton, engaged Japanese air units over Shanghai—China's first aerial battle with a foreign power. On 28 February, superior Japanese forces attacked the Hangzhou air base near Shanghai. The CAF withdrew from Shanghai, as it did not want to risk losing more aircraft.

With unofficial American assistance, China aviation developed greatly from 1932 to 1936. China sought airpower to compensate for weak ground forces, tenuous loyalty of several warlords, and lack of training resources—a decision that was reinforced by the strength of Japan's airpower. Nanking diverted $11 million intended for the navy to the air force and announced a five-year program (1932–1936) to establish advanced aviation schools for pilots and mechanics, build the air force to 27 squadrons, and establish three aircraft factories and additional repair shops.

An observer of the Shanghai air battle of 1932, Captain George C. Westervelt, a leading U.S. naval aviator in World War I, wrote to T. V. Soong that if China had a larger air force the Japanese occupation of Shanghai could have been prevented. Westervelt suggested that China secure a high-ranking officer to advise on aeronautical matters.

China asked the United States to send an air mission to China. Colonel John Jouett, formerly in charge of U.S. Army Air Corps training, assembled flight instructors and a small staff of mechanics in 1932 to train military pilots for the CAF.

The Chinese cadets followed a program based on the sequence used by the USAAC: four months each of primary, basic, and advanced training. The program was a success—335 qualified cadets graduated under Jouett. By 1937, the graduates of the 1932 class were captains and squadron leaders. Nanking asked Jouett to reorganize the Nationalist Air Corps, and Jouett was given authority over all foreign aviation personnel in China.

The Jouett mission also aided American military aircraft sales to China. The five-year aviation program called for expenditures of more than $32 million. For 1933–1934, $2.333 million was appropriated for aircraft purchases. Major James H. Doolittle, the famous racing and stunt pilot, demonstrated the Curtiss P-40 Hawk in China, which resulted in an order for 15 Hawk pursuits. In 1933, China imported 90 percent of its planes from the United States—in the amount of $5.634 million. By 1934, China purchased 215 American planes: Northrop bombers, Douglas aircraft basic trainers, observation planes, Dolphin flying boats, a DC-2 transport, a Curtiss Condor transport bomber, Boeing pursuit planes, and Corsair observation/light bombers.

Italy emerged as a rival to the United States in training the Chinese after 1933, but in general the Chinese preferred American methods and aircraft. General Chou Chih-jou (Zhou Zirou), commander of the CAF, asked Roy Holbrook, an American adviser with the Central Trust of China, to help obtain American former military pilots as replacements. Holbrook wrote to his friend, Captain Claire L. Chennault of the USAAC, seeking recommendations for pilots.

In August 1936, a contingent of Americans whom Chennault recommended arrived and assumed direction of the assembly and repair departments at Hangzhou. Despite the efforts of the Nanking government, the political unity of China was tenuous during these years. In addition to the communist insurrection, Nanking had to deal with several "allied" warlord defections. After suppressing Canton's "independence" in 1936, the Nanking government assimilated Canton's air force and aviation school, where American instructors continued to teach. By December 1936, the Nationalist government had nearly consolidated its control over China's factions (except the CCP). All provincial air arms were under the control of the CAF, which had a total of 645 aircraft in 12 tactical squadrons, several modern aircraft factories and aviation schools, as well as 262 useable airports.

Japan denounced U.S. aviation activity in China and criticized the construction of air bases on China's coast opposite Taiwan (a Japanese colony taken from China in 1895) and of the aircraft factory at Hangzhou. The attempted kidnapping of Chiang Kai-shek in December 1936 led to talks in 1937 between communists and Nationalists that hinted at collaboration against Japan. This threat to Japan's economic ambitions in China prompted the so-called Marco Polo Bridge Incident, the pretext for Japan's attack on China in July 1937—the start of the Sino-Japanese War.

In July 1937, the CAF comprised 700 planes, approximately 440 of U.S. manufacture, and most CAF group commanders had trained under Americans. Japan had about 1,530 army and navy aircraft and deployed about 400 in the Chinese theater. After hostilities erupted, Chinese aircraft attacked Japanese ships in Shanghai Harbor, and there was intense fighting over Shanghai and Nanking. In the last half of 1937, the American-trained pilots of the CAF strongly resisted Japan; in more than 50 skirmishes they shot down or destroyed about 150 Japanese planes. By December the CAF had lost a reported 131 planes—most of its combat aircraft—without acquiring replacements to match Japan's.

After the Sino-Japanese War began, the United States continued to export aircraft and war materials to both China and Japan. U.S. willingness to sell modern aircraft to China led Tokyo in August 1937 to blockade Chinese ships in most Chinese coastal waters, with assurance that "peaceful commerce" carried by third parties would be respected. Japan's blockade was challenged by U.S. Secretary of State Cordell Hull, who noted that neither country had declared a state of war and that only belligerents could impose a blockade effecting third-party nations.

President Franklin D. Roosevelt, sympathetic to China, sought to avoid a clash with Japan, and on 18 September 1937 Washington forbid U.S. government ships from transporting arms to China or Japan and warned other U.S.-registered vessels of the risks in such trade. Roosevelt allowed the Chinese to purchase arms in the United States with delivery effected via Hong Kong or Vietnam.

American policy thus weakened the CAF. Between 1 July 1937 and October 1940, the United States exported only 279 aircraft to China. The need for aircraft and aviation personnel—especially trained military pilots—led China to accept a Soviet offer of help, and from November 1937 to July 1940 the Soviet Union sold 885 aircraft including about 200 SB-type bombers. Four Soviet *eskadrilii* (squadrons), about 250 pilots, flew Polikarpov I-15bis and I-16 fighters with Chinese units and out of northern bases in China. When France fell in June 1940, the Soviet Union withdrew from China to prepare for its defense against Germany. This loss of aid came at the time of Japan's intensive bombing of Chungking (Zhongqing) in seeking to force China's surrender.

In August 1937, Claire L. Chennault arrived in China and accepted Madame Chiang's offer as adviser to the CAF, a position that placed him in command of China's aerial warfare with Japan. Chennault and several aviation business organizations recruited American and foreign pilots for the CAF. On 5 August, Tokyo protested that America aided in procuring more than 180 pilots and many aviation technicians for the CAF. In 1939, H. H. Kung, China's minister of finance, proposed sending American volunteer pilots similar to the Lafayette Escadrille of World War I. In the summer of 1940, China pressed America to increase aircraft sales. U.S. Secretary of the Navy Frank Knox recommended a $100 million loan and the sale of 500 airplanes to China. In October 1940, Chiang suggested that because the U.S. government could not send military pilots it might be permissible for China to recruit pilots in America. Chiang sent an air mission to the United States, composed of General P. T. Mow (Mao Pangzhu) of the CAF and Claire Chennault, to investigate the purchase of new fighter aircraft and recruitment of American pilots. Secretary of Treasury Henry Morgenthau discussed the possible deployment of U.S.-made bombers, to be used by China to bomb Japan, with T. V. Soong, P. T. Mow, and Chennault. Chiang then appealed directly to Roosevelt for 500 airplanes, including some B-17 bombers to bomb Japanese cities, just as Japanese gains in Southeast Asia increased Roosevelt's concern for China.

Dissention continued among Washington officials. Knox's request that American volunteer pilots be allowed to serve China was denied by Hull on the grounds of the earlier policy. Chinese and American officials proposed that American volunteer pilots go to China under passports that misstated their purpose for travel, and by December 1940 Washington agreed to provide China with many of the latest aircraft and authorized Chennault to solicit American military aviators, who would resign their commissions and volunteer to serve in the CAF. In the eyes of Japan, the United States had allied itself with China in a war against the empire.

Richard C. DeAngelis

References

Chennault, Claire L. *Way of a Fighter: The Memoirs of Claire Lee Chennault.* New York: Putnam's, 1949.

Pickler, Gordon K. "United States Aid to the Chinese Nationalist Air Force, 1931–1949." Ph.D. diss., Florida State University, 1971.

Xu, Guangqiu. "The Eagle and the Dragon's War Wings." Ph.D. diss., University of Maryland, 1993.

Chinese-American Composite Wing

In the six months following Japan's attack on China in July 1937, the best units of the Chinese Air Force (CAF) were destroyed. In 1938, Claire L. Chennault, a civilian adviser to the CAF, assembled an international squadron of pilots as flight leaders for Chinese units. The Japanese A6M2 Zero, introduced in 1940, was superior to CAF aircraft. In October 1940, Chennault visited the United States in search of planes and pilots; the result was the American Volunteer Group (AVG)—military pilots who resigned their commissions to fly for China—and 100 P-40 aircraft.

The AVG was disbanded on 4 July 1942 and replaced by the China Air Task Force (CATF) under then-commissioned Brigadier General Chennault. The CATF consisted of four P-40 squadrons of the 23d Fighter Group plus the B-25s of the 11th Bomb Group. Their performance convinced General Henry H. "Hap" Arnold, chief of the U.S. Army Air Corps, of the benefits of providing combat aircraft for Chinese pilots.

The Chinese-American Composite Wing (CACW) was conceived by Chennault when the U.S. Fourteenth Air Force was formed in March 1943. As Chinese pilots lacked training and confidence to engage the enemy, the plan was to have an American commander, assisted by a staff of Chinese officers, head a special unit composed of Chinese and American pilots and crews. CACW plans called for a four squadrons of fighters (80 planes) and four squadrons of bombers (40 planes), all units of the CAF, to be under Chennault's command.

The 1st Bomb Group and the 3d Fighter Group of the CAF were formed on 31 July 1943, after American pilots arrived at Malir, India. One hundred Chinese cadets returned from training in the United States at Luke Air Advanced School to fly for the CACW. Training began at Malir using old AVG P-40s and B-25s that had been used in China. The Chinese and American officers had segregated facilities, and each maintained separate quarters and mess from enlisted personnel. The CACW was activated on 1 October 1943, shortly after 24 new P-40Ns and 12 B-25s were deployed to China; three additional squadrons of the CACW trained at Malir.

In November 1943, the 2d Bomb Squadron began combat operations; a Thanksgiving Day raid on Japan's largest air base in Formosa (Taiwan) shot down 14 Japanese planes and destroyed more than 50 without loss of any CACW planes. CACW pressure on Japanese forces in eastern China prompted Japan's Operation ICHI-GO to capture Chennault's eastern China airfields employed for B-29 bombing raids on Japan after June 1944. By late December 1944, as CACW pilots began the transition to the longer-range P-51C Mustangs, the CACW had lost 20 fighters to Japanese pilots and 35 fighters and eight bombers to enemy ground fire; no bombers were lost to Japanese interceptors, a tribute to the B-25 crews and the fighter escorts.

The CACW unofficial combat record included 190 Japanese aircraft destroyed in the air, 301 on the ground; more than 2,500 vehicles were damaged or destroyed; many bridges, railroads, and enemy facilities and troops were destroyed; and several hundred thousand tons of shipping was sunk. The CACW produced eight air aces, including three Chinese aces. Chennault's experiment yielded substantial results before it was disbanded on 19 September 1945.

Richard C. DeAngelis

References

Chennault, Claire L. *Way of a Fighter: The Memoirs of Claire Lee Chennault.* New York: Putnam, 1949.

Molesworth, Carl, and S. Mosely. *Wing to Wing: Air Combat in China, 1943–1945.* New York: Orion Books, 1990.

Chinese Communist Air Force (People's Liberation Army Air Force [PLAAF])

Despite the end of the Cold War, even historical information about airpower in the People's Republic of China remains sparse and contradictory. Although the PLAAF traces its origins to 1924, when several individuals were trained at Whampoa and later received minimal training from the Soviet Union, there were no aircraft to speak of. Upon the 1945 defeat of the Japanese in World War II, the PLAAF was established, using captured Japanese aircraft and Japanese pilots as instructors. However, only about 200 pilots were trained, there was little in the way of structure, and there is no information about use of these aircraft during the civil war between communist and Nationalist forces.

Genuine organization began in July 1949 using 159 aircraft of 21 types abandoned by the Nationalists. The first commander was Liu Yalou with Commissar Xiao Hua, both men being chosen from the ground forces and signifying a strict subordination to the army that continues today. A Soviet mission to China in 1950 marked the start of massive assistance. Initially, this involved supplying Soviet units (which had fought air combat over Shanghai in April 1940 while wearing Chinese markings), followed by the dispatch of more than a dozen air divisions to provide interim air security and train the Chinese, who handed over their aircraft upon departure.

By mid-1951, the PLAAF had 1,050 aircraft in 17 divisions, including 445 modern MiG-15s. By the end of 1954, the Soviet Union had provided 3,000 combat aircraft, including jet and propeller fighters, propeller-driven bombers and attack aircraft, and at least 100 Il-28 jet bombers. These were organized into 28 air divisions comprising 70 regiments. A dozen academies and schools trained at least 6,000 pilots and many more support and maintenance staff.

China's first air operation came in January 1950 during the occupation of Tibet, when 12 C-47 and C-46 transports dropped supplies to the advancing infantry. This unit received Russian aircraft and was expanded into the 13th Transport Air Division, remaining active in Tibet through the end of 1952, flying 1,282 sorties. Later during 1953, the PLAAF also used Tu-2 bombers and La-9 fighters against "bandit" resistance in Sichaun and Gansu Provinces.

Contrary to widespread belief, Soviet pilots, not Chinese, flew the first MiGs to intervene in the Korean War at the end of 1950 and flew the great majority of sorties throughout the war. The first Chinese air regiment entered combat only in January 1951, attached to the Soviet 50 IAD (Fighter Aviation) and flew for only a few weeks before being relieved. In December 1951, the PLAAF finally committed the 1st Unified Air Army, with a strength of three fighter air divisions, commanded by Liu Zhen. This organization controlled all PLAAF assets committed to Korea, swelling to seven air divisions, including seldom-used propeller-driven fighters, bombers, and attack aircraft, as well as the units of the newly recreated North Korean Air Force. The Soviet pilots considered their Chinese comrades brave but poorly trained and completely unsuited for jet combat.

By July 1953, the 1st OVA (Unified Air Arm) flew 22,300 sorties (versus 63,229 for the Soviets) and fought 366 air combats, claiming 271 air victories with the loss of 231 of their own aircraft and 126 pilots. Eight Chinese pilots are known to have been credited with five or more air victories; their top ace was Deng Wang, with 10 victories.

Korean operations had barely ceased when the PLAAF resumed action against the Nationalist Chinese, evidence that they may not have been so badly punished in Korea as the West believed. During the successful Yijiangshan Campaign to seize Nationalist-held coastal islands, from 1 November 1954 to 18 January 1955 the PLAAF flew 288 sorties against Dachen and other islands, losing 19 aircraft to antiaircraft fire. The next combat went differently when the People's Liberation Army decided to capture the offshore islands of Quemoy and Mastu, precipitating the Taiwan Strait Crisis of July 1958.

The PLAAF was assigned the tasks of establishing local air superiority and of bombing the heavily fortified Nationalist islands; for the first time, they committed their new MiG-17F fighters. However, the Nationalists had also begun to receive modern F-86 fighters and had a significant advantage (they also had a monopoly of new heat-seeking Sidewinder air-to-air missles). The Sidewinder and the superior training of the Taiwanese pilots gave them a decisive edge. They claimed 32 MiGs shot down with a loss of four of their own, against a PLAAF claim of 14 Nationalist aircraft shot down with a loss of five MiGs. Though the truth is unknown, it is probably closer to the Nationalist version. The last air battle was fought on 14 October 1958.

During the 1960s, the PLAAF continued modernizing. From the mid-1950s, the Chinese had begun to build the MiG-17 fighter and Il-28 bomber aircraft under license, soon joined by the medium-range Tupolev Tu-16 bomber and other aircraft. From the early 1960s, they received the MiG-19, which they placed into mass production, including several original modifications. At the end of the century this aircraft, known to the Chinese as the J-6, remains the most numerous aircraft in service. They also received the first SA-2 SAMs from the Soviet Union, as well as helicopters and transports. Shortly before China's rupture with the Soviet Union, the PLAAF received a small number of MiG-21Fs, which were placed into production without a license—but only much later due to the dislocations of the Great Leap Forward and the Cultural Revolution, which disorganized the Chinese industrial base and military.

Also during the 1960s, the Chinese began a policy of providing military aid, particularly in aviation, to anti-Western Third World countries, a practice that continues. In 1962, China fought a serious border conflict in the Himalayas with India, but aviation was notably absent on both sides, probably due in part to lack of suitable bases, partly to lack of appropriate targets in the high mountains. During the Vietnam War, the PLAAF provided much training and assistance to the North Vietnamese, in return gaining experience, a chance to observe the developments in modern air warfare, and access to captured U.S. technology. According to the Vietnamese, the Chinese also stole modern Soviet equipment being transshipped to Vietnam, substituting their own older equipment. On a number of occasions, the PLAAF shot down U.S. aircraft that had strayed into Chinese airspace in the course of operations. Also, between 1962 and 1967 they shot down a number of Taiwanese U-2 and other reconnaissance aircraft over the Chinese mainland.

During the 1960s and 1970s, relations between China and the Soviet Union steadily worsened, reaching a nadir in 1969 with a major border engagement along the Ussuri River. Although there are no reports that either side used airpower (except for some transport helicopters by the Soviets), this period marked the end of Russian assistance. There are also murky hints in Russian sources that during the 1960s and 1970s the Soviets shot down a number of Chinese aircraft for violating Soviet airspace.

China also had a falling out with communist Vietnam, culminating in the so-called Punitive Invasion of 1979. The PLAAF provided major air support for this venture, and though details are lacking, it is generally known that even though Vietnamese air forces refrained from battle, their experienced and well-equipped antiaircraft defenses taught the PLAAF a sharp lesson.

The Chinese began to open to the West from the early 1980s, and the PLAAF began to benefit, receiving new Western technology, particularly modern helicopters from the United States, Britain, and France, new transport aircraft, and improved aviation missiles and avionics, the latter particularly from Israel. This has led China to develop expertise in modernizing obsolete systems, producing such aircraft as the J-7-III, essentially a 1960s-era MiG-21F airframe with 1980s-vintage engines, avionics, and weapons.

During the 1990s, alliances shifted once again, and the Chinese reestablished cordial relations with post-Soviet Russia, leading to new defense agreements and contracts. This includes the supply of 72 modern Su-27 and 30 Su-30MK jets, Il-76MD transports, and manufacturing licenses. There has been no real air combat, but the PLAAF and the PLAN-AF (naval air force) have been aggressive over the Taiwan Strait and the disputed Spratley and Paracel Islands in the South China Sea.

Information remains uncertain, but it seems that at the turn of the century the PLAAF consisted of about 45 air divisions of some 3,350 aircraft, the PLAN-AF 9 divisions and about 540 aircraft, including 180 J-8s, 570 J-7s (MiG-21), 2,100 J-6s (MiG-19), 450 Q-5s (MiG-19 derivative) fighters; 140 H-6 (Tu-16) and 260 H-5 (Il-28) bombers; and about 450 transports. Much of the equipment is obsolete, and the air transport and helicopter resources are inadequate. Chinese pilots are also believed to fly far fewer hours per year than is considered minimally acceptable in the West and in modern noncommunist Asian nations. Although Chinese airpower has taken remarkable strides, for the foreseeable future it will remain an unbalanced force, 40 years out of date but with gradual advancement in cutting-edge technology.

George M. Mellinger

See also

Fighter Air Corps; Ilyushin Aircraft; Korean War; Lavochkin Aircraft; Mao Tse Tung, and Airpower; Mikoyan-Guryevich Aircraft; Tupolev Aircraft; Yakovlev, Aleksandr S.

References

Allen, Kenneth W., Glenn Krumel, and Jonathan D. Pollack. *China's Air Force Enters the 21st Century.* Santa Monica, CA: RAND, 1995.
Shu Guang Zhang. *Mao's Military Romanticism: China and the Korean War, 1950–1953.* Lawrence: University Press of Kansas, 1995.

Chkalov, Valeri Pavlovich (1904–1938)

Soviet test pilot and aviation pioneer. V. P. Chkalov was born in the village of Vailevo (since renamed Chkalovsk) on 15 December 1904. Chkalov joined the Red Army as an aircraft mechanic in 1919 and, despite being underaged, completed the Yegorevsk Military-Theoretical School for Aviators in 1922 and was commissioned as a captain. He quickly demonstrated extraordinary skill in aerial acrobatics.

In 1929, after a minor flying accident, Chkalov was briefly imprisoned and cashiered from the air force. Nearly two years later he was hired as a test pilot by the air force's Scientific Research Institute. In 1936, he led a team of three in completing a nonstop flight from Moscow to Petropavlovsk (Kamchatka) to Udd Island (now Chkalov Island).

In 1937, the same crew, headed by Chkalov, flew nonstop from Moscow over the North Pole to Vancouver. These exploits made Chkalov a national hero, and he was immediately named a deputy to the Supreme Soviet of the USSR. The following year he was killed in an air crash while flying the prototype I-180 fighter. Although it was officially ruled an accident, many questions have been raised about his death. According to Georgi Baidukov, his copilot on the transpolar flight, it resulted from the Polikarpov Design Bureau's deliberately submitting a substandard aircraft for testing in order to meet a deadline. Family members allege that the aircraft he was flying was sabotaged on Stalin's order, because Chkalov had spoken up on behalf of victims of the Great Purges.

William B. Green

References

Abramov, Aleksey. *U kremlevskoy steny* (By the Kremlin Wall). Moscow: Izd. Politicheskoy literatury, 1980.
Baudukov, Georgiy F. *Chkalov.* Moscow: Izd. Molodaya gvardiya, 1977; translated as *Russian Lindbergh: The Life of Valery Chkalov.* Washington, DC: Smithsonian Institution Press, 1991.
Chkalova, Olga E., and Igor V. Chkalov. *Fotoal'bom V.P. Chkalov* (V.P. Chkalov: A Photographic Album). Moscow: Izd. Planeta, 1984.
Chkalova, Valeriya V. *Chkalov bez grifa* "sekretno" (Chkalov Declassified). Moscow: Poligraphresursy, 1999.

Churchill, Winston S. (1874–1965)

Britain's prime minister during World War II and a longtime student of airpower. To the despair of his wife and friends, Churchill actively sought his own pilot's license in the years leading up to World War I when serving as First Lord of the Admiralty, feeling he would better understand the growing naval concern with aviation if he himself could fly. He halted his efforts only shortly before he would have soloed, an action taken in the face of several fatal crashes by others. He returned briefly to flying in 1919 but gave it up for good after a crash that could easily have killed him.

But it was Churchill's actions while in various ministerial roles that demonstrated his interest; by the end of World War II, one authority concluded that he alone among the world's prime ministers had shown a real understanding of the meaning of air power. He promoted naval aviation and formed the Royal Naval Air Service just before World War I.

He even claimed to have invented the term "seaplane." From 1919 to 1920, he served as secretary of state for air (under Prime Minister David Lloyd George) while holding down the War Office. Upon taking that post, he stated that the Royal Air Force would remain independent (it had only become so the year before) and that "given superior thinking power and knowledge it must obtain the primary place in the general conception of war policy." He brought back Sir Hugh Trenchard as Chief of the Air Staff (he would remain for a decade), as both agreed military aviation needs should be paramount over civil transport concerns. He proved his point by supporting RAF supervision of British-occupied territories in the Middle East (in part to cut costs) and by supporting Trenchard's quest for a thriving air force equal to the army and navy.

During the 1930s, out of office, Churchill made his living by writing books and articles, some of the latter on aviation. Just a year before World War II began, he asked in a magazine piece whether airpower was decisive and concluded that the Spanish civil war demonstrated that Britain had to "acquire at the earliest possible moment an air force at least equal to that of any Power within striking distance of her shores." Out of power until after the war began, however, Churchill could only berate Parliament about the parlous state of British air defense in the face of the growing German air threat.

On taking the prime ministership in May 1940, Churchill's energies were pulled in many directions. Nonetheless, he was always open to ideas and means for supporting the hard-pressed RAF. His famous speech at the time of the Battle of Britain—"never have so many owed so much to so few"—even today brings home his view of the RAF's central position in Britain's survival. But he did more than use words or wear his air commodore uniform or visit front-line air units. By appointing his longtime friend Lord Beaverbrook as minister of aircraft production, he revitalized the British air industry to manufacture even more fighters (the top priority) and bombers. He had to determine the priority between Coastal Command and Bomber Command, almost always deferring to the latter in an attempt to get at the heart of German wartime production ability. Churchill was unerring in his support of Fighter Command's Hugh Dowding and Bomber Command's Arthur Harris, even when both were under attack from rivals.

During Churchill's second term as prime minister (1951–1955), the Air Ministry expanded more rapidly among the three services; air was the means by which Britain would deliver its growing nuclear capability. But that policy had been set by the previous Labour administration and was merely continued under Churchill. In 1952, however, the Churchill government promoted development of jet bombers over a fighter force—a decision to depend more on deterrence rather than defense.

Winston Churchill will live in history as one of the great defenders of freedom, a staunch advocate of air warfare during Britain's most perilous moment.

Christopher H. Sterling

See also

Beaverbrook, Lord; Britain, Battle of; Dowding, Hugh C.T.; Harris, Arthur T.; Royal Flying Corps/Royal Naval Air Service/Royal Air Force; Spanish Civil War; Ten-Year Rule; Trenchard, Hugh

References

Churchill, Winston S. *"Bombs Don't Scare Us Now." Collier's* (17 June 1939).

Ferte, Sir Philip Joubert de al. "Churchill the Airman." In Charles Eade, ed. *Churchill by His Contemporaries.* New York: Simon and Schuster, 1954, pp. 127–140.

Gilbert, Martin, *Winston S. Churchill, Volume 4: The Stricken World, 1916–1922.* Boston: Houghton Mifflin, 1975.

Grey, C. G. "Winston Churchill and Air Power." *The Aeroplane* (8 June 1945).

Civil Air Patrol (CAP, in World War II)

Established on 1 December 1941 for U.S. civilian air defense. The CAP searched for lost aircraft, provided emergency radio communication, exposed youngsters to aviation, and provided disaster relief. It was open to citizens 18 and over of good moral character and proven loyalty. The first volunteers were competent in flying, radio, mechanics, office work, and guard duty.

From bases ranging from New Jersey to Florida, the CAP watched for U-boats and either bluffed them by diving or reported them to military aircraft. In early summer 1942, CAP planes began carrying bombs and depth charges. Planes of the CAP actually sank two submarines before the Navy began protecting the sea lanes in August 1943. Over 18 months, the CAP flew 24 million miles over water, spotted 173 subs, attacked 82 with bombs or depth charges, and reported 17 floating mines. It spotted 363 survivors of ship sinkings or aircraft wrecks and reported 91 ships in distress. Twenty-six CAP personnel lost their lives in coastal patrol. After 1943, search and rescue missions flew 24,000 hours and located 100 aircraft.

From October 1942, CAP tracked infiltrators from Mexico; its 4,720 missions reported 176 unidentified aircraft and 6,874 unusual activities. CAP also managed and maintained 215 airfields, serving as guards, mowing grass, patching potholes, and so on. Building 81 new airfields, CAP also lengthened runways, installed lights, and built hangars on 108 others. Other support included courier service, towing targets, and flying for searchlight practice.

By war's end, 135,000 people served in the CAP.

John Barnhill

References

Glines, Carroll V., and Gene Gurney. *Minutemen of the Air: The Valiant Exploits of the Civil Air Patrol in Peace and War.* New York: Random House, 1966.

Civil Air Patrol Headquarters Website. http://www.capnhq.gov.

Civil Aviation: Impact of Military Advances

Civil aviation has gained more from military advances than vice versa, due largely to the high cost of and government support for military priorities in wartime. The exigencies of war increase the pace of technical advances and aviation.

World War I saw great advances. The aircraft of 1914 were outclassed in every way by those flying in 1918. This was true in virtually all measures—speed, load-carrying capacity, range and effective ceiling, and especially in the reliability of engines and aircraft structures. The trend toward air-cooled rather than water-cooled engines and the increasing use of metal in aircraft structures were two important steps. So was the introduction of mass production of aircraft, which greatly increased efficiency and quality standards.

Most airliners (and thus airlines) developed after World War I with government support (except in the United States and Britain, where Minister of Aviation Winston Churchill felt companies should literally fly on their own). This led to several commercial operations in 1920 that had foundered by 1923. The British government then played a central role in starting and supporting Imperial Airways (1924–1940) to catch up with European airline expansion. U.S. reluctance to put government funds into air transport in the early 1920s meant that Europe led in airline innovation for much of the interwar period.

Yet mainland Europe took a different route, drawing from the wartime precedent of government support for military aviation. In France, Holland, and other European countries, government subsidies for fledgling air transport operations were usually assumed and forthcoming. Likewise, when the German Lufthansa firm developed out of several earlier airlines in 1926, it was substantially supported by the government, which owned more than a quarter of the airline.

Simultaneously, many early airliners were modified from military models because they were readily available, and it was soon evident that bombers and transports have parallel aims—to carry a heavy load as cheaply as possible over a long distance. In Britain, the first airliners used by Imperial's short-lived commercial predecessors were modified from D.H. 4 and D.H. 9 single-engine biplane bombers; the four-engine HPW 8 transport of 1920 was based on the Handley Page 0/400 bomber. Germany and France also used lightly modified single-engine military models, though the French were able to introduce a larger transport based on the Farman "Goliath" bomber.

Military flying was starved for funds between the wars, and U.S. military services undertook some spectacular endurance flights in an attempt to regain public support while testing their capabilities. The U.S. Navy's 1919 transatlantic flight with four NC flying boats was the first, though soon eclipsed by the British nonstop flight with a Vickers Vimy aircraft later the same year. In 1922, the U.S. Army created a 4,400-mile model airway covering 35 cities and used it for training and transport purposes. The army, which allowed some civil pilots to use the airway as well, included 12 weather stations in a pioneering attempt to strengthen the connection between accurate weather forecasting and flight safety. A year later, two Army fliers using a Fokker T-2 twin-engine monoplane flew nonstop in 27 hours from Long Island to San Diego, demonstrating that such air distances were possible even with the crude equipment of the time (of course, the only cargo carried was fuel). And in 1924, four U.S. Army Douglas World Cruisers took off from Seattle in an attempt to fly clear around the world; two of them were the first to accomplish the feat weeks later. All of these pioneered what would become commercial routes when aircraft and facilities were up to the task of scheduled routes for passengers.

World War II had even more dramatic effects on postwar civil aviation. Development of radar by Allied and Axis powers would eventually be of tremendous value to civil flying and military and civil air-traffic control. Jet propulsion was first applied during the war but was applied to pioneering airliners only four years after the war ended. Swept-wing design and engines mounted in pods beneath the wing were ideas drawn from Junkers wartime designs that would prove important to postwar U.S. jet bomber and then jet airliner design.

Military development or improvement of numerous airports, combined with development of efficient long-range landplanes (bombers, patrol craft, and transports) spelled the doom of flying boats for civil and military applications. Expensive to maintain and less efficient than landplanes, flying boats served through and after the war for naval patrol purposes but could not survive airline efficiency demands past the 1940s, with only minor exceptions. Regular transatlantic flying became commonplace thanks to ferrying flights of men and aircraft. Improved means of all-weather flying, long-range navigation, and instrumentation all contributed. So did pressurization, applied in an airliner (the Boeing 307 "Stratoliner") in 1940 but first widely used in high-altitude long-range bombers during World War II (indeed, the Model 307 itself had developed from Boeing's B-17 bomber).

Many immediate postwar airliners grew directly from military designs. British interim transports included the York and Lancastrian, both based on the Lancaster bomber (same engines, wing, undercarriage, and tail) and the Halton, based on the Halifax bomber. But they offered too little payload for the expense of running their military engines and were soon phased out. In the United States, the B-29 heavy bomber led directly to the C-97 military transport and Boeing 377 "Stratocruiser" airliner (all three shared engines, wing, undercarriage, and tail).

Military leadership in civil aviation development continued after 1945, pushed by fear and the arms race brought about by Cold War tensions. Unlike the period after World War I, when military spending all but disappeared in the United States for two decades, post-1945 military aviation spending (save for a brief drop 1945–1950) continued at high levels.

USAF development of jet bombers, especially the Boeing B-47, had a direct impact on later jetliner development in at least two ways. First, the engine layout developed by Boeing (drawn in considerable part from German prototype development late in World War II) was followed in the company's pioneering Dash 80 prototype for the 707 airliner series. Engines slung in pods below the wing had several advantages over other options (such as buried in the wing roots, as with Britain's pioneering Comet, or hung on the back, as with the French Caravelle) that were made clear in wind-tunnel tests and actual experience with the B-47 bomber fleet. When the B-47 was joined by the B-52, the Air Force needed an aerial refueling tanker faster than the four-piston-engine KC-97. In 1954, the Air Force ordered the KC-135 derivation from the basic 707 airframe, providing badly needed support to Boeing, which had financed the prototype on its own. Boeing soon obtained government permission to launch the 707 airliner using some of the same rigs in the government-owned Renton manufacturing facility.

Closer cooperation was evident elsewhere. The Soviet Union made a pattern of developing early jet airliners from existing bomber designs, thus saving time and expense in getting the civil versions into service. The Tu-16 twin-jet bomber (called "Badger" by NATO) became, with only marginal changes, the pioneering Tu-104 jetliner in 1955. Likewise, the huge turboprop Tu-95 long-range bomber (dubbed "Bear" by NATO) was the forebear of the Tu-114 long-range airliner. Both aircraft—and several later Soviet airliners—retained the overall bomber airframe and glazed nose windows originally intended for bombsighting.

Since its earliest days, military aviation has provided impetus to the development of airlines worldwide.

Christopher H. Sterling

See also

Civil Aviation: Impact on the Military

References

Jarrett, Philip, series ed. *Biplane to Monoplane: Aircraft Development, 1919–1939.* London: Putnam, 1997.

______. *Modern Air Transport: Worldwide Air Transport From 1945 to the Present.* London: Putnam, 2000.

Lofton, Laurence K. Jr. *Quest for Performance: The Evolution of Modern Aircraft.* Washington, DC: National Aeronautics and Space Administration, Government Printing Office, 1985.

Stroud, John. *Soviet Transport Aircraft Since 1945.* London: Putnam, 1968.

Civil Aviation: Impact on the Military

Although military advances generally guide those in civil aviation, there have been important exceptions. In Germany, the DELAG firm was formed in 1909 to provide passenger airship service but also provided training for military Zeppelin crews. But the most significant developments occurred during the 1919–1939 period, between the world wars. Aviation development, especially pure research, was driven more by commercial than military priorities during this time. Military budgets were small in many countries until the eve of World War II.

U.S. aeronautical research centered on the Department of Commerce's National Bureau of Standards and focused on improving engine reliability and aircraft instrumentation and, in the 1920s, developing an airborne radio direction finder for the War Department. The National Advisory Committee for Aeronautics, formed in 1915, focused on the continued shift to manufacture aircraft from metal rather than wood; away from biplane and more to monoplane structures; development of stressed-skin construction; devising retractable undercarriages; improving wing design; and refining controllable-pitch propellers. Results of this government work were soon applied by civil and military fliers alike.

Policy changes helped place civil aviation in the aviation vanguard. The Kelly Air Mail Act of 1925 shifted air mail from government to fledgling airlines that needed the business and revenue. (Indeed, when the Army briefly took back airmail flights in 1934, its terrible performance illustrated how civil aviation loomed over the military.) Then the presidentially appointed Morrow Board of 1925 led to passage of the Air Commerce Act of 1926, the first federal regulation of civil aviation and the source of funding for five-year development programs for struggling army and navy aviation programs.

Most of the important research during this era was accomplished with private support. Public attention was drawn to the annual Detroit Aviation Society/Ford Reliability Tours (held from 1925 to 1931, when the Depression brought them to a halt). Publicity and the chance for a prize led to concerted efforts to improve airplane reliability on all levels, and submissions came from Europe as well as the United States. The army often provided fliers to accompany the contestants on some legs. The participating airplanes were far more capable than most military models of the period.

The Daniel Guggenheim Fund for the Promotion of Aeronautics spent $2.8 million from 1926 to 1930 in a multifaceted program of immense importance to civil and military flying. Although focused at first on civil aviation needs, it turned in 1928 to more fundamental problems in aerodynamics. Its grants to eight universities improved aviation engineering education. Guggenheim's Model Air Line project allowed Western Air Express to purchase Fokker trimotors to use between Los Angeles and San Francisco. As with the Army model airway that preceded it by four years, this airway focused on the importance of an organized aviation weather service to regular air operations, whether civilian or military. With Army pilot James Doolittle doing the legwork, Guggenheim supported vital research into blind and instrument flying. The fund also supported an international safe-aircraft competition and helped to promote the image of aviation in national air tours by Richard E. Byrd (1926) and Charles Lindbergh (1927).

Racing was a focus of public interest and helped to improve airplane design during the interwar period. Various air races in the United States often featured military as well as civilian pilots. Internationally, the Schneider Cup Trophy air races of 1913–1931 (they were suspended during World War I) were a major spur to seaplane development, attracting both private and government-supported military entries. The annual competition prompted substantial improvement in engines, aerodynamics, and streamlining. The series was finally won definitively by the British with the graceful Supermarine racers designed by R. J. Mitchell, which were immediate predecessors of the Spitfire fighter.

In structure and streamlining, civil air transports outpaced military designs. The process began with the classic Junkers F.13 of 1919, perhaps the most widely used airliner in the 1920s. Of all-metal construction, the F.13 was a four-passenger monoplane in a biplane era. And unlike converted bombers, it was designed for passenger service from the start. More than 300 were built. Leadership then moved to the United States, with the pathbreaking work of William Stout and then the Ford Motor Company with its famous 1926 Tri-Motor, an all-metal aircraft with substantial load capabilities and steady flying characteristics. Nearly 200 were made before production ceased in 1932; there was even a bomber version, though it was not successful. The similar Junkers Ju 52/3m appeared the same year; thousands of copies of the German airliner were manufactured, half of them during World War II. Both of these aircraft emphasized reliability and strength over beauty.

The early 1930s saw a breakthrough when airliners' designs as well as airspeeds were far ahead of military aircraft. The value of streamlining was demonstrated with a number of handsome single-engine U.S. airliners built from 1927 through the 1930s. Northrop's Alpha (1930), Delta (1933), and Gamma (1932) aircraft represented one approach. The Lockheed single-engine airliners—the Vega, Sirius, Altair, and Orion series—were even better known and used by several airlines.

Boeing manufactured the first modern twin-engine airliner, the Model 247, in 1933. This plane was far ahead of its civilian rivals, let alone any military aircraft. Lockheed's twin-engine Electra series (the L-10 first flew in 1934) expanded the lead, figuring in important long-distance flying feats, including Amelia Earhart's and Howard Hughes's around-the-world flights. Refined L-14 (1937) and L-18 Lodestar (1938) models served in a variety of airline and then military roles in the 1940s.

Britain's Imperial Airways lagged with lumbering biplanes until the handsome S.23 C-class all-metal Empire flying boats of 1936, which opened many routes to British colonies in Africa and Asia. The design led directly to the wartime Sunderland naval patrol boat.

The ultimate airliner of the period—the Douglas DC-2/3 series—was an established standard around the world by 1941. At the same time, most military aircraft were aging biplanes. The developing DC-4 and Constellation four-engine airliners demonstrated that the military could rely on civil designs for military air transport. And so they did until after World War II, when purpose-built military transport designs became important.

British, French, and Dutch airlines pioneered service into and across Africa and Asia in the 1930s, developing needed airports, hot-and-high take-off procedures, means of navigation in regions with little infrastructure, and regular schedules for people, mail, and some freight over long distances. Their airliners, at first biplanes of marginal reliability but soon all-metal aircraft with vastly improved range and carrying capacity, paved the way for wartime military routes.

U.S., British, and German efforts to span the all-important Atlantic barrier likewise developed the expertise needed for wartime ferry flights and postwar airline use. U.S. and British efforts focused on long-range flying boats, with the inception of regular (and highly expensive) passenger flights in mid-1939. The 1937 Focke-Wulf Fw 200 Condor was the first four-engine landplane to fly the Atlantic (in 1938) and also tested a Lufthansa route to Tokyo. Only briefly in airline service, the handsome aircraft could fly better than 200 mph, faster and farther than most military planes of that time.

Likewise, Pan American's transpacific flights of the late 1930s helped pave the way for regular military transoceanic transport flights during the war. The ever-larger and more capable Sikorsky S.42 (1934), Martin 130 (1935), and Boeing 314 (1938) flying boats were far beyond anything operated by the U.S. and most foreign military services. Although none directly led to military models, the techniques and procedures used to fly them long distances were of immense wartime value.

Christopher H. Sterling

See also

Civil Aviation: Impact of Military Advances

References

Gray, George W. *Frontiers of Flight: The Story of NACA Research.* New York: Knopf, 1948.

Leary, William M., ed. *Aviation's Golden Age: Portraits from the 1920s and 1930s.* Iowa City: University of Iowa Press, 1989.

Miller, Ronald, and David Sawers. *The Technical Development of Modern Aviation.* New York: Praeger, 1970.

Civil War (U.S.) and Use of Balloons

The first use of airpower for military purposes in the United States occurred in the Civil War. Union and Confederate forces used balloons for a variety of purposes such as artillery spotting, observing troop movements, estimating enemy strength, and observing construction of fortifications.

The Union Army organized a balloon department led by civilians from August 1861 through July 1863. It had seven balloons under the control of Thaddeus Lowe and two under John LaMountain. Lowe and LaMountain were bitter rivals and never joined forces. Lowe employed notable aeronauts of the day such as John H. Steiner, Ebenezer Seaver Jr., James Allen, Ezra Allen, and John B. Starkweather; LaMountain operated as a solo aeronaut. Both balloon teams used military troops who were detailed from the closest corps to where the balloons were stationed. These troops supported balloon maintenance and operations. Approximately 30 men were used to operate each balloon. By the end of the war, more than 300 troops had been trained to support the balloons.

Lowe was an inventive genius. He developed a system of successful telegraph operations from his tethered balloons. He conceived and constructed the first specifically designed flat-top aircraft carrier, called the *G. W. Park Custis,* and at least twelve portable gas generators that were used in the field and on the *Park Custis.* Lowe would launch a tethered balloon from the carrier, which was originally a coal barge, and had it towed up and down the Potomac, James, and York Rivers, allowing observations of the enemy from a mobile platform.

Operationally, the Union balloons did not use hot air, but hydrogen or city utility gas. The balloons were deployed at a variety of strategic locations, ascending to heights of about 1,000 feet and tethered to the ground in order to make observations lasting many hours. More than 3,000 flights were made in this manner. Union balloons were used extensively around Washington, D.C., in the Peninsula Campaign right after Antietam, and at the Battles of Fredericksburg, Chancellorsville, and Island No. 10.

Although LaMountain would mostly make observations from a tethered balloon, he occasionally performed a number of sensational "free" (untethered) flights over Confederate positions, relying on oppositely directed wind currents at different layers of the atmosphere to bring his balloon back to the Union lines. LaMountain is also credited with the first tethered balloon observations from a moving steamer around Fortress Monroe, Virginia.

The Confederates would occasionally operate a few balloons but never established an infrastructure to support them. It is believed that they did not use professional balloonists but pressed into service novices such as John Randolph Bryan and Potter Alexander. Confederate ballooning was performed largely in response to the Union effort.

James L. Green

References

Haydon, F. Stansbury. *Military Ballooning During the Early Civil War.* Baltimore: Johns Hopkins University Press, 2000.

Civil Wars

A domestic conflict between military forces of the same state or political entity is known as a civil war. Airpower has played an important role in civil war, beginning in the nineteenth century. There have been roughly 40 intrastate, political, secessionist, or ethnic conflicts in which airpower was employed. Airpower, since its introduction into warfare, has emerged as an integral and decisive part of these conflicts and has been employed in diverse strategic, climatic, and terrain conditions. Additionally, the air dimension of civil wars stimulated or emphasized some significant changes in air technology, organization, strategy, and tactics.

In 1849, Austrian troops unsuccessfully experimented with the balloon bombing of the rebellious Venetians. Balloons were also used in 1862 during the U.S. Civil War, where Union and Confederate forces used balloons for a variety of purposes: artillery spotting, observing troop movements, estimating enemy strength, and observing construction of fortifications. During the war in France in 1871, the Commune of Paris tried to use balloons for reconnaissance and propaganda purposes.

In most civil wars during the first half of the twentieth century, government troops and foreign interventionist forces employed airpower for machine-gunning, bombing attacks, and reconnaissance.

In some important cases, domestic antagonists used aircraft for air-to-air combat (Russia in 1918–1920, China in the 1920s, Spain in 1936–1939). Civil wars also emphasized the critical importance of air dominance and developed sophisticated air operations. Examples of this include the use of railroads for massive transport of air units and strategic maneuver between the fronts; combined operations, including seaplane support to ground troops (Russia); air strikes on naval targets and the dissemination of propaganda by air (Russia, Spain); and interdiction of enemy supply lines (Spain).

The second half of the twentieth century witnessed large-scale employment of airpower in civil conflicts. These include China in 1945–1949; Congo/Katanga in 1960–1967; Ethiopia/Eritrea in 1961–1991; Iraq/Kurdistan since 1963; Rhodesia in 1965–1980; Nigeria/Biafra in 1967–1970; Angola and Mozambique in 1975–1991; and elsewhere.

The guerrilla nature of many civil wars made helicopters with light automatic weapons and grenades a useful tool for attacking rebel formations. The guerrillas in turn developed a new generation of antiaircraft weapons, especially surface-to-air missiles.

The historical and military experience of air operations in civil wars saw significant developments, including massive airlift of troops, weapons, and supplies (China); the first use of air-to-air guided weapons during the 1958 air battles between communist and Nationalist Chinese aircraft (Taiwan Strait); the introduction of mixed antiguerrilla fire forces with the extensive use of antipersonnel bombs (Rhodesia); the use of chemical weapons by government air forces (Iraq/Kurdistan; Laos since 1975); the rise of helicopter gunships to a dominant role in air operations (Angola, Mozambique, Sri Lanka, Nicaragua, and El Salvador); and the use of aircraft for large-scale refugee movements (Biafra).

Since the use of aircraft during the U.S. expeditions into Mexico in 1914–1916, foreign airpower interventions have been an important pattern of civil wars. There were many decisive and crucial air interventions by third parties in civil wars: the Italians, Germans, and Soviets in Spain in 1936–1939; the RAF in Greece in 1944–1949; the French in Chad in 1983–1984; the Turks in Cyprus in 1974; and India in Sri Lanka in 1987–1990.

Additionally, some interventions of the twentieth century demonstrated important operational and tactical decisions in the use of airpower. These include the first air operation in support of naval attack (U.S. flying boats for mine searching in Vera Cruz, Mexico, 1914); the first combined air-naval operation (the Allied seizure of Archangel, Russia, 1918); the first successful dive-bombing (U.S. Marines in Nicaragua, 1927); the first massive and decisive airlift of troops (Germans into Spain, 1936); the first decisive airborne assault in civil war (U.S.-Belgian rescue operation in Congo, 1964); and the use of gas attacks (Egyptian intervention in Yemen, 1962–1970).

Some foreign military interventions in civil wars, involving large-scale use of airpower, evolved into major local wars, as with U.S. involvement in Vietnam and the Soviet intervention in Afghanistan.

Peter Rainow

See also

Chinese Communist Air Force; Counterinsurgency Operations; Gunships; Helicopters, Military Use; Somalia; Soviet Air Force; Spanish Civil War

References

Brown, David, Christopher Shores, and Kenneth Moskey. *The Guinness History of Air Warfare.* Enfield, UK: Guinness Superlatives, 1976.

Flintham, Victor. *Air Wars and Aircraft: A Detailed Record of Air Combat, 1945 to Present.* New York: Facts on File, 1990.

Haighan, Robin. *Air Power: A Concise History.* New York: St. Martin's, 1972.

Clark, Joseph J. "Jocko" (1893–1971)

World War II aircraft carrier commander and Korean War fleet commander. Clark was born in Pryor, Oklahoma, on 12 November 1893 and attended the U.S. Naval Academy, graduating in 1917 with the original class of 1918. His career followed the standard path; he served on destroyers, saw convoy duty at the end of World War I, and commanded USS *Bulmer.* Clark volunteered for flight training, becoming a naval aviator in 1925. He commanded Fighting Squadron 2-B, embarked on USS *Lexington,* served as *Lexington*'s air officer from 1936 to 1937, commanded Patrol Wing Two, and was executive officer of USS *Yorktown.* Following the outbreak of war with Japan, he quickly gained tactical experience in carrier warfare. In 1943, Clark became the first commanding officer of the new *Yorktown.* He subsequently led carrier formations around Saipan, Iwo Jima, and Okinawa.

In 1946, Clark became assistant Chief of Naval Operations (Air). He next commanded Carrier Division Four, his post at the outbreak of the Korean War. He led Task Force 77 during initial combat operations and subsequently headed naval air bases (Eleventh and Twelfth Naval Divisions), as well as Carrier Division Three. In 1952, he was promoted to vice admiral, became commander of First Fleet, and almost immediately moved to command of Seventh Fleet.

Clark worked closely with his Air Force counterpart, Lieutenant General Glenn Barcus, integrating naval aviation into the overall air campaign. Offensively oriented, Clark took the war to his land-based enemy whenever possible, winning the trust of United Nations Commander General Mark Clark. He later successfully shifted the focus of naval air strikes to interdict communist supply lines.

Clark was promoted to full admiral upon retirement from active duty in 1953. Following a career in the corporate world, Clark died in St. Albans, New York, on 13 July 1971.

Michael S. Casey

See also

Iwo Jima; Korean War; Okinawa; STRANGLE

References

Clark, Joseph J., and Clark G. Reynolds. *Carrier Admiral.* New York: McKay, 1967.

Reynolds, Clark G. *The Fast Carriers: The Forging of an Air Navy.* Huntington, NY: Robert Krieger, 1978.

Clark, Mark W. (1896–1984)

U.S. Army general; liberated Rome during World War II and terminated the war in Korea. Also a strong advocate of large-scale use of airpower in support of ground operations.

Mark Clark was born in Watertown, New York, on 1 May 1896. After graduating from West Point in April 1917, he served in France as commander of an infantry company and then a battalion. After World War I, he took various army assignments, attended the Fort Leavenworth Command and General Staff College (1933) and Army War College (1936), and was promoted to commander, 3d Infantry Division. Clark obtained the reputation as an extremely effective trainer of his troops, conducting exercises in realistic and innovative manner.

In 1942, General Clark was appointed commander of the U.S. II Corps in England. He contributed enormously to the success of Operation TORCH in 1942 as one of its main planners and as the chief Allied negotiator with the Vichy administration in Algeria.

As a commander of the U.S. Fifth Army and later the Fifteenth Army Group in Italy, Lieutenant General Clark skillfully managed the multinational military formations and provided effective interservice coordination, including employment of airpower for isolating the battlefield. Winston Churchill was deeply impressed by Clark's command ability and called him "the American Eagle."

At the same time, Clark's attempt to reach Rome by frontal advance led to the bitterly fought Battle of Monte Cassino (January-May 1944) and destruction of its medieval monastery by massive bombing. Although demonstrating the spectacular power of strategic bombing, this action's operational effect was limited and remains a matter of controversy.

After World War II, Clark took several command positions: commander of U.S. troops in Austria (1945–1947), commander of the U.S. Sixth Army (1947–1949), and chief of Army field forces (1949–1952). During the Korean War, Clark supported the idea of retaliatory bombing of military targets in Manchuria and China. In 1952, he was appointed commander in chief of U.S. troops in the Far East as well as UN troops in Korea. Clark undertook a bombing campaign to regain success on the ground and bring about the ceasefire with the North Koreans and the Chinese.

After the war, Major General Clark served as president of the Citadel in Charleston, South Carolina (1954–1965); he retired from the Army in 1965. During the Vietnam War, he supported President Richard Nixon's decision to resume the air campaign over North Vietnam. Clark died in Charleston on 17 April 1984.

Peter Rainow

See also

Anzio, Battle of; Cassino, Battle of; Italian Campaign; Korean War

References

Blumenson, Martin. *Mark Clark.* New York: Congdon and Weed, 1984.

Clark, Mark W. *Calculated Risk.* New York: Harper and Brothers, 1950.

______. *From the Danube to the Yalu.* New York: Harper and Brothers, 1954.

Clark, Wesley K. (1944–)

U.S. Army general. Wesley K. Clark was born in Little Rock, Arkansas, on 23 December 1944. A 1966 graduate from the U.S. Military Academy at West Point and career armor officer, Clark made his greatest contribution to airpower history as Supreme Allied Commander Europe during the bombing of Yugoslavia by the North Atlantic Treaty Organization (NATO) in Operation ALLIED FORCE (23 March–9 June 1999).

Clark's rise to prominence in U.S. policy regarding the former Yugoslavia stems from his involvement in the 1995 Dayton Peace Accord. At Dayton, Clark forged relationships with many of the leaders of Yugoslavia, whom he would go to war against during ALLIED FORCE in 1999. Clark believed he had a special insight into the mindset of Yugoslav President Slobodan Milosevic, which influenced his employment of airpower in ALLIED FORCE.

During ALLIED FORCE, Clark found himself at odds with his Allied Air Forces Southern Europe commander, U.S. Air Force Lieutenant General Michael C. Short, who was in direct command of ALLIED FORCE air operations. Short, who also had met with Milosevic on several occasions, wanted an air campaign that would inflict massive damage on the Yugoslav hierarchy and infrastructure, compelling the Yugoslav government to sue for peace in Kosovo. Clark, by contrast, feared a strategic bombardment would bring world condemnation and unravel the fragile NATO coalition. Instead, he believed that the Yugoslav Third Army in Kosovo was the true center of gravity in the conflict and demanded interdiction strikes against fielded forces as well as close air support for Kosovo Liberation Army rebels. This disagreement in strategy led to much verbal sparring between Clark and Short throughout the conflict, as well as a campaign strategy that seemed to wander from one objective to the next for the entire 78-day effort.

In the aftermath of ALLIED FORCE, both Clark and Short would claim their strategy was the one most responsible for Milosevic's capitulation to NATO demands. Short claimed the attacks on key Yugoslav government buildings and the electric power grid ended the war. Clark, ever the Army officer, credited the show of NATO will for the victory. To Clark, bombing the Yugoslav Third Army and threatening a ground invasion of Serbia convinced Milosevic he could not prevail. In the end, ALLIED FORCE would become the final accomplishment in the military careers of both men.

Mark D. Witzel

References

Daalder, Ivo H., and Michael E. O'Hanlon. *Winning Ugly: NATO's War to Save Kosovo.* Washington, DC: Brookings Institute Press, 2000.

Holbrooke, Richard C. *To End a War.* New York: Random House, 1998.

Clay, Lucius D. (1897–1978)

U.S. Army general who served as military governor of occupied Germany and directed the Berlin Airlift in 1948–1949. Born on 23 April 1897 in Marietta, Georgia, Clay graduated from the U.S. Military Academy in 1918. He served in Army engineer assignments before becoming head of the first national civil airport program (1940–1941). Soon after the U.S. entered World War II, he became a specialist in war production and supply and in 1942 was placed in charge of the Army procurement program.

When the war was over, Clay became the deputy military governor in Germany under General Dwight D. Eisenhower. Two years later, he was elevated to commander in chief of U.S. forces in Europe and military governor of the U.S. Zone. As such he had to direct the support for a devastated civilian population and, simultaneously, supervise a denazification and deindustrialization. In 1948, when the Soviets blockaded Berlin, Clay directed a successful Allied airlift of food and supplies into the city.

Following his retirement in May 1949, Clay entered private business and became active in politics as a supporter and adviser to President Eisenhower (1953–1961). In 1961 and 1962, President John F. Kennedy asked Clay to serve as his personal representative in Berlin, with the rank of ambassador, to help deal with the critical situation that had developed among the four occupying powers concerning that city's future status. Clay died on 16 April 1978 in Cape Cod, Massachusetts.

James H. Willbanks

See also

Berlin Airlift

References

Clay, Lucius D. *Decision in Germany.* Garden City, NY: Doubleday, 1950.

Gimbel, John. *The American Occupation of Germany: Politics and the Military, 1945–1949.* Stanford: Stanford University Press, 1968.

Close Air Support

Air attacks conducted in support of friendly ground forces, normally when directly engaged with enemy surface forces. Close air support (CAS) operations emerged during World War I as pilots sought to use the advantage of altitude to identify and attack enemy forces and key positions. Attacks were initially conducted with machine guns, eventually termed "strafing," and by dropping a variety of explosive devices such as grenades, modified artillery shells, and eventually specially designed bombs.

Initially, armed observation and fighter aircraft performed ground attack missions. With experience, the air forces developed specialized ground attack aircraft, normally characterized by protective armor, multiple machine guns, and the ability to drop bombs. All sides in World War I recognized the value of using the speed and flexibility of airpower to provide timely, powerful, concentrated attacks against enemy ground forces, with special appreciation for the psychological effects on troops subjected to heavy air attacks. The close-attack aviation experience during World War I identified the major challenges for this type of mission. Night and poor weather conditions severely limited operations; enemy air defenses were especially intense at the front lines; command and communications systems were needed to quickly identify the most appropriate targets and to task attack aircraft for timely missions; and distinguishing between friendly and enemy forces was often difficult, especially in fluid tactical situations.

CAS concepts and capabilities evolved significantly during the interwar period and were further improved during World War II. CAS developments during the interwar period were strongest in those militaries that were creating mechanized ground forces that required mobile and flexible sources of firepower, such as the German army and Luftwaffe team or the Red Army and Red Air Force team in the Soviet Union. CAS capabilities were also important for light forces that did not have significant assigned firepower resources, such as the U.S. Marine Corps or British units controlling the extensive empire.

Although existing fighter designs were used extensively for ground attack missions during this period, air forces also developed specialized attack aircraft—such as dive-bombers—and developed tactics and procedures for the use of light and medium bombers in direct support missions. Combat operations during World War II provided the refining experience for CAS, with the Luftwaffe demonstrating considerable skill and success early in the war; British and American tactical air forces, as well as the Russian Frontal Aviation forces, developed significant capabilities as the war progressed. These wartime developments included improved aircraft performance—both in multirole fighters and specialized attack aircraft—and new munitions, such as cannons and high-velocity rockets.

However, the most significant developments were the evolution of effective air-ground organizations for improved planning and coordination and the creation of effective communications systems for command and control of attack missions. Control of air strikes also was improved by assigning trained observers (often pilots) equipped with tactical radios to front-line combat units to direct attack aircraft. These observers, known as forward air controllers (FACs), helped the attack pilots identify targets and ensured that the location of friendly units was clearly established before weapons were delivered. In Korea, Vietnam, and Operation DESERT STORM, the U.S. military built on the experience of World War II, adding the use of airborne FACs to improve flexibility and to enhance the effectiveness of air attacks. After Korea, the U.S. Army, as well as many other military forces, developed specialized attack helicopters that provided a responsive close-attack capability that was normally assigned directly to the ground commander as a firepower resource.

Technological developments also significantly improved CAS capabilities in the late twentieth century, including the use of improved navigation systems, marking beacons to identify friendly and enemy locations, enhanced communications systems, laser designators, and other guidance systems that allowed precise weapons delivery close to friendly forces.

CAS operations often have been the focus of significant interservice disagreement over the allocation of airpower in combat. After air superiority, ground force personnel tend to view CAS—attacks on the most immediate threat—as the best use for airpower. Air Force leaders accept the value of CAS, especially in emergencies or in fluid offensive operations, but tend to believe that other uses of scarce air assets, especially air superiority, interdiction, or strategic attack missions, are more effective in accomplishing the strategic and operational (i.e., theater) objectives. Senior air commanders often argue that deeper missions can have a greater impact on theater operations by destroying enemy forces and supplies before they can engage or maneuver against friendly forces. Additionally, enemy forces and supplies will normally be more vulnerable to attack and less protected in the rear, and enemy resources devoted to protecting the rear area will further reduce the combat potential at the front. Deep air operations also avoid the heavier defenses on the front, reduce the complex coordination requirements with friendly ground forces, and eliminate the potential for fratricide (inflicting damage and casualties on friendly forces). To reduce fratricide and control concerns, some military forces developed ground support tactics that attacked the enemy slightly behind the line of contact, often assigning another mission title, such as battlefield air interdiction.

CAS operations can be highly structured, preplanned attacks, or they can be responsive to a changing tactical situation from ground or airborne alert positions. CAS missions must be tightly controlled and well integrated into the ground force commander's scheme of maneuver and fire-support plan, and a strong command and control system is necessary for effective CAS operations.

Jerome V. Martin

See also

Air Interdiction; Defense Suppression; Frontal Aviation; German Air Force (Luftwaffe); Tactical Air Warfare

References

Cooling, Benjamin Franklin, ed. *Case Studies in the Development of Close Air Support.* Washington, DC: U.S. Government Printing Office, 1990.

Momyer, William W. *Airpower in Three Wars.* Washington, DC: U.S. Government Printing Office, 1982.

Warden, John A. *The Air Campaign: Planning for Air Combat.* Washington, DC: National Defense University Press, 1988, and New York: Pergamon-Brassey's, 1989.

Cold War

Tense standoff between the two global superpowers in the East (Soviet Union) and West (United States) that lasted some 45 years after World War II until the collapse of communism. Airpower played a critical role in the Cold War. When the specter of global thermonuclear war dominated military planning for a half-century, aviation provided the primary means of nuclear attack and defense. The skies were also the most frequent arena for direct military clashes between the superpowers and their allies. Given that the Cold War was as much about economic competition and international prestige as purely military concerns, the importance of airpower in operations other than war is too often overlooked.

Atomic warfare was associated with aviation from the very beginning. The first and last nuclear weapons ever used in anger were dropped by U.S. B-29 bombers in August 1945 on the Japanese cities of Hiroshima and Nagasaki. These actions represented the end of World War II (Japan soon surrendered) and the beginning of the Cold War (erstwhile allies aligned against one another). As postwar tensions mounted, the United States clung to its monopoly on atomic weapons as its trump card in any future conflict. In the late 1940s and early 1950s, the U.S. Air Force developed the newly created Strategic Air Command into an elite force of medium- and long-range bombers capable of delivering nuclear weapons to targets throughout the Soviet Union, a strategy of massive retaliation in the event of war with the communist nation. Though the Soviet Union tested its first atomic bomb in 1949—years earlier than expected—the United States remained well ahead in its capacity for nuclear attack throughout the 1950s. In the early 1950s, the superpowers added thermonuclear weapons to their arsenals; some explosive yields were 1,000 times more powerful than early atomic bombs. By the mid-1950s, it had become possible to kill an entire nation in a matter of days. U.S. military planners hoped their nuclear superiority would deter any war, but should it come they continued to believe they could "win" a nuclear exchange by undertaking a massive first strike, thereby preventing Soviet retaliation. These hopes began to fade following the first Soviet tests of intercontinental ballistic missiles in August 1957 and the subsequent deployment by both sides of an increasing number of nuclear-tipped ICBMs and submarine-launched ballistic missiles. By the mid-1960s, U.S. nuclear theorists, recognizing that a global nuclear war would mean the obliteration of both protagonists, dubbed this strategy one of mutual assured destruction (known by its apt acronym MAD). It was now possible to kill an entire nation in a matter of hours.

Though neither side gave up trying to develop antimissile defenses capable of hitting a bullet with a bullet (i.e., intercepting incoming ICBMs), the problem was never solved. The resulting nuclear danger posed to the U.S. and Soviet homelands provided the single greatest deterrent against the Cold War becoming "hot." Because the bomber (or at least missiles) would always get through, airpower played a critical role in deterring World War III.

The absence of global war did not mean, however, that there were no direct and violent interactions between the armed forces and intelligence services of the superpowers. Early in the Cold War, incidents most often took the form of Soviet attacks on U.S. and British aircraft as they gathered intelligence by flying near, and sometimes over, Soviet airspace. By far the most famous incident was the May 1960 downing of a U-2 spyplane piloted by Francis Gary Powers, but this was not the only incident. By one count, 40 U.S. aircraft were shot down by Soviet and their allies' aircraft between 1947 and 1977, most while on intelligence-gathering Ferret flights. Of the 356 men involved in these 40 flights, 187 survived, 34 bodies were returned to the United States, and the fate of 135 remains unknown. There is evidence that some were captured alive. Another indication of the scope of these missions comes from the secretive U.S. National Security Agency, which stated in one of its few official publications, an eight-page pamphlet entitled "Dedication and Sacrifice," that 152 cryptologists lost their lives during the Cold War, 64 of them while engaged in aerial reconnaissance.

Direct conflict also took place during wars fought by one superpower against a proxy of the other. During the Korean War, for example, Soviet pilots, flying their own aircraft in Chinese markings, battled U.S. fighters over North Korea, a fact reportedly known to the United States through signals intercepts. Some captured U.S. pilots were probably taken to China and the Soviet Union for interrogation and never returned. By the late 1960s during the Vietnam War, there were more than 1,000 Soviet military technicians in North Vietnam maintaining and operating surface-to-air missile sites against U.S. aircraft. Similarly, though on a smaller scale, U.S. CIA officers in the 1980s delivered surface-to-air Stinger missiles to Afghan mujahideen rebels, trained them in their use, and at least once traveled with them inside Afghanistan and pointed out Soviet Hind helicopters to be shot down. And in 2001, U.S. aircraft faced the possibility of taking fire from U.S.-provided weapons in air strikes against Afghanistan.

Given the secrecy that continues to surround these Cold War encounters, the full truth may never be known.

Finally, since its inception aviation has held a certain mystique, especially within the Soviet Union (now Russia) and the United States. Given that the Cold War was as much a struggle over hearts and minds as it was about weapons and territory, airpower naturally was caught up in the competition. When the Soviet Union cut off ground access to West Berlin in the summer of 1948, it was the symbolism of benign Western technology feeding a hungry city for an entire year through airpower alone that made the Berlin Airlift such a devastating propaganda defeat for the Soviet Union. It is hard to appear to the world as the good guy when a nation finds itself literally lodging diplomatic protests objecting to the dropping of candy to children (over East Berlin); it is no coincidence that the symbolic end of the Cold War is generally taken to be the scene of Berliners (East and West) dancing together on the Berlin Wall in November 1989.

The superpowers and their allies also raced to claim various aeronautical records, such as the breaking of the sound barrier by a U.S. X-1 in October 1947 and the Soviet deployment of the world's first supersonic airliner, the ill-fated Tu-144, which first exceeded the speed of sound in June 1969. (In keeping with the Cold War motif, the design of the Tu-144 owed much to the illicit acquisition by Soviet intelligence agents of blueprints for the Franco-British Concorde; and the famous June 1973 crash of a Tu-144 at the Paris Air Show was due in large part to a bungled French attempt to have a Mirage fighter clandestinely photograph the Soviet jet in midflight.) The competition in space was even more intense, with the Soviet Union placing into orbit the first satellite (Sputnik, October 1957) and the first human (Yuri Gagarin, April 1961), and the United States winning the race to the moon (July 1969). Even such scientific achievements were offshoots of military projects, especially the desire of both sides to deploy the first ICBMs (the Soviet R-7 series) and the first spy satellites (the U.S. CORONA satellites). It is a fitting symbol of the post–Cold War era that at the turn of the century the largest project in aerospace exploration would be the International Space Station, the two primary sponsors being Russia and the United States. The countries continue to bicker, and Russia continues to play the poor cousin, but the end of the Cold War—as well as the disruption caused by unexpected world events—have led to more cooperative efforts.

David Rezelman

See also

Air Defense Command; Antimissile Defense; Atomic Bomb; Cold War, and Commercial Aviation; CORONA Spy Satellites; Cuban Missile Crisis; Electronic Warfare; Ferrets; Korean War; LeMay, Curtis E.; Massive Retaliation; Mutual Assured Destruction; National Security Council; North American Air Defense Command; North Atlantic Treaty Organization; Powers, Francis Gary; Satellites; Single Integrated Operational Plan; Soviet Air Force; Space Stations; Sputnik; Strategic Air Command; Strategic Arms Limitation Talks; Strategic Arms Reduction Talks; Strategic Defense Initiative; Suez Crisis; Tactical Air Command; Vietnam War; Warning Systems

References

Boyne, Walter J. *Beyond the Wild Blue: A History of the United States Air Force, 1947–1997.* New York: St. Martin's Press, 1997.

Bundy, McGeorge. *Danger and Survival: Choices about the Bomb in the First Fifty Years.* New York: Random House, 1988.

Friedman, Norman. *The Fifty-Year War: Conflict and Strategy in the Cold War.* Annapolis, MD: Naval Institute Press, 1999.

McDougall, Walter A. *"Between the Heavens and the Earth": A Political History of the Space Age.* New York: Basic Books, 1985.

Cold War and Commercial Aviation

The Cold War dramatically affected international commercial aviation, as governments on both sides of the Iron Curtain agreed on the desirability of limiting East-West travel and contact. Washington made denying communist access to Western travel networks an essential part of its doctrine of containment, fearing Soviet leaders would pervert aviation's benefits: Aircraft intended to bring people closer could simultaneously transport communist spies; technologies necessary for air transit could enhance communist military capabilities; and communist airlines "showing the flag" around the world could enhance communist prestige abroad.

This air-containment philosophy was codified in 1948 with National Security Council Resolution 15 (NSC-15), which cut off American air ties to communist states. Soviet officials, eager on their own to limit Western access to Eastern Bloc countries, agreed with Washington's goals if not its underlying motives. Limits imposed in Washington and Moscow only retarded East-West travel, however, as other countries, especially those on the Cold War's dividing lines, hesitated to enforce such harsh restrictions. East-West transit remained a difficult but feasible option for travelers willing to fly through neutral or less belligerent states. Faced with détente and the growing conviction that travel could improve East-West ties, Washington approved direct flights from America to Eastern Europe in the late 1960s and to mainland China in the 1970s, though American flights to Cuba remained banned well after the fall of the Berlin Wall.

The bipolar conflict also altered international aircraft sales and development, as NSC-15 additionally barred the export of Western commercial aircraft to communist states. Washington sought to limit communist access to aeronautical technologies present on civil airliners, since most technical advances in commercial aviation began as military projects. Indeed, military procurements were crucial to the dramatic strides made by commercial aviation during these decades. For example, Britain's first jet airliner, the Comet, carried engines developed for bombers, and Boeing's 707 developed from production of an Air Force tanker, the KC-135. Air-traffic control technologies also gained immeasurably from Pentagon-funded research in electronics, computers, and radar systems. America's allies once more took a less rigid stance than Washington, however, and in 1958 Great Britain began exporting aircraft across the Iron Curtain. France soon followed, and by the mid-1960s even U.S. firms could sell in Eastern Europe; China remained off-limits until 1972. By the 1970s, détente eased travel and business between the Cold War's belligerents.

Jeffrey Engel

College Eye Task Force (CETF)

Airborne radar platforms sent to Southeast Asia in April 1965 by the U.S. Joint Chiefs of Staff. Once the decision was made, the 552d Airborne Early Warning and Control Wing provided five EC-121Ds with VHF voice capability, crews, and some 100 support personnel. This detachment, initially known as the Big Eye Task Force, was rechristened the College Eye Task Force in July 1967.

CETF's main support base was in Taiwan, with a forward operating base initially at Tan Son Nhut in South Vietnam and, later, at Thailand bases in Ubon, Udorn, and Korat. CETF aircraft over the Gulf of Tonkin controlled airstrikes against North Vietnam, relayed information between strike aircraft and Seventh Air Force headquarters, warned of enemy fighter activity, vectored friendly interceptors, helped friendly aircraft find tankers, and assisted in search-and-rescue operations. CETF aircraft over Laos prevented friendly aircraft from violating Chinese airspace and directed strike, escort, and combat air patrols on the border between North Vietnam and Laos.

EC-121Ds carried 6 tons of surveillance equipment and a crew of 31. The twin radomes on the aircraft fuselage could sweep a 40,000-square-mile area. The radar could not, however, "look down" over land, because ground clutter obscured radar returns.

From 1965 to 1973, CETF EC-121Ds flew 13,921 combat missions (for 98,777 combat hours). Aircraft were on station 24 hours a day every day and assisted more than 135,000 fighters and bombers to reach their targets and return. CETF was credited with 25 MiG kill assists, the first in July 1965. CETF participated in the successful rescue of 80 downed aircrew members. CETF was sometimes able to place rescue aircraft over downed aircrews before they even reached the ground. CETF also prevented 3,297 friendly aircraft from violating Chinese airspace. CETF flew its last combat mission on 15 August 1973 and deactivated for return to McClellan AFB in June 1974.

James D. Perry

References

Boys, Dean. "History of the 552nd Airborne Early Warning and Control Wing" and "History of the College Eye Task Force." Available online at http://www.dean-boys.com/552/552nd.htm and http://www.dean-boys.com/552/college_eye_task_force.htm.

Colonial Wars

Military force, especially airpower, was used by colonial powers to conquer, dominate, and preserve control over their territories despite resistance and struggle for independence by local populations. There were some 40 wars, conflicts, and military actions of this kind in the twentieth century. The most distinctive feature was their one-sided character: the indisputable air dominance of colonial powers. In the two exceptions (the Italo-Ethiopian War of 1935–1936 and the First Chechen War of 1994–1996), the European powers rapidly and decisively eliminated their potential air opponents.

The colonial experience also had a significant influence on technological development, organizational evolution, and expansion of major world air forces as independent services, as well as their air doctrines, combat performances, tactics, and operations.

The first recorded attempt to use airpower in colonial conflicts was by Napoleon in Egypt in 1799, with he used balloons to undermine the morale of the hostile population. Britain and Spain also used balloons in military campaigns in Africa in the late nineteenth and early twentieth centuries.

Aircraft surpassed balloons as an instrument of colonial control. As opposing forces usually lacked any air force, reconnaissance and ground strafing were the primary tactics. However, some expeditions introduced important operational and tactical novelties to the air warfare. These include aerial bombing (the Italian war in Tripolitania, 1911; the French campaign in Morocco, 1912–1914); casualty evacuation (U.S. Marines occupation of Haiti, 1915–1924); evacuation of populations (RAF action in Kirkuk, Mesopotamia,

1924); and combined use of airpower and mechanized units, as well as gas attacks (the Italian war in Abyssinia, 1935–1936).

Aerial bombing, ground support, and reconnaissance were used extensively during the British war in Afghanistan in 1919, the Spanish and French campaigns against the Rifs in Morocco in 1919–1926, the Soviet operations against Muslim rebels in Central Asia in 1920–1933, and the Italian expeditions in Libya and Italian Somaliland during the 1920s.

Colonial wars also stimulated the development of multipurpose aircraft (bomber/transport/reconnaissance) as well as general-purpose planes. The colonial experience, as well as the effectiveness of airpower over costly ground expeditions, propelled the emergence and development of the most important contribution of colonial air operations to the history of airpower: the theory and practice of an air constabulary and aerial policing.

The Royal Air Force invented this new function and was successful in performing air raids, support, communications, air cover, and evacuation in Iraq, British Somaliland, Aden, Sudan, India's Northwest Frontier, Palestine, and Transjordan during the 1920s–1930s. These demonstrated the RAF's ability to control disturbances, tribal warfare, and border disputes and proved its effectiveness in garrisoning the empire—and thereby proved its own indispensability as an autonomous and unified service.

After World War II, the overall strategic pattern of colonial air warfare had changed dramatically. Although the Western colonial powers enjoyed improvements and innovations in air technology (jets, helicopters, power projection, and airlift capacity), they remained dependent on U.S. military and financial aid and logistic support.

Nationalist forces challenged European air superiority with antiaircraft weapons from their new communist patrons and Third World allies. An active air strike on rebel external bases and supply lines usually led to the internationalization of colonial war and further isolated the colonial power. No example could better serve as a symbol of this radical shift in the balance of power than the 1961 conflict in Portuguese Goa, when the oldest colonial army in the world was swiftly overwhelmed by Indian air assaults.

In addition to traditional functions (bombing raids, reconnaissance, troop transport, search and rescue), the use of airpower in colonial wars of 1945–1974 demonstrated some operational and tactical innovations. These included large-scale aircraft carrier assaults (the French in Indochina, 1947–1954; the British in Malaya, 1948–1960 and South Arabia, 1958–1963); the first operational use of helicopters for casualty evacuation (Malaya, 1950); the largest airlift since Berlin (the British evacuation from Aden in 1967); the first large-scale combat use of helicopters (French in Algeria, 1954–1962); large-scale decentralization of air operations control (Malaya, Algeria); use of air chemical attacks to eliminate jungle cover for rebels (Malaya) and food resources for insurgents (the Portuguese in Mozambique, 1961–1974); and psychological warfare (Malaya, Indochina).

Although the introduction of helicopters and improvements in air mobility led mostly to success in counterinsurgency in colonial and dependent territories, they could not change the unfavorable pattern of rising nationalism and decolonization. Neither could they provide an answer to the growing urban guerrilla and terrorist operations, which developed into a dominant feature of irregular warfare, as the Russian air campaign in Chechnya in 1994–1996 demonstrated. The use of airpower against terrorist elements in the harshest conditions was again put to the test in 2001 during the U.S. air strikes against Afghanistan.

Peter Rainow

See also

Algeria; Churchill, Winston; Counterinsurgency Operations; Ethiopian War; French Air Force; French Army Light Air Force; French Naval Air Force; Gunships; Helicopters, Military Use; Parachutes; Royal Flying Corps/Royal Naval Air Service/Royal Air Force; Russian Air Force (Post-Soviet)

References

Armitage, M. J., and R. A. Mason. *Air Power in the Nuclear Age, 1945–1982.* London: Macmillan, 1983.

Flintham, Victor. *Air Wars and Aircraft: A Detailed Record of Air Combat, 1945 to Present.* New York: Facts on File, 1990.

Lee, David. *Flight from the Middle East.* London: Ministry of Defence, Air Historical Branch, 1980.

Omissi, David E. *Air Power and Colonial Control: The Royal Air Force, 1919–1939.* Manchester, UK: Manchester University Press, 1990.

Combat Cargo Command

U.S. Air Force airlift organization at the beginning of the Korean War. Combat Cargo Command was formed on 10 September 1950 as a response to theater airlift requirements in the Far East that were created by the Korean War. Led by airlift specialist Major General William H. Tunner, the new organization assumed operational control of all troop carrier assets in the theater. Tunner quickly brought centralized direction and standardized procedures to the airlift, replacing the earlier ad hoc arrangements. As a result, efficiency shot up.

Combat Cargo supported General Douglas MacArthur's landing at Inchon on 15 September 1950, flying urgently needed cargo into Seoul's Kimpo airfield only hours after its capture. Tunner's airmen then played a key logistical role in sustaining the Eighth Army's northward drive toward the Yalu River, including the airdrop of the 187th Regimental Combat Team near Pyyongyang in late October.

In late November 1950, the UN forces' advance turned into a retreat when massive Chinese forces entered the war. Combat Cargo was forced to conduct an airlift in reverse, flying out wounded soldiers and tons of materiel in the face of the rapid Chinese advance southward toward Seoul.

Combat Cargo was also called upon to sustain the beleaguered forces of X Corps in northeastern Korea. In some of the most challenging flying of the war, Combat Cargo's pilots air-dropped supplies to surrounded U.S. Marine Corps outposts adjacent to the Chosin Reservoir and evacuated wounded from tiny airstrips at Hagaru-ri and Koto-ri. At one point, the airlifters attracted national press attention in the United States when they air-dropped four sections of an M-2 treadway bridge to the Marines, enabling them to escape the Chinese trap with their heavy equipment intact.

In January 1951, as the military situation in Korea stabilized around the 38th Parallel, Combat Cargo Command, a temporary organization, turned over its airlift responsibilities to the 315th Air Division. It left behind an impressive record. In four and a half months, Tunner's airlifters had flown 32,632 sorties, carried more than 130,000 tons of cargo and 155,294 passengers, and were responsible for transporting 72,960 casualties to hospitals in Korea and Japan.

William M. Leary

See also

Airlift Operations, U.S.; Tunner, William H.

References

Leary, William M. *Anything, Anywhere, Any Time: Combat Cargo in the Korean War.* Washington, DC: Office of Air Force History, 2000.

Tunner, William H. *Over the Hump.* New York: Duell, Sloan, and Pearce, 1964.

Combat Search and Rescue (CSAR)

Known simply as "search and rescue" in the past, CSAR continued to be a key capability of U.S. air forces, special forces, and other services. General Henry H. "Hap" Arnold realized in World War II that the U.S. Army Air Forces needed to develop a capability to recover downed aircrews. This was based on two realities. First, training aircrews required a significant investment in terms of costs and time. And second, an expectation of recovery was key to the morale of the crews themselves. He directed the creation of rescue squadrons that had some success in both the Pacific and European theaters. Almost 5,000 men were rescued.

In the Korean War, helicopters were assigned to the rescue squadrons. Limited initially by range and load capability, these agile aircraft added a new dimension to rescue and made it theoretically possible to recover anyone from anywhere—including enemy-controlled territory. During this conflict, 340 American and Allied airmen were rescued, half of them from behind enemy lines.

During the Vietnam War, rescue capabilities continued to improve. New helicopters like the HH-53 were developed that had the range and load capability to rescue a downed airman from any part of that extensive theater. Additionally, task forces of supporting A-1 strike aircraft and forward air controllers were organized and perfected to locate downed airmen and protect the lumbering helicopters. In that long and bitter conflict, 3,883 airmen were recovered by the rescue forces.

In the 1991 Gulf War rescue duties were performed by specially modified helicopters of the Special Operations Command. During the seven-week campaign, there were three successful rescues from enemy territory. These efforts were duplicated in Bosnia during Operation ALLIED FORCE in 1999, when two downed American pilots were recovered again by helicopters of the Special Operations Command.

Today, every service has forces capable of rescuing American or Allied personnel from enemy territory. Every reasonable effort will be made to recover personnel who are at risk of capture.

Darrel Whitcomb

Combined Bomber Offensive

Allied bombing strategy in World War II. The Combined Bomber Offensive (CBO) is the term describing the strategy of nighttime area-bombing by the Royal Air Force combined with daytime precision bombing by the U.S. Army Air Forces in Europe in June 1943 to May 1944. The objective of this campaign was to destroy the German military, industrial, and economic systems and undermine the morale of its people.

The CBO was actually a strategy born of the opposing doctrines of the RAF and USAAF. The Americans, possessing many heavily armed "self-defending" long-range high-altitude B-17 and B-24 heavy bombers equipped with the extremely accurate Norden bombsight, had long advocated the concept of strategic bombing, or precision bombing of specified military targets.

RAF Bomber Command had quickly discovered that its lightly gunned and armored bombers were unable to fly daylight precision bombing raids without incurring unacceptably high losses. They were thus forced to revert to nighttime area-bombing, or blanket dropping of bombs over a broad target area. The round-the-clock bombing of Axis targets resulting from these combined bombing strategies became known as the CBO.

The CBO has generally been accepted as a successful campaign that achieved its objective; however, its true effectiveness and morality are still debated today. The *U.S. Strategic Bombing Survey* conducted at the end of the war showed a surprising lack of significant damage to heavily bombed German targets; furthermore, the Germans' will to fight was never shown to be significantly weakened by the bombing raids. In addition, the idea that mass formations of highly armed bombers were self-defending unfortunately proved to be a myth. Finally, even precision bombing in 1943–1944 was relatively indiscriminate, resulting in high numbers of German civilian casualties and destruction of cities.

Even so, there is little doubt that the CBO was the best strategy available at the time, a major contribution to the Allies' ultimate victory.

Steven A. Ruffin

See also

Casablanca Conference; U.S. Strategic Bombing Survey

References

Copp, Dewitt S. *Forged in Fire: Strategy and Decisions in the Air War Over Europe, 1940–1945.* Garden City, NY: Doubleday, 1982.

Hansell, Haywood S. Jr. *The Air Plan That Defeated Hitler.* New York: Arno Press, 1980.

Command of the Air (Giulio Douhet, 1921)

Early airpower treatise promoted by Italian artillery officer Giulio Douhet (1869–1930). Douhet was one of the very first to think and write critically about the role of airpower in warfare. By 1915, the year Italy entered World War I, he had already formulated his theories, which included bombing campaigns directed against the morale of an enemy's population. However, his ideas were rejected; moreover, he was court-martialed and imprisoned for criticizing the Italian military's conduct of the war. He was eventually exonerated and promoted to general officer in 1921, the same year he published his most famous work, *Command of the Air.*

Making the assumption that future wars would be total and that defenses would never be capable of stopping a determined bomber offensive, *Command of the Air* advocated a national strategy relying upon control of the air to destroy an enemy's vital centers. In order to mount such an effort, air forces would have to be independent of ground and naval forces, and early airmen used Douhet's writing to argue for an independent air force. Although some of his predictions turned out to be incorrect, many of Douhet's principles proved timeless and, as such, are still seriously studied today.

Paul G. Gillespie

See also

U.S. Air Force Doctrine

References

Meilinger, Phillip S. "Giulio Douhet and the Origins of Airpower Theory." In *The Paths of Heaven: The Evolution of Airpower Theory.* Maxwell AFB, AL: Air University Press, 1997.

COMMANDO HUNT (1968–1972)

Code name for the quintessential aerial interdiction campaign of the Vietnam War. Operation COMMANDO HUNT lasted from 10 November 1968 until 10 May 1972 and involved seven distinct consecutive campaigns of six months' duration. It was aimed at cutting the Ho Chi Minh Trail, running some 250 miles through eastern Laos into South Vietnam and Cambodia.

COMMANDO HUNT involved attacks against four target categories. First there was the attack on trucks moving along the 200 miles of paved roads and hundreds of more miles of dirt roads. Gunships, including four-engine AC-130s armed with an array of 20mm Gatling guns, 40mm Bofors cannons, and, in later models, 105mm computer-aimed howitzers, emerged as the primary aircraft in the war on trucks. Second, bombers and fighter-bombers attacked the trail complex to include roads, pathways, waterways, repair depots, rest facilities, and storage areas. The trail complex was a logistical corridor that could handle an estimated 10,000 trucks at any one time.

A third aspect of COMMANDO HUNT was the attack on the terrain. Laser-guided bombs blasted the cliffs in Mu Gia, Ban Karai, and Nape Passes leading from North Vietnam into Laos in an attempt to cause landslides to close those roads. B-52 strikes, along with occasional C-123 Ranch Hand defoliation sorties, stripped away the jungle foliage. Bombs rained down on rivers and streams in an attempt to alter their courses. Fourth, there was the attack on the trail's defenses: the estimated 1,200 23mm, 37mm, 57mm and the occasional 85mm and 100mm radar-guided antiaircraft guns that blasted away at the attacking aircraft. Beginning in 1969, laser-guided bombs were first used to blast antiaircraft guns from the relative safety of 10,000 feet.

What made COMMANDO HUNT work was the Igloo White sensor system consisting of acoustical and seismic sensors dropped from aircraft and implanted in the ground and hanging from trees disguised as flora. Transmissions from the sensors were analyzed at a secret base known as Task Force Alpha (TFA) located on the Mekong River at Nakhon

Phanom Royal Thai Air Force Base, Thailand. At TFA, analysts developed targets and directed missions against all aspects of the trail as the attack continued day and night for nearly as long as ROLLING THUNDER.

In the end, the impact COMMANDO HUNT was difficult to estimate. Around 3 million tons of bombs and ordnance were expended, and many in the Air Force claimed it was another in an unbroken string of unmitigated airpower victories. Although many trucks were destroyed and the movement of supplies was by Vietnamese historians' own admission most difficult, the bombing never closed down the trail. In fact, North Vietnam moved the war from what was basically a guerrilla war to a conventional war in the period 1968–1972, culminating in a massive, 14-division offensive originating in Laos and Cambodia and out of the Central Highlands of South Vietnam, with most of those forces having traversed the Ho Chi Minh Trail.

Earl H. Tilford Jr.

References

Ballard, Jack S. *Development and Employment of Fixed-Wing Gunships, 1962–1972.* Washington, DC: Office of Air Force History, 1982.

Littauer, Raphael, and Norman Uphoff, eds. *The Air War in Indochina.* Rev ed. Air War Study Group, Cornell University. Boston: Boston Publishing Company, 1971.

Commonwealth of Independent States (CIS)

Air forces of the former Soviet socialist republics, including Armenia, Azerbaidjan, Belarus, Georgia, Kazakhstan, Kyrgizstan, Moldova, Russia, Turkmenistan, Ukraine, and Uzbekistan. One other member of the CIS—Tajikistan—has no independent air force. In terms of airpower, strength, manpower, training, and experience of air personnel, as well as the aviation industry potential, there is no air force within the former Soviet Union (with the possible exception of Ukraine) that can match Russian airpower.

Some fundamental factors are also influencing the shape and development of non-Russian CIS air forces. These are: the multifaceted heritage of the Soviet air force, endemic strategic instability, deep and long-term economic disarray in Eurasia, as well as the airpower limitations envisioned by the Treaty on Conventional Forces in Europe (for the European members of the CIS).

The CIS air forces have predominately Soviet inventories of combat aircraft and other planes. This includes MiG-23, -25, -27, -29, -31 and Su-17, -24, -25 fighters, interceptors. and ground attack planes; Il-76, An-12, -24, -26 and Tu-134 transports; and Mi-2, -6, -8, -24, -26 helicopters. There are also a number of Czech-designed L-29 and -39 trainers.

Only the Ukrainian and Georgian air forces acquired some aircraft of Western design. By 1991, the remnants of Soviet airpower were deployed unevenly among the non-Russian republics, with 69 percent of the force stationed in Belarus, Ukraine, and Kazakhstan.

The CIS air forces are almost totally dependent on Russia for design, production, and maintenance of aircraft and personnel training. Only Ukraine is self-sufficient in training and maintenance, and it has some aircraft production capacity (the Antonov transport series is mainly of Ukrainian design). Thus, airpower remains a valuable tool for prolonging Russia's influence within the former Soviet empire.

Following the Soviet breakup, former commanders of the Red Air Force tried to preserve the centralized command and control network within the common military-strategic space of the CIS. This was to serve Russian attempts to develop the Commonwealth into an institutionalized military and political entity. As the projected CIS military functions did not materialize, the post-Soviet republics established some multilateral frameworks for airpower cooperation.

At the same time, the air forces of Moldova, Turkmenistan, Ukraine, and Uzbekistan emphasize bilateral technical cooperation. The air and air defense forces of Armenia, Belarus, Kazakhstan, and Russia conducted several exercises for the combined CIS air defense system. Ukraine and Russia are developing a collaborative project on a heavy transport plane of the next generation due to the production interdependence and growing cost of domestic aircraft design and development even for the largest CIS countries.

Since 1992, CIS air forces experienced organizational diversity: whereas Belarus, Georgia, Kazakhstan, and Turkmenistan choose to retain the Soviet-style separation of air forces and air defense, Armenia, Azerbaijan, Moldova, Ukraine, and Uzbekistan joined the services. Yet fundamental problems, aggravated by deep economic crisis, remain: widespread shortage of fuel, lack of spare parts, inadequate training of flying personnel, and inoperable aircraft.

Additionally, the bulk of the close-support aircraft (Su-24, -25) has limited tactical capacity due to obsolete navigational and combat control systems. To overcome the widespread shortcoming of tactical strike aircraft, there are attempts to use jet trainers as light close-support planes.

Peter Rainow

See also

Antonov Aircraft; Mikoyan-Guryevich MiG-29; Russian Air Force (Post-Soviet); Soviet Air Force; Sukhoi Su-24; Sukhoi Su-27

References

Aviation and Aerospace Almanac 2000. Washington, DC: Aviation Week, 2000.

International Institute for Strategic Studies. *The Military Balance 2000–2001.* London: Oxford University Press, 2001.

Lambeth, Benjamin S. *Russia's Air Power at the Crossroads.* Santa Monica, CA: Rand, 1996.

Coningham, Arthur "Mary" (1895–1948)

RAF Air Marshal. Sir Arthur "Mary" Coningham was the architect of modern tactical airpower, creating a doctrine based upon his World War II achievements in North Africa and Europe. Born in Australia in 1895 and raised in New Zealand, Coningham endured 20 months of undistinguished World War I service in the infantry and mounted cavalry before joining the Royal Flying Corps in April 1916. He flew DH-2 and SE-5 fighter aircraft, earning distinction as commander of No. 92 squadron and his unusual nickname, "Mary," a corruption of "Maori," for his New Zealand roots.

Coningham remained in the RAF after the war and flew in England, Iraq, and Egypt, including an extraordinary round-trip flight from Cairo to Nigeria and back in 1925. From 1939 to 1941, he commanded No. 4 Group of Bomber Command in early strategic bombing efforts against Germany.

With the support of Air Chief Marshal Arthur Tedder, Coningham revamped RAF operations in the Western Desert from 1941 to 1943. He argued for prioritizing air superiority and a centralized air command coequal with ground forces, and he developed a viable air-ground support network. After the disaster at Kasserine Pass, the U.S. Army Air Forces incorporated Coningham's ideas in Field Manual 100-20, *Command and Employment of Air Power.*

Coningham's mastery of tactical air operations culminated in his command of the Second Tactical Air Force supporting the Normandy invasion and drive across France. Although Coningham was appointed head of the RAF Flying Training Command, a bitter feud with Field Marshal Bernard L. Montgomery marred his postwar service. On 30 January 1948, Coningham died in an airliner crash.

References

Black, Adam, and Charles Black, eds. *Who Was Who, 1961–1970.* Vol. 4. London: Adam and Charles Black, 1951.

Orange, Vincent. *Coningham: A Biography of Air Marshal Sir Arthur Coningham KCB, KBE, DSO, MC, DFC, AFC.* Reprint. Washington, DC: Center for Air Force History, 1992.

Consolidated Aircraft Corporation (CONVAIR, Convair)

Formed by Major Reuben H. Fleet in East Greenwich, Rhode Island, on 29 May 1923 when certain aviation assets of the Dayton Wright Airplane Company and the Gallaudet Engineering Company were combined into a new company. It moved to Buffalo, New York, in 1925, then to San Diego in 1934. At the time, it had 900 employees. By 1939, the company employed 6,000 and, by the middle of 1940, had grown to more than 40,000 employees to help with the war effort. During this period, Consolidated was selected to operate a new government-built production plant in Fort Worth, Texas.

On 17 March 1943, the Consolidated Aircraft Corporation merged with Vultee Aircraft, Inc., becoming the Consolidated Vultee Aircraft Corporation. This name was often truncated to "Convair," although this did not become official until 29 April 1954, when Consolidated Vultee Aircraft Corporation became the Convair division of the General Dynamics Corporation after the two companies merged. In between, the company referred to itself alternately as CVAC or CONVAIR.

It is often reported that Consolidated was "owned" by the Atlas Corporation. As far as can be determined, Atlas was the single largest shareholder of Consolidated stock (about 430,000 of 2.4 million shares) but otherwise did not control the company. Atlas sold 400,000 of its shares to General Dynamics in April 1953, making General Dynamics the largest single shareholder. Subsequently, it purchased a majority of the stock, becoming the de facto owner of Consolidated.

The company built both civilian and military aircraft, including everything from fighters to bombers to flying boats. Among the more notable were the famed B-24 Liberator of World War II, as well as the first operational supersonic bomber—the B-58 Hustler—and the first operational swing-wing aircraft—the F-111 Aardvark. Convair was also instrumental in developing the first intercontinental ballistic missile (the Atlas), which later went on to a very successful space-launch career. In May 1994, Martin Marietta acquired the Space Systems Division (primarily Atlas and Centaur) of General Dynamics Corporation. A year later, in 1995, Lockheed and Martin Marietta merged to form Lockheed Martin Corporation. The Lockheed Martin Corporation now controls all of the defense aspects of the General Dynamics Corporation, including the San Diego and Fort Worth assembly plants that built most of the famous Convair aircraft. The last Convair aircraft—the F-16 Fighting Falcon—is still in production by Lockheed Martin in Fort Worth.

Dennis R. Jenkins

References

Wegg, John. *General Dynamics Aircraft and Their Predecessors.* Annapolis, MD: Naval Institute Press, 1990.

Consolidated B-24 Liberator

U.S. heavy bomber during World War II; manufactured in greater numbers than any U.S. warplane. During late 1938, the U.S. Army Air Corps saw a need for additional heavy bombardment aircraft and approached Consolidated Aircraft to supplement B-17 Flying Fortress production by Boe-

Never given the public adulation accorded Boeing's Flying Fortress, the Consolidated B-24 Liberator was nonetheless a gallant warplane that served well in all theaters. (U.S. Air Force)

ing, Douglas, and Vega. When Consolidated president Reuben Fleet was approached, he stated that his company could build a better airplane. Consolidated began design of its Model 32 in January 1939.

By coincidence, Reuben Fleet had been approached by David R. Davis in 1937 to discuss wing-design theory. Not an aerodynamicist, Fleet insisted on having his chief engineer, Isaac Machlin "Mac" Laddon, and aerodynamicist George S. Schairer listen to the proposal. Extensive testing of the design in Cal Tech's Guggenheim wind tunnel proved Davis's concept to be far better than expected. The result was a high-aspect-ratio wing that offered excellent long-range cruise characteristics. This wing that was applied to the design of the Model 32, which became the B-24 Liberator.

The B-24 was powered by four Pratt and Whitney R-1820 engines. It had an 8,800-pound bombload, a service ceiling of 28,000 feet, a cruising speed of 215 mph, and a range of 2,100 miles. Manned by a crew of 10, the B-24H thru B-24J models mounted 10 .50-caliber machine guns for defensive armament.

The B-24 was a stablemate of the B-17 in the European theater during World War II; however, its vulnerability to battle damage and dissimilar performance compared to the B-17 led Brigadier General Curtis E. LeMay, then commander of the 3d Air Division, to remove the Liberators completely in favor of B-17s. The result was that the 1st and 3d ADs were equipped with B-17s and the 2d AD with only B-24s.

The first raid on the Ploesti oil fields was flown by 13 B-24s from the Halverson Provisional Group on the night of 11/12 June 1942, marking the first Allied heavy bombardment mission against Fortress Europe. On 1 August 1943, the famed Ploesti raid was flown under Operation TIDAL WAVE with a force of 177 B-24s from five bomb groups (three of which were loaned from the Eighth Air Force in Europe).

In the Mediterranean theater of operations, B-24s far outnumbered B-17s. Of the 21 heavy bombardment groups in the Mediterranean late in the war, 15 were equipped with B-24s. The airplanes performed well on the long-range missions deep into Germany and Austria. B-24s did far better in the Pacific theater. The missions were long, over water, with no mountainous obstacles as were encountered in the European and Mediterranean theaters, and enemy resistance was not as intense.

B-24s were also modified for specialized roles as Ferrets, photoreconnaissance platforms, fuel tankers, clandestine operations, and radio/radar jamming.

The B-24 was built in greater numbers than any other U.S. combat aircraft. A total of 19,257 B-24s, RAF Liberators, C-87 transports, and Navy PB4Y-2 Privateers were built at two Consolidated plants as well as Douglas (Tulsa), North

American (Fort Worth), and Ford (Detroit). Ford produced 6,792 complete aircraft and another 1,893 knockdown kits that were shipped by road to other plants for assembly and completion.

Alwyn T. Lloyd

See also

Ferrets

References

Blue, Alan G. *The B-24 Liberator.* Shepperton, UK: Ian Allan, 1967.

Lloyd, Alwyn T. *Liberator: America's Global Bomber.* Missoula, MT: Pictorial Histories, 1993.

Consolidated B-36 Peacemaker

Begun in 1941 when it appeared that the United States would have to conduct bombing missions against Europe from bases in the United States, the prototype Consolidated-Vultee XB-36 did not make its first flight until 8 August 1946. The aircraft was the ultimate expression of a piston-engine bomber, using six Pratt and Whitney R4360 Wasp radial engines, each developing 3,500 hp. Beginning with the B-36D, a pair of General Electric J47 jet engines were added under each outer wing panel to provide additional speed over the target.

The B-36 was probably the most controversial weapon developed in the immediate postwar period, with the U.S. Navy and many members of Congress arguing that the aircraft was too slow to be an effective deterrent. The Air Force countered that no current fighter aircraft could reach the bomber's 45,000-foot altitudes, and in any case it was the only aircraft available that could carry the early thermonuclear weapons (hydrogen bombs). Eventual production totaled 386 aircraft in 13 distinct versions; almost half of them were configured to conduct long-range reconnaissance and signals intelligence, in addition to retaining a nuclear delivery capability.

The B-36 never dropped a bomb in anger, but the reconnaissance versions flew numerous overflight and peripheral missions around China and the Soviet Union. The last B-36 was retired on 12 February 1959, replaced by the Boeing B-52 Stratofortress.

Dennis R. Jenkins

References

Jacobsen, Meyers K., et al. *Convair B-36: A Comprehensive History of America's Big Stick.* Atglen, PA: Schiffer, 1999.

Jenkins, Dennis R. *Convair B-36 "Peacemaker."* WarbirdTech Series Volume 24. North Branch, MN: Specialty Press, 1999.

Consolidated PBY Catalina

An American amphibious aircraft noted for its distinctive shape and great versatility. The Catalina, probably the most famous flying boat in history, first flew in 1935. Early models had low production runs, but with the outbreak of war de-

Noted for its role in reconnaissance missions, the Catalina was probably the most famous flying boat in history. (Walter J. Boyne)

mand rose dramatically. Australia, Canada, the Netherlands East Indies, the United Kingdom, and the United States operated Catalinas, and the Soviet Union produced a license-built version. The PBY-1 through PBY-5 were flying boats. In 1941, an amphibious version, the PBY-5A, was introduced and became the standard. Armament and speed varied between the versions, but generally Catalinas did far better to hide in a cloud rather than try to outrun or outfight an enemy. Range was generally over 2,000 miles.

Catalinas were used in an antisubmarine role and became a welcome sight to downed aviators as air-sea rescue planes. The Catalina had its greatest impact in its reconnaissance role, however. A British Catalina found the German battleship *Bismarck* after surface vessels lost contact, resulting in that ship's destruction. A U.S. Catalina located the Japanese aircraft carriers off Midway, allowing the nearby U.S. carriers to launch a crippling first strike.

Grant Weller

See also

Air Rescue; Antisubmarine Warfare; Bismarck, Air Operations Against; Consolidated Aircraft Corporation; Flying Boats; Midway, Battle of

References

Angelucci, Enzo, ed. *The Rand McNally Encyclopedia of Military Aircraft, 1914–1980.* New York: Military Press, 1980.

Munson, Kenneth. *Fighters and Bombers of World War II, 1939–1945.* London: Peerage Books, 1969.

Continental Air Command (CONAC)

Major USAF continental command from 1948 to 1968. (CONAC is not to be confused with the Continental Air Defense Command, a joint headquarters that coordinated the air defense operations of each of the services from 1954 to 1975.) In the atmosphere of severe budgetary restraint prevalent in the late 1940s, the Air Force decided that Strategic Air Command should continue for the time being to receive first priority for resources. CONAC was therefore created in November 1948 to combine the limited resources of both Tactical Air Command (TAC) and Air (later Aerospace) Defense Command (ADC), along with related elements of the Air Force Reserve. By pooling the limited tactical assets the Air Force possessed, all under one headquarters, units could be more easily shifted to whichever mission was deemed most urgent at any given time. It soon became clear that in practice CONAC's first priority would be the air defense mission, a shift reinforced by the first test of a Soviet atomic device in August 1949.

By late 1950, following the massive expansion in defense spending associated with the Korean War and National Security Council Resolution 68, the rationale for the consolidation of TAC and ADC had disappeared. Accordingly, in November 1950 TAC was reconstituted as a major command, followed shortly in January 1951 by ADC. The remaining mission for CONAC was now to administer the Air Force Reserve and the Air National Guard and to otherwise fulfill any other miscellaneous Air Force responsibilities within the continental United States. In 1968, CONAC was inactivated, and the Air Force Reserve became a separate operating agency.

David Rezelman

See also

Air Defense Command; Air National Guard; Strategic Air Command; Tactical Air Command

References

Schaffel, Kenneth. *The Emerging Shield: The Air Force and the Evolution of Continental Air Defense, 1945–1960.* Washington, DC: Office of Air Force History, United States Air Force, 1991.

CONVAIR (Convair)

See Consolidated Aircraft Corporation

Convair B-58 Hustler

The world's first supersonic bomber. Convair's beautiful B-58 Hustler made its maiden flight on 11 November 1956. Powered by four General Electric J79 turbojet engines, the B-58 was capable of extended Mach 2 flight and set no fewer than 19 world records during its service career. The B-58 and its crews would also win the Thomson Trophy, Blériot Trophy, Mackay Trophy, Bendix Trophy, and Harmon Trophy. The B-58 was a tremendously advanced aircraft for its time but proved to be a maintenance nightmare in operational service. Nevertheless, it provided the United States with an extraordinary capability to deliver nuclear weapons during the height of the Cold War.

The B-58 was never used in combat, although some planning was accomplished toward using it in Southeast Asia. Only 116 of the bombers were produced, and they would serve operationally until they were retired in 1970.

Dennis R. Jenkins

References

Wagner, Ray. *American Combat Planes,* 3rd ed. Garden City, NY: Doubleday, 1982.

The Convair B-58 Hustler was the world's first supersonic bomber, but it proved to be expensive to operate, and many were lost in crashes. (Walter J. Boyne)

Convair F-102 Delta Dagger and F-106 Delta Dart

U.S. fighters that used the delta-wing planform that Dr. Alexander Lippisch began promoting in Germany during World War II. The concept promised high airspeeds and decent stability from a relatively lightweight airframe. When Lippisch came to the United States after the war, Convair began building an experimental fighter—the XP-92—around his delta-wing principles. The XP-92 made the first flight of an American delta-wing aircraft on 18 September 1948 and eventually conducted 118 research flights that largely validated the design.

Convair was subsequently selected to build a larger and much more sophisticated delta-wing interceptor as part of Weapons System 201A, the key defensive system designed to protect the continental United States from Soviet bomber attack. The YF-102 made its first flight on 24 October 1953, but by this time analysis had shown that the design would not attain anywhere near its proposed maximum speed because of excessive transonic drag. What saved the F-102 (and several other contemporary aircraft) was the application of National Advisory Committee for Aeronautics scientist Richard Whitcomb's so-called area-rule principle. This resulted in a characteristic fuselage, with a shape similar to a Coca-Cola bottle, and allowed the F-102A to easily achieve its design speeds.

The F-102A was not totally successful, mostly because the advanced fire-control system never lived up to expectations. This had become evident fairly early, and plans were made to proceed to an even more advanced F-102B version as soon as possible. The first operational F-102A was finally delivered on 1 May 1956, almost three years behind schedule. Convair built 875 F-102As and 63 two-seat TF-102A trainers. In 1960, the aircraft were being transferred to Air National Guard squadrons, and a few even rotated to Vietnam during 1964. By 1969, the aircraft was largely withdraw from U.S. service, and 40 were transferred to Turkey and 20 to Greece. Others were converted into PQM-102 drones.

In the meantime, Convair was developing the ultimate interceptor—the F-102B, subsequently redesignated F-106A. The airframe was unmistakably related to the F-102 but had been optimized for greater performance and to accommo-

The Convair F-106 took a long time to mature, primarily because of the sophistication of its fire control system, but it was an effective interceptor for many years. (U.S. Air Force)

date a much more powerful engine. Perhaps most important, the fire-control system was significantly improved and was well integrated into the Semiautomatic Ground Environment (SAGE, a defense network meant to provide all-weather control for the interceptor force). The first F-106A made its maiden flight on 26 December 1956, and the type began joining operational units in May 1959. Convair built 277 F-106As and 63 two-seat F-106B trainers, with the last being delivered on 20 July 1960.

The F-106 became the first front-line fighter to serve with the U.S. Air Force for more than 20 years. Interestingly, a world speed record of 1,525 mph set by an F-106A on 15 December 1959 remained unbroken during the period. From 1972 onward, the McDonnell Douglas F-15 Eagle gradually began to replace the F-106A as the continental defense interceptor. As they were removed from Air Force service, they were passed along to the Air National Guard, which flew the type until August 1988.

Dennis R. Jenkins

References

Holder, William. *F-106 Delta Dart in Action.* Fallbrook, CA: Aero, 1986.

Mutza, Wayne, *Convair F-102: Delta Dagger.* Atglen, PA: Schiffer, 1999.

Wagner, Ray. *American Combat Planes,* 3rd ed. Garden City, NY: Doubleday, 1982.

Coppens, Baron Willy (1892–1986)

Belgium's "Ace of Aces." Willy Coppens transferred from the grenadiers to aviation in 1915. Delayed in training, it was not until 1917 that he made it to the front, flying the BE.2c. Finally getting a chance to fly fighters later that year, Coppens managed two unconfirmed victories plus one forced landing by the end of the year.

On 8 May 1918, he brought down the first of 35 balloons for which he would receive credit, a total that would make him the most successful balloon-buster of all time. His ultimate score of 37 put him at the head of the short list of Belgian aces. During his last mission, on 14 October 1918, he was shot down and wounded, losing a leg. His nation rewarded him with a barony, his title being Baron de Houthulst, after the forest over which many of his victories had occurred.

James Streckfuss

References
Coppens, Willy. *Days on the Wing.* London: John Hamilton, 1932.
Franks, Norman, Russell Guest, and Gregory Alegi. *Above the War Fronts.* London: Grub Street, 1997.
Pieters, Walter. *Above Flanders Fields.* London: Grub Street, 1998.

Coral Sea, Battle of the (1942)

The first setback for Japan in World War II and the first naval battle where opposing surface ships did not sight each other. In April 1942, the Japanese decided to capture Port Moresby on the southern coast of New Guinea. Taking Port Moresby would drive Allied forces out of New Guinea and isolate Australia. The invasion fleet included the light carrier *Shoho* and the fleet carriers *Shokaku* and *Zuikaku.*

Warned by intelligence of Japanese intentions, Admiral Chester Nimitz ordered all available forces, including the fleet carriers *Lexington* and *Yorktown,* to concentrate and repel the attack. Between 3 and 8 May 1942, the two forces jockeyed for position, launching a series of air searches and air attacks. The Americans sank *Shoho* but lost the larger *Lexington,* plus an oiler and a destroyer, giving the Japanese a tactical victory.

However, the Americans achieved their strategic goal of defending Port Moresby when the Japanese withdrew after *Shokaku* was damaged and *Zuikaku* suffered heavy aircraft losses. The long-term importance of the Battle of the Coral Sea was its impact on the Battle of Midway in June 1942. The U.S. repaired *Yorktown* in time to take part, but the Japanese could not prepare *Shokaku* and *Zuikaku* for the battle, significantly reducing Japan's potential strength at that decisive battle.

Grant Weller

See also
Aircraft Carriers, Development of; Douglas SBD Dauntless; Grumman F4F Wildcat; Hara, Chuichi; Inouye, Shigeyoshi; Japanese Naval Air Force, Imperial; Midway, Battle of; Mitsubishi A6M Reisen; Nimitz, Chester William; Pearl Harbor; United States Navy, and Aviation; Yamamoto, Isoroku

References
Maclean, Anne, and Suzanne Poole. *Fighting Ships of World Wars One and Two.* London: Peerage Books, 1986.
Sherman, Frederick C. *Combat Command.* New York: Bantam Books, 1950.

CORONA Spy Satellites (Discoverer)

The world's first successful spy satellites, launched initially under the public cover name DISCOVERER. In the early years of the Cold War, the United States, spurred by fears of a thermonuclear Pearl Harbor, was desperate for information on Soviet strategic nuclear weapons programs. Beginning in the summer of 1956, the high-flying U-2 spy plane began to produce some overhead imagery of the Soviet Union, but the loss of Francis Gary Powers's aircraft on 1 May 1960 led to cancellation of direct overflights of the Soviet Union. Fortunately, an alternative—and more effective—means of collecting overhead imagery was in work.

The RAND Corporation had been studying the intelligence potential of earth-orbiting satellites since 1946, but these reports were greeted with skepticism by the U.S. Air Force. Following advances associated with early intercontinental ballistic missile (ICBM) programs, however, the Air Force in October 1956 awarded the Lockheed Corporation a contract to develop the Advanced (satellite) Reconnaissance System, dubbed WS-117L. At the heart of this program was the SENTRY (later SAMOS) satellite, which would transmit digitized images directly to ground stations. Concerns over its slow progress, however, led President Dwight D. Eisenhower in February 1958 to approve an interim spinoff system that would physically return its images on film via a recoverable capsule. This program, to be run jointly by the Air Force and the Central Intelligence Agency, was given the code name CORONA.

Though the first test of the new system was ready to go in less than a year, the project was plagued with problems from the start. The first launch attempt to get off the ground, known to the public under the cover name DISCOVERER I, did place a test vehicle into orbit, but once there it was never heard from again. The 11 tests that followed, from April 1959 through June 1960, resulted only in an embarrassing series of often public failures that even included the deaths of two "crews" of four mice each, included in the flights in support of the DISCOVERER cover story.

Though it contained test instruments instead of film, the capsule from DISCOVERER XIII was successfully recovered on 11 August 1960. Finally, exactly one week later, CORONA Mission 9009 (DISCOVERER XIV) succeeded in exposing 20 pounds of film over the Soviet Union and returning it to earth, the recovery capsule being snatched literally in midair by an Air Force C-119 flying 8,500 feet over the Pacific Ocean.

Though the first CORONA satellite (later designated KH-1) took lower resolution images than did a U-2, this very first mission by itself photographed more of the Soviet Union than had all of the previous 24 U-2 overflights combined, revealing in the process 64 new airfields and 26 new surface-to-air missile sites.

Although four of the next five CORONA launches did fail, by the latter half of 1961 the system had become fairly reliable, with seven of the 11 missions from June through the end of 1961 succeeding. During this period the CORONA satellites incorporated a succession of camera upgrades, improving the ground resolution of their images from 40 feet for the KH-1, to 25 feet for the KH-2, to 10 feet for the KH-3. To manage the new influx of imagery, Director of Central Intelligence Allen Dulles on 9 August 1960 established the Committee on Overhead Reconnaissance to set CORONA target priorities, and the following year the National Reconnaissance Office was established to centralize management of all U.S. reconnaissance satellites.

In early 1962, the DISCOVERER cover story was dropped, and the workhorse of the CORONA program emerged—the KH-4. Over the next decade, 95 KH-4s (including the variants KH-4A and KH-4B) would be launched, with a success rate above 90 percent. As their service life expanded, from several days in 1960–1961 to 18 days, the quality of their now stereoscopic cameras also improved, culminating in 1967 with the J-3 camera of the KH-4B, with ground resolution of about 5 feet. (The wide-area coverage provided by KH-4s was supplemented beginning in 1964 by the first of the "close-look" GAMBIT satellites, the KH-7, with ground resolution of approximately 18 inches.) Though the KH-5 ARGON (an Army-sponsored mapping satellite) and the KH-6 LANYARD (what was left of the failed SAMOS project) did make brief appearances in 1961 and 1963, respectively, neither produced much usable imagery, and both were retired by 1964. Thus, against the initial expectations of many, it was the "interim" CORONA satellites, and especially the KH-4s, that ultimately dominated early U.S. satellite reconnaissance (along with their close-look partners, the KH-7s and KH-8s of the GAMBIT series).

The importance of these early "keyhole" satellites is difficult to overstate. In the absence of hard intelligence that prevailed in the late 1940s and well into the 1950s, the United States had been surprised several times by unexpected Soviet technological advances, such as the 1949 atomic test and the 1957 ICBM test, each occurring years earlier than had been predicted. This ambiguity regarding Soviet capabilities allowed the military services, and especially the U.S. Air Force, to indulge fears that the Soviet Union might be progressing ahead of the United States in bomber and then missile production—the so-called bomber and missile gaps. The U-2 imagery of the late 1950s strongly suggested that both of these American weaknesses were myths, but it was the images produced by CORONA satellites that definitely proved by 1961–1962 that any missile gap favored the United States.

By continuing to monitor Soviet bomber and missile deployment throughout the 1960s, CORONA imagery provided the hard data that allowed civilian policymakers within the U.S. Department of Defense essentially to freeze the size of U.S. strategic nuclear forces at those levels already reached by the early 1960s. In short, it was largely due to the CORONA satellites, and their successors, that former Director of Central Intelligence Robert Gates could boast in November 1999 that, for the United States, "during the last two-thirds of the Cold War . . . there were no more strategic surprises."

David Rezelman

See also

Antisatellite Capability; Cold War; KOSMOS; Lockheed U-2; Mutual Assured Destruction; Powers, Francis Gary; Satellites; SENTRY (SAMOS) Reconnaissance System; Sputnik

References

Day, Dwayne A., John M. Logsdon, and Brian Latell, eds. *Eye in the Sky: The Story of the CORONA Spy Satellites.* Washington, DC: Smithsonian Institution Press, 1998.

Lindgren, David T. *Trust but Verify: Imagery Analysis in the Cold War.* Annapolis, MD: Naval Institute Press, 2000.

McDonald, Robert A. CORONA *Between the Sun and the Earth: The First NRO Reconnaissance Eye in Space.* Bethesda, MD: American Society for Photogrammetry and Remote Sensing, 1997.

Peebles, Curtis. *The CORONA Project: America's First Spy Satellites.* Annapolis, MD: Naval Institute Press, 1997.

Counterinsurgency Operations

The use of airpower for purposes of counterinsurgency can be divided into two sometimes overlapping approaches. The first and older approach is based upon directly attacking the supply lines of insurgent forces or the forces themselves. This can be accomplished by aerial bombing for interdiction purposes and the use of rockets and machine guns in a close air support (CAS) role of ground forces. Operation ARC LIGHT in Vietnam is an unusual example because B-52 carpet-bombing raids were used for CAS purposes. The second and newer approach relies upon the transport of ground forces by helicopters, the air mobility concept (pioneered by the U.S. Army in the 1960s), and, to a declining extent, the use of airborne (parachute) forces.

Counterinsurgency operations were carried out in the Middle East by the British in the 1920s, the French in Algeria and the British in Malaya after World War II, the United States in Vietnam, and the Soviet Union in Afghanistan. Typically, airpower alone will have greater counterinsurgency value in open terrain, such as deserts and scrublands, as opposed to jungles and urban zones, where much of its value is negated. With the rise of man-portable air defense systems (i.e., shoulder-fired Stinger-type surface-to-air missiles), these operations have become increasingly difficult to carry out.

Robert J. Bunker

References

Berger, ed., Carl. *The United States Air Force in Southeast Asia, 1961–1973: An Illustrated Account.* Washington, DC: Office of Air Force History, 1984.

Venter, Al. J. *The Chopper Boys: Helicopter Warfare in Africa.* London: Greenhill, 1994.

Coventry Air Raids

On the night of 14 November 1940, more than 500 German bombers staged the biggest air raid up to that time. The target, Coventry, was a historic British city with factories that produced bombers and military vehicles. Coventry had been bombed earlier, first on 25 June and again on 25 August, with 16 deaths. In October, many small raids killed 176. Operation MOONLIGHT SONATA, the Luftwaffe's November raid, was different. Hitler wanted revenge for the RAF's bombing of Munich, the birthplace of the Nazi Party.

At 7:00 P.M. the attack began with parachute flares followed by phosphorus incendiaries to light the way for the bombers that came at 7:30, dropping 30,000 incendiaries and 500 tons of high explosives and landmines attached to parachutes. The attack was against both the industrial outskirts and the center of the city, where a huge fire erupted. When the all-clear sounded at 6:15 A.M., 4,330 homes were destroyed and three-fourths of the factories were damaged. The raid killed 554 men, women, and children and injured 865. The level of destruction was such as the world had never before seen, and the Germans coined the word "coventrized" to describe it.

By the time of the last raid on Coventry in August 1942, the city had been through 41 actual raids and 373 siren alerts. Death by air raid in Coventry came to 1,236 people during World War II.

John Barnhill

References

See related articles by David McGrory in *Coventry Warwickshire News.* Available online at http://www.cwn.org.uk/heritage/blitz/index.html.

Keegan, John. "War in the West." Available online at Dan's History Website, http://www.danshistory.com/ww2/west.html.

Kurki, Allan. *Operation Moonlight Sonata: The German Raid on Coventry.* Westport, CT: Praeger, 1995.

Crete, Battle of (1941)

In 1941, the first seizure of a strategic target by airborne forces. The German assault of Crete on 20 May 1941 served as the culmination of a lightning campaign to drive the British from the Balkans and secure a southern flank for the German invasion of Russia. It also bolstered Italy's fortunes in the Eastern Basin of the Mediterranean Sea. Luftwaffe forces included some 650 aircraft—280 level bombers, 150 dive-bombers, 180 single- and twin-engine fighters, and 40 reconnaissance aircraft. Carrying in some 15,750 paratroops and air-landed infantry were nearly 500 transports and 100 gliders. Another 7,000 mountain troops planned to follow by sea.

Opposing them were approximately 30,000 British and Imperial troops recently driven from the mainland or dispatched from Egypt, tough fighters but lacking in artillery, tanks, and air cover.

Ferocious combat began with the first of the airborne landings. German forces were very hard pressed but enjoyed good air support. Though annihilating the Germans' attempted seaborne reinforcement, the British command began evacuation on 28 May. In the fighting on and around the island, Luftwaffe forces sank three Royal Navy cruisers and six destroyers and damaged other vessels, including an aircraft carrier.

The Germans suffered grievously. Of a total of 22,000 men involved in Operation MERCURY, some 7,000 were killed and 3,400 wounded. Fully 272 transports were destroyed or damaged beyond repair. Though the paratroops' morale remained high, the Battle of Crete marked the end of large-scale Luftwaffe airborne operations.

D. R. Dorondo

See also

German Air Force (Luftwaffe); Junkers Aircraft; Junkers Ju 52/3m, Ju 87 Stuka, and Ju 88

References

Price, Alfred. "Luftwaffe: Birth, Life, and Death of an Air Force." In Barrie Pitt, ed., *Ballantine's Illustrated History of World War II.* New York: Ballantine Books, 1970.

Quarrie, Bruce, and Mike Chappell. *German Airborne Troops, 1939–1945.* Men-at-Arms Series. Ed. Martin Windrow. London: Osprey, 1983.

Whiting, Charles. *Hunters from the Sky: The German Parachute Corps, 1940–1945.* London: Leo Cooper, 1974.

CROSSROADS (1946)

Code name for a gigantic peacetime exercise following World War II. The 509th Bombardment unit had dropped the two atomic bombs that brought World War II to a rapid conclusion. After World War II, the 393d Bomb Squadron, 509th Bombardment Group, was stationed at Roswell Army Air Base, New Mexico. With the postwar demobilization, the unit could barely keep its B-29s in the air for routine pilot proficiency training. Its only redeeming asset was its knowledge of atomic weapons.

In early January 1946, U.S. President Harry Truman had approved Operation CROSSROADS. This exercise required some 42,000 people, including Army, Navy, and civilian scientists. The object was to determine the effects of an air-dropped and underwater-detonated atomic weapon on naval surface vessels anchored near Enewetak Atoll. Around 2,000 USAAF personnel participated in the test with 44 aircraft.

On 1 July 1946, *Dave's Dream* (a B-29–40-MO, serial number 44–27354) from the 393d Bomb Squadron took off from Kwajalein Island under the command of Major Woodrow P. Swaincutt. Unfortunately, the day's weather forecast did not provide accurate winds, thereby leaving the crew's new bombardier, Major Harold E. Wood, to make his own assessment.

The bomb dropped that day was an Mk.2 type (codenamed "Fat Man") with a complicated set of fins. The bomb was short of the predicted area and 2,000 feet to the left. The detonation, however, was at the prescribed altitude of 500 feet. *Dave's Dream* was flown back to Albuquerque for a checkout of the bombsight. A problem with the airplane was ruled out. An analysis of the photographs taken during the drop revealed that the bomb's trajectory was not as planned, leading to the belief that one of the bomb's fins had departed the weapon.

Although the results of the airdrop were not quite as desired, the effects were substantial. The USS *Nevada* was still afloat, but five ships were sunk and another nine were severely damage. Had the ships been manned, there would have been no survivors because of the blast wave and the thermal and radiological effects.

Alwyn T. Lloyd

References

Bright, Charles D., ed. *Historical Dictionary of the U.S. Air Force.* New York: Greenwood Press, 1992.

Lloyd, Alwyn T. *A Cold War Legacy: A Tribute to Strategic Air Command, 1946–1992.* Missoula, MT: Pictorial Histories, 2000.

CRUSADER (1941)

British code name for support of Allied ground operations in a desert environment during World War II. German Afrika Korps commander Erwin Rommel's first offensive in Africa recaptured most of Cyrenaica in the spring of 1941, but the Allies maintained control of the coastal fortress of Tobruk, cut off by land from the main Allied army. Through the summer of 1941, the Axis and Allied armies opposed each other along a line approximating the Egypt-Libya frontier. RAF bombers repeatedly struck the Italian-held ports of Benghazi and Tripoli, and RAF aircraft on Malta struck shipping and ports on the Italian mainland. Both sides rushed to gather the necessary supplies for an offensive, a race won by the British, who launched Operation CRUSADER on 18 November 1941 with the intent of relieving the Tobruk fortress.

The RAF under Air Marshal Arthur W. Tedder fielded 700 aircraft that faced only 437 Axis aircraft at forward bases, but the proximity of Italian bases in Tripolitania, Italy, and the Balkans made Axis reinforcement easier. The RAF gained a margin of air superiority for much of the battle and successfully harassed and attacked Axis columns. The open desert terrain helped considerably in successful target acquisition, particularly in attacks against German columns during the bold move by Rommel to the Egyptian frontier (the so-called Dash to the Wire).

After hard fighting, Tobruk was successfully relieved. In mid-December, the Afrika Korps and its Italian allies retreated toward El Aghelia. CRUSADER was the first significant British ground success against German forces.

Frank E. Watson

References

Playfair, I.S.O., et al. *History of the Second World War: Meditterranean and Middle East, Volume 3: British Fortunes Reach Lowest Ebb.* London: HMSO, 1960.

Cuban Missile Crisis

Perilous events surrounding the construction of Soviet missile sites in Cuba. At no time in U.S. history had the importance of aerial reconnaissance been demonstrated more dramatically than during the Cuban Missile Crisis of 1962. In September and October of that year, Soviet officials had persistently denied their intent to install offensive weapons in Cuba, only 90 miles from U.S. shores, despite intelligence reports to the contrary.

On 14 October 1962, two USAF high-flying U-2 reconnaissance aircraft photographed portions of Cuba, and analysis confirmed that bases were being constructed for intermediate-range missiles within striking distance of the United States. On 16 October 1962, President John F. Kennedy reviewed reconnaissance photos of Soviet missile installations under construction in Cuba.

President Kennedy placed the U.S. armed forces on alert for whatever action might be necessary as USAF U-2 and RF-101 flights over Cuba continued, the latter aircraft sometimes flying at treetop level. The USAF Tactical Air Command (TAC) was completely mobilized as a combat force for the first time in history. In only two days, it had more than 1,000 airplanes and 15,000 personnel in southern Florida, ready for any conflict that might have developed. While Strategic Air Command (SAC) airplanes photographed Cuba from high altitude, TAC airplanes flew a constant vigil over the island at low level, obtaining photographic evidence of the communist buildup of offensive weapons.

On 22 October, President Kennedy publicly announced details of the critical situation and declared that "a strict quarantine on all offensive military equipment under shipment to Cuba is being initiated."

Meanwhile, USAF aircraft kept the island of Cuba as well as the Caribbean and Atlantic Ocean under constant surveillance, providing the U.S. Navy with data on scores of ships at sea apparently en route to Cuba. On 28 October, Soviet Premier Nikita Khrushchev agreed to remove the offensive missiles as well as the medium-range twinjet Il-28 "Beagle" bombers being assembled in Cuba. USAF reconnaissance aircraft then monitored communist compliance with the agreement.

Henry M. Holden

References

USAF Musuem Website. "Tactical Air Command Cuban Crisis." Available online at http://www.wpafb.af.mil/museum/history/postwwii/tac-cc.htm.

Cunningham, Randall "Duke" (1941–)

U.S. Navy lieutenant, F-4 pilot, and first ace in Vietnam War (five MiG kills). Born in Los Angeles on 8 December 1941, Randall Cunningham graduated from the University of Missouri in 1964 and the following year earned a master's degree in education.

Cunningham joined the U.S. Navy in 1967 and received his wings the next year. He took his operational training at the Naval Air Station at Miramar, California, then joined Fighter Squadron 96. His first combat deployment was aboard the carrier *America* (1969–1970).

On 19 January 1972, during his second Vietnam deployment with the *Constellation,* Lieutenant Cunningham shot down a MiG-21 and, on 8 May 1972 a MiG-19. On 10 May 1972, he downed three MiG-17s. On the way back to the carrier, his plane was hit by a surface-to-air missile and downed. Cunningham and his radar intercept officer, Lieutenant (junior grade) Bill Driscoll, were picked up at the mouth of the Red River by a search-and-rescue helicopter. In all, Cunningham flew 300 Vietnam combat missions. His decorations include the Navy Cross, two Silver Stars, and the Purple Heart. Cunningham retired from the Navy in 1988, and in 1990 he was elected on the Republican ticket to the U.S. House of Representatives from California.

James H. Willbanks

References

Cunningham, Randy. *Fox Two.* Mesa, AZ: Champlin Fighter Museum, 1984.

Eastman, James N. Jr., Walter Hanak, and Lawrence J. Paszek. *Aces and Aerial Victories—The United States Air Force in Southeast Asia, 1965–1973.* Washington, DC: U.S. Government Printing Office, 1976.

Curtiss Aircraft

U.S. manufacturer of aircraft and aircraft engines. Glenn Curtiss's lightweight, high-powered, air-cooled engines found favor among aeronautical pioneers, leading to his involvement in aviation and, in 1910, his establishment of the Curtiss Aeroplane Company.

Curtiss initially produced pusher biplanes. By 1914 that design was obsolete and tractor biplanes, designed by B. Douglas Thomas, replaced them. Curtiss also developed successful pusher flying boats and, with John C. Porte, a large multiengine example for a proposed transatlantic crossing.

War in Europe brought Curtiss substantial orders for JN trainers, large and small flying boats, and engines. America's entry into the war added still more orders. By 1918, Curtiss operated seven plants (plus a Canadian subsidiary) manufacturing aircraft and engines and accounted for more than one-third of America's wartime production.

The Curtiss firm survived postwar industry contraction because of its financial resources and management, design, and engineering talent. The superb D-12 engine, a series of racers, and the Hawk and Falcon lines of military single- and two-seaters brought the company substantial orders from 1923 onward. By 1929, the company had more than 3,000 employees.

On 26 June 1929, Curtiss merged with the Wright Aeronautical Corporation to form the Curtiss-Wright Corporation, adding an important range of air-cooled radial engines to the firm's products. The company survived the Depression, largely thanks to export orders, and transitioned to all-metal monoplane construction with its Shrike and Hawk 75 military models, ordered by both the USAAC and foreign air forces. All-metal biplane Seagulls and Helldivers for the U.S. Navy, and a successful range of small single- and twin-engine commercial aircraft produced in St. Louis, rounded out its 1930s product line.

Conflicts in China and Europe, as well as U.S. military expansion in response to the threat of international disorder, renewed demand for Curtiss products. Contracts for almost 14,000 P-40 fighters and well over 5,000 SB2C/A-25 dive-bombers formed the majority of some 28,000 Curtiss aircraft produced for U.S. and Allied forces between 1935 and 1945.

At the end of World War II, Curtiss-Wright, like all U.S. aircraft manufacturers, was hit by massive contract cancellations. Unlike some other firms, however, the only Curtiss design suitable for the postwar civil market was its twin-engine Commando, readily available in the war-surplus market. The firm's two new military prototypes, the XF15C-1 for the Navy and the four-jet XP-87, failed to attract production orders. In 1949, Curtiss-Wright closed its Aeroplane Division and sold the assets to North American Aviation.

Paul E. Fontenoy

See also

Curtiss JN-4 "Jenny"; Curtiss P-40 Warhawk; Curtiss, Glenn Hammond; Porte, John C.

References

Bowers, Peter M. *Curtiss Aircraft, 1907–1947.* London: Putnam, 1979.

Curtiss Biplane Fighters

Although Curtiss was the largest manufacturer of aircraft during World War I, it did not produce a fighter until the end of that period (the 18-T "Wasp" triplane, of which only two were built). Curtiss built 50 Orenco D fighters in 1920, one U.S. Army Engineering Service PN-1 biplane fighter in 1920, and 34 U.S. Navy Bureau of Aeronautics TS-1 biplane fighters in 1921 under the competitive procurement program, but none was a Curtiss design or added to Curtiss's technology. In 1924 Curtiss built two TS-1s as all-metal aircraft (the original used much wood); these were designated F4C-1s.

Curtiss fighter technology got a boost from the design of racers for the Army and Navy, starting in 1921. These aircraft, the CR-1 and -2, the R-6, and the R2C/R3C, dominated Pulitzer Trophy racing, greatly influenced fighter aircraft design, and caused the diversion of the Schneider Trophy races from a sportsman's game to serious international rivalry between governments.

The PW-8 was Curtiss's first production fighter design, being rolled out January 1923, and used much of the race plane technology, including the D-12 engine, flush wing-mounted radiators, and the parallel leading and trailing edges on single-bay wings. A few months later, Boeing rolled out a similar design, the PW-9, having tapered wings that Curtiss quickly adopted for the P-1; this began a 10-year era of Army and Navy use of both companies to supply their fighters. It was not a competition, as the services desired to have two manufacturers for fighter aircraft.

The airframe was enlarged slightly to accept the larger Curtiss V-1400 and V-1570 Conqueror engines as they became available. The Army's need for trainers, which used the "AT" designation, was satisfied by fitting Hawk airframes with lower-powered Wright Hisso 200-shp engines. Most of these were later refitted with D-12s and again designated fighters.

When the Navy decided to stop using liquid-cooled en-

The Curtiss P-6 was modified over the years but retained the same basic formula of World War I fighters as an open cockpit biplane with fixed landing gear and fixed propeller. (U.S. Air Force)

gines it ordered Hawks with Pratt and Whitney R1340 Wasp radial engines. The Army briefly tried the Wasp in the P-3 series but found it unsatisfactory. Early in Navy Hawk production, the F6Cs had stiffened landing gear and arresting gear. The F7C was the first Curtiss airplane designed specifically for carrier operation.

From the beginning, the Hawks had welded-steel-tube, fabric-covered fuselages and used wooden wings. The later series of biplane Hawks was built with steel wings that suffered from sympathetic vibration; these were exchanged for wooden wings. Curtiss also exploited the design in the Falcon and Helldiver lines of attack and fighter-bomber aircraft that were basically stretched and rewinged Hawks.

Douglas G. Culy

References

Bowers, Peter M. *Curtiss Aircraft, 1907–1947.* London: Putnam; Annapolis, MD: Naval Institute Press, 1979.

Shamburger, Page, and Joe Christy. *The Curtiss Hawks.* Kalamazoo, MI: Wolverine Press, 1972.

Curtiss, Glenn Hammond (1878–1930)

One of America's pioneer aviators. Glenn Curtiss was born in 1878 in Hammondsport, New York. Like the Wright brothers, Curtiss started a bicycle shop but quickly moved into the arena of motorcycles and mechanical engines. His talent with gasoline engines brought him to the attention of Alexander Graham Bell, who asked Curtiss to join his Aeronautical Experiment Association (AEA) in Canada. Joining Bell and Curtiss in the AEA were Frederick Casey Baldwin, soon to be Canada's first aviator, J.A.D. McCurdy, and Lieutenant Thomas Selfridge, who became the airplane's first casualty. (On 17 September 1908, Selfridge died from his injuries after a crash as a passenger in Orville Wright's plane; his was the first death to occur from a heavier-than-air aircraft accident.) Bell required each of the members to build a successful heavier-than-air craft of his own design. Every aircraft built by the AEA was powered by an engine designed by Curtiss.

His flair for design and talent with engineering soon propelled Curtiss into leadership in the burgeoning field of aviation. In 1908, Curtiss introduced the AEA's third aircraft, the June Bug. He later toured with the June Bug and won the Scientific American Trophy. Curtiss often toured and competed in aviation meets worldwide. In 1909, with the help of Baldwin and McCurdy, Curtiss opened the first aircraft manufacturing company. His business partner was A. Herring, a former employee of Octave Chanute. In 1910, Curtiss opened a flying school in Hammondsport, and America's first female aviator, Blanche Stuart Scott, learned to fly there in the fall of that year.

Curtiss's career was marred by his court battles with the Wright brothers over patent infringement. The Wright brothers claimed Curtiss had stolen their ideas while visiting them in 1906 with Baldwin. In 1906, the Wrights believed Curtiss's interest in aviation was a passing interest, and they were not threatened by his interest and questions. The Wrights gave the AEA advice and offered sources where their work had been published. Apparently many of the Wrights' published suggestions were found on "June Bug," but the Wrights were not given credit. The battle was drawn out and hostile, but with the threat of World War and the need to increase production of warplanes, the case was finally settled in 1917.

Curtiss continued advancing his work by employing skilled designers, some from Great Britain, and creating one of the most popular American aircraft of World War I—the JN-4 "Jenny." Due to postwar surplus, many aviators were able to purchase the Jenny, becoming barnstormers. This aircraft was responsible for training a majority of America's war-time pilots and was equally important in the postwar years.

Court battles so sapped Curtiss's creative energy that he moved to Florida and became a real estate developer. He died in Florida at the age of 52.

Wendy Coble

See also

Curtiss JN-4 "Jenny"

References

Longyard, William H. *Who's Who in Aviation History.* Novato, CA: Presidio Press, 1994.

Whitehouse, Arch. *The Early Birds: The Wonders and Heroics of the First Decades of Flight.* Garden City, NY: Doubleday, 1965.

Curtiss JN-4 "Jenny"

World War I U.S. training aircraft. The Curtiss JN-4, affectionately referred to as the "Jenny," was the first mass-produced aircraft in America. The Jenny was without a doubt this country's most famous aircraft during World War I and remained so for several years afterward.

The idea behind the birth of the Jenny arose from concerns by U.S. military aviation officials over the dismal safety record of existing pusher-type aircraft. As a consequence, the Curtiss Aeroplane and Motor Company hired British aircraft designer B. Douglas Thomas to develop a tractor-type aircraft to replace the deadly pushers. Thomas, who had experience with both the Avro and Sopwith aircraft companies in England, soon came up with the Model J. The best characteristics of this aircraft were combined with those of the Curtiss Model N, culminating in a docile yet attractive two-seater aircraft designated the JN, which quickly evolved to Jenny. The JN promptly went into production at various locations throughout the United States, progressing through several designations, the most common of which was the JN-4.

The Jenny soon became the standard military trainer in the United States during World War I and for several years afterward. In addition to its use by all three major service branches of the U.S. military, Canada, England, and Spain also used various models of the Jenny as a basic trainer during 1917–1918. The most common version was powered by the 90-hp OX-5 engine.

Although most Jennies were used as basic flight trainers, some were equipped for more advanced training with machine guns, bomb racks, and the more powerful 150-hp Wright-Hispano engine. By the time production finally ended, more than 8,000 Jennies of several variants had been manufactured in the United States and Canada, and it had taught tens of thousands of aspiring aviators to fly. Indeed, 95 percent of all U.S. wartime pilots learned to fly in a Jenny. This adaptable aircraft remained in the U.S. military inventory until late 1927.

The wartime significance of the Jenny is undisputed, but it did not reach immortality status until after the war, when thousands of surplus aircraft were put on the public market. Selling well below cost—in some cases less than $100—the Jenny became America's premier barnstorming aircraft. Hundreds of former wartime pilots wandered like flying gypsies throughout America during the 1920s, stunting, giving rides, and putting on impromptu aerial demonstrations with their surplus Jennies.

Steven A. Ruffin

References

Bowers, Peter M. *Curtiss Aircraft, 1907–1947.* London: Putnam, 1979.
Lincke, Jack R. *Jenny Was No Lady: The Story of the JN-4D.* New York: W. W.Norton, 1970.

Curtiss P-40 Warhawk

World War II U.S. fighter. The Curtiss P-40 Warhawk, made famous by the legendary Flying Tigers, was one of America's most important fighter aircraft of World War II. The P-40 originated in 1938 as the XP-40, a derivation of the mid-1930s Curtiss radial-engine design, the P-36 Hawk. Unlike the Hawk, however, the P-40 was equipped with a liquid-cooled Allison V-1710-33 inline engine, which greatly reduced frontal area and increased performance.

Although the P-40 was sturdy, with good diving characteristics and an attractive, sleek-looking design, it exhibited only mediocre performance compared to most other fighters of the day. By the start of the war, in fact, the P-40 was virtually obsolete. Still, it continued to be produced in great numbers, as it was one of the few fighters already in full production and readily available from war's outset.

The P-40's chief claim to fame was its use by General Claire Chennault's American Volunteer Group (AVG), immortalized as the Flying Tigers. The AVG operated in China under the control of General Chiang Kai-shek in the early months of World War II. With the colorful but intimidating shark's teeth painted on their noses, the P-40 fighter aircraft flown by the flamboyant and highly capable pilots of the AVG were extremely successful in intercepting and destroying invading Japanese aircraft. Although consistently outnumbered, pilots flying the P-40 registered a kill ratio of 25 Japanese aircraft for every P-40 destroyed in aerial combat. Because of its effectiveness, as well as the popular cause the AVG supported, the P-40 became one of the most recognized aircraft in history.

The P-40 saw extensive service throughout World War II—beginning with the actual attack on Pearl Harbor. In addition to its use by the United States, the P-40 was used by 28 Allied nations, including the British in North Africa, the Australians in the South Pacific, and the Russians on the Eastern Front. Indeed, even as late as 1943 the P-40—in combination with the Bell P-39—still represented over half of the total fighter strength in the U.S. Army Air Forces.

The P-40 underwent numerous design modifications throughout the war, but when the far superior P-38, P-47, and P-51 fighters arrived on the scene, the P-40 was quickly relegated to roles other than air-to-air combat, such as ground support. By the end of the war, only one U.S. squadron was still equipped with the P-40.

The rugged P-40 played a significant role in winning the war because it was available at a time when most other World War II fighters were still in the planning stages, and it performed dependably and effectively until more advanced fighters became available. Even though a total of 13,738 P-40s were built from May 1940 through 1944, only a handful of these classic and historic aircraft are still flying today.

Steven A. Ruffin and Daniel A. Ruffin

See also

American Volunteer Group; Bell P-39 Airacobra and P-63 Kingcobra

References

Bowers, Peter M. *Curtiss Aircraft, 1907–1947.* London: Putnam, 1979.

The Curtiss P-40 achieved its greatest fame with the Flying Tigers, but it also proved itself in every theater of war. Rarely the fastest or most maneuverable aircraft in a combat, it was often the most rugged and served its nation well. (U.S. Air Force)

Rubenstein, Murry, and Richard M. Goldman. *To Join with the Eagles: Curtiss-Wright Aircraft, 1903–1965.* New York: Doubleday, 1974.

Curtiss-Wright Corporation

U.S. aircraft manufacturing company. The Curtiss-Wright Corporation was one of the largest aircraft manufacturing companies in the United States before and during World War II. Its contribution to the war effort was so significant that it was said to be second only to General Motors as a manufacturer of war goods.

Curtiss-Wright was founded in 1929 with the somewhat unlikely merger of two old enemies, the Curtiss Aeroplane and Motor Company and the Wright Aeronautical Corporation. Throughout the 1930s, the company flourished, producing airframes, propellers, and engines for both military and commercial aircraft in the United States, as well as for numerous foreign countries.

As the buildup for World War II began, Curtiss-Wright rapidly expanded to several locations throughout the United States, increasing plant capacity tenfold from 1939 to 1941. By the time the United States entered the war, the company operated 15 factories, occupying 11 million square feet of space and employing 50,000 workers, and it had a backlog of orders totaling $1 billion.

During its heyday, Curtiss-Wright manufactured numerous types of aircraft, many now regarded as classic, such as the Curtiss Helldiver and the Curtiss C-46 Commando transport. But without a doubt the most famous and successful Curtiss aircraft was the P-40 Warhawk, immortalized as the shark-nosed fighter flown by the famed Flying Tigers. Already in full-scale production at the start of the war, this aircraft was produced continuously until the end of 1944. By the end of the war, Curtiss-Wright had produced more than 140,000 aircraft engines and propellers and nearly 30,000 aircraft.

When the war ended, military aircraft orders came to a virtual standstill, and even though Curtiss-Wright was financially sound, the company went into a decline. Unlike other aircraft companies, which were able to transition to new technologies, a peacetime economy, and civilian aircraft production, Curtiss-Wright lagged in the development of successful postwar civilian aircraft designs. Instead, the company opted to concentrate its efforts on engine and propeller production alone. By 1950, Curtiss-Wright was in effect no longer in the aircraft manufacturing business.

The company continued to manufacture engines until 1983, when that part of its operation was discontinued as

One of the most beautiful biplane fighters ever built, the Curtiss P-6E appeared at its best in the colors of the 17th Pursuit Squadron of the 1st Pursuit Group. (U.S. Air Force)

well. Once a world giant in the field of aviation, the Curtiss-Wright Corporation has continued to survive by diversifying its efforts into a variety of ventures, not all of which are related to aviation. And even though today the company's name is the only remaining hint of its aviation heritage, the Curtiss-Wright Corporation still continues to prosper.

Steven A. Ruffin

References

Bowers, Peter M. *Curtiss Aircraft, 1907–1947.* London: Putnam, 1979.

Eltscher, Louis R., and Edward M. Young. *Curtiss-Wright: Greatness and Decline.* New York: Twayne, 1998.

Fausel, Robert W. *Whatever Happened to Curtiss-Wright?* Manhattan, KS: Sunflower University Press, 1990.

Rubenstein, Murry, and Richard M. Goldman. *To Join with the Eagles: Curtiss-Wright Aircraft, 1903–1965.* New York: Doubleday, 1974.

D

Dargue, Herbert A. (1886–1941)

Major general in the U.S. military. Herbert Arthur "Bert" Dargue was born in New Jersey on 17 November 1886. After a brief career as a schoolteacher, he entered the U.S. Military Academy in 1907, graduating in 1911 as a lieutenant of coast artillery. He was rated a military aviator in 1913 after transferring to the Signal Corps and taking flight training in the Philippine aviation school.

In December 1914, Dargue and Lieutenant J. O. Mauborgne became the first Army airmen to both transmit and receive inflight radio messages, operating a wireless unit they had designed and built. Soon afterward, Dargue was transferred to San Diego, California, as a flight instructor. Following that tour, he was assigned to the 1st Aero Squadron in San Antonio, Texas. He participated in the campaign of 1916 that pursued the rebel leader Pancho Villa deep into the interior of Mexico. Forced landings were frequent, and Dargue and his observer once hiked for three days back to friendly territory after crashing behind Villa's lines.

During World War I, Dargue first helped establish, and then commanded, the Aerial Observer School at Fort Sill, Oklahoma. He later went to France at the direction of the chief of the Signal Corps as a special observer to report on the readiness of training and combat air units.

After the war, he graduated from both the Army and Navy War Colleges. He and Hap Arnold were close friends of General Billy Mitchell, whom they counseled in vain to stay within the military chain of command in his fight for an independent air force; both were strong proponents.

In 1926, Dargue was chosen to lead the record-setting Pan-American Goodwill Flight, which circumnavigated the South American continent in Loening 0A-1A amphibians. He and his copilot parachuted to safety after a midair collision over Buenos Aires that killed the crew of the other aircraft. He led the flight back to the United States in a replacement Loening, and in 1927 he and the other surviving members of the Goodwill Flight were awarded the first Distinguished Flying Crosses by President Calvin Coolidge.

He was later assigned to Langley Field, Virginia, as commanding officer of the 2d Bombardment Group, flying Keystone B-3A aircraft. While there, he conceived and developed many of the strategic bombing plans and aircraft formations used by the U.S. Army Air Forces in World War II.

During the 1930s, he led development and testing of the Norden precision bombsight, a top-secret weapon that contributed greatly to the success of World War II USAAF bombing missions in Europe and the Pacific.

In late 1941, Major General Dargue commanded the First Air Force at Mitchell Field, New York. After the Pearl Harbor attack, he was chosen by Secretary of War Henry Stimson to take command of Army forces in Hawaii; en route, the B-18 he was piloting crashed in the Sierra Nevada Mountains of California, killing all aboard.

James Snyder

Dassault, Marcel (1892–1986)

French aircraft designer and industrialist, born Marcel Bloch in Paris on 22 January 1892. Dassault companies built the most successful military aircraft in Europe in the decades after World War II.

The son of a Jewish physician, Bloch obtained degrees in aeronautical design and electrical engineering. In addition, he worked as an aircraft designer for France during World War I. There, he engaged in real estate in the 1920s but returned to aeronautics in 1930, starting his own company

The Dassault Mirage IIIC all-weather interceptor, one of the many variants of the successful Mirage design. (Walter J. Boyne)

and building military and civilian airplanes with notable success and profitability. During World War II, he refused to work for the Germans, and as a consequence Bloch was sent to the Buchenwald concentration camp.

After the war, Bloch changed his last name to Dassault (a nom de guerre of one of his brothers in the Resistance) and converted to Roman Catholicism. His aircraft manufacturing company, Générale Aéronautique Marcel Dassault, led the postwar revival of the French aircraft industry, producing Europe's first supersonic plane, the Mystère, as well as the highly successful Mirage line of delta-winged military aircraft in 1956. The Mirage symbolized modern aerial combat and brought additional trade to France and incalculable prestige, especially in defense hardware. The various Mirage warplanes proved very popular among neutral and Third World nations and became some of the most widely used military aircraft in the world.

In 1967, Dassault's company merged with Breguet Aviation, a manufacturer of transport aircraft, to form Avions Marcel Dassault–Breguet Aviation. In addition, Dassault was a deputy in the National Assembly from 1951 to 1955 and from 1958 to 1986.

In January 1976, Marcel Dassault announced that he was launching a private venture to build the Delta Super Mirage as a long-range multirole aircraft for export, but it was canceled. As a replacement, the French government announced a decision to award a study contract with Marcel Dassault for a smaller and simpler single-engine delta fighter outwardly very much like the Mirage III of 20 years earlier. The result was the Mirage 2000, currently in service with a number of foreign countries. Marcel Dassault died in Paris on 18 April 1986. The Lycée Marcel Dassault, a famous technological and scientific institute in Rochefort, France, carries his name.

Albert Atkins

See also

Dassault Mirage III; Dassault Mystère IVA

References

Gunston, Bill. *Modern Fighters and Attack Aircraft.* New York: Arco, 1980.

Dassault Mirage III

One of the most successful European military aircraft of its generation. The French Mirage has been adopted by the air arms of many overseas customers, as well as by the Armée de l'Air (the French air force). Equally adaptable for the low-level ground attack or high-altitude intercept roles, the Mirage began life as an attempt to produce the smallest practicable all-weather interceptor capable of attaining an altitude of 60,000 feet in six minutes and fulfilling an Armée de l'Air specification. The first model, the MD.550 Mirage I, which flew on 25 June 1955, was intended essentially to prove the practicability of the tailless delta configuration; it was powered by two 1,640–pound/thrust Bristol-Siddeley Viper turbojets. Weighing only 7,341 pounds empty and 11,177 pounds loaded, the Mirage I attained Mach 1.15 in a shallow dive. With additional power, Mach 1.3 was attained in level flight on 17 December 1956.

The Mirage II was also hampered by insufficient engine power and was succeeded by the Mirage III. Considerably larger than the Mirage I and some 30 percent heavier, the Mirage III retained the 5 percent thickness-to-chord ratio, with a leading edge sweep of 60 degrees, and used a single SNECMA Atar 101G.1 turbojet offering an afterburning thrust of 8,818 pounds. The Mirage III-001 flew for the first time on 17 November 1956, attaining Mach 1.6 in a dive on 30 January 1957. With afterburning, maximum level speed was raised from Mach 1.52 to Mach 1.65. A speed of Mach 1.8 (1,188 mph) was later attained with the aid of an SEPR 66 rocket.

The Mirage III was, in its initial form, intended solely for the intercept role, and a demand for a wider versatility resulted in a multipurpose Mirage IIIA, which differed from its immediate predecessor in a number of respects. Wing area was increased, and the leading edge was provided with conical camber and an axial "notch." The fuselage was lengthened to accommodate the Atar 09, a supersonic engine with additional compressor and turbine stages to those of the Atar 101G rated at 9,370 pounds/thrust and 13,230 pounds/thrust with afterburning, and provision was made for a detachable SEPR 841 rocket pack offering 1,500 pounds/thrust for 160 seconds or 3,000 pounds/thrust for 80 seconds.

The first "preseries" aircraft the Mirage IIIA-01 flew on 12 May 1958, and in six months, on 24 October, the aircraft attained Mach 2.0 in level flight without the rocket motor mounted, the SEPR 841 being first tested on the Mirage IIIA-02. The Mirage IIIA-05 was the first aircraft to be completed to full production standard, effectively being a prototype for the initial production model, the Mirage IIIC, which was visually almost indistinguishable from the preseries aircraft.

Albert Atkins

References

Green, William. *The World's Fighting Planes.* London: MacDonald, 1964.

Dassault Mystère IVA

The French Mystère series of aircraft was among the most important to appear in the West and maintained France's indigenous aircraft industry. A variety of Mystère aircraft was produced to meet many different national needs.

The Mystère IVA remained in service with the Armée de l'Air (the French air force) until 1964. Dassault built 421 examples of this interceptor before production ended in 1958. One hundred and ten were delivered to India, 60 to Israel, and the remainder to the Armée de l'Air.

Bearing more than a general aerodynamic resemblance to its immediate predecessor, only 150 production examples of the Mystère IIC saw limited service with the Armée de l'Air. The Mystère IVA featured a more robust, oval-section fuselage, a wing of increased sweepback and reduced thickness-to-chord ratio, and a more powerful turbojet. The Mystère IVA-01 flew for the first time on 28 September 1952. The first 50 Mystère IVA fighters manufactured for the Armée de l'Air were powered by the 6,280-pounds/thrust Hispano Suiza Tay 250A turbojet, and the type entered service in 1955. All subsequent Mystère IVAs received the more powerful Verdon 350.

The first prototype of the Super Mystère B.1 flew on 2 March 1955, powered by a Rolls-Royce Avon R.A. 7R turbojet. The first of five Atar-powered preproduction Super Mystère B.2s followed on 15 May 1956. The primary role of the Super Mystère B.2 was that of day interceptor, but a variety of underwing stores made it suitable for the fighter-bomber role. The Super Mystère B.2 equipped two squadrons of the 5th Armée de l'Air and one squadron of the Israeli Air Force. One hundred and eighty Super Mystère B.2s were completed when production terminated in 1959.

Albert Atkins

References

Aeroflight Website.
http://www.aeroflight.co.uk/waf/israel/sqns/101sqn.htm.

Green, William. *The World's Fighting Planes.* London: MacDonald, 1964.

Davis, Benjamin Oliver Jr. (1912–)

U.S. general. Benjamin Oliver Davis Jr. was born in Washington, D.C., on 18 December 1912 to Benjamin Oliver and Elnora Davis. His father had been the first African American to attend the United States Military Academy (USMA) and later, in 1940, the first African American to become an Army brigadier general.

Davis was only the second African American accepted at West Point, his father being the first. Once at the USMA, Davis had to endure four long years of what cadets called "the silent treatment." His classmates and instructors never spoke to him except to give him orders or instructions. Davis persevered and graduated in June 1936, thirty-fifth out of a class of 276.

Soon after graduation, he married Agatha Scott, who became his life partner and strongest supporter. Upon graduation, Davis applied for pilot training but was instead assigned to the infantry. Captain Davis was sent to the Tuskegee Institute in Alabama to teach military science. Soon, the need for personnel brought on by the war in Europe led to Davis and 12 other black cadets receiving flight training at Tuskegee. Davis and three others received their wings in March 1942. This group formed the cadre of the all-black 99th Pursuit Squadron formed later that year.

The 99th was deployed to North Africa in June 1943, flying older Curtiss P-40 Warhawks, and was not allowed to fly combat missions. After four months, Davis rotated home. White officers argued that the black pilots were too cowardly to fly combat. Davis countered that they had not been given a fair chance. After a tense several weeks, U.S. Army Air Forces leaders, no doubt pressured by the White House, directed that select black pilots be allowed to fly combat missions.

In late 1943, Davis took command of the 332d Fighter Group and was promoted to lieutenant colonel. In January 1944, the 332d deployed to Italy and by May had transitioned to Republic P-47 Thunderbolts.

On 9 June, Davis led 39 P-47s escorting Consolidated B-24s on a raid on Munich. Over the target they engaged more than 100 Messerschmitt Bf 109 fighters, downing five and damaging many others. For his leadership Davis won the Distinguished Flying Cross, which was pinned on by his father. During the raid the 332d continued a tradition it maintained throughout the war. During 200 escort missions it never lost a bomber under its protection.

By 1945, the 332d had transitioned to North American P-51 Mustangs, which were painted with a distinctive red tail and nose. As such, the unit became known as the "Red Tails." By the end of the war in Europe, the unit had flown 15,000 sorties, downed 111 enemy planes, and destroyed 150 on the ground with a loss of 66 aircraft. It received the Presidential Unit Citation.

After the war, Colonel Davis became an influential advocate for integration of the U.S. military and an example of making it happen. In 1946, he assumed a difficult assignment when he became commander of Lockbourne AFB, Ohio. While he gained the distinction of being the first African American to command an air installation, the local community in Columbus was not happy with a black unit and a black commander. It was to Davis's credit that by the time he left in 1949 local relations had dramatically improved.

In the early 1950s, Davis commanded the 477th Composite Group and 332d Fighter Wing. In 1953, he again saw combat as commander of the 51st Fighter-Interceptor Wing flying North American F-86 Sabre jets in Korea. In late 1953, following the war, Davis became the first African American to become an Air Force brigadier general.

In 1959, he became a major general and then made lieutenant general in 1965. In 1967, Davis took command of the Thirteenth Air Force stationed at Clark AFB in the Philippines, flying combat sorties during the Vietnam War. His final assignment was a concurrent position as deputy commander in chief (CINC), U.S. Strike Command, and Deputy CINC, Middle East.

General Davis retired in late 1970 after 34 years in service. President Richard M. Nixon appointed him director of civil aviation security. In June 1971, he was promoted to assistant secretary of transportation for environmental, safety, and consumer affairs.

Davis retired from the Department of Transportation in 1975 and received its National Gold Medal. Among his many awards he received the Distinguished Flying Cross, the Army and Air Force Distinguished Service Medals, Silver Star, Croix de Guerre, Air Medal with five Oak Leaf Clusters, three Legions of Merit, the UN Service Medal, Langley Medal from the Smithsonian Institution, and the Thomas D. White National Defense Award.

In 1991, Davis published his memoir (*Benjamin O. Davis, Jr., American: An Autobiography*), detailing his trials and successes. On 15 February 1997, the U.S. Post Office issued a stamp honoring Davis and all African American service personnel. On 8 December 1998, President Bill Clinton, during a ceremony at the White House, promoted Davis to the rank of four-star general. General Daniel "Chappie" James had been the first black Air Force four-star, but many believed that Davis should have been and that this was a long-overdue honor for a pioneer of airpower and equal rights.

At this writing, the Davises live in the Washington, D.C., area. He remains an active advocate for strong national defense, a strong Air Force, and equal opportunity for all Americans.

William Head and Brian Head

References

Davis, Benjamin O. Jr. *Benjamin O. Davis, Jr., American: An Autobiography.* Washington, DC: Smithsonian Institution Press, 1991.

Gropman, Alan L. "Benjamin O. Davis, Jr.: History on Two Fronts." In John L. Frisbee, ed., *Makers of the United States Air Force.* Washington, DC: Office of Air Force History, 1987.

______. *The Air Force Integrates, 1945–1964.* Washington, DC: Office of Air Force History, 1978.

The de Havilland Vampire was first flown in September 1943 and remained in use with the Swiss air force into the 1990s. Shown here is Geoffrey de Havilland, Jr., who would be killed in the 1946 crash of the de Havilland D.H. 108 Swallow. (Walter J. Boyne)

De Havilland Aircraft (Early Years and World War I)

British aircraft manufacturer. George Thomas had acquired the British rights to Farman aircraft in 1911 and used the interest to found the Aircraft Company, Ltd. (Airco). In 1914, at Geoffrey de Havilland's urging, Holt undertook the manufacture of original designs and hired de Havilland to head the design department.

Throughout the war, Airco designs were prefixed with the letters "DH," indicating their designer, Geoffrey de Havilland. By war's end, the fame of this prefix had eclipsed the name of the manufacturer, and the aircraft were known everywhere as de Havillands.

De Havilland's early designs were pushers, a layout dictated by the lack of a workable interrupter gear. His first success was the D.H. 2, the single-seat pusher that, along with the Nieuport 11, ended the reign of the Fokker Eindecker.

The D.H. 3 was intended as a heavy bomber but never made it past the prototype stage. It did, however, serve as the basis for the later D.H. 10.

His next effort, the D.H. 4, was a tractor design powered by a Rolls-Royce engine. One of the most successful types to come out of Airco, the de Havilland D.H. 4 first appeared in 1917. It was a two-seat light daytime bomber powered by a 375-hp Rolls-Royce Eagle VIII engine. Intended for use against tactical targets, it could carry four 100-pound bombs on external racks under the lower wing. Defensively, it was equipped with a synchronized Vickers .303-caliber machine gun for the pilot and one or two .303-caliber Lewis guns mounted on a rotating Scarff ring for use by the observer. Its real defense, however, lay in its great speed, which allowed it to outrun pursuing German fighters.

Replaced in due course by the D.H. 9 and D.H. 9a, the D.H. 4 got a new lease on life in 1918, when it entered service with the U.S. Air Service. Powered in that role by the new Liberty engine, the DH-4 (its American designation) became the only aircraft manufactured in the United States to see action in World War I.

The D.H. 5 was a departure for de Havilland. A single-seater, its layout employed negative stagger to maximize the pilot's view so the aircraft could be used for ground attack.

The next product, the D.H. 6, was an inexpensive trainer, its "wings built by the mile and cut off by the yard." Its angular wings and control surfaces enabled easy, inexpensive construction. As it happened, the aircraft also proved useful on coastal patrol duties.

The D.H. 9 was a revised D.H. 4, intended for the Siddeley Puma engine. When the engine did not live up to its potential, however, the design was re-engined with the Rolls-Royce Eagle VIII or the American Liberty and emerged as the D.H. 9a.

De Havilland's last wartime effort was the D.H. 10, a second attempt to produce a heavy bomber. Had the war continued, this aircraft would have competed with the Handley Page and Vickers Vimy.

James Streckfuss

References
Bruce, J. M. *British Aeroplanes, 1914–1918.* London: Putnam, 1957.
______. *The Aeroplanes of the Royal Flying Corps (Military Wing).* London: Putnam, 1982.

De Havilland Aircraft (Post–World War I)

Geoffrey de Havilland formed De Havilland Aircraft Company on 25 September 1920, following the closing of the wartime Airco, for which he was chief designer and where he designed the classic de Havilland D.H. 4, among others.

A whole series of aircraft flowed from the de Havilland plant, including bombers, fighters, sportplanes, racers, trainers, transports, and ultra-lightweight aircraft. The first military aircraft produced by the de Havilland plant was the D.H. 27 Derby, a large, single-engine bomber prototype that did not receive any production orders.

The most prominent design of the 1920s and 1930s was the D.H. 60 Moth series, which was sold all over the world to both civil and military customers and led directly to the classic de Havilland D.H. 82A Tiger Moth, which became the RAF's standard basic trainer for many years; more than 8,000 were built.

Other classic designs included the twin- and four-engine biplane transports, the famous Puss Moth sportplane, and the de Havilland D.H. 88 Comet that won the 1934 London-to-Australia race. The Comet featured wooden stressed-skin construction that would appear again on the elegant D.H. 91 Albatross four-engine transport and the incomparable D.H. 98 Mosquito.

De Havilland design and construction lent itself to the jet age, and there appeared a series of fighters, including the Vampire, Venom, and Sea Vixen. Commercial aircraft included the twin-engine Dove and four-engine Heron.

The most brilliant, if also the most tragic, de Havilland effort in the postwar years was undoubtedly the stunning D.H. 106 Comet, the first jet airliner to see service. Although an otherwise masterful design, it fell prey to the lack of experience in building large airliners with pressurized cabins and encountered fatigue problems that caused crashes and forced its withdrawal from service. Later-model Comets were built that had overcome the design flaw, but the design never recovered its initial momentum and was superseded by Boeing and Douglas airliners.

De Havilland built the successful Trident, which sold in small numbers but was succeeded by the highly successful Hawker-Siddeley H.S. 121 after de Havilland was absorbed by that corporation. It also built the de Havilland D.H. 125 executive jet, which was also built in greater numbers by Hawker-Siddeley.

De Havilland also built aircraft in Australia and Canada. In Canada, the company became famous for its Chipmunk trainer and the Beaver and Otter bush transports. The DHC-4 Caribou was used extensively by the United States Army (and later by the USAF) and led to a whole series of designs including the DHC-5 Buffalo, DHC-6 Twin Otter, DHC-7 Dash 7, and DHC-8 Dash 8. The company was acquired by Boeing, which in turn sold it to Bombardier Aerospace.

Walter J. Boyne

See also
de Havilland D.H. 82 Tiger Moth; de Havilland D.H. 98 Mosquito

References
Donald, David, gen. ed. *The Complete Encyclopedia of World Aircraft.* New York: Barnes and Noble, 1997.
Gunston, Bill. *World Encyclopedia of Aircraft Manufacturers.* Sparkford, UK: Patrick Stephens, 1993.
Jackson, A. J. *De Havilland Aircraft Since 1909.* London, Putnam, 1962.

De Havilland D.H. 98 Mosquito

Classic British multimission aircraft from World War II. The de Havilland D.H. 98 Mosquito was a private venture of the De Havilland Aircraft Company, building on their experience in wood construction gained on the de Havilland Comet and other aircraft. It was built mainly of plywood molded to complex shapes. A pair of Merlin engines powered the Mosquito, which was fast and maneuverable.

Successive variants appeared, each with increased power, improved propellers, and a wide variety of equipment. Some aircraft were pressurized for operation at extreme altitudes.

The final two variants of the Mosquito remained in Royal Air Force operational service until replaced by the Canberra PR.3 in 1955. Some examples remained in use as target tugs until 1961.

The Mosquito bomber role first entered RAF service in November 1941. It was employed in both day and night operations and often performed diversionary raids. Further changes of operation saw the Mosquitos flying at night in the Pathfinder target-marking role where they dropped incendiaries to mark targets for the following bomber fleets. Although target-marking was the primary mission, the Pathfinders also carried high-explosive weapons to supplement the main load.

Its speed and maneuverability made the Mosquito effective as a fighter. Three distinct versions were employed—for ground attack, antishipping, and as a night-fighter.

One of the most successful aircraft of the war, the de Havilland Mosquito combined high speed, long range, and good load capability in a single aircraft. (Kev Darling)

The Mosquito was also deployed to the Far East theater of operations, where it replaced the Bristol Blenheim. During the war the USAAF flew the reconnaissance version over Italy. Surplus aircraft also entered service with the air forces of Belgium, Norway, and Sweden and others.

Kev Darling

References

Franks, Richard A. *The de Havilland Mosquito.* London: SAM, 1998

De Havilland Tiger Moth

British trainer during World War II. De Havilland's Tiger Moth served the Royal Air Force in a training role for more than 15 years before being replaced by the Percival Prentice and the de Havilland Canada Chipmunk.

Developed from the earlier Gypsy Moth, the Tiger Moth featured staggered and slightly swept wings, mainly to aid better egress from the front cockpit while wearing a parachute. The engine was mounted in the inverted position to improve forward vision, and other detail improvements aided stability and handling. After acceptance testing, the Tiger Moth was cleared for full blind flying and the full range of aerobatics.

A first production batch was delivered to the Central Flying School in early 1932. These were followed by Mk.II versions, which were fitted with a slightly more powerful Gypsy Major engine rated at 130 horsepower. Slightly later in their career they were fitted with antispin strakes to improve stability.

When war was declared against Germany in September 1939, more than 1,000 aircraft had been delivered to elementary and reserve training schools. Eventually, 4,200 Tiger Moths were built in Britain; large quantities were also built in Canada, Australia, and New Zealand for use in the Commonwealth Air Training plan. The Tiger Moth was eventually phased out in 1951. There was one other variant of the Tiger Moth, the Queen Bee, which was a radio-controlled pilotless target used for live firing practice. The Bee was available in both landplane and floatplane versions.

Kev Darling

References

McKay, Stuart. *De Havilland Tiger Moth.* London: PSL, 1999.

Defense Advanced Research Projects Agency (DARPA)

Manages and directs selected basic and applied research and development projects for the U.S. Department of Defense. It also pursues research and technology where risk and payoff are both very high and where success may provide dramatic advances for traditional military roles and missions.

U.S. Secretary of Defense Neil H. McElroy created the Advanced Research Projects Agency (ARPA) on 8 February 1958 as a new agency for space technology and development with complete authority for direction of the growing space program. Today ARPA is best known as the creator of the Internet. ARPA Director Roy W. Johnson intended ARPA to be a "fourth service," in effect a national space agency. In 1950, the Department of Defense had assigned military satellites to the Air Force. Now program direction came from ARPA. Another government agency had taken over the Air Force's plans for a space program. However, that proscriptive role was very short-lived.

In October 1958, the National Aeronautics and Space Administration (NASA) became a reality, inheriting existing scientific satellites and planetary missions from the National Science Foundation and ARPA. The act creating NASA divided U.S. space activities between the public NASA civilian world and the private ARPA military world. ARPA lost its dominant role in December 1959 when the Department of Defense divided the responsibility for the various military satellite missions among all three services, redesignating ARPA as a research and development agency. In 1961, the department assigned research, development, test, and engineering for all space programs back to the Air Force, except for "unusual circumstances." Any defense department agency, however, could conduct preliminary research.

In 1972, the name was changed to the Defense Advanced Research Projects Agency. In 1993, DARPA was re-redesignated ARPA. In 1996, the Defense Authorization Act directed an organizational name change to DARPA.

David C. Arnold

Defense Support Program (DSP) and Missile Detection

A space-based system operated by the United States for detecting ICBM launches. The roots of the DSP extend to World War II and branched outward during the following decade. At U.S. Air Force headquarters in the Pentagon during the early 1950s, electrical engineer Joseph Knopow pondered the use of infrared technology for detecting aircraft and submarines. Examining literature captured at the end of World War II, Knopow studied the German Luftwaffe's Kiel IV—a nighttime air-to-air infrared detection system—and considered the possibility of using properly equipped satellites to detect the hot exhaust plumes from ballistic missiles and high-altitude jet aircraft. Shortly after joining Lockheed Aircraft Corporation in June 1995, Knopow convinced his bosses to adopt the infrared-sensing satellite concept, which appeared as Subsystem G of Weapon System 117L (WS-117L) in the March 1956 advanced reconnaissance satellite proposal that Lockheed submitted to the USAF. Meanwhile, Sidney Passman and William Kellogg from the USAF-funded RAND Corporation had written a research memorandum in October 1955 identifying infrared techniques that might be applied to space-based detection of ICBM launches. Their study caught the attention of various science advisory committees and doubtless contributed to the Air Force's selection of Lockheed as prime contractor for WS-117L in June 1956. Knopow became the company's manager for Subsystem G, which he informally dubbed the ICBM Attack Alarm System.

Control of WS-117L and all other military satellite programs shifted to the newly created Advanced Research Projects Agency (ARPA) in March 1958. Although Knopow found himself defending the feasibility of Subsystem G more vigorously than before, the success of experimental payloads aboard aerial test flights in mid-1958 excited Air Force officers. They convinced ARPA officials to separate it from the WS-117L program. On 17 November 1958, the space-based infrared detection system became an independent program identified as the Missile Defense Alarm System (MIDAS). Given the prospect that MIDAS could warn Strategic Air Command (SAC) bomber crews of an impending attack 15 minutes earlier than any other system, Air Force leaders pressed enthusiastically in February 1959 for additional funds to accelerate the program. On 18 September 1959, Secretary of Defense Neil McElroy removed ARPA's oversight and assigned the Air Force direct responsibility for MIDAS.

Although early versions of the development plan had projected an operational space-based warning system by 1962, formidable technical challenges and grossly inadequate funding retarded Lockheed's progress. The first attempt to launch a MIDAS spacecraft failed on 26 February 1960 due to improper separation of the Agena upper stage from the Atlas first stage. After a successful launch of the second MIDAS satellite into a low-inclination, 300-mile orbit on 24 May 1960, problems with the Agena communication link prevented operation of the payload. By August, skepticism on the part of high-ranking Defense Department officials compelled Colonel Quentin Riepe, the first Air Force MIDAS program director, to reorient efforts away from an operational focus toward further developmental and flight tests. Unfortunately, the MIDAS 3 mission on 12 July 1961 terminated prematurely when one of two solar arrays failed to deploy and the satellite ran out of power after only five orbits. An Atlas booster failure on 21 October doomed MIDAS 4. Consequently, on 30 November 1961 a group of experts chaired by ARPA director Jack Ruina recommended to Secretary of Defense Harold Brown that no further consideration be given to an operational system until Lockheed and the Air Force adequately demonstrated the technical feasibility of space-based infrared detection and warning. Hinting at serious program misdirection and mismanagement, the Ruina Report estimated it could take 10 years to achieve an operational version.

Not surprisingly, the MIDAS program was lengthened, wrapped in tighter security restrictions, and renamed Program 461. Disaster continued to plague development efforts in 1962, however, with the loss of MIDAS 5 in April due to a massive onboard power failure on only its sixth orbit, and the destruction of MIDAS 6 in December due to an Atlas launch failure. Shortly after the loss of MIDAS 5, an exhausted Joe Knopow had undergone surgery for a bleeding ulcer, leaving his deputy, John Solvason, to take over program management. Finally, on 9 May 1963 MIDAS 7 successfully achieved a nearly circular 2,250-mile polar orbit. Carrying an improved Aerojet-General infrared payload and a Bouwers concentric telescope with an 8-inch aperture, it detected nine missile launches during 47 days of operation. After yet another launch failure destroyed MIDAS 8 on 12 June, the last satellite with a Program 461 payload—MIDAS 9—went successfully into orbit on 18 July 1963. During its 11-day life span, MIDAS 9 detected one missile as well as some Soviet ground tests. Lockheed and the Air Force had established the feasibility of using infrared-sensing satellites for detection and early warning of ICBM launches.

To support design of the next generation of early warning satellites, the director of defense research and engineering, Harold Brown, on 3 November 1963, approved a three-flight MIDAS research test series for enhancement of longevity and payload reliability. Identified as Research Test Series 1 (RTS-1), these Lockheed satellites had a six-month operational lifetime and carried an improved sensor package produced by Aerojet Corporation for real-time detection and launchpoint determination of low-radiance submarine-launched ballistic missiles and ground-launched, intermediate-range ballistic missiles. The Air Force launched the RTS-1 satellites during 1966, the first on 9 June into an improper, highly elliptical orbit and the others on 19 August and 5 October, respectively, into nearly circular 2,300-mile polar orbits. Their performance far surpassed design standards. Operations continued for a year, capturing data on 139 U.S. and Soviet launches.

Meanwhile, in early 1964 the Air Force had initiated competitive procurement of a follow-on multimission RTS-2 satellite system that would operate in geosynchronous orbit 22,300 miles above the equator. On 15 November 1965, the service redesignated the new system Program 266 (later 949, then 647). Eventually, on 14 June 1969 it would receive the unclassified label of Defense Support Program. Three bidders—Hughes, TRW, and Lockheed—submitted DSP proposals in June 1966. The Air Force awarded TRW the spacecraft contract on 15 December. During the next three and a half years, as TRW worked to deliver the first DSP satellites, the Air Force dispatched survey teams to study possible Large Processing Station (LPS) locations. The United States and Australia signed an agreement in November 1969 to create the Joint Defence Space Communications Station at Nurrungar, near Woomera, which became known as the Overseas Ground Station (OGS). Before the end of June 1970, Buckley Air National Guard Base east of Denver, Colorado, had been selected for the Continental Ground Station (CGS). Those sites, under the direction of Aerospace Defense Command (later Strategic Air Command, then Air Force Space Command), would control the DSP satellites and process in real time all data on missile launches that were transmitted.

The first four launches of DSP satellites, each weighing approximately 2,000 pounds and known collectively as Phase I, occurred during the period 1970–1973. That established an initial operational constellation. Those satellites lasted much longer than their 15-month design life but were replaced with three slightly heavier, more powerful Phase II models during 1975–1977. As the nature of the Soviet missile threat changed, DSP satellites evolved to handle complicated scenarios. Flights 8–11, launched during 1979–1984, had the capability to orbit in either a geosynchronous or highly elliptical path. They also carried external electronic packages for greater survivability, as well as more attitude control system fuel to extend their operational life to three years. Two upgraded Phase II satellites, carrying lead sulfide sensors with improved resolution and new mercury cadmium telluride detectors, entered the picture in December 1984 and November 1987. Finally, in 1989 the on-orbit constellation began to take its present form with introduction of DSP-1 satellites, which weighed more than 5,000 pounds, had a power output more than three times that of the Phase I model, and were designed to last five years.

As DSP satellites improved, the ground segment also evolved to accommodate new mission requirements. Proliferation of ground stations was one way to fulfill a perceived need for greater survivability. Consequently, in December 1974 the Air Force selected IBM Corporation to develop a Simplified Processing Station (SPS). A number of such stations would allow dispersal of receiving capability, as well as backup for the LPSs. During the early 1980s, both OGS and CGS underwent hardware and software upgrades to support future DSP satellite capabilities, and a third fixed site—the European Ground Station—was activated. At the same time, the high cost of the SPS, combined with the perceived need for survivability during and after a nuclear or terrorist attack led the service to acquire a Mobile Ground System (MGS) that became operational in 1985. The latter included six Mobile Ground Terminals (MGTs), along with Mobile Communication Terminals (MCTs) and an MGS Operating Base. Each MGT and MCT had the appearance of an 18-wheel tractor-trailer rig and was entirely roadworthy.

Although the Air Force originally developed DSP to meet a global strategic threat, the system proved its tactical value during Operation DESERT STORM in early 1991. The DSP satellites detected the launch of every Iraqi Scud missile—a total of 88—between 17 January and 25 February. Command centers in Colorado Springs, Colorado, assessed the launch data and provided timely warning to civilians and Coalition forces, including Patriot missile batteries, in Saudi Arabia and Israel. Having demonstrated that the DSP early warning capability worked in the face of theater-level ballistic missile attacks, Air Force Space Command established TALON SHIELD, which officially transitioned to an operational Attack and Launch Early Reporting to Theater (ALERT) capability in September 1994. The ALERT Control Center at Schriever Air Force Base, Colorado, gained responsibility for processing DSP tactical data and warning friendly forces around the globe of potentially hostile launches.

Even as DSP personnel basked in the system's triumphant performance during the Gulf War, Air Force planners struggled to evolve DSP into a far more sophisticated capability—the Space-Based Infrared System (SBIRS)—to support an even broader range of requirements early in the twenty-first century. The complete SBIRS satellite constellation would include sophisticated sensors in geosynchronous, highly elliptical, and low-earth orbits. Among the contractors that teamed up to demonstrate and develop the high and low components of SBIRS were Lockheed Martin, Aerojet, TRW, Boeing, and Raytheon. Alterations in the ground segment would include an SBIRS control station proximate to the old CGS and reduction of overseas sites to Relay Ground Station (RGS) status. In fact, the Nurrungar facility ceased operation in 1999, and a joint U.S.-Australian RGS opened at Pine Gap. A coordinated system-of-systems approach would integrate previously separate space-based infrared sensor programs from the Air Force and national intelligence organizations, thereby eliminating duplication of effort and saving money. Without SBIRS, which would provide critical midcourse tracking and discrimination data, the goals of creating effective theater, national, and global missile defenses would remain illusory.

Rick W. Sturdevant

See also

Missiles, Intercontinental Ballistic; Satellites

References

Ball, Desmond. *A Base for Debate: The U.S. Satellite Station at Nurrungar.* Sydney, Australia: Allen and Unwin, 1987.

Hall, R. Cargill. *Missile Defense Alarm: The Genesis of Space-Based Infrared Early Warning.* Chantilly, VA: NRO History Office, July 1988.

Richelson, Jeffrey T. *America's Space Sentinels: DSP Satellites and National Security.* Lawrence: University Press of Kansas, 1999.

Rosolanka, James J. *The Defense Support Program (DSP): A Pictorial Chronology 1970-1998.* Los Angeles: Los Angeles Air Force Station, Space and Missile Systems Center, 1998.

Defense Suppression

Action taken by military forces to reduce the capability of antiaircraft defenses and allow the highest probability of success for friendly air operations. Defense suppression missions emerged during World War I as military forces sought ways to reduce the effectiveness of enemy aircraft in a range of missions, especially ground attack. In World War I, machine guns and heavier weapons used against aircraft became known as antiaircraft artillery (AAA). These defenses were complemented by fighter/interceptor aircraft that operated on standing patrols or were launched upon warning of enemy attack.

Offensive forces attempted to counter defenses through a combination of tactics (e.g., surprise, night operations, or mission profiles) and defense suppression missions. Defense suppression operations normally involved attacks on the defensive positions near the selected target immediately prior to the actual attack. The attacks included strafing and/or bombing, or artillery fire if close to the front, with the intent of either destroying the defensive position or forcing the defenders to abandon their position, thereby preventing them from engaging the attacking aircraft. These basic approaches of tactics, combined with suppressive attacks on defensive positions, remained in effect through the post–Cold War period, although the effectiveness improved with advances in weapons such as cluster bomb units and precision-guided munitions.

As air defenses became more sophisticated, the defense suppression efforts also evolved to meet the challenge. During World War II, the addition of radar for early warning and for controlling AAA fire increased the threat to attacking aircraft. These increased threats were met by new concepts of electronic warfare and the use of chaff—metal strips dropped from the air to reflect any radar beam and thereby hide the location and direction of travel of the threatened aircraft.

After World War II, the sophistication of defensive systems evolved rapidly and included the addition of surface-to-air missiles (SAMs) and improved warning and targeting radars. Air forces developed new combinations of tactics and suppression capabilities to ensure offensive success. During the Cold War, planned defense suppression in front of strategic bomber attacks included nuclear strikes by escort fighters or missiles fired to precede the bombers (e.g., the Hound Dog, SRAM, and air-launched cruise missile). In theater war settings, the ability to attack AAA and SAM sites was improved by the creation of specialized defense suppression systems. Airborne jamming of radar and communications systems—either by standoff (such as the USAF Lockheed EC-130) or escort (such as the USN Grumman E-A6 and USAF General Dynamics EF-111A) platforms—and improved chaff systems degraded both early warning and target tracking radar capabilities. The USAF developed modified fighters (e.g., the Vietnam-era North American F-100D, Republic F-105G, and McDonnell F-4G Wild Weasels) with threat-detection sensor packages and the ability to attack air defense systems with conventional weapons or antiradiation missiles (ARM) that home in on the radar signal (such as the U.S. Shrike and Standard ARM and later the HARM and the British ALARM).

Late in the Cold War, the much improved AAA and SAM threats and enhanced detection, warning, and tracking capabilities were melded with ground-directed interceptors and complex command and control systems to create integrated air defense systems (IADS), which presented serious challenges for attacking air forces. But an enemy IADS could be successfully attacked based on good intelligence, careful planning, and disruptive attacks on key points in the system, followed by the skillful application of traditional tactical and technical responses to individual air defense threats. The opening phase of Operation DESERT STORM involved the successful disruption of the Iraqi IADS followed by aggressive offensive counter air attacks and continuous tactical adjustments and ongoing defense suppression missions, resulting in minimal Coalition losses throughout the campaign.

Jerome V. Martin

See also

Air Superiority; Defense Suppression; DESERT STORM; Electronic Warfare; Missiles; Tactical Air Warfare

References

Hallion, Richard P. *Storm over Iraq: Air Power and the Gulf War.* Washington, DC: Smithsonian Institution Press, 1992.

______. *Strike from the Sky: The History of Battlefield Air Attack, 1911–1945.* Washington, DC: Smithsonian Institution Press, 1989.

Lambeth, Benjamin S. *The Transformation of American Air Power.* Ithaca: Cornell University Press, 2000.

DELIBERATE FORCE (1995)

NATO code name for peacemaking air campaign in Bosnia-Herzegovina under the command of USAF Lieutenant General Michael E. Ryan. Operation DELIBERATE FORCE was the first NATO military campaign in alliance history and was designed to force the Bosnian Serb army to cease shelling UN-designated "safe areas" throughout Bosnia. In concert with other events of late 1995, DELIBERATE FORCE played a decisive role in bringing the Bosnian Serbs to the negotiating table and ending three years of civil war in Bosnia-Herzegovina.

DELIBERATE FORCE received its mandate from Operation DENY FLIGHT, an air operation approved by UN Security Council Resolution 816 on 12 April 1993 to protect UN peacekeepers. After several Bosnian-Serb actions in July-August 1995, UN and NATO leaders concluded the piecemeal nature of DENY FLIGHT was ineffective and began planning an air campaign to protect UN safe havens in Gorazde and Sarajevo. NATO made the decision to begin the bombing 48 hours after a mortar attack against a Sarajevo market killed 37 civilians on 28 August.

The UN/NATO Joint Targeting Board approved 87 targets for DELIBERATE FORCE, including integrated air defense systems, fielded heavy weapons, supply and munitions depots, command and control relay sites, and key lines of communications for the Bosnian Serb Army. DELIBERATE FORCE involved 15 nations flying 3,535 sorties and 1,026 munitions expenditures, 70 percent of which were precision-guided. More than 400 hundred aircraft, including 222 fighters, were poised at 18 air bases across Europe for the operation. The operation was complemented by U.S. Tomahawk missile strikes and Predator unmanned aerial vehicles.

Although DELIBERATE FORCE spanned only 16 days of bombing, it was decisive in ending the civil war in Bosnia. Along with a successful Bosniak-Croat Federation ground campaign and an aggressive U.S. diplomatic strategy, DELIBERATE FORCE paved the way for eventual peace talks in Dayton, Ohio, in December 1995.

Mark D. Witzel

References

Beale, Michael O. *Bombs over Bosnia: The Role of Airpower in Bosnia-Herzegovina.* Maxwell AFB, AL: Air University Press, 1997.

Holbrooke, Richard C. *To End a War.* New York: Random House, 1998.

Owen, Robert C., ed. *Deliberate Force: A Case Study in Effective Air Campaigning.* Maxwell AFB, AL: Air University Press, 2000.

Deptula, David A. (1952–)

USAF general. David Albin Deptula was born in Dayton, Ohio, on 11 June 1952. He earned a bachelor's degree (1974)

and master's degree (1976) from the University of Virginia and, in 1994, a master's degree in national security strategy from the National War College. A distinguished graduate of the Air Force Reserve Officer Training Corps program, he completed pilot training in early 1977.

He has taken part in air operations, defense planning, and joint warfighting from unit to unified command and service headquarters levels, in addition to serving on two congressional commissions charged with outlining the nation's future defense needs. His aviation career includes more than 3,000 flying hours (more than 400 combat) in operational fighter and training assignments. He is a graduate of the USAF Fighter Weapons School and has served as an operational instructor pilot, F-15 aerial demonstration pilot, commander of an F-15 operations group, and commander of a joint and combined task force. In August 1990, he participated in the original design of the Coalition air campaign against Iraq.

During Operation DESERT STORM he was the principal offensive air campaign planner for the Joint Force Air Component Commander. As the commanding general, Joint/Combined Task Force Operation Northern Watch (1998/1999), he flew more than 80 combat missions leading a coalition of Turkish, British, and U.S. forces in enforcing the no-fly zone over northern Iraq. He has served in a variety of staff positions, including legislative liaison for the Air Staff's War Fighting Concepts Development Division and on the Secretary of the Air Force's policy group, where he was a principal author of the white paper *The Air Force and U.S. National Security: Global Reach—Global Power.*

More recently he has served on the 1994 Commission on Roles and Missions, as the Air Force representative to the 1997 National Defense Panel, as director, Expeditionary Aerospace Force Implementation, and as director, Air Force Quadrennial Defense Review (2001). Among his many awards and decorations is America's highest peacetime award, the Defense Distinguished Service Medal.

John Andreas Olsen

See also

DESERT STORM; INSTANT THUNDER

DESERT FOX (1998)

Code name for post–Gulf War air campaign against Iraq to thwart its capability to produce weapons of mass destruction. At the end of the Gulf War of 1991, the United Nations Security Council demanded that Iraq fully disclose and dismantle its program to build biological, chemical, and nuclear weapons and the missiles to deliver them. By December 1998, the United Nations Special Commission concluded that Iraq had not met those requirements, and as diplomatic efforts failed to solve the ongoing inspection problems, the U.S. and British governments decided to resolve the crisis by the use of military force. Operation DESERT FOX sought to strike military and security targets in Iraq that were contributing to Iraq's ability to produce, store, maintain, and deliver weapons of mass destruction.

The declared objectives were "to degrade Saddam Hussein's ability to make and use weapons of mass destruction, to diminish his ability to wage war against his neighbors, and to demonstrate the consequences of flouting international obligations." The combined air strikes lasted four nights (16–19 December 1998), ending as the Muslim holy month of Ramadan started. The United States and the United Kingdom suffered no losses; Iraqi casualty figures remain unknown. Approximately 600 sorties and 400 cruise missiles were launched against some 100 targets in the lowland areas between the Tigris and Euphrates Rivers from Tikrit in the north to the southern port city of Basra. The key targets were suspected weapons production sites, air defense systems, command and control facilities, Republican Guard bases, and other presidential elite units.

In military terms, Operation DESERT FOX is regarded as a success: The bomb-damage assessment indicates that smart bombs and improved cruise missiles resulted in one of the most accurate bombing campaigns in the history of warfare. The political effects of the air campaign are disputed. U.S. and British leaders claimed that the air strikes achieved their mission, whereas others speculate that Saddam Hussein succeeded in weakening the cohesion of the 1991 Coalition and halting UN inspections (such inspection operations have yet to resume). Considered together with the no-fly zones and UN-imposed economic sanctions against Iraq throughout the 1990s, Operation DESERT FOX represented the culmination of tension between Iraq and the United Nations in the aftermath of Operation DESERT STORM.

John Andreas Olsen

See also

DESERT STORM; Iraqi Air Force

DESERT SHIELD (1990)

Operation by the U.S. military and the international Coalition to deter further Iraqi aggression and, if necessary, defend Saudi Arabia during the Gulf War. The operation was originally known as PENINSULA SHIELD. On 2 August 1990, six divisions of the elite Iraqi Republican Guard Corps invaded Kuwait. Five days later, U.S. military forces started deploying to Saudi Arabia to establish a credible deterrence capability.

Airpower played an important role in DESERT SHIELD. The first two service branches able to move assets to the Persian Gulf were the U.S. Navy and Air Force. Aircraft from U.S. carriers and elements of the 1st Tactical Fighter Wing, which began arriving on 8 August, were the first credible military assets ready to defend Saudi Arabia.

By 2 September, the United States had approximately 600 aircraft in place. With the necessary assets, U.S. Air Force Lieutenant General Charles Horner began to create a plan to integrate the various types of aircraft into a coherent strike force.

During this time, high-level U.S. military leaders were debating strategy for the possible air war. Air Force planners put together a strategic bombing concept that was intended to destroy Baghdad's command and control, critical "centers of gravity" (petroleum and electrical targets), and the country's infrastructure in order to cripple Iraq's ability to wage war.

Airpower enthusiasts thought the plan to be exactly what was needed to keep Coalition casualties to a minimum. Others in the military hierarchy were not so supportive. It would not be until DESERT STORM that the debate would be resolved.

Craig T. Cobane

See also

DESERT STORM; Horner, Charles A.; Strategic Bombing

References

Atkinson, Rick. *Crusade: The Untold Story of the Persian Gulf War.* New York: Houghton Mifflin, 1993.

DESERT STORM (1991)

International military operation undertaken in early 1991 to expel Iraqi forces from Kuwait; the offensive portion of the Gulf War. Airpower played a vital role in deterring Iraq during Operation DESERT SHIELD, paving the way for one of the most decisive military victories in history. Many analysts believe that the Gulf War was the first in history to be decided by airpower.

DESERT STORM can be divided into two phases: the air war and the ground war. The Coalition strategy was to take advantage of its superior airpower. On 17 January, the air war began when a flight of U.S. Apache helicopters destroyed early warning radar installations, allowing U.S. F-117 stealth aircraft, using laser-guided bombs, to cripple Iraq's sophisticated air defense system.

Early in the war, the Coalition's air superiority became clear. Iraq possessed nearly 800 combat aircraft and an integrated air defense system controlling more than 3,000 surface-to-air missiles. Due to Coalition air supremacy, however, Iraq was unable to win a single air-to-air engagement and lost 35 aircraft (total Iraqi losses exceeded 200 aircraft).

The air war continued for five weeks, with more than 109,000 combat sorties (40,000 against Iraqi ground forces). The Coalition lost only 38 aircraft—the lowest loss rate of any air combat in history and less than the normal accident rate per sortie in combat training. By the cease-fire, Coalition airplanes had dropped 88,500 tons of ordnance (6,500 tons precision-guided). As the air phase of the war ended, it was clear that Coalition airpower had significantly degraded Iraq's military capability.

Craig T. Cobane

See also

DESERT SHIELD; Horner, Charles A.

References

Hallion, Richard. *Storm Over Iraq: Air Power and the Gulf War.* Washington, DC: Smithsonian Institution Press, 1992.

Watson, Bruce, ed. *Military Lessons of the Gulf War.* London: Greenhill Books, 1991.

Dewoitine Aircraft

Emile Dewoitine (1892–1979), innovative engineer, designed an all-metal parasol fighter in 1919. The D.1 flew in 1922 and was bought in quantity by the French services and Serbia; Italy produced 120 units under license. After improvements, the second-generation D.27 arrived in 1927 and was selected by Yugoslavia, Switzerland, and France, which also bought the D.53 derivative. Launched in 1932, the D.500 series was a success in France, with 350 fighters built. The D.370 and its derivatives were a step backward as the last parasol fighters, their production reaching only 87 units. The Dewoitine D.520, a modern design that flew in October 1938, became the best French fighter of its time. Only 403 examples had been accepted before France collapsed in June 1940. As good as the German fighters, they were not in a sufficient number to play a decisive role. More were built for occupied France. After the war, Emile Dewoitine was accused of active collaboration. He never built aircraft in France again, but he did assist in designs in Argentina.

Stéphane Nicolaou

References

Danel Raymond, and Jean Cuny. *Les Avions Dewoitine.* Paris: Larivière, 1982.

Dien Bien Phu, Battle of (1954)

Viet Minh victory at Dien Bien Phu in 1954, the first achieved by a Third World nationalist uprising against a great colonialist power like France. Located near the Laotian border, Dien Bien Phu had been selected to change from a moving to static war. The reinforcement started on 20 November 1953. Air transportation was the only way of access, first by dropping parachutists, then by using a former Japanese landing strip.

The Viet Minh placed 130,000 men and a quantity of artillery without being detected by French aerial reconnaissance. The siege began on 13 March 1954, and the Vietnamese immediately overran several strong points where they put antiaircraft artillery, limiting the strip to night use only.

The tactical pilots of the Aéronavale (the French naval air force) fought bravely when morale was low among Armée de l'Air crews, but the transporters proved to be equally important. Their task was vital for the troops, as all support was coming from the air. Bombing missions were mainly against antiaircraft artillery to make C-47 and C-119 drops less dangerous. The United States, fearing a Chinese reaction, rejected the French plea for B-29 bombing. On 7 May 1954, the last defenders surrendered. Dien Bien Phu showed that aerial weaponry by itself couldn't secure a victory—a lesson U.S. politicians forgot 10 years later in Vietnam.

Stéphane Nicolaou

References

Gras, Philippe. *L'armée de l'Air française dans le conflit indochinois.* Paris: L'Harmatant, 2001.

Dieppe, Battle of (1942)

First major European amphibious operation of World War II. On 19 August 1942, a landing force of 5,000 Canadian and 1,000 British troops, plus a token force of 60 U.S. Army Rangers, raided the German-held French channel port of Dieppe. The raid was launched because the Allies needed to demonstrate to the people of occupied Europe that they could mount an operation against the Germans, who had marched unimpeded across Europe. Additionally, the raid would provide needed experience in modern landing techniques.

Operation JUBILEE, as the raid was called, ran into trouble early when the approaching assault boats were discovered and fired on by five armed German trawlers. All hope for surprise was lost as the German defenders established a deadly crossfire on the beach in the predawn darkness.

By 9 A.M., the beachhead was a site of carnage, and British commanders decided to withdraw the surviving troops. Allied destroyers escorted rescue boats under murderous German fire to pull out the survivors.

By early afternoon, the rescue boats were headed back to England with the remnants of the Dieppe raiders, leaving 24 officers and 3,164 men behind, killed or captured. Of the 5,000 Canadian troops, some 900 were dead and almost 2,000 captured.

James H. Willbanks

References

Robertson, Terrence. *Dieppe.* New York: Harcourt, Brace, 1943.
Thompson, R. W. *At Whatever Cost: The Story of the Dieppe Raid.* New York: Coward-McCann, 1957.
Whitehead, William. *Dieppe, 1942: Echoes of Disaster.* Toronto: Personal Library, 1979.

Distant Early Warning (DEW)

A series of radar installations, stretching just above the Arctic Circle from Alaska across Canada to Greenland, designed to give early warning of attacks from air and space on North America. Construction of the DEW Line was initially approved by President Harry Truman in late 1952. Despite a contentious public debate throughout 1953 and 1954, testing and construction commenced, and the initial network of 57 sites became operational during the summer of 1957.

Construction was funded by the United States and carried out under extremely harsh Arctic conditions by U.S. and Canadian contractors. Duty for the U.S. civilian and military personnel manning DEW installations was both arduous and tedious. In theory they would provide the first warning of any Soviet attack coming in over the Arctic Ocean, then relay that information to the Combat Operations Center, North American Air Defense Command, in Colorado Springs, Colorado. The Air Force hoped that the resulting 3–6 hours of warning would allow them to scramble air defenses to intercept Soviet bombers and, more important, allow the bombers of the Strategic Air Command to be dispersed and protected from attack.

The DEW Line evolved throughout the rest of the Cold War to match the changing threat. The number of DEW sites peaked at 78 in the early 1960s, by which time it was supplemented not only by the Mid-Canada and Pinetree radar networks that had preceded it to the south but also by seaward extensions of radar coverage provided by a variety of permanent radar platforms (so-called Texas Towers), naval picket ships, and early warning aircraft. As the threat from intercontinental ballistic missiles slowly eclipsed that of bombers throughout the 1960s, most of these supplementary systems were gradually decommissioned, but the DEW Line continued in service for the duration of the Cold War. From the late 1980s through the mid-1990s, it was gradually replaced by the North Warning System, build largely on old DEW sites.

David Rezelman

See also

Air Defense Command; Antimissile Defense; Ballistic Missile Early Warning System; Cold War; Missiles, Intercontinental Ballistic; North American Air Defense Command; Radar; Satellites; Soviet Aircraft Development and Production; Sputnik; Strategic Air Command; Strategic Defense Initiative

References

Morenus, Richard. *DEW Line: Distant Early Warning, The Miracle of America's First Line of Defense.* New York: Rand McNally, 1957.

Schaffel, Kenneth. *The Emerging Shield: The Air Force and the Evolution of Continental Air Defense, 1945–1960.* Washington, DC: Office of Air Force History, United States Air Force, 1991.

The great Jimmy Doolittle, sitting on the edge of the cockpit of his Wedell Williams racer. (Walter J. Boyne)

Doolittle, James H. (1896–1993)

Pioneer American aviator, engineer, scientist, and military officer; his career spanned aviation's first century. He spent his early childhood in Nome, Alaska, while his father prospected for gold. Educated in Southern California, he was an excellent amateur boxer and at times fought for money.

When the United States entered World War I, Doolittle enlisted as a flying cadet in the Signal Corps Reserve, attended flying school, and soloed after 7 hours and 4 minutes of flight instruction. After commissioning as a second lieutenant, he served as a flight gunnery instructor at Rockwell Field in San Diego, California. His request and hope for an overseas assignment to the war zone were denied because of the Armistice of November 1918.

Following the war, he had several flying assignments and received some excellent hands-on engine and airplane construction experience from several superb instructors at Kelly Field, Texas. In September 1922, he made a cross-country flight in an elapsed time of 22 hours and 30 minutes, a feat that gained him instant notoriety.

Doolittle spent the next several years in academia, earning a bachelor's degree from the University of California and a master's and a Ph.D. from the Massachusetts Institute of Technology. In 1925, he won the Schneider Trophy for testing a Curtiss R3C-2 float biplane, bettering both domestic and international competitors at an average speed of 232.573 mph over a straightaway course. At the age of 28, James Doolittle was considered the most qualified, most experienced, and best-educated test pilot in the United States.

Taking several leaves of absence from the Army, Doolittle flew many dangerous demonstration flights for various U.S. aviation companies while working on flight instrumentation and blind flying at Mitchell Field's Full Flight Laboratory in New York. On 24 September 1929, he made a flight using the Kollsman precision altimeter, the Sperry gyrocompass, the Sperry artificial horizon, and rudimentary radio navigation aids. Besides piloting the historic flight, Doolittle had much to do with the aircraft's engineering, offering suggestions to the contractors, helping them refine their thinking and improve their designs, and furnishing them with vital input from a cockpit perspective.

In February 1930, Doolittle decided for personal financial reasons to resign from the Air Corps to work for Shell Petroleum Corporation, where he coordinated the company's aviation departments in San Francisco, St. Louis, and New York. In addition, he kept the company in the public's eye by continuing to participate in air shows and races.

In January 1940, he was appointed president of the Institute of Aeronautical Sciences, one of the most prestigious and influential technical societies in the world, but this was not satisfying enough. Doolittle wanted to be in the action, and he requested recall to active duty. On 1 July 1940, he returned to active-duty status, went to Great Britain on an inspection tour, and tested new aircraft like the B-26 Marauder.

In early 1942, the United States, still tormented by the shock of Pearl Harbor and the continuing succession of Japanese victories, needed some type of victory to raise morale. General Henry H. "Hap" Arnold, the commanding general of the Army Air Forces, chose Doolittle to lead an air strike of Army B-25 bombers from the Navy aircraft carrier *Hornet* against the Japanese mainland. On the morning of 18 April 1942, the Japanese observed the carriers *Hornet* and *Enterprise,* compelling higher command to schedule the raid a day earlier. All 16 B-25s dropped their bombs, but as a consequence of the 150-mile extended flight path all but one aircraft, which landed in the Soviet Union, ran out of fuel and went down in Japanese-occupied China. Most of the pilots, including Doolittle, maneuvered their way to friendly lines. Although the damage from the Doolittle Raid was slight, the psychological effect on the Japanese was significant: Imperial forces had failed to protect the homeland. Doolittle was made a brigadier general following the raid and received the Congressional Medal of Honor. Promotion to major general soon followed.

He went to Europe to command the 4th Bombardment Wing (Medium) of the Eighth Air Force and subsequently the Twelfth Air Force for the invasion of French North Africa, before commanding the Northwest African Strategic Air Forces (NASAF). As NASAF commander, his forces concentrated on Axis logistics and supply. Doolittle flew at least a half-dozen combat missions during this period.

During his stint in the Mediterranean theater, Doolittle underwent a crash course in large-scale military administration. He introduced imaginative new fighter tactics by encouraging his fighters to employ loose escort, instead of close escort, of bomber formations. On 6 January 1944, Doolittle assumed command of the mighty Eighth Air Force, the largest and most prestigious air force, with no fewer than 26 heavy bomber groups, 12 fighter groups, 42,000 combat aircraft, and 150,000 personnel. He again changed the role of his fighters from escort to killer, allowing his fighters to chase German fighters instead of waiting for the enemy to come to them.

After V-E Day, Doolittle moved his Eighth Air Force to the Pacific, where he was present for the unconditional Japanese surrender aboard the battleship *Missouri* on 2 September 1945. Following the war, he worked hard to promote a separate U.S. Air Force through speech-making and congressional testimony. He was a founder of the Air Force Association and its first president. He left active duty but remained in the Air Force Reserve until retiring as a lieutenant general in 1959. After leaving active duty, he returned to his position at Shell as a vice president and director, holding that position until 1967. In 1985, President Ronald Reagan and Senator Barry Goldwater pinned on his fourth star, promoting him to full general.

Known as the master of the calculated risk, this scientist-aviator and man of many talents and accomplishments died peacefully in his sleep on 27 September 1993, at the age of 96. The Air Force gave him a full-honors funeral and an elaborate ceremony reserved for dignitaries and top officers that included a 21-gun salute and a flyover by 11 aircraft.

George M. Watson Jr.

References

Doolittle, James H., with Caroll V. Glines. *I Could Never Be so Lucky Again: An Autobiography by General James H. "Jimmy" Doolittle.* Bantam Books. New York: 1991.

Nalty, Bernard C., ed., and Russ A. Prichard, tech. adv. *War in the Pacific: Pearl Harbor to Tokyo Bay.* New York: Salamander Books Limited, 1991.

Thomas, Lowell, and Edward Jablonski. *Doolittle: A Biography.* Garden City, NY: Doubleday, 1976.

Dornier Aircraft

Claude Dornier (1884–1969) began his aviation career with the Zeppelin Airship Company in 1910. From 1915 to 1918, he directed manufacture of several all-metal aircraft, including large flying boats.

Prohibited by the victorious Western allies from making aircraft in Germany after World War I, Dornier moved work to Switzerland and Italy and initiated manufacture of the Wal (Whale) flying boats, which pioneered mail and passenger services in the 1920s and 1930s; more than 260 were made. The huge 12-engine Do X flying boat of 1929 undertook a four-continent tour in 1931.

The Do17 Flying Pencil and the Do 24 (more than 200 were made and in service in some countries until the 1970s) and Do 26 flying boats developed for Lufthansa Airlines saw extensive military work in World War II. Dornier also manufactured products of other firms. The Do 335 twin-engine fighter-bomber, at 450 mph, was one of the fastest wartime aircraft, though few were built before the war ended.

Having undertaken other manufacturing after 1945, Dornier resumed civil and training aircraft manufacture a decade later. The company was taken over by Daimler Benz in 1985.

Christopher H. Sterling

References

Dornier: A Documentation on the Dornier Company History, and Dornier Aircraft. 2 vols. Friedrichschafen, Germany: Dornier, 1983.

"Dornier." In William Green, *The Warplanes of the Third Reich.* Garden City, NY: Doubleday, 1970, pp. 109–162.

Dornier Do 217

German twin-engine bomber and night-fighter during World War II. Dornier designed the Do 217 as a successor to the Do 17. Design began in 1937, a prototype flew in 1938, and 1,541 bombers and 364 night-fighters served from 1940 to 1945.

Do 217s were initially envisioned as dive-bombers, and technical difficulties delayed the program until this requirement was waived. Twelve preproduction Do 217A/Cs began clandestine reconnaissance of the Soviet Union in late 1940. At that time, Do 217Es commenced level-bombing, reconnaissance, and antishipping tasks. After initial operational experience, one 20mm cannon, two machine guns (for a total of seven), and cockpit armor plating were added. By late 1941, 300 Do 217Es were flying antishipping missions from the Netherlands, where they remained until late 1944. At 17,000 feet cruising altitude, Do 217Es carried 8,818 pounds of bombs at 258 mph for 1,430 miles.

Do 217J night-fighters were Do 217Es with four additional 20mm cannons, four machine guns, and a Liechtenstein radar in the nose. Do 217N night-fighters were Do 217Js modified with Schräge Musik (jazz music): two (later four) 20mm cannons mounted in the fuselage at a 70-degree angle to fire upward into the unprotected bellies of enemy bombers. Some Do 217Ns received Flensburg and Naxos devices that homed on to emissions from British bombers. Do 217J/Ns operated from May 1943 until mid-1944.

Do 217K/M night-bombers employed Fritz-X radio-guided bombs and Hs 293A wire-guided bombs to attack Allied shipping in the Mediterranean and Bay of Biscay in late 1943. They sank or seriously damaged three battleships, three cruisers, and several destroyers. Three Do 217P high-altitude (43,960-feet) reconnaissance aircraft and five Do 217R guided-bomb carriers never saw active service.

James D. Perry

References

Green, William. *Warplanes of the Third Reich.* New York: Galahad Books, 1986, pp. 143–156.

Douglas, William Sholto (1893–1970)

Held several high offices in the Royal Air Force during World War II and in commercial aviation in the postwar period. William Sholto Douglas, later Lord Douglas of Kirtleside, joined the Royal Flying Corps in 1914, having learned to fly before the war. He served in a reconnaissance squadron, flying the BE.2a, and rose to command Nos. 43 and 44 Fighter Squadrons. He became an ace, with five German aircraft shot down.

After the war, he became chief test pilot for Handley Page (and held commercial license number four), then returned to the RAF to command forces in the Sudan. Douglas became head of Fighter Command in 1940 on the retirement of Hugh Dowding. He moved on to head the RAF in the Middle East in 1943, then commanded Coastal Command from 1944 to 1945.

After serving as military governor of the British zone of occupation in Germany after the war, he became a director of British Overseas Airways Corporation, one of the two state-owned airlines, and finally served for 15 years as chairman of the other, British European Airways (1949–1964).

Christopher H. Sterling

See also

Britain, Battle of; Dowding, Hugh C.T.

References

Douglas, Sholto, with Robert Wright. *Sholto Douglas—Combat and Command: The Story of an Airman in Two World Wars.* New York: Simon and Schuster, 1966.

Douglas A-4 Skyhawk

Often called "Heinemann's Hot Rod," after the Douglas chief engineer Edward Henry Heinemann. The diminutive A-4 served as the primary U.S. Navy light attack aircraft for nearly 30 years. The design originated in 1952 when the Navy asked for the minimal aircraft that could deliver a tactical nuclear weapon: The A-4 (originally designated A4D-1) designed by Heinemann was less than 40 feet long, spanned less than 28 feet, and only weighed 8,500 pounds empty. The wing was so small that it did not require folding during carrier storage. The XA4D-1 made its first flight on 22 June 1954, and operational A4D-1s were accepted beginning in August 1954.

The A-4 was heavily involved in bombing missions in Southeast Asia, although it was limited to daytime operations in relatively good weather. The first A-4 strike against Vietnam was on 5 August 1964, with the last occurring on 28 June 1973. Eventually, 2,960 A-4s of all types would be manufactured, with the last being delivered on 27 February 1979. This included 555 two-seat trainers, a type that would not be retired until 20 October 1999.

The Blue Angels aerobatic team flew A-4s from 1974 to 1986, and a few TA-4J Skyhawks equipped with special electronics gear are expected to remain in service with the U.S. Navy until 2004. The A-4 proved to be popular with operators other than the United States, mainly because it was inexpensive to acquire and operate and was still a relatively capable daylight attack aircraft. In addition to the U.S. Navy and Marines, Argentina, Australia, Brazil, Indonesia, Kuwait, Malaysia, New Zealand, and Singapore operated the type.

Dennis R. Jenkins

Popular around the world because of its low price tag and ease of operation, the Douglas Skyhawk served as the primary U.S. Navy light attack aircraft for nearly 30 years. (Walter J. Boyne)

References

Kinzey, Bert. *A-4 Skyhawk in Detail and Scale.* Carrollton, TX: Squadron/Signal, 1990.

Francillon, Rene J. *McDonnell Douglas Aircraft Since 1920.* Annapolis, MD: Naval Institute Press, 1988.

Douglas A-20 Havoc

Douglas Aircraft developed the Model 7B twin-engine light attack bomber in the spring of 1936. The prototype flew for the first time in October 1938. However, due to budget constraints U.S. Army Air Corps officials decided not to purchase the aircraft.

French officials had no such hesitation. In 1939, they ordered 270 of what was now designated the DB-7. Belgium also ordered an unspecified number. When France fell to Germany in 1940, the DB-7s as well as remodeled DB-7As and Bs were shipped instead to Great Britain and redesignated the Boston I, II, and III.

Ironically, Air Corps leaders had already changed their minds by late 1939 following the passage of the bountiful Military Appropriations Act of April 1939. They ordered 63 DB-7s as high-altitude attack bombers with turbosupercharged Wright Cyclone radial engines. The Air Corps redesignated this aircraft the A-20.

After initial flights of the aircraft, the Air Corps decided it did not need a high-altitude light attack bomber but rather a low-altitude medium attack aircraft. To this end, only one A-20 was built and delivered. The final 62 contracted aircraft were built as P-70 night-fighters, A-20A medium attack aircraft, or F-3 reconnaissance aircraft. The lone A-20 was used later as a prototype XP-70 for the development of the P-70 night-fighter version of the Havoc.

Construction of the A-20A, the first production model, began in early 1940. By April 1941, 143 had been built and delivered to the 3d Bomb Group (Light; 3BG). The aircraft was 47 feet, 7 inches long with a wingspan of 61 feet, 4 inches. It had a gross takeoff weight of 20,711 pounds. Powered by two Wright R-2600-3 or -11 Cyclone radial engines producing 1,600 hp, it had a maximum speed of 347 mph, a cruising speed of 295 mph, and a maximum ferry range of 1,000 miles. It had nine .30-caliber machine guns: four forward-firing in a fuselage blister, two in a flexible dorsal position, one in a ventral position, and two rear-firing guns in the engine nacelles. It had a maximum bombload of 1,600 pounds.

In October 1940, Douglas and Air Corps officials concluded a contract for 999 B models. Although it used the same Wright 2600-11 engines as the last 20 -A models, it was lighter and armed like the DB-7A. The A-20B had two .50-caliber machine guns in the nose and only one .50-caliber gun in the dorsal mount. Its fuselage was 5 inches longer; it had a 2,400-pound maximum bombload, a maximum speed of 350 mph, a cruising speed of 278 mph, and a 2,300-mile ferry range. Eight were sent to the Navy as DB-2 target-towing aircraft, and 665 were delivered to the Soviet Union as Lend-Lease aircraft.

Douglas built 948 C models, 808 at the Douglas plant in Santa Monica, California, and 140 under contract at the Boeing plant in Seattle, Washington. The C was patterned after the A model. Its Wright R-2600-23 Cyclone radial engines provided this heavier aircraft a maximum speed of 342 mph. Like all Havoc models, it had four crew members—a pilot, navigator, bombardier, and gunner. Originally built to be Royal Air Force and Soviet Lend-Lease aircraft, the Cs were diverted to the U.S. Army Air Forces once the United States entered World War II.

More G models were produced than any other A-20 version. Douglas built 2,850 in 45 block runs. The major differences were new and varying armaments, most notably the addition of four forward firing 20mm cannons in the nose. After block run number five, these were again replaced with six .50-caliber machine guns.

Douglas built 412 H models, 450 J models, and 413 K models. They were heavier at 2,700 pounds and had Wright R-2600-29 Cyclone supercharged radial engines producing 1,700 hp and flying at 339 mph. They carried 2,000 pounds of bombs internally and 2,000 externally.

A-20 production ended in September 1944. Douglas and other plants built 7,230 A-20s. They served in every theater of war and with the USAAF, the RAF, as well as the Australian, Soviet, and several other Allied air forces. More A-20s were built than any other attack-designated aircraft to serve in World War II.

William Head and Brian Head

References

Hess, William. *A-20 Havoc at War.* New York: Scribner's, 1979.

Swanborough, Gordon, and Peter M. Bowers. *U.S. Military Aircraft Since 1909.* Washington, DC: Smithsonian Institution Press, 1989.

Douglas A/B-26 Invader

In June 1941, Douglas Aircraft contracted with the U.S. Army Air Corps to produce two prototype twin-engine medium attack aircraft to replace the Douglas A-20 Havoc—the XA-26 attack version, and the XA-26A night-fighter, which was later canceled in favor of the Northrop P-61.

The XA-26 first flew on 10 July 1942 and was accepted by the U.S. Army Air Forces on 21 February 1944. It had twin Pratt and Whitney R-2800-27 radial engines producing 2,000 hp each. It was 51 feet, 2 inches long with a wingspan of 70 feet. Its gross weight was 31,000 pounds and had a maximum bombload of 5,000 pounds. Its maximum speed was 370 mph, its cruising speed 212 mph, and it had a range of 2,500 miles. It had a crew of three, a clear nose structure, two forward-firing .50-caliber machine guns, and two aft barbettes (dorsal and ventral).

As testing continued, the USAAF ordered a third prototype designated the XA-26B that featured a solid nose. After numerous experiments with various nose armaments, the early production A-26Bs had six .50-caliber machine guns, and later Bs had eight guns mounted in the nose.

The first production model was the A-26B. Douglas built them at Long Beach, California, and Tulsa, Oklahoma, delivering 1,355 from 1943 to 1945. The production model was similar to the prototypes, except it carried 6,000 pounds of bombs, could reach a maximum speed of 355 mph, cruise at 284 mph, and had a range of 3,200 miles. Deliveries began in August 1943. The first B models saw combat on 19 November 1944. In 1945, Douglas made minor armament and engine changes to the A-26, and later production models were designated A-26C. Once in combat, all 2,502 A-26B/Cs produced by the time contract ended in the mid-1945 used the nickname Invader.

The B models remained in service after the war, and in 1948 the U.S. Air Force dropped the attack designation and redesignated them the B-26. During the Korean War (July 1950–July 1953), between 90 and 111 B-26s stationed in Japan flew nearly 70,000 sorties, dropping nearly 100,000 tons of bombs on enemy targets.

The B models were also converted into CB-26B cargo transports, TB-26B trainers, VB-26B staff transports, DB-26Bs (which towed the Ryan Q-2A Firebee drone), the EB-26B Wingless Wonder drag parachute test aircraft, and the RB-26B reconnaissance aircraft. Some flew until the 1970s.

In the early 1960s, the Air Force, realizing the advantages of the B-26 design in reconnaissance and counterinsurgency roles, employed B models in Vietnam. Crashes due to structural failure forced the Bs to be retired. To fill the void, a B-26C (S/N 44-35684) was modified with Pratt and Whitney R2800-103W engines, larger propellers, and a 8,000-pound bombload. It was designated the YB-26K Counter Invader.

The test program was so successful that the Air Force ordered 40 modified B-26Ks. On Mark Engineering Company produced the K models in 1963 and 1964. They first saw combat in 1966. Based in Thailand, they proved highly effective flying interdiction and counterinsurgency missions over the Laotian Panhandle in support of Operation STEEL TIGER. Since the Thai government restricted the number of bombers using Thailand's bases, the Air Force redesignated the Ks A-26As.

Throughout three major wars, the Douglas A/B-26 models performed their various roles effectively. Whether as an attack aircraft, medium bomber, or light bomber, they were

Although bought out by McDonnell Aircraft in 1967, the Douglas Aircraft Company was one of the top airplane manufacturers in the United States, producing such influential designs as the Douglas Havoc. (Douglas Aircraft Company, Inc.)

one of the longest-serving and best aircraft in U.S. Air Force history.

William Head

References

Johnsen, Frederick A. *Douglas A-26 Invader.* North Branch, MN: Specialty Press, 1999.

Mesko, Jim. *A-26 Invader in Action.* Carrollton, TX: Squadron/Signal, 1993.

Douglas Aircraft

U.S. aircraft manufacturer. For seven decades, the Douglas Aircraft Company produced 80 types, fully nine generations of successful commercial aircraft. Donald Douglas graduated from the Massachusetts Institute of Technology in 1915 and remained for a year as an assistant instructor in aeronautical engineering.

After Douglas left MIT, he went to the Connecticut Aircraft Company, where he worked on the first Navy dirigible, the DN-1, and then briefly for the Glenn Martin Company. In 1918, he went to work for the U.S. Army Signal Corps. He went back to Martin briefly and designed the Martin MB-1 bomber.

In 1920, he moved to Santa Monica, California, invested his entire savings of $600, and formed his first company (Davis Douglas Company), with 18 square feet of desk space in the rear of a barbershop. His first aircraft design was a large, two-place wood-and-fabric biplane called the "Cloudster." The first flight was on 24 February 1921, becoming the first aircraft to lift off the ground with a combination of payload and fuel equal to its own empty weight.

Douglas reformed his company in 1921 as the Douglas Company (in 1928 it became the Douglas Aircraft Company); Douglas served as president until 1957, when he became chairman and chief executive officer.

On 6 April 1924, four Douglas "World Cruisers" took off for the first successful round-the-world flight. Many civil and military developments of the World Cruiser followed.

On 17 December 1935, the Douglas DC-3 made its first flight, and no single aircraft has influenced air transportation as much since. Some historians regard it as the most important transport aircraft ever built. The DC-3 was the first commercial aircraft that could make money carrying passengers alone, without a mail subsidy. In the United States between 1935 and 1985, at least 355 civilian airlines and corporations used DC-3s; this does not take into account all the individual private owners. The DC-3 became the C-47 in military service.

By 1944, Douglas was the fourth largest aircraft company in the United States. It had six factories in three states, 160,000 employees, and a payroll of $400 million. It produced the SBDA-20 and A-26 and built B-17s for Boeing.

Through a series of strategic miscalculations on the part of the Douglas company, Boeing fielded the first commercial passenger jet—the 707. Douglas followed up with the DC-8, but this led to a decline in profits, despite its marketing of many successful military designs, including the A-4.

The McDonnell Aircraft Company acquired Douglas in 1967, becoming McDonnell Douglas. The 1990s saw an additional decline in sales and profits. In 1998, Boeing acquired the McDonnell Douglas Corporation.

Henry M. Holden

See also

Douglas World Cruiser; Douglas A/B-26 Invader; Douglas A-20 Havoc; Douglas C-47 Transport; Douglas SBD Dauntless

References

Holden, Henry M. *The Legacy of the DC-3.* Niceville, FL: Wind Canyon, 1997.

Douglas C-47 Transport

Ranked as one of the five most important pieces of equipment assisting in the Allied victory in Europe in World War II by General Dwight D. Eisenhower, commanding general of the Allied forces in Europe.

The C-47 was one of more than 50 variants of the Douglas DC-3. It was used mainly as an ambulance and transport aircraft. The C-47 was the primary aircraft used for every paratroop invasion during World War II. During that war, the C-47 carried 22 million tons of goods and flew 67 million passenger-miles. It was responsible for the evacuation of more than 750,000 wounded.

The total military variants of the DC-3/C-47 were 10,291, or 96.79 percent of DC-3 production (10,632 total). Additionally, 487 Japanese variants and 6,157 Russian Li-2s were manufactured from the Douglas plans, bringing the grand total for the type to 17,276. It was nicknamed the "Gooney Bird" and the "Dakota."

Henry M. Holden

References

Holden, Henry M. *The Legacy of the DC-3.* Niceville, FL: Wind Canyon, 1997

Douglas D-558

U.S. research plane; significant because it helped to provide design data for future transonic and supersonic aircraft with both straight and swept wings. The D-558 flight research

The Douglas C-47 was one of the most important airplanes in World War II, used primarily for transport and evacuation. (Walter J. Boyne)

program, carried out in a partnership between Douglas Aircraft, the U.S. Navy, and the National Advisory Committee for Aeronautics at the High-Speed Flight Research Station at Edwards Air Force Base, California, was divided into two phases, each having three aircraft.

A single-place straight-wing jet-powered aircraft—the D-558-1 Skystreak—was manufactured by Douglas Aircraft and designed to investigate jet aircraft characteristics at transonic speeds, including stability and control and buffet. Unlike the Bell XS-1 (X-1), it took off and landed under its own power.

The first flight of the aircraft was on 14 April 1947, with Gene May as the Douglas test pilot. Its maximum speed of 650.8 mph, then a world record for turbojet-powered aircraft, was achieved by U.S. Marine Corps Major Marion Carl on 25 August 1947. The three D-558-2 Skyrockets had the mission to investigate flight characteristics of a swept-wing aircraft at high supersonic speeds, with particular attention to the problem of pitch-up, a phenomenon often encountered with swept-wing aircraft.

The first of the D-558-2s had a Westinghouse J34-40 jet engine and took off under its own power. The second was equipped with a turbojet engine, replaced in 1950 with a Reaction Motors LR8-RM-6 rocket engine. This aircraft was modified so it could be air-launched from a P2B-1S (a Navy B-29) carrier aircraft. The third Skyrocket had jet and rocket engines and could be air-launched.

The D-558-2 was first flown on 4 February 1948 by Douglas test pilot John Martin. National Advisory Committee for Aeronautics pilot Scott Crossfield became the first person to fly faster than twice the speed of sound when he piloted the D-558-2 to its maximum speed of 1,291 mph on 20 November 1953. Its peak altitude, 83,235 feet, a record in its day, was reached on 21 August 1953, with Lieutenant Carl behind the controls.

J. D. Hunley

See also

Research Aircraft

References

Crossfield, A. Scott. *Always Another Dawn: The Story of a Rocket Test Pilot.* Cleveland: World, 1960.

Hallion, Richard P. *Supersonic Flight: Breaking the Sound Barrier and Beyond. The Story of the Bell X-1 and the Douglas D-558.* Rev. ed. London: Brassey's, 1997.

Hunley, J. D. ed. *Toward Mach 2: The Douglas D-558 Program.* SP-4222. Washington, DC: NASA, 1999.

Douglas SBD Dauntless

U.S. carrier-borne dive-bomber; responsible for many of the early losses suffered by the Imperial Japanese Navy in the Pacific War. Variations of the SBD (for "Scout Bomber, Douglas") were used by the U.S. Army Air Forces, Royal New Zealand Air Force, British Fleet Air Arm, and the French navy and air force, but it was most successful with the U.S. Navy and Marine Corps.

The SBD Dauntless went through six major versions before production ended in 1944. Perforated dive flaps characterized all versions. Despite its primary role as a dive-bomber, the Dauntless had good air-to-air combat characteristics and was credited with 40 of 91 enemy aircraft shot down during the Battle of the Coral Sea. Its rugged design gave it the lowest attrition rate of any U.S. carrier-based aircraft in the Pacific War.

In 1942, Dauntlesses crippled Japanese striking power, sinking four fleet carriers at Midway. Beginning in mid-1943, they were phased out in favor of the Curtiss "Helldiver." Dauntlesses flew off escort carriers in antisubmarine and close air support roles for the rest of the war.

Grant Weller

See also

Antisubmarine Warfare; Close Air Support; Coral Sea, Battle of the; Douglas Aircraft; Midway, Battle of

References

Angelucci, Enzo, ed. *The Rand McNally Encyclopedia of Military Aircraft, 1914–1980.* New York: Military Press, 1980.

Munson, Kenneth. *Fighters and Bombers of World War II, 1939–1945.* London: Peerage Books, 1969.

Douglas World Cruiser

By achieving the first aerial circumnavigation of the world on 6 April 1924, the Douglas World Cruiser set an aviation milestone. The press called it the greatest achievement in aviation history. Douglas aircraft thus became the first to fly the future routes of the global network of air commerce.

The Douglas World Cruiser was a conventional-looking biplane with a 50-foot wingspan and was powered by a 420-hp Liberty engine. Top speed was 103 mph and maximum range was 2,200 miles.

The four-plane flight of the *Seattle, Chicago, Boston,* and *New Orleans* ran into the worst weather of the century along the route. Rain, sleet, snow, and strong headwinds plagued the pilots. Clever logistics and good planning enabled them to overcome the hazards.

The flight took 175 days and covered 27,553 miles. The actual flying time was 15 days, 11 hours, and 7 minutes, averaging 74.2 mph. The *Seattle* went down off Alaska, and the *Boston* went down off the coast of Iceland, but each crew

The Douglas World Cruiser was a simple, sturdy design that had the stamina to undertake the first successful flight around the world. (U.S. Air Force)

survived. The two remaining World Cruisers flew over 28 countries and were the first to cross the Pacific Ocean. A fifth plane, the prototype *Boston II,* joined up with the flight at Nova Scotia. The *Chicago* may be seen in the National Air and Space Museum, the *New Orleans* in the Museum of Flying in Santa Monica, California.

Henry M. Holden

References

McDonnell Douglas. *First Around the World.* Privately published, 1974.

Dowding, Hugh C. T. (1882–1970)

Air vice marshal and head of RAF Fighter Command during the Battle of Britain. "Stuffy" Dowding is credited with much of the planning and leadership that staved off defeat in 1940 from the German Luftwaffe.

He entered the British army in the late nineteenth century, transferring to the new RAF upon its formation in 1918, having paid for his own flight training. He was knighted in 1935 for his important work in aircraft procurement. A year later, he became head of the new Fighter Command and strongly encouraged the development and use of radar as a key part of the defense of Britain.

Along with the Ground Observer Corps, complex command and control facilities, the new Hurricane and Spitfire interceptors, and the welding of the whole into a highly trained and cohesive weapons system, Dowding's preparations created the successful edge over Germany in the 1940 Battle of Britain. But despite support from Air Vice Marshall Keith Park about the use of smaller groups of fighters meeting invading German aircraft as early as possible, Dowding lost out in the late-1940 policy debate to Air Vice Marshall Trafford Leigh-Mallory's support of "big wings" of defense aircraft; he was replaced in November 1940.

He headed an unsuccessful British mission to the United States seeking more aircraft and then retired in mid-1942. In recognition of his efforts for the RAF, Dowding was made a lord in 1943 (the first from the RAF since Hugh Trenchard).

Christopher H. Sterling

See also

Britain, Battle of; Royal Flying Corps/Royal Naval Air Service/Royal Air Force; Trenchard, Hugh

References

Wright, Robert. *The Man Who Won the Battle of Britain: Hugh Dowding, RAF.* New York: Scribners, 1969.

Dresden, Bombing of (1945)

Controversial Allied combined bombing mission late in World War II that has become a symbol for the excesses of strategic bombing. Much of this reputation is based on Cold War distortions of the facts. Britain's RAF Bomber Command and the U.S. Eighth Air Force mounted coordinated attacks on the German city on 14 and 15 February 1945.

Contrary to popular beliefs, the city did contain valid military targets, and the mission was prompted by Russian requests for attacks on transportation centers like Dresden to assist their advance into Germany. But the raid was also related to Operation THUNDERCLAP, a British-inspired plan to break German morale from the air by destroying Berlin, and the large RAF formation succeeded in igniting a firestorm at night that degraded the accuracy of supporting USAAF daylight attacks. The bombing and its aftermath confirmed American misgivings about THUNDERCLAP.

According to official German records, 25,000–35,000 people died in the conflagration. This was the third deadliest bombing raid of the war in Europe, ranking behind only the 1943 Allied attack on Hamburg and the 1942 German assault on Stalingrad.

Reports of the destruction and a briefer's offhand remark that the Allies were adopting terror bombing caused a serious backlash, especially in Britain, and contributed to the end of strategic bombing in Europe. After the war, German and Russian propaganda propounded much higher casualty figures, which were reinforced by David Irving's influential book that settled on a death toll of 135,000. Irving later recanted and accepted the lower total from German records, but his earlier high claim is still widely cited.

Conrad C. Crane

See also

Berlin Air Battles; GOMMORRAH; Hamburg Bombing Campaign; Stalingrad, Battle of; Terror-Bombing

References

Angell, Joseph W. "Historical Analysis of the 14–15 February 1945 Bombing of Dresden." File K239.046-38. Maxwell AFB, AL: Air Force Historical Research Agency.

Crane, Conrad. *Bombs, Cities, and Civilians: American Airpower Strategy in World War II.* Lawrence: University Press of Kansas, 1993.

Irving, David. *The Destruction of Dresden.* New York: Ballantine Books, 1965.

Dunkirk

The Luftwaffe dominated the skies over France during the May 1940 blitzkrieg. Within days, the Royal Air Force stationed in France had lost half of its combat-ready bombers. Its Hurricane fighters fared no better. Fighter Command was quickly down to 39 squadrons, less than the required 60 for defense of Great Britain. The Germans were just across the English Channel, in Holland, threatening to overwhelm Belgium as well. By 20 May, the British were exploring options for evacuating from Calais to Dover. Then Adolf Hitler halted the ground effort. Still, the British Expeditionary Force at Dunkirk endured heavy air and artillery attacks as well as strafing by Messerschmitts, bombing by Dorniers and Heinkels, and dive-bombing by Stukas.

The assignment of Sir Hugh Dowding's RAF Fighter Command's was to patrol the beach for three miles on each side of Dunkirk from daylight to dark while continuing to protect the retreat and escort the British Fairey Battles and Bristol Blenheims. British forces also had home defense duties, so the 200 planes had as little as 20 minutes over Dunkirk before they withdrew. The German fleet included 300 bombers and 550 fighters. The outnumbered British routinely sent eight to 20 plane sorties against up to 50 of the enemy. At that point, the RAF pilots lacked experience, their communications were monitored, and they came in too low, giving the altitude advantage to the Germans, who gladly swooped down from the sun. Still, the RAF disrupted the attacks enough that the retreat and evacuation succeeded. At the end of the evacuation the RAF was outnumbered 8:1, but when Operation DYNAMO ended on 4 June, 364,628 Allied troops had been evacuated, and only 30,000–40,000 French had to surrender. Dunkirk cost 106 RAF fighters, 80 pilots, and 77 bombers. The fighter force was reduced to a total of 524 aircraft for the coming Battle of Britain.

John Barnhill

See also

Dowding, Hugh C.T.; German Air Force (Luftwaffe); Royal Flying Corps/Royal Naval Air Service/Royal Air Force

References

Carse, Robert. *Dunkirk, 1940: A history.* Englewood Cliffs, NJ: Prentice-Hall, 1970.

Gelb, Norman. *Dunkirk: The Complete Story of the First Step in the Defeat of Hitler.* New York: William Morrow, 1989

E

Eagle Squadrons

America was still at peace in 1940, but some American young men were very much at war. They were the transport pilots, cropdusters, washed-out cadets, students, and other adventurous youths who had gone to Canada and enlisted in the Royal Canadian Air Force. After basic training, they had been sent to England for operational training and assignment to Royal Canadian Air Force or Royal Air Force units.

In October 1940, these Americans transferred to the newly organized RAF No. 71 Squadron, the first of the Eagle Squadrons. They wore the RAF uniform with the distinguishing Eagle Squadron patch on the left shoulder. The No. 21 and No. 133 Squadrons were formed as more Americans signed up.

In September 1942, after the U.S. Army Air Forces began operations in England, the Eagle Squadrons were transferred to U.S. control. However, Squadron Leader J. C. Nelson of Denver, Colorado, one of the first Americans to fly for Britain and who fought in the Battle of Britain, elected to remain with the RAF. Flight Lieutenant Chesley Peterson of Utah and Flying Officer Gregory Daymond of California, both Eagle Squadron commanders, became aces in the Battle of Britain. Peterson later became known as the "21-year-old colonel."

After transferring to the USAAF, the three Eagle Squadrons were organized into the 4th Fighter Group stationed at Debden. They retained their Spitfires under a reverse Lend-Lease arrangement.

Albert Atkins

References

Gurney, Gene. *The War in the Air: A Pictorial History of World War II Air Forces in Combat.* New York: Crown, 1964.

Nesbit, Roy C. *An Illustrated History of the RAF.* London: Colour Liberty, 1996.

Eaker, Ira C. (1896–1987)

American aviation pioneer and general. Born in Field Creek, Texas, on 3 April 1896, he enlisted in the Army in 1917 following graduation from school and was accepted to officer training and commissioned as an infantry officer. He did not serve overseas during World War I; instead he was sent to the Aviation Section of the U.S. Army Signal Corps, where he learned to fly and earned his pilot's wings in October 1918. Over the next several decades, he participated in some of the most daring and innovative flights of the time. In 1926, Captain Eaker was second in command of a 22,000-mile goodwill tour by Army planes that circled Central and South America. Three years later, he piloted the Army Air Corps's "Question Mark" flight, which established a world endurance record by remaining aloft more than 150 hours in a series of pioneering airborne refueling operations. Besides these monumental fights, Eaker's name ranks with such prominent air advocates such as William "Billy" Mitchell, Henry H. "Hap" Arnold, and Carl "Tooey" Spaatz in the fight for the enhancement of airpower as the most important strategic arm of the military.

Eaker progressed through the ranks until earning two-star status as a major general just prior to World War II. It was in this war that he established his reputation as an airman. He commanded the famed Eighth Air Force in Britain in 1942 and 1943, then went on to command the Allied air forces in the Mediterranean in 1944 and 1945. During the last months of the war, he became deputy commander of the Army Air Forces and chief of the Air Staff in Washington, D.C.

During the war, General Eaker personally led the first U.S. B-17 bomber strike against German occupation forces in France (against Rouen on 17 August 1942). As commander of the Fifteenth Air Force in the Mediterranean, he flew the first bombing raid from Italy into Germany, landing in the Soviet Union after striking a series of military targets. He advocated precision daylight bombing, a tactic that most Allied leaders were skeptical about. In addition, he also developed the plan to bomb enemy targets around the clock using U.S. B-17s to strike by day and Royal Air Force bombers to attack by night.

Before he retired from Air Force service in June 1947, General Eaker worked closely with General Spaatz and Assistant Secretary of War W. Stuart Symington to establish a separate U.S. Air Force. Awards would follow. He received the Silver Star, the Distinguished Flying Cross, and myriad other military awards from other countries as well as the United States, including a special Gold Medal from Congress in 1979.

After his Air Force retirement, General Eaker worked at the Hughes Tool Company and Hughes Aircraft until 1957. For almost two decades, he wrote a column on military affairs that was syndicated to 180 newspapers. He died in 1987, two years after President Ronald Reagan awarded him his fourth star. The wartime hero and aviation pioneer is buried at Arlington National Cemetery.

George M. Watson Jr.

References

Copp, DeWitt S. *A Few Great Captains: The Men and Events That Shaped the Development of U.S. Air Power.* McLean, VA: EPM, 1980.

Parton, James. *"Air Force Spoken Here": General Ira Eaker and the Command of the Air.* Bethesda, MD: Adler and Adler, 1986.

Ira Eaker and Carl Spaatz were two brilliant officers whose careers intertwined, from before the famous flight of the Question Mark *in 1929 to the sending of the Eighth Air Force against Germany. Here Spaatz is pinning another well-earned decoration on Eaker. (U.S. Air Force)*

Eastern Solomons, Battle of the (1942)

Carrier engagement during the Guadalcanal Campaign in August 1942. A Japanese fleet under Admiral Nobutake Kondo (carriers *Ryujo, Shokaku,* and *Zuikaku*) moved south from Truk to cover resupply and reinforcement operations to Guadalcanal. The fleet was spotted by reconnaissance, and a U.S. force under Admiral Jack Fletcher steamed to intercept (carriers *Enterprise* and *Saratoga,* with *Wasp* refueling to the south).

The Americans struck first, at a force acting as bait, and sank *Ryujo* with a 38-plane strike. Shortly after that force was launched, reconnaissance discovered the main Japanese carrier force, but poor radio communications, due in part to weather conditions, made it impossible to divert the strike force to the more attractive target.

The Japanese strike force scored three bomb hits on *Enterprise,* but successful damage control allowed the ship to continue to operate aircraft. A follow-up U.S. strike sunk the seaplane tender *Chitose;* a subsequent Japanese strike was unsuccessful in locating the U.S. fleet. Both sides then retired. Although usually considered an American victory for the sinking of *Ryujo,* Japanese resupply of Guadalcanal was successful.

The Battle of the Eastern Solomons showed the importance of communications with air units in flight to allow reaction to changing situations. It also illustrates the importance of effective damage control in allowing a carrier to maintain flight operations. This was an area where the Japanese were initially deficient, and became progressively more so, while the Americans entered the war with a high degree of proficiency that was steadily improved.

Frank E. Watson

See also

Guadalcanal

References

Hoffman, Carl W. *Carrier Clash: The Invasion of Guadalcanal and the Battle of the Eastern Solomons.* Pacifica, CA: Pacifica Press, 1997.

Morison, Samuel Eliot. *The Two Ocean War.* Boston: Little, Brown, 1963.

Ebro 33: Rescue Efforts

Demonstration of NATO efforts to rescue downed aircrew members. On 30 August 1995, a French Mirage 2000K aircraft, call sign Ebro 33, was shot down by Serbian forces as it was attacking an arms storage area 20 miles southeast of Pale, Bosnia-Herzegovina. This mission was part of NATO Operation DELIBERATE FORCE.

The Mirage was hit by a Serbian surface-to-air missile. The missile severely crippled the aircraft, and the crew of Captain Frederic Chiffot and Lieutenant Jose Souvignet ejected. The two pilots were immediately captured by an armed civilian and passed to Serbian army forces. But NATO commanders were unaware of this and began immediate planning for rescue operations.

Early on the morning of 6 September, Admiral Leighton Smith, commander of NATO's southern forces, ordered the USS *Roosevelt* to execute a search-and-rescue mission. It launched a task force consisting of HH-60 helicopters from Helicopter Squadron 3 (HS-3) and U.S. Navy SEALs from Delta Platoon, SEAL Team-8, onboard for just such emergencies. But bad weather in the recovery area prevented the force from searching for the two Frenchmen.

Admiral Smith determined that the collected intelligence warranted another attempt. This time, he tasked the mission to the Joint Special Operations Task Force (JSOTF) at Brindisi, Italy. Early on the morning of 7 September, it launched a package consisting of two MH-53 "Pave Low" helicopters, AC-130 gunships, A-10s, and other supporting aircraft. Onboard the two helicopters were both U.S. and French personnel trained to search for and recover the missing airmen. But once again, the horrible Bosnian weather precluded a comprehensive search of the area. Admiral Smith ordered the JSOTF to launch a third attempt on the evening of 7 September. This time the weather was perfect for the mission. AC-130 aircraft entered the area and began the search. Two more MH-53s launched as the recovery aircraft.

The search was fruitless. But it did catch the attention of Bosnian Serb forces in the area. An estimated eight antiaircraft guns of varying sizes began firing at them. Both the AC-130 and helicopters returned fire. Additionally, supporting A-10s and F-18s attacked the enemy guns. As the helicopters turned to depart the area, both were hit numerous times. Onboard, two sergeants, Randy Rutledge and Dennis Turner, were wounded, although neither seriously.

Reviewing the negative results of the three efforts, Admiral Smith decided against any further missions. Subsequently, it was revealed that some of the signals received and objects observed by the rescue forces had been fakes purposely created by the Bosnia Serb forces. In October, the French government determined through other sources that the two men had been captured by the Bosnians and were being held in an undisclosed location. They were eventually released to French authorities as an initial step in the Paris Peace Agreement and the Dayton Accords, which ended the conflict.

The rescue attempts for the crew of Ebro 33 had been unsuccessful. But the level of effort sent a powerful message to all of the NATO aircrews. They knew that if they were shot down, they could count on the rescue crews to try to get them. It bonded together the men from the various allied nations into one unified force.

Darrel Whitcomb

Egyptian Air Force

The roots of Egypt's air forces run back to 1912, when an improvised Egyptian antiaircraft battery brought down an Italian Nieuport. During World War I, the Egyptian army engaged in some operations in cooperation with the Royal Flying Corps.

The direct antecedent of the current Egyptian Air Force was established in 1932, as a political gesture on the part of the British who still dominated Egypt, nominally an independent kingdom. The first Egyptian airmen were trained by the Royal Air Force and operated RAF aircraft. When World War II began, the Royal Egyptian Air Force (REAF) operated a single fighter squadron, flying Gloster Gladiator biplane fighters.

The REAF was beset by internal problems, including subversive action by a number of officers, one of whom was Anwar Sadat, later president of Egypt. The REAF was essentially grounded because of this and did not emerge as a fighting force until after the Axis powers had been driven from Africa.

After World War II, the REAF was given more autonomy and equipped with modern aircraft, including Supermarine Spitfires. By 1947, it included three fighter squadrons, as well as a mixed bag of transport and liaison aircraft. These were used in the series of battles that culminated in the Israeli War of Independence in 1948–1949.

When in 1952 Egypt rebelled against British influence and established itself as a sovereign state, it created the Egyptian Air Force, with six squadrons of fighters, including three equipped with Gloster Meteor and de Havilland Vampire jets. It turned to the Soviet bloc for more modern arms and eventually received MiG-15 fighters. By 1967 it had grown greatly in strength and had several hundred MiG fighters, including MiG-15s, -17s, and -21s as well as about 65 bombers, including Ilyushin Il-28s and Tupolev Tu-16s.

Israel destroyed this formidable force in the Six Day War of October 1967. Egypt rebuilt its air forces during the so-called War of Attrition and the October War of 1973 but was never able to achieve the training and level of proficiency of its opponent, the air arm of the Israeli Defense Force.

After 1973, Egypt developed a larger and more diverse air force, operating aircraft from the Soviet Union, the United States, France, and China. Emphasis is now being placed on the acquisition of Lockheed Martin F-16s. Egypt's Air Defense Command is a separate organization, responsible for operation of surface-to-air missiles and antiaircraft weapons. The Air Defense Command was notably successful during the 1973 October War. The expansion of Egypt's air forces may be due in part to the fact that Egypt's president, Hosni Mubarak, was formerly commander in chief.

Walter J. Boyne

References

Nordeen, Lon, and David Nicolle. *Phoenix over the Nile: A History of Egyptian Air Power, 1932–1994.* Washington, DC: Smithsonian Institution Press, 1996.

Willis, David, ed. *Aerospace Encyclopedia of World Air Forces.* London: Aerospace, 1999.

Ejection Seats

Rapid egress from stricken aircraft. Ejection seats came into common use soon after World War II, with the increased dangers of inflight evacuation from high-performance jet aircraft.

Early designs for ejection seats date back to 1910, but significant progress was not made until the 1930s. The first successful ejection occurred in 1934, when a German pilot inadvertently triggered the spring-loaded ejection seat of his Dornier 23 monoplane. The first deliberate ejection seat escape was also made by a German pilot in 1943. By the end of World War II, German airmen had employed ejection seats more than 60 times.

Early seats were purely ballistic, being activated by springs, compressed air, or an explosive device. Unfortunately, the extreme acceleration forces they created often resulted in pilot injury. To lessen these forces, as well as achieve zero-zero seat capability—the ability to eject while sitting motionless on the ground—rocket sustainers were added. These softened the shock of ejection and propelled pilots to sufficient altitude for safe parachute deployment. Other features, such as automatic parachute deployment, computer-controlled ejection functions, and vectored, variable thrust rockets, have further increased ejection survivability.

To date, ejection seats have been used more than 12,000 times and are standard equipment in high-performance military aircraft.

Steven A. Ruffin

References

Robinson, Douglas. *The Dangerous Sky: A History of Aviation Medicine.* Seattle: University of Washington Press, 1973.

van Patten, Robert. *A History of Developments in Aircrew Life Support Equipment, 1910–1994.* Bellbrook, OH: Privately printed, 1994.

El Alamein, Air Battles of (1942)

Crucial element of the successful British breakthrough in the Western Desert. The British Eighth Army's effort to prevent an Italo-German descent on Alexandria and Suez culminated successfully at El Alamein (24 October–4 November 1942).

At the battle's outset, Axis forces fielded some 675 aircraft. The Luftwaffe's contribution was 275, Italy's Regia Aeronautica 400. Of these, approximately 350 were serviceable. Royal Air Force and attached U.S. Army Air Forces aircraft numbered 750, including some 530 serviceable machines. They comprised an Anglo-American Desert Air Task Force (DATF) under U.S. command. The DATF's fighters and light bombers would be used against Italo-German forces in the battle itself while RAF and U.S. Army Middle East Air Force heavy bombers struck lines of communication and reinforcement stretching back to Tobruk, Benghazi, and Tripoli. Additionally, aircraft based on Malta and the Royal Navy's carriers successfully continued their interdiction of Axis maritime reinforcement.

From the opening barrage, preceded by a wave of 125 medium bombers blasting German and Italian artillery batteries, Allied airpower dominated the skies. Of particular note was the USAAF's 57th Fighter Group's aerial victory on 27 October. Sixteen of the Group's Curtiss P-40 "Warhawks" decisively scattered—with no loss to themselves—a force of some 60 German and Italian fighters and dive-bombers, downing seven in the process. All the while, 12th Medium Bombardment Group's North American B-25 "Mitchells" and RAF Douglas DB-7 "Bostons" savaged Axis armored formations, infantry positions, and assembly areas. These constant attacks helped disrupt Axis counterattacks and forced German Field Marshal Erwin Rommel to initiate a withdrawal on 3–4 November. The British advance to Tunisia had begun.

D. R. Dorondo

See also

North African Campaign

References

Hammel, Eric. *Air War Europa: America's Air War Against Germany in Europe and North Africa. Chronology, 1942–1945.* Pacifica, CA: Pacifica Press, 1994.

Heckmann, Wolf. *Rommel's War in Africa.* Trans. Stephen Seago. Garden City, NY: Doubleday, 1981.

Young, Peter, ed. *Atlas of the Second World War.* New York: Paragon/G. P. Putnam's Sons, 1979.

EL DORADO CANYON (1986)

Code name for attack by United States Navy and Air Force aircraft on targets in Libya during the night of 14–15 August

1986. The operation was a response to Libyan support for terrorist activities, especially the bombing of a Berlin discotheque that was frequented by U.S. servicemen. The raid was preceded in March 1986 by skirmishes between the U.S. Navy and the Libyan military over the international status of the Gulf of Sidra and Libyan leader Muammar Qaddafi's declared "Line of Death."

The Sixth Fleet, including the aircraft carriers USS *America* and USS *Coral Sea,* and the 48th Tactical Fighter Wing (48th TFW) stationed at RAF Lakenheath in the United Kingdom, performed the mission against five military and terrorist training targets. Eighteen General Dynamics F-111Fs from the 48th TFW hit three targets in the Tripoli area, and 14 Grumman A-6Es from the two carriers struck the two targets near Benghazi. The attack aircraft were supported by EA-6Bs and EF-111As for radar-jamming, Vought A-7Es and McDonnell Douglas F/A-18Cs for defense suppression, and Grumman F-14s to counter any Libyan fighter response. Navy Grumman E-2Cs provided AWACS support during the raid. The F/EF-111s were also supported by Boeing KC-135 and McDonnell Douglas KC-10 tankers that provided multiple aerial refuelings in their 13-hour, 5,500-nautical-mile round-trip. One F-111F and its two crewmen were lost to enemy action during the raid. Although not all aircraft successfully hit the assigned targets, EL DORADO CANYON inflicted substantial damage. The raid was considered a success based on the clear demonstration of U.S. willingness to respond to state-sponsored terrorism and the apparent effect of reducing aggressive Libyan support for terrorist actions. The Navy considered the raid to be a clear demonstration of the ability to project power from the sea, and the Air Force viewed the raid as an example of the ability to project power using aircraft from long ranges.

Jerome V. Martin

References

Bolger, Daniel P. *Americans at War, 1975–1986: An Era of Violent Peace.* Novato, CA: Presidio Press, 1988.

Stanik, Joseph T. *Swift and Effective Retribution: The U.S. Sixth Fleet and the Confrontation with Qaddafi.* Washington, DC: Naval Historical Center, 1996.

Venkus, Robert E. *Raid on Qaddafi: The Untold Story of History's Longest Fighter Mission by the Pilot Who Directed It.* New York: St. Martin's, 1992.

Electronic Warfare (EW)

Includes electronic countermeasures (ECM) and electronic reconnaissance/intelligence (ER, or ELINT). ECM includes jamming to disrupt radar, communications, and other systems, both in missiles and in satellites. An enemy may counterjam with electronic counter-countermeasures (ECCM). During the Vietnam War, the U.S. Air Force used the term *electronic support measures* to describe the collection of signal data to ease jamming of North Vietnamese air defenses. The term *electronic reconnaissance* covers all forms of electronic data-gathering, whether or not it is used for jamming purposes.

ER provides a battlefield advantage. If accurate and timely, it allows the attacker the use of jammer aircraft or other means to blind the enemy's electronic eyes. A stronger transmitter can blank out the enemy's radarscope. Spot-jamming blocks a single frequency, whereas barrage-jamming blocks an entire band. A jammer aircraft that does not accompany the attackers to the target can still use powerful equipment from outside the battle area (standoff jamming). Chaff (small metal fibers dropped from an airplane) is also good for jamming, causing enemy radar to read aircraft-sized returns. Chaff also blinds radar, dropping slowly to provide hours of deception. Use of a signal generator to make the enemy radar show a false target is called "deception jamming." This process requires the perpetrator to know in great detail the enemy's frequencies.

ECM never gives unequivocal superiority. The enemy always has the capability of applying electronic counter-countermeasures. ECCM generates new ECM methods, active or passive, which in turn generate new ECCM in an ongoing technological seesaw.

Electronic warfare, especially signal intercepts, was first used in the 1904 Russo-Japanese War. Russian failure to jam Japanese radio was one factor in the Russian defeat at Tsushima. In World War I, because radios were too heavy for airplanes, EW consisted of direction-finding, jamming, and intelligence analysis of ground forces' radio, telephone, and Morse transmissions, whether encoded or clear signal.

Between the world wars, radar developed rapidly, with Germany having the edge. Germany also had the edge in radar detection. Britain managed to trap the *Graf Spee* in 1939 and sink the *Bismarck* in 1941 despite the Germans' apparent edge. Britain had accelerated its own radar and radio intercept development, gaining EW superiority in the 1940 Battle of Britain.

By World War II, radios were lighter, planes were stronger, and radar was available to detect and track aircraft. ELINT collection requires sensitive receivers, direction-finding equipment, and sophisticated equipment to measure the operating characteristics of electronic systems. Specially equipped B-17 and B-24 bombers traced enemy signals and, tuned to the right frequencies, jammed enemy radar and electronics during bombing missions.

With postwar reduction of military spending, by 1950 the United States had ER but no jamming capability. The Air

Force used ER to map electronic radar sites so its planes could get through radar-controlled guns and searchlights; fighters had to rely on speed, maneuverability, and the cover of night. After the Korean War, ECMs developed as the enemy introduced new types of radar and communications systems.

By the late 1950s, modern air defense systems used complex command and control communications to link weapons, radar, and command posts. ER flights continued to track and identify enemy resources. This information was needed to steer attacking friendly aircraft away from enemy missile sites and radar. It also supported intelligence. Failures, such as the capture of Francis Gary Powers in 1960 with his 1950s-vintage U-2, and the ERB-47 shot down the same year, demonstrated that electronic intelligence–gathering missions were not risk-free.

In Vietnam, the Air Force used a mix of ECM and surface-to-air missile suppression aircraft to protect the B-52s during LINEBACKER I and II. Up to 85 aircraft supported each nightly bomber raid. Chaff dropped by F-4s and EB-66s blinded North Vietnamese early warning and acquisition raiders. Jamming EB-66s and EA-6Bs blocked North Vietnamese ground-controlled intercept radar. The North Vietnamese countered with band-switching, frequency changes, and quickly shutting off radar to hide its location and to cut down the time EB-66s had to learn the radar's capabilities.

For a time, the U.S. Air Force believed that pod jammers, carried by the fighters themselves, would provide adequate protection. Sufficient during the Vietnam War, pod protection failed during the 1973 Arab-Israeli War. Pods failed to jam the SA-6 Gainful SAMs. Israeli Air Force pilots had to fly below radar, opening themselves to antiaircraft (AA) fire.

During the Vietnam War, the U.S. Air Force developed the Wild Weasels, a series of fighters modified to find the electronic emissions of SAM and AA raiders and attack the sites (suppression of enemy air defenses, or SEAD). When the military focus shifted back to the Central Front in West Germany after the Vietnam War, it faced a Soviet integrated air defense system of such magnitude that, for SEAD to work, a part of the radar network would have to be jammed. First, the Air Force had to map the Soviet capability. Similar problems existed in Korea. Times called for an ELINT collector.

The Air Force conceived the tactical electronic reconnaissance sensor (TEREC)–equipped RF-4 in 1970, but the sensor system did not arrive in United States Air Force Europe (USAFE) and the Pacific Air Forces (PACAF) until 1975. The ALQ-125 pod determined precisely the enemy's electronic order of battle. It had automatic detection, classification, and location of hostile ground-based emitters and was preprogrammed to seek out systems defined as the highest threat. It tracked quickly, then sent data real-time to ground-based intelligence facilities.

Once a radar had been identified, tracking continued just long enough to permit its precise location to be determined. A real-time data link sent relevant information to ground-based intelligence facilities. Twenty-four TEREC pods were deployed to USAFE and PACAF on RF-4Cs. They were not replaced as the RF-4Cs retired. Another tool, the U-2R (TR-1) precision location strike system, operated briefly in Europe before the collapse of the Soviet Union. This tool had passive detection capabilities and real-time data links.

The Vietnam-era EB-66s tried to jam communications between radar sites and SAM launchers and between MiGs and their ground controllers.

The 1973 Arab-Israeli War produced a new Air Force system, the EC-130H "Compass Call," that performed basically the same missions. Compass Call used C-130s carrying complex computers and electronics. Input to Compass Call came from antennas placed on the plane's fuselage in front of the wings. An antenna array behind the wings transmits powerful jamming signals. The aircraft also uses its on-board computers to prevent enemy jamming of its signals or friendly frequencies. The EC-130H crew of specialists adjust jamming parameters in flight. This is "person-in-the-loop" versatility.

The EC-130H breaks complex and interdependent enemy systems into smaller pieces, then destroys or disrupts them by spot-jamming of selected frequencies, not broad-band barrage-jamming. Its on-board crew can assess and improve its operations on the fly. The EC-130H is the best jammer in the sky.

Stealth, the Air Force believed, was a better way to get an aircraft to its target. Instead of jamming and thereby alerting the enemy, stealth would allow the aircraft to sneak in. Slowly, in the 1990s, the EW planes went away. The F-4G Wild Weasel retired in 1992 and was replaced by the F-16CJ with the HARM targeting system. The EF-111 saw action in Libya in 1986, DESERT STORM in 1991, and the Southern and Northern no-fly zones over Iraq until 1998. Then the final dozen EF-111s retired. The Air Force and Navy then pooled their EW in the EA-6B Prowler.

Operations after Iraq and Yugoslavia demonstrated that Third World countries using air defense weapons similar to those used in Vietnam from 1965 to 1973 could still down U.S. aircraft or hamper air operations. While the EB-66s were flying over Vietnam, the Navy had begun working on carrier-based jammers—the piston-engine EA-1F, then the EKA-3 (an enhanced A-3D, the predecessor of the USAF EB-66). Wanting just one type of aircraft, the Navy looked into an EW A-6. The first variant was the two-seat EA-6A flown by the U.S. Marine Corps from Da Nang. The Navy wanted more capability. An elongated A-6 accommodated two additional electronic warfare officers . This version, the EA-6B Prowler, flew combat missions over North Vietnam in 1972. The aircraft received continuous updates to its electronic equipment. When the EF-111s were phased out of service in 1998, four new "purple" (joint) USN/USAF-manned Prowler squadrons picked up the Air Force electronic warfare mission.

Contemporary EW includes threats to satellites. Computer hackers can penetrate communications networks that guide satellites and receive their data. Hiding or disguising targets is easy once satellite orbital and sensor characteristics are known. Jamming devices can be as small as a cigarette pack. Ground lasers can blind sensors and cameras. And microsatellites or nanosatellites can spy on other satellites or, if armed, damage or destroy them. Countermeasures include antisatellite missiles fired from F-15s, hardening and stealth technology, antijamming, and antilaser deflector. Yet human intervention—sabotage of ground-based stations—remains a viable counter to EW.

John Barnhill

See also

Defense Suppression; DESERT STORM; Wild Weasel

References

De Arcangelis, Mario. *Electronic Warfare: From the Battle of Tsushima to the Falklands and Lebanon Conflicts.* New York: Sterling, 1985.

Van Nederveen, Gilles. "Sparks Over Vietnam: The EB-66 and the Early Struggle of Tactical Electronic Warfare." Airpower Research Institute Research Reports No. 3. Available online at the *Air Chronicles* website (electronic journal edited by Luetwinder T. Eaves), http://www.airpower.maxwell.af.mil/airchronicles/new.html.

Ellyson, Theodore Gordon (1885–1928)

American aviation pioneer. Theodore Gordon "Spuds" Ellyson was born on 27 February 1885 in Richmond, Virginia. After graduating from the Naval Academy in 1905, he was assigned to the battleship *Texas.* Serving for several years aboard various battleships and cruisers, Ellyson was assigned to the submarine *Shark* in 1908. On 23 December 1910, his request for duty in connection with aeronautics was accepted. He was ordered to the Glenn Curtiss Company training field at Dominguez Field, south of Los Angeles. On 2 July 1912, Ellyson took and passed his aero test and became Aero Club License No. 28, Military Aviator No. 26, and Naval Aviator No. 1.

On 7 September 1911, the first naval aviation unit was organized, with Lieutenant Ellyson as its commanding officer. For the next 18 months, Ellyson trained naval aviation volunteers and conducted various experiments associated with aircraft. However, at this time promotion within the Navy depended upon time spent at sea. Therefore, on 29 April 1913 he was detached from aviation and assigned to the USS *South Carolina.* In January 1918, Ellyson was transferred to subchasing duty. Following the war, Ellyson transferred to destroyer duty. In January 1921, Commander Ellyson returned to aviation, and he became executive officer of the Hampton Roads Naval Air Station. Ten months later he joined the Navy's Bureau of Aeronautics in Washington, D.C.

Wishing to get back to sea in an aviation role, Ellyson got himself appointed commanding officer of Squadron VT-1 in July 1922. In September 1928, Ellyson reported to the inspector of machinery at Boston for duty aboard the USS *Lexington.* On 25 February 1928, Ellyson learned that his daughter had a serious infection. He received permission to fly home in a Loening OL-7 amphibian from Hampton Roads to Annapolis. The aircraft crashed at the mouth of Chesapeake Bay, and Ellyson was killed.

Noel C. Shirley

References

van Deurs, George. *Anchors in the Sky: "Spuds" Ellyson, the First Naval Aviator.* Novato, CA: Presidio Press, 1978.

Shirley, N. C. *U.S. Naval Aviation 1910–1918.* Atglen, PA: Schiffer, 2000.

Ely, Eugene (1886–1911)

Early U.S. pilot. Eugene Ely was raised on an Iowa farm, graduated from Iowa State University, and became a chauffeur and one of the first race-car drivers. In 1909, he moved to San Francisco to sell cars. He married and relocated to Portland, Oregon, where he taught himself to fly. Then he moved to Minneapolis, joined Glenn Curtiss's fledgling aircraft company, and received pilot's license no. 17.

On 14 November 1910, Ely took off in a 50-hp Curtiss plane from a specially constructed wooden platform built over the bow of the light cruiser USS *Birmingham,* anchored in Hampton Roads, Virginia. A few minutes later he landed on Willoughby Spit. On 18 January 1911, at 11:01 A.M., Ely landed a Curtiss pusher on a specially built platform on the armored cruiser USS *Pennsylvania* anchored in San Francisco Bay. Ely was so cold from his hour-long effort that he was literally blue, but Navy coffee brought his color back. Ely's landing and takeoff marked the birth of naval aviation.

After his landmark feats, Ely continued exhibition flying. At the Georgia State Fairgrounds in Macon on 11 October,

Ely's plane crashed. Thrown from his seat, he died of a broken neck. The crowd stripped souvenirs from the plane and clothing from Ely's body.

John Barnhill

References

Bauman, Richard. "Eugene Ely." Available online at http://www.usspennsylvania.com/flattop.htm.

U.S. Navy, Office of Information. "A Brief History of U.S. Navy Aircraft Carriers, Part I: The Early Years." Available online at http://www.chinfo.navy.mil/navpalib/ships/carriers/cv-hist1.html.

ENDURING FREEDOM

Operation ENDURING FREEDOM is the name for the U.S. military response to the 11 September 2001 terrorist attacks. That morning, Al Qaeda–backed terrorists hijacked four U.S. commercial airliners. Two of the planes were slammed into the twin towers of the World Trade Center in New York City, a third hit the Pentagon outside Washington, DC, and the fourth crashed in the Pennsylvania countryside near Pittsburgh when the passengers attacked their hijackers, sacrificing themselves in the process. The total loss of life from the day's tragedies has not been established but is expected to exceed 3,000.

The immediate reaction of the U.S. government was to suspend all air traffic within the United States and establish combat air patrols (CAP) over several major U.S. cites. President George W. Bush, declaring the attacks "an act of war," announced the commitment of the full resources of the United States against the terrorists and the elimination of any distinction between the terrorists and those who harbor them.

The United States quickly began establishing an international coalition, at the same time mustering U.S. forces to attack the Al Qaeda terrorist organization to which the Taliban government gave a safe haven in Afghanistan. The obstacles to a successful campaign were formidable, for the United States possessed no military bases near Afghanistan, and the deplorable condition of the Afghan economy ruled out a bombing campaign similar to those used on Iraq in 1991 and Serbia in 1999. At the same time, many political and military commentators warned about involvement in an Afghan war, citing the debacle of the Soviet Union's invasion of the country in 1979. Despite the lean years of the Clinton administration, which had seen military budgets reduced time and again, the armed forces of the United States nonetheless had at the ready a whole generation of new weapons to be employed with entirely new tactics. The responsibility for utilizing these forces fell to the commander of U.S. Central Command, Army General Tommy Franks, who planned Operation ENDURING FREEDOM. The objective of the operation was simple: carry out the president's promise to destroy Al Qaeda in Afghanistan and elsewhere.

The United States opened the bombing campaign in early October with Northrop Grumman B-2s staging from Whiteman AFB, Missouri. The 44-hour missions flown by the B-2s were the longest combat sorties in the history of air power. Joining the CONUS-based bomber in the opening phase of the campaign were Boeing B-52 and B-1B bombers staging from Diego Garcia in the Indian Ocean as well as a sizable naval contingent. The Navy's F/A-18s and F-14s were called on to fulfill the primary fighter bomber role. Additionally, the Navy utilized the ship-launched Tomahawk land attack missile (TLAM) to strike targets that posed a potential threat to manned aircraft.

The United States pitted high-technology weaponry against an enemy that use obsolete weapons but took advantage of the exceptionally rough terrain. The vast majority of munitions dropped were precision-guided. These included laser-guided munitions such as the GBU-10 (2,000 pounds), GBU-12 (500 pounds), and GBU-24 (2,000 pounds), electrooptically guided munitions such as the GBU-15 (2,000 pounds) and AGM-130 (2,000 pounds), and GPS-guided weapons such as the GBU-31 (2,000 pounds). The GPS-guided joint direct attack munition (JDAM) became the weapon of choice for the entire bomber fleet.

In addition to advanced munitions, the United States also made extensive use of unmanned aerial vehicles (UAV). Both the Predator and the next-generation UAV, the Global Hawk, were used as reconnaissance platforms to provide real-time video to the intelligence community. The Predator made history when it employed the Hellfire missile in combat, thus becoming the first unmanned strike aircraft.

The United States also introduced a limited number of Special Forces personnel, who scouted targets and identified them for precision bombing. Special Forces aircraft played a role when the venerable AC-130 gunship was called in to pound Al Qaeda positions with its 25mm, 40mm, and 105mm cannons. Additionally, MC-130s dropped the 15,000-pound BLU-82, which was originally designed as an area weapon to clear a hilltop for a firebase.

The final effects of Operation ENDURING FREEDOM are not yet known, but the initial result was the establishment of a provisional Afghan government that will undertake to establish order and prepare the country for a transition to a democratically elected government. In the meantime, selective anti–Al Qaeda operations continue in an effort to destroy any of the organization's leadership remaining in the country.

Walter J. Boyne and Troy D. Hammon

Energy Maneuverability

Concept used in air combat to compare the capability of opposing aircraft by assessing the ability of an aircraft to accelerate or climb at a given load factor (g). It is expressed as specific excess power (SEP—feet per second or meters per second) and defined as excess thrust multiplied by speed and then divided by weight.

The aim of air combat is to gain a position advantage over an opponent so that the fighter's weapons can be employed. Two basic approaches to air combat are available. First, a pilot can try to gain a position advantage at the expense of some energy ("angles" tactics) with the intent of further improving his advantage until he has a firing solution. For example, a maximum-rate turn toward an opponent's rear quarter will gain an immediate position advantage but may sacrifice some speed and altitude. Alternatively, a pilot can attempt to gain an energy advantage over his opponent at the expense of some position ("energy" tactics), with a view toward converting the energy advantage to a decisive position advantage. For example, a vertical zoom will favor an aircraft with higher energy, as it will be able to delay pitching back downward until after the opposing aircraft.

Both these approaches require the fighter to expend some energy. The fighter that has a significantly higher SEP or higher initial speed or height will have the advantage.

The pilot of a lower wing-loaded aircraft (e.g., MiG-17) will tend to favor angles tactics because the turn rate will be higher. A fighter with higher thrust-to-weight ratio (e.g., F-4) will to climb and accelerate better and will tend to favor energy tactics. Angles tactics are inherently more aggressive and instinctive; energy tactics are generally safer but require a higher degree of pilot training.

Andy Blackburn

References

Shaw, Robert L. *Fighter Combat Tactics and Maneuvering.* Annapolis, MD: Naval Institute Press, 1985.

Whitford, Ray. *Fundamentals of Fighter Design.* Shrewsbury, UK: Airlife, 2000.

Engine Technology

Although many early aircraft engines derived from the automotive experience, the rigorous demands of flying meant that an entirely new industry had to be created, one devoted to building engines of relatively high power and low weight and of maximum reliability. The development and manufacture of aircraft engines proved to be expensive and time-consuming; only those companies with demonstrated records of success could survive over the long term.

Although engine designs were proprietary, much of the technology of the industry quickly became generally available, so that most nations were able to build competitive aircraft engines for most of the century. Many of the technologies that go into the design and manufacture of aircraft engines are frequently developed by suppliers to the engine companies rather than by the primary engine manufacturer. As engines became more sophisticated, the number of types of engines and the number of manufacturers declined, and many companies were forced either to merge together or to enter into cooperative partnerships.

The goals of improving power and weight were usually the factors that drove the development process, with improvement in weight, size, and specific fuel consumption being beneficial side effects. Reciprocating engines and turbine engines each followed their own development paths, and each had specific challenges that had to be overcome. The pace of reciprocating engine development lagged behind that of airframe development for many years. After a slow start, jet-engine development proceeded at a much swifter pace, so much so that engine development led airframe development.

Just as reciprocating engines began to reach their practical peak of power in terms of weight and mechanical complexity, the jet engine arrived on the scene. Although the early jet engines generated a level of power roughly equivalent to reciprocating engines of the time, it was soon evident that they were capable of reaching far higher levels of power.

Beyond the benefit of ever greater power, the difference between the reciprocal motion of piston engines and the rotary motion of turbine engines carried important implications for maintenance that were not initially obvious. In the very earliest days, piston engines were far more reliable and could be run safely for many more hours than a jet. However, in a very short time the jet engine proved to be more reliable and to have greater endurance. Whereas piston engines required inspections and overhauls at frequent intervals, jet engines soon were able to run for thousands of hours with great reliability. And while the practicality of jet engines was initially doubted because of high fuel consumption, later jet engines were able to operate at high speeds and altitudes with remarkable fuel economy.

Reciprocating Engines

The development of the aircraft piston engine from the Manly Balzer liquid-cooled five-cylinder radial of 1903 to the Napier Nomad liquid-cooled 0-12 of 1954 was the result of the development and interaction of the many technologies influencing engine design and operation. These included the following factors:

Materials: Higher-strength alloys led to lower weight, longer life, and greater power.

Fabrication techniques (casting, forging, machining, joining): Better processes led to longer life, lower cost, and greater strength.

Cylinder inlet and exhaust aerodynamics: Internal aerodynamic improvements led to greater volumetric efficiency (air-breathing capacity).

Cylinder cooling: Improved fin spacing, baffling, and cowling allowed more power per cylinder.

Valve cooling: Sodium-cooled valves allowed longer life and higher compression ratios.

Piston and ring design: Better materials and special shapes allowed longer life and higher compression ratios through better sealing.

High-power gearing: Better precision in manufacture, design of optimal tooth shapes, and better materials allowed higher engine speeds to match slow propeller speeds.

Journal bearings (material, configuration, fabrication, lubrication): The steel-backed bearing allowed higher engine speed and longer life.

Mechanical dynamics (balance and harmonics): The addition of crankshaft counterweights and bifilar dampers (harmonic counterweights) allowed higher engine speeds.

Vibration control (dynamics plus engine mounting): Strategic location of engine mountpoints and use of hydraulic mount pads reduced vibration input to the airframe.

Fuel formulation and production: Development of higher-octane fuels as well as different and improved means of formulating them was the biggest single contributor to improved engine power and efficiency.

Fuel metering: The addition of hydraulic computational mechanisms and altitude- and temperature-sensing features to carburetors/fuel controls allowed more precise matching of fuel delivery to the engine's needs.

Fuel combustion: Continuing studies of the combustion process lead to higher efficiency and reduced emissions.

Supercharging: Engine-driven compressors (mechanical supercharging) and exhaust-driven turbosuperchargers (turbochargers) allowed rated engine power to be maintained to high altitudes; aerodynamic analysis of the centrifugal compressor impeller, diffuser, and inlet/discharge ducting led to major improvements in efficiency and air breathing capacity.

Water-alcohol injection: Takeoff and emergency power was augmented by injection of large amounts of water and/or alcohol to cool the combustion chamber as well as to supercharge (by means of expansion of the water to steam) the engine.

Turbine compounding: The last step in evolution of the aircraft piston engine was the use of an exhaust-driven turbine geared to the engine crankshaft to extract greater power from the energy of the burned fuel.

Propeller aerodynamics: The improvement of propeller aerodynamic and mechanical design for a while allowed engines to operate at higher speeds without the need for reduction gearing.

Propeller mechanical design and control: The development of variable- and controllable-pitch propellers allowed the better matching of engine power and speed to the needs of the aircraft, leading to improved operating speed range, operating altitude, and overall propulsive efficiency.

Control and accessory size and effectiveness: Engine controls and accessories have become an increasingly significant fraction of the size, weight, and cost of the engine installation and have therefore become a very important driver of engine reliability.

Much of the time, these technologies were developed by companies other than engine manufacturers and became generally available to all manufacturers simultaneously. Sometimes the engine manufacturers had to force development of technologies when the normal suppliers refused to do so. Similarly, governments maintained engine development laboratories to investigate, guide, and evaluate technologies that the free market was not undertaking. Frequently, development was pointed in a needed direction by these government laboratories.

Sometimes, individual persons had an unusually large influence on the course of events—none more so than Samuel D. Heron, who had major roles in government laboratory development in Britain and then in the United States, as well as also in fuel development in the United States. Roy Fedden of Bristol Engines almost single-handedly developed the sleeve valve; Stanley Hooker of Rolls-Royce advanced engine aerodynamics tremendously; many others made major contributions.

Gas-Turbine Engines

The technologies supporting gas-turbine engines had a more important role in their development because the gas turbine would not even run until enough power could be generated

Aircraft engine developments took a great deal of time, and the superchargers that enabled the B-17s and B-24s to live over Germany derived from these early experiments with Sanford Moss's supercharger on a Liberty engine. (Walter J. Boyne)

in the combustor to drive a turbine that was efficient enough to drive a compressor efficient enough to not consume all of the turbine's power and have enough remaining to drive a propeller or develop thrust on the aircraft. Many early gas turbines fell short of their power goals because of these difficulties, in addition to the problems of containing (sealing) the high-pressure flows along the appropriate path. Thermodynamics dictates that efficiency is driven by the maximum temperature and pressure at the turbine entrance and the minimum temperature at maximum pressure at the compressor exit. The exposure of the combustor and turbine sections to continuous high temperatures demanded new materials that combined strength at temperature with resistance to oxidation and corrosion from impurities in the fuels. The component technology development situation for turbine engines was much the same as that for reciprocating engines except for the different perspective from there being many blades and vanes, higher rotating speeds, and higher average metal temperatures. One unique problem of turbine engines is that scaling down the size of the blades and vanes presents much more difficulty in the manufacture of the smaller and thinner parts. Sealing of leakages is also a problem, as the running clearances and boundary layers become a greater fraction of the total flowpath.

Following are examples of some of the major manufacturers of aircraft engines along with information on a few of their most famous products.

Allison

Allison began in Indianapolis as a rebuilder of used Liberty engines in 1924. Its most famous piston engine was the Allison V-1710, a monoblock V-12, which began development in

1930 as an airship power plant for the Navy, first giving 750 shp. Its development was retarded by the termination of the Navy airship program and by the Army's decision, during the Depression, that the lower system cost of air-cooled radials was most appealing. In 1935, the premonitions of war caused the pace of power development to increase, and the V-1710 was qualified at 1,000 shp in March 1937, ahead of the Rolls-Royce Merlin to that power but behind the Pratt and Whitney R-1830. Low-rate production started in 1938 for the Bell YFM "Airacuda" and prototype Lockheed P-38, Bell P-39, and Curtiss P-40 fighters. By 1940, the production rate was able to match the orders for these fighters.

Development of the V-1710 continued to improve durability and increase power to 1,325 shp for single-stage-supercharged engines, 1,500 shp for engines with a turbocharger as the second stage of supercharging, and up to 2,300 shp for engines with two mechanical superchargers and intercooling. The ultimate version had turbocompounding (exhaust turbine shaft driving into the crankshaft) in addition to a two-stage supercharger and demonstrated 2,800 shp in initial tests, with 3,000 shp expected after development; 70,033 V-1710s were built.

Allison produced thousands of the General Electric J33 and J35 jet engines by September 1946 and built more than 15,000 of its own T56 turboprop engines. It continued in the jet engine business and was particularly successful in supplying engines to the helicopter industry. More than 22,000 of its A-5 turboshaft model were supplied for the Bell Jetranger and the Hughes 500.

BMW

Founded in Germany in 1916, BMW (Bavarian Motor Works) came into prominence after 1929, when it licensed the Pratt and Whitney Hornet for production, modifying it with fuel injection. It became the basis for development of a long series of engines, which powered such famous aircraft as the Focke-Wulf Fw 190. BMW excelled in the close cowling of its engines, which reduced drag, and in the time required to change a complete engine package.

After the normal development problems, BMW created a turbojet engine that delivered 1,760 pounds/thrust. Intended primarily for the Heinkel He 162, about 3,500 had been built by the end of World War II.

Bristol

In July 1920, the Bristol Aeroplane Company was persuaded by the British Air Ministry to buy Cosmos Engineering (formerly Brazil Straker), which in mid-1917 had already started development of the Jupiter nine-cylinder single-row radial air-cooled engine at 1,753 cubic inches, with a goal of 500 shp at 650 pounds. Led by Roy Fedden, the new firm developed the Jupiter into a great success, for it came to be used on 262 different types of aircraft. More than 7,100 were built, and it was licensed in 17 foreign countries. It also inspired many descendants, including the Mercury and Pegasus, which were widely used in World War II aircraft.

The most distinctive Bristol engineering feature was the Burt-McCollum type of sleeve-valve engine, which was used on the Perseus, Hercules, and Taurus engines. The Hercules 14-cylinder two-row geared and supercharged radial engine was eventually developed to 2,080 shp at takeoff (2,140 shp emergency) at 2,355 pound-weight. The Short Stirling and Vickers Wellesley bombers were the first applications of the Hercules, which was used on many other aircraft of the era. The Taurus was a scaled-down Hercules that developed 1,050 shp at takeoff and was used on early Bristol Beaufort and Fairey Albacore aircraft.

The 18-cylinder two-row air-cooled Centaurus derived from the Perseus and was developed to 2,980 shp at takeoff. It was used to power the Hawker Tempest fighter and other aircraft. Some 5,330 Centaurus engines were produced through 1959.

In December 1940, Bristol began studies of turboprop engines and in July 1943 began development of the 1,975-shp Theseus free-turbine. In September 1944, design of the Proteus free-turbine turboprop began under Stanley G. Hooker. Some 400 flying Proteuses were built, but it achieved more importance when it was successfully applied to warship propulsion and electrical power generation.

In March 1947, Hooker began the design of a two-spool axial flow turbojet, the BE.10 Olympus. It first ran in May 1950, delivering 9,140 pounds/thrust but ultimately was developed to an astounding 38,400 rating with afterburner. At the other end of the power scale, Bristol developed the Orpheus for the Fiat G91 and Folland Gnat fighters, with an initial 3,285-pound thrust rating. It ultimately developed 8,170 pounds/thrust with afterburner.

One of the most innovative Bristol engines was the Pegasus, developed for the series of vertical-takeoff-and-landing fighters that culminated in the Harrier, achieving thrust of 23, 620 pounds. The company entered the helicopter field with the Gem, developed after it was absorbed by Rolls-Royce in October 1966 and used in the Westland Lynx and Augusta. Previously, the firm had joined Hawker-Siddeley to become Bristol-Siddeley in 1958.

Curtiss, Wright, and Curtiss-Wright

The early Curtiss aircraft engines came from motorcycle engines that founder Glenn Curtiss had designed. These were soon followed by an air-cooled V-8 in 1907. The OX-5 V-8, designed in 1910, developed 90 shp from 503 cubic inches and weighed 320 pounds. By World War I, it was suitable only as a trainer engine, but it was mass-produced for the Curtiss JN trainer and other aircraft until a larger engine became available. The K-12 was one of the first technologically superior American V-12s, with a water-cooled cast block and head (monoblock), producing 400 shp from 1,145 cubic inches and 679 pounds. The K-12 ran in October 1916 and had no significant production. For unknown reasons, Curtiss was not included in the Liberty engine planning of 1917.

The Curtiss 400-shp D-12 evolved in 1922 from the K-12, C-12, and CD-12 monoblock engines and revolutionized the engine industry in the early 1920s with its compactness, efficiency, and reliability. It was the dominant power source for U.S. fighters and smaller bombers in the 1920s and was succeeded by the Conqueror V-12 1,570-cubic-inch engine (initially 1,550) in 1926 at 575 shp. The Conqueror gained many military and some civil applications and was in production until 1932. It also influenced the design of the Rolls-Royce Merlin.

The aircraft engine industry in the United States began with the 16-shp Wright four-cylinder 201 cubic inches 152-pound-weight water-cooled inline for the Wright Flyer. Design was started in November 1902 and the engine ran in February 1903, flying in December. The Wrights sought help from auto-engine suppliers but, for lack of response, designed their engines with no known major outside influences. The Wrights developed the four-cylinder engine to 30 shp by 1911 and had a 50-shp six-cylinder by 1912 (this being uprated to 60 shp by 1914), but that line ended when the Wrights merged with Glenn Martin in 1915.

The Wright-Martin Company obtained rights to manufacture the 150-shp, 718-cubic-inch Hispano V-8 that year and spent several millions of dollars to design and tool for its manufacture. This engine, the Wright-Hispano, was one of the first examples of the monoblock design and was built in large quantities. For unknown reasons, Wright was not included in the 1917 Liberty engine planning. Wright-Martin was succeeded by the Wright Aeronautical Corporation in October 1919. On 26 June 1929, the two greatest names in American aviation, long antagonists, merged into the Curtiss-Wright Corporation.

Wright continued development of both the 718-cubic-inch and 1,127-cubic-inch V-8 Hispanos until 1923, when the Navy said it would not buy any more. In 1921, Wright started the T series V-12s of 1,947-cubic-inch displacement and 1,000 pounds. These began at 350 shp, ending with the T-4 of 675 shp in 1923, and competed with the D-12; 264 were built between 1921 and 1926 for many Navy aircraft, including two Schneider Trophy racers.

The U.S. Navy in the early 1920s, and the airlines in the late 1920s, announced a preference for air-cooled engines because of their lighter weight and greater reliability; the liquid cooling system accounted for 25–30 percent of engine failures. The first practical large air-cooled radial, the nine-cylinder Lawrance J-1, ran in 1921, and produced 200 shp from 787 cubic inches and 476 pounds. In 1925, this became the Wright J-5 Whirlwind of 220 shp that later powered the Ryan *Spirit of St. Louis* flown by Charles Lindbergh across the Atlantic. The Whirlwind was the engine of choice in its power range. Wright's engine of that era, the R-1, developed 350 shp from 1,454 cubic inches and was a failure; with redesigned cylinder heads and designated the R-2, it was satisfactorily demonstrated, but production was awarded to Curtiss. The Lawrance firm and Wright were then encouraged by the Navy to merge for the purpose of further developing and producing Lawrance designs.

In 1924, Wright had started work on the P-1/P-2, nine-cylinder, 1,654-cubic-inch supercharged radial, later designated the Cyclone, which was qualified in 1925 at 435 shp. This led to a long and successful series of Wright Aeronautical Corporation radial engines, including the R-2600 Cyclone 14, with cylinders from the R-1820 Cyclone 9, in late 1935. R-2600 power ranged from 1,500 shp at 1,950 pounds for the single-stage supercharged engine to 1,900 shp for the two-stage engines at about 150 pounds more weight. Next was the R-3350 Duplex Cyclone 18-cylinder radial, which began development in early 1936 with the same bore and stroke as the R-2600 with a goal of 2,000 shp and was qualified at 2,200 shp in March 1942, having been delayed by several development problems. Major problems were suffered in most of the R-3350's early applications, due partly to poor cylinder cooling and cylinder head design. Power had reached 2,750 shp by the end of World War II.

In 1946, Wright started the turbocompounding program for the R-3350, which was qualified in 1949 at 3,500 shp. In the jet field, Wright had its first and almost only major success with the J65, a derivative of the Armstrong-Siddeley Sapphire. The reliability of this engine was greatly improved by Wright in the course of development for qualification, obtained in February 1954; and few parts remained common with the Sapphire. Later, thrust was boosted to 7,800 pounds, and thousands were used on a variety of aircraft. Thousands were built, saving the Wright Corporation for a while longer; it was the corporation's last significant engine. Wright disappeared from the aircraft industry with the same rapidity as Curtiss.

Daimler Benz

Daimler was the parent company of Mercedes, which with Benz had been one of the two premier German aircraft engine manufacturers during World War I. A merger in 1926 created Daimler Benz. The company built large engines for aircraft and airships but is most famous for the line of engines it created for use in World War II. These included the DB-600 and DB-601 series, the principal inline engines for German fighters and bombers at the beginning of the war. The Messerschmitt Bf 109 was a principal user and saw its Daimler Benz engines grow from 1,100 hp in the 601A to 2,000 hp in the 605.

De Havilland

Geoffrey de Havilland built his first engine in 1903 for a motorcycle and designed his first aero engine in 1908 (a four-cylinder design built by Iris Motor Company). In 1927, de Havilland collaborated with Frank Halford to design the 319-cubic-inch upright Gipsy four-cylinder inline air-cooled direct-drive engine delivering 98 shp (135 shp for racing) at 285 pounds for a large number of small pleasure and training aircraft; 19,548 were installed. The Gipsy was inverted, bored, and stroked to 415 cubic inches, delivering up to 220 shp at 410 pounds when turbocharged. It was developed into the Gipsy 6 and Gipsy 12 engines.

In January 1941, de Havilland began studies of gas-turbine engines and had completed design of the 3,000-pound-thrust Goblin engine in August, with the engine running in April 1942. It was flown in March 1943 in the Gloster Meteor fighter. It flew in the prototype Lockheed P-80 in January 1944 and was licensed to Svenska Flygmotor as the RM1 for the Saab J-21 fighter; 2,688 Goblins were built.

The Goblin was scaled up to become the Ghost, a 5,200-pound-thrust engine used on the de Havilland Venom series of fighters. It was licensed to Svenska Flygmotor as the RM2 for the Saab J-29 fighter; 2,035 Ghosts were built.

De Havilland built versions of the Gyron engine in small numbers before being absorbed into Bristol-Siddeley Engines in November 1961.

General Electric

In September 1941, the U.S. Army negotiated with the British government for rights to the Whittle engine and awarded that program to the General Electric (GE) turbocharger group in September 1941. General Electric developed the J33 and J35 engines. The J33 ran on 9 January 1944. It delivered 4,200 pounds/thrust and flew in the Lockheed XP-80A and other aircraft. The J35 ran first on 2 April 1944 and was installed in a variety of fighter and bomber aircraft. GE delivered 300 production J33s and 140 production J35s by September 1946, when responsibility for both engines was shifted to Allison.

GE's more advanced J47 program was a huge success, with 36,500 being produced through 1956 for the Republic F-84, North American F-86, Boeing B-47, and many other aircraft. A whole series of single-spool axial-flow engines followed, including the J53, J73, J79, T58, J85, T64, J87, J93, and J97. By 1960, GE had established itself as one of the world's premier engine manufacturers.

One notable success was the J79 for supersonic aircraft, started in October 1952 under the leadership of Gerhard Neumann. It featured variable vanes, which became a feature of all future GE engines. The J79 was selected for the Lockheed F-104, Convair B-58, Grumman F11F-1F, McDonnell F-4, and Douglas A-5 aircraft, as well as the Regulus II missile. The greatest production was for the F-4 and F-104; 17,309 engines being built by GE, plus others in Europe and Japan. The last engines were rated at 17,900 pounds/thrust.

The T58 started development in June 1953 as a rear-drive free-turbine. The T58 was qualified in November 1957 at 1,024 shp and was selected for the Kaman UH-2A, Sikorsky SH-3A, Boeing-Vertol CH-46A, the Bell UH-1F, and other military and commercial variants of these helicopters. The T58 was developed to 1,870 shp and 440 pounds; the last of 8,536 T58s was produced in 1988.

At the time GE started the T58, it also started studies of a 2,500-shp engine, finalizing the design in 1957 as the T64. The development program was started that May for both prop- and shaft-drive versions with a goal of 2,650 shp at 1,161, 887, and 723 pounds for the prop-, shaft-, and direct-drive versions. The T64 flew in the de Havilland Caribou in May 1960, and power was increased to 2,850 shp prior to qualification in June 1963. It was also selected for the CH-53, de Havilland Buffalo, Fiat G.222, Lockheed AH-56 helicopter, and Shin Mei Wa PS-1 flying boat and reengined the Japanese P-2 patrol aircraft. Although problems delayed initial qualification, the T64 was uprated to more than 5,000 shp with little weight change; 3,215 engines having been built.

In late 1954, GE began the J85 program as a low-cost lightweight single-spool missile engine with a new six-stage compressor and combustor and two-stage turbine derived from the T58. It flew first as an engine for the Quail missile and was then rated for use in the Northrop F-5 and T-38 programs. It became a popular engine for executive aircraft.

GE participated in the 1962 USAF studies that defined the C-X transport, later to become the Lockheed C-5, for which the TF39 was built. GE built 469 TF39s, which were later uprated to 43,000 pounds/thrust; the TF39 became the basis for the civil CF6 series of engines, of which only a few were in military service as the F103 for the McDonnell Douglas KC-10 and Boeing E-4.

In 1963, GE began studies of the two-spool turbofan that became the TF34. It was selected for the Lockheed S-3A patrol and (slightly derated for improved life) Fairchild-Republic A-10 attack aircraft. More than 2,100 TF34s were built; the civil version, the CF34, has significant production for larger business and regional jet aircraft, extending well into the twenty-first century.

The GE F101 afterburning two-spool turbofan engine started development in August 1968 as the GE9 (X370) demonstrator for the advanced bomber study that became the B-1, running in 1969. This lead to the F101 program, kicked off in 1970, with a goal of 30,750 pounds/thrust. The F110 engine was a redeveloped F101 for the fighter mission. It was initially rated at 27,846 pounds/thrust and 3,980 pounds/weight and was selected for reengining the Grumman F-14 and General Dynamics F-16 fighters. Some 2,800 of the F101/F110/F118 family had been built by mid-1994. The F118 engine for the Northrop B-2 bomber was a non-afterburning version of the F110, with a new fan, and rated at 19,000 pounds/thrust at 3,363 pounds/weight. About 100 F118 engines were produced for the B-2. It has been proposed to re-engine the U-2/TR-2 aircraft with F118 engines.

Another derivative of the F101 was the CFM56 engine, the program starting in December 1971 as a joint venture with SNECMA; it was used in many civil transport aircraft and to re-engine (as the F108) the Boeing KC-135 fleet. The CFM56 substituted a high-BPR (bypass ratio) fan for the F101's low-BPR fan and was certified at 24,000 pounds/thrust and 4,610 pounds/weight in November 1979. Growth versions had reached 34,000 pounds/thrust at 5,700 pounds/weight by the time CFM56 no. 10,000 was produced in June 1999.

GE's two-spool axial-flow afterburning J101 turbojet engine was started in April 1971 and first ran in July 1972. It was intended for the lightweight fighter program; only flight-test quantities were built to fly in the YF-17, but this became the core for the F404 engine, started in March 1975 for the F-18. Volvo further developed the F404 to 18,100 pounds/thrust and 2,315 pounds/weight for Saab's JAS 39 "Gripen" fighter; U.S. development has continued as the F414 for the F18E/F, at 22,000 pounds/thrust and 2,445 pounds/weight (with 150-hour test qualification in October 1996).

GE started the T700 front-drive free-turbine helicopter engine after having run the GE12 demonstrator in 1969, with the T700 started in March 1972 at a goal of 1,500 shp at 400 pounds/weight. This was the first Army engine to have high priority set on maintainability. First run was in February 1973; more than 10,000 engines of the T700/CT7 family have been produced.

General Electric was contracted in 1990 to continue slow-paced further development of the F120 as a backup/alternate engine for the F119 for the next-generation fighter; and when the studies began, GE participated. In 1996, GE was contracted to develop the F120-FX as a backup for the JSF119, but at a slower pace. The F120 development was to focus on engine core technologies during the 1990s and include the same fan and exhaust system variants as the F119 in a demonstration program to start in 2000. It is expected that the GE effort will also tailor the F120 more directly for the needs of the F-24.

Napier

The firm D. Napier and Son manufactured automobiles and engines when, in 1915, the British Air Ministry requested it begin building Royal Aircraft Factory 3a V-12 liquid-cooled engines and Sunbeam Arab V-8 liquid-cooled engines. Believing it could do better, Napier initiated its own engine program in 1916. The first engine was the E64 Lion, developed by A. J. Rowledge. It was of advanced design, being a geared, naturally aspirated (unsupercharged), liquid-cooled engine of W-12 configuration (three banks of four cylinders each, one bank vertical, the others 45 degrees from it). It had double-overhead camshafts, four valves per cylinder, individual cylinders (the first prototypes had monoblock cylinders), and a single cylinder head for each bank. Some 800 Lions were produced through 1932 and were selected for 59 different military and civil aircraft models, including bombers, transports, seaplanes, fighters, and racers.

In 1928, Napier contracted Frank B. Halford to design three air-cooled engines—the H-16 Rapier, the I-6 Javelin, and the H-24 Dagger. Production in small quantities continued into World War II. In 1935, Halford designed the E107 Sabre H-24 double-crankshaft supercharged liquid-cooled sleeve-valve monoblock engine of 2,238-cubic-inch displacement. It was selected for the Hawker Typhoon, Tempest, and Fury fighters, ultimately developing 3,500 shp with water-methanol augmentation. In January 1945, Napier began design of the ultimate in piston-engine efficiency, a 5,000-shp H-24 diesel of 4,571-cubic-inch displacement. Six engines were built and 1,370 test hours were run before the program was canceled in 1955.

After some early disappointments with turbine-engine development, Napier began production of the Eland single-spool turboprop for a rating of 2,750 shp. The initial applications were for reengining of piston-engine aircraft, and the Eland was selected for the Convair 340 (renamed 540), having been demonstrated in the Avro Tudor, Airspeed Ambassador, and Vickers Varsity transports. Later, the Eland was selected for the Fairey Rotodyne and Westland Westminster helicopters. Another helicopter engine was the Gazelle, used in the Bristol Belvedere. Napier was absorbed into Rolls-Royce in the early 1960s.

Pratt and Whitney

In mid-1925, Wright's reluctance to invest in research and development caused its president, F. W. Rentschler, to resign and form Pratt and Whitney Aircraft (named after its benefactor, the Pratt and Whitney Machine Tool Company of

In 1935, Frank B. Halford designed the E107 Sabre H-24 double-crankshaft supercharged liquid-cooled sleeve-valve monoblock engine of 2,238 cubic-inch displacement. It was selected for the Hawker Typhoon, Tempest, and Fury (shown here), ultimately developing 3500-shp with water-methanol augmentation. (Walter J. Boyne)

Hartford, Conn.). Pratt and Whitney's first product was the nine-cylinder R-1340 Wasp, the largest and most powerful U.S. radial engine in 1926 at 425 shp and 650 pounds/weight. Pratt and Whitney immediately followed this with the nine-cylinder R-1690 and R-1860 Hornets; the Navy and then the Army quickly replaced liquid-cooled engines and/or installed these air-cooled engines in as many of their aircraft as practicable. By 1932, the services were primarily using air-cooled engines.

Pratt and Whitney embarked on twin-row radial development in late 1929, leading to the R-1535 and R-1830 twin-row 14-cylinder radial engines. The R-1535 Twin Wasp Jr. began at 600 shp and was produced into World War II at powers up to 825 shp; 2,880 were built. It powered the Grumman biplane fighters, the Hughes Racer, the Vought Vindicator, and others. The R-1830 Twin Wasp had the greatest production run (173,618) of any aircraft engine. It started at 750 shp and quickly grew to 1,000 shp with single-stage supercharging in 1936 for the Seversky P-35 and Curtiss P-36. The basic R-1830 powered most of the C-47s produced. The R-1830, with a single-stage supercharger and a turbocharger, powered 19,000 B-24 bombers and the B-17 prototype. It ran with two-speed, two-stage supercharging before 1940, being qualified before the Allison V-1710 and Rolls-Royce Merlin two-stage programs had started; production versions with intercooling powered the first production Grumman F4F-3 Wildcat at 1,200 shp.

Pratt and Whitney followed the R-1830 with the R-2180 Twin Hornet (a bored and stroked R-1830) at 1,150 shp for the DC-4E and the R-2000 Twin Wasp D (an overbored R-1830) at 1,200 shp for the C-54 (DC-4). These were early examples of engines tailored for a specific airframe; 10,448 R-2000s were built.

The R-2800 Double Wasp 18-cylinder twin-row radial ran in August 1937 and was qualified in 1940 at 1,850 shp at 2,150 pounds/weight. In six months it was rated at 2,000 shp and reached 2,500 shp by the end of World War II. R-2800s were built until 1960 and were in airline service through the 1960s. The R-2800 was an evolutionary design, using improved cylinder design, materials, and baffling to get significant improvement in cylinder cooling technology and was the first air-cooled engine to deliver more than 100 shp per cylinder. The R-2800 used a two-stage supercharger in most fighter applications, and one model used two first-stage superchargers mounted on each side of the engine. More than 114,000 R-2800s were built during World War II.

The R-4360 Wasp Major 28-cylinder four-row radial was the only successful large air-cooled engine to be started by the United States in the 1940s. The Pratt and Whitney R-4360 Wasp Major was the largest piston engine to be mass-produced (larger engines were built elsewhere but did not have significant production). Its four rows of seven cylinders were of conventional design, and the engine drew much from the R-2800. Its development was difficult in spite of the conservative approach, and it was not qualified until August 1943. The R-4360 was selected for the many large aircraft, including the Boeing B-50 and Consolidated B-36.

In July 1946, Pratt and Whitney started negotiations with Rolls-Royce and obtained licenses in May 1947 for the Nene and the Tay. The Nene became the J42 at 5,000 pounds/thrust, with 1,139 built for the Grumman F9F Panther. The Tay became the J48 at 6250 pounds/thrust (with 4,108 built for the F9F-6 Cougar, North American F-86D, and Lockheed F-94C over 11 years). Pratt and Whitney spent significant effort making them suitable for production and used its own design for the accessory section and controls in the J48. Later, Pratt and Whitney developed an afterburner for the J48, raising its thrust to 8,750 pounds.

Pratt and Whitney's next great success was the two-spool J57 that powered fighters, bombers, and transports. The last of 21,186 J57s was built in 1965. It was scaled up to the J75, which was also used in advanced fighters and airliners. After building several very large engines, including the J58 for the Lockheed A-12, Pratt and Whitney began the JT3D/TF33 program in 1958. Although only 8,600 JT3Ds were produced (most of them conversions), this engine revolutionized the airline industry and greatly extended the life of the B-52 and, later, the C-135. The TF33 was developed to 21,000 pounds/thrust and was in limited production into the 1990s. Pratt and Whitney started the JT8D engine program in April 1960, which was followed by the JT9D in August 1965 for the Boeing 747. This was followed by the Pratt and Whitney F100 afterburning two-spool turbofan that was selected for the General Dynamics F-16 fighter in 1972. More than 6,000 F100s had been built by the early 1990s. These engines were followed by the Pratt and Whitney F117 (PW2037) transport engine for the Boeing 757 and the McDonnell-Douglas C-17, the Pratt and Whitney F119 (PW5000) afterburning two-spool turbofan engine, with a thrust-vectoring exhaust nozzle, for the Lockheed Martin F-22 and Northrop Grumman F-23, and the development of technology for an engine for the next-generation F-24 fighter in the early 1990s

Rolls-Royce

Rolls-Royce was ordered by the British War Office to start building aero engines—the V-8 designs of the Royal Aircraft Factory and Renault—in August 1914. Believing that a better engine could be built, and with encouragement from the British Admiralty, Rolls-Royce started design of its first aero engine, the Eagle, with a goal of 200 shp. It was a separate-cylinder liquid-cooled V-12 of 1,283-cubic-inch displace-

The Pratt and Whitney F119 engine powers the Lockheed Martin F-22 Raptor and, with augmented power, puts out 39,000 pounds of thrust. (U.S. Air Force)

ment, had epicyclic reduction gear, and was not supercharged. The Eagle first ran in late February 1915, flew in December, and was delivered in production by June 1916 at ratings of 225–255 shp at 820 pounds/weight. Its first applications were the FE-2d patrol plane and the 0/100 bomber. The Eagle was later selected for the 0/400 and V/1500 bombers, the D.H. 4 patrol plane, Felixstowe large flying boats, and numerous other aircraft. After World War I, the Eagle was further developed and was applied to bombers, flying boats, and transports, including the Vickers Vimy. Its highest rating was 375 shp at 847 pounds/weight; 4,675 Eagles were built, some staying in service until 1930.

The Falcon engine was a scaled-down Eagle, having all of its features and displacement of 867 cubic inches. It was intended for fighters and initially rated at 190 shp. The Falcon was initially installed in the Bristol F.2B two-seat fighter, its principal application (more than 3,500 built with Falcons), which remained in service until 1932. Falcons were also installed in Avro, Blackburn, de Havilland, Fairey, Martinsyde, Parnall, Royal Aircraft Factory, Vickers, and Westland fighter, seaplane, and transport aircraft.

The Condor engine was a scaled-up Eagle, at 600 shp the world's most powerful engine. The Condor was the first Rolls-Royce engine with four valves per cylinder, and it went into service in 1920. It powered many aircraft and the R-100 airship. Postwar Condors were redesigned. This effort reduced weight, which declined in steps to 1,200 pounds/weight; 327 Condors were built, the last rated at 750 shp. Two experimental diesel versions were built, as was a turbocharged version, neither leading to production.

The supremacy of the Curtiss D-12 engine shook the British engine establishment, with Fairey obtaining a license to produce it in Britain. The Ministry of Supply refused to support Fairey's endeavor, buying a token amount for the Fairey Fox bomber, which was faster than the fighters of the time. Rolls-Royce was persuaded to develop a D-12 look-alike, named the Kestrel; the last Kestrel (of 4,750 total) was produced in 1938; it had been used in 80 different aircraft.

Rolls-Royce began design of the R engine for Schneider Trophy racing planes in November 1928. For the 1931 Schneider race, the R was thoroughly redesigned to uprate it to 2,350 shp, taking the trophy in September.

To provide still greater power for fighter and bomber aircraft, the Kestrel was scaled up to become the famous Merlin. Design started without government sponsorship in October 1932 as the PV-12. The first production engine, delivered in August 1937 for the Hawker Hurricane, was rated at 890 shp for takeoff, 990 shp at 12,250 feet altitude, and 1,030 shp emergency/combat at 16,250 feet.

A switch from 87 octane to 100 octane fuel in March 1940 allowed the Merlins to be uprated by approximately 30 percent. In a 15-minute 1944 demonstration, a Merlin gave 2,640 shp. Including U.S. production by Packard, approximately 150,000 Merlins were built through 1949.

The Griffon was a growth version of the Merlin and first ran in November 1939, entering service at 1720 shp. Further development of the Griffon resulted in takeoff rating at 2,500-shp with water injection; some 8,100 Griffons were produced through 1955.

Rolls-Royce entered the jet age supporting the Whittle W.2 program and accepted a subcontract for six W.2B engines as WR-1s in the Spring of 1942, running two in November 1942. Then, Rolls-Royce took over the Rover program for the Whittle W.2B engine in January 1943 and improved it as the Welland for the Meteor fighter.

When Rolls-Royce learned that GE was developing the J33 and J35 engines for 4,000 pounds/thrust, it started the Nene program in May 1944. The Nene powered the Supermarine Attacker and Hawker Sea Hawk fighters, several U.K. and foreign prototype and research aircraft, and was licensed to the United States (Pratt and Whitney) as the J42. It served as the basis for the Soviet Union's jet-engine program when export versions were copied as the RD-45.

In April 1945, design began for a single-spool turboprop called the RB.53 Dart. It was selected for the Vickers Viscount airliner and many other aircraft; the last of 7,100 Darts was delivered in 1987.

The Dart was followed by the Tyne, a more powerful two-spool turboprop that powered large transport aircraft, including the Canadair CL-44. It was still being produced in 1994 after more than 900 engines had been delivered.

The Rolls-Royce Avon first saw service in 1950, when it was produced for the English Electric Canberra. Uprated to 7,500 pounds/thrust, it was used in the Vickers Valiant bomber, Hawker Hunter fighter and de Havilland Comet II, among many others. The Avon was adaptable and ultimately developed more than 16,000 pounds/thrust with afterburner; 10,433 Avons were built for aircraft propulsion, plus many more for industrial and marine power.

By now confident in its approach, Rolls-Royce developed the Conway bypass (turbofan) engines. After trial periods, it was certified in September 1958 at 17,500 pounds/thrust, the world's first production turbofan. Production began for the large airliners; 907 Conways were produced.

In the early 1950s, Rolls-Royce began working with vertical-takeoff rigs to understand their control problems—looking toward vertical takeoff and landing of manned aircraft—and designed a long series of lift engines, including the RB.108, RB.145, RB.162, RB.189, RB.198 and RB.202. This series of engines showed what was possible in achieving high thrust-to-weight ratios and benefited later programs.

In June 1961, development continued on the Rolls-Royce Spey engine, which ultimately powered both fighter and patrol aircraft. The engine was licensed to the People's Republic of China in the mid-1970s, where it was built as the WP-9. Approximately 5,500 Spey and derivative engines have been produced.

The RB.172 Adour first ran in May 1967 and was selected for the British Aerospace Hawk trainer and light attack aircraft in 1975. It has been developed to 6,300 pounds/thrust.

In September 1969, after several years of studies, Rolls-Royce started development of the RB.199 three-spool afterburning turbofan (the engine chosen for the Panavia Tornado fighter-attack aircraft, in a joint venture with Moteren und Turbine Union, München Gmbh [MTU], and Fiat, called Turbo-Union). The RB.199 was uprated in steps to 16,900 pounds/thrust with afterburner. Approximately 1,900 RB.199s were produced.

In September 1986, after several years of studies, Rolls-Royce started development of the EJ.200 two-spool afterburning turbofan engine (for the Eurofighter Typhoon fighter) in a joint venture with MTU, Fiat, and Senera, called Eurojet Engines. The first engine run was in November 1988. and the 150-hour type-test was completed in October 1999, illustrating the long development period required for modern jet engines.

Douglas G. Culy

See also

Liberty Engine

References

Eltscher, Louis R., and Edward M. Young. *Curtiss-Wright/Greatness and Decline.* New York: Twayne, 1998.

Gunston, Bill. *Fedden: The Life of Sir Roy Fedden.* Derby, UK: Rolls-Royce Heritage Trust, 1998.

Heron, S. D. *History of the Aircraft Piston Engine.* Detroit: Ethyl Corp., 1961.

Holder, Bill, and Scott Vadnais. *The "C"Planes.* Atglen, PA: Schiffer, 1996.

Hooker, Stanley. *Not Much of an Engineer.* Shrewsbury, UK: Airlife, 1984.

Lumsden, Alec. *British Piston Aero-Engines and Their Aircraft.* Shrewsbury, UK: Airlife, 1994.

Schlaifer, Robert, and Samuel D. Heron. *Development of Aircraft Engines and Fuels.* Boston: Harvard University Press, 1950.

St. Peter, James. *The History of Aircraft Gas Turbine Engine Development in the United States: A Tradition of Excellence.* Atlanta: ASME International Gas Turbine Institute, 1999.

Smith, Herschel. *Aircraft Piston Engines: From the Manly Baltzer to the Continental Tiara.* New York: McGraw-Hill, 1981.

Sonnenburg, Paul, and William A. Schoneberger. *Allison: Power of Excellence.* Malibu, CA: Coastline, 1990.

Stevenson, James P. *The Long Battle for the F-22. Aerospace America* (November 1998).

Stokes, Peter. *From Gipsy to Gem—With Diversions, 1926–1986.* Derby, UK: Rolls-Royce Heritage Trust, 1987.

Taylor, C. Fayette. *Aircraft Propulsion.* Smithsonian Annals of Flight No.4. Washington, DC: Smithsonian Institution, 1977.

Vessey, Alan. *Napier Powered.* Stroud, UK: Chalford, 1997.

Wagner, Ray. *American Combat Planes.* 3rd ed. Garden City, NY: Doubleday, 1982.

White, Graham. *Allied Aircraft Piston Engines of World War II.* Warrendale, PA: Society of Automotive Engineers, 1995.

Whitney, Daniel D., *Vee's For Victory: The Story of the Allison V-1710 Aircraft Engine, 1929–1948.* Atglen, PA: Schiffer, 1998.

English Electric Aircraft

British aircraft manufacturer. The English Electric Company was founded in 1918 by three disparate companies that had produced aircraft for the Royal Flying Corps and the Royal Naval Air Service during World War I. Its first products were a series of flying boats and a single-seat ultralight, the Wren, in 1923.

In 1926, the company suspended aircraft-building operations. However, the threat of war saw the resumption of manufacturing when subcontracts were placed for various types. Throughout World War II, the company built and repaired Hampden and Halifax bombers for the RAF. After the war, English Electric landed contracts to produce various versions of the de Havilland Vampire under license.

The company finally moved into the design business with the Canberra bomber. Designed by W. E. W. Petter, the prototype first flew in May 1949. A total of 631 aircraft were built by the parent company, with others being assembled under contract, including some in Australia. Such was the success of the Canberra that it was chosen to be built for the USAF as the Martin B-57.

English Electric next designed the Lightning supersonic fighter, which managed to evade the cuts imposed by the 1957 Defence White Paper that advocated replacing manned aircraft with missiles. Eventually, the Lightning went on to serve with the RAF in six different variants. Overseas, the Lightning served with the air forces of Saudi Arabia and Kuwait.

The company's final military project was the TSR.2 (Tactical Strike Reconnaissance). The aircraft proved successful, although political interference and cost overruns finally saw the project canceled. The English Electric name finally disappeared when the company was absorbed by the British Aircraft Corporation in 1964.

Kev Darling

References

Ransom, Stephen, and Robert Fairclough. *English Electric Aircraft and Their Predecessors.* London: Putnam, 1981.

The English Electra Canberra proved to be one of the most efficient and longest-lived attack aircraft in history. (Kev Darling)

English Electric Canberra

The first jet bomber to be produced in Britain and the first to enter military service. In common with its RAF predecessor, the de Havilland Mosquito, the Canberra flew its missions unarmed at high altitude and at high speed.

Originally intended for radar bombing, the Canberra eventually emerged as a three-seat visual bomber. The prototype, VN799, made its maiden flight in April 1953. Service deliveries began to No. 101 Squadron in May 1951. Such was the demand for the aircraft that subcontracts were placed with Avro, Handley Page, and Short. Eventually, 25 squadrons received the Canberra.

There were many developments of the aircraft, including the T.4 trainer and various upgrades of the bomber versions for use in the Far East and Middle East. An intruder version complete with gunpack was later deployed to Germany.

The Canberra also conducted photoreconnaissance. First developments were based on the bomber, although the final variant featured modified wings and fuselage complete with fighter-type canopy. This final variant was known as the PR.9 and is still in RAF service.

Possibly the greatest coup for any British aircraft was the Canberra's sale to the United States. Built under license by Martin Aircraft, the B-57 Canberra went on to see war service in Vietnam in numerous guises and also served with Pakistan's air force.

Sales overseas for English Electric were also extensive, with countries such as Australia, India, and Sweden, as well as numerous Latin American nations, purchasing quantities. Most are now retired.

Kev Darling

References

Delve, Ken, Peter Green, and John Clemons. *English Electric Canberra.* Leicester, UK: Midland Counties, 1992.

Beamont, Roland and Arthur Reed. *English Electric Canberra.* London: Ian Allan, 1984.

English Electric Lightning

British fighter. In common with a great many aviation projects during the 1950s, the English Electric Lightning was dogged throughout its development and service career by political interference. However, so correct was the design that it eventually won through.

The Lightning concept owes its birth to German aviation-industries research into swept-wing technology during World War II. Another factor that influenced the design was the lack of a fighter in RAF service that could counter the bombers of the potential enemy, the Soviet Union.

Development of the Lightning began in 1947 when a team led by W.E.W. Petter began research into a supersonic research aircraft. The fruits of their labor first flew as the P.1A in August 1954. Judged successful, the design was further developed into the service version via the P.1B interim experimental fighter.

The RAF received its first service aircraft in July 1960 when No. 74 Squadron was equipped. As the type was developed through the various marks, more squadrons replaced their outdated equipment with the Lightning. Not only were the units of Fighter Command (later Strike Command) equipped; aircraft were also deployed to squadrons in Germany, the Middle East, and the Far East.

Developments to the design included changes to the wing planform that improved stability and allowed an increased fuel load. Improvements to the radar, weapons, and guidance systems extended the Lightning's capabilities. As the aircraft was originally designed for point-defense work, range was extremely short. To counteract this, an underwing refueling probe was installed, as were overwing wing fuel tanks on the last mark, the F.6.

Sales overseas were eventually limited to Saudi Arabia and Kuwait, attempts to sell to such countries as Nicaragua and Venezuela failing for various reasons. Saudi Arabia eventually replaced its Lightnings with the Tornado F.3; Kuwait reequipped with the easier to operate French Mirage F.1.

The RAF rundown of its Lightning fleet was gradual as squadrons reequipped with the Phantom and later the Tornado. By the early 1980s, only two units flew the type until they too changed to the Tornado F.3.

Kev Darling

References

Darling, Kev. *English Electric Lightning.* London: Specialty Press, 2000.

Philpott, Bryan. *EE/BAC Lightning.* London: Patrick Stephens, 1984.

Enlisted Pilots in U.S. Military Services

Enlisted and noncommissioned pilots were prominent in many of the world's major air forces. However, the vast majority of pilots in the United States military have been commissioned officers. Nonetheless, enlisted pilots played a significant role in the U.S. military in the years through World War II.

Sergeant William Ivy was probably the first enlisted pilot. In June 1898, during the Spanish-American War, he took an observer aloft in a balloon to report on the Spanish fleet in the harbor of Santiago, Cuba. In 1907, the Army created an aeronautical division to work with "all matters pertaining to military ballooning, air machines, and kindred subjects." At least two enlisted men were part of this earliest incarnation of today's U.S. Air Force.

In 1912, Captain Frank P. Lahm, commander of a newly opened U.S. Army air school in the Philippines, had trouble finding enough officers to train; Corporal Vernon L. Burge, who had been assigned to the aeronautical division earlier, volunteered and became certified as the first enlisted pilot. That same year, it is believed that Harold H. Karr became the first U.S. Navy enlisted pilot, though he did not receive an official naval aviation pilot (NAP) rating until 1920. Some undeterminable, though small, number of Army, Navy, and U.S. Marine Corps pilots served in combat during World War I; many received commissions during their tour of duty.

During the interwar years, two enlisted pilots, Alva Harvey and Henry Ogden, participated in the Army's 1924 round-the-world flight. Harvey, flying with expedition commander Frederick Martin, crashed in Alaska and did not complete the trip; Ogden's plane went down in the North Atlantic, but he completed the circumnavigation. The 1926 National Defense Act required that 20 percent of pilots assigned to tactical squadrons in the Army Air Corps be enlisted; 30 percent of Navy pilots were supposed to be enlisted, though this figure was reduced to 20 percent in 1932. In neither service did the actual number of enlisted pilots come close to those percentages.

As the nation's leaders prepared for World War II, Congress passed Public Law 99 in June 1941 specifically authorizing the creation of a wartime enlisted pilot training program. A few months later, the first class of Army enlisted pilots, who gained popularity as "flying sergeants," reported to primary flying school. The enlisted students of Class 42-C finished their training and graduated on 7 March 1942, one half from Kelly Field, near San Antonio, and the other from Ellington Field, near Houston. They all went on to fly P-38s during World War II. Subsequent classes were assigned to various types of aircraft in both combat and support units.

The Army's sergeant pilot program ended in July 1942 with the passage of Public Law 658. This legislation created the title of "flight officer" in an attempt to lessen the divide between officer and enlisted pilots. Qualification standards for both the enlisted pilot and aviation cadet programs were made equal, and enlisted flying training graduates gained the rank of flight officer or second lieutenant at graduation, depending on class standing. Between 1912 and 1942, nearly 3,000 enlisted pilots, ranging from private through master sergeant, earned their wings and flew for the Army. Of these, 155 were killed in action during World War II. Seventeen became aces, and 11 went on to attain the rank of general officer. At the time of the creation of the USAF in 1947, two pilots reverted to their enlisted ranks and became the only flying sergeants in the new service.

Over the years, as many as 5,000 enlisted men may have served as pilots with the Navy, Marines, and Coast Guard. Legislation ended the enlisted naval pilot program in 1947. Master Chief Robert K. Jones, the last enlisted NAP and the last serving enlisted pilot in the U.S. military, retired in 1981 after 38 years of service. Among the Navy's World War II heroes, Machinist Donald E. Runyon was credited with eight kills during World War II, including four on one day, before he became a commissioned officer. Runyon finished the war with 11 victories. Marine Corps Medal of Honor winner Ken Walsh started his career as an enlisted pilot and went on to become one of the leading American aces of World War II with 21 kills.

Many notable pilots started out in the enlisted ranks. William Ocker, an enlisted pilot during World War I, helped pioneer instrument flying. Walter Beech, cofounder of Beech Aircraft Corporation and a member of the National Aviation Hall of Fame, served as a sergeant pilot in World War I. Another Aviation Hall of Fame pilot, Bob Hoover, served as an enlisted pilot during World War II and is considered one of the great test pilots of any era. Sergeant pilot Ralph Bottriell earned the Distinguished Flying Cross for his work with parachutes.

Bruce A. Ashcroft

See also

Aces, leading; U.S. Army Aviation (Operations); U.S. Marine Corps Aviation; United States Navy, and Aviation; World War I Aviation; World War II Aviation

References

Airmen Memorial Museum, comp. *Heroes: A History of the Enlisted Airmen.* Washington, DC: Airmen Memorial Museum, 1997.

Arbon, Lee. *They Also Flew: The Enlisted Pilot Legacy, 1912–1942.* Washington, DC: Smithsonian Institution Press, 1992.

Martin, Robert J. *Enlisted Naval Aviation Pilots: USN, USMC, USCG 1916–1981.* Paducah, KY: Turner, 1995.

Enola Gay

The U.S. heavy bomber that dropped the first atomic weapon over Japan. A Boeing B-29-46-MO, serial number 44-76292, *Enola Gay* was one of a block of Martin-Omaha B-29s that were especially built without fuselage turrets to lighten the airframe and permit higher airspeeds. Curtiss electric propellers were installed in lieu of the usual Hamilton Standard hydromatics. The forward bomb bay was modified by the addition of an H-frame support and a British-designed C-mount used to carry massive 22,000-pound conventional Tallboy bombs. These airplanes were all assigned to the 393d Bomb Squadron, 509th Bombardment Group (Very Heavy).

The unit trained at Wendover Field, Utah, where it practiced dropping massive dummy bombs (known as "pumpkins") in preparation for dropping the large and heavy atomic bombs. The *Enola Gay* was the personal aircraft of the group commander, Colonel Paul W. Tibbets, and was named for his mother.

The 509th Bombardment Group deployed to North Field, Guam, where it was attached to the 313th Bombardment

The most famous Boeing B-29 in the world is the Enola Gay. *The combination of the B-29 and the atomic bomb was the ultimate expression of air power. (U.S. Air Force)*

Wing. Crews flew in formation with other bomb groups in the Mariana Islands for familiarization.

On 6 August 1945, Colonel Tibbets and his crew flew the *Enola Gay* to the Japanese home islands and dropped the world's first atomic weapon—code-named "Little Boy"—on the city of Hiroshima.

The *Enola Gay* is now in the collection of the National Air and Space Museum of the Smithsonian Institution.

Alwyn T. Lloyd

References

Lloyd, Alwyn T. *A Cold War Legacy: A Tribute to Strategic Air Command, 1946–1992.* Missoula, MT: Pictorial Histories, 2000.

Ethiopian War

Italian attack on Ethiopia on 3 October 1935; the last European drive to gain African colonies. Italy had prepared thoroughly, its Regia Aeronautica (the air force) receiving massive funding for new aircraft and a huge logistic organization. To preserve home forces, each squadron sent to Ethiopia left behind a so-called *bis* unit with older aircraft. Thus, the 27th *Stormo* fought in East Africa with Caproni Ca.111s while in Italy a 27th Bis flew Ca.74 and Ca.102s. By May 1936, Italy sent to East Africa 389 aircraft and 309 spare engines; Ethiopia fielded five Potez 25 general-purpose biplanes, four Fokker F.VII transports, and a handful of other types.

The surface campaign was launched from the neighboring Italian colonies of Eritrea (northern front) and Somalia (southern). The Ethiopian capital, Addis Ababa, fell on 5 May 1936; four days later, Mussolini proclaimed the Empire.

The Regia Aeronautica was a decisive factor in the victory. The lack of aerial opposition allowed Italian reconnaissance to track enemy moves. Bombers hit troop concentrations, and airdrops allowed the army to advance through inhospitable terrains. Wherever a lack of refrigerators made it impossible to store meat, live animals were dropped. This close air-ground cooperation relied largely on visual signals—white sheets deployed in conventional patterns, thus obviating the lack of direct radio links.

Ethiopian antiaircraft fire was very effective, hitting about two-thirds of all Italian aircraft. This explains the relatively high aircrew casualties (110 dead, more than 150 wounded), although many resulted from accidents—very dangerous in the harsh environment.

On 27 October 1935, Mussolini authorized the use of gas "as an extreme measure to overcome enemy resistance and in case of counterattacks." The orders were repeated on 16 and 28 December 1935 and on 5 January, 29 March, and 27 April 1936. Gas sorties (132) and bombs dropped (272 tons) represented only 2.6 percent and 18.8 percent of the total, but their effect was often critical: On 19 January 1936, only gas prevented an Ethiopian breakthrough at Uarieu. It is important to note that the decision to use gas was made at the highest political level and not by individual air commanders.

Italy overestimated its African victory, which relied on a superiority unlikely to be repeated; thus the campaign offered more training than stimulus for technological evolution. The war ended officially in May 1936, but extensive insurgency committed the Regia Aeronautica to a long and costly "colonial police" campaign.

Gregory Alegi

References

Gentilli, Roberto. *Guerra aerea sull'Etiopia, 1935–1939.* Florence, Italy: EDAI, 1992.

Mockler, Anthony. *Haile Selassie's War.* New York: Random House, 1984.

Eurofighter Typhoon

Joint project between the United Kingdom, Germany, Italy, and Spain, with each country being responsible for areas of development and construction. It is intended that the Typhoon will replace various aircraft in the air forces of the participating countries. The types destined to be retired include various versions of the Tornado and Jaguar.

The quest for the Typhoon, regarded as a fourth-generation fighter, began in 1977 when tentative discussions were held between the defense ministers of Britain, France, and Germany. Although these talks did not result in a cooperative venture, they did lay the foundations for the Tornado partners—Britain, Germany, and Italy—to start looking at the so-called Agile Combat Aircraft in 1982 to replace the Tornado. These early discussions resulted in permission to build two test aircraft for the Experimental Aircraft Program (EAP).

Before metal was cut or carbon fiber autoclaved, the project had run into trouble. The German government, caught between two sets of political loyalties to two sets of partners, eventually voted to do nothing. This left British Aerospace to develop the EAP alone. Incorporating all the latest technology advances, including an unstable fly-by-wire system, the single aircraft flew in August 1986. A series of 259 sorties proved the concept of the aircraft before it was grounded in 1991.

The usual intergovernmental wrangling was finally completed in 1985 before the aircraft had flown. The service aircraft was to be known as the "European Fighter Aircraft" and

Due to enter service in 2003, the Eurofighter Typhoon is the result of an uncommon partnership between Spain, the United Kingdom, Germany, and Italy. (Kev Darling)

was planned to consist of 760 units. Work division by percentage was: United Kingdom (33), Germany (33), Italy (21), and Spain (13). Total orders for each nation are: United Kingdom (250), Germany (250), Italy (160), and Spain (100).

Even with program agreement, there were to be political problems, mainly in Germany, as the project underwent evaluation, rejection, and reinstatement almost on a monthly basis. Fortunately, this most advanced of aircraft has not succumbed to the political furor that has occasionally surrounded it. There has also been some export interest with both Greece and Norway, both of whom have made firm commitments. Also looking closely at the Typhoon are Australia and Saudi Arabia. The Eurofighter Typhoon is due to enter service by 2003.

Kev Darling

F

Fairchild A-10 Thunderbolt II

Attack plane; entered USAF operational service in March 1976. It has two General Electric turbofan engines, each capable of 9,064 pounds/thrust. It is 53 feet, 3 inches long, 14 feet, 8 inches high, and has a 57-foot, 6-inch wingspan with a gross weight of 51,000 pounds. Its combat speed is about 440 mph, with a range of 650–800 miles. Its maximum ordnance load is 16,000 pounds. Employing depleted uranium armor-piercing shells, the seven-barrel 30mm GAU-8A rotary cannons mounted in the nose are capable of firing 2,100–4,200 rounds per minute. During the Gulf War, the 144 deployed A-10s flew 8,624 sorties in extreme climate conditions and still maintained a 95.7 percent mission-capable rate.

It has self-sealing fuel tanks, redundant wing spars, widely separated tail-mounted engines, and a manual backup flight control system. These features, as well as 1-inch-thick titanium armor covering vital flight control elements, allowed many A-10s to survive direct hits from Iraqi missiles.

Also nicknamed the "Warthog," the A-10 proved its lethality during Operation DESERT STORM, consistently chewing up Iraqi armor. In one operation, two A-10s destroyed 23 armored vehicles (mostly tanks) in one day. All total, A-10s destroyed 967 tanks, 1,026 pieces of artillery, 1,306 trucks, 281 military structures, 53 Scud missiles, 10 aircraft on the ground, and two in the air.

Besides the GAU-8A cannons, the A-10 can carry a wide variety of "dumb" ordnance on eight underwing and three underfuselage pylon stations. It can also carry laser-guided/electrooptically guided bombs, infrared countermeasure flares, electronic countermeasure chaff, jammer pods, 2.75-inch rockets, and illumination flares.

Today, there are two variants of the Thunderbolt II, the A-10 and the OA-10. The latter is an airborne forward air control platform.

William Head

References

Boyne, Walter J. *Beyond the Wild Blue: A History of the United States Air Force, 1947–1997.* New York: St. Martin's, 1997.

Smallwood, William L. *Warthog: Flying the A-10 in the Gulf War.* Washington, DC: Brassey's, 1993.

Fairchild Aircraft

U.S. aircraft manufacturer. Growing out of Sherman Fairchild's interest in aerial photography, the Fairchild manufacturing firm experienced many name and ownership changes in its history (1925–1988). Known primarily for its trainers and transport aircraft, it operated a Canadian subsidiary in 1922–1948.

The company's first big success was the PT-19/23/26 series of basic trainers, first flown in 1939 and of which more than 7,000 were built (Cornells in Commonwealth service). The C-61 Forwarder single-engine utility aircraft saw some 1,665 built from 1941 to 1944, of which about half went to the RAF. From 1944 to 1948, some 220 C-82 Packet twin-engine cargo aircraft were manufactured. It was followed by the improved C-119 Flying Boxcar, of which 1,087 were manufactured from 1948 to 1953. The smaller C-123 Provider originated as a Kaiser-Frazer design in 1954, but the contract was turned over to Fairchild, which made more than 300 in 1954–1955.

Fairchild had a successful regional airliner project when it purchased a license from Fokker to manufacture the F-27. From 1956 to 1971, the F-27 Friendship and the stretch ver-

Form followed function in the Fairchild A-10 Thunderbolt II, but if the aesthetic result was not the highest, the practical results were. The "Warthog," as it is affectionately known, gained a new lease on life in the Persian Gulf War and will be part of the U.S. Air Force for many years to come. (U.S. Air Force)

sion, the FH-227 (of which 79 were made) totaled 205 aircraft by the time production ceased in Hagerstown, Maryland, in 1971.

Fairchild took over Hiller Helicopter in 1964 and Republic Aviation in 1965 (becoming Fairchild Republic). With the latter purchase came the A-10 Thunderbolt II ground support aircraft, of which more than 700 were manufactured in the 1970s. But after the loss of several further contracts, the firm closed in 1988.

Christopher H. Sterling

References

Gunston, Bill. *The Plane Makers.* London: New English Library, 1980, pp. 32–35.

Jacks, Maston M., ed. *Yesterday, Today, Tomorrow: Fifty Years of Fairchild Aviation.* Frederick, MD: Fairchild Hiller Corp., 1976.

Fairchild C-82 Packet and C-119 Flying Boxcar

U.S.-manufactured cargo haulers. Through to the end of World War II, Allied airlifters were constrained by aircraft that were not designed for swift onloading and offloading of cargo.

Fairchild Aircraft of Hagerstown, Maryland, designed and developed America's first endloading aircraft. Known as the C-82 Packet, the aircraft had tricycle landing gear, thereby offering a level cargo floor. In addition, a pair of clamshell doors were installed at the aft end of the fuselage. With the doors wide open, a special truck with a bed equal to the height of the cargo floor offered unrestricted loading and unloading. For troop carrier operations, the C-82 had troop doors within the sides of the clamshell doors that permitted two sticks of paratroops to jump simultaneously from the aircraft. For heavy cargo drops, the clamshell doors could be removed prior to flight and the cargo could be extracted in flight. Frangible pallets and rigging equipment developed by the U.S. Army Quartermaster Corps permitted heavy cargo, small vehicles, and howitzers to be dropped without sustaining any damage.

Despite some shortcomings, C-82s served well with U.S. forces in post–World War II Europe and permitted the USAF and Army to perfect their airdrop capabilities during exercises within the United States. The C-82s also flew numerous humanitarian missions during natural disasters such as floods and blizzards.

The C-119 Flying Boxcar was developed from the C-82. Both were twin-engine, twin-boom aircraft with a fuselage pod suspended beneath the wing center section. The C-119 was slightly larger but could carry 22,000 pounds more than its predecessor. Problems persisted due to marginal engine-out performance and stability. The stability problems were rectified by the addition of dorsal, and later ventral, fairings on the tailbooms. Engine and later propeller problems continued to plague the aircraft throughout its service life.

When the Korean War erupted in June 1950, only Curtiss C-46s and Douglas C-47s were available as transports in the theater. By August 1950, C-119s began arriving in Japan and were able to fly their first aerial supply missions. Throughout the war, the C-119s bore the brunt of the tactical airlift assignments, performing airlift, airdrop, and paratroop drop missions. One of the most significant missions of the war was flown on 7 December 1950, when eight C-119s each dropped a section of treadway bridge to the "Chosen Frozen," a force of the 1st Marine Division and the remnants of the Army's 31st Infantry Regiment, which had been pinned down and cut off for 13 days. This was the first time a bridge was ever dropped from an aircraft. Of all the aircraft in the USAF inventory, only the C-119 had the capability to perform this mission.

After the Korean War, C-119s became the backbone of the Air Force Reserve troop carrier force, with 45 squadrons equipped with the aircraft. The aircraft served with the Reserve for 19 years.

A new mission was developed for the Flying Boxcar to meet the requirements of the Vietnam War. Fifty-two were converted into AC-119 gunships to fly night interdiction missions with USAF special operations units. Though arriving late in the war, the aircraft performed remarkably well and were most appreciated by friendly forces on the ground.

Alwyn T. Lloyd

See also

Douglas C-47; Special Operations

References

Ballard, Jack S. *The United States Air Force in Southeast Asia—Development and Employment of Fixed-Wing Gunships.* Washington, DC: Office of Air Force History, 1982.

Futrell, Robert F. *The United States Air Force in Korea, 1950–1953.* Rev. ed. Washington, DC: Office of Air Force History, 1983.

Fairchild, Muir Stephen (1894–1950)

U.S. Air Force vice Chief of Staff, airpower theorist, and founder of Air University. Muir "Santy" Fairchild was born on 2 September 1894 in Bellingham, Washington, and began his military career in the Washington National Guard in 1916. Beginning flight training as a flying cadet at Berkeley, California, in 1917, Fairchild completed his training overseas in Europe and earned a commission as a second lieutenant in the Aviation Section in 1918. He flew bombing missions over the Rhine with French forces until the Armistice. Fairchild received a regular commission as a first lieutenant in the Air Service, serving as a test pilot, flight instructor, and engineering officer. Fairchild earned the Distinguished Flying Cross for his participation in the Pan American Goodwill Flight (1926–1927).

Over the course of the 1930s, Fairchild graduated from the Air Corps Tactical School (ACTS, 1935), Army Industrial College (1936), and the Army War College (1937). Fairchild became a member of the ACTS faculty in 1937 and was appointed director of the Department of Air Tactics and Strategy in 1939. During his time at ACTS, Fairchild participated with Donald Wilson in the theoretical development of strategic precision daylight bombing. A colonel at the commencement of World War II, Fairchild experienced rapid promotion to the rank of major general as a result of his contributions in developing U.S. military strategy during the war. Valued for his vision and thinking abilities, Fairchild received prominent assignments that included secretary to the newly created Air Staff (1941), assistant chief of the Air Corps (1941), director of military requirements at the U.S. Army Air Forces Headquarters (1942), and member of the Joint Strategic Survey Committee in the Office of the Combined Chiefs of Staff (1942–1946). After the war, he was also one of the few officers to provide input into the formation of the United Nations. In 1945, Fairchild also successfully lobbied for the creation of a separate military educational system for the USAAF that was designed to study air strategy in a preventative context. Fairchild's reputation as a critical thinker and airpower theorist made him the overwhelming choice to become the first commandant of the USAAF School in February 1946, soon renamed Air University (AU).

During his tenure as AU commandant (1946–1948), Fairchild forged an enduring educational philosophy that integrated the elements of air warfare with both ground and naval warfare in order to create a prevailing military strategy that allowed the United States to influence world affairs. Fairchild's service as AU commandant ended in May 1948 with his appointment to USAF vice Chief of Staff and promotion to four-star general. For this period, Fairchild concentrated on the creation of the Air Force's air defense system, an assignment that became more pertinent with the Soviet Union attaining atomic capabilities. General Fairchild suffered a massive heart attack and died on 17 March 1950 at Fort Myers, Virginia.

Mark R. Grandstaff

References

Grandstaff, Mark R. "Muir Fairchild and the Origins of Air University, 1945–1946." *Airpower Journal* 11, 4 (1997): 29–38.

Schaffel, Kenneth. "Muir S. Fairchild: Philosopher of Airpower." *Aerospace Historian* 33, 3 (1986): 165–71.

Fairey Aircraft

Founded by Charles Richard Fairey (1887–1956), who worked as an electrical engineer and first entered aviation by building award-winning models. After a stint as chief en-

The Fairey Swordfish, though by the 1940s slow and obsolete, was nonetheless a major factor in World War II, with its strike on the German battleship Bismarck *and its part in the brilliant victory at Taranto. (Big Bird Aviation)*

gineer at the Short aircraft firm, he formed his own company in 1915. Initial output focused on successful seaplanes.

The Fairey III family of biplane fighters was manufactured in various marks from 1917 into the 1930s. The Fairey Fox daytime fighter of 1926 was a handsome metal biplane for the Royal Air Force. From 1930 until 1945, Fairey operated from the Great West Aerodrome at what is now Heathrow Airport outside London. The Swordfish biplane torpedo-bomber of 1934 sank 1 million tons of enemy shipping in World War II; more than 2,400 were manufactured by Fairey and Blackburn. The Battle bomber and Seafox fighter for the Fleet Air Arm were late-1930s products.

During World War II, Fairey manufactured some 2,500 Barracuda torpedo-bombers and well over 1,000 Firefly carrier fighters. Postwar activity centered on the turboprop Gannet antisubmarine and early warning aircraft for the Royal Navy. The two F.D. 2 research aircraft were the world's first to take the absolute speed record over 1,000 mph and were later used in research for the Concorde airliner. The Rotodyne transport of 1957 combined helicopter and normal airplane operation but was terminated before reaching production. Fairey was taken over by Westland in 1960.

Christopher H. Sterling

References

Fairey Aircraft: The Archive Photographs Series. Stroud, UK: Chalmers, 1997.

Macmillan, Norman. "Fairey's Four Decades." *The Aeroplane* (22 July 1955): 138–150.

"Sir Richard Fairey: A Great Designer and Industrialist." *The Aeroplane* (5 October 1956): 573.

Taylor, H. A. *Fairey Aircraft Since 1915.* Rev. ed. London: Putnam, 1988.

Fairey Swordfish

British dive-bomber and torpedo-bomber. Regarded as obsolete at the beginning of World War II, the Swordfish nevertheless went on to serve in the Fleet Air Arm and the RAF until the end of hostilities. The reason for such longevity was its superb handling, especially during landing, torpedo attack runs, and dive-bombing.

A follow-up to the earlier TSR.I, the Swordfish was developed as the TSR.II by Fairey Aircraft, the first one flying in April 1934. Fairey delivered 692 aircraft before handing over production to Blackburn to make way for production of the Albacore, hailed as the replacement for the Swordfish.

Service deliveries of the Swordfish I began in February 1936, with deployments to the various fleet carriers occurring soon after. A further development of the Swordfish, the Mk.II, began to enter service in 1943 and featured a strengthened lower mainplane that was stressed for the carriage of rocket projectiles. The final major production variant was the Swordfish III, which had an uprated Pegasus engine and an air-to-surface-vessel radome located between the main undercarriage legs. A further upgrade saw the appearance of the Swordfish IV, which had an enclosed cockpit for use in Canada.

The Swordfish first came to prominence during the Battle of Narvick when a battleship-launched aircraft spotted a U-boat for the fleet before destroying it itself. In November 1940, the Swordfish was involved in the most famous torpedo attack of all: the immortal strike against the Italian main battle fleet at Taranto Harbor. The Italian fleet suffered great losses that rendered it almost useless for the rest of the war. Further escapades involved the hunting of the German battleship *Bismarck.* For the last three years of the war, the Swordfish operated from the smaller fleet carriers in support of operations during convoy work.

The Swordfish also operated with the RAF for Coastal Command patrol duties. All operational Swordfish flying duties finished with the FAA in June 1945. A few aircraft remained in use for trials and communications use before final retirement ceremonies in 1953.

Kev Darling

Falaise-Argentan Pocket

Support of ground operations and interdiction of enemy retreat during World War II. By mid-August 1944, the American breakout from the western section of the Normandy bridgehead threatened to create a massive encirclement of German forces. The British Second Army and Canadian First Army moved south in an attempt to join with the U.S. First Army and pocket up to 16 German divisions, including the primary remaining mobile forces in France. The defeated German units tried desperately to escape the developing encirclement and moved by daylight along roads and in the open. This offered pilots of the Allied tactical air forces lucrative targets that had been uncommon in recent months.

For an entire week, Allied fighter-bombers and medium bombers pounded the retreating columns at will, wreaking havoc with the German withdrawal and destroying much of the German Seventh Army. Rocket-firing Hawker Typhoons were particularly effective. The Allied advances on the ground were not as successful, however, and German forces that were not destroyed from the air largely escaped.

Scenes of the Falaise killing ground graphically show the awesome effect of airpower on exposed ground targets. Although Allied air attacks caused enormous amounts of destruction, the battle can also show the difficulty in isolating and destroying a retreating army from the air, since the German armies, using cadres that escaped from Falaise-Argentan, were soon able to reform along the German frontier.

Frank E. Watson

Falkland Islands War

Also called the Falklands War, Malvinas War, or the South Atlantic War—a brief undeclared war fought between Argentina and Great Britain in 1982 over the control of a group of islands approximately 300 miles east of the Argentine coast.

The war was the first use of modern cruise missiles against warships of a major naval power. The Argentine Air Force (AAF), using French-built Exocet missiles, sank several British ships, including the destroyer HMS *Sheffield* and the container ship *Atlantic Conveyor.* The Exocet threat to British shipping would have been greater but for the fact that the AAF possessed only five missiles; an arms embargo kept Argentina from purchasing more.

The air war in the Falklands was the first time since World War II that sustained air attacks were made against naval forces at sea. The AAF demonstrated that brave pilots flying less-than-state-of-the-art or unsuitable aircraft could penetrate modern missile defenses and inflict major or even fatal damage on warships. The British were saved the loss of numerous other ships because, by one account, almost 75 percent of Argentine bombs failed to detonate. Four 1,000-pound bombs, none of which exploded, hit the British frigate HMS *Plymouth.*

The Falklands air campaign was the first known use of vertical/short takeoff and landing (V/STOL) aircraft in combat. The British Harrier jump jets, operating off of small carriers, emerged from the conflict with a greatly enhanced reputation. During the war, there were never more than 25 Harriers available in the theater of operations, and therefore the British were outnumbered at least three-to-one by the AAF.

In air-to-air combat, Harriers destroyed 23 aircraft with no Harriers shot down. This discrepancy is a result of several factors, including superior British training, poor tactics on the part of the AAF, and superior British equipment—especially the U.S.-made Sidewinder missile.

Craig T. Cobane

References

Ethell, Jeffrey L., and Alfred Price. *Air War South Atlantic.* New York: Berkley Publishing Group, 1983.

Hastings, Max, and Simon Jenkins. *The Battle for the Falklands.* New York: W. W. Norton, 1984.

Far East Air Forces (FEAF)

U.S. Army Air Forces and U.S. Air Force organization controlling forces in the Pacific region. The Far East Air Force (singular) designation was originally assigned to the U.S. Army Air Forces units in the Philippines in October 1941. This organization moved to Australia in February 1942 and was subsequently redesignated the Fifth Air Force.

The structure of the Far East Air Forces (plural) was first created in August 1944 to serve as the senior air headquarters controlling the Fifth and Thirteenth Air Forces in the Southwest Pacific Theater. HQ FEAF also served as headquarters for Allied Air Forces Southwest Pacific. FEAF provided support for Army and Navy forces in the liberation of the Philippine Islands. FEAF operations in the Southwest Pacific emphasized seizing air superiority, disrupting enemy logistical operations, and providing support to Allied surface forces. The Seventh Air Force was reassigned to FEAF from Army Air Forces, Pacific Ocean Areas, on 14 July 1945 as part of the consolidation of all Army forces in the Pacific under General Douglas MacArthur in preparation for the planned invasion of Japan. General George C. Kenney commanded FEAF during World War II.

After World War II, HQ FEAF was assigned to Japan as the Army Air Forces component of Far East Command (FECOM), which was responsible for U.S. military forces in Japan, Korea, the Philippines, and Ryuku, Mariana, and Bonin Islands. When the National Defense Act of 1947 created the Department of Defense and the independent United States Air Force, FEAF became a major command of the USAF while retaining its role as a component of FECOM under the Joint Chiefs of Staff Unified Command Plan. Prior to the Korean War, the major FEAF subordinate units were the Fifth Air Force in Japan, the Twentieth Air Force in Okinawa, and the Thirteenth Air Force in the Philippines.

When the Korean War erupted on 25 June 1951, FEAF assumed responsibility for Air Force combat operations under FECOM and the United Nations Command, working with the other U.S. components—Army Forces Far East and Naval Forces Far East (NAVFE)—and with the Allied forces. General George E. Stratemeyer was the FEAF commander at the start of the war, and after Stratemeyer suffered a heart attack in May 1951, General Otto P. Weyland assumed command for the remainder of the conflict. The major FEAF subordinate combat commands for Korean War operations were Fifth Air Force and FEAF Bomber Command, with airlift operations controlled by the FEAF Combat Cargo Command (designated the 315th Air Division in February 1951) and logistical support provided by Far East Material Command (designated the Far East Air Logistics Force in July 1952). The Fifth Air Force controlled the interceptors, fighters, fighter-bombers, light bombers, and reconnaissance and liaison aircraft.

FEAF Bomber Command controlled the B-29 medium bombers, as well as RB-29 and RB-45 reconnaissance aircraft, provided by the Strategic Air Command. FEAF also controlled the Allied fighter aircraft provided to the UN Command. Conflicting service doctrines on the employment of airpower complicated the task of controlling air activities during the Korean War.

The FEAF commanders followed USAF doctrine and sought centralized control of all air operations to provide the greatest amount of flexibility in the use of all available airpower. However, Navy and Marine leaders resisted this approach and fought to maintain independent operational control of their air assets. Coordination between FEAF and NAVFE and Marine aviation assets evolved through the war, with Naval and Marine operations increasingly integrated into the FEAF/Fifth Air Force plans. Formally, the FECOM Targeting Committee provided broad direction for air operations throughout the conflict, but eventually the FEAF Targeting Committee and the Fifth Air Force Joint Operations Center, which included Navy and Marine representatives, essentially directed all air operations.

After the Korean War, FEAF continued to serve as the air component for FECOM. In 1957, Far East Command was merged into Pacific Command (PACOM), and FEAF became Pacific Air Forces (PACAF), a USAF major command and PACOM's air component. In support of this realignment, the PACAF HQ transferred from Japan to Hawaii.

Jerome V. Martin

See also

Cactus Air Force; Kenney, George C.; Korean War; Leyte Gulf, Battle of; MacArthur, Douglas, and Airpower; Pacific Air Forces; Weyland, Otto P. "Opie"

References

Craven, Wesley F., and James L. Cate, eds. *The Army Air Forces in World War II.* 7 vols. Chicago: University of Chicago Press, 1948–1957 (reissued Washington, DC: U.S. Government Printing Office, 1983).

Futrell, Robert F. *The United States Air Force in Korea, 1950–1953.* Rev. ed. Washington, DC: Office of Air Force History, 1983.

Ravenstein, Charles A. *The Organization and Lineage of the United States Air Force.* USAF Warrior Studies. Washington, DC: Office of Air Force History, 1986.

Farman Aircraft

Founded by Henri Farman (1874–1958), who had purchased the second aircraft manufactured by the Voisin firm. After painful tests, he successfully took off. Developing the machine, he obtained great success and received an order for two biplanes (designated H.F.) from the French navy in July 1909 and four from the Armée de l'Air. Simultaneously, brother Maurice Farman (1877–1964) built his own models (designated M.F.). Due to the absence of a clear designation system, however, the history of early Farman aircraft is very confusing, as more than 1,500 were produced before World War I for civilian and military purposes.

Used for observation and bombing, the HF.20, HF.30, and many MFs were used extensively by France, Belgium, Great Britain, Italy, Japan, and Russia. The F.40 arrived in 1915 and replaced the former types in 1916. The only advanced bomber designed by Farman, the F.50, was built (171 units) before the end of the war. Thirteen were later obtained by Mexico. A total of 4,164 Farman aircraft were produced during World War I in France alone.

The first F.60 "Goliath" flew just before the Armistice. Launched as a twin-engine big bomber, it was quickly developed as a major commercial aircraft, but many versions were built for military purposes. No less than 600 left the Farman works, being used mostly by French services. They were highly successful in the 1926 Morocco operations. It was followed by the F.220 series, long-range four-engine bombers, 59 of which were delivered to the Armée de l'Air. It was the Farman N.C. (Nord Centre) 223-4—the *Jules Verne*—that achieved the very first raid over Berlin, launching 2 tons of bombs over the city on 8 June 1940 in a symbolic action forecasting more raids to come.

The Farman works had been nationalized in 1936 and became part of Nord Centre. The Farman name disappeared from military aviation after World War II.

Stephane Nicolaou

Farman Pushers

Farman was one of the many French firms that began operations prior to World War I. Another effort by a pair of brothers, Maurice and Henri, Farman aircraft came in two varieties: the H.F. series, designed by brother Henri, and M.F. aircraft, the work of brother Maurice.

The firm manufactured pusher aircraft, featuring large, bathtublike nacelles for the crew; they were used as bombers both in French escadrilles and in British two-seater squadrons. Although the pusher configuration was effective early in the war, Farman held on to it long after its useful days were over. As a consequence, not much was heard of the company in the war's later years, that is, at the front. The training fields were another matter. There the Farman's easy handling characteristics made it a useful primary training machine, and in this role it soldiered on until the Armistice.

James Streckfuss

References

Davilla, Dr. James, and Arthur M. Soltan. *French Aircraft of the First World War.* Mountain View, CA: Flying Machines Press, 1997.

Ferrets

Aircraft specifically designed to detect, analyze, and sometimes jam enemy radio and radar stations. During World War II, modifications and training were conducted at Boca Raton, Florida. B-17s and B-24s were converted for this mission. Passive sensors and associated antennas were installed, along with specialized operator stations.

The first Ferret operation was flown against a Japanese radar at Kiska in the Aleutian Islands on 6 March 1943 using a B-24. The Ferret operators were able to define and plot the enemy radar pattern so that a successful P-38 strike could be launched with minimal risk from antiaircraft fire.

Section 22, in the Southwest Pacific, utilized data from a B-24L Ferret assigned to the Thirteenth Air Force. By 1944, Ferret tactics now included detection and plotting as well as jamming with both and radio.

During Operation HUSKY, one of several B-17 Ferrets assigned to the Ninth Air Force was flown to suppress German antiaircraft fire for the parachute invasion of Sicily.

Strategic Air Command continued using Ferrets during the Cold War. RB-29s and RB-50s from the 55th Strategic Reconnaissance Wing regularly probed Soviet defenses around the world. These were followed by RB-47s from that wing.

Unique were the seven RB-69 Neptunes (former USN P2V-7s) procured by the USAF for use by the CIA. The basic production aircraft were modified in the famed Lockheed Skunk Works. The specialized equipment was so heavy that each aircraft was individually built for a specific mission. Though painted Navy blue, the aircraft carried USAF markings, operated out of USAF bases, and were flown by CIA crews.

The U.S. Navy also used Ferrets during World War II, converting PB4Y Privateers and supplementing them with P4M Mercators and P2V Neptunes.

Alwyn T. Lloyd

See also

HUSKY; Strategic Air Command

References

Lloyd, Alwyn T. *A Cold War Legacy: A Tribute to Strategic Air Command, 1946–1992.* Missoula, MT: Pictorial Histories, 2000.

______. *Liberator: America's Global Bomber.* Missoula, MT: Pictorial Histories, 1993.
Mutza, Wayne; *Lockheed P2V Neptune: An Illustrated History.* Atglen, PA: Schiffer, 1996.

Fiat

Founded in Turin, Italy, in 1899 as an automobile manufacturer. Today Fiat is a leading multinational group. FiatAvio, its $1 billion aviation subsidiary active in engine manufacture and overhaul, space propulsion, and energy, traces its origins to 1908.

Before World War I, Fiat built several experimental aircraft and airship power plants. The first production engine was the 100-hp A.10 (1915), patterned upon the Mercedes-Daimler D.I; the more powerful A.12 family (1916) accounted for more than one-half of all World War I engine production in Italy. In 1915, the Italian army invited Fiat to build the Farman M.F. 11 biplane, and in 1916 the new SIA company was formed for aircraft production. The large SIA 14 bomber was a failure, and the single-engine SIA 9 proved disappointing. Worse, the SIA 7, ordered in quantity trusting on the prototype's remarkable performance, suffered fatal structural failures in squadron service and was withdrawn. Enraged, the army in June 1918 called for the withdrawal of all SIA types "past, present, and future" but allowed a new Fiat "Aviazione" to operate under the technical direction of Celestino Rosatelli (1885–1945).

In 1925, Fiat bought Aeronautica Ansaldo, which was renamed Aeronautica d'Italia and became its aircraft division. Aero engines were still built under the Fiat name, powering all Fiat types as well as the Macchi C.72 speed-record seaplane.

Rosatelli conceived 60 types for Fiat, and some 6,000 aircraft were built. They ranged from racers to bombers to transports, but Rosatelli is best known for the CR fighters, which began with the all-wood CR.1 (1923). He introduced metal construction with the CR.20 (1926) and peaked with the CR.32 (1935).

A second design office was established in 1931 for Giuseppe Gabrielli (1903–1987), whose first production type was the lackluster G.50 fighter of 1937. Gabrielli also designed transports that served initially with the airline ALI, a Fiat subsidiary like the CANSA and CMASA factories.

At the outbreak of World War II, Fiat was the largest Italian aviation firm, and its parent company wielded enormous influence. Nevertheless, its contribution to the Italian war effort was disappointing. In the engine field, the inability to go beyond the 1,000-hp A.80 radial forced it to belatedly acquire a license for the Daimler Benz DB.605. The BR.20 twin-engine medium bomber (1935) proved adequate, but the obsolete CR.42 fighter biplane (1938) remained in production until 1943 to become the most widely produced Italian design of World War II. The G.55 monoplane (1942) offered better performance, but only a handful were completed before the Italian armistice. Aircraft production was stopped by U.S. air raids in March–April 1944, although Fiat supplied engines and subassemblies to German industry.

After the war, Fiat rapidly regained its industrial preeminence. Gabrielli designed two jet trainers, the G.80 (1951—the first Italian turbojet aircraft) and G.82 (1954), which did not go beyond the prototype phase, but Fiat was able to enter the jet age by building under license the de Havilland D.H. 100 Vampire and North American F-86K fighters. The importance of this experience was evident in the G.91 (1956), selected to fulfill the light attack role by Italy and Germany, where it was built by Dornier. Possessing limited combat value but delightful handling, the G.91 equipped the Frecce Tricolori display team for 13 years. Its variants comprised the two-seat advanced trainer (G.91T, 1960) and the twin-engined Y attack aircraft (1966).

In 1961, Fiat became the main contractor for the Italian Group in the F-104G program, leading five other Italian participants and coordinating with the West Group in Belgium. Fiat took over even greater responsibilities for the F-104S, launched in 1966 and built until 1979. Conceived in 1962 as a vertical/short-takeoff-and-landing tactical transport, the G.222 flew in conventional form in 1970.

In 1969, Fiat became the Italian industrial partner for the nascent Tornado program, but a few months later Fiat merged its aircraft business with Aerfer and Salmoiraghi to form Aeritalia. In 1976, with the auto market in severe crisis, Fiat withdrew from airframe manufacture, selling its 50 percent share of Aeritalia to IRI-Finmeccanica and concentrating aero engine production in a new Fiat Aviazione (FiatAvio from 1989), which later absorbed the Fiat energy division (1987), the BPD space propulsion activities (1994), and Alfa Romeo Avio (1997).

Gregory Alegi

See also

Aeritalia; Ansaldo; Italian Air Force; Italian Aircraft Development; Lockheed F-104 "Starfighter"; Panavia Tornado; Regia Aeronautica (Pre–World War II); Regia Aeronautica (World War II)

References

Castronovo, Valerio. *Fiat, 1899–1999: Un secolo di storia italiana.* Milan, Italy: Rizzoli, 1999.
Vergnano, Piero and Gregory Alegi. *Fiat G.55.* Turin, Italy: La Bancarella Aeronautica, 1998.

Field Manual 100-20 (U.S. Army)

Helped define the proper role of airpower in war, a thorny subject within the U.S. Army prior to World War II. Ground officers tended to see the air weapon as a useful, perhaps even necessary, tool that would help them gain their tactical objectives. As a consequence, they insisted on controlling those air assets themselves and, indeed, apportioning them out to various ground commanders for their specific use.

Airmen, by contrast, saw aircraft as an inherently strategic weapon that should be used not only to assist ground operations but also to operate at the strategic level of war as well. They therefore favored a centralized system in which theater air assets would be controlled by a single airman; some assets would be designated for use in strategic air operations and others for tactical cooperation. Existing U.S. Army doctrine, not surprisingly, endorsed the ground view.

The North Africa campaign of 1942–1943 forced a reevaluation. Airpower was not viewed as having been overly responsive or flexible in that campaign. Six months of combat experience, reinforced by contact with British forces that had been at war far longer, dictated a change. The War Department therefore directed that a new doctrine manual be written. The task was given to two airmen and an armor officer, and their product was War Department Field Manual (FM) 100-20, *Command and Employment of Air Power,* published in July 1943.

FM 100-20 began by stating in bold capital letters: "LAND POWER AND AIR POWER ARE CO-EQUAL AND INTERDEPENDENT FORCES; NEITHER IS AN AUXILIARY OF THE OTHER." The manual then stated that flexibility was airpower's greatest asset, and that asset could only be ensured if airpower was centralized and controlled by the air commander. It posited a command arrangement in which the theater commander exercised authority through two component commanders—one for air forces and one for ground forces. The manual warned that the theater commander should not attach air units to ground commanders except in rare cases where units were geographically isolated. Thus, in the first two pages the two top issues of airpower's basic function, as well as who should control it, were addressed and decided in terms that favored airmen.

Perhaps in an attempt to soften the message, the manual then stated that because air and ground operations were interdependent, joint planning and joint training were absolutely essential to success.

The basic tasks of airpower were listed as the destruction of hostile air forces; denial of establishing hostile airbases; operations against land and sea forces; offensive air operations against an enemy's sources of military and economic strength; service in joint task forces, and in conjunction with or in lieu of naval forces.

Strategic air operations were described in the manual as those that aimed to defeat the enemy nation by striking at its "vital centers." Strategic air forces would be controlled by an airman, but the selection of their objectives would be the responsibility of the theater commander. Thus, in certain circumstances, strategic air forces could be used to achieve tactical objectives.

When discussing the role of tactical air forces, the manual listed three functions in order of priority. The first priority was to gain and maintain air superiority over the theater. This was an intensive and continuous process that required offensive actions against the enemy's air force and aviation infrastructure as well as strong air defenses. The second priority was to isolate the battlefield by preventing the movement of hostile troops and supplies—"air interdiction" in today's parlance. The third priority was the destruction of selected targets in the battle area, generally in the immediate front of friendly ground forces. Today this would be termed "close air support."

Air and ground officers alike saw FM 100-20 as a "declaration of independence" by the air arm. Although the manual was approved by the Army hierarchy, including the Chief of Staff, General George C. Marshall, most ground officers thought it went too far. They feared it would result in a decrease in the amount of tactical air assets committed to the ground battle. Conversely, many airmen felt the manual did not go far enough and objected to the statement of interdependency: Strategic air operations, they believed, could be conducted independently, and simultaneously, with tactical air operations. In addition, some airmen rejected the designation of strategic and tactical air forces. They thought airpower was indivisible, and that to divide it arbitrarily into separate forces would result in a loss of flexibility—airpower's greatest attribute.

Subsequent events would give fodder to both points of view. Despite its controversial nature, FM 100-20 remained official Army doctrine for the remainder of the war. Seen in the broader context, FM 100-20 was a stepping-stone on the path to an independent United States Air Force, which was created in 1947.

Phillip S. Meilinger

See also

Air Interdiction; Close Air Support; North African Campaign; Tactical Air Warfare; U.S. Air Force Doctrine

References

Futrell, R. Frank. *Ideas, Concepts, Doctrine: Basic Thinking in the United States Air Force, 1907–1960.* 2 vols. Maxwell AFB, AL: Air University Press, 1989.

Mortensen, Daniel R. "The Legend of Laurence Kuter." In Vincent Orange et al., *Airpower and Ground Armies.* Maxwell AFB, AL: Air University Press, 1998.

A captured Fieseler Storch, perhaps the most efficient liaison plane of World War II. It was in a Storch that Otto Skorzeny flew Mussolini to "freedom" in 1943. (U.S. Air Force)

Fieseler Fi 156 Storch

German liaison plane. Following its failure to successfully compete for the Stuka contract in 1935 (its model 98 prototype having crashed and killed the pilot), the Fieseler factory moved to compete aggressively to win a new contract, this time for a light liaison aircraft. Using experience acquired with the F-97 four-seater, an engineering team designed the Storch (Stork) in six months and flew the first of three prototypes in 1936.

One of the pre-series aircraft made a stunning impression at the Dübendorf meeting in Switzerland in 1937 by taking off short and hovering in a headwind. Various models from reconnaissance to air ambulance were ordered, and early versions saw service in the Spanish civil war. Almost 2,600 were built until the end of World War II and served on all German fronts. In the meantime, two prototypes of a bigger version, the Fi 256, were assembled by Morane-Saulnier in occupied France, but they were abandoned. The latter company used the experience to assemble its MS 500 Criquet, a French version of the Storch, after the war.

The Fieseler firm gained notoriety through the development of the Fi 103 flying bomb, better known as the V-1.

Guillaume de Syon

See also

V-1 Missile and V-2 Rocket

References

Fieseler, Gerhard. *Meine Bahn am Himmel.* Munich: Bertelsmann, 1979.

Piekalkiewicz, Janusz. *Der Fieseler Fi 156 "Storch" im Zweiten Weltkrieg.* Stuttgart, Germany: Motorbuch, 1999.

Fighter Air Corps, 64th (Soviet Air Force)

The 64th Fighter Air Corps (64 IAK—Isrebitelnyi Aviatsionnyi Korpus) was established in northeastern China on 26 November 1950 and headquartered in Mukden (Shenyang). Its purpose was to control fighter units of the Soviet VVS (Air Forces) sent to assist the North Korean and Chinese forces in the Korean War, by preparing those units to operate the MiG-15 and providing air defense against UN air attacks.

During the war, the units of 64 IAK flew the great majority of communist sorties and scored a disproportionate share of their victories. Initially, 64 IAK consisted of three fighter divisions that began operations on 1 November 1950. In March 1951, these divisions rotated home and were replaced by new units. A second rotation of units occurred during the summer of 1952. This cycling of units allowed more pilots to gain experience in jet combat but also had the effect of depressing experience and skill in the combat zone. The 64 IAK also was assigned the night interception role. It was initially equipped with the La-11, then the MiG-15, along with two antiaircraft artillery divisions, two searchlight regiments, and support units. In 1953, two regiments of naval MiG-15s were added to the night interception task.

According to Soviet sources, units of 64 IAK flew 63,229 sorties (60,450 day, 2,779 night), participated in 1,790 air combats (1,683 day, 107 night), and shot down 1,309 enemy aircraft, including 1,097 by fighter aviation (1,067 day, 30 night), and 212 by antiaircraft artillery. The Soviets lost 13 pilots killed in noncombat accidents and 111 pilots killed in combat, in addition to about 350 aircraft. Even allowing for additional Chinese and North Korean air activity, these figures remain at variance with UN loss and victory claims, suggesting that overclaiming occurred on both sides.

George M. Mellinger

See also

Korean War; Kozhedub, Ivan; Pepelyaev, Evgenii Georgievich; Sutyagin, Nikolai

References

Gordon, Yefim, and Vladimir Rigmant. *MiG-15: Design, Development, and Korean War Combat History.* Osceola, WI: Motorbooks International, 1993.

Sarin, Oleg, and Lev Dvoretsky. *Alien Wars: The Soviet Union's Aggressions Against the World, 1919–1989.* Novato, CA: Presidio Press, 1996.

Finletter Commission

The Air Policy Commission, established by President Harry Truman in July 1947 with Thomas K. Finletter serving as chair. Its charter was to make an objective inquiry into national aviation policies and problems. After three months of study and the interviewing of 140 witnesses from the military services, industry, and commercial aviation, the commission issued a report, *Survival in the Air Age.* Its main conclusion was that the security of the United States in the nuclear age would rest on airpower and that the Air Force, as well as naval aviation, should be greatly expanded to meet future threats.

Phillip S. Meilinger

See also

Cold War; National Security Act of 1947; Truman, Harry S.

References

Moody, Walton S. *Building a Strategic Air Force.* Washington, DC: Air Force History and Museums Program, 1996.

Rearden, Steven L. *History of the Office of the Secretary of Defense, Volume 1: The Formative Years, 1947–1950.* Washington, DC: U.S. Government Printing Office, 1984.

Survival in the Air Age: A Report by the President's Air Policy Commission. Washington, DC: U.S. Government Printing Office, 1948.

Finnish Air Force (Early Years)

The Ilmailuvoimat, Finland's air force, is one of the oldest official independent aviation forces in the world. During the revolution in 1917, the Finns saw a chance to break away from the Russian empire and become an independent country. Their war of independence began in December 1917 under General Gustaf Mannerheim. In February 1918, the first of two donated aircraft arrived to assist Finland's White Army. The first aircraft was a Nordiska Aviatik–built Albatros two-seater. It arrived in Kokkola from Sweden on 25 February 1918. The second donated aircraft, a Thulin D, came from Count Eric Von Rosen, a Swedish explorer. His donation, flown by Lieutenant Nils Kindberg, arrived on 4 March 1918. Rosen had painted a blue swastika, his personal good-luck symbol, on the fuselage of the plane. This blue swastika became the Ilmailuvoimat's official insignia, an unfortunate resemblance to Nazi Germany's black swastika. By 10 March 1918, the Ilmailuvoimat was officially formed and given its own commander.

Shortly thereafter, the Ilmailuvoimat acquired a rather motley collection of aircraft, but enough to complete two flying divisions. These aircraft were Thulin Ds, Nodiska-built Albatros B.Is and C.IIIs, several captured Russian Nieuport 10 and 23s, as well as Shchetinin M5, M9, M15, and M16 hydroplanes—a total of 47 aircraft of 19 different types. During World War I, the aircraft were used for reconnaissance and limited bomb-dropping. Recruits went to Germany for training until June 1919, when a French military mission arrived with 12 pilots under the command of Major Raoul Etienne to initiate training at home.

The Finns spent 20 million Swiss francs to purchase 20 Breguet 14 B-2 reconnaissance planes and 12 Georges Levy hydroplanes, but they soon recognized the need for an indigenous aircraft factory. In 1920, the same year as the peace treaty with Russia, the Ilmailuvoimien Lentokonetehdas (Aviation Force Aircraft Factory) was created and concentrated on Hansa Brandenburg W 33 monoplane floatplanes. Floatplanes and hydroplanes predominated during the years between the wars, upon the advice of a British mission that arrived in 1924. Early in the 1920s, the Ilmailuvoimat was also tasked with aerial photographic survey duties, a mission it carries out today.

Wendy Coble

References

Aeroflight Website. Available online at http://www.aeroflight.co.uk/waf/finland/finaf2.htm.

Divone, Louis, and Judene Divone. *Wings of History: The Air Museums of Europe.* Oakton, VA: Oakton Hills, 1989.

Green, William, and John Fricker. *The Air Forces of the World: Their History, Development, and Present Strength.* New York: Hanover House, 1958.

Finnish Air Force (in Russo-Finnish Wars)

Seeds of tradition were sown in the Ilmailuvoimat (the Finnish Air Force) during the Winter War (30 November 1939–12 March 1940) against the Soviet Union. Finnish air operations hit their stride during the Continuation War, so called because it continued the conflict begun by the Soviets in 1939. The first real combat for the Ilmailuvoimat occurred during the Soviet invasion of Finland. In this war, the Finns scored 190 confirmed kills and more than 100 probables. They achieved a 16:1 ratio with the Soviets—in aerial combat, the Finns shot down 16 Soviets for every one of theirs the Soviets downed.

The small and ill-equipped Ilmailuvoimat followed certain principals to ensure success. First, by concentrating its fighter power and using the element of surprise, it achieved temporary air superiority. Second, it flew in small, flexible formations. Next, it demanded that its pilots be skilled in aerobatics and combat maneuvers. Finally, Finnish pilots were continuously trained until they were masters in shooting accuracy.

Although Finland did not share the Nazi political ideology, it still formed an alliance with Germany to defend itself against the Soviet Union. When Hitler invaded the Soviet Union on 22 June 1941, Finland went to war. The air force began the Continuation War with 120 fighters (Brewsters, Fiats, Curtisses, Morane-Saulniers, and Hurricanes) and 58 mostly obsolete reconnaissance planes.

Initially, the Finns were quite successful against the Soviets, achieving a 32:1 exchange ratio. As the war went on, the Finnish forces became less effective despite the acquisition of limited numbers of German Messerschmitt Bf 109Gs and Junkers Ju 88s.

The Battle of the Gulf of Finland is the best example of air operations during the war. The Finnish fighter pilots were successful, attaining an average exchange ratio of 25:1. Their strategy of focusing on aerial combat made the difference; raids on Soviet air bases were not worth the risk. The Soviets had no shortage of aircraft but lacked experienced pilots. By focusing on eliminating these trained Soviet pilots, the Finns achieved air superiority.

The Soviets did not wish to spend what was necessary to defeat the Finns militarily, so on 4 September 1944 a peace agreement was signed. The Ilmailuvoimat again finished a war with more fighters than it started with. Finland ended with the largest proportion of aces in the world in relation to population. Most of the Finn aces survived the war.

Scott R. DiMarco

References

Nikunen, Lieutenant General (ret.) Heikki. *The Finnish Air Force (FAF): A Historical Review.* Helsinki: Finnish Air Force, 1993.

Finnish Air Force (Recent History)

The heroism that the Finnish Air Force exhibited during the Winter War with the Soviet Union in 1939–1940 was displayed again in the Continuation War, which it fought from 22 June 1941 to 4 September 1944, when once again overwhelming Soviet numbers forced a Finnish surrender.

After World War II, activity of the Finnish Air Force was greatly restricted, being limited in size to 60 aircraft, usually of Soviet manufacture. Over time, it began to reassert its independence from the Soviet Union and built up a modern air force, initially supplementing its MiG-21 aircraft with Swedish Saab J-35 Draken fighters. A major modernization program began in 1995 with the acquisition of 64 McDonnell Douglas (Boeing) F/A 18 Hornets. The Finnish squadrons are also equipped with flights of the British Aerospace "Hawk," which is used as an economical proficiency trainer and light fighter.

The Finnish Air Force is noted today for its high standards of training and maintenance.

Walter J. Boyne

References

Willis, David, ed. *Aerospace Encyclopedia of World Air Forces.* London: Aerospace, 1999.

First Aero Squadron

Founded prior to World War I at a time when the United States could have remained competitive in military aviation with Europe. Instead, Europe went to war and the United States involved itself in border problems with Mexico.

As a rehearsal for later U.S. intervention in World War I, the fighting in Mexico proved ineffective. The heat was the real enemy. It melted the glue binding the laminated wood propellers and kept the 1st Aero Squadron's few Curtiss aircraft grounded most of the time. When the United States entered World War I in 1917, however, the pilots of the 1st Aero Squadron provided a personnel nucleus, which went on to command positions in the United States Air Service.

James Streckfuss

First Marine Air Wing

U.S. Marine close air support force during the Korean War. By the end of World War II, the Marines had almost perfected the art of close air support by fighters. As the Cold War heated up, the Marines became specialists in rapid deployment. The era of close support from the Navy's battleships and heavy cruisers was drawing to a close. The Marines now had to provide close air support from their own Marine aircraft.

When the Korean War started on 25 June 1950, all of the Marine forces were stateside. President Harry Truman's call to arms was answered by the 1st Marine Division. Forming up with the division was a group of aviators that flew the Chance-Vought F4U Corsair, the Douglas AD Skyraider, and a host of other support types. This became the 1st Marine Air Wing, and its only objective was to support the ground troops without regard to the cost. At the time of their entry into combat, their commanding officer was Major General Field Harris.

The 1st Marine Air Wing's entry into the war coincided with its counterpart, the 1st Marine Division, in early September 1950. Both were in place to support the successful amphibious landing at Inchon that cut the supply lines of the North Korean army between the Pusan perimeter and the North. It proved to be the most decisive military ground action of the war.

The 1st Marine Air Wing flew Corsairs as well as the night-fighter version (the F4U-5N) along with the heavy-hauling Skyraiders. During the Chosin Reservoir action, VMF-311 became the first Marine squadron in history to fly jets in combat, using the Grumman F9F Panther. The Grumman F7F-3N Tigercat was assigned night interdiction duties.

The 1st Marine Air Wing was tasked with dangerous low-level close air support missions against a myriad of small arms and heavy antiaircraft fire. Protecting the Chosin Reservoir retreat was perhaps the most difficult assignment because of severe weather conditions. Soon after the war ended on 27 July 1953, the 1st Marine Air Wing received one of the highest awards that could be earned in combat during this period, the Presidential Unit Citation. This was signed by South Korean President Syngman Rhee. The most significant statistic in this citation was that between 27 February 1951 and 11 June 1953 the 1st Marine Air Wing flew more than 80,000 combat sorties.

Warren E. Thompson

References

U.S. Marine Operations in Korea. Vol. 2. Historical Division HQ, USMC, 1972.

U.S. Marine Operations in Korea. Vol. 5. Historical Division HQ, USMC, 1972.

Fleet Air Arm

Aerial striking force of the British Royal Navy (RN). Early in the twentieth century, RN aviators duplicated Eugene Ely's feat of launching aircraft from ships. In 1911, a successful launch occurred from the battleship HMS *Africa.* Subsequently, the period after 1914 saw further development of RN seaplane tenders and attempts at carrier conversions. The RN commissioned its first aircraft carrier, HMS *Argus,* in 1918.

The Royal Naval Air Service of World War I became the Fleet Air Arm (FAA) in 1924. Initially it remained integral to the Royal Air Force. Consequently, problems concerning personnel and procurement of suitable aircraft hampered the FAA's growth. Adopting the RAF's squadron structure, the FAA possessed only 232 aircraft by 1939, most of them technically obsolescent. That condition changed dramatically under the pressures of war. By mid-1945, the FAA counted more than 1,600 aircraft in 73 squadrons. These aircraft flew from more than 50 fleet, light, and escort carriers.

The FAA's aircraft included several well-received U.S. types: the Grumman F4F Wildcat (Martlet in RN service) and F6F Hellcat as well as the TBF Avenger; the FAA also operated the Chance-Vought F4U Corsair.

British-made aircraft also supplied the FAA. The venerable Fairey Swordfish biplane torpedo-bomber (the "Stringbag"), though obsolete, was remarkably versatile and long-lived. Fairey also supplied the Barracuda torpedo-bomber and the Firefly reconnaissance-fighter. Hawker contributed the Sea Hurricane (the RN's first single-seat monoplane carrier-borne fighter). Supermarine modified its immortal Spitfire as the Seafire, and Blackburn Aircraft supplied Skua dive-bombers and the Firebrand fighter/torpedo-strike aircraft. Though making a significant contribution to the Allied victory, the FAA suffered severe reductions after 1945 as the Royal Navy was reduced to a peacetime establishment.

D. R. Dorondo

See also

Royal Flying Corps/Royal Naval Air Service/Royal Air Force

References

Chesneau, Roger. *Aircraft Carriers of the World, 1914 to the Present: An Illustrated Encyclopedia.* London: Arms and Armour, 1992.

Grove, Eric J. *Vanguard to Trident: British Naval Policy Since World War Two.* Annapolis, MD: Naval Institute Press, 1987.

Fletcher, Frank Jack (1885–1973)

Admiral and carrier task force commander. Born in Marshalltown, Iowa, on 30 October 1882, Fletcher attended the Naval Academy. He won the Medal of Honor at Veracruz in 1914 and the Navy Cross as a destroyer commander during World War I. Never an aviator, Fletcher followed a typical surface career, was promoted to rear admiral in 1939, and had command of Cruiser Division Six when World War II began.

Fletcher's task force participated in air strikes on Japanese forces in the Gilbert and Marshall Islands and New Guinea. At the Battle of the Coral Sea (May 1942), Fletcher's planes turned back the Japanese in the first battle fought solely between carriers and embarked aircraft.

Fletcher next deployed his carriers to defend Midway Island. Though Admiral Raymond Spruance took command when Fletcher's flagship was battered, the carriers Fletcher led into that battle scored a major victory over Admiral Chuichi Nagumo, who lost four carriers to Fletcher's one. Fletcher was rewarded by immediate promotion to vice admiral.

He was also victorious in the Eastern Solomons (August 1942), but charges of undue caution began to affect Fletcher's reputation, especially after he withdrew his vulnerable carriers from Guadalcanal, leaving the expeditionary force without adequate air support. After his flagship was torpedoed, Fletcher was relieved pending recuperation.

Fletcher returned to command the North Pacific Area, but he never again commanded carriers at sea. He later chaired the Navy's General Board, was promoted to admiral, and retired in 1947. Fletcher died in Bethesda, Maryland, on 25 April 1973.

Michael S. Casey

See also
Coral Sea, Battle of the; Eastern Solomons, Battle of; Guadalcanal; Halsey, William F.; Midway, Battle of; Nagumo, Chuichi; Spruance, Raymond A.

References
Heaton, Dean R. *Four Stars: The Super Stars of United States Military History.* Baltimore: Gateway Press, 1995.
Lundstrom, John B. *The First South Pacific Campaign: Pacific Fleet Strategy, December 1941–June 1942.* Annapolis, MD: Naval Institute Press, 1976.

Flight Refuelling Ltd.

Pioneered the use of aerial refueling. Based on his own experiments beginning in 1932, British pilot Sir Alan Cobham (1894–1973) formed Flight Refuelling Ltd. in 1934, with initial support from Imperial Airways, to develop technologies for air-to-air refueling of aircraft. The company's hose refueling techniques were deemed essential to development of long-distance air routes and were tested on Imperial flying boats in 1938–1939.

These tests included transatlantic flights and achieved refueling rates of 120 U.S. gallons per minute. During the war, Flight Refuelling personnel assisted the U.S. Army Air Forces in developing aerial refueling techniques. Further trials in 1946–1948 employed wartime bomber aircraft modified as tankers to test the use of radar in bringing the tanker and receiver aircraft together on various routes and weather conditions.

The first round-the-world nonstop flight (February-March 1949 by the B-50 bomber *Lucky Lady II*) employed methods pioneered by Flight Refuelling. The company expanded and diversified its operations after the 1950s and became central to Royal Air Force capabilities in the Falklands War (1982) and the Gulf War (1991), in which distance flights were essential. By 2000, Flight Refuelling Ltd. had 1,300 employees in three divisions: military systems (drones, air-to-air refueling, weapons release, and drop tanks), FR Digital Systems (primarily air traffic control systems), and FR Hi-Temp (aircraft fuel systems and equipment). It is part of the Cobham PLC group of companies.

Christopher H. Sterling

See also
Aerial Refueling

References
Cruddas, Colin. *In Cobham's Company: 60 Years of Flight Refuelling Ltd.* Winborne, UK: Cobham PLC, 1994.
Latimer-Needham, C. H. *Refuelling in Flight.* London: Pitman, 1950.

Flying Boats

Flying boats were important to early aviation because water was widespread, whereas land airports took money and time to build. Henri Fabre was the first person to successfully take off from and land an aircraft on water—in 1910 near Marseilles.

Just a year later, Glenn Curtiss interested the U.S. Navy in the flying boat's potential. Curtiss developed the boat-shaped hull with a break, or "step," on its bottom to ease takeoffs, an innovation that was soon featured on all flying boats.

The first airliners were Benoist flying boats of the St. Petersburg–Tampa Airboat line in early 1914. A Curtiss H-12 flying boat became the first American aircraft used in combat in mid-1917. A Navy Curtiss NC-4 flying boat was the first aircraft to cross the Atlantic just two years later.

In the 1930s, a few dozen large flying boats opened up world airline service for Imperial and Pan American, including the first transpacific service in 1935 and transatlantic routes by 1939. Though nearly 8,000 flying boats were built (chiefly by Britain, Japan, and the United States) for patrol, rescue, and antisubmarine use during World War II, construction of more efficient long-distance aircraft and airports to serve them spelled the eventual end of the flying boat. Most airline use ended in the 1940s; naval flying boats were phased out by the mid-1960s, replaced by more reliable and economic land- or carrier-based aircraft. Only a handful of patrol and fire-fighting flying boats remain in service.

Christopher H. Sterling

See also

Balbo, Italo; Beriev Aircraft; Blohm and Voss Aircraft; Consolidated PBY Catalina; Fleet Air Arm; Saro Aircraft; Short Sunderland; U.S. Coast Guard Aviation

References

Duval, G. R. *British Flying-Boats and Amphibians, 1909–1952.* London: Putnam, 1966.

Nicolaou, Stephane. *Flying Boats and Seaplanes: A History from 1905.* Bideford, UK: Bay View Books, 1998.

Focke-Wulf Aircraft

German aircraft manufacturer; originated in the work of Heinrich Focke (1890–1979) He designed light aircraft together with his friend and colleague, Georg Wulf, including the Ente (Duck), which had canard-configured stabilizers and was intended for use as a trainer. Flight-testing it in 1927, however, Wulf crashed the machine and lost his life. The company kept the name of the joint collaboration and continued to produce light aircraft while competing for civilian contracts.

Focke functioned as head of the company until 1931, when he was eased out by financial backers, though he remained a member of the board of directors. A new technical director, Kurt Tank, was hired to oversee development of most factory prototypes. Focke, meanwhile, devoted time to pet projects, in particular helicopter experimentation. The Focke Achgelis factory turned out several prototype helicopters, including the Fa 61, test-flown by Hanna Reitsch before an audience in the Deutschland-Halle.

Meanwhile, Kurt Tank's key role in the development of Focke-Wulf machines grew considerably. The factory began producing a series of prototypes while manufacturing aircraft for other companies due to the dearth of production capacity in the mid-1930s. Some Focke-Wulf machines were nonetheless produced successfully and included the Fw 44 Stieglitz, a two-seat trainer, and the Fw 58 Weihe.

Tank pushed for the production of prototypes in response to various army contracts. These included "unlucky" entries submitted in response to Luftwaffe requirements. Among them were the Fw 157, a single-engine fighter, and the Fw 187, a twin-engine fighter; they were bested by the Messerschmitt Bf 109 and Bf 110 respectively.

Among the successful developments of the company was the Fw 200 Condor, a civilian long-range transport that also saw service in the Luftwaffe as a long-range patrol. The FW 189 model, a twin-engine plane, was used principally on the Russian front. By the time production ceased in 1944, more than 800 machines had been built, many in Czech and French subsidiary factories.

The Fw 190 is probably the best-known production of the factory. It went through a series of versions, with new designs bearing the designation "Ta" as of 1943. Thus, later versions of the Fw 190 (like the Ta 152) bore that designation. Tank developed a twin-engine fighter out of wood intended for the night-fighter program, but it lost out to the Heinkel 219 "Uhu" (Owl). A series of paper designs followed, which never saw the light of day. However, some may have influenced early jet designs, and one, the Ta 183, served as a base for the construction of the Argentine Pulqui II jet prototype in 1950.

After World War II, the Focke-Wulf firm, like all German manufacturers, was forbidden from producing aircraft for a period of 10 years. Its management focused on license production of the Piaggio 149 trainer. Later productions followed, but by then Focke-Wulf was part of a growing German aerospace concern that first included VFW-Fokker, then MBB, and eventually became part of Daimler Aerospace, itself now part of the European consortium EADS.

Guillaume de Syon

See also

Focke-Wulf Fw 190; Focke-Wulf Fw 200 Condor; Heinkel Aircraft; Messerschmitt

References

Beiträge zur Geschichte von VFW-Fokker. Bremen, Germany: VFW-Fokker, 1974.

Smith, J. Richard. *Focke-Wulf—an Aircraft Album.* New York: ARCO, 1973.

Focke-Wulf Fw 190

Designed by Kurt Tank, the Focke-Wulf 190 was the epitome of deadly elegance. It was engineered for mass production, employing subassemblies from many widely dispersed factories. Multiple panels and excellent cowl design afforded quick access and easy maintenance.

A BMW radial engine provided 1,700 hp at takeoff and 1,440 at 19,000 feet. At the pilot's choice, movement of the throttle controlled an ingenious apparatus that automatically adjusted supercharger blower, propeller pitch, and fuel flow and mixture. A semireclining seat facilitated high-G maneuvering. Controls were light to the touch and beautifully harmonized. Visibility in flight was outstanding.

One of the most popular and efficient fighters of the German Luftwaffe, the Focke-Wulf Fw 190 was extremely effective in close air support work. (U.S. Air Force)

In July 1941, the Fw 190 entered combat, inflicting heavy losses on its Spitfire VB opponents. The sleek machine also became a Luftwaffe workhorse on the Russian front and in the Mediterranean theater. In the course of the war, 20,051 Fw 190s were manufactured.

The Fw 190 was fast at 408 mph at 20,600 feet with methanol water boost. Acceleration was swift and speed in the dive fast. The Fw 190 excelled in roll rate and sharp aileron turns. Heavily armed, it eventually featured two heavy 13mm machine guns and four 20mm cannons. A stable weapons platform, the Fw 190 was a very effective fighter-bomber. Rugged and well protected with armor, it carried a substantial payload. Of all the Fw 190s constructed, 6,634 were especially built for the ground support role.

The Fw 190 was not without flaws. High wing loading led to abrupt stalls and inverted spins, discouraging tight turns. Radius of action, even with two external fuel tanks, remained less than 500 miles. Best performance was obtained from 18,000 to 23,000 feet. Above 25,000 feet performance deteriorated sharply, a shortcoming that proved fatal against the P-47 Thunderbolt and P-51 Mustang. Nonetheless, the Focke-Wulf 190 was a versatile warplane and a formidable adversary.

Sherwood S. Cordier

See also
Focke-Wulf Aircraft; Tank, Kurt

References

Brown, Captain Eric. "Flying the Fu 190." *Flight Journal* (October 2000).

Mizrahi, Joe. "In the Devil's Workshop." *Airpower* 30, 6 (November 2000).

Focke-Wulf Fw 200 Condor

Aircraft based on a feasibility study ordered in 1936 by Lufthansa for a plane capable of crossing the Atlantic; first flew on 27 July 1937. Designed to carry 26 passengers and four crewmembers, this cantilevered low-wing four-engine plane first proved its capacity on a series of long-distance flights for publicity. The longest was a 48-hour flight from Berlin to Tokyo. (The plane crash-landed in Manila Bay on the return leg due to pilot error.) The aircraft was used mostly on European medium-range routes. Sixteen civilian Condors were completed by September 1939, and several more were under construction.

Meanwhile, the Luftwaffe was having trouble defining its long-range aircraft needs. The Junkers Ju 89 and Dornier Do 19 aircraft were canceled, and the Heinkel He 177 project was delayed. By October 1939, 12 civilian Condors (six of which were initially scheduled for delivery to Japan) had been taken over by the Luftwaffe for training in long-range sea reconnaissance. Focke-Wulf received an order for the development of a military version, the Fw 200C series, of which 243 were produced until the closing of production in 1943. The C-4, which was built in the largest numbers, sported additional machine guns and a bomb/torpedo bay. Its primary mission in the Luftwaffe became long-range reconnaissance and the spotting of Allied convoys in the Atlantic. Positions were then relayed to submarines and an attack coordinated. The Condor also saw service on the Eastern Front, even bringing supplies to encircled troops in Stalingrad. A few specially modified versions were also used as VIP transports (a V3 S-9 version replaced a Ju 52 as Hitler's personal transport).

Two civilian Condors survived World War II and were used in Brazil but were written off by 1947. A few military machines flew in Spain, Denmark, and with the Royal Air Force, but the lack of spare parts quickly ended their careers.

Guillaume de Syon

See also

Focke-Wulf Aircraft

References

Nowarra, Heinz J. *Focke-Wulf Fw 200 Condor.* Koblenz: Bernard and Graefe, 1988.

Wagner, Wolfgang. *Kurt Tank: Konstrukteur und Testpilot bei Focke-Wulf.* Munich: Bernard and Graefe, 1980.

Fokker Aircraft (Early Years, World War I)

Aviation pioneer Anthony Fokker (1890–1939) emigrated from Holland to Germany in the years before World War I to further his interest in aircraft. With financial help from his wealthy father, he began experimenting in the design of his own aircraft. He soon taught himself to fly and established a factory and flying school at Schwerin, outside Berlin.

After having supplied a moderate number of conventional aircraft, Fokker's fortunes improved during the war, in 1915. Roland Garros's French aircraft used a wedge deflector on the propeller to permit firing through it; one had been captured, and Fokker was tasked to emulate the installation. Instead, Fokker's engineers developed one of the first working interrupter gears, a synchronizing mechanism, and installed it on one of his monoplanes. Acceptance of the aircraft and gun led to deployment of the first true fighter plane, the Fokker E.I "Eindecker" (literally "single wing," i.e., monoplane).

The "Fokker scourge"—the period when the German fighter wreaked havoc on its French and British opponents—began with the introduction of the E.I. The most numerous of the Fokker Eindecker designs was the E.III. Powered by the Oberursel 100-hp rotary engine, lateral control was by wing-warping, and firepower came in the form of a LMG 108 (Spandau) gun synchronized to fire through the propeller. Between 120 and 150 examples of the type were built.

Operationally, the early Fokker was deployed in ones and twos to the *feldflieger-abteilungen* (battalions) until several were grouped together in *staffeln* (squadrons) at Sivry and Vaux. In the hands of pilots like Max Immelmann and Oswald Boelcke, the Fokker was a powerful weapon, but the Nieuport 11 and the de Havilland D.H. 2 soon surpassed it. By autumn it was disappearing from the force in favor of the Albatros and Halberstädt.

Billed as the first true fighter plane, the Fokker Eindecker was equipped with a LMG 108 (Spandau) gun synchronized to fire through the propeller. (Walter J. Boyne)

Considered by many to be the best fighter of World War I, the Fokker D.VII stands behind a row of extremely well-equipped German pilots. (Walter J. Boyne)

Fokker's standing slid for a while after rival designs passed by the Eindecker in the summer of 1916. He recovered his position with the Dr.I "Dreidecker" (triplane). Hailed as one of the most maneuverable dogfighters ever, the triplane achieved immortality in the hands of aces like Werner Voss and Manfred von Richthofen.

Rotary powered and equipped with two LMG 08/15 (Spandau) guns, the triplane was highly maneuverable and climbed quickly. The first two examples were delivered to Jagdgeschwader I (von Richthofen's Flying Circus) in August 1917 as personal gifts for Richthofen and Voss, the two leading German aces.

Early wing failures caused the type to be withdrawn temporarily until the shoddy workmanship at the root of the problem was solved. This delay resulted in a total of only about 320 aircraft being produced. Triplanes returned to the front in 1918 and served as the principal equipment of the elite fighter groups during the great German offensive that spring. By summer, the triplane began to be replaced by the new Fokker D.VII, although it continued in use for a while longer.

In January 1918, the Luftstreitkräfte (Air Service) decided to hold an open competition for the next single-seat fighter. The clear winner was a single-bay biplane with thick cantilevered wings powered by the six-cylinder Mercedes engine. It would become the Fokker D.VII, generally regarded as the best single-seat fighter of World War I.

In May, early examples of the new fighter arrived at the front. Impressive as the first version was, the D.VII was even better when it was coupled with the new BMW high-compression 185-hp engine, which added 3,000–5,000 feet to its ceiling and improved its speed.

The D.VII reequipped most of the *jagdstaffeln* (fighter squadrons) in German service, revitalizing the fighter force despite the shortage of fuel that kept it grounded much of the time. In September, it inflicted a record number of casualties on the British. The reputation of the D.VII was such that it was specifically named for surrender in the Armistice agreement.

Following the war, Fokker returned to Holland, smuggling most of his inventory with him, and was able to remain in aviation.

James Streckfuss

See also

Garros, Roland; Richthofen, Manfred von

References

Hegener, Henri. *Fokker: The Man and His Aircraft.* Letchworth, UK: Harleyford, 1961.

Weyl, Alfred R. *Fokker: The Creative Years.* London: Putnam, 1965.

Fokker Aircraft (Post–World War I)

After World War I, Anthony Fokker (1890–1939) moved his aviation concern from Germany to the Netherlands to begin again in July 1919 as a Dutch company, based at the former Dutch Naval Air Service base in Veere, Zeeland, until 1924 and then at Amsterdam. Initially, company output was divided among fighter aircraft for several nations and early airliners. The Dutch airline KLM, founded the same year, became an important purchaser of Fokker airplanes. The first U.S. transcontinental flight was accomplished with a Fokker F.IV (T-2 to the Army Air Service) in May 1922. Two years later, a KLM Fokker F.VII made a multistop 8,000-mile flight from Amsterdam to Batavia (now Jakarta) in the Dutch East Indies (now Indonesia). By this point, Fokker transports used two or three engines, wooden construction, and thick cantilevered wings. Increasingly large and complex airliners would range from the single-engine F.I to the four-engine F.XXXVI by 1939.

During the 1930s, a U.S. arm of the Fokker firm built civil aircraft as well. Military output ranged from the biplane C series of the 1920s (of which the C.V family served into early World War II) to the D.XXIII of 1939, a low-wing monoplane with fixed landing gear, and the twin-engine G.1 heavy fighter.

But Fokker had fallen behind in airplane technology, sticking with wood when others moved to all-metal construction. Germany occupied the Fokker facilities during World War II (just months after the pioneer aviator's death) and compelled manufacture of German aircraft, hindered to some degree by the passive resistance of Dutch workers. A new factory was developed at the Schipol airport outside Amsterdam by 1951.

The company manufactured a variety of trainers (including the S.14, the first jet trainer designed as such and the first Fokker jet) and in 1955 first flew the F.27 "Friendship" twin-engine regional airliner that would remain in production for many years and became a great success worldwide. The F.28 "Fellowship" twin-jet transport followed in 1967 and was improved and stretched to become the F.100 jet transport, which first flew in 1986. With increasing consolidation, however, the limited line of Fokker products could not survive marketplace competition from industry giants, and after several attempts to save it, the company declared bankruptcy in late 1996 and closed down production shortly thereafter.

Christopher H. Sterling

References

de Leeuw, René. *Fokker Commercial Aircraft from the F.1 of 1918 to the Fokker 100 of Today.* Amsterdam: Fokker Public Relations, 1994.

Dierikx, Marc. *Fokker: A Transatlantic Biography.* Washington, DC: Smithsonian Institution Press, 1997.

Young Anthony Fokker had much to smile about. A great pilot and salesman, he was able to use the talents of good engineers to create high-performing aircraft. (Walter J. Boyne Collection)

Folland, Henry Phillip (1889–1954)

Important early British aircraft designer, primarily of fighter and racing aircraft. "HPF" (as Folland was widely known) had a generally conservative approach, remaining throughout most of his career strongly antimonoplane, anti–metal structure, and anti–variable-pitch prop.

He came into his own as the chief designer during World War I at the Royal Aircraft Factory, where he was primarily responsible for a fighter series culminating in the classic SE.5a, widely regarded as the supreme fighter of the war. Folland's glory days peaked in the 1920s with his series of racing and fast fighter biplanes. His 1921 Bamel won its first races, the beginning of a three-year stretch of success, just as Folland moved on to Gloucestershire (later Gloster) Aircraft as chief designer and engineer. There he turned to floatplanes for the Schneider Trophy races: the ill-fated Gloster II and III-A, which came in second in the 1925 race; the handsome Gloster IV for 1927; and Folland's first monoplane, the Gloster VI, which placed in 1929. He also designed the Gloster Grebe, the water-cooled Grebe-like Gorcock, the Gauntlet, and the Gladiator (1934).

Folland's last design was a fighter built to specification F.5/34, but as an air-cooled design in a water-cooled era it could not compete with the Spitfire and Hurricane. Folland left Gloster after Hawker (Thomas Sopwith) took over the firm and he felt overshadowed by designer Sidney Camm. British Marine Aircraft attracted Folland in May 1937, and the firm was renamed Folland Aircraft with a factory at Hamble near Southampton. It was a subcontractor during World War II and, after the war, for de Havilland and Bristol. Folland retired in 1951.

Christopher H. Sterling

References

Foxworth, Thomas G. *The Speed Seekers.* London: Macdonald and Jane's, 1975.

Penrose, Harald. *British Aviation: The Adventuring Years.* London: Putnam, 1973.

Fonck, René Paul (1894–1953)

The Allies' "ace of aces" during World War I. Going to war at its start, Frenchman René Fonck managed a transfer to pilot training in February 1915. Completing flight training in May, he was assigned to Escadrille C 47, flying Caudrons. There he showed the aggression necessary to be a fighter pilot, gaining his first two victories. He transferred to fighters in April 1917, going to Escadrille Spa 103, a part of the famous Stork unit.

With the Storks, Fonck increased his score at lightning speed, having 19 kills before the end of 1917. During 1918, the pace quickened further, and twice Fonck was credited with six victories in a single day, the only pilot to do this during World War I. Though his score eventually reached 75, the highest of any Western Allied pilot, a boastful personality kept Fonck from achieving the beloved status that his predecessor, Georges Guynemer, had earned in the hearts of the French.

James Streckfuss

References

Fonck, Rene. *Ace of Aces.* Garden City, NY: Doubleday, 1967.

Robertson, Bruce, ed. *Air Aces of the 1914–1918 War.* Letchworth, UK: Harleyford, 1959.

Football War

More accurately, the name for this July 1969 conflict between El Salvador and Honduras is the Hundred Hours' War, as fighting ended after four days due to diplomatic efforts by the Organization of American States. But popular disorder stirred up by harassment of opposing fans and players in a qualifying match for the 1970 soccer World Cup provided a vivid name for the conflict. The primary trigger was the harsh expulsion of thousands of Salvadoran small farmers from Honduran borderlands (the precise boundary being disputed in small areas).

Densely populated El Salvador was reputed to have the best army in Central America. Geographically fragmented, Honduras reputedly had the best air force (the Fuerza Aerea Hondureña—FAH) in Central America. The FAH would provide the means to neutralize an otherwise stronger opponent. Given the recent success of Israel (in 1967), the Salvadorans hoped to destroy the FAH while its planes were still on the ground.

Honduras had steadily emphasized its military aviation since the 1930s. The lack of road and rail alternatives had also caused the republic to be the headquarters of the famed TACA airlines, which for a decade or more provided commercial service throughout Central America. Politically, air force officers were not subordinate to army generals.

The Chance-Vought F4U Corsair was the standard fighter of the FAH in 1969. North American T-28s also played an offensive role, as did a few North American T-6s and transport aircraft. No dedicated bombers were available to either side.

The Salvadoran strike involved two Douglas C-47 aircraft dropping bombs at the principal FAH base in the capital, Tegucigalpa. The Hondurans, however, had noted war preparations; most aircraft were ready the north. The FAH was able to provide considerable air support to the Honduran army, helping to blunt the Salvadoran invasion on several fronts. The Hondurans struck back at the Salvadoran air base and damaged oil storage facilities at a coastal port. On the third day of combat, an FAH Corsair pilot shot down three Salvadoran fighter aircraft, two Goodyear FG-1D Corsairs and a North American F-51 Mustang.

Airpower enabled less-populated and poorer Honduras to achieve a standoff in a sudden conflict. Many years of development made a difference when a crisis arose.

Gary Kuhn

References

Henriquez, Orlando. *En el Cielo Escribieron Historia.* Tegucigalpa, 1972.

Ford Motor Company

Entered aviation during World War I, when its factory produced 3,950 Liberty engines for the war effort. This engine later powered the U.S.-designed NC-4 planes in the first Atlantic crossing and was used in many other historic U.S.

flights of the postwar period. During the war, Ford-built Liberty engines were installed in the U.S.-made, British-designed de Havilland DH-4 bombers.

Henry Ford set out to prove that commercial aviation was practical. In 1924, Ford Motor Company purchased the Stout All-Metal Airplane Company. William Stout had designed an all-metal single-engine monoplane, and it would be from this 2-AT design that the Ford Tri-Motor 4-AT model evolved. Sometimes called the "Tin Goose," it made its first flight on 11 June 1926. The Ford Tri-Motor became the foundation for the passenger airline system in America.

More than 100 airlines flew the 199 Tri-Motors that Ford built. The "Tin Goose" found its way throughout North America, Central America, South America, Europe, Australia, and China. Ford ended Tri-Motor production on 4 June 1933.

It did not take long for people to discover that the 14-passenger airliner had a remarkable ability as a heavy-duty freight carrier. When it came to hauling freight, the Ford Tri-Motor surpassed every other prewar American commercial transport except the Douglas DC-3.

During World War II, Ford Motor Company reentered aviation by building Consolidated B-24 "Liberator" bombers at the famous Willow Run industrial complex.

Henry M. Holden

References

Holden, Henry M. *The Fabulous Ford Tri-Motors.* New York: Tab/McGraw-Hill, 1992.

Ford, William Wallace (1898–1986)

U.S. Army brigadier general. One of the key figures in the development of modern U.S. Army aviation, Ford was born on 2 October 1898 in Waverly, Virginia. He graduated from West Point in 1920 and joined the field artillery. The experience of observing fire from Air Corps observation planes in the early 1930s reawakened his boyhood interest in flying. He purchased a light aircraft and became an enthusiastic pilot in his spare time.

Ford commanded a battery during the 1940 maneuvers and criticized the Air Corps for its failure to provide timely aerial observation. He wrote an article calling for the field artillery to fly and maintain its own organic light aircraft to serve as air observation posts for the firing batteries. In December 1941, he was selected to organize and command a detachment to test the concept. He subsequently became the first director of the Department of Air Training at the Field Artillery School in Fort Sill, Oklahoma, serving from August 1942 until October 1943. Promoted to full colonel in June 1942, he advanced to brigadier general in August 1944 (both temporary ranks) and subsequently commanded the 87th Infantry Division (Artillery) in combat.

Although Ford held a number of other aviation-related assignments before he retired as a brigadier general in 1954, his wartime service constituted the period of his greatest influence on the organic aviation program. By insisting on high standards and then living up to them himself, Ford ensured that the organic aviation program got off to a solid start in the field artillery. This man came close to being indispensable.

Edgar F. Raines Jr.

References

Bergerson, Frederic A. *The Army Gets an Air Force: Tactics of Insurgent Bureaucratic Politics.* Baltimore: Johns Hopkins University Press, 1980.

Ford, William Wallace. *Wagon Soldier.* North Adams, MA: Excelsior Printing, 1980.

Raines, Edgar F. Jr. *Eyes of Artillery: The Origins of Modern U.S. Army Aviation in World War II.* Army Historical Series. Washington, DC: Center of Military History, Department of the Army, 2000.

Foss, Joseph J. (1915–)

U.S. Marine colonel and leading fighter ace of World War II. Joseph J. "Joe" Foss was born in South Dakota in 1915. At the age of 25, he hitchhiked to Minneapolis to join the U.S. Marines, then thumbed his way to Florida for flight training.

Foss entered combat as executive officer of Marine Fighter Squadron 121 (VMF-121) when it arrived on Guadalcanal in October 1942. Flying the Grumman F4F Wildcat, he shot down his first Japanese Zero on 13 October. For more than a month, Foss and the other pilots of VMF-121 engaged almost daily in aerial combat against Japanese planes attacking U.S. Marines on the island. Foss was credited with 23 planes shot down during this period.

On January 15, after his squadron was given a brief respite from combat, Foss shot down three more Japanese planes to raise his score to 26, matching the aerial record of Eddie Rickenbacker, who shot down 26 German planes during World War I.

President Franklin Roosevelt presented Foss the Medal of Honor for his skill as a fighter pilot and combat leader. After the war, Foss left the Marine Corps and entered private business. He became a brigadier general in the Air National Guard, a state legislator, governor of South Dakota, commissioner of the fledgling American Football League, and head of the National Rifle Association.

James H. Willbanks

See also

Guadalcanal; Rickenbacker, Edward Vernon

References

Foss, Joseph J. (as told by Walter Simmons). *Joe Foss, Flying Marine: The Story of His Flying Circus.* New York: Pocket Books, 1993.

Foss, Joseph J., with Donna Wild Foss. *A Proud American: The Autobiography of Joe Foss.* New York: Pocket Books, 1992.

Foulois, Benjamin D. (1879–1967)

One of America's earliest airpower pioneers and pilots. Benjamin D. "Benny" Foulois was born on 9 December 1879 in Washington, Connecticut. In 1898, he enlisted in the U.S. Army Corps of Engineers. He participated in the campaign in the Philippines and in 1899 transferred to the infantry, where he received his commission as a second lieutenant in 1901.

On 19 June 1908, he graduated from the Army Signal School and was detailed to the Signal Corps's Aeronautical Board, which was conducting airplane and dirigible performance trials. In August, Foulois and two other officers learned to fly Dirigible No. 1.

In 1909, Foulois served on the official board evaluating the Wright Flyer. During the speed qualification tests, he flew with Orville Wright to meet the passenger requirements of their contract. Army leaders selected Foulois and Lieutenant Frank P. Lahm to become their first pilots. In preparation, Foulois was sent to France as America's official delegate to the International Congress of Aeronautics.

Next, Foulois took the Wright Military Flyer and a small group of enlisted men by train to Fort Sam Houston, San Antonio, Texas. Aided by written instructions and letters from the Wright brothers, he taught himself to fly. By September 1910, he had made 61 flights totaling 9 hours. He crashed so much that the worn-out plane had to be retired. It was donated to the Smithsonian Institution on 4 May 1911. Foulois's heroic effort eventually led to the acquisition of $125,000 for additional development and training.

Benny Foulois taught himself to fly in the Wright Military Flyer, then went on to become Chief of the Air Corps in 1931. He died at 85, beloved by all, in 1965. (U.S. Air Force)

In 1911, Foulois designed the first airplane radio receiver. Following tours at the Signal Corps Aviation Schools in San Diego, California, and Galveston, Texas, Foulois became commander of the 1st Aero Squadron stationed at Fort Sill, Oklahoma.

In 1916, he led the squadron during the Punitive Expedition against Pancho Villa in Mexico. Their planes were so poor that they could not fly over the Sierra Madre Mountains to deliver mail and messages to General John Pershing's troops. Afterward, Captain Foulois lobbied for better equipment and more pilots.

In 1917, Foulois went to Washington, D.C., to chair the Army-Navy Technical Aircraft Committee. When the United States entered World War I, he was advanced to the rank of brigadier general and named Chief of the Air Service for the American Expeditionary Force and later Chief, First Army Air Service. Although Foulois and Billy Mitchell, Pershing's brash young airpower visionary, did not get along, Foulois recognized Mitchell's brilliance and allowed him to have operational control of U.S. air forces in Europe.

Following the war, Foulois reverted to his permanent rank of major. By 1927, he had once again become a brigadier general and assistant to the Chief of the U.S. Army Air Corps. He served as chief of the materiel division from June 1929 to June 1930. In 1931, he commanded the highly successful USAAC annual exercises, for which he won the MacKay Trophy.

On 20 December 1931, Major General Foulois became the third USAAC chief, serving during four tumultuous years. The high point came with the creation of General Headquarters Air Force, the offensive arm of Army airpower. The low point came when Foulois misjudged USAAC ability to deliver U.S. airmail. Dozens of mishaps and the death of several pilots during the bitter winter of early 1934 created one of the worst public relations disasters in the history of the U.S. air forces. Under public and congressional pressure, Foulois retired on 31 December 1935.

Foulois remained an influential airpower and Air Force advocate until his death in 1967. His memoirs were published after his death in 1968.

William Head

References

Copp, DeWitt S. *A Few Great Captains: The Men and Events That*

Shaped the Development of U.S. Air Power. Garden City, NY: Doubleday, 1980.
Foulois, General Benjamin D., with Carroll V. Gilnes. *From the Wright Brothers to the Astronauts: The Memoirs of Major General Benjamin D. Foulois.* New York: McGraw-Hill, 1968.
Head, William P. *Every Inch a Soldier: Augustine Warner Robins and the Building of U.S. Air Power.* College Station: Texas A&M University, 1995.

France, Battle for (1940)

Airpower played a decisive role in the Battle for France. The Allies had more men, tanks, aircraft, and artillery than Germany. But Germany had a superior doctrine and operational concept and deployed better-trained forces.

On 10 May 1940, most Allied aircraft were in Great Britain or Africa, not in northeastern France. Therefore, Germany enjoyed numerical superiority at the decisive point. German and British aircraft were approximately equal qualitatively. Most French aircraft were obsolete, and squadrons receiving modern equipment in early 1940 had low operational readiness.

The Luftwaffe trained intensively for close air support (CAS). Many personnel had combat experience in Spain and Poland. Luftwaffe headquarters were located with the headquarters of the army units they supported. Air liaison teams attached to Panzer divisions provided CAS within 45–75 minutes of a request. In contrast, the Allies had no specialist CAS aircraft, training, or doctrine. Allied air-ground communications and liaison were very poor. Superior logistics enabled German aircraft to fly more than four sorties a day, whereas French fighters and bombers flew 0.9 and 0.25 sorties a day, respectively.

Germany began with diversionary thrusts into Holland and Belgium that drew Allied forces forward to be cut off by another German thrust through the Ardennes to the English Channel. In three days, the Luftwaffe secured air superiority, annihilating the Belgian and Dutch air forces and destroying 229 French aircraft on the ground.

German airborne troops neutralized Belgium's Eben Emael Fortress and seized Dutch airfields and bridges. Holland surrendered after a rapid German ground advance and a brutal air raid on Rotterdam. Meanwhile, the Luftwaffe shielded German forces in the Ardennes from Allied reconnaissance.

On 13 May, 1,000 sorties of the VIII Fliegerkorps supported the crossing of the Meuse (principally by suppressing French artillery). Airlifted supplies enabled Luftwaffe units at rough forward airfields to follow directly behind advancing ground units and maintain the fighter/CAS umbrella. VIII Fliegerkorps permitted Panzergruppe to advance rapidly and disrupted the French Ninth Army's counterattack on the Panzergruppe Kleist's southern flank. Two flak corps repelled desperate Allied air strikes on the Meuse bridges.

The British sent no more fighters to France after May 15 but mounted several ineffectual raids on the Ruhr that week. When German forces halted on the Channel on May 24, Luftwaffe chief Hermann Goering promised to destroy trapped British forces with airpower. Royal Air Force units based in England then clashed with German aircraft at the limit of their ranges. In nine days, Britain lost 177 aircraft and Germany 280, but the British Expeditionary Force escaped via Dunkirk.

France's position was hopeless, and Germany quickly forced its surrender. However, during May-June 1940 Germany had lost 19 percent of its single-engine fighters, 30 percent of its twin-engine fighters, bombers, and dive-bombers, and 40 percent of its transports. These painful losses exacerbated the Luftwaffe's difficulties in the skies over Britain later that year.

James D. Perry

See also

Dunkirk; German Air Force (Luftwaffe)

References

Bekker, Cajus. *The Luftwaffe War Diaries.* New York: Da Capo, 1994.
Maier, Klaus, et al. *Germany and the Second World War, Volume 2: Germany's Initial Conquests in Europe.* Oxford: Clarendon Press, 1991.
Murray, Williamson. *Luftwaffe.* Baltimore: Nautical and Aviation, 1985.

Franco, Francisco (1892–1975)

Born in El Ferrol, Spain, to a middle-class family. Franco went to the Military Academy of Toledo (1907–1910), graduating 251st in a class of 312. He rose rapidly, with consistent promotions for battlefield service, and became brigadier at age 33. A strong Spanish patriot-nationalist, he believed the army was the last line of defense and had the right to intervene in politics to save the fatherland. He was contemptuous of the constitutional monarchy (1876–1923) that had lost the 1898 war and was hostile to the Second Republic (1931–1936).

In 1936, he led other generals in a conspiracy and insurrection that became the Spanish civil war. Hitler supplied Junkers Ju 52/3m transport planes to transport Franco's Moorish troops from Africa to Spain, a decisive event in the war.

Franco's Falangists had support from the German Kondor Legion (about 100 planes) and 70,000 Italian soldiers and airmen. The Republicans had help from the Soviet Union and international volunteers, totaling about 60,000 troops. The war ended in 1939 with defeat of the Second Republic. Franco established an authoritarian regime that lasted until his death in 1975.

In 1939, Spain joined Italy and Germany in the Anti-Comintern Pact, which Franco reaffirmed for five years in 1941. Franco's Spain was repressive, having exiled about 300,000 and imprisoned another 300,000 between 1939 and 1945. Estimates on the number shot vary between 28,000 and 200,000.

In 1946, the United Nations found Franco guilty of conspiring with Mussolini and Hitler to bring on World War II; Franco's Spain became an outcast in the community of nations. By 1955, however, Spain was back in the good graces of the western powers. Its Catholicism won over the Vatican, and its anticommunism won over the United States and its Cold War allies. Toward the end of his life, Franco made provisions for a peaceful transition to a constitutional monarchy in Spain. He died in 1975.

John Barnhill

References

Beaulac, Willard L. *Franco: Silent Ally in World War II.* Carbondale: Southern Illinois University Press, 1986.

Fusi, J. P. *Franco: A Biography.* Trans. Felipe Fernandez-Armesto. New York: Harper and Row, 1987.

FRANTIC (1944)

Code name for unsuccessful Soviet-U.S. strategic bombing operation during World War II. U.S. bombers and their escorts would take off from England and Italy, bomb Germany, and recover at bases in Ukraine. After refueling and rearming, the strike force would depart for their home bases, bombing Germany again en route. The objectives of this shuttle bombing were to attack targets previously untouched due to their location deep in the Reich, divert Luftwaffe defensive assets from the West, and foster Allied cooperation. It was hoped that FRANTIC would lead to similar U.S. air bases in Siberia from which to bomb Japan.

FRANTIC was unsuccessful. Because of constant bickering and delay over targets and procedures, only six shuttle missions were flown. There is no indication that any Luftwaffe units were diverted to defend against them. On the night of 22 June 1944, German bombers attacked the major base at Poltava and destroyed or damaged 73 B-17s, leading to further recriminations and delay. The last mission was flown on 19 September 1944.

Phillip S. Meilinger

See also

Combined Bomber Offensive; Lend-Lease Aircraft

References

Conversino, Mark J. *Fighting with the Soviets: The Failure of Operation FRANTIC, 1944–1945.* Lawrence: University Press of Kansas, 1997.

Infield, Glenn B. *The Poltava Affair: A Russian Warning, an American Tragedy.* New York: Macmillan, 1973.

Lukas, Richard C. *Eagles East: The Army Air Forces in the Soviet Union, 1941–1945.* Tallahassee: Florida State University Press, 1970.

Franz, Anselm (1900–1994)

German aircraft turbine propulsion pioneer; designer of the first mass-produced turbojet engine and of the first helicopter turboshaft engine. Anselm Franz was born on 21 January 1900 in Schladming, Austria, where he spent his youth. He attended and graduated from Graz Institute of Technology, Austria, in 1924 with a master's degree in mechanical engineering. Much later, in 1940, Franz received his doctor of aeronautical engineering from the Technical University, Berlin.

Anselm Franz joined the Junkers Engine Development Division in 1936. In July 1939, two months before the world's first flight of a gas turbine–powered aircraft, Junkers received a contract for the 109-004 turbojet engine. Because of his experience in turbines, Franz was given full responsibility for design and development. Realizing the need for new engine concepts and practices, he insisted on being separated from the existing piston-engine organizations in order to be free from their traditions and influence.

The results of his efforts was the first successful turbojet engine using an axial compressor, air-cooled turbine blades, automatic control of the exhaust area, and afterburning for increased thrust. Construction of the Jumo 004 engine began in 1939, and the first engine was test-run in October 1940. The first flight of the engine, in a Messerschmitt Me 262 on 18 July 1942, was only 30 months after engine design had commenced. It was a remarkable achievement, especially for a new design.

The Junkers Jumo 109-004B went into production at a static thrust rating of 2,000 pounds and a weight of 1,640 pounds. More than 6,000 engines were produced before the end of World War II. They powered the Messerschmitt Me 262 fighter-bomber, the Arado Ar 234 reconnaissance-bomber, the Junkers Ju 287 bomber, and the Horten Ho IX flying-wing fighter. It was the selected engine for many other planned aircraft in development when the war ended. Many of the examples of the engines were taken for study by the

Anselm Franz designed the Junkers Jumo engine used on the Messerschmitt Me 262 and Arado Ar 234, then went on to a distinguished career in the United States. (Kenneth Collinger)

Allied countries, and Russia copied the design and manufactured a large number with the designation RD-10.

Franz came to the United States and worked for the U.S. Air Force at Wright-Patterson Air Force Base in Dayton, Ohio. From 1946 to 1950, he consulted with U.S. turbojet engine manufacturers and realized that there was a potential for medium-power gas-turbine engines for helicopters, propeller aircraft, ground vehicles, and stationary pumps and generators.

In 1950, with the support of the Air Force, he approached the Avco Corporation and proposed developing medium-power gas-turbine engines in a range to complement their piston aircraft engines being produced in Williamsport, Pennsylvania. After being given full authority and responsibility for development, he gathered a small group of specialists to begin the design. Soon after, the group moved from the Williamsport facility to the newly established Lycoming Division in Stratford, Connecticut. After a major competition with many established turbine engine manufactures, the group was successful in winning an Air Force contract for the T53 turboshaft engine in July 1952.

The T53 was contracted at 600 hp to power the Bell XH-40 helicopter. The YT53-L-1 engine made for Bell delivered 860 hp and powered the YH-40 for its first flight on 22 October 1956. Further engine development resulted in versions of the T53 to 1,700 hp. The subsequent production was more than 20,000 engines for more than 12,000 HU-1/UH-1 "Iroquois"/"Huey" helicopters, formerly designated the H-40.

The T53 was closely followed by the T55 turboshaft engine that produced 2,200 hp in its first production version and has been developed to nearly 5,000 hp for the CH-47 "Chinook" helicopter and other applications. Both the T53 and T55 have been produced in turboprop and marine and industrial versions, powering a variety of applications, including aircraft, boats, hydrofoils, hovercraft, trucks, trains, pumps, compressors, and generators.

Another major achievement of Franz was the PLF1A-2, the world's first high-bypass turbofan engine. The engine, first tested in February 1962, was composed of a T55 engine core and a 40-inch-diameter geared fan stage and produced a static thrust of 4,320 pounds. The PLF1A-2 was developed into the ALF502 and LF507 engines at up to 7,200 pounds/thrust, powering the Canadair CL-600 Challenger business aircraft and the British Aerospace 146 and RJ series Avroliner commuter transports. The original PLF1A-2 engine is in the National Air and Space Museum in Washington, D.C.

During the Gulf War, the United States depended on Lycoming engines in the M1 Abrams tank, as well as the UH-1 Huey and Cobra and CH-47 Chinook helicopters and the LCAC hovercraft. Those Lycoming engines were all designed by Franz.

After he retired in 1968 as vice president of engineering and assistant plant manager, he continued as a consultant to Lycoming for several years. On 18 November 1994, Franz died in Bridgeport, Connecticut.

Kenneth S. Collinge

See also

Arado Ar 234 Blitz; Messerschmitt Me 262

References

Franz, Anselm. *From Jets to Tanks: My Contribution to the Turbine Age.* Stratford, CT: Avco Lycoming Stratford Division, 1985.

Franz, Dr. Anselm. *50 Years of Jet Powered Flight.* Munich: Deutsch Gesellschaft fur Luft- und Raumfahrt e.V., 1989.

Schlaifer, Robert, and S. D. Heron. *Development of Aviation Fuels and Development of Aircraft Engines: Two Studies of Relations Between Government and Business.* Boston: Harvard University Press, 1950.

French Air Doctrine

French air doctrine has roots dating to the earliest years of aviation; it evolved significantly during and between the two world wars.

World War I

Before World War I, the French army recognized the need for some kind of air arm based on ballooning units. Thus, by the time conflict broke out, some 20 dirigibles were on hand to conduct reconnaissance and artillery support missions. Airplanes were also added, though their role remained limited to observation.

At the outbreak of World War I, the French army possessed 162 aircraft, which Aeronautics Commander Edouard Barrès reorganized into observation and bombing groups. The former were also responsible for chasing enemy observation aircraft. This notion of specific missions for different squadrons and aircraft was not unique (Clément Ader had thought of it, too), but its application was unique at the time. Meanwhile, General Louis Hirschauer, who had organized ballooning units before the war, was named chief of the air arm. However, his rank and position did not allow him to initiate any clear reform in how the high command thought of aviation. Indeed, although acknowledged as a valuable tool of observation, the airplane was seen as having little value other than engaging similar machines belonging to the enemy.

Operations over the next three years slowly made the high command aware of the advantages of a specialized air arm. General Joseph Joffre (who led the Marne counteroffensive against the Germans) initiated a reprisal air attack on Karlsruhe only after several Zeppelin attacks on French soil in March 1915. When he began considering the best use of aviation, he remained convinced that it should be used in support of ground operations alone, yet he suggested that there should be three types of squadrons: artillery assistance and photography; reconnaissance and bombing; and fighter engagement. Joffre's retirement in 1916 may have put reforms on hold. Things changed in 1917 when, under the impulse of a new organizational structure put forward by Colonel Charles Duval, aircraft became available in quantity. The French high command, desperate for weaponry that might break the stalemate, started sending aircraft over and beyond enemy lines, but this aggressive campaign cost men and materiel, for no fighter escort had been devised to protect the observation aircraft that were used by the French army over its own trenches. This hard-learned lesson explains why, after World War I, squadrons increased in size and were assigned multiple functions.

Interwar Years

However, the air arm remained subordinated to the army. Marshall Henri Pétain, who had led the French army from the Battle of Verdun onward, would not conceive of a separate air force, either. Despite several studies and memoranda in the early 1920s that called for an autonomous "air army" (sometimes termed "national aviation" to avoid antagonizing ground-forces officers), Pétain remained suspicious. The creation of an air ministry in 1928 to oversee both military and commercial aviation further complicated matters, for it added one more level to the French military system. Pétain would finally allow for the hypothesis of an air force only once a new ministry of defense, in charge of overseeing the three other military ministries (war, navy, army), was allowed to coordinate all operations. Thus, a new Territorial Air Defense came into existence in 1931.

Air thinking had evolved starting in 1928. Instead of an offensive air arm, strategists and politicians conceived of the airplane as a way to fill gaps over the projected Maginot Line, a fortified construction intended to check any German advances. In this realm, there was considerable disagreement between airmen and ground commanders over the future war. Some argued that it would begin with massive air bombardments, whereas others claimed the tank would be used first. Pétain seemed sympathetic to the interpretation of Colonel P. Vauthier, who followed the arguments of air strategy pioneer Giulio Douhet and suggested using the threat of massive air attack in case of enemy threats. Yet Pétain and several others rejected the Douhet notion that the army and navy were defensive arms and the air force, the sword. Thus, when the air force was indeed created and formalized as a separate arm, there remained confusion about its precise functions.

In 1934, Plan I of the air force (which confirmed independence from the army) called for aerial bombing, reconnaissance, and interception missions. However, there was now less rigidity in the definition of each unit's purpose. At the top, aerial regiments were replaced by air fleets, each divided into air groups, each of those split into squadrons. These groups were assigned to cover one of the five aerial regions of France and Algeria. With Germany's announcement that it was creating the Luftwaffe, Plan II was enacted, calling for the establishment of a 1,500-aircraft first line of defense. This would be superseded by two other plans, as well as a modification of the air force's basic structure. In addition, an aerial mobilization plan was put together. However, the World War I notion of bomber units also acting as reconnaissance confused the effective development of an air doctrine.

World War II

Pierre Cot, who acted as air minister during the left-wing Popular Front government of 1936–1938, sought to clarify the French air doctrine by having Plan V emphasize fighters. Yet by the time he left office, there was considerable confusion in what an air force should truly do. This had an important impact on later events and may have even affected

The simple, clean lines of the Deperdussin racer were the key to its high 127 mph speed in 1913. (Walter J. Boyne)

Prime Minister Edouard Dalladier's decision to accept Hitler's demands in Munich in 1938: Not only did the Luftwaffe appear better equipped, but the specificity of missions and machines suggested that the French air force, still missing hundreds of fighters from its projected inventory, might not be able to effectively engage it even in a defensive role. This was, unfortunately, the case when the Luftwaffe attacked in May 1940. Combined with the confusion that reigned among the air force officer corps, the confusion over a proper air doctrine gave Germany a decisive advantage.

Guillaume de Syon

See also

French Air Force

References

Cain, Anthony Christopher. "Neither Decadent, nor Traitorous, nor Stupid: The French Air Force and Air Doctrine in the 1930s." Ph.D. diss., The Ohio State University, 2000.

Christienne, Charles, and Pierre Lissarague. *A History of French Military Aviation.* Washington, DC: Smithsonian, 1986.

Kirkland, Faris R. "French Air Strength in May 1940." *Air Power History* 40, 1 (1993): 22–34.

French Air Force

Although technically in existence in 1914, the French Air Force (Aviation Militaire/Armeé de l'Air) underwent a series of changes in the first two decades of its existence; it did not acquire legal status until passage of the Organization Law of 2 July 1934. Until then, it had a semiautonomous status that nonetheless depended heavily on the wants and needs of the army.

By the time World War I began, the air arm was composed of some 162 aircraft facing off against some 250 German airplanes. By fall 1914, under the management of General Joseph Bares, a new standardization procedure was under way, designed to ensure more efficient use of aircraft for observation, interception, and bombing purposes. Several modifications and reorganizations occurred during the conflict in response to increases in men, machines, and technological progress. By 1918, the air arm had almost 20,000 aircraft, tops in the world; the French navy had another 1,000 hydroplanes and several dirigibles.

With the end of World War I hostilities, the air arm now required a permanent structure, which took four years to get approved. New training methods and new squadron structures appeared, designed to streamline the use of the 2,600 aircraft in 186 squadrons in operation by 1926. Still, the aeronautical structure remained fairly complicated, prompting calls for the creation of an air ministry that would manage navy and army air branches. In 1928 such a ministry appeared, headed first by Laurent Eynac. This was the initial step of a five-year effort toward the creation of a general air staff in 1933 and the confirmation of the French air force as its own independent air arm a year later.

Consequently, a new structure appeared, consisting of

five aeronautical regions (four in France, one in Algeria). Further modifications followed, few of which took into account the number of aircraft needed in response to the growing threat of the German Luftwaffe.

The air force saw service in the 1920s in the so-called Pacification War in Morocco (also known as the Rif War), and orders were placed with both French and foreign manufacturers for new fighters and bombers. By August 1939, the air force had more than 700 fighters, some 440 bombers, and 400 reconnaissance aircraft. Its budget had steadily been increased, doubling, in fact, between 1937 and 1939.

This was insufficient to hold off the German Luftwaffe and Wehrmacht, which brought France to its knees in six weeks. On 15 June 1940, an armistice was declared, with much of the air force now under control of the Vichy government. A small group of Free French Air Force staff was based in England. This latter force would merge with the French air units stationed in North Africa in 1942 and be involved in various air operations, from fighter escort to bombers and reconnaissance. In addition, some French pilots were incorporated into Soviet units.

French efforts included 67,000 air missions and about 600 air victories, of which only 277 can be officially confirmed. The French air force suffered the heavy toll of 557 losses.

Nonetheless, the French air force, through its efforts, was among the first organizations to be reformed in France's Fourth Republic (1944–1958). With the aeronautical industry almost nonexistent, the air force faced considerable challenges. Not only was its role in future defense planning ill-defined, but the serious economic crisis that affected France also prevented effective modernization. Consequently, the early role military commanders carved out for themselves was that of guardians of the declining French empire, as they sought to stave off rebellions in Indochina and then in Algeria.

The French air force was also involved in the 1956 Suez Crisis, committing F-84s and Noratlas transports to the joint British-French-Israeli force that won the air battle during the campaign.

With the beginning of the Fifth Republic and constitutional democracy in 1958, France's new president, General Charles de Gaulle, made several changes to the status of the air force. The functions of secretaries of state for an arm were abolished, as were the posts of deputy ministers, in favor of greater power to the armed forces minister and the Chief of Staff of each arm. President de Gaulle also called for the development of a French atomic bomb.

With the concept of a triad in mind (sea-, air-, and land-based nuclear weapons), the air force established in 1964 a nuclear section known as the Strategic Forces Command, which oversaw all elements of the triad. First equipped with modified SO-4050 "Vautour" bombers, it soon received supersonic Mirage IV aircraft intended to act as a stopgap until missiles could be produced. The Mirage IV remained in service, in modernized form, until the 1990s, its intended targets in the Soviet Union to be reached by aerial refueling with Boeing KC-135s. French technological and political independence still required, paradoxically, a nudge from a product of the U.S. military-industrial complex.

A review of the French air force's structure in the mid-1960s kept the four aerial regions in existence but called for base commanders to have greater operational autonomy and responsibility. By then, the air force included some 104,000 men and more than 2,300 aircraft, 900 of which were considered front-line machines. With France's exit from NATO's integrated command in 1966, however, the air force's mission changed. Now it would place greater emphasis on the preservation of French interests in the former colonies and participation in various air operations, from interdiction of Libyan incursions into Chad in 1984 to Operation DESERT STORM in 1991.

In the 1950s, a series of prototypes were funded by the French state, yet few led to successful programs. The most successful ones eventually equipped the French air force and included a series of Dassault machines (Ouragan, Mystère, Super Mystère), which culminated in the series of Mirage fighters, from the model III and its variants to the F-1 and 2000 N in the 1990s. Several international programs involving France resulted in the supplying of the SEPECAT Jaguar ground attack jet and the Dassault-Dornier Alpha Jet.

The air force is also responsible for troop and VIP transport. Transports have included the Noratlas twin-engine (in use from the 1950s until the late 1980s) and the C-160 Transall. Longer-range aircraft have included DC-8s, later replaced by Airbus A-310s. Acquisition of the new Airbus A-400M transport is under consideration.

Women play a role, albeit a limited one, in the French air force. Female convoy pilots served in World War II and continued the practice afterward, adding medical evacuation to female duties during the Indochina War. Pilot Valérie André became the first female general in all the French armed forces in 1976. By the 1980s, women were also undergoing training as fighter pilots.

Guillaume de Syon

See also

Algeria; Dassault Mirage III; Dassault Mystère IVA; Indochina; Suez Crisis

References

Bénichou, Michel. *Un siècle d'aviation française.* Paris: Larivière, 2000.

Christienne, Charles, and Pierre Lissarague. *A History of French Military Aviation.* Trans. Frances Kianka. Washington, DC: Smithsonian Institution Press, 1986.

French Aircraft Development and Production (World War I–Early World War II)

The development of French aircraft up to World War II depended initially on aviation pioneers who became aircraft builders. The first company established as such, in 1905, was that of Gabriel Voisin, who oversaw the building a full-fledged aircraft factory near Paris. Other companies soon appeared, such as Blériot, Breguet, and Farman.

At the beginning of World War I, the French aircraft industry consisted of a mix of small aircraft factories producing fragile machines of varying quality. Under the leadership of Commander Edouard Barrès, by October 1914 a new streamlined plan of production was put in place that included license production, aircraft design according to specific missions, and the opening of new factories as the economy shifted to support the war effort. However, the lack of priority given to air armament affected the development of new aircraft, and it was not until 1917, when Colonel Charles Duval was called in to help solve such problems, that the aircraft industry gained priority. With the end of the war, however, the end of standing orders for machines placed such pressure on aircraft manufacturers that several went out of business (Voisin closed in 1920 and shifted to automobiles and some engine production). Still others, however, slowly began to enter the scene, as was the case of Marcel Bloch, a young aeronautical engineer who had gained prominence after designing the éclair propeller. Others, such as Henri Potez, produced remarkable machines in response to state contracts, yet by the 1930s the French aeronautical industry was in a funk.

Failures in innovation combined with increased foreign competition meant that from 1918 to 1928 the number of aeronautical firms had shrunk from 40 to 28, with another 10 making motors. Attempts to remedy this problem with the creation of an air ministry in 1928 yielded limited results, as the world economic crisis dried up foreign orders and political instability shook France. Some notable progress did occur, however, in the establishment of a flight-test center (CEMA, a rough equivalent to the U.S. NACA) at Villacoublay. Its recommendations, however, were often overlooked by constructors. With the change of government in 1936 to a left-wing coalition, a massive wave of nationalization ensued, led by Air Minister Pierre Cot and designed in part to save the French aircraft industry. This affected both research and production programs. No attention was paid to organizational culture and specialty, and in several cases companies had to fight hard to retain some control over their research laboratories, whose innovative processes would otherwise have been limited.

Six major groups fell under the umbrella of the Société Nationale de Constructions Aéronautiques (SNCA, for National Aircraft Building Company):

- N (nord/north): ANF Les Mureaux, CAMS, and a part of Breguet
- O (ouest/west): Another part of Breguet as well as Loire-Nieuport
- SO (sud-ouest/southwest): Bloch, Blériot-SPAD, and a section of Lioré and Olivier
- SE (sud-est/southeast): Potez, SPCA, and a section of Lioré and Olivier
- C (centre/center): Farman and Hanriot
- M (midi/south): Dewoitine

Other private manufacturers who specialized in light aviation were able to survive (such as Amiot and Caudron), though contracts often dried up for them. The impact of such a nationalization process was immeasurable. Companies that declined the initial buyout offer (such as Breguet) saw contract attributions reversed. (The Bre-690, though initially selected as a fighter, was then rejected in favor of the less able Potez 63.) New processes of engine allocations, contracts, and subcontracts meant slippage in schedules and slow workmanship, although some remarkable projects still appeared. The Amiot 370, for example, was a brilliantly designed twin-engine machine derived from the Amiot 340 bomber and successfully bested several speed records in 1938. Only one was built, however, and the bomber from which it had been extrapolated was never properly tested.

When France was invaded in 1940 and the Third Republic fell, Germany took over French factories in its zone of occupation and began production of its own machines and parts (such as the Fi 156 Storch). In the Vichy zone, production of aircraft was authorized only to fill in the ones lost in combat to the British by the Vichy air force. As for transport projects, these were the only ones whose production was fully authorized (such as the SE 200 giant hydroplane). A couple of projects underwent secret development (i.e., on paper), such as the SO 6000 Triton, which after 1945 became the first French jet aircraft to fly. Overall, however, the French aeronautical industry was dead in the water, producing barely 8,000 aircraft (compared to 35,000 in Germany). More than a decade would be necessary to effect a recovery.

Guillaume de Syon

See also

French Aircraft Development and Production (Post–World War II); Vichy French Air Force

References

Chapman, Herrick. *State Capitalism and Working Class Radicalism in the French Aircraft Industry.* Berkeley: University of California Press, 1991.

Danel, Raymond. *Emile Dewoitine.* Paris: Larivière, 1982.

French Aircraft Development and Production (World War II–Present)

The state control of major French aircraft factories after 1936 had shown a lack of understanding for efficient industrial and technological development. The high costs associated with regional aircraft constructors as created before World War II affected the rebirth of the French aircraft industry after World War II. Combined with socioeconomic hardship, the French aircraft industry lagged behind other nations. Although the government awarded contracts for local production, the lack of immediate availability of French machines forced a reliance on U.S. and British productions.

However, the French government also wished to regenerate its own aircraft industry and to replace the 6,000 aircraft lost to war, obsolescence, and attrition. There was a split, however, between the need to keep government-owned factories going by producing proven German designs, and that of encouraging private companies. Such was the case of constructor Marcel Bloch, who, upon returning from a German concentration camp, faced opposition from communist members of the government regarding his restarting his factory. However, he was able to capitalize on the French air force's needs for a more rationalized fleet that could replace the ragtag surplus aircraft obtained from Allied (and even German) sources. Thus, while the Morane-Saulnier factory manufactured a French version of the Fieseler 156 Storch liaison plane (the MS-500 Criquet), Bloch, who had changed his name to Dassault, bid and won a contract for the twin-engine MD 315 Flamant transport. In the meantime, a new trend affected all French aircraft manufacturers, whereby the government, based on experience from the war bombings, now required that aircraft factories be moved outside of cities and placed near airports.

In engine production, France lagged behind the United States and Great Britain and required several years to catch up to the standards developed during World War II. In jet development, however, all countries involved had a roughly equal start. France, using the services of Hermann Oestrich, formerly of BMW, began the study of the Atar jet engine program. Consequently, the French government encouraged its factories to develop jet prototypes, but the requirements placed on these projects were often far too optimistic, prompting the production under license of the de Havilland Vampire and of the Rolls-Royce Nene jet engine. It was not until Dassault produced the Ouragan jet fighter in the early 1950s (acquired by the French, Indian, and Israeli air forces) that the French aerospace industry slowly began to catch up to its competitors.

In the meantime, the experience of the Korean War prompted the French high command to identify two new programs, one for a light attack aircraft, the other for a NATO-standard supersonic interceptor, which would later become the Mirage.

The trends that had characterized French aerospace production before World War II changed rapidly in the 1950s. Several pioneer names disappeared from the rosters. Some, like Morane-Saulnier, went bankrupt by the early 1960s and were acquired by other aircraft producers (in this case, by Sud Aviation). Others, like Latécoère, ceased production of major aircraft projects to focus on parts manufacturing and subcontracts. A third category—private designers who hoped to emulate the practices of early pioneers—generally failed in their attempts to secure full state support and left the scene. For example, René Leduc designed a series of ramjet aircraft prototypes but lost funding in the late 1950s in the wake of the political and economic crisis that characterized the end of the Fourth Republic. Others, like Hurel-Dubois, producer of the twin-engine HD-34 survey aircraft, went into subcontracting.

With the advent of the Fifth Republic under the initial leadership of President Charles de Gaulle, the French aerospace industry experienced a new wave of financial backing and new project development. Several of these had begun years before, as was the case for the Mirage prototype and the atomic bomb feasibility study, but funding, coupled with a more clearly defined foreign policy that emphasized French independence, boosted such projects. These included the Dassault Mirage IV nuclear bomber as well as SLBM and ICBM development (by a national factory known as SEREB) for the newly developed French atomic bomb (first tested in 1960). There also appeared international cooperation programs like the SEPECAT Jaguar ground attack jet, the Dassault-Dornier Alpha Jet trainer, and, on the civilian level, the Concorde and Airbus projects.

At the industrial level, further consolidations occurred, notably with the forced acquisition of Breguet by Dassault (prearranged by the French state). Other companies, including previously nationalized ones, eventually joined with SNCASE (also known as Sud Aviation) and SNCAN (Nord Aviation). Both giants eventually underwent their own integration when, on 1 January 1970, the Société Nationale Industrielle Aérospatiale became the new entity and included the SEREB.

A similar process affected engine manufacturers, which earlier had become part of the nationalized SNECMA, builder of the Atar engine used on many jet fighters. Several private companies continued to prosper, such as Dassault, Messier (landing gear), and Matra (missiles), but the lion's share of contracts went to Aérospatiale, which became heavily involved in several international construction projects, notably Airbus Industrie and Eurocopter (a result of the fusion of its helicopter division with the German firm MBB). However, by the turn of the millennium, things had evolved once again toward pan-European integration, and Aérospatiale, after merging with the Matra concern, became part, along with the major other European manufacturers, of the EADS consortium.

Of the few independent companies that remain, Dassault Aircraft continues to prosper in both aircraft and avionics development. Attempts at cooperation in the design of a new Eurofighter (the Typhoon) failed in the 1980s, primarily on political grounds, and led to the design of a new Dassault fighter, the Rafale.

By 2000, the French aerospace industry had become a major player on the commercial and military market, helping maintain France in the top-five weapons-exporting nations. New avenues of prosperity, first chartered in the 1980s, began to yield considerable returns in the communications and observation satellites business as well as the booster market (Arianespace).

Guillaume de Syon

See also

Dassault; French Air Force; French Aircraft Development and Production (World War I–Early World War II); Potez Aircraft

References

Bénichou, Michel. *Un siècle d'aviation française.* Paris: Larivière, 2000.

Leroy, François. "The Elusive Pursuit of Grandeur and Independence: Mirage Diplomacy, French Foreign Policy, and International Affairs, 1958–1970." Ph.D. diss., University of Kentucky, 1997.

French Army Light Air Force

The French army's interest in aviation dates from the nineteenth century, with ballooning. The Revolutionary Army had made use of a balloon at the Battle of Fleurus in 1792, and a century later several pioneers considered the use of military dirigibles.

As of 1909, however, with the flight of Louis Blériot over the English Channel, military circles began to focus anew on the potential of military aviation. Several dirigibles were involved in military maneuvers during the 1910–1914 period. When World War I broke out, airplanes and dirigibles were responsible primarily for observation. One such airplane patrol allowed General Joseph Galliéni to shift his troops to meet German forces making their way toward the Marne River. In time, artillery support became more important, and by the end of the conflict the army had 1,600 planes specifically assigned to that task.

During the interwar years airpower doctrine evolved considerably, and in 1934 the Armeé de l'Air (French Air Force) was formally established as a separate arm. This shift meant that the army was on its own to devise a new air support and intelligence doctrine, as the air force was focusing more and more on bombing and air interception. Further disagreements on the use of light aviation in the French army and air force were suspended by France's defeat in 1940.

The appearance of U.S. light aircraft (Piper L-4s in particular) to support the U.S. naval artillery in Operation TORCH in North Africa, so impressed members of the Free French Forces that they demanded their ground forces be equipped with their own aviation support units.

Although French army air units saw service in the liberation of France, it was during the summer of 1945 that the newly formed Ministry of Defense, in light of the French air force's professed limited interest in observation missions, ordered the creation of an artillery aviation capability for the army. However, the air force failed to carry out the order, and the army found itself dependent on a few observation machines—but without any operational structure.

France's colonial wars would soon force the problem to resurface. In Indochina, artillery planes would be used heavily for VIP transport and reconnaissance purposes, hardly ever for artillery fire. Soon, Cessna L-19 aircraft replaced aging Morane-Saulnier 500 Criquet machines (French versions of the Fi 156 "Storch"). Meanwhile, the first helicopters appeared and were used for medevac purposes. They included Hiller UH-12As, H-19s, and H-23s and Sikorsky S-53s and S-55s. However, the moment the French Indochina War ended in 1954, the French air force, mindful of budgetary constraints, took over all rotary-wing aircraft, creating considerable tension with the French army.

However, based on lessons learned in Indochina, the French army started defining a new operational doctrine that included air mobility, antitank capacity, and general combat. Consequently, on 22 November 1954, the army's light aviation observation unit merged with its first helicopter group to form the Army Light Air Force (ALAT). It was immediately put to work in Algeria, where helicopters were used for tactical troop drops (using formations of six H-21s in a "helicopter intervention detachment"). Other operations included ground attack, using modified Bell 47 G-2s carrying either machine guns or wire-guided French SS-10 missiles, later Alouette 2 platforms with SS-11s. Other technical experiments in the field would include arming H-21s with rockets and guns and even an H-34 with a 20mm cannon. By the 1960s, ALAT had almost 700 planes and close to 400 helicopters at its disposal.

The effective use of helicopters and planes during the Algerian War proved that the army did not need the air force to effectively deploy an aviation force; this would be confirmed in 1962, when the French government gave the army autonomy in the formation of its pilots. Two army aviation groups were then stationed in Germany while another two remained in France, each comprising about 20 planes and 20 helicopters.

In 1977, in response to new technologies and military requirements, five combat helicopter regiments were created and divided into reconnaissance, attack, and maneuver squadrons. The helicopters used include an assortment of Aerospatiale/Eurocopter Dauphin, Ecureuil, and Puma machines, with plans for the acquisition of the Tiger attack helicopter.

Guillaume de Syon

See also
Algeria; French Air Force

References

Christienne, Charles, and Pierre Lissarague. *A History of French Military Aviation.* Trans. Frances Kianka. Washington, DC: Smithsonian Institution Press, 1986.

Parotte, Claude. *Historique des aéronefs en service dans l'ALAT de 1955 à 1997.* Self-published, 1998.

Shrader, Charles R. *The First Helicopter War: Logistics and Mobility in Algeria, 1954–1962.* Westport, CT: Praeger, 1999.

French Missile Production and Development

The first consideration of missile development in France came about through the suggestions of René Lorin, an artillery officer, whose description of an "aerial torpedo" in 1915 would have involved a remotely controlled piston-engine machine. A variant applying the principle of the ramjet engine was also discussed but never developed. In the meantime, in 1916, aerial rockets of the "Le Prieur" type were put to use against tethered observation balloons.

In the interwar years, little attention was paid to the potential of missiles and rockets, other than through the theoretical work of pioneer Robert Esnault-Pelterie and the tests of rocket bombs in 1936 by Camille Rougeron. In fact, applied missile development in France began only after World War II—based on German results. Consequently, production followed several tracks in relation to the demands of each service.

The French navy became very interested in the potential of sea-launched antiship missiles and acquired antisubmarine Malafon missiles for the defense of its carrier battle groups, adding the Masurca surface-to-air system in the late 1960s. In 1967, when Soviet-built SSN2-A Styx missiles, fired by Egypt, destroyed the Israeli frigate *Eilath,* the idea of a sea-launched antiship missile came to prominence in France.

Although a series of short-range rockets also entered service, the major industrial production in the 1970s and 1980s was the Aérospatiale Exocet missile, which first entered service in 1974. Available in several versions, including surface-to-surface and air-to-surface, this missile was sold to several navies throughout the world, including Germany, the United Kingdom, and France. It gained notoriety when an Argentine fighter fired an Exocet at HMS *Sheffield* and sank it during the Falklands War in 1982. Meanwhile, the French army ordered the development of several antitank missiles, using the SS-10 and SS-12 systems. Other systems included the internationally procured MILAN.

The French air force also commissioned the construction of several missiles, particularly air-to-ground and air-to-air missiles for various missions. The first French air-to-air missile was Matra's R 511. Variants of the American Sidewinder were also used, alongside the Matra 530 and later the Matra 550 Magic. The AS 30 air-to-ground vector, developed by Nord Aviation (later part of Aérospatiale), entered service in 1961 and was based on the air-to-air AA 10 and AA 20 missiles. It was followed by the Franco-British AS 37 Martel antiradar unit, which equipped both Mirage IIIEs and Jaguar aircraft.

Other French missile developments grew as part of international programs designed to cut costs as well as ensure equipment compatibility wherever possible among European forces. For example, France and Germany worked together on the development of the infantry antitank MILAN missile system, designed to succeed the SS 10, SS 11, and Cobra systems. Begun in the 1960s, the MILAN concept entered service a decade later. Several other projects are the result of Franco-German teamwork, through such companies as the Euromissile Corporation, in which groups from Aérospatiale and Germany's MBB work together updating MILAN and developing other projects. The most recent consortium work revolves around the Apache missile, for which the French air force placed a $225 million order in 1997. Equipped with the French-built Prométhée radar, the Apache uses Inertial Guidance System/Global Positioning System navigation to reach the target, then switches to radar for the final phase of its flight.

As for ballistic missiles, the French government began feasibility studies in the late 1950s, partly in response to Soviet and U.S. efforts in that field. Eight types of experimental missiles were tested between 1960 and 1965, leading, among other things, to the first orbiting of a French satellite atop a Diamant rocket in 1965. The other result was the knowledge accumulated toward the development for ground-to-ground strategic ballistic missiles. The first such machine was the S112 two-stage rocket, tested seven times (with four failures) between 1965 and 1967. Tests of other models, the S01 and S02, were more successful. A similar path came about in the development of submarine-launched ballistic missiles (SLBMs). At the same time, the French army began considering the use of tactical missiles, which eventually included the Hades and Pluton rockets, designed to carry tactical nuclear weapons.

The production of France's ballistic missiles was initially assigned to the National Society for Explosives and Powder for the propulsion material and to Aérospatiale for the missiles themselves. Eighteen S2 missiles were placed in silos on the Albion Plateau in 1972, replaced eight years later by S3 types. As for SLBMs, M1 missiles first equipped submarines starting in 1972, followed by M20 vectors in 1977. The most recent missile, the M4, carrying six warheads, began operation in 1985. An upgraded M4, the M40 SLBM, is scheduled to enter service; ground-launched ballistic missiles were retired from service in the late 1990s.

In parallel, Aérospatiale developed a new cruise missile, the ASMP (medium-range air-to-ground), for use onboard the Mirage IV and later the Mirage 2000N. Capable of carrying a 200-kiloton nuclear warhead, the ASMP can cruise over a maximum distance of 250 kilometers if released from high level. A newer version, with longer range, should enter service around 2008.

Guillaume de Syon

See also

French Air Force; French Naval Air Force

References

Benecke, Theodor, et al. *Flugkörper und Lenkraketen.* Koblenz, Germany: Bernard and Graefe, 1987.

Estival, Bernard. *Les missiles navals.* Paris: Larivière, 1990.

French Naval Air Force (Aéronavale)

From the very beginning of military aviation, the French navy considered using aircraft to further carry the missions it was assigned. In World War I, it used a number of planes for coastal patrol and convoy escorts. Pilot training initially took place at a naval base as well as the French army's Istres airfield. Soon, however, a new naval air base was set up at Berre. Most machines were hydroplanes from the Georges Lévy factory, which were soon replaced by the float-modified Farman 60 "Goliath" and various other types.

In the interwar years, the navy's air arm also played a role in enforcing French control over its colonies, for example, by setting up bases in Indochina.

By the mid-1930s, the navy used several squadrons of torpedo-bomber hydroplanes, among them the Levasseur PL 15 and Latécoère 290. These were then replaced by the Latécoère 298, a torpedo-bomber, which first flew in 1936, entered the service in 1939, and remained active until 1950. In the meantime, the navy placed into service the *Commandant Teste,* a hydroplane carrier, which launched machines from special catapults and collected them through an access hangar near the ship's waterline.

In World War II, the navy also used the *Béarn* as an aircraft carrier. After 1945, the navy reorganized its aeronautical section, dividing it into squadrons for maintenance and training and flotillas for combat. Under this system, neither was automatically linked to an aircraft carrier, as had been the case with the *Béarn* and *Commandant Teste* carrier groups.

As part of its plans to fulfill its NATO-assigned duties, France first used aircraft carriers obtained from the United States and United Kingdom. However, these carriers (*La Fayette, Bois-Belleau, Dixmude,* and *Arromanches*) were also used to support air operations in the Indochina War and later in Algeria. There, the navy deployed squadrons of Grumman Hellcats, Curtiss Helldivers, and Chance-Vought Corsairs.

In addition, Grumman Goose amphibians were used to drop French commandos while Consolidated Privateers ensured air surveillance. Other aircraft, some used for carrier training, included Spitfires and Grumman Bearcats. With the advent of the jet age, training of naval pilots was first done in CM 175 "Zephyr" jets. Later, qualifications were done in Dassault Etendard IVMs (until 1990) and then in the Super Etendard.

Aware of the shortcomings of World War II–era carriers, France opted for new ships in the late 1950s rather than refurbishing of older ones. Two French-built attack aircraft carriers, R98 *Clémenceau* and R99 *Foch* (25,000 metric tons, equivalent to the U.S. *Essex* class) entered service in 1961 and 1963 and served as the main vector of power projection until retired in the 1990s.

During that time, the de Havilland Aquilon, a French naval version of the de Havilland Sea Venom used for both defense and attack purposes, reached retirement. There were no acceptable French replacements for the machine, so France purchased 46 Vought F-8E(FN) "Crusaders," which remained in service until 1999. The Dassault Etendard, used for attack purposes, was replaced by navalized Jaguar jets. Although both R98 and R99 served French interests with great distinction, their lack of nuclear power and limited size suggested that they would eventually be unable to support power projection in any meaningful way. Indeed, during the Balkan crisis of the late 1990s, R98 was retired, leaving R99 to do the work and requiring it to return regularly to port. In the meantime, the French parliament approved funding for a new nuclear-powered ship, the *Charles de Gaulle,* that began sea trials in 1999 and will carry the first squadrons of navalized Dassault Rafales. Though the new ship will allow for effective power projection on European seas and in the context of UN and NATO operations, the French navy finds itself at a crossroads, currently lacking the means to fund a second aircraft carrier.

Nonetheless, the Aéronavale continues to render great service, as it can use other vectors to ensure its goals are carried out. These include nuclear-powered submarines that carry France's nuclear missile deterrent, as well as various battle cruisers equipped with Exocet missiles. Furthermore, several coastal bases are available from which to launch air patrols, notably in the form of Dassault-Breguet 1150 Atlantic submarine hunters.

Guillaume de Syon

See also

French Air Force; French Missile Production and Development

References

Gall, Jean-Marie. *Les Crusader français en action.* Boulogne-sur-Mer: LELA Presse, 1997.

Ménès, Louis. *Sous l'aile du Calao.* Paris: ARDHAN, 1997.

FREQUENT WIND (1975)

U.S. code name for the final evacuation operation from Saigon, South Vietnam (Republic of Vietnam, RVN). In the early morning of 29 April, a People's Army of Vietnam (PAVN, the North Vietnamese Army) rocket and artillery barrage against Tan Son Nhut Air Base announced the final assault on the RVN capital. As the last U.S. fixed-wing aircraft departed the battered air base, Major General Homer D. Smith, head of the U.S. Defense Attaché Office (DAO), informed U.S. Ambassador Graham A. Martin that the runway at Tan Son Nhut was unusable. He recommended the execution of Option IV, in which U.S. and Vietnamese refugees would be evacuated by helicopter to U.S. Seventh Fleet ships waiting 80 miles offshore.

Martin decided to come to Tan Son Nhut for a firsthand inspection. At 10:51 A.M., he issued orders to begin Option IV. This was followed by radio broadcasts of Bing Crosby singing "White Christmas," the signal for Americans to proceed to evacuation points. At 2:53 P.M., with the temperature reaching 105 degrees, 865 Marines arrived via CH-53s to cover the evacuation.

Over the next seven hours, 4,500 Vietnamese and 395 Americans were flown out. Around 11:00 P.M., the last Marines departed, destroying classified equipment and facilities as well as $3.6 million in U.S. currency.

Originally, no plans had been made for a major rescue from the U.S. Embassy. By late afternoon, the embassy Marine commander, Brigadier General Richard E. Carey, reported that several thousand stranded Vietnamese and Americans had gathered in or around the embassy compound. Quickly, 130 additional Marines were flown in to defend the area. Since only one CH-53 at a time could land in the compound's parking area, they were augmented by CH-46s flying off the embassy's rooftop.

Except for a brief delay to evacuate the DAO, a steady stream of helicopters made hundreds of round-trips to the waiting ships. By 4:30 the next morning, with growing concerns that the embassy might be overrun by PAVN forces, Carey gave orders that thereafter only Americans were to be airlifted. Around 5:00 P.M., Ambassador Martin and the last American departed. About 420 Vietnamese were left waiting in the parking area.

Elsewhere in Saigon, hundreds of other Vietnamese who had worked for the U.S. military, embassy, and Central Intelligence Agency were left behind. All told, 1,500 Vietnamese and 978 Americans were rescued from the embassy. At daybreak, only the Marine security forces remained inside. Nine CH-46s finished evacuating them at 7:53 A.M., the last man to leave being Master Sergeant Juan Valdez aboard *Lady Ace 09.*

U.S. helicopters flew 662 sorties. They lost two Marine guards to ground fire and two CH-46s that crashed at sea. About 8,800 evacuees were eventually brought to Subic Bay, in the Philippines, including 989 Marines. Some 675,000 Vietnamese refugees eventually made their way to the United States after the Vietnam War.

William Head

References

Boyne, Walter J. "The Fall of Saigon." *Air Force Magazine* 83, 4 (April 2000).

Herrington, Stuart. *Peace With Honor?* Novato, CA: Presidio Press, 1983.

Isaacs, Arnold R. *Without Honor: Defeat in Vietnam and Cambodia.* Baltimore: Johns Hopkins University Press, 1983.

Frontal Aviation

Branch of the Red Air Force that controlled tactical air assets supporting ground operations. The concept for Frontal Aviation evolved during the interwar period and the Great Patriotic War (the Soviets' name for World War II) as the Soviet military developed its concepts for rapid, deep offensive operations. The designation was based on the fact that the Frontal Aviation units were assigned directly to a front commander—a senior Red Army officer—for conducting combined arms operations.

A front (roughly equivalent to a group in a Western army) was a Soviet command echelon subordinate to a theater of military operations. A front controlled multiple armies, including Frontal Aviation units formed into an air army. Normally, a single air army was assigned to each front, although more could be assigned if the front was the main axis of attack. Additionally, strategic resources from Long Range Aviation forces (and later nuclear missiles) could be assigned to augment the Frontal Aviation effort.

During the Cold War period, each military district and each Soviet group of forces outside the Soviet Union included an air army in its military structure. Air armies normally included several air divisions, each of which controlled three regiments, each containing three squadrons. Frontal Aviation played an important role in the successful campaigns in the latter portion of the Great Patriotic War and in the planning for operations during the Cold War. Frontal Aviation operational concepts emphasized preparation for and then support of combined arms ground offensives. Preparation operations would begin with an air offensive that was designed to gain air superiority by attacks on the airfields, air defense assets, and command and control facilities.

The preparation phase would also provide reconnaissance on enemy dispositions, suppress enemy firepower capabilities (especially in the nuclear era), and disrupt enemy movement to the main axis of attack. Support for ground offensive operations emphasized air superiority, reconnaissance, and providing mobile firepower to enhance the offensive penetration and movement of offensive thrusts. In the post-Soviet period, the tactical resources of the Russian air force were organized under the Frontal Aviation Command, one of four commands of the Russian air force.

Jerome V. Martin

See also

Russian Air Force (Post-Soviet); Soviet Air Force; Tactical Air Warfare

References

Erickson, John, Lynn Hanson, and William Schneider. *Soviet Ground Forces: An Operational Assessment.* Boulder: Westview Press, 1986.

Lambeth, Benjamin S. *Russia's Air Power at the Crossroads.* Santa Monica, CA: RAND, 1996.

Murphy, Paul J., ed. *The Soviet Air Forces.* London: McFarland, 1984.

Fuchida, Mitsuo (1903–1973)

Led the Japanese air attack on Pearl Harbor on 7 December 1941. After World War II, he converted to Christianity and became a globetrotting evangelist.

In 1941, Fuchida was one of Japan's most experienced aviators. Although his comrades were killed off as the war progressed, he survived many close calls, including being recalled from Hiroshima the day before the atomic bombing. At the war's end, Fuchida took up farming.

On the way to testify at a war-crimes trial, Fuchida accepted a pamphlet written by Jacob DeShazer, a member of the Doolittle Raid. The Japanese had captured and tortured DeShazer, but he became a Christian from reading the bible in prison and returned to evangelize Japan. Fuchida realized DeShazer's forgiveness was like that of Peggy Covall, who had helped Japanese POWs even though Japanese soldiers had beheaded her missionary parents. Intrigued, Fuchida purchased a bible and, after reading it, also became a Christian.

Eventually, Fuchida traveled the world as an evangelist. Once he shared the platform at a West Berlin crusade with Billy Graham. He regretted ever leading the Pearl Harbor raid.

Emerson T. McMullen

See also

Pearl Harbor

References

G. W. Prange. *God's Samurai.* New York: Brassey's, 1990.

G

Gabreski, Francis S. (1919–2002)

Top-ranking U.S. World War II ace in Europe. Francis S. "Gabby" Gabreski was born in Oil City, Pennsylvania, the son of Polish immigrants. In 1940, after attending college for two years at Notre Dame, he joined the U.S. Army Air Corps. In March 1941, he was commissioned a second lieutenant in the U.S. Army Air Corps and was assigned to the 45th Fighter Squadron of the 15th Fighter Group at Wheeler Field, Hawaii, where he flew the Curtiss P-40 Warhawk.

Gabreski was anxious to get into the European conflict, so he volunteered to transfer to one of the Polish squadrons flying with the Royal Air Force. Because he was fluent in Polish, his application was accepted and he was assigned to Northolt, the home of six Polish Spitfire squadrons. He was attached to No. 315 Squadron, flying the highly regarded Spitfire Mk.IX fighter in several missions with the Poles.

On 27 February 1943, Gabreski was assigned to the 61st Fighter Squadron of Hub Zemke's famed 56th Fighter Group, flying the Republic P-47 Thunderbolt. He was soon appointed commander of B flight, and on June 9 he was promoted to major and given command of the 61st Fighter Squadron.

On 24 August 1943, Gabreski scored his first aerial victory. From then on, kills came more frequently, often by doubles and triples, until he recorded his twenty-eighth victory on 5 July 1944. He was the leading U.S. ace in Europe and, after almost 200 missions and 500 combat hours, had earned a rest.

On 20 July 1944, while waiting to depart for the United States, Gabreski abruptly decided to fly one last mission. After encountering no fighter opposition, he elected to strafe a German airfield near Coblenz. On his second very low pass, Gabreski's propeller contacted the ground, forcing him to crash-land in a nearby field. He evaded capture for five days before the Germans finally apprehended him. He spent the remainder of the war as a POW in Stalag Luft I.

After the war, Gabreski stayed in the military, gaining further experience flight-testing and commanding fighter units. When the Korean conflict erupted, Gabreski—now a colonel—once more went to war, this time flying the North

Gabby Gabreski shot down 31 planes in Europe before becoming a prisoner of war. As wing commander of the 51st Fighter Group, he scored six-and-a-half victories flying F-86s in Korea, becoming one of the few who were aces in both wars. (U.S. Air Force)

American F-86 Sabre Jet. He was once again a phenomenally successful fighter pilot, with 6.5 MiG-15s to his credit. This ensured his membership in the very select club of pilots who achieved ace status in two wars.

In 1967, after 34.5 total confirmed aerial victories in two wars and numerous command positions, Gabreski—now the third-ranking U.S. ace of all time—finally ended his distinguished military career. After retirement from the Air Force, he served as an executive with Grumman Aircraft Corporation and as president of the Long Island Railroad.

His numerous decorations include the Distinguished Service Cross, and in 1978 he was honored by being elected to the National Aviation Hall of Fame in Dayton, Ohio. He died of a heart attack on 31 January 2002.

Daniel Ruffin and Steven A. Ruffin

References

Bright, Charles D., ed. *Historical Dictionary of the U.S. Air Force.* New York: Greenwood Press, 1992.

Gabreski, Francis S., and Carl Molesworth. *Gabby: A Fighter Pilot's Life.* Atglen, PA: Schiffer Military History, 1998.

Gagarin, Yuri (1934–1968)

First person to orbit Earth. Born in Klushino (Russia), Gagarin was trained as a major in the Red Air Force. Chosen for the historic space flight on 8 April 1960, Gagarin lifted off on 12 April 1961 aboard a Vostok capsule. The flight lasted 108 minutes. Following his success, Gagarin became a great hero in the Soviet Union whose appeal to the public was comparable to that of Charles Lindbergh in the United States.

Although Gagarin stated several times that he wished to fly again into space, Soviet authorities preferred to keep him on the ground, where his value as a symbol of the Soviet Union at home and abroad continued to grow. Officials eventually conceded that they might allow him another orbital flight if Gagarin completed his engineering studies, interrupted in 1961.

In 1967, to his surprise, he was also allowed to fly aircraft again. Gagarin finished an honors thesis (the title of which remains classified), received his diploma on 8 February, then undertook jet training. On 27 March 1968, Gagarin was flying a two-seater MiG-15 UTI with instructor-pilot Colonel Vladimir Seryogin when the plane crashed, killing both occupants. The accident report, classified for 20 years, concluded that the crash was the result of pilot error combined with atmospheric conditions. He was buried with full military honors; an obelisk was erected at the site of the crash.

Guillaume de Syon

See also

Korolyov, Sergei; Vostok

References

Bond, Peter. *Heroes in Space: From Gagarin to Challenger.* New York: Basil Blackwell, 1987.

Golowanow, Jaroslaw. *Our Gagarin.* Moscow: Progress, 1979.

Kowalski, Gerhard. *Die Gagarin-Story.* Berlin: Schwarzkopf and Schwarzkopf, 1999.

Gallai, Mark (1914–1998)

Soviet military test pilot. Mark Lazarevich Gallai was born on 16 April 1914 in Saint Petersburg, Russia. After graduating from an engineering institute and flight school, he became a test pilot for TsAGI (Central Aerodynamics and Hydrodynamics Institute), where he remained for his entire career except for three brief periods of combat flying during World War II, primarily for the sake of field-testing. He was honored as a Hero of the Soviet Union on 1 May 1957 and in 1959 was given the title Honored Test Pilot of the Soviet Union. In 1957, he retired from the air force and thereafter continued his test-flying and research as a civilian focusing on flight dynamics. In 1972, he was awarded a Doctorate of Technical Sciences. He died on 14 July 1998.

George M. Mellinger

Galland, Adolf (1912–1996)

Legendary German fighter pilot and commander; undoubtedly the best-remembered veteran of the Luftwaffe. Galland joined the still-secret German air force in 1934. He gained an excellent reputation in the Spanish civil war as the leader of a squadron of ground attack aircraft, and he fought in the Polish campaign in that capacity. He transferred to fighters and was named commander of Jagdgeschwader 26 (JG 26; 26th Fighter Wing) in August 1940, one of the first of the younger generation of fighter pilots to be promoted to that level of command. By the end of the Battle of Britain, Galland's innovative escort formations had become standard doctrine, and JG 26 had earned a reputation as the best fighter unit in the Luftwaffe.

Galland led JG 26 in France until December 1941, when he was summoned to Berlin to replace Werner Moelders as General der Jagdflieger (General of the Fighter Arm) after the latter's death. He was soon awarded the Oak Leaves with Swords and Diamonds to the Knight's Cross of the Iron Cross, the second member of the Wehrmacht (after Mölders) to receive this new highest decoration. At age 30, Galland became the youngest general in the Wehrmacht. His new job was a staff rather than a command position, and Galland spent three frustrating years attempting to defend the interests of the fighter force within the Luftwaffe High Command.

Reichsmarschall Hermann Goering tended to blame the failures of his fighter arm on the cowardice of his pilots rather than deficiencies in numbers, training, and equipment. Galland, although a favorite of Hitler's, gradually lost all credibility and influence in his position, and he resigned in January 1945. He requested and was granted permission to form a small unit of Me 262 jet fighters, Jagdverband 44, and led it until he was wounded in April 1945. Galland ended the war as a lieutenant general. His final victory total was 103, all scored against the Western Allies.

Galland served after the war as a technical adviser to the Argentine air force, and after his return to Germany he became a consultant to the German aviation industry. He remained active until his death in 1996. His classic memoir, *The First and the Last,* established his reputation in the English-speaking world and remains in print in several languages nearly a half-century after its original publication.

Donald Caldwell

See also

German Air Force (Luftwaffe)

References

Caldwell, D. *JG 26: Top Guns of the Luftwaffe.* New York: Orion Books, 1991.

Galland, A. *The First and the Last.* New York: Henry Holt, 1954.

Garros, Roland (1888–1918)

Pioneer French aviator. Roland Garros was part of the cadre of pilots who achieved fame at air shows, races, and aviation contests in the days prior to World War I. And like his comrades, when war was declared he volunteered.

Over the war's first winter, he began collaborating with Raymond Saulnier on the problem of firing a gun through the propeller. Settling on the attachment of steel wedges to the propeller as protection, Garros tested the device in the spring of 1915. His "tests" resulted in three victories over German aircraft before he became the victim of engine failure over enemy lines. Along with his secret weapon, Garros was captured and became a POW.

Escaping in 1918, Garros returned to the front flying SPADs. He was shot down on 5 October 1918, this time losing his life. A Paris sports stadium is named in his honor.

James Streckfuss

See also

Morane-Saulnier Aircraft

References

Franks, Norman, and Frank Bailey. *The Storks: The Story of France's Elite Fighter Groupe de Combat 12 (Les Cigognes) in WWI.* London: Grub Street, 1998.

Woodman, Harry. *Early Aircraft Armament: The Aeroplane and the Gun up to 1918.* Washington, DC: Smithsonian Institution Press, 1989.

Gasoline

A liquid hydrocarbon extracted from crude oil. Gasoline has also been produced from natural gas and coal. The energy content of gasoline is 18,500–19,000 btu/lb, and it weighs 5.9–6.0 lbs/gal.

Early straight-run (distillation process) gasolines were of varied and limited quality, quite prone to "knock" or detonation in high-performance aircraft piston engines. World War I experience soon demonstrated that the knocking tendency was related to the crude oil characteristics from which it was derived. The increased aromatic content in crude oils from the Dutch East Indies and Southern California fields resulted in greater knock resistance than gasolines distilled from Pennsylvania crudes, for instance.

The dreadful quality of early gasolines, typically having an octane rating of around 50, resulted in the use of fuel blends to improve knock resistance. Benzol, a mixture of benzine, toluene, and a small amount of xylene blended with gasoline, derived from California oil fields was frequently used in pursuit and racing aircraft engines of the 1920s and early 1930s.

High-performance aviation gasolines available to the United States and its Allies during World War II were due in no small part to the earlier discovery that tetraethyl lead was a very effective knock inhibitor. This additive, together with improved refining methods and blending such compounds as iso octane with gasoline, led to development of 100-octane aviation fuel.

Development of aviation fuels was a vital factor in the dramatic progress achieved by the aviation industry during the 1920–1940 period. It was absolutely essential to the aircraft engine industry and facilitated ever larger and more powerful piston engines. The adoption and use of high-quality aviation fuels by the Allies was a major contributing factor to victory in World War II.

Birch Matthews

Gavin, James Maurice (1907–1990)

U. S. Army general who charted a new course for Army aviation. As commander of the 82d Airborne Division in World

War II, Gavin learned about air mobility. Service after the war in a group evaluating nuclear weapons development and as commander of VII Corps in Germany convinced him that the Army had to prepare for tactical nuclear warfare. Knowing that the Soviet Union was developing tactical nuclear weapons, Gavin exercised VII Corps in nuclear scenarios. He found it necessary to disperse and assemble the corps rapidly to avoid nuclear annihilation. The corps could not perform these exercises satisfactorily using its ground transportation and communications.

Assigned to the Army staff as the deputy for operations and later director of Army research and development, Gavin spent the remainder of his career seeking solutions to the problems of tactical nuclear warfare. The solution that he found was to develop new missions for Army aviation so that troops could disperse, assemble, and resupply rapidly by using helicopters and light transport airplanes. To scout enemy lines, he proposed mounting cavalry in helicopters. To acquire enemy targets suitable for nuclear weapons, he desired Army reconnaissance airplanes transmitting real-time intelligence to commanders. To enable helicopter-borne troops to attack hostile targets, Gavin sought to arm helicopters and procure light bombers under Army control. Gavin also created the position of director of army aviation to assure that the Army moved in these new directions.

As director of research and development, Gavin helped develop tactical missiles, new and better helicopters, vertical takeoff and landing aircraft, and equipment suitable for the nuclear battlefield.

Gavin's ideas pushed the Army into conflict with the Air Force over roles and missions. The services compromised in the 1960s, the Army securing armed helicopters but giving up light transport airplanes and light bombers.

Although Gavin retired in 1958, his ideas came to fruition later with the integration of Army aviation into the combat arms and the creation of Army divisions integrating air cavalry and air assault missions. Never used in nuclear war, these units have proven effective in counterinsurgency and conventional warfare.

John L. Bell

References

Biggs, Bradley. *Gavin: A Biography of General James M. Gavin.* Hamden, CT: Archon Books, 1980.

Booth, T. Michael, and Duncan Spencer. *Paratrooper: The Life of James M. Gavin.* New York: Simon and Schuster, 1994.

Geisler, Hans-Ferdinand (1891–1966)

German general. Hans-Ferdinand Geisler was born in Hannover on 19 April 1891. He entered the German navy as a cadet in 1909 and was promoted to *Leutnant (*second lieutenant) on 19 September 1912. He served in the navy throughout World War I and the Weimar era, rising to the rank of commander, then transferred to the new Luftwaffe on 1 September 1933. Geisler was promoted rapidly from *Oberst* (colonel) on 1 March 1934 to *Generalleutnant (*lieutenant general) on 1 April 1939, and finally to *General der Flieger* (general of fliers) on 19 July 1940. He was awarded the Knight's Cross on 4 May 1940. He commanded Fliegerdivision 10 (redesignated X Fliegerkorps one month later) from September 1939, until his retirement. Geisler's first wartime command was in Hamburg, against British naval forces in the North Sea. He was later transferred to Sicily in support of Mussolini's troops. From 24 August to his retirement on 31 October 1942, Geisler was posted as special duty officer to the Air Ministry and commander in chief of the Luftwaffe. For his service, he received the German Cross in Gold on 9 November 1942. Geisler died in Köln-Kalk on 25 June 1966.

Suzanne Hayes Fischer

Gemini Space Program

The second manned U.S. space project. Gemini bridged the Mercury and Apollo programs and worked out most of the technical problems needed to reach the moon. Goals such as extravehicular activity, rendezvous and docking, the use of fuel cells instead of batteries, and spacecraft maneuverability—all necessary aspects of lunar missions—were achieved. The program additionally gave two new classes of astronauts a chance to fly with the original seven veterans.

Between 23 March 1965 and 15 November 1966, U.S. astronauts spent 1,940 hours in space—a far cry from the 54 hours accumulated during Mercury. Significant advancements in only four additional missions came with the development of better spacecraft able to support the two-man crew for much greater lengths of time. The Gemini 7 crew set a record: 14 days in space. Such extended trips would be vital for the 250,000-mile lunar journeys planned for Apollo.

In addition to its extended duration, Gemini 7 also participated in a space first as Gemini 6 (actually launched nine days after Gemini 7) met up and flew within a few yards of Gemini 7. This difficult rendezvous was the most vital part of a lunar mission.

Another requirement, such as the ability to work outside in space, was met with Edward White's Gemini 4 spacewalk, a first for America. Skeptics' theories that a man would perish in an atmosphere-void space environment were disproved.

U.S. astronauts were now ready to go to a place man had always dreamed of: the moon.

Erich Streckfuss

References

Collins, Michael. *Liftoff.* New York: Grove Press, 1988.

Genda, A. Minoru (1904–1989)

Commander and later captain in the Imperial Japanese Navy. Genda was born in Hiroshima on 16 August 1904 and graduated from the Japanese naval academy in 1924. He attended flight school from December 1928 to November 1929 at Kasumigaura and graduated with honors in the nineteenth class. Genda later spent a year in England as the assistant naval air attaché, which helped him to become an expert on fighter aircraft and tactics as well as one of the navy's most respected officers. In 1941, Genda was picked by Admiral Isoroku Yamamoto to plan the air attack on Pearl Harbor. Genda served throughout the war in many capacities. In 1944, he took command of the 343d Air Corps, an elite flying group based at Matsuyama Air Base that was the cream of the remaining Japanese fighter pilots.

Postwar, Genda served as Chief of Staff of the Japanese Air Self-Defense Force (1959–1962); he also served in the House of Councilors (the Japanese parliament) from 1962 until 1986.

David A. Pluth

References

Hata, Ikuhiko, and Yashuho Izawa. *Japanese Naval Aces and Fighter Units in World War II.* Annapolis, MD: Naval Institute Press, 1989

Prange, Gordon W. *God's Samuri—Lead Pilot at Pearl Harbor.* Prange Enterprises, 1990.

General Dynamics

U.S. aircraft manufacturer and major defense contractor. General Dynamics has a complex history, with many firms and some famous names: Thomas-Morse, Dayton Wright, Stinson, Vultee, Convair. The company was founded in 1952 when Electric Boat, the Connecticut-based maker of submarines for the U.S. Navy, voted to change its corporate name to better represent its widening acquisitions. The company was involved with aviation ever since it purchased control of Canadair in 1946.

General Dynamics moved to the forefront of U.S. aviation with its takeover of Consolidated Vultee in 1953 to become the Convair Division. Convair had just completed the manufacture of the huge B-36 for the Air Force and was manufacturing jets, including the F-102 and later F-106 delta-wing fighters. San Diego operations were closed down after 1961. Fort Worth manufactured the B-58 and then the controversial F-111, though that program was curtailed in scope. By 1990, the firm and its predecessors had manufactured more than 100 basic types of airplane and produced more than 62,000 aircraft.

Because of declining Pentagon weapons purchases and general industry consolidation, as well as changing company interests, General Dynamics began to move out of aviation. Canadair was sold to the Canadian government in 1976. It took control of Cessna (private and business aircraft) in 1985 but sold that company to Textron just seven years later. Most important, it sold the huge Fort Worth division (formerly Convair) to Lockheed in 1993 for $1.5 billion and the remainder of its aircraft structures business to McDonnell Douglas the next year. The Space Division (which included the Atlas rocket fundamental to many space launches, among other missile and space products) was sold to Martin Marietta in 1994. With those sales, General Dynamics was essentially out of the aviation business for five years, concentrating instead on land and amphibious combat systems, information systems and technology, and marine products. Then, in mid-1994, it purchased control of Gulfstream Aerospace, a 1978 spinoff from Grumman that manufactured jet executive aircraft; this purchase returned the firm to aviation.

Christopher H. Sterling

See also

Cessna Aircraft; Consolidated Aircraft Corporation; Convair B-58 Hustler; Convair F-102 Delta Dagger and F-106 Delta Dart; General Dynamics F-111 Aardvark; Grumman Aircraft; Lockheed Aircraft; Lockheed Martin F-16 Fighting Falcon; Martin Aircraft

References

General Dynamics Website. Available online at http://www.generaldynamics.com.

Wegg, John. *General Dynamics Aircraft and Their Predecessors.* Annapolis, MD: Naval Institute Press, 1990.

General Dynamics F-111 Aardvark

A technically advanced multimission aircraft, perhaps the most controversial fighter ever procured by the U.S. Air Force. Conceived as the TFX by Secretary of Defense Robert McNamara—a "common" aircraft that could fulfill fighter, attack, reconnaissance, and bomber roles for both the Air Force and Navy—the F-111 suffered from numerous technical and political problems during its development and initial service. The F-111 was the first operational fighter equipped with variable-geometry wings (so-called swing wings that could sweep forward and back depending on conditions), afterburning turbofan engines, and an escape capsule for the crew. It was also the first operational attack aircraft capable of supersonic performance while flying less than 100 feet from the ground. The Navy bowed out of the program when the resulting aircraft was deemed too heavy to operate safely from aircraft carriers.

Eventually, the F-111 developed into a highly successful long-range interdiction aircraft—its early Vietnam experience notwithstanding—and saw limited service during several strikes against Middle East targets. An electronic warfare variant also proved remarkably effective, especially during Operation DESERT STORM in 1991. The first F-111A was flown on 21 December 1964, and 573 aircraft had been completed when production ended in November 1976. These included 79 FB-111As for the Strategic Air Command. An order for 50 F-111Ks for the Royal Air Force was canceled in January 1968 before any aircraft were delivered, but 24 F-111Cs were completed for the Royal Australian Air Force, which subsequently accepted six modified F-111As and 15 F-111Gs (formerly FB-111As) as attrition aircraft. Interestingly, the F-111 did not have an official name until 27 July 1996, the same day the type was retired from U.S. service. The Australians intend to continue operating their aircraft for the foreseeable future.

Dennis R. Jenkins

References

Davies, Peter E. and Anthony M. Thornborough. *F-111 Aardvark.* Wiltshire, UK: Crowood, 1997.

Wagner, Ray. *American Combat Planes.* 3rd ed. Garden City, NY: Doubleday, 1982.

George, Harold Lee (1893–1986)

U.S. general who oversaw the military's transport command. Harold Lee George was born on 19 July 1893 in Somerville, Massachusetts. He delayed his studies when World War I began, becoming a second lieutenant of cavalry in the Officers Reserve Corps. In October 1917, he resigned his commission to enroll as a cadet in the Army Signal Corps Aviation Section flying school at Love Field near Dallas, Texas. He received his wings on 29 March 1918.

In September, he joined the 7th Aviation Instruction Center, American Expeditionary Forces Air Service, in Clermont, France. During the Meuse-Argonne Offensive in October-November 1918, George flew bombers for the 163d Bomb Squadron. During this time, he became an adherent of General William "Billy" Mitchell's theories of airpower.

In June 1921, First Lieutenant George was one of a select group of young airmen who participated with Billy Mitchell in his famous aerial demonstration attack and sinking of the German prize battleship *Ostfriesland.* It galvanized George's belief in strategic bombing.

Captain George matriculated to the Air Corps Tactical School (ACTS), Maxwell Field, Alabama, where in 1934 he became the director of the Department of Air Tactics and Strategy. It was at ACTS that George expressed and developed his theories of institutional independence and offensive airpower: massed bomber formations carrying the battle to the enemy's heartland and destroying its ability and will to wage war.

Promoted to major in July 1936, George went to the Air Corps General Staff School for one year before going to Langley Field as commander of General Headquarters Air Force's 96th Bombardment Squadron and later its only B-17 unit, the 2d Bombardment Group. In February 1941, George was promoted to lieutenant colonel and in July was appointed assistant Chief of Staff for war plans in the newly created Air Staff in Washington. George chaired a board of officers developing Air War Plans Division (AWPD) Plan-1.

In April 1942, he was promoted to brigadier general and assigned command of the Air Corps Ferrying Command (ACFC). In June, ACFC became the now famous Air Transport Command. Major General George took a command of 130 antiquated transports and 11,000 personnel and built it into a force of more than 3,000 modern aircraft and 300,000 personnel.

For his dedicated service George received the Distinguished Service Medal, Legion of Merit, Distinguished Flying Cross, and Air Medal. He died on 24 February 1986 at age 92.

William Head

See also

AWPD/1 and AWPD-42

References

Copp, DeWitt S. *A Few Great Captains: The Men and Events That Shaped the Development of U.S. Airpower.* Garden City, NY: Doubleday, 1980.

Finney, Robert T. *History of the Air Corps Tactical School, 1920–1940.* Maxwell AFB, AL: Research Studies Institute, USAF Historical Division, Air University, 1955. Reprint: Washington, DC: Air Force History and Museum Program, 1998.

German Air Force (Luftwaffe, World War II)

Germany's revitalized, semisecret air arm that came to dominate the skies over Europe during the early blitzkriegs of World War II. After the Armistice to end World War I, the Al-

Junkers Ju 52/3m aircraft specialized in dropping paratroopers early in the war. (Walter J. Boyne)

lied victors limited Germany to a 100,000-man military. With no more than a token force and with enemies on its borders, Germany quickly established research programs in whatever areas it could—particularly rocketry—deemed militarily insignificant by the victors; it also established clandestine programs in areas prohibited by treaty. German civilian aviation was preeminent in Europe during the interwar years.

With the assumption of power by Adolf Hitler in the mid-1930s, remilitarization began in earnest. To create a viable air force, Germany had to develop synthetic fuels, establish a military organization from scratch, and find money to pay for multiple simultaneous programs. All programs suffered from funding shortages, but the Luftwaffe had a strong advocate in Hermann Goering, a World War I hero. Germany then used the Spanish civil war as a testing ground for close air support and other innovative tactics and gained hands-on education for Luftwaffe pilots and commanders.

By 1938, the Germans were more technologically advanced than their enemies in many areas, including the Knickebein blind-bombing system. The German leadership elected to maintain a Luftwaffe of about 5,000 aircraft but did not pursue research and development as they might have done. By 1942, German leaders realized—all too late—that they had fallen behind; they were forced to use updated versions of planes they had used against Poland years before.

Leaders had been deceived by the fact that in the battles of 1939 and 1940 (e.g., Poland, the Low Countries, France, Britain) the Luftwaffe appeared to have the edge, for it won relatively easy victories. But because the Luftwaffe was stretched thin, it fell victim to stagnation and then attrition. The Allies had better resources, more research and development, industrial capacity, manpower, technology, money, leadership, and plans. The Allied forces quickly surpassed the Luftwaffe in sheer numbers and, eventually, technical capability in most areas.

The Luftwaffe met its first defeat at the hands of Air Marshall Sir Hugh Dowding's Fighter Command over Dunkirk during the heroic evacuation of Allied troops in mid-1940. Another defeat was administered in the Battle of Britain—the opening move in a planned German invasion—shortly thereafter. Then by staking everything on the invasion of the Soviet Union, Hitler plunged Germany into a war it could no longer win. As early as 1942, German flight schools were turning out barely enough pilots to replace those lost, even though their training was half the length of Allied training. When it was apparent that Allied airpower was growing at a pace the Luftwaffe could not match, Germany turned to the production of "wonder weapons" as a last-ditch alternative. The resources devoted to the V-1 and V-2 rocket weapons would have been better spent on revamping the German aircraft industry.

When the United States entered the war, it was only a matter of time before Germany lost. By 1944, the Allies possessed long-range fighters to escort their bombers, took command of the air, forced the Luftwaffe to protect German airspace, and were able to control the air over the beaches of Normandy. German night-fighter resistance continued almost unabated through March 1944, but day-fighter resistance was overcome by then.

The Luftwaffe was unable to cope with the massive bombing by day and night, and German industry was forced to disperse. Then, when tactical fighters could roam over Germany, the German transport system collapsed. By the second half of 1944, the Allies could select targets by category—synthetic-fuel plants, for instance—and systematically reduce their capacity to less than 50 percent.

The Luftwaffe's failure to repel the Allied air offensive was costly. Antiaircraft batteries absorbed 10,000 guns that could have been used as airborne antitank weapons, and the half-million artillerists could have been better used in the workforce or at the battle fronts. Battered by the Allied fighter force, the Luftwaffe by June 1944 was reduced to only 1,375 fighters on all fronts. This number was insufficient to hold back the invading Soviet forces in the East or repel the Allied bombers from the West. The Luftwaffe had been bankrupted, thanks in great part to inept leadership. The collapse of the German homeland was inevitable.

John Barnhill

See also
Britain, Battle of; Dunkirk

References
Murray, Williamson. *Strategy for Defeat: The Luftwaffe, 1933–1945.* Maxwell AFB, AL: Air University Press, 1983.

German Air Service (Luftstreitkräfte, World War I)

Germany began organizing an aviation service during the last few years of peace prior to the outbreak of World War I. At the beginning, there were two types of units making up the Luftfahrtruppe (Aviation Troops): the *Feld Flieger-Abteilung* (Field Flying Section), a mobile unit equipped with two-seat aircraft, and the *Festungs Flieger-Abteilung* (Fortress Flying Section), a similar force attached to a fortress. Each unit had six aircraft.

The Festungs Flieger-Abteilung quickly disappeared from the German order of battle, but the Feld Flieger-Abteilung remained, the number expanding over the years, but the mission remaining the provision of the entire range of aviation services.

By 1916, it was clear that the self-contained air force approach in vogue at the beginning of the war was not an efficient way to run military aviation. The situation had been evolving gradually, with such innovations as the spinoff of single-seaters into independent *staffeln* (squadrons) previewing the coming reorganization of units around their intended mission. During the Battle of the Somme, the Luftfahrtruppe was reorganized and became the Luftstreitkräfte (Air Service) under the command of a former cavalry officer, General Ernst von Hoeppner.

Two other features distinguish the German service from that of the Allies; one was political, the other doctrinal. On the political level, Germany was made up previously independent and still semiautonomous states, and the larger of those other entities had to be accommodated by the creation of their own units. Thus, the years 1917 and 1918 saw the creation of Bavarian, Saxon, and Württemburg units.

On the doctrinal level, the Germans adopted a defensive posture. Having to conserve assets in consideration of a two-front war and the British blockade, such a policy made sense. Occasionally, it cost opportunities—notably at Verdun, where an aggressive approach against the *voie sacre* (sacred road) may have proven a tactical advantage.

The Luftstreitkräfte continued as an effective force until the end of the war despite the fuel and equipment shortages that plagued its final months.

James Streckfuss

References
Hoeppner, Ernst von. *Germany's War in the Air.* Nashville, TN: Battery Press, 1994.
Kilduff, Peter. *Germany's First Air Force.* London: Arms and Armour Press, 1990.

German Aircraft Development and Production, Post–World War II

In 1945, the victorious Allies dismantled and banned Germany's ability to produce civil and military aircraft as well as other implements of war, presumably for all time. By 1955, however, the Cold War had ushered in a radical change. Two separate German states now existed, and each had been drawn into the orbits of the two remaining superpowers: the Soviet Union and the United States. The Federal Republic of Germany (West Germany) voluntarily joined NATO; the German Democratic Republic (communist East Germany) entered the Warsaw Pact.

In West Germany, the establishment of armed forces meant the resumption of aircraft production. Initially (and for many years thereafter), the resurrected Luftwaffe operated primarily U.S. aircraft. These included the Republic F-84F Thunderstreak fighter-bomber, the Luftwaffe's first jet. Following closely were North American F-86K Sabres and, in the 1960s, Lockheed F-104G Starfighters and McDonnell F-4s and later F-4Fs.

From the beginning, however, indigenous production also contributed to the Luftwaffe's strength. Given sharply rising costs of development, many of the domestically produced aircraft came from international consortia involving German firms. For example, German-French programs produced the Nord Noratlas in the 1950s and, a bit later, the Nord-MBB C-160 Transall (in 2000 only on the verge of replacement). These hard-working twin-engine transports supplied airlift for infantry, paratroops, and cargo. A complementary German-Italian program produced the nimble Aeritalia (FIAT) G91 ground attack/reconnaissance jet, which resembled a scaled-down version of the F-86K.

Another program involving the veteran German manufacturer Dornier and the French company Dassault resulted in the Alpha Jet. This nimble trainer/ground attack fighter did yeoman's service in the Luftwaffe. In more recent years, a European consortium with heavy German participation, Panavia, has produced the very successful and combat-tested Tornado in several variants. They include the Tornado ADV (Air Defense Variant), the terrain-following Tornado IDS (Interdictor/Strike; Gr.Mk.I), and the German Tornado ECR, which is used for wild-weasel missions.

A next-generation replacement for the Tornado is yet another consortium-produced aircraft, the Typhoon. Produced by Eurofighter GmbH, which includes Germany's leading aerospace manufacturer, DASA, the Typhoon first flew in 1994.The Luftwaffe confidently expects the Typhoon to be Europe's leading air superiority/strike aircraft as it enters operational service.

The aerial war over Kosovo in 1999 demonstrated several of Germany's—and Europe's—military deficiencies. These included a lack of airlift, aerial refueling, and command and control aircraft. In part to redress the balance, Airbus Industrie, which includes major German participation, has established the Airbus Military Company to produce the A-400M, a four-engine turboprop-driven tactical transport. The A-400M will replace the Luftwaffe's remaining C-160 Transalls and complement the A310–304 multirole twinjet airlifters already in service. In addition, DASA has joined AirTanker, a new European company bidding to produce the Future Strategic Tanker Aircraft (FSTA). Aircraft such as the FSTA and A-400M will, it is hoped, decrease future German (and European) dependence on combat support elements of the U.S. Air Force.

D. R. Dorondo

References

Aircraft of the World: The Complete Guide. Groups 4, 5, and 6. Pittsburgh, PA: International Masters, 1997–1998.

German Imperial Naval Air Service (World War I)

The Imperial German Navy took an early interest in aviation. The Danzig Imperial Dockyard began seaplane research in early 1911 on orders from Grossadmiral Alfred von Tirpitz and soon issued broad specifications, initially for amphibians. Domestic industry responded poorly, at first forcing purchase of foreign machines, but later supplied indigenous aircraft.

When World War I started, the navy operated only nine seaplanes and a single airship, deployed to protect approaches from the North Sea and the Baltic, but soon expanded its air arm. Grossadmiral Prince Heinrich, the kaiser's younger brother and an ardent naval-aviation advocate, took command of forces in the Baltic. There he aggressively used aviation, deploying seaplanes with the fleet for forward reconnaissance, torpedo attack, and aerial minelaying.

North Sea commanders also appreciated aviation's value. Airships significantly enhanced the fleet's reconnaissance capabilities. Senior commanders viewed seaplanes as important not only as scouts but also for offensive operations and antisubmarine patrol. The Zeebrugge air station soon became a key base for German offensive and defensive operations in the North Sea.

The navy generally eschewed flying boats, although Dornier developed some very large examples late in the war. Industry supplied rugged patrol seaplanes, large twin-engine torpedo carriers, single-seat fighters, and the excellent Hansa Brandenburg two-seater biplane and monoplane fighters that were serious threats to patrolling British airships and flying boats, submarines, and small craft. By war's end, the German navy deployed more than 1,100 seaplanes at 32 naval air stations along the coastlines of the Central Powers.

The navy also built up a substantial land-based front-line force in Flanders to defend its bases, expand reconnaissance coverage of the English Channel, and eventually support naval infantry at the front. By late 1918, it deployed more than 100 modern landplanes, roughly divided between single-seat fighters of the Marinefeldgeschwader (Marine Field

Squadron) and two-seaters in reconnaissance and ground support units.

During World War I, the Imperial German Naval Air Service grew from nine seaplanes to more than 1,500 aircraft (excluding airships). Aircrew increased from 20 officer pilots to more than 2,100 officers and men supported by a further 14,000 ground personnel (another 6,000 officers and men served with 16 airships). The service significantly enhanced the fleet's capabilities throughout the conflict. After the air service demobilized (1919–1920), Germany's navy never again operated its own organic air arm.

Paul E. Fontenoy

See also
Aircraft Carriers, Development of; Airships; Dornier Aircraft; German Naval Airship Division; Gotha Aircraft; Heinkel Aircraft; Zeppelin, Ferdinand von

References
Franks, Norman L.R., Frank W. Bailey, and Russell Guest. *Above the Lines: The Aces and Fighter Units of the German Air Service, Naval Air Service, and Flanders Marine Corps, 1914–1918.* London: Grub Street, 1993.
Imrie, Alex, *German Naval Air Service.* London: Arms and Armour Press, 1989.
Layman, R. D. *Naval Aviation in the First World War: Its Impact and Influence.* Annapolis, MD: Naval Institute Press, 1996.
Morrow, John H. Jr. *Building German Air Power, 1909–1914.* Knoxville: University of Tennessee Press, 1976.

German Naval Airship Division

Created in 1912 to exploit a new weapon: the rigid airship. The brainchild of Ferdinand von Zeppelin, these giant lighter-than-air craft served two purposes. The more valuable, though less colorful, task performed by airships was fleet reconnaissance. The long endurance of airships provided an uninterrupted aerial platform and a third dimension to naval operations, lengthening the range of view to unprecedented distances.

The other mission was the bombing of England. This campaign, the obsession of Commander Peter Strasser, counts as history's first attempt at strategic bombing. Results achieved were less than impressive, a final accounting documenting slightly more than £1.5 million in damage and minimal loss of life. The losses incurred and the expense of the Zeppelins led to their being abandoned as a primary weapon and replaced by large bombing aircraft. Zeppelins conducted almost 1,000 reconnaissance missions over the North Sea in support of the Imperial German Navy.

A vital lesson that was not learned from the failure of the bombing—by both Zeppelins and aircraft—was that civilian morale rises to the occasion rather than breaking under attack. This hard lesson was learned a second time in the 1940 Battle of Britain.

James Streckfuss

See also
Airships; Balloons; World War I Aviation

References
Raleigh, Sir Walter, and H. A. Jones. *The War in the Air: Being the Story of the Part Played in the Great War by the Royal Air Force.* Oxford: Clarendon Press, 1922–1937.
Robinson, Douglas. *The Zeppelin in Combat.* London: G. T. Foulis, 1962.

German Rocket Development

Both sides used rockets in World War I. Afterward, the Allied victors lost interest, focusing research efforts on tanks, planes, and the other successful weapons from that war. But Germany continued its rocket research, and the Verein für Raumschiffahrt (Society for Space Travel) was established in 1927 in Breslau. The first successful rocket test took place in 1930, with other tests following, but by 1934 the amateur society was defunct. The German army took over rocket testing, consistent with its practice from the 1920s of working illegally with Russia on weapons research. The army sought a better artillery weapon, so the research was in the ordnance department.

In 1932, Wernher von Braun joined army rocket research at Kummersdorf. The first test of a 650-pound/thrust motor fueled with alcohol and liquid oxygen fed into the combustion chamber by nitrogen failed when the engine blew up. Undaunted, von Braun and staff designed the Aggregate 1 (A-1) rocket.

The A-1 was 4.5 feet long with a 1-foot diameter and a takeoff weight of 330 pounds. The engine developed 650 pounds/thrust for 16 seconds. Stabilization was built in as a design factor; the nose of the rocket spun, serving as a gyroscope. Before launch, an electric motor revved it to 9,000 rpm, and it ran down during flight. The first three A-1 tests at Kummersdorf failed.

Even before the first A-1 test, the A-2 was designed with the same 650-pound/thrust engine but separate fuel and liquid oxygen tanks with a gyroscope in the middle close to the rocket's center of gravity. A-2 tests relocated from Kummersdorf to preserve secrecy (by this time the Nazis were in power and suppressing information and amateurs). Von Braun's 1934 Ph.D. thesis called his work "combustion experiments."

In December 1934, two A-2s were launched successfully

at Borkum (and were named *Max* and *Moritz,* after the Katzenjammer Kids) from a 40-foot launch platform. They attained 1.4 miles of altitude and landed, with a parachute assist, approximately 800 meters from the launch point. When the army asked him about the weapon potential of the A-2, von Braun noted that conventional artillery had the same capability.

In March 1935, Hitler repudiated the Versailles Treaty and the buildup was on, including at Kummersdorf (renamed Experimental Station West). The A-3 was on the drawing board, and the Army Ordnance Office began a cooperative effort with the Luftwaffe that eventuated in the center at Peenemünde.

Peenemünde was in northern Usedom. Its conversion to a test center began in 1936. By 1937, the Kummersdorf contingent could relocate except for engines, which remained at Kummersdorf until 1940. Peenemünde provided a clear 300-kilometer firing range, harbors, and all other required facilities. Most noteworthy was its supersonic wind tunnel, which initially was smaller than the one at Aachen that tested up to Mach 3.3. By 1942, the capability of the wind tunnel at Peenemünde exceeded Mach 4.4, the best in the world until after the war. Peenemünde also had a small rocket production facility.

The A-3 was 21 feet, 8 inches long and 28 inches in diameter; its takeoff weigh was 1,650 pounds. Inside the nose was a telemetry package to measure heat and pressure in flight. There was a guidance system to control attitude, a liquid oxygen tank and nitrogen reservoir, and a parachute container. In the rear was the 6-foot-long motor, encased in the alcohol tank, with 1.5 tons/thrust. The rocket had four fins and jet vanes in the nozzle for better early-flight control and in the thin upper atmosphere, where fins were ineffective.

The A-3 took nearly two years to build because of difficulties developing a guidance system. A combination of four gyroscopes spinning at 20,000 rpm to control yaw and pitch helped keep the rocket level. The 1937 test on the island of Greifswalder Oie failed because the gyro system could not control beyond 30 degrees and could not correct the A-3's tendency to turn into the wind. Because the A-3 had not burned or exploded, the group felt confident enough to develop a small A-5 to refine the new technologies. The A-4 was the designation for the military rocket that became the V-2.

John Barnhill

References

Johnson, David. *V-1/V-2: Hitler's Vengeance on London.* New York: Stein and Day, 1981.

King, Benjamin, and Timothy J. Kutta. *Impact: The History of Germany's V-Weapons in World War II.* Rockville Centre, NY: Sarpedon, 1998.

Germany and World War II Air Battles (1940–1945)

Greatest aerial campaign in history, involving the air forces of the United States, Great Britain, Germany, and the Soviet Union. As early as 1939–1940, Royal Air Force units executed reconnaissance and leaflet-dropping raids over Hitler's Reich. The RAF began more serious operations even as the Luftwaffe blitzed the home islands. On the night of 15–16 May 1940, RAF bombers struck targets in the Ruhr Valley. These operations culminated in raids on Berlin itself in August. Flown primarily by Vickers Wellington, Armstrong Whitworth Whitley, and Handley Page Hampden twin-engine machines, the raids caused little actual damage but did help boost British morale and heralded things to come.

These early British attacks were hampered by several factors. The RAF lacked long-range escort fighters; the bombers had insufficient defensive firepower; bombsights were inaccurate, as was navigation; and the bomb-carrying capacity was low. These inadequacies forced RAF Bomber Command to turn to area-bombing, or city-busting. The subsequent introduction of four-engine Handley Page Halifax and Avro Lancaster heavy bombers and the leadership of Sir Arthur "Bomber" Harris enabled Bomber Command to overcome some of these handicaps.

These developments occurred in the face of a German air force whose greatest strength in interceptors would not be reached until the summer of 1944. The German fighter force would include some formidable aircraft, including the Messerschmitt Bf 109, 110, and 410, the Focke-Wulf Fw 190, and a handful of Messerschmitt Me 262 jets late in the war.

Meanwhile, Bomber Command's efforts slowly intensified through 1941. Bremen, Hamburg, and Kiel were bombed, in part because they were easily located at night. As for specific targets, the RAF concentrated first on oil production facilities and, later, rail centers in the Ruhr. The Luftwaffe, however, countered with the introduction of the Liechtenstein air-to-air radar system, and Bomber Command's losses increased.

New equipment, such as the Gee radar system, allowed relatively accurate all-weather bombing by night, and losses temporarily fell. Essen, Lübeck, and Rostock were all successfully attacked in March and April 1942. On 30–31 May, the RAF's first 1,000-plane raid took place, made possible by Harris's scraping together every available aircraft, including those from training units. Cologne was heavily bombed, and only 41 bombers were lost, a manageable rate of 3.8 percent. This raid's size surprised the Germans and equally heartened the British.

More important, it gave Bomber Command a new lease

on life just as the U.S. Eighth Air Force became active against Germany from bases in the United Kingdom. The consequent accretion of Allied strength, coupled with the Luftwaffe's growing commitments in North Africa, over the Mediterranean, and in Russia, would eat into the latter's reservoir of aircrews, the training establishment, and, eventually, the production of aircraft. The initiation of the Allies' Combined Bombing Offensive took shape at the Casablanca Conference in January 1943.

It was first manifested in the RAF's Battle of the Ruhr. On 5 March, 442 heavy bombers attacked Essen. Twin-engine de Havilland Mosquitos equipped with Oboe direction-finding radar led the way. These were the first of more than 18,500 sorties flown against targets in the Ruhr by the termination date of 14 July. Of the bombers dispatched, 872 failed to return; another 2,126 suffered damage.

In the meantime, U.S. Eighth Air Force bombers made their first daylight raid on Germany on 27 January 1943. Of 91 bombers dispatched, 55 Boeing B-17 Flying Fortresses attacked the German navy's U-boat facilities at Wilhelmshaven. Others bombed Emden. Consolidated B-24 Liberators accompanying the mission, unable to find their targets due to weather, returned to base with their bombs. No aircraft were lost. It seemed an auspicious first use of heavily armed four-engine daylight raiders over Germany.

Before 1943, the Luftwaffe's principal task lay in devising effective night-fighting techniques to counter British operations. This was largely accomplished through the development of radar-directed flak batteries and searchlights using two variants of a system called Würzburg. This system could also be used for vectoring night-fighters to their targets. A subsequent, complementary device (Freya) came to be used for early warning. The resulting combined system, Himmelbett, was eventually arranged in a north-to-south line through northwestern Germany and the Low Countries to provide the so-called Kammhuber Line (named after Major General Josef Kammhuber, its principal advocate).

Although attacks by Bomber Command and the Eight Air Force continued almost daily thereafter, two high points were reached in the summer and fall of 1943. In the first instance, combined daytime and nighttime assaults on Hamburg in late July resulted in the first-ever devastation of a city by firestorm. Unusually good weather and the use of radar-jamming foil strips (Window, or chaff) allowed Allied bombers to swamp the Germans' defenses and burn out the heart of the city. Some 50,000 Germans were killed, another 40,000 injured, and yet another 1 million driven out. But that same month also saw the Luftwaffe's first use of a new aerial weapon. On 28 July, interceptors fired 210mm air-to-air rockets into Eighth Air Force bomber formations, knocking three B-17s from the sky. German night-fighters also began to overcome the RAF's radar-jamming efforts as the summer waned.

The second high point witnessed the Eighth Air Force's attacks on ball-bearing factories at Schweinfurt and the Messerschmitt aircraft plant at Regensburg. In two separate efforts in August and October 1943, the USAAF lost 120 heavy bombers. Hundreds of others were damaged, and thousands of air crewmen were killed and wounded. Though U.S. fighter escorts had first entered German airspace in July, deep-penetration raids were flown without cover due to the escorts' limited combat radius. Appalling losses to the bombers were the result. Despite the activation of the USAAF's Fifteenth Air Force in Italy in November (for attacks on southern Germany, Austria, and the Balkans), the Allies appeared to lose the initiative in the air war as 1943 drew to a close.

In part to offset any resulting ill effects, Bomber Command launched the Battle of Berlin on the night of 18 November 1943. As over Hamburg, the RAF bombed at night while the Eighth Air Force eventually attacked by day, its first raid over the city occurring on 4 March 1944. U.S. bombers assaulted the Reich capital three more times that month, flying 1,700 sorties and being accompanied now by long-range escort fighters, most notably North American P-51 Mustangs. Although reduced in strength, the Luftwaffe could still fight back. On 6 March, for example, 69 U.S. bombers were lost to flak and interceptors. Although Berlin was badly damaged, the destruction did not cost Germany the war, as planners (especially British planners) had assumed it would. Nevertheless, by early 1944 the Luftwaffe had stationed 75 percent of its fighter strength in the West within Germany proper as a result of the bombing campaign. That disposition helped denude fighter forces from other theaters, despite an actual increase in total German fighter strength through the summer of that year.

The USAAF's BIG WEEK attacks of 20–27 February 1944 broke the back of the Luftwaffe fighter arm. Combined with the raids on Berlin and other cities, these attacks by Allied bombers and escorts cost the Luftwaffe approximately 1,000 pilots from January to April. This critical loss could not be overcome. Bomber production ceased and the Luftwaffe stripped its remaining fighter strength to skeletal remnants on all fronts to place 1,260 of an available 1,975 remaining fighters and fighter-bombers in the home-defense role as 1944 progressed. The turn of the year 1944–1945 saw the Luftwaffe hounded from every quarter.

The Luftwaffe's last offensive action, Operation BODENPLATTE (1 January 1945) achieved tactical surprise at enormous cost in attacks on Allied airfields across the Low Countries and northeastern France. Subsequent engagements over the Remagen bridgehead in March and Bavaria in April saw the frequent appearance of the Me 262 as well as the Arado Ar 234 Blitz, the world's first operational jet bomber. But even remarkable aircraft like these proved too little, too late to prevent the ultimate demise of Germany and the Luftwaffe.

D. R. Dorondo

See also

Berlin Air Battles; German Air Force (Luftwaffe); Hamburg Bombing Campaign; Kammhuber, Josef; Royal Flying Corps/Royal Naval Air Service/Royal Air Force

References

Craven, Wesley, and James Lea Cate. *The Army Air Forces in World War II, Volume 3: Europe: ARGUMENT to V-E Day, January 1944 to May 1945.* Washington, DC: Office of Air Force History, 1983.

Frankland, Noble. *Bomber Offensive: The Devastation of Europe.* In Barrie Pitt, ed., *Ballantine's Illustrated History of World War II.* New York: Ballantine Books, 1971.

Gibson, Guy P. (1918–1944)

RAF commander. Guy Penrose Gibson was born in Simla, India, on 12 September 1918; he joined the RAF in August 1936.

During a successful flying career with the RAF, Wing Commander Gibson was quickly recognized to be an outstanding operational pilot and leader. He served with conspicuously successful results, mainly as a nighttime bomber pilot. Gibson is best known for commanding the famous No. 617 Squadron—the Dam Busters—formed for special tasks. Under his inspiring leadership, this squadron executed one of the most devastating attacks of World War II: the breaching of the Möhne and Eder dams. During the attack Gibson, showing leadership, determination, and valor of the highest order, flew a Lancaster bomber to within 50 feet of the water in order to deliver the bomb precisely. Gibson then circled very low for 30 minutes to draw enemy fire, thus permitting his squadron a free run to the target. Gibson received the Victoria Cross in 28 May 1943.

On 19 September 1944, at age 26, Gibson flew out of Woodhall Spa on a bombing mission in a Mosquito from No. 627 Squadron. After completing the bombing raid, Gibson went on to check antiaircraft positions and his Mosquito crashed, killing himself and his navigator, Squadron Leader J. B. Warwick. Gibson is buried at Steenbergen-en-Kruisland, the Netherlands.

Albert Atkins

References

Nesbit, Roy C. *An Illustrated History of the RAF.* London: Colour Liberty, 1996.

Gilbert Islands

Air operations in the Central Pacific to prepare for and support U.S. Marine amphibious invasion in 1943. The Gilberts, taken by the Japanese in early 1942, provided the first step in the Allied offensive in this theater. Throughout the fall of 1943, Allied land-based medium and heavy bombers attacked targets in the Gilberts from bases in the Ellice Islands and farther south. Task Force 50 of six heavy and five lighter carriers, the largest carrier force yet assembled, directly supported the landings and destroyed the remaining Japanese air forces on the islands. They also struck Japanese bases in the Marshalls, suppressing support from those islands. Another carrier task force raided air bases in the Solomons, preventing reinforcement from that theater.

U.S. Marines landed on Tarawa (Betio) and Makin on 20 November 1943 and took the islands with heavy casualties after three days of difficult fighting (Operation GALVANIC). Japanese attempts at air support from bases in the Marshalls were unsuccessful. There were no Allied naval losses to Japanese aircraft, although a Japanese submarine torpedoed and sank the escort carrier *Liscombe Bay.*

The Allied victory in the Gilberts provided the first solid validation of the ability of mobile carrier-based airpower to concentrate and overwhelm local land-based air forces.

Frank E. Watson

References

Morison, Samuel Eliot. *United States Naval Operations in World War II, Volume 3: The Aleutians, Gilberts, and Marshalls.* Boston: Little, Brown, 1951.

Global Navigation Satellite Systems (GNSS)

A system employing one or more satellite constellations for the purposes of navigation. The requirement for a civil GNSS is rooted in the aviation community's worldwide need for precise navigation and a more efficient aircraft surveillance system.

Two GNSS constellations exist today: the Global Positioning System (GPS), built and maintained by the United States; and Russia's Global Navigation Satellite System (GLONASS). Eurocontrol, the European Union's civil aviation authority, made use of both the Russian and U.S. systems by employing geosynchronous satellites to form a third hybrid system: the European Global Navigation Overlay System (EGNOS). More recently, the European Space Agency, the European Community, and Eurocontrol have formed the Tripartite Group for the purposes of building an independent European GNSS. Named Galileo, this planned system will consist of both geostationary (GEO) and middle-earth (MEO) orbiting satellites owned and operated by the European Union.

GPS

The concept of a worldwide satellite navigation system for the United States began in the early 1960s with three governmental organizations: the National Aeronautics and Space Administration, the Department of Defense, and the Department of Transportation. The first attempt, Transit, became operational in 1964; however, it was limited to low dynamic, or slow-moving, transportation platforms such as ships. The Navy began its own program, Timation, to improve the concept of space-based terrestrial navigation. The Air Force, building on the Timation and Transit programs, began experimenting with a satellite system it named System 621B. In 1969, the secretary of defense established the Defense Navigation Satellite System (DNSS). DNSS created a single joint-use satellite system—NAVSTAR GPS—managed by the Joint Program Office (JPO).

The JPO maintains the current GPS constellation, ground-control equipment, satellite production, and maintenance functions; policy decisions are made by the Interagency GPS Executive Board formed 28 March 1996.

GLONASS

Russia's Scientific Production Association of Applied Mechanics began development of GLONASS under the auspices of Russia's Ministry of Defense in the mid-1970s. The system, originally designed for the navy, was applied to other military and civilian aviation missions. Within the Military Space Forces, the State Department of Space Means maintains and manages all aspects of the GLONASS system.

The first three satellites were launched on the same SL-12 Proton rocket from Kazakhstan on 12 October 1982. The system has yet to reach its planned constellation of 24 satellites due to the breakup of the Soviet Union and subsequent economic crises.

EGNOS

A feasibility study by the European Space Agency, Inmarsat, and the French National Center for Space Studies led to testing a concept using GEO satellites, such as INMARSAT-3, to augment both the GPS and GLONASS constellations. Testing proved the soundness of this concept, and INMARSAT began procurement of INMARSAT-3 satellites with the required navigation packages in 1989.

GNSS Navigation Fundamentals

GNSS satellites provide position, altitude, and velocity by utilizing time-of-arrival (TOA) and ranging concepts. The distance between the satellite and receiver is determined by measuring the elapsed time between transmission to receipt of the signal. Accurate positioning using the TOA concept requires that at least three satellites be in view, e.g., accessible by the receiver during use.

Both the GLONASS and GPS systems, originally built for military use, were designed with selective availability (SA) and antispoofing capabilities. SA denied precise navigational accuracy to anyone other than the military. However, both Russia and the United States have since ended SA, and both systems' precise positioning service is available for use by anyone with the appropriate receiver. Additionally, the Federal Aviation Administration has been developing terrestrially based Wide Area Augmentation Systems and Local Area Augmentation Systems to overcome inherent GPS inaccuracies and increase precision for aviation applications. The Europeans, however, have looked to a GEO satellite overlay system to provide increased accuracy.

Randy Johnson

References

European Space Agency. "The European Global Navigation Overlay System and Galileo." Available online at http://www.esa.int/navigation/index.html.

Kaplan, Elliot D., ed. *Understanding GPS: Principles and Application.* Boston: Artech House, 1996.

Russian Space Science Internet [Ministry of Defense of the Russian Federation, Scientific Information Coordination Center (KNITS)]. "The Russian Global Navigation Satellite System." Available online at http://www.rssi.ru/SFCSIC/SFCSIC_main.html.

Gloster Aircraft

British aircraft manufacturer. Originally named the Gloucestershire Aircraft Company, the more marketable name "Gloster" came into use in 1926. The first vestige of the company had appeared in 1917 and built aircraft under license for the war effort.

Glosters suffered with others from the Great Depression, although it stayed in business and began to resume aircraft production with the Grebe in 1923. This was followed by the Gamecock, Gauntlet, and the famous Gladiator biplane fighter.

Gloster Aircraft became part of the Hawker-Siddeley Group in 1935, although it was to retain its individual identity. Throughout World War II, the company built many Hawker products before building the first jet-powered aircraft in the United Kingdom. The Pioneer was soon followed by the Meteor fighter. Supplied to the RAF, the Fleet Air Arm, and numerous overseas air forces, the Meteor was made in 14 different versions before production ceased.

The Gloster Meteor became a work horse for the RAF, serving many test purposes, including inflight refueling. (Walter J. Boyne)

Gloster was also the first company to address Britain's lack of a decent nighttime/all-weather fighter with the Javelin two-seater. The first flight of the prototype Javelin was undertaken in November 1951, with the type entering RAF service in 1956. The company identity finally disappeared in 1965 when it was fully integrated into the Hawker-Siddeley Group.

Kev Darling

References

James, Derek N. *Gloster Aircraft Since 1917.* London: Putnam, 1987.

Gloster E.28/39 (G.40) Pioneer

The first gas turbine/turbojet–powered airplane to be designed, developed, and flown in Great Britain. After its initial static engine runs and taxi tests, RAF Flight Lieutenant Philip E. G. "Jerry" Sayer successfully took the Pioneer into the air for the first time on 15 May 1941. He performed speed runs at 2,500 and 4,000 feet during the 17-minute test hop at Hucclecote, hitting a top speed of 380 mph. Known as "Squirt," the radical plane had been developed under a strict RAF requirement (designated E.28/39), which called for a single-engine prototype to prove the feasibility of jet propulsion for a fighter-type aircraft. It was powered by a single Power Jets Incorporated 850-pound/thrust W.1 turbojet engine that was closely based upon a design patented by RAF Air Commodore Frank Whittle.

The chief of the United States Army Air Corps, General Henry H. "Hap" Arnold, set the wheels in motion for America to have its own jet-powered airplane. The E.28/39 paved the way for Gloster Aircraft to create Britain's first operational jet-powered fighter plane: the Gloster Meteor. It may be seen today at the Science Museum in London.

Steve Pace

References

James, Derek N. *Gloster Aircraft Since 1917.* London: Putnam, 1987.

Gloster Meteor

Britain's first operational jet-powered fighter. The design of the Meteor began in 1940. A twin-engine layout was chosen due to the low power output of the available centrifugal jet engines. An initial batch of eight development aircraft was ordered, the first flying in March 1943. By this time an extended order for 100 production aircraft had already been placed.

First service deliveries to the RAF took place in July 1944 to equip No. 616 Squadron. Based at Manston, the Meteors joined the Tempests, Mustangs, and Spitfires of Air Defence forces in combating the menace of the V-1 flying bomb. Further developments of the Meteor resulted in the appearance of the Meteor III and Meteor IV, both of which featured improved engines as their main area of improvement. It was a clipped-wing Meteor IV that set a new world air speed record of 606 mph on 7 November 1945.

These early aircraft were followed by the definitive Meteor day-fighter: the F.8. More than 1,000 of this variant were delivered and stayed in RAF service until the final aircraft was retired in 1977. Two other single-seat versions were built: the FR.9, based on the F.8 fighter, and the PR.10, which owed more to the F.4 but with improved engines. The FR.9 was intended for low-level usage while the PR.10 replaced the reconnaissance versions of the Spitfire and Mosquito. The Meteor T.7 was the trainer version.

The final development of the Meteor married the center section and twin cockpit of the Meteor T.7 to the tail section of the F.8. The outer wing panels were borrowed from the earlier Meteor III, and the nose grew even more elongated with each mark. Built by Armstrong Whitworth Aircraft, the Meteor night-fighter encompassed four versions (Mks.11–14).

Meteors found many new roles, including target tug and navigation training tasks. The Fleet Air Arm operated the T.7 and the TT.20. Prior to settling upon the use of the Meteor for secondary tasks, the Fleet Air Arm had operated a small quantity of navalized Meteor IIIs.

As the first jet fighter to enter regular squadron service, the Meteor also attracted the attention of many foreign air forces. One of these was the Royal Australian Air Force, whose aircraft became embroiled in the Korean War. Other operators included Belgium and Holland in Europe; in Latin America, Brazil and Ecuador were among those to operate the type.

Kev Darling

References

Bond, Steven J. *Meteor Gloster's First Jet Fighter.* Leicester, UK: Midland Counties, 1983.

Gnôme/Gnôme-Rhône Rotary Engines

There were two major types of aircraft engines in World War I, serving two purposes. The water-cooled inline engine powered aircraft designed for missions that allowed time for advance preparation; the air-cooled rotary engine was designed for aircraft that had to be off the ground in a hurry. Gnôme-Rhône manufactured air-cooled rotary engines.

The rotary differed from inlines in that its cylinders spun with the propeller and its crankshaft remained stationery. Early versions also lacked a throttle so that it always ran either full-on or full-off.

Gnôme-Rhône products powered the entire range of Allied rotary-engine aircraft, including Nieuports, Sopwiths, and Caudrons. They also occasionally equipped German aircraft. The Fokker triplane, for example, which normally used a copy of the French LeRhône rotary engine, Oberursel, is reported to have sometimes been fitted with captured Allied engines. This occurred most often in the last months of the war, when the Allied blockade was making supply problems increasingly severe in Germany. Such hardships prompted German ace Joseph Jacobs to offer a case of champagne to soldiers who brought him a captured rotary.

Rotaries were limited in their development because of the torque effect of the mass of rotating cylinders. They reached their peak during World War I and disappeared from military inventories as technology progressed in the 1920s.

James Streckfuss

References

Gunston, Bill. *World Encyclopedia of Aircraft Engines.* London: Patrick Stephens, 1986.

Goddard, Robert H. (1882–1945)

Father of U.S. rocketry and inventor of the liquid-fuel rocket. Born in Worcester, Massachusetts, in 1882, as a youth Robert H. Goddard suffered from tuberculosis. Enforced rest gave the young man time to daydream and read science-fiction works by Jules Verne and H. G. Wells. One daydream about spaceflight proved so vivid that Goddard noted the date, 19 October 1899, in his diary and celebrated "Anniversary Day" thereafter. Four years behind his contemporaries when he entered Worcester Polytechnic Institute in 1904, he studied physics and tested solid-fuel rockets. After graduation in 1908, Goddard earned an M.A. and Ph.D. in physics from nearby Clark University. He completed a postgraduate fellowship at Princeton and then returned to Clark, where he held various academic ranks and positions for the next three decades.

As a faculty member, Goddard continued testing rockets, building stronger combustion chambers, and improving thermal efficiency. He patented (1914) the multistage rocket and proved experimentally rocket thrust in a vacuum (1915). The Smithsonian Institution awarded him a grant in support of his research. His experiments during World War I were also funded by the U.S. military. The latter resulted in a rocket field weapon, precursor to the bazooka.

Goddard's 1919 Smithsonian report, "A Method of Reaching Extreme Altitudes," established his preeminence in the field. Shortly after its publication, he began experiments using liquid fuels as propellants. In 1924, he married Esther C. Kisk, who helped document his accomplishments via home movies. At his aunt's farm outside Worcester, Goddard launched the first liquid-fuel rocket on 16 March 1926. Subsequent tests drew complaints from neighbors and a desist order in 1929 from the local fire marshal.

National notoriety over the issue attracted the attention of Charles A. Lindbergh, who visited and then supported Goddard. Through Lindbergh, the rocket scientist gained grants (1930–1932; 1934–1942) from the Daniel and Florence Guggenheim Foundation to conduct research near Roswell, New Mexico. In this phase of his career, Goddard created pumps for rocket propellants, techniques for using rocket fuel to cool reaction motors, and guidance systems by employing gyroscopes and deflector vanes. He published a second Smithsonian report, "Liquid-Propellant Rocket Developments," in 1936. During World War II, Goddard served as a consultant to the Curtiss-Wright Corporation and directed research on behalf of the U.S. Navy's Bureau of Aeronautics. The latter contributed to the idea of jet-assisted takeoff (JATO) technology—i.e., rocket power—for aircraft. He died from throat cancer in 1945. In 1960, his widow later sold Goddard's 214 rocket-related patents to the National Aeronautics and Space Administration for $1 million.

James K. Libbey

See also

Bureau of Naval Aeronautics; Curtiss-Wright Corporation; National Aeronautics and Space Administration; United States Navy, and Aviation

References

Goddard, Esther C., ed. *The Papers of Robert H. Goddard: Including the Reports to the Smithsonian Institution and the Daniel and Florence Guggenheim Foundation.* 3 vols. New York: McGraw-Hill, 1970.

Lehman, Milton. *This High Man: The Life of Robert H. Goddard.* New York: Farrar, Straus, 1963.

German ace Hermann Goering in his World War I uniform. (George M. Watson, Jr.)

Goering, Hermann (1893–1946)

Second in importance only to Adolf Hitler in the foundation and government of the Third Reich. Goering was a successful fighter pilot in World War I, winning the Pour le Mérite and succeeding Manfred von Richthofen in command of the world's first multisquadron fighter unit, Jagdgeschwader 1 (1st Fighter Wing).

Goering left Germany after the Armistice and upon his 1922 return quickly fell under the influence of Adolf Hitler. Goering was badly injured in the unsuccessful Munich Beer Hall Putsch of November 1923, resulting in a lifelong addiction to morphine and other painkillers. In 1927, he returned from Italian exile to rejoin Hitler and soon became the Nazis' spokesman to the German upper classes. He was elected to the Reichstag as a delegate from Bavaria and in 1932 was chosen its president. After Hitler became chancellor, Goering was named to his cabinet, becoming the Prussian minister of the interior and national commissioner of aviation. He used the former position to cement the Nazis' hold on power by establishing the Gestapo and the concentration-camp system. His second role gave him responsibility for all aspects of German aviation, and when the Luftwaffe was established in March 1935, he became its commander in chief.

In 1936, Goering became the national commissioner for the four-year plan for the German economy. His ruthlessness, energy, and intelligence enabled him to carry out all of his official roles with a high degree of success while participating in the prewar interservice intrigues that ended when Hitler took over direct command of the Wehrmacht.

The September 1939 invasion of Poland ended Germany's string of bloodless territorial acquisitions, and the subsequent declarations of war by Britain and France took Goering completely by surprise; he had believed Hitler's statement that no major war would begin until 1942. Within four years of its official formation, the Luftwaffe had become one of the world's largest, best-organized, and best-equipped air forces, but one that was extremely thin in infrastructure and talent. Goering took full credit for its early successes, and Hitler promoted him to a unique high rank, *Reichsmarschall,* and awarded him a unique medal, the Great Cross of the Iron Cross.

But in the summer of 1940, the Luftwaffe failed to win the quick air victory over England that Goering had promised Hitler. Goering blamed his pilots for this failure rather than taking responsibility for any deficiencies in planning or equipment, and he withdrew almost completely from active command of "his" Luftwaffe, leaving this to deputy Erhard Milch and to the Luftwaffe Chief of Staff, Hans Jeschonnek. He remained active in his role as commissioner of the German economy during the invasion of the Soviet Union in mid-1941, approving plans to loot Ukraine and Byelorussia, starve most of the Slavic inhabitants of the region, and exterminate its Jews.

In early 1943, Goering's broken promise to the Führer—to maintain the Sixth Army at Stalingrad by aerial supply—cost him the last of his credibility, and he spent most of the last two years of the war at his various estates, hunting and admiring his looted art collection. He made only token appearances at Hitler's staff meetings, and most of his infrequent requests were vetoed or ignored.

In April 1945, after Hitler announced his intention to fight to the last in Berlin, Goering radioed Hitler to inquire if this meant that Goering was to take over the government. An enraged Hitler ordered Goering arrested and stripped him of all his duties, turning the Luftwaffe over to General Robert Ritter von Greim. Goering spent the remaining few days of the war under SS house arrest and turned himself over to the U.S. Army on 8 May.

Goering, the highest-ranking German prisoner of war, became the principal defendant in the 1945–1946 Nuremberg war-crimes trials. Unclouded by drugs for the first time in 20 years, his intelligence and arrogance reasserted themselves, and his aggressive, forceful defense dominated the proceedings. Found guilty and condemned to death by hanging, he committed suicide the night before his scheduled execution by swallowing cyanide.

Donald Caldwell

References

Cooper, M. *The German Air Force, 1933–1945: An Anatomy of Failure.* London: Jane's, 1981.

Corum, J. *The Luftwaffe: Creating the Operational Air War, 1918–1940.* Lawrence: University Press of Kansas, 1997.

Golovanov, Aleksandr (1904–1975)

World War II Soviet bomber commander. Aleksandr Evgenevich Golovanov was born on 7 August 1904 in Nizhnii Novgorod, Russia. Following the 1917 revolution, he fought in the civil war and then worked for the security police. In 1933, he completed pilot training and was assigned to Aeroflot, flying long-range aircraft. He spent the 1930s flying prominent political prisoners between Moscow and the Gulag. In 1941, he organized the first bomber regiment to specialize in long-range night-flying. A favorite of Stalin and a sycophant, he was promoted in March 1942 to general and given command of Long Range Aviation (redesignated the Eighteenth Air Army in December 1944) and reported directly to the Supreme High Command. He held that position until 1947, when he was assigned other command duties. After Stalin's death in 1953, Golovanov was retired from the air force. He died on 22 September 1975.

George M. Mellinger

References

Hardesty, Von. *Red Phoenix: The Rise of Soviet Air Power, 1941–1945.* Washington, DC: Smithsonian Institution Press, 1982.

Kozhevnikov, M. N. *The Command and Staff of the Soviet Army Air Force in the Great Patriotic War, 1941–1945: A Soviet View.* Moscow: All-Union, 1977. Trans. and publ. United States Air Force.

GOMORRAH (1943)

Allied code name for six air raids on Hamburg, Germany, in mid-1943. This city was chosen for its large size, proximity to the coast, easy identification from the air, and production of U-boats, warships, and aircraft.

The first RAF raid on 24 July involved 791 aircraft and employed Window (air-dropped metal strips) to baffle Ger-

Notorious for the raids in which they were used, the German Gotha aircraft were capable of firing on targets below them, taking the British by surprise. (Smithsonian Institution)

man radar. The attack caused severe damage, and only 12 planes were lost. The Americans struck twice in the next two days and suffered heavy losses. Smoke from the RAF raid impeded the U.S. attacks, but the U-boat yards were damaged.

The RAF returned on 26 July with 787 planes. The Pathfinder force (which marked targets for the following bombers) was exceptionally accurate, and 45 percent of the bombs fell within 3 miles of the aimpoint. Most of the bombs were incendiary, and weather conditions resulted in the first firestorm—one huge, extremely hot fire—that killed more than 40,000 people.

The next RAF raid—777 aircraft on 28 July—focused on areas unharmed by the firestorm. The final raid—737 aircraft on 2 August—was scattered by bad weather and achieved little. In total, Bomber Command launched 3,091 sorties, dropped 8,344 tons of bombs, and lost only 100 planes. Hamburg's industries lost 1.8 months of production and 26–27 U-boats.

The Germans were initially panicked but soon adopted new defensive tactics to counter Window. Other German cities of comparable importance were too far inland and too well defended, and thus the Allies could not repeat their Hamburg performance in many other cities in rapid succession.

James D. Perry

References

Levine, Alan J. *The Strategic Bombing of Germany, 1940–1945.* Westport, CT: Praeger, 1992.

Middlebrook, Martin. *The Battle of Hamburg: The Firestorm Raid.* London: Penguin, 1980.

Gotha Bombers

German World War I–era bomber. In the language of World War I, the word "Gotha"—much like the word "Zeppelin"—described not only an aircraft type but also the raids on which Gotha bombers were used. In the summer of 1917, then, it was not sufficient to say the Germans had attacked London; one had to add whether it was a "Zeppelin raid" or a "Gotha raid." As it happened, if the raid involved airplanes, rather than airships, the Germans might have employed any of several types, *Friedrichshafens, Riesenflugzeugen,* or Gothas, but to the British upon whom the bombs fell they were all Gothas.

The principal Gotha types were the G IV and G V, the "G" standing for *Grossflugzeug,* or large aircraft, the German classification for twin-engine bombers. The aircraft spanned 77 feet, 9 inches, were 38 feet, 11 inches long, and stood 14 feet, 1 inch in height. Powered by twin Mercedes engines, they carried a crew of three and a bombload ranging from 660 to 1,100 pounds.

For defense, the Gotha had two Parabellum machine guns, one in the nose, the other in the tail. The fuselage contained a plywood tunnel that allowed the rear gunner to fire his weapon downward at fighters attacking from below, a feature that early British defenders learned about the hard way. But the Gotha's primary protection, at least in its early days, was its high ceiling—21,320 feet—which put it out of reach of the fairly obsolescent types that flew home defense during 1917. When the British began operating more capable aircraft, the Gotha stopped coming during daylight hours and switched to nighttime raids.

Like other attempts at strategic bombing during World War I, the Gotha raids' principal value was not the damage done but the precious resources that defending against them diverted from the front.

In addition to its heavy bombers, Gothaer Waggonfabrik (the Gotha factory) also manufactured a line of seaplanes. The most famous was the WD (water biplane) 14. The WD 14 was originally used as a *wasser doppeldecker* (biplane seaplane) torpedo-bomber, but it suffered from the same deficiency that hampered most World War I experiments with that type. It lacked the power necessary to lift a really effective load off the water. When attacks against enemy shipping proved unimpressive, the WD 14 was modified for use in long-range reconnaissance, its partially faired torpedo bay being converted to a fuel tank.

James Streckfuss

See also
Airships; Independent Bombing Force

References
Gray, Peter, and Owen Thetford. *German Aircraft of the First World War.* London: Putnam, 1962.
Grosz, Peter M. *The Gotha GI-GV.* Leatherhead, UK: Profile, 1966.

Great Britain, Missile Development and Production in

The United Kingdom's guided weapons industry had its origins in a number of early experiments conducted during World War II by various establishments. Progress in this work was assisted by an agreement on the transfer of classified U.S. weapons design data that was the result of the Tizard Mission, which visited Washington in 1940.

The first formal staff requirement for guided weapons issued by the Admiralty Signals Establishment in late 1943 proposed a surface-to-air missile (SAM) that would be guided by a radar beam. The Guided Anti-Aircraft Projectile Committee, an interservice committee, was formed in March 1944 to control and direct antiaircraft projectile research. The operational requirements of the army's Anti-Aircraft Command (later transferred to the RAF) and the Admiralty were sufficiently compatible to be jointly investigated, and preliminary work eventually gave rise to the Sea Slug, Bloodhound, and Thunderbird missile systems. Toward the end of hostilities, the Tizard Agreement was reviewed by the United States and the flow of new scientific information was curtailed. This had a serious effect on the progress of British guided weapons development.

By the end of World War II, the British economy was on the verge of collapse and the sudden termination of Lend-Lease forced an immediate reappraisal of substantial defense spending. The Chiefs of Staff made the assumption that there would be no war for the next 10 years. Yet a number of guided weapons research projects were initiated. In the light of the perceived threat from atomic weapons and the realization that the densely populated country might not be capable of surviving a nuclear conflict, priority was given to Fighter Command and antiaircraft defense. In 1948, the Ministry of Supply decided to curtail research into long-range missiles to concentrate on the defensive missile program.

In January 1950, the U.S.-U.K. transfer of guided weapons technology was formalized by the Burns-Templer Agreement, which provided for the full and frank interchange of military information and guided weapons technology. The first batch of information on new U.S. weapons projects arrived during the second half of 1950, and weapons such as the Terrier II, Hawk, and Sparrow missiles were assessed to determine whether they could be accommodated within the U.K. guided weapons program.

The outbreak of the Korean War in June 1950 came as an unpleasant surprise to strategic planners. A drastic rearmament program was initiated, and the defense budget was approximately doubled, assisted by U.S. aid. Although this was a prudent precaution in the light of international events, it exerted a strain on the economy that would have unfortunate consequences before the end of the decade.

In 1955, Sir Anthony Eden initiated a wide-ranging review of defense strategy with a view toward reducing defense spending. Duncan Sandys continued the review through 1957, when a famous white paper on defense was published. It placed great emphasis on the nuclear deterrent, initially delivered by V-bombers and later by the Blue Streak missile fired from underground silos. V-bomber bases were to be protected initially by fighter defenses and later solely by a surface-to-air missiles system. This doctrine was discredited within a few years as it became clear that Britain could not afford to pay for the research and technology necessary to make the deterrent sufficiently safe from attack.

In the late 1950s, the projects that had been initiated in the 1940s began to enter service. The Fairey Fireflash was the first air-to-air guided weapon to be deployed by the RAF, albeit on a very limited scale in August 1957. The Fireflash was a radar beam–rider and had a limited capability against piston-engine bombers.

The first fully operational guided weapon to be deployed was the Bristol Bloodhound SAM, in 1958. It used semiactive Doppler radar guidance and was typically deployed with four mobile launchers controlled by target-illuminating radar. An improved Bloodhound Mk.II entered service in 1964. The Thunderbird SAM debuted with the British army in 1960 and had a similar performance to the Bloodhound.

The first effective air-to-air missile was the de Havilland Firestreak. It was a rear-aspect weapon and was deployed by the Royal Navy and RAF in August 1958. The later Red Top was based on the Firestreak Mk.IV. It was faster, had a longer range, and was capable of all-aspect homing against supersonic targets. It entered service in 1964.

The Armstrong-Whitworth Sea Slug was a naval SAM. Guidance was by radar beam, and it had solid fuel strap-on boosters and a solid fuel sustainer. It entered service in 1962 aboard County-class destroyers after a protracted development period.

The Avro Blue Steel nuclear missile entered service in December 1962 and was carried by Vulcan and Victor V-bombers. It was designed to deliver a nuclear warhead to a target 100 miles from launch using inertial guidance.

The de Havilland Blue Streak was intended to be an intermediate-range ballistic missile. Development relied heavily on U.S. assistance, as the design was based on the Atlas. Following extreme pressure from the treasury, the Blue Streak program was canceled in April 1960 in favor of the U.S. Skybolt missile (which was subsequently canceled by U.S. Defense Secretary Robert McNamara in November 1962).

In 1977, a long period of industrial amalgamation concluded with the formation of British Aerospace (BAe), a large entity that included every remaining British aerospace company with the exception of Short.

The BAe Skyflash missile was the only successful radar-guided air-to-air missile to enter service in the twentieth century and was an adaptation of the Raytheon AIM-7E2 Sparrow with a new monopulse semiactive seeker. It entered service with the RAF in 1980.

Many other missile systems were developed and entered service between the late 1960s and 1980s, including the Sea Dart naval SAM (1967), the Sea Wolf naval SAM (1979), the land-based point-defense Rapier (1970), and the antiship Sea Skua (1982). All of these weapons were used during the Falklands War of 1982 with reasonable success.

In 1996, BAe Dynamics and Matra Defense joined forces to create a new defense company. Matra BAe Dynamics has an extensive and very capable product portfolio and research capability and at the turn of the century is developing the Storm Shadow conventional stand-off missile and the Meteor beyond-visual-range air-to-air missile for the RAF.

Andy Blackburn

See also

Missiles, Air-to-Air; Missiles, Intermediate-Range Ballistic; Missiles, Surface-to-Air

References

Gunston, Bill. *The Illustrated Encyclopedia of Aircraft Armament,* London: Salamander, 1987.

Pretty, R. T., and D.H.R. Archer. *Jane's Weapon Systems, 1971–1972.* London: Sampson Low, 1971.

Twigge, Stephen R. *The Early Development of Guided Weapons in the United Kingdom, 1940–1960.* London: Harwood, 1993.

Greece

Site of protracted World War II air campaign in support of ground operations. On 28 October 1940, Italy invaded northwestern Greece from Albania, well supported by aircraft and expecting a quick victory.

The Elleniki Vassiliki Aeroporia (Royal Hellenic Air Force) was armed with the Polish-built PZL P.24 fighter and a mixed variety of light bombers, liaison, and reconnaissance aircraft. The RAF soon established bases in Greece, and British Gladiator fighters and Blenheim bombers began flying missions on the Epirus front. British Wellington medium bombers also flew in support from bases in Egypt, bombing ports in Albania. It was against Italians flying from Albania that the RAF's highest-scoring ace, South African Marmaduke St. John Pattle, in a Gladiator, scored most of his 40-plus victories.

The Italian air force maintained a steady presence over the front in spite of losses and bad Greek winter weather, and mounted several raids on Athens. An Italian offensive in March met with heavy air losses.

Otherwise something of a sideshow, the Greco-Italian War took on increased importance because of airpower. If the war in the Balkans continued and British involvement increased, British bombers based in Greece and Crete could threaten the vital German oil installations at Ploesti. This fact and the threat of an Allied force operating on the flank of the German armies, which would soon invade the Soviet Union, led Germany to take an active role in the theater. German forces started moving into Romania and Bulgaria in March. The Allies responded with Australian, New Zealander, and British ground forces.

On 6 April 1941, Germany intervened in the Balkan conflict by invading Yugoslavia and moving into Greece through southern Yugoslavia and directly from Bulgaria. More than 1,200 aircraft of General Alexander Löhr's Luftflotte 4 (Fourth Air Force) supported the attack. The complexion of the conflict changed completely.

The Yugoslav air force was quickly eliminated and German bombers made a devastating attack on Belgrade. Yugoslavia signed an armistice on 17 April.

The small RAF contingent, commanded by Air Vice Marshal J. H. D'Albiac, and the remainder of the Greek air force were quickly swept from the skies. Squadron Leader Pattle was shot down and killed on 20 April. The Allied army in Greece fought a series of delaying actions as they withdrew down the peninsula, harried by the Luftwaffe.

In Piraeus Harbor near Athens, German aircraft destroyed the ammunition ship *Clan Fraser,* and secondary explosions closed this important port. As a result, Commonwealth troops were forced to use beaches and small harbors of the Peloponesus for their evacuation. German airborne troops attempted to capture the vital bridge over the Corinth Canal but were unsuccessful. The last RAF aircraft departed Greece on 24 April, and the last of the 50,000 Allied troops to evacuate left by 29 April. Axis operations against Crete followed.

Frank E. Watson

See also
Crete, Battle of

References
Papagos, Alexander. *The Battle of Greece, 1940–1941.* Athens: Hellenic, 1949.
Shores, Christopher. *Air War for Yugoslavia, Greece, and Crete.* Carrollton, TX: Squadron/Signal, 1987.

Greek Air Force

Greek mythology tells of Daedelus and Icarus, a father and son who escaped tyranny by making wings of feathers and wax and flying off their island prison to the Greek mainland. Greek aviators honor those roots and carry on that tradition.

In 1910, the Hellenic government visited France to witness aerial exhibitions and to consider purchasing aircraft. Immediately upon their return they announced that Greece would send officers to France to learn aviation. Although 60 officers applied, only three were chosen. Several months later, three more joined them at the Farman school at Etampes. These six men became the pioneers of military aviation within Greece. The men obtained first their civil, then their military licenses. When they returned a year later to assist in the Balkans conflict, they brought with them Greece's first military aircraft. By May 1912, Dimitrios Kamperos flew the first military aircraft in Greece, a Henri Farman, participating in army maneuvers. During this flight Prime Minister Eleftherios Venezelos joined him as the first passenger in Greece. The prime minister was a great supporter of military aviation and through his example helped assuage the superstitions and fears of a skeptical public.

The first combat air unit of the Royal Hellenic Army was established at Larissa in September 1912. This unit consisted of four Farman biplanes and four officer-pilots. The unit was one of the world's earliest aggressive air forces, preferring to act rather than merely observe. During the Balkan wars in October 1912, the aviators dropped improvised bombs on enemy positions and brought supplies to besieged cities. In January 1913, the first naval air operations began over the Dardanelles. First Lieutenant Michael Moutousis and Ensign Aristidis Moraitinis dropped four bombs on the Turkish fleet from their Farman-adapted hydroplane.

Kamperos envisioned a separate naval air force and adapted one of the Farmans into a hydroplane in June 1912, christening the craft *Daedelus.* Because of the work of Kamperos and Moraitinis, the first Greek naval air force school began in 1914. Despite limited funds, Moraitinis established the Naval Air Force School and Corps in 1914. Moraitinis also established the first aircraft factory, which became the forerunner of the Hellenic aerospace industry. Unfortunately, jealousy over Moraitinis's success induced Kamberos to desert the dream of Greek naval aviation. In 1916, his bid for a separate army air force was supported, which brought the end of naval aviation in Greece.

The Hellenic Army Air Force was established in 1917. During World War I, naval aviation units were also formed. The air force fought valiantly when Italy invaded in 1941. After the war, it became an important part of NATO's strength. The independent air force is now called Polemiki Aeroporia (the Greek air force). The force is divided into three commands: tactical, air support, and air training.

Wendy Coble

References
Aeroflight Website. Available online at http://www.aeroflight.co.uk/waf/greece/greekaf2.htm.
Green, William, and John Fricker. *The Air Forces of the World: Their History, Development, and Present Strength.* New York: Hanover House, 1958.
Helenic Air Force Website. Available online at http://www.haf.gr/gea_uk/istoriauk2.htm.
Katralamakis, Elias D. *Greek Wings, 1912–1932.* Athens: 1983.
Taylor, John W.R., Michael J.H. Taylor, and David Mondey. *Air Facts and Feats.* New York: Two Continents, 1973.

Greim, Robert Ritter von (1892–1945)

The last commander in chief of the Luftwaffe. An outstanding fighter pilot in World War I, during which he won the Pour le Mérite, von Greim had a successful career in civil aviation before rejoining the German armed forces in 1934. He was named the first commander of the first fighter squadron of the new Luftwaffe. During World War II, he was given successively more responsible field commands and higher decorations and gained a reputation as an inspirational leader. Von Greim was the last general promoted to field marshal by Hitler. This took place in a bizarre *Führerbunker* ceremony in besieged Berlin, to which von Greim had been summoned at great personal risk to be told that he was to replace Hermann Goering as Luftwaffe commander in chief. An ardent Nazi to the end, von Greim committed suicide on 24 May 1945 while in U.S. captivity.

Donald Caldwell

See also
German Air Force (Luftwaffe)

References

Corum, J. *The Luftwaffe: Creating the Operational Air War, 1918–1940.* Lawrence: University Press of Kansas, 1997.

Muller, R. *The German Air War in Russia.* Baltimore: Nautical and Aviation, 1992.

Grizodubova, Valentina Stepanova (1910–1993)

The only woman commander of a wing of Soviet airmen. Grizodubova had flown an ANT-37 from Moscow to the Pacific nonstop (6,450 kilometers) on 24–25 September 1938. For this pioneering flight, she became a Hero of the Soviet Union, along with copilot Polina Osipenko (1907–1939) and navigator Marina Raskova (1912–1943), the first Soviet women to be thus honored.

Born in Kharkiv, she graduated from the Penza Flying Club (1929), Kharkiv Flying School, and Advanced Flying School in Tula (1933). Grizodubova flew many types of aircraft, setting seven world records.

In May 1942, she was appointed commanding officer of the 101st Long-Range Air Regiment (renamed 31st Krasnoselsky Guards Bomber Regiment in 1944), where she demonstrated the suitability of her Li 2 (a modified DC-3) for use as a night-bomber. In June 1942, she led her unit in delivering supplies to blockaded Leningrad. She was noted for flying more than her male colleagues did and flew at times as copilot to monitor her pilots' performance. Due to her intervention a troublesome general—her superior—was demoted.

In September 1942, her unit was placed at the disposal of Central Partisan HQ. Overcoming dense enemy flak and engaging enemy fighters, her aircrews flew more than 1,850 supply missions and on their way back evacuated wounded partisans and children. In 1943, she successfully resisted her superiors' orders to decrease these flights.

She flew about 200 wartime missions and overall spent 18,000 hours in the air and was awarded many prestigious military decorations. A senior official of civil aviation, after the war she served on the executive of several veterans' organizations. More unusual, as a member of the Supreme Soviet she courageously criticized Stalin's reign of terror.

Kazimiera J. Cottam

See also
Raskova, Marina Mikhaylovna

References

Cottam, Kazimiera J. *Women in War and Resistance.* Nepean, Canada: New Military, 1998.

Toropov, L. F., ed. *Heroines* (in Russian). Vol. 1. 2nd ed. Moscow: Politizdat, 1969.

Verkhozin, A. M. *Aircraft Depart Toward Partisans* (in Russian). 2nd ed. Moscow: Izdatel'stvo politicheskoy literatury, 1966.

Groves, Leslie Richard (1896–1970)

U.S. general who played an important role in the development of the atomic bomb. Leslie Richard Groves was born in Albany, New York, on 17 August 1896. He attended the University of Washington for one year and the Massachusetts Institute of Technology for two years before entering the U.S. Military Academy. He graduated in June 1918 and became a second lieutenant of engineers. From 1918 to 1921, Groves took courses at the Engineer's School at Camp Humphreys (today Fort Belvoir), Virginia, with a brief stint in France during World War I. During the 1920s, he had assignments in places such as San Francisco, Delaware, Hawaii, and Nicaragua.

In 1931, Groves went to the Office of the Chief of Engineers in Washington, D.C., where in October 1934 he was promoted to captain. Groves graduated from the Army Command and General Staff School in Fort Leavenworth, Kansas, in 1936 and the Army War College in 1939. In 1939, he was assigned to the General Staff in Washington.

Assigned to the Office of the Quartermaster General in 1940, Groves was promoted to major in July. Later, he returned to the Office of Chief of Engineers as deputy chief of construction and was promoted to temporary colonel in November. He oversaw several projects, including the construction of the Pentagon.

In September 1942, he was promoted to temporary

brigadier general and placed in charge of the Manhattan District Engineering Project. Best known as the Manhattan Project, it was the code name for the production of three atomic bombs. Groves was an aggressive manager and an involved leader. Most of the research was done at Columbia University and the University of Chicago by world-famous physicists, including Groves's assistant, J. Robert Oppenheimer, of the University of California and the California Institute of Technology.

Project plants were established in remote parts of the United States to assure secrecy. These included Clinton Laboratory in Oak Ridge, Tennessee, the Hanford Engineering Works near Pasco, Washington, and Oppenheimer's converted summer camp near Los Alamos, New Mexico. Oak Ridge scientists gathered U-235 uranium to form a nuclear chain reaction while their Hanford colleagues made artificial plutonium detonators. At Los Alamos, Oppenheimer's team fashioned the components into three bombs, each able to fit into a B-29 of the 509th Composite Wing.

The project cost $2 billion, most of which came from blind appropriations. The money was spent on the secret purchase and delicate transport of scarce materials, the careful hiring of the workforce (125,000 at its height), and the construction of the worksites. All of this was done under tight security. Perhaps Groves's greatest success was dealing with the many scientists and technicians who were not used to such security.

The project culminated on 16 July 1945, with the detonation of the first device at Trinity Site, Alamogordo, New Mexico. Afterward, President Harry Truman okayed its use on Japan. On 6 August 1945, Colonel Paul W. Tibbets dropped a gun-type device (Little Boy) from the B-29 *Enola Gay* flying at 31,600 feet and destroyed Hiroshima, Japan. Three days later, Major Charles W. Sweeney aboard *Bock's Car* dropped an implosion bomb (code-named "Fat Man") on Nagasaki with equal devastation. As a result Japan surrendered, ending World War II.

Promoted to temporary major general in October 1944, Groves's role in the project cannot be overstated. The confidence U.S. leaders had in his command skills are mirrored by the fact that he remained in charge of U.S. atomic energy development until January 1947. He was then made chief of the Army's Special Weapons Project and promoted to temporary lieutenant general in January 1948.

Groves retired on 1 March 1948 and spent the next 13 years as vice president of Sperry Rand Corporation. He died on 13 July 1970 and was buried in Arlington National Cemetery.

William Head

References

Groves, Leslie R. *Now It Can Be Told: The Story of the Manhattan Project.* New York: Harper, 1962. Reprint New York: Da Capo, 1975, 1983.

Lawren, William. *The General and the Bomb: A Biography of Genera Leslie R. Groves, Director of the Manhattan Project.* New York: Dodd, Mead, 1988.

Rhodes, Richard. *The Making of the Atomic Bomb.* New York: Simon and Schuster, 1986.

Stoff, Michael B., Jonathan F. Fanton, and R. Hal Williams. *The Manhattan Project.* New York: McGraw-Hill, 1991.

Grumman A-6E Intruder

Twin-engine all-weather two-seat subsonic carrier-based attack aircraft. In spite of its 60,400-pound maximum gross weight, it has excellent slow-flying capabilities with full-span slats and flaps. The crew—a pilot and bombardier-navigator sitting side by side—can see in all directions through a broad canopy. The aircraft is equipped with a microminiaturized digital computer, a solid-state weapons-release system, and a single integrated track-and-search radar. The Intruder is armed with laser-guided weapons and equipped with a chin turret containing a forward-looking infrared system and laser designator and receiver.

In 1956, the U.S. Navy requested a carrier-borne all-weather attack aircraft. In size it was to be bigger than the A-4 Skyhawk but smaller than the A-3 Sky Warrior. The requirement also emphasized the ability to fly a long-range mission at low altitude and be capable of performing its mission in bad weather. The aircraft must also be capable of navigating through terrain without help of external sources such as beacons. The A-6E met those requirements.

The A-6 flew round the clock in Vietnam, conducting attacks on targets with pinpoint accuracy unavailable through any other aircraft at that time.

The A-6E proved that it is the best all-weather precision bomber in the world in the joint strike on Libyan terrorist-related targets in 1986. A-6s were used extensively during Operation DESERT STORM, providing precision bombing on a wide range of targets.

Henry M. Holden

References

Rendall, James. *Jane's Aircraft Recognition Guide.* New York: Harper Collins, 1999.

Grumman Aircraft

U.S. aircraft manufacturer. Leroy Grumman and partners William T. Schwendler, Ed Poor, E. Clint Towl, and Leon A.

The two-seat Grumman SF-1 was faster than any Navy single-seat fighter, thanks to its clean design and manually retractable landing gear. (U.S. Navy)

Swirbul founded the Grumman Aircraft Engineering Corporation in December 1929. Grumman and his partners had worked for Loening Aircraft Engineering Corporation when Keystone Aircraft Corporation bought it out. The decision was made to move the operation from New York to Pennsylvania. Grumman and his partners decided to stay in New York and start their own company. They acquired a small garage on Long Island and opened for business in January 1930.

Shortly thereafter, Grumman was contracted by Vought Aircraft to build floats for their Navy Scout planes. With that success, Grumman began work on a design for a fighter aircraft, the FF-1, a leap forward in technology. An enclosed cockpit and retractable landing gear made it unique for its time. Over the course of the next four years, Grumman would move to three new facilities for additional production and development space. The final move was to Bethpage, Long Island.

Grumman's success in producing biplanes (F2F and F3F) and Amphibians (JF and J2F Duck) continued through the mid-1930s, when its attention turned to monoplane fighters. In 1937, Grumman competed against Brewster for the right to produce the U.S. Navy's first monoplane fighter. The Brewster F2A Buffalo won the competition, but not the trust of the U.S. Navy, and Grumman was asked to continue work on its F4F Wildcat. The Wildcat's performance was determined to be superior to the Buffalo's, and an order was taken for 54 Wildcats. It would go on to become immensely popular with pilots and effective in the Pacific against the Japanese during World War II.

The Navy Wildcat would eventually be replaced by one of Grumman's own designs, the F6F Hellcat. Speed, maneuverability, and durability would make the Hellcat America's top ace-maker. Its performance in the Pacific brought its pilots an impressive 19:1 favorable kill ratio.

Grumman also was asked to design a Navy torpedo-bomber, the TBF Avenger. Again, Grumman put forth a simple but rugged design that would serve its crewmen well. The Avenger took part in the sinking of 12 Japanese aircraft carriers, six battleships, and nineteen cruisers during World

No sight was sweeter to a downed airman than that of a Grumman HU-16 Albatross on its way in for a pickup. (U.S. Air Force)

War II. In 1942, Grumman turned over production of Avengers and Wildcats to the Eastern Aircraft Division of General Motors so it could concentrate on the development and production of the Hellcat at the Bethpage facility.

After World War II, Grumman continued to produce aircraft. During the Korean conflict, Grumman developed the F9F Panther for the U.S. Navy. In Vietnam, the A-6 Intruder was used by the Navy and Marines. Finally, Grumman produced the F-14 during the close of the Vietnam War. This aircraft is still in service today. Grumman also expanded its scope to the aerospace industry, working with NASA on the Lunar Module that would help land the first man on the moon in the 1960s.

Grumman was bought out by Northrop in 1994 and operates today as Northrop Grumman.

David A. Pluth

References

Britannica.com. "Leroy Grumman." Available online.

M.A.T.S. Website [Grumman, F-14 Reference]. Available online at http://www.anft.net/f-14/grumman.htm.

Grumman Biplane Fighters

American aircraft series that began with the FF-1, FF-2, SF-1, and GG-1. Beginning operations in December 1929, the Grumman Corporation's first products were monocoque aluminum floats for observation floatplanes, designed with retractable landing gear.

In February 1930, the U.S. Navy asked Grumman if its retractable landing gear mechanism could be adapted to existing fighter aircraft. This motivated Grumman to respond in March to a procurement request for a two-seat fighter, proposing an all-metal (except for fabric wing covering) biplane aircraft with enclosed cockpits as well as retractable landing gear and powered by a Wright R-1820 575-shp Cyclone engine. The estimated performance was greater than any fighter in Navy service; the Navy purchased only drawings to construct a wind-tunnel model. It then ordered one prototype of the fighter in March 1931, designating it XFF-1, which flew on 29 December 1931 and was delivered the same day. It was 7 mph faster than the F4B-4, the fastest Navy fighter at the time. Board of Inspection and Survey flight trials resulted in minor changes, and 27 production aircraft, armed with two forward-firing machine guns and one swiveling gun, all .30-caliber, in the rear cockpit. The first was delivered in April 1933 and the last in November. VF-5B, on the USS *Ranger,* was the only squadron to completely equip with the FF-1, which remained in frontline service until April 1936, being redesignated FF-2, a reversion to the trainer role, the last of which was stricken July 1942. A parallel development, the SF-1, was a scout aircraft using one fewer gun and increased fuel tankage, of which 34 were built, deliveries being from February through July 1934. Only one squadron (VS3B) was completely equipped with SF-1s, and they were removed from front-line service in mid-1935. Other squadrons used single examples of both the FF and SF aircraft.

In 1934, Grumman built a single GG-1 (Grumman G-23) for use as a company demonstrator for export sales. It initially was powered by an R-1340 but was later reengined with an R-1820 of 890 hp, giving it a top speed of 242 mph. Canadian Car and Foundry obtained a license and produced 52 aircraft (having built components for 70) and sold one to Japan, one to Nicaragua, and 50 initially to Spain (erroneously thinking that they were for Turkey). The last 16 of these were taken over by the Canadian Air Force. The ones remaining in Spanish service were scrapped in 1955.

In the fall of 1932, Grumman proposed a new single-seat biplane fighter to the Navy, which had decided to abandon two-seat fighters. This would lead to the F2F, XSF-2, and XSBF-1. The proposal for the F2F, powered by a twin-row R-1535 of 625 shp, was accepted in November, and the only prototype flew on 9 October 1933. This design featured a watertight compartment beneath the pilot and a variable-incidence tailplane for trimming in flight. Flight trials revealed a top speed of 229 mph and the need for only minor changes. Fifty-four production F2F-1s were ordered in May 1934. The first was delivered in January 1935 and the last in August. They were again the fastest Navy fighters in service. Six squadrons operated F2Fs, and the last was withdrawn in 1942. The last aircraft of the SF-1 order was modified to accept the engine and cowling of the F2F, and in early 1935 Grumman built a single prototype XSBF-1 for a fighter-bomber competition that embodied further improvements to the SF airframe, including F2F and F3F design elements.

In October 1934, Grumman was awarded a contract for a single prototype XF3F-1, an evolutionary improvement of the F2F focusing on stability and retaining the same engine while increasing the length and wingspan. It flew on 20 March 1935 and crashed during dive-tests two days later. A second prototype was ordered and flew on 9 May 1935 and crashed during dive-tests eight days later. A third prototype was ordered and flew on 7 June 1935; it passed trials in March 1936. Fifty-four production F3F-1s were ordered, with the first delivered in January 1936 and the last in September. Armament of the F3F was two .50-caliber machine guns. Four squadrons were equipped with F3F-1s, and the last was withdrawn from squadron service in February 1941.

The F3F-2 received the more powerful R-1820 engine of 865 shp. This was a competitive response to Brewster's being awarded the F2A contract. The F3F-2, using the same engine as the F2A, achieved nearly the same performance. The XF3F-2 was ordered in June 1936 as a modification of the last -1, and flew on 21 July 1936. In March 1937, 81 production F3F-2s were ordered, the first being delivered in July, having a 950-shp Cyclone and other evolutionary improvements. Three new F3F-2s were built in 1993 by the Texas Aircraft Factory for museum and air-show use.

The XF3F-3, ordered in May 1938, was to fill a need resulting from delays in the F2A and F4F programs and featured further minor improvements in the F3F design. It was the last of the biplane Navy fighters ordered. The Cyclone engine had a two-speed supercharger to raise its operating altitude ceiling nearly 5,300 feet, to 30,000 feet. Twenty-seven were built and were used to augment various Navy squadrons. One- and two-seat versions of the F3F were built for Al Williams as the Gulfhawk II and III, and one two-seat demonstrator was built for Grumman's use.

Douglas G. Culy

References

Dann, Richard S. *Grumman Biplane Fighters in Action,* Carrollton, TX: Squadron/Signal, 1996.

Green, William, and Gordon Swanborough. *The Complete Book of Fighters.* London: Salamander, 1994.

Treadwell, Terry. *Ironworks—Grumman's Fighting Aeroplanes.* Osceola, WI: Motorbooks International, 1990.

Grumman EA-6B Prowler

Twin-engine midwing aircraft manufactured as a modification of the basic A-6 Intruder airframe. Its first flight was on 25 May 1968, and it became operational in July 1971. Designed for carrier and advanced base operations, the Prowler's primary function is electronic countermeasures. It is a fully integrated electronic warfare system combining long-range all-weather capabilities with advanced electronic countermeasures. A forward equipment bay and pod-shaped faring on the vertical fin house the additional avionics equipment. The side-by-side cockpit arrangement gives maximum efficiency, visibility, and comfort.

Early experiences with the EA-6A led to the development of a lengthened four-seat advanced EA-6B. Instead of two-man crews in the EA-6A, the B variant deploys four-man crews (one pilot and three electronic warfare officers) to manage the sophisticated array of systems.

The EA-6B first saw action in the Vietnam War in July 1972. The EA-6B has gone through many upgrades. The most recent is the ADVCAP configuration. The basic type has a new jammer system and an expanded AN/ALE-39 chaff dispenser. The other will have new displays, radar improvements, and an improved tactical support jamming system and digital autopilot.

Henry M. Holden

The Grumman EA-6B Prowler is one of the most important aircraft in the U.S. inventory, providing electronic countermeasures support for both the Navy and Air Force. (U.S. Navy)

References

Rendall, James. *Jane's Aircraft Recognition Guide.* New York: Harper Collins, 1999.

Grumman F-14 Tomcat

U.S. Navy's primary fleet defense fighter for more than 25 years. The first prototype made its maiden flight on 21 December 1970; unfortunately, the aircraft crashed on its second flight nine days later.

The F-14 was embroiled in controversy almost from the beginning. It was a large, expensive aircraft designed to replace the even more controversial Navy version of the General Dynamics F-111. The Total Procurement Package concept (fixed-price development contract) under which the F-14 was procured almost drove Grumman into bankruptcy. The crash of the first prototype did not help. But in the end the Tomcat developed into a very capable and long-lived aircraft.

A total of 710 aircraft were manufactured, including 80 for the Imperial Iranian Air Force before the fall of the shah. Many are still in service in the year 2000, and recently the F-14 has been fitted for ground attack missions using advanced LANTIRN targeting systems. A TARPS system is also available to selected F-14s and provides the fleet's primary reconnaissance asset.

Dennis R. Jenkins

References

Jenkins, Dennis R. *Grumman F-14 Tomcat: Leading U.S. Navy Fleet Fighter.* Leicester, UK: Aerofax/Midland Counties, 1997.

Grumman F4F Wildcat

U.S. Navy World War II fighter. Prior to World War II, a competition was held to select the Navy's first monoplane fighter. The Brewster XF2A Buffalo won out based on some engine and instability problems that the Wildcat possessed. The Navy, however, was not satisfied with the performance of the Buffalo and authorized Grumman to continue work on the Wildcat. An order for 54 F4F-3 Wildcats was submitted to Grumman on 8 August 1939. In October 1939, France submitted an order for 100 aircraft. This order was diverted to England when France was taken over by Germany. In British service, the Wildcat would become the Martlet I. On 25 December 1940, it would become the first of the F4F line

The swept-back wings of these Grumman F-14 Tomcats reveal that they are making a high-speed pass. Complex and not easy to fly, the Tomcat gained its greatest public acclaim in the film Top Gun, *but it was already highly regarded by professionals. (U.S. Navy)*

From its first flight on 21 December 1970, the Grumman F-14 Tomcat has been one of the most advanced aircraft in the world. In the war against terrorism, it has extended its fleet defense role to include reconnaissance and ground assault. (U.S. Navy)

The Grumman F4F Wildcat proved to be a rugged fighter. The Zero could best it in one-on-one combat, but two F4Fs flown together, using the Thach weave, could handle up to four of the enemy. (U.S. Navy)

to score an air victory when a Martlet I shot down a German Ju 88 bomber over Scapa Flow near Scotland.

In December 1940, U.S. Navy squadrons began to receive the Wildcat. The carriers USS *Ranger* and USS *Wasp* received the first shipment. The Wildcat's first service for the United States was in defense of Wake Island, when two shot down three Japanese bombers that were part of a 30-plane raid.

Lieutenant Edward "Butch" O'Hare became the U.S. Navy's first ace on 20 February 1942, shooting down five Japanese bombers that were attacking the USS *Lexington.* Many aces would follow. In all, 34 Marine pilots and 27 Navy pilots would become aces flying the Wildcat. The top-scoring ace was Joe Foss, with 26 air victories, all in Wildcats.

In January 1942, General Motors switched over several factories from producing cars to producing aircraft. Shortly thereafter, the production of the Wildcat was shifted from Grumman in order to allow Grumman continue development of the F6F Hellcat, which would replace the Wildcat.

Although the Wildcat was replaced as a front-line fighter in mid-1943, it did gain distinction as the only U.S. fighter to serve from the bombing of Pearl Harbor through war's end.

David A. Pluth

References

Donald, David. *American Warplanes of World War II.* London: Aerospace, 1995.

Kinzey, Bert. *F4F Wildcat in Detail and Scale.* Carrollton, TX: Squadron/Signal, 2000.

Grumman F6F Hellcat

The direct replacement for the F4F Wildcat, the U.S. Navy's frontline carrier fighter in 1942. The Navy's order for the first two prototypes was taken on 30 June 1941. The first prototype flew on 26 June 1942. The first production version of the Hellcat was the F6F-3, which first flew on 4 October 1942 and was carrier-qualified on the USS *Essex* in February 1943.

The Hellcat first saw combat on 31 August 1943 when groups from *Yorktown, Independence,* and *Essex* raided Marcus Island. Its first large air battle was in the Kwajalein-Roi area on 4 December 1943. Ninety-one Hellcats met 50 Japanese Zeros, shooting down a total of 28 while losing only two.

The next major version of the Hellcat, the F6F-5, first flew in April 1944. Production began in April 1944 and continued until November 1945. In all, 12,275 Hellcats were produced for the U.S. Navy, France, England, and even Uruguay.

By war's end, 5,156 enemy planes were shot down by Hellcats, for a 19:1 favorable kill ratio. Hellcat pilots accounted for 4,947 of the 6,477 total aircraft shot down by U.S. Navy pilots. The Hellcat was America's number one acemaker, with 307 Hellcat pilots claiming the title.

The Hellcat ended its distinguished military career during the Korean War, where it was used as a target drone and drone bomb.

David A. Pluth

Ordered by the British navy to replace the F4F, the Grumman F6F Hellcat had a 19-to-1 kill ratio over all enemy planes. (Philip Makanna)

References
Donald, David. *American Warplanes of World War II.* London: Aerospace, 1995.
Kinzey, Bert. *F6F Hellcat in Detail and Scale.* Squadron/Signal, 1996.
Tillman, Barrett. *Hellcat Aces of World War 2.* Oxford, UK: Osprey 1996

Grumman F9F Panther/Cougar

U.S. Navy jet fighter. The Grumman F9F was ordered in April 1946 as a straight-wing fighter using four 1,500-pound/thrust Westinghouse J30 engines. Grumman quickly decided that it was more efficient to use a single 5,000-pound/thrust Rolls-Royce Nene—interestingly, the same engines were provided to power the Soviet MiG-15 prototypes.

The straight-wing XF9F-2 made its first flight on 24 November 1947, powered by a British-built Nene. Production models would be equipped, alternately and almost interchangeably, by Pratt and Whitney J42s (F9F-2) or Allison J33s (F9F-3). An improved J33-A-16 powered the F9F-4 while a new Pratt and Whitney J48-P-6 was used in the F9F-5, both distinguished by slightly higher and more pointed vertical stabilizers. A total of 1,388 Panthers were manufactured; at least 715 of them saw service during the Korean War. On 9 November 1950, an F9F-2 became the first Navy jet to shoot down another jet fighter, a swept-wing MiG-15 that also used a version of the same Rolls-Royce engine design.

The successful development of the swept wing caused Grumman to redesign the Panther. Three XF9F-6 prototypes were converted from F9F-5s, renamed Cougar, and first flown on 20 September 1951. The design proved successful, being roughly 50 mph faster than the straight-wing variant. A total of 645 F9F-6 fighters and 70 F9F-6P reconnaissance aircraft were delivered by mid-1954, all using Pratt and Whitney J48-P-8 engines. The Allison J33-A-19 was used in 168 similar F9F-7s. Cougars joined operational squadrons beginning in November 1952, but only 18 were deployed to Korea before hostilities ended.

A longer fuselage, larger wing, and more powerful Pratt and Whitney J48-P-8A engine were incorporated into the F9F-8, first flown on 18 December 1953. Provisions were also incorporated for four Sidewinder air-to-air missiles. Grumman delivered 601 F9F-8s between February 1954 and March 1957, with most of them being modified to the

F9F-8B configuration capable of delivering tactical nuclear weapons. The last Cougars were 110 F9F-8P reconnaissance aircraft and 400 two-seat F9F-8T trainers. The trainer version, later redesignated TF-9J, remained in service until 1974.

Dennis R. Jenkins

References

Wagner, Ray. *American Combat Planes.* 3rd ed. Garden City, NY: Doubleday, 1982.

Grumman TBF/TBM Avenger

U.S. Navy World War II torpedo-bomber. In 1939, the U.S. Navy decided that a new torpedo-bomber was required to replace the Douglas TBD Devastator in the U.S. arsenal. Specifications were written, and two companies, Grumman and Vought, entered competition for the contract. Two XTBF-1 prototypes were ordered on 8 April 1940, and Grumman received a contract for 286 TBF-1s in December 1940.

Delivery of the Avenger began in January 1942 to VT-8 (torpedo squadron from the USS *Hornet*). In May, VT-8 headed to Hawaii to board the *Hornet.* The group missed the departing ship by one day. On 1 June, six Avengers were flown to Midway Island. On 4 June, these six Avengers would be the first Avengers in combat against the Japanese fleet at Midway. Five of the six were shot down in the battle while doing little or no damage to the Japanese.

The first carrier-based Avenger attack occurred on 24 August 1942 when two Avengers discovered the Japanese aircraft carrier *Ryujo* during a scouting mission. They dropped their four 500-pound bombs, with none hitting the mark. They did, however, report their findings back to the U.S. carrier *Enterprise,* which launched an attack with Avengers and Dauntlesses. The Avengers carried torpedoes while the Dauntlesses carried bombs. The coordinated attack sank the *Ryujo.*

In November 1942, production of the Avenger shifted to the Eastern Aircraft Division of General Motors with the first TBM (note the designation change) coming off the production line in mid-1943. Grumman ceased production of the Avenger completely by the end of 1943 to concentrate on the Hellcat.

The Avenger had many roles during World War II. In the Atlantic, it was used on escort carriers to protect convoys of troops and supplies headed for Europe. Some 950 Avengers served in the Royal Navy's Fleet Air Arm as the Tarpon (eventually becoming the Avenger I) in various roles from submarine patrol to escort duty.

The Avenger's biggest role of the war, however, was that of attack-bomber. The Avenger took part in sinking 12 of Japan's 26 aircraft carriers, six of 11 battleships, and 19 of 41 cruisers. The Avenger was the U.S. Navy's last torpedo-bomber ever ordered into production, with the role deemed no longer necessary after World War II.

The Avenger remains in service today. It is a very successful firefighting bomber that works to control forest fires in the United States and Canada.

David A. Pluth

References

Aero Data International. *U.S. Navy Carrier Bombers of World War II.* Carrollton, TX: Squadron/Signal, 1987.

Kinzey, Bert. *TBF and TBM Avenger in Detail and Scale.* Carrollton, TX: Squadron/Signal, 1997.

Guadalcanal

The opening U.S. offensive of World War II in the Pacific, the first fought by land, sea, and air. The clash of contending airpowers, in all their manifestations, dominated the campaign. Operation WATCHTOWER's primary objective was control of an air base, Henderson Field, whose construction by Japanese forces precipitated its launch.

Japanese airpower throughout the campaign rested upon the Eleventh Air Fleet at Rabaul. Approximately 50 G4M bombers and an equal number of A6M Zero fighters for escort and base defense formed its core. Small numbers of D3A dive-bombers and a few flying boats supplemented its strength. On Guadalcanal itself, U.S. Marine Corps and Army units with fighters and dive-bombers provided most local support and defense. Army, Navy, and ANZAC aircraft flew long-range offensive and reconnaissance missions from more distant bases.

Pacific Fleet carriers covered the beach landings on 7 August 1942 but withdrew after two days, forcing the transports to depart. Henderson Field was ready to receive Marine Air Group 23, its first aircraft, on 20 August, followed by Army Bell P-400s of the 67th Fighter Squadron two days later and, temporarily, Navy SBD-3s from the *Enterprise* on 24 August. Over the next six months, the Marines deployed to Guadalcanal eight scout-bomber and seven fighter squadrons, the Army six fighter and two bombardment squadrons, supported by reconnaissance aircraft, temporary Navy detachments, and two RNZAF bomber units.

From the operation's outset it was clear that command of the sea would determine its outcome—and that the contest for air superiority would decide that command. Two large-scale carrier actions, the Battles of the Eastern Solomons and Santa Cruz, demonstrated airpower's significance most dramatically. On 24–25 August, and again on 26 October, U.S. Pacific Fleet carriers engaged their Combined Fleet counterparts in tactically indecisive battles that nevertheless achieved the U.S. aim of preventing large-scale reinforcement of Japanese forces on Guadalcanal. On both occasions the Japanese carriers' withdrawal left the transports they were covering vulnerable to devastating attacks, primarily by aircraft from Henderson Field but also from the U.S. fleet.

Dramatic though these battles were, the principal struggle in the air was between contending Japanese and U.S. land-based air forces. This soon became a battle of attrition as each side struggled to replace combat and operational aircraft and aircrew losses sustained in continuous action while attempting to increase their total deployed forces. Eleventh Air Fleet launched almost daily raids, using two dozen or so bombers with fighter escort, losing 15–30 percent of their number to U.S. defenders. By the end of September, more than 200 Japanese aircraft had been lost since the campaign began.

Marine Corps scout-bombers raided Japanese positions on the island, provided close support for the infantry, and scoured a 200-mile radius from Henderson field for enemy shipping. Air raids and accidents, however, took their toll. Despite enjoying a 6:1 victory-to-loss ratio, U.S. fighter strength also diminished rapidly as conditions at Henderson Field took their toll (67th Fighter Squadron's strength, for example, fell from 14 to three aircraft in four days, largely due to operational losses).

By mid-September, several important features of the aerial campaign at Guadalcanal were clear. U.S. air forces ashore had wrested sufficient local control of the air to ensure continued supply and reinforcement of U.S. forces on the island, albeit at a significant cost. Japanese surface forces endeavoring to reinforce their position could operate only during the 12-hour-long tropical nights or risk annihilation from U.S. airpower; their own air forces generally could simultaneously inhibit substantial U.S. offensive surface movement, so both navies became nocturnal combatants. Finally, Japanese airpower was too distant and insufficient to offset its army's numerical inferiority on the island, its navy's inability to land large-scale reinforcements and supplies, and growing U.S. ground, air, and naval strength at Guadalcanal.

By late December it was clear that Japan could not break the U.S. hold on Guadalcanal. Even its navy's reinforcement missions became perilous as night-flying radar-equipped PBY flying boats began directing torpedo-boats and destroyers against them. Nevertheless, the Imperial Japanese Navy was able to pull off one final success in the face of U.S. airpower: the evacuation, with relatively little loss, of its surviving garrison from the island.

Paul E. Fontenoy

See also

Eastern Solomons, Battle of; Halsey, William F.; Japanese Naval Air Force, Imperial; McCain, John S.; Santa Cruz, Battle of; U.S. Marine Corps Aviation

References

Craven, Wesley F., and James L. Cate, eds. *The Army Air Forces in World War II, Volume 4: Pacific: Guadalcanal to Saipan, August 1942–July 1944.* Chicago: University of Chicago Press, 1950.

Frank, Richard B. *Guadalcanal.* New York: Random House, 1990.

Lundstrom, John B. *The First Team and the Guadalcanal Campaign.* Annapolis, MD: Naval Institute Press, 1994.

Sherrod, Robert. *History of Marine Corps Aviation in World War II.* 2nd ed. San Rafael, CA: Presidio Press, 1980.

Guam, Battles of (1944)

Site of air operations to support of U.S. amphibious invasion. Japanese forces occupied U.S.-owned Guam, in the Mariana Islands, on 10 December 1941.

In 1944, the Allies moved against the Marianas. U.S. Marines landed on Saipan on 15 June, but after the approach of the main Japanese fleet was detected, Admiral Raymond A. Spruance called off landings on Guam and dispersed the transport fleet until the Japanese had been defeated in the Battle of the Philippine Sea. After the delay, landings by III Amphibious Corps commenced on 21 July 1944, and the island was secure by 10 August. U.S. airpower supported ground operations for the duration of the fighting.

The postponement of the Allied landings on Guam showed the importance that Japanese carrier-based airpower still held in U.S. naval operations as late as mid-1944.

Frank E. Watson

Guernica

Site of air attack during the Spanish civil war. In 1931, Spain became a constitutional republic with much opposition from conservatives, who wanted a return to monarchy. In Catalonia and the Basque region, separatists desired to form their own government. When the Republicans won the election of 1936, a conspiracy of generals supported the rebellion of Francisco Franco and fascism.

The civil war lasted for three years. Adolf Hitler's Germany and Benito Mussolini's Italy sent troops and aircraft to the Nationalists. Stalin's Russia sold supplies, including aircraft, to the Loyalists. Britain and France stayed officially neutral, but their citizens flocked to the Republican cause.

In early 1937, after the first months of fighting had given

A direct descendant of the German Wasserfall missile, the Soviet Union's SA-2 Guideline was one of the most important surface-to-air missiles ever built. (Lon Nordeen)

neither side a clear advantage, General Emilio Mola led 40,000 troops into the Basque country and threatened to raze Vizcaya if the loyalist Basques did not surrender. Backing his threat was the Kondor Legion of 100 German bombers and fighters.

Mola attacked Guernica, the refugee-flooded traditional center of the Basque region, on market day when the streets were full of people. The Kondor Legion, in a three-hour attack, first dropped incendiaries, then strafed the people. The city was in flames and the dead and wounded (elderly, women, children) were everywhere. This was the most effective air assault that had attempted to destroy a city and its civilian population.

When world opinion became outraged the Nationalists denied responsibility, then claimed that the Basques fired their own city. Pablo Picasso immediately began painting his commemorative masterpiece, which hung at a 1937 international exposition. By 1939, the Nationalists had won the civil war.

John Barnhill

References

Anderson, Dale. *Battles That Changed the Modern World.* Austin, TX: Steck-Vaughn Company, 1994.

Guideline (SA-2) Surface-to-Air Missile

The Soviet Union's Lavochkin Design Bureau began developing the SA-2 Guideline in 1952. Testing commenced in 1954, and deployment began in 1957. Many countries (Warsaw Pact nations, China, Cuba, Egypt, Iraq, and Vietnam) acquired the SA-2. Improved and indigenously produced versions are still used today.

Lavochkin designed the SA-2 to defend cities and fixed installations from high-altitude U.S. bombers. SA-2 sites consist of six revetted launch positions surrounding a command post, a Fan Song missile control radar, a Spoon Rest early warning radar, and reload missiles on trailers. All components are road/rail mobile, but setup time is lengthy. The two-stage missile is 10.6 meters long, 0.7 meters wide, and weighs 2,300 kilograms at launch. Maximum range is 35–50 kilometers, maximum altitude is 27–40 kilometers, and maximum velocity is Mach 3.5. The 195-kilogram high-explosive warhead has a 65-meter kill radius, with severe damage at 100–250 meters.

More than 13,000 SA-2s have been fired in combat. SA-2s shot down U-2s over Sverdlovsk in 1960 and over Cuba in 1962. From 1965 to 1972, North Vietnamese SA-2s shot down about 150 U.S. aircraft and forced U.S. pilots to fly lower, where antiaircraft artillery was more effective. Later in the war, jamming and suppression missions kept SAM kill rates low.

James D. Perry

References

Zaloga, Steven J. *Soviet Air Defence Missiles: Design, Development, and Tactics.* Coulsdon, UK: Jane's Information Group, 1989.

Gulf of Tonkin Resolution

U.S. Public Law 88–408, which gave President Lyndon Johnson power to take whatever actions he deemed necessary—including the use of armed force—to defend Southeast Asia. This resolution was passed by Congress in reaction to two allegedly unprovoked attacks by North Vietnamese torpedo boats on the U.S. destroyers *Maddox* and *C. Turner Joy* in the Gulf of Tonkin on 2 August and 4 August, respectively.

The resolution passed 82-2 in the Senate, where Democrats Wayne K. Morse of Oregon and Ernest Gruening of Alaska were the only dissenting votes; the bill passed 416-0 in the House of Representatives. President Johnson signed it into law on 10 August. The resolution gave Johnson broad authority to conduct the war in Vietnam. It became the legal basis for every presidential action taken by the Johnson administration during its conduct of the war. Despite the initial support for the resolution, it became controversial as Johnson used it to increase U.S. commitment to the war in Vietnam. Several years later, as the war became even more controversial, President Richard Nixon drew upon the resolution to justify the incursion into Cambodia in April 1970. Many congressmen came to see the resolution as giving the president a blanket power to wage war; it was repealed as of December 1970.

James H. Willbanks

See also

Vietnam War

References

Herring, George C. *America's Longest War.* New York: Alfred A. Knopf, 1979.

Moise, Edwin E. *Tonkin Gulf and the Escalation of the Vietnam War.* Chapell Hill: University of North Carolina Press, 1996.

Gulf War (1991)

On 2 August 1990, Iraqi forces under the command of Saddam Hussein invaded and occupied Kuwait, an action that precipitated the Gulf War. Disputes between Kuwait and Iran stemmed from one primary issue: money. Iraq, having financed its recent war with Iran, amassed an $80 billion debt, a portion of which was owed to Kuwait. Iraq also claimed that the Kuwaiti government continued to pump oil from a field along their common border without sharing the revenue and that Kuwait continued to produce more oil than agreed to by OPEC, thereby depressing the price of the commodity, which was Iraq's main export. Within hours the Iraqi forces captured Kuwait City, where all movable assets were confiscated and returned to Iraq. Kuwait's ruling family appealed to the United Nations Security Council and the Arab League for assistance. An embargo against Iraq resulted in Hussein declaring that Kuwait had been annexed on 8 August. An international coalition with troops from Saudi Arabia, the United States, the United Kingdom, France, Egypt, Syria, Senegal, Niger, Morocco, Bangladesh, Pakistan, the United Arab Emirates, Qatar, Oman, and Bahrain assembled forces primarily in Saudi Arabia. Other countries made significant contributions of ships, forces, and medical supplies in support of the Coalition's war against Iraq. When attempts to pressure the Iraqi forces into withdrawing failed, the United Nations passed a resolution allowing for the use of all necessary means to restore the country of Kuwait to its people. The U.S. Congress passed a resolution on 12 January 1991 allowing President George Bush the authority to use force against Iraq.

The expiration of a UN deadline for withdrawal by 12 January 1991 resulted in the commencement of air assaults designed to disrupt command-and-control operations and to weakened the Iraqi forces. The United States Air Force, along with British pilots, dominated the skies over the country. Using precision bombing, the Air Force targeted electrical plants, command centers, roads, bridges, and government structures with a minimum impact on civilians. Bombing continued for five and a half weeks, with more than 100,000 flights by Coalition forces. Iraq responded by attacking Israel with Scud missiles in an attempt to draw Israel into the war, an action calculated to divide the Arab nations from the rest of the Coalition.

The USAF flew more than 65,000 missions with 35 kills against fixed-wing aircraft. Officials utilized a flexible response policy deploying a variety of aircraft to accomplish war goals. Initial attacks on Baghdad required the combined stealth and precision of the F-117 fighter-bomber. Flying 1,300 combat missions and dropping 2,000 tons of bombs within 6,900 hours, these planes achieved air superiority for the Coalition forces. During Operation DESERT SHIELD, prior to the attack on Iraq, the F-15 was deployed as a defensive shield; after fighting broke out it was used to help establish air superiority. Forty-eight F-15Es, utilizing the Joint Altitude Navigation and Attack Radar System, proved effective in locating and destroying Scud missile sites. The deploy-

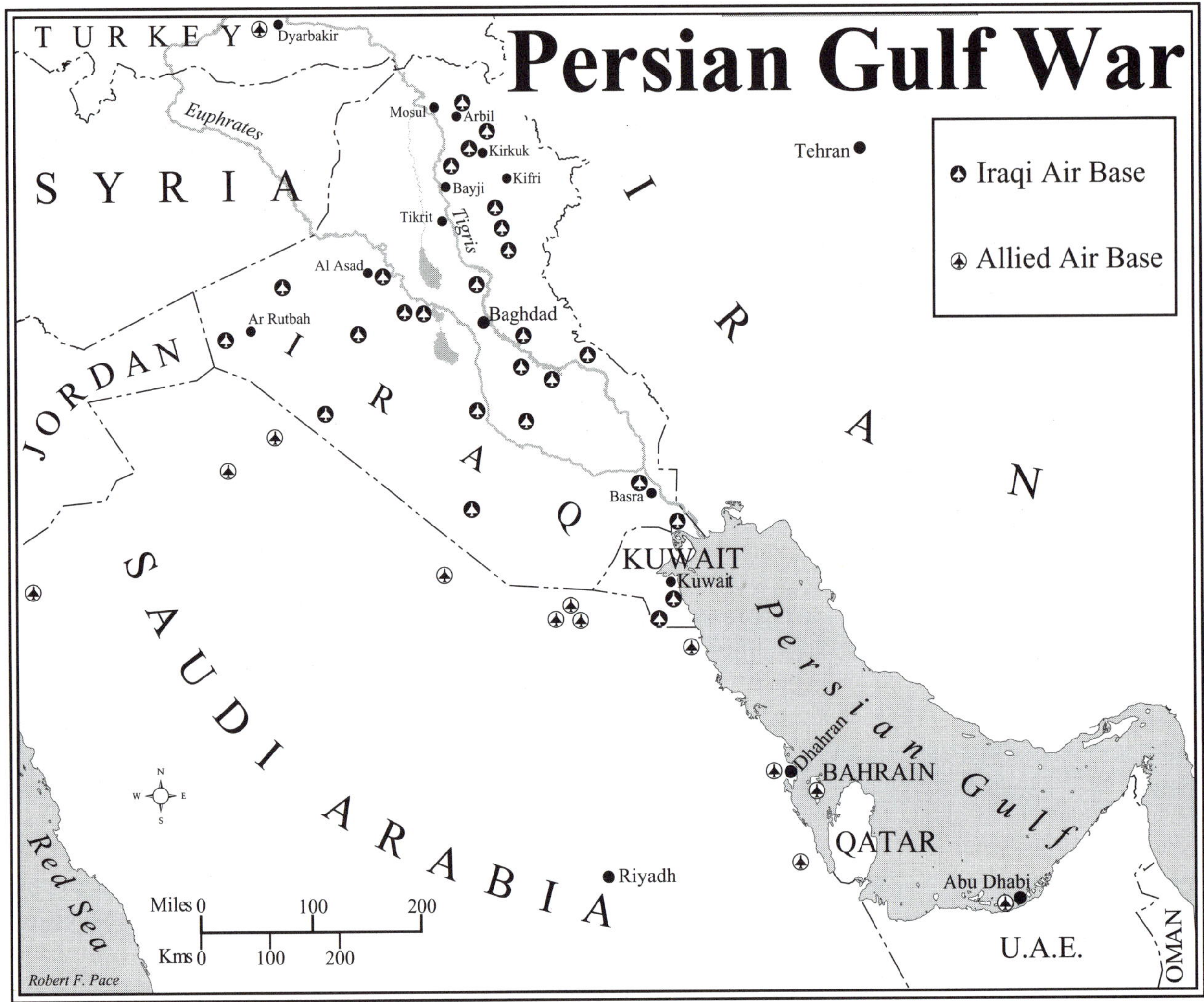

ment of 144 A-10s resulted in 8,100 missions primarily against tanks. The F-111 targeted military production facilities by utilizing its forward-looking infrared and laser-designation systems. EF-111s and F4-Gs effectively jammed Iraqi radar capabilities. F-16s attacked ground forces in the Kuwaiti Theater of Operations while B-52s dropped 25,700 tons of munitions on airfields and industrial targets within Iraq. AH-64 Apache helicopters, designed to destroy tanks and armored vehicles, and Drones, remote-controlled pilotless planes designed for intelligence-gathering, also operated effectively. By using precision-guided munitions, or smart bombs, the USAF reduced collateral damage to civilian structures as well as civilian casualties. The Maverick missile, used by the F-16s and A-10s, proved its accuracy by destroying one tank for each missile deployed. AIM-7s and AIM-9s proved to be effective air-to-air missiles.

Land forces launched an attack on 24 February, focusing on the Iraqi port of Al Basrah, a maneuver designed to surround Kuwait. Iraqi troops quickly surrendered as the Coalition forces moved rapidly toward Kuwait City. Retreating back to Iraq, Hussein's forces destroyed oil wells by setting them afire, producing an environmental disaster. On 26 February, Iraq announced it was withdrawing from Kuwait. The land war lasted only 100 hours.

After the signing of a cease-fire, the United Nations Security Council outlined necessary measures for lifting the embargo against Iraq, including payment of damages, destruction of all biological and chemical weapons, and international inspection. A secondary issue arose over Iraqi treatment of Kurds within Iraq. Throughout the remainder of the decade, U.S. and British forces repeatedly patrolled a no-fly zone and struck Iraqi missile launch sites. Iraq's role in the terrorist attacks against the United States in September 2001 was unclear at the time, although Saddam Hussein was still suspected of trying to develop weapons of mass destruction.

Cynthia Clark Northrup

The Boeing air-launched cruise missile gave a standoff capability to the venerable Boeing B-52 bomber in the Gulf War. (Walter J. Boyne)

References

Andrews, William F. *Airpower Against an Army: Challenge and Response in CENTAF's Duel with the Republican Guards.* Maxwell AFB, AL: Air University Press, 1998.

Murray, Williamson. *Air War in the Persian Gulf.* Baltimore: Nautical and Aviation, 1995.

Reynolds, Richard T. *Heart of the Storm: The Genesis of the Air Campaign Against Iraq.* Maxwell AFB, AL: Air University Press, 1995.

Gun Sights

Devices that allow a pilot or gunner to aim weapons at an enemy aircraft. Air-to-air gunnery entails hitting a moving target with projectiles that are constantly decelerating and subject to gravity and are fired from a platform that is also moving. The pilot or gunner must aim ahead of the target by some angle (the deflection angle) and allow for gravity drop, wind, and the like so that bullets and target arrive at the same point simultaneously.

The problem reduces as muzzle velocity increases and as range reduces. Many aces (e.g., Erich Hartmann) closed to pointblank range before firing in order to reduce deflection to a minimum.

Throughout the initial part of World War I, most gun sights were simple ring-and-bead types that worked reasonably well but required accurate head positioning from the pilot. An optical (Aldis) sight was introduced during the latter part of the war and was much easier to use. A further advance was the reflector sight, which projected an aiming mark appearing at infinity on a sloped piece of glass through which the pilot sighted the target; a patent for a reflector sight was filed by Sir Howard Cribb as early as 1900, and in 1918 some Fokker Dr.Is of Jasta 12 were equipped with a German Oigee reflector sight for operational trials. The reflector sight came into wide use during the interwar years, although fixed optical sights continued to be used well into the 1940s.

Some air arms recognized the importance of deflection shooting and trained accordingly—the U.S. Navy being a prime example—but the training syllabus of many air forces did not emphasize air-to-air gunnery.

In 1936, Dr. L. Cunningham had suggested a "predictor" gun sight using the principle that a gyroscope resists any rotation of its axis. If one is attached to a normal gun sight, any attempt to follow a crossing target will be resisted with a force proportional to the crossing speed. This idea was adopted and developed by scientists at Royal Aircraft Establishment Farnborough, and the first preproduction Mark I Gyro Gun Sights (GGS) were installed on Spitfire and Defiant aircraft for trials in 1941. The tests were very promising, but there were a number of operational problems, and a redesigned Mark II GGS was rushed into production late in 1943. The pilot selected the type of enemy aircraft on a dial, then adjusted the sighting graticule to match the target's wingspan while tracking it. An analog computer in the sight calculated target range and offset the graticule to give the correct deflection.

The importance of the GGS is difficult to overestimate;

operational experience showed that it approximately doubled the effectiveness of the average squadron pilot. The GGS Mark II was formally accepted into the U.S. Army Air Forces as the K-14 and the U.S. Navy as the Mark 18.

A radar-ranging gun sight (the Davis-Draper sight) was tested by the U.S. Air Force between 1945 and 1948 and eventually went into production as the A-1B computing sight. The A1-CM was used on F-86 fighters during the Korean War and enabled hits to be scored at quite high deflection angles and ranges. However, it was quite fragile and suffered from inadequate maintenance.

In 1955, the U.S. Navy experimented with a head-up display (HUD). The flight-navigation and weapon-aiming symbology was generated electronically and projected onto a reflector glass in front of the pilot. The first production HUD was developed by Ferranti in 1962, and the Blackburn Buccaneer became the first operational aircraft to be fitted with it. HUDs initially used analogue computers to generate data, and the first digital HUD appeared in 1966.

The latest generation of helmet-mounted displays project HUD symbology onto the pilot's visor and track head movement, giving a look-and-shoot capability and allowing off-boresight engagements with short-range air-to-air missiles.

Andy Blackburn

See also

Aircraft Armament; Hartmann, Erich; Missiles, Air-to-Air

References

Clarke, R. Wallace. *British Aircraft Armament.* 2 vols. London: PSL/Haynes, 1993, 1994.

Gunston, Bill. *The Illustrated Encyclopedia of Aircraft Armament.* London: Salamander, 1987.

Gunships

Side-firing airborne weapons platform. The gunship was a totally new weapons system at the time of its development. The concept originated in 1926 with a .30-caliber Lewis machine gun mounted on the wing of a de Havilland DH-4; it flew pylon turns to keep the gun on target.

The idea for the modern gunships came in 1964 from a U.S. Air Force officer, Captain Ronald W. Terry, who had heard of aircraft delivering mail and supplies to remote jungle areas in South America. The plane would circle in a steep pylon turn, lowering a bucket on a long rope. The bucket would orbit in a tight circle, suspended from the cargo door, and someone on the ground placed mail in it. Captain Terry suggested replacing the rope with a line of machine-gun fire.

Terry was assigned to see if the concept worked in practice, and he became one of the few individuals in military history who helped create a new weapons system and then tested it in combat himself.

The idea was tried with 10 .30-caliber machine guns mounted in an FC-47. Testing proved the concept, and the Air Force replaced the machine guns with three General Electric six-barrel rotating miniguns, reminiscent of Civil War–era Gatling guns. The 7.62mm guns were capable of covering every square foot of a football field with one round in one minute. The first of several successful day missions occurred on 15 December 1964; eight days later the first night missions were flown.

Although the gunship was effective, a better nighttime illumination system was needed. The standard flares, some dating to World War II, often did not work. The furious gunfire of the FC-47 raised South Vietnamese morale. The aircraft soon acquired affectionate nicknames such as "Puff" and "Dragonship." The call sign "Spooky" was assigned to early gunship operations in Vietnam.

The 7.62mm miniguns were excellent weapons but were in short supply. Terry got authorization to take 300 old M-2 .30-caliber machine guns and install them, 10 at a time, in four C-47s.

In 1965, Spooky's mission expanded to include interdiction of roads, trails, and rivers. The gunships—now designated AC-47s—had to operate low, slow, at night, and in bad weather. Forty-seven AC-47s went to Vietnam, and 12 were lost.

The United States had to try to interdict the flow of supplies from North Vietnam, and the obvious tool for the job was an improved gunship. Terry proposed a converted C-130A with improved sensors, weapons, and more ammunition. Four 7.62mm miniguns and four M-61 Vulcan 20mm cannons were installed in Gunship II, along with side- and forward-looking radar. A computerized fire-control system linking sensors and guns, and "inerted" fuel tanks protected against ground fire.

Although Secretary of the Air Force Harold Brown had authorized the C-119G as the AC-47's replacement, a costly compromise led to the creation of three types of gunships in the fleet: AC-47s, AC-119s, and AC-130s.

As the Air Force gained experience, the success of the gunships continued to rise. In 1969, AC-119Gs flew more than 3,700 sorties over 14,251 combat hours, fired almost 35 million rounds of ammunition, and expended 22,000 flares. They killed some 1,500 enemy troops and, most important, allowed no outpost to be overrun while they were overhead.

In the spring of 1972, North Vietnam began a major offensive. The gunships worked from Thai and South Vietnamese bases against targets in Cambodia, South Vietnam, and Laos. As North Vietnam stepped up its efforts, the work of the gunships expanded to provide more close support of the South Vietnamese army. There were many instances reported when the heavy fire from gunships halted overwhelming assaults on South Vietnamese positions.

Henry M. Holden

References

Boyne, Walter J. "The Awesome Power of Air Force Gunships." *Air Force Magazine* 82, 4 (April 1999)

Larry, Davis. *Gunships: A Pictorial History of Spooky.* Carrollton, TX: Squadron/Signal, 1982.

Gurevich, Mikhail I. (1892–1976)

Military aircraft designer of the former Soviet Union. Born in a small village in the Kursk Oblast, Mikhail I. Gurevich finished high school and attended Kharkov University, studying physics and mathematics before being expelled for political reasons.

He temporarily emigrated to France in 1913 and took classes in mathematics at Montpellier University. After the Russian Revolution, Gurevich returned to Kharkov, where in 1925 he completed his studies at the Kharkov Technological Institute. He organized among fellow students a youthful faculty of aviation at the institute, which became an important center of aeronautical studies in the Soviet Union. After a period of sketching and building gliders, Gurevich in 1928 joined the Soviet aircraft industry and served as an assistant to various foreign and Russian engineers. Later, in the early 1930s, he participated in the Soviet think-tank for designing airframes, TsAGI (Central Aero-Hydrodynamics Institute). His facility with languages, diplomatic demeanor, and knowledge of airplane construction led to his appointment as a member of the Soviet team that in 1936–1937 negotiated with Douglas Aircraft the licensed transfer of DC-3s and DC-3 plans to the Soviet Union.

After assisting Boris P. Lisunov in setting up the DC-3 (Li 2) production line, Gurevich became a member of Nikolai N. Polikarpov's design bureau at the end of 1938. He applied his knowledge from the DC-3 experience to help Artem I. Mikoyan in devising a more effective production line for the Polikarpov fighter, the I-153. Late in 1939, Gurevich (deputy) and Mikoyan (chief) directed a new experimental department that had the approval and encouragement of the highest levels of party and government, including Soviet dictator Joseph Stalin. The experimental bureau focused on creating a high-performance fighter aircraft, the I 200. A prototype flew in March 1940, but extensive changes were necessary before the aircraft was ready for a small production run in December 1940. By then the model name had changed to the MiG-1, a designation based on the initials of the last names of the designers connected by an "i" (the Russian word for "and"). The most successful of the early models was the MiG-3, which enjoyed a production run of 3,300 and provided interceptor defense for the Soviet Union's metropolitan centers during World War II.

After the war, Gurevich and Mikoyan examined German technology and merged two BMW 003 turbojet engines with the MiG-9 airframe to create one of the Soviet Union's first successful jet fighters in April 1946. The MiG-9 entered full production and became the precursor for an array of famous fighter aircraft, ranging from the MiG-15 to the MiG-31. At the time of his retirement in 1964, Gurevich held the official post of chief constructor of the MiG OKB (Experimental Design Bureau). He received numerous Soviet awards and honors for his outstanding design achievements in military aviation, including the prestigious Lenin Prize in 1962.

James K. Libbey

See also

Douglas Aircraft; Mikoyan, Artem I.; Mikoyan-Guryevich Aircraft; Polikarpov, Nikolai N.; Soviet Air Force

References

Belyakov, R. A., and J. Marmain. *MiG: Fifty Years of Secret Aircraft Design.* Annapolis, MD: Naval Institute Press, 1994.

Great Soviet Encyclopedia. 3rd ed. Vol. 7. New York: Macmillan, 1975, p. 485.

Gunston, Bill, and Yefim Gordon. *MiG Aircraft Since 1937.* London: Putnam; and Annapolis, MD: Naval Institute Press, 1998.

Guynemer, Georges (1894–1917)

The Hero of France during World War I. Frail in appearance and thought to be consumptive, Georges Guynemer nevertheless volunteered immediately upon the war's declaration and became an aviation mechanic. After pilot training in 1915, he was assigned to Escadrille 3, a unit that would become famous largely due to his performance. Over the next two years, his stork-emblazoned Nieuports and SPADs became the symbol of French aerial success as he ran his victory total to 53. He remained active in combat despite being injured several times.

Guynemer was one of a few pilots to fly the cannon-armed SPAD XII operationally, his four victories on the type making him its greatest exponent.

Guynemer was killed in action on 11 September 1917 under mysterious circumstances. He may be buried in Rumbeke, although this remains uncertain. The French air force is called out in his memory each year on the anniversary of his death.

James Streckfuss

See also
Nieuport Aircraft; SPAD Aircraft

References

Franks, Norman L.R., and Frank W. Bailey. *Over the Front.* London: Grub Street, 1992.

Vanoverbeke, Lothair. "Is Guynemer Buried in Rumbeke?" In *Over the Front* 15, 1, pp. 4–9. Cincinnati: League of World War I Aviation Historians, 2000.

H

Haiphong Air Attacks

U.S. air campaign to close an important North Vietnamese port. North Vietnam relied on the Soviet Union, China, and other communist countries for war materials, all of which had to be imported, mostly by sea. By 1971, because of the Sino-Soviet rift and the warming relations between the United States and China, 85 percent of all military supplies entered North Vietnam through Haiphong Harbor.

Haiphong is located 10 miles north of the Gulf of Tonkin at the mouth of the Red River, the silt of which would close access were it not for dredges. As a kind of metaphor for the air war, these dredges were off-limits to U.S. bombing throughout the war. From 1964, the Joint Chiefs of Staff called for mining of the harbor, but the White House ruled that out for two reasons. First, President Lyndon Johnson feared that a mistakenly sunken Soviet merchant ship might lead to World War III. Second, Britain, France, and other U.S. allies traded with North Vietnam, and their ships regularly visited Haiphong Harbor.

Due to interservice rivalries between the U.S. Air Force and Navy, North Vietnam was divided into a system of route packages (known as "route packs") to evenly portion out the bombing. Haiphong was in Route Pack 6b and reserved primarily for naval air action, although Air Force sorties were sometimes targeted there. In June 1967, Air Force F-105s flying over the Cam Pha Peninsula north of Haiphong strafed the *Turkestan,* a Soviet freighter. The local USAF wing commander tried to cover up the incident and Washington denied that it had happened, but when Premier Alexei Kosygin presented President Johnson a 20mm slug with U.S. markings on it at the Glassboro, New Jersey, summit in July, denial turned to embarrassment.

Haiphong became fair game during Operation LINEBACKER. On 8 May 1972, as a part of a concerted air effort aimed at stemming North Vietnam's Easter Offensive, President Richard Nixon ordered Haiphong and the port at Dong Ha closed by mining. During his televised address on the evening of 8 May, Nixon announced that as he was speaking A-7 Corsairs and A-6 Intruders were sowing acoustical and magnetic mines across the harbor entrance. He gave shipping 72 hours to vacate the harbor, and then the mines would be activated. After 11 May, the harbor remained closed until the Navy started clearing the mines away on 5 February 1973, after the Paris Peace Accords brought an end to U.S. involvement in the war.

Like Hanoi, Haiphong suffered very little damage from U.S. bombing during either ROLLING THUNDER or the two LINEBACKER operations. For most of the war, the docking facilities and storage areas around the harbor were rarely targeted because of fear of collateral damage to Soviet or allied merchant vessels. But the closing of Haiphong Harbor during the critical days of the Easter Offensive of 1972 probably did more to turn the war in the favor of the United States than any other single operation. This one act effectively denied the North Vietnamese Army the supplies it needed to sustain a 14-division offensive inside South Vietnam. Given the increased pace of U.S. bombing along the infiltration corridors, and the stiff resistance offered by a better-trained and better-led Army of the Republic of South Vietnam, North Vietnam's big offensive was made to pay a price it could not afford.

Earl H. Tilford Jr.

References

Momyer, William. *Airpower in Three Wars: World War II, Korea, and Vietnam.* Washington, DC: U.S. Government Printing Office, 1978.

Morrocco, John. *The Vietnam Experience: Rain of Fire—The Air War, 1969–1973.* Boston: Boston Publishing Company, 1984.

Tilford, Earl H. Jr. *Crosswinds: The Air Force's Setup in Vietnam.* College Station: Texas A&M University Press, 1993.

One of the finest close assault weapons of World War I was the Halberstädt CL.IV. Its success influenced German thinking on the coordination of air and ground attack in World War II. (Walter J. Boyne)

Halberstädt Aircraft

German aircraft manufacturer. The Halberstädter Flugzeugwerke firm designed and built a conventional line of single- and two-seat aircraft. Over the winter of 1916–1917, its D.II single-seat fighter was used alongside the Albatros D.II in the early *jagdstaffeln* (fighter squadrons), but the Albatros became the favored mount, and the Halberstädt soon disappeared from the front. Manfred von Richthofen used the type for a brief period following a lower-wing failure in his Albatros.

The company's primary claim to fame is associated with its line of light two-seaters, the CL.II and CL.IV. The CL class was originally conceived as a two-seat escort fighter that would protect the larger and heavier C-class two-seaters on bombing and artillery registration flights. With that assignment, the CL.II equipped the *schutzstaffeln* (protection flights) formed in 1917. When the units were redesignated *schlachtstaffeln* (battle flights) in 1918, their role was also switched to ground attack, and Halberstädt issued the slightly modified CL.IV. Both the CL.II and CL.IV were single-bay Mercedes-powered biplanes that carried a crew of two in a large, bathtublike cockpit designed for close communication. Pilot and observer each had a machine gun, and a small load of bombs was carried for use against ground targets.

James Streckfuss

See also

German Air Force (Luftwaffe)

References

Gray, Peter, and Owen Thetford. *German Aircraft of the First World War.* London: Putnam, 1962.

Halsey, William Frederick (1882–1959)

U.S. admiral and fleet commander during World War II. Born in Elizabeth, New Jersey, on 30 October 1882, Halsey attended the U.S. Naval Academy, graduating in 1904. His initial assignments were on surface ships, leading to command of two destroyers. Changing warfare specialties late in his career, Halsey became a naval aviator in 1935 and later commanded the carrier USS *Saratoga,* Pensacola Naval Air Station, and two separate carrier divisions. When Pearl Harbor was attacked, Halsey commanded all aircraft carriers in the Pacific Fleet.

President Harry Truman and Admiral William Frederick Halsey, Jr., confer on 19 October 1945. Halsey's smile may not have been sincere, because he had not received his promotion to Fleet Admiral, and would not until December of that year. (U.S. Navy)

In early 1942, his carrier forces struck deeply at the Japanese around the Marshall Islands and later escorted Colonel Jimmy Doolittle's B-25 bombers within striking distance of Japan, resulting in needed propaganda victories for the United States. Having Admiral Chester Nimitz's total confidence, Halsey commanded forces in the South Pacific and took over operations around Guadalcanal after efforts had stalled and success was in doubt. Halsey's aggressive approach turned the campaign around, and Guadalcanal was soon in U.S. hands. Illness forced Halsey to step down temporarily, turning command over to Admiral Raymond Spruance.

Halsey—dubbed "Bull" by the press—was later appointed to command Third Fleet. With carrier-based airpower, his forces won an overwhelming victory at Leyte Gulf in the Philippines, virtually eliminating the Imperial Japanese Navy as a fighting force. In the heat of combat, however, Halsey typically decided to seek out and destroy what was, in reality, a Japanese decoy force. His decision to split his forces deprived the vulnerable amphibious force of critical air cover, courting disaster. Halsey's carriers decisively engaged the Japanese at Cape Engano, destroying four carriers, but a Japanese surface force threatened the entire landing operation before being neutralized without Halsey's expected air support. Halsey's performance has been criticized ever since, and his professional reputation has suffered accordingly.

He was retained in command, and planes from Halsey's carriers struck the Japanese home islands in 1945. At war's end, Halsey was rewarded by promotion to five-star rank as fleet admiral. Due to poor health, Halsey retired from the Navy in 1947 and died at Fishers Island, New York, on 16 August 1959.

Halsey had been an early advocate of naval airpower, recognizing the preeminence of the carrier over the battleship in contemporary warfare. Throughout the war in the South Pacific, he effectively isolated Japanese strongpoints and outmaneuvered or outfought the Imperial Japanese Navy by relying on his own carrier-based airpower. His unswerving objective of hitting the enemy "hard, fast, and often" made him one of the most bellicose and colorful of America's wartime military leaders.

Michael S. Casey

See also

Cape Engano, Battle of; Doolittle, James H.; Gilbert Islands; Guadalcanal; Iwo Jima; Leyte Gulf, Battle of; Nimitz, Chester

William; Okinawa; Rabaul; Santa Cruz, Battle of; Spruance, Raymond A.

References

Keating, Lawrence A. *Fleet Admiral.* Philadelphia: Westminster Press, 1965.

Merrill, James M. *A Sailor's Admiral.* New York: Crowell, 1976.

Potter, E. B. *Bull Halsey.* Annapolis, MD: Naval Institute Press, 1985.

Hamburg Bombing Campaign

Allied bombing of Hamburg (Operation GOMORRAH), one of the most destructive operations of World War II and ranking among the most devastating conventional bombing operations of all time. The vast scale of the bombing led to the first firestorm, an immense conflagration typically associated with nuclear weapons today. More than 50,000 people died in a week-long campaign against Hamburg in July 1943.

The RAF had carried out increasingly successful raids over many cities in the Ruhr and western Germany, reaching 1,000-plane strength against Cologne in May 1942. Area-bombing was thus far Britain's most potent weapon, and the chief of Bomber Command, Sir Arthur Harris, sought to bring the Nazis to their knees. He recognized that massive bomb tonnages must fall on German cities to achieve victory from the air. The success of these increasingly large strikes led planners to attempt concentrated attack campaigns against major cities. At the same time, technical advances made such large-scale attacks feasible. These included H2S, an early airborne radar system; Window (aluminum strips, or chaff, dropped from the air to confuse enemy radar); Pathfinder aircraft to mark targets; and the massing of sufficient four-engine bombers, primarily the Handley Page Halifax and Avro Lancaster bombers, to put enormous fleets in the air on a nightly basis. During this campaign, the United States continued to emphasize precision strikes but also contributed to the destruction of Hamburg, targeting shipyards, U-boat works, and electric generation plants.

Hamburg was a prime target. The second largest city in Germany and its leading port, Hamburg was home to shipyards, refineries, and other essential industries. Eliminating its many capabilities would greatly affect the German war effort.

On 24 July 1943, the RAF launched more than 700 bombers carrying a mix of high-explosive and incendiary bombs against the city. From their experience, British planners knew that a mix of bombs caused greater destruction and hindered damage-control efforts. After more than 100 raids, Hamburg had a well-trained, well-equipped civil defense program. However, the GOMORRAH bombing overwhelmed all possible countermeasures. General Harris intended to saturate Hamburg's fire and defensive services. If these could be inundated, then the effects of bombing could not be repaired; thus the offensive could move on instead of requiring repeated attacks.

Window rendered the strike force nearly invulnerable to radar interception, leaving German flak and fighters blind. Shortly after midnight, British bombers began dropping their bombs on Hamburg. Only 12 RAF bombers were shot down. Hamburg was pounded in one of the worst raids seen up to that point, leaving hundreds dead. The port was hit especially hard. U.S. daylight raids followed on 25 and 26 July.

The RAF returned on the night of 26–27 July. In two waves, the British again pounded the urban area with incendiary and high-explosive bombs. Water mains were ruptured, making firefighting nearly impossible. The thousands of unbridled fires created a never-before-seen phenomenon—the firestorm. As the air became heated, convection occurred, feeding the blaze with fresh air. Taking place in numerous places simultaneously, this generated hurricane-force winds, fanning the flames before it, spreading into unbombed areas, and consuming everything flammable. The city was destroyed. Those who found refuge in bomb shelters were often suffocated. The temperatures exceeded 1,500 degrees Fahrenheit, setting asphalt ablaze and melting glass, brick, and steel. The RAF would hit Hamburg twice more in the coming week, but the city was already a ruin. More than 50,000 people were dead, hundreds of thousands left homeless. More than half the city's buildings were rubble. Albert Speer reported to Hitler that war production would stop if the Allies carried out such raids on six more German cities.

The bombing of Hamburg heralded the enormous power of the aerial bomber and was a harbinger of the destructive conventional bombing raids such as those against Berlin and Dresden in February 1945 and the firebomb raids that wreaked devastation on more than 50 Japanese cities in 1945. Hamburg demonstrated that the most well-organized defenses could be overrun, the most regimented society broken by airpower. The incredible power of the air arm forecast by Douhet, Mitchell, and Alexander de Seversky in prewar writings had become reality. The airplane could bring about decisive results far from the battlefields by crippling the forces that sustained the armies in the field. Hiroshima, Nagasaki, and the advent of nuclear weapons would only make certain the potential for annihilation from the air.

James M. Pfaff

References

Caidin, Martin. *The Night Hamburg Died.* New York: Ballantine Books, 1960.

Harris, Arthur. *Bomber Offensive.* New York: Collins, 1947.
Morrison, Wilbur H. *Fortress Without a Roof.* New York: St. Martin's, 1982.
Overy, Richard. *Why the Allies Won.* New York: Norton, 1996.

References

Bruce, J. M. *British Aeroplanes, 1914–1918.* London: Putnam, 1957.
______. *Aeroplanes of the Royal Flying Corps (Military Wing).* London: Putnam, 1982.
Henshaw, Trevor. *The Sky Their Battlefield.* London: Grub Street, 1995.

Handley Page Aircraft (Early Years/World War I)

Frederick Handley Page was one of many aviation pioneers who founded a company on the hope that aircraft manufacturing would become a thriving business. Starting in 1908, Handley Page first concentrated on the production of monoplanes and, in 1912, offered flight instruction at Hendon. The firm's entry in the 1912 military trials, the Type F, ended in a crash that took it out of the competition. The company did not lose its competitive spirit, however, and in 1913 responded to the offer of £10,000 by the London *Daily Mail* to the first to fly across the Atlantic with the design of the L/200. The contest was interrupted by the outbreak of World War I before anyone could claim the prize. But the L/200 had given Handley Page experience in the design of large aircraft, and in December 1914, when the Admiralty issued a request for a large patrol bomber, the company began work on what would become the O/100.

The firm seems to have been the victim of more than a little bad luck with respect to its first big design. The O/100 first took to the air on 17 December 1915 but suffered from tail flutter in its initial tests. Engineering problems were worked out, and a year later the O/100 was ready for delivery to France. On 1 January 1917, O/100 No. 1463, crewed by Lieutenants H. C. Verker and S. R. Hibbard and three air mechanics, was on its way when the crew became lost in the fog and landed at Chalandry, on the aerodrome occupied by German Flieger Abteilung 208, providing the enemy with the bomber before the British. Later, on one of its first patrols over the English Channel, another O/100 crashed in the water and was lost. Following this, it was decided to switch the mammoth aircraft to night-bombing duties.

In mid-1917, the O/100 was replaced in government contracts by the O/400, which differed only in the design of its engine nacelle. The HP finally made it to operations in France in 1918 with the RAF Independent Force, but a decision was made early in the year to replace it with the Vickers Vimy. The Vimy had not yet appeared at the front, however, before the Armistice eliminated the need for large bombers. Meanwhile, Handley Page had produced the new V/1500, which served in the postwar Royal Air Force.

James Streckfuss

Handley Page Aircraft (Post–World War I)

The large Handley Page bombers of World War I were suitable for conversion to airliners, and Handley Page Transport began operations in August 1919. A long line of derivative aircraft followed, many of them being tested and adapted to the harsh climatic conditions of the Middle East and India. Most of these had the typical wood, metal, and fabric construction of the wartime aircraft, but some aircraft had all-metal structures.

Sir Frederick Handley Page was an aerodynamicist, the inventor (with R. O. Boswell) of the slotted wing. He patented both the fixed and the movable slot, which were used in many Handley Page aircraft and under license in others. (In Germany, Gustav V. Lachman also invented, in parallel, a similar slotted wing.)

The company manufactured a long line of advanced aircraft, including the Hendon torpedo plane and the very sleek Type S fighter, a low-wing cantilever monoplane. Many of Handley Page's advanced ideas came together in the oddly named Gugnunc, which placed second to the Curtiss Tanager in the 1929 Guggenheim Safe Aircraft Competition.

Handley Page continued in the bomber business with the Hyderabad biplane heavy bomber and the much more advanced—and very unusual-appearing—Heyford. The Heyford's biplane arrangement had the top wing faired into the fuselage, with the lower wing suspended well below on struts. The aircraft had a good performance for the time, and the 124 that were procured became the equipment of no less than 11 RAF squadrons.

The Handley Page biplane/slot formula was also used by Imperial Airways in the four-engine HP 42 airliner. Stately rather than swift, the HP 42 carried its passengers in comfort over the long routes that connected Great Britain to its empire. The 18 passengers were well served by a cabin crew that could produce seven-course dinners. Best of all, the eight aircraft in the series never had a fatal accident in a decade of service.

When World War II came, Handley Page contributed two important bomber designs—the Hampden and the Halifax. The twin-engine Hampden was a complete departure from past Handley Page practice, being streamlined, fast, and equipped with closely cowled engines, an enclosed cockpit, and retractable landing gear. Although its 254-mph top speed was fast for its time, it was not well armed and was vulnerable to German fighters. It served best at night, as a mine-laying aircraft, and in antisubmarine work. Some of the 1,432 Hampdens that were built were converted for use as torpedo-bombers.

After World War II had ended, Handley Page built 147 of its four-engine Hasting transports. This was followed by the very advanced four-engine Hermes, a sleek transport that was competitive with the contemporary Lockheed Constellation. One model was fitted with turboprop engines, becoming the largest and fastest four-engine transport flying at the time.

The Handley Page firm had great success with the Victor bomber and continued to experiment with very advanced projects, including supersonic airliners and flying jeeps. Despite some great designs, including the twin-turboprop Herald and the very modern Jetstream executive aircraft, the fire had gone out of the company with the death of Sir Frederick in 1962. He had seen the company grow from his first experimental gliders in 1909 to the 640-mph Victor of 1952. Only eight years after his death, the company was dissolved, unable to obtain the necessary financing to compete in the dwindling marketplace.

Walter J. Boyne

See also
Handley Page Halifax; Handley Page Victor

References
Barnes, C. H. *Handley Page Aircraft Since 1907.* London: Putnam, 1976.
Donald, David, gen. ed. *The Complete Encyclopedia of World Aircraft.* New York: Barnes and Noble, 1997.
Gunston, Bill. *World Encyclopedia of Aircraft Manufacturers.* Sparkford, UK: Patrick Stephens, 1993.

Handley Page Halifax

British four-engine bomber; served at the heart of Royal Air Force night attacks on Germany as part of the Combined Bomber Offensive, as well as in several special mission roles. Large, almost rectangular, twin tailplanes and a smooth Perspex nose distinguished the later and more numerous versions.

Like its better-known cousin, the Avro Lancaster, the Halifax was a redesign of a twin-engine plan. Early versions used Merlin inline engines, though later models had Hercules radials. Various subcontractors produced or converted variants of the Halifax for coastal patrol, transport, glider-towing, and paratroop-drop missions.

Halifaxes made their first strike on occupied Le Havre, France, in March 1941. Operations continued through the war and after, with the last operational flight by an RAF Coastal Command Halifax in 1952.

The Halifax was a workhorse, noted for it smooth flying characteristics, at least in the later versions. Far more successful than its immediate predecessor, the Short Stirling, the Halifax was never modified to carry the extremely heavy blockbuster bombs that made the Lancaster more famous.

Grant Weller

See also
Avro Lancaster; Berlin Air Battles; Combined Bomber Offensive; Harris, Arthur T.; Royal Flying Corps/Royal Naval Air Service/Royal Air Force

References
Angelucci, Enzo, ed. *The Rand McNally Encyclopedia of Military Aircraft, 1914–1980.* New York: Military Press, 1980.
Munson, Kenneth. *Fighters and Bombers of World War II, 1939–1945.* London: Peerage Books, 1969.

Handley Page Victor

One of the triumvirate of British V-bombers that also included the Valiant and Vulcan. Designed to the same specification as the Vulcan, the Victor was unique in that it featured swept crescent wings and a T-shaped tail.

The prototype made its maiden flight in December 1952, with the first production aircraft flying three years later. Squadron service began in November 1957. Eventually, four units in RAF Bomber Command were equipped with the Victor B.1. Initially, the aircraft were finished in overall anti-flash white, although the switch to lower-altitude operations required that an upper surface finish of gray and green be applied.

Following on from the first version of the Victor came the more advanced B.2, which was later optimized to carry the Blue Steel standoff weapon. Primary changes to the airframe included an extended span that sported large underwing tanks. On the wing trailing edge were two aerodynamic fairings that were to eventually house electronic countermeasures equipment. Fitted from the outset was an inflight refueling probe. The Victor B.2 entered service in 1962 with No. 139 Squadron. With their arrival, earlier aircraft were withdrawn from service. However, the Victor B.1s were to gain a new lease on life when they were converted to tankers to replace the Valiants that had been grounded on short notice due to fatigue failure of the wing mainspar.

Not all the later Victors were completed as bombers; a handful emerged as SR.2s for the strategic reconnaissance role. This entailed the fitting of customizable pallets into the bomb bay to match mission requirements. During the mid-1970s, the aircraft of No. 543 Squadron were replaced by upgraded versions of the Vulcan designated B.2(MRR).

As with the Victor B.1, the surviving bombers and reconnaissance aircraft were converted into K.2 tankers. Their service spanned 20 years and involved operational flying in support of operations during the Falkland Islands War and the Gulf War.

Kev Darling

References

Brookes, Andrew. *V Force*. London: Jane's Information Group, 1982.

Hannover Aircraft

Hannoverische Waggonfabrik had been a manufacturer of railroad rolling stock when, like other firms in related businesses, it was called upon by the government to make aircraft. Again like others, during the first half of World War I, the German firm built other manufacturer's designs under license until establishing a company drawing office and developing a type of its own. The Hannover CL.II was designed against the Luftstreitkräfte's request for a light two-seater for protection and, later, ground attack work. Light and strong, due to its plywood-covered fuselage, the Hannover ("Hawa," or "Hannoverana," as it was variously nicknamed) was powered by the ubiquitous Mercedes engine. It was a single-bay biplane, with a biplane empennage that made the tail quite compact, increasing the observer's field of rearward fire. Forward fire was provided to the pilot by a Spandau gun synchronized to fire through the propeller. The pilot's view was excellent, the deep fuselage almost filling the gap between the wings, putting the upper wing at eye level. The crewmen were seated in separate cockpits set close together. That similarity to the Bristol Fighter, along with the Hannover's small size, gave it a great advantage in combat. Enemy pilots would often lunge into the attack before realizing it was a two-seater they were up against, fire from the rear gun being their first warning.

Introduced at the end of 1917, the CL.II was refined during 1918 through the subsequent CL.III and CL.IIIa models. The difference between the III and IIIa was the engine, the latter having an Argus rather than the Mercedes, which, due to priority use, was being committed to single-seat fighters.

Along with Halberstädts, Hannovers equipped the *schlachtstaffeln* (battle flights) during the German spring offensive, performing dangerous ground attack missions then and throughout the remainder of the war.

James Streckfuss

See also

Bristol Beaufighter

References

Gray, Peter, and Owen Thetford. *German Aircraft of the First World War*. London: Putnam, 1962.

Hanoi Air Attacks

U.S. air campaign against what was considered to be the most heavily defended city in the history of aerial warfare. When they flew to Hanoi, U.S. pilots dubbed it "going downtown." Although Hanoi proper was never a target as major European and Japanese cities had been during World War II, U.S. Air Force and Navy aircraft struck bridges, petroleum storage facilities, and railyards in and around the city. At the height of Operation ROLLING THUNDER, one out of every 40 USAF fighter-bombers that "went downtown" did not return.

Hanoi, the capital of North Vietnam (now the capital of the Socialist Republic of Vietnam), sits astride the Red River about 75 miles inland from the Gulf of Tonkin. Although Hanoi was heavily defended, U.S. planes struck only intermittently, and the city itself was lightly damaged. From the start of ROLLING THUNDER on 2 March 1965 until June 1966, most of the bombing was in the panhandle. The White House assumed, and the State Department agreed, that bombing Hanoi posed two risks. First, it might prompt Chinese and Soviet intervention and escalation. Second, some thought if Hanoi lost its industrial base—consisting of three major factories—the effect would be like "killing the hostage." With no industrial base and nothing else to lose, Hanoi could not be threatened with losing what it no longer had. This Alice in Wonderland reasoning dominated civilian strategizing throughout ROLLING THUNDER.

Airpower advocates called for concerted bombing in and around Hanoi to destroy major targets like the Paul Doumer Bridge, the railways and highways leading the China, the petroleum, oil, and lubricant (POL) storage facilities, and railyards. Although an elaborate system of dikes and levies protected Hanoi from the seasonal flooding of the Red River, there was no consideration given to breaching those dikes as a way of destroying the city.

In June 1966, the first strikes hit Hanoi and Haiphong. For 30 days, Air Force and naval aircraft pounded POL storage facilities. Estimates are these strikes cost Hanoi 110,000 of its 185,000 tons of POL, leaving 75,000 tons stored at major airfields—which remained off-limits to bombing—and scattered about in small storage areas consisting of 55-gallon-drum caches placed in the center of small towns and villages. Because North Vietnam dedicated almost all POL to the war effort, losing even 60 percent of it had little effect on an army that moved more supplies on foot than in trucks.

Hundreds of antiaircraft guns, SA-2 surface-to-air missiles, and three major MiG bases formed a netted air defense system that made going downtown dangerous. Typically, Air Force crews, flying F-105 Thunderchiefs ("Thuds") with F-4 Phantoms as escorts, approached Hanoi from the northwest, below 1,500 feet along a spine of the Annamite Mountains consecrated as "Thud Ridge." Although low altitudes provided crews some protection against radar detection and surface-to-air missiles, they remained vulnerable to thousands of Vietnamese civilians firing rifles and to antiaircraft fire. Over Hanoi, they climbed above 10,000 feet, where SAMs and MiGs became the threat. Then the crews dove back into intense antiaircraft fire to release their bombs at around 6,000 feet and pull out below 3,000 feet. Even a single bullet from an AK-47 or a few fragments from an antiaircraft round could tear apart a jet engine, ripping off turbine blades that could sever fuel lines to start a fire or rip into hydraulic systems that negated use of controls. If the pilot survived the burning and exploding aircraft and high-speed ejection, he would be captured by angry villagers. If he made it to the Hanoi Hilton—the infamous POW installation—he faced years of barbaric torture. In 1966, 1967, and for most of 1968, an F-105 pilot assigned to Southeast Asia had about a 50-50 chance of surviving the tour. That is what "going downtown" meant.

In 1967, bombing focused on degrading the electrical power grid and bombing bridges. Neither was very successful. Backup gasoline generators provided sufficient power, and pontoon bridges, put in place at dark and removed before dawn, replaced the concrete spans over the Red River. In October 1968, ROLLING THUNDER came to an end, and Hanoi received a nearly four-year respite from bombing.

On 8 May 1972, President Richard Nixon, responding to North Vietnam's Easter Offensive, ordered targets struck throughout North Vietnam. The Paul Doumer Bridge, the Yen Vien railyards, and POL storage facilities were hit. For the first time, B-52s were used to bomb targets in and around Hanoi and Haiphong Harbor. Operation LINEBACKER lasted until the North Vietnamese leadership negotiated seriously, coming to an end when a peace agreement seem within reach on 23 October 1972. It was the most successful bombing campaign of the war in that it brought Hanoi to the brink of peace. But it took one more bombing campaign to clinch the deal.

When in December 1972 Hanoi recalled its negotiators from the Paris peace talks, Nixon unleashed airpower with a vengeance. During the 11 days of Operation LINEBACKER II, 739 B-52 sorties and 1,200 fighter-bomber sorties struck 334 targets in and around Hanoi, Haiphong, Vinh, and Thanh Hoa. The 20,000 tons of bombs dropped during the so-called Christmas bombing battered railyards and storage facilities. But most important, airpower rendered North Vietnamese air defenses useless by destroying its air-control headquarters and SAM assembly area. By December 29, North Vietnam was helpless against U.S. airpower. They agreed to negotiate, and the bombing stopped.

Antiwar activists claimed that the Air Force had carpet-bombed Hanoi, and North Vietnam's propaganda mill produced vivid photographic "evidence" to support those claims. But in reality damage to the city was light, as confirmed by aerial reconnaissance and visitors to the city.

Earl H. Tilford Jr.

References

Clodfelter, Mark. *The Limits of Air Power: The American Bombing of North Vietnam.* New York: Free Press, 1989.

Emerson, Gloria. *Winners and Losers: Battles, Retreats, Gains, Losses, and Ruins from a Long War.* New York: Harcourt, Brace, 1976.

Morrocco, John. *The Vietnam Experience: Thunder From Above—The Air War, 1941–1968.* Boston: Boston Publishing Company, 1984.

Tilford, Earl H. Jr. *Crosswinds: The Air Force's Setup in Vietnam.* College Station: Texas A&M University Press, 1993.

Hansell, Haywood S., Jr. (1903–1988)

USAF general. Born to Colonel Haywood S. Hansell in Fort Monroe, Virginia, in 1903, Heywood Shepherd Hansell Jr. graduated from the Georgia School of Technology in 1924 with a degree in mechanical engineering and was commissioned a second lieutenant in the Army Air Corps Reserve upon completing advanced flight training at Kelly Field, Texas, in 1929. He was assigned to the Second Bombardment Group at Langley Field, Virginia, in June 1930 and later served as armament officer of the Air Corps Tactical School. In August 1931, Lieutenant Hansell was transferred to Maxwell Field, Alabama, where he served with Captain Claire L. Chennault on the Army aerobatic team (Three Men on a Flying Trapeze).

Hansell graduated from the Air Corps Tactical School at Maxwell Field in June 1935. He stayed on as an instructor there, becoming affiliated with a group of young officers who espoused the belief that strategic long-range aircraft could destroy an enemy's industrial infrastructure. In 1939, upon completing the Command and General Staff School at Fort Leavenworth, Kansas, he was assigned to the office of the chief of the Air Corps, where he became assistant executive officer in September 1939. In November, Captain Hansell was transferred to the Intelligence Division and became chief of the Operations Planning Branch, Foreign Intelligence Section.

After a stint in London as a special observer in July and August 1941, he returned to the Air Staff War Plans Division in Washington, D.C. He transferred to the Operations Division of the War Department General Staff in April 1942 and served on the Joint Strategic Committee. Brigadier General Hansell commanded the 3d Bomb Wing and later the 1st Bomb of the Eighth Air Force in Europe and flew combat missions before becoming deputy commander in chief of the Allied Expeditionary Air Force. Hansell returned to Army Air Forces HQ as air planner on the Joint Planning Staff until he was given command of the new XXI Bomber Command on Saipan in August 1944, where he directed bombing raids on Tokyo.

Reassigned to the United States to head the 38th Flying Training Wing at Kirtland Field, New Mexico, in January 1945, he was later transferred to Air Transport Command HQ in Washington, D.C. At the war's end, he was commanding general of the Caribbean Wing, Atlantic Division, Air Transport Command, and retired from the USAAF on 31 December 1946. In July 1951, during the Korean War, Hansell was recalled to active duty and served as chief of the Mobilization Division, Directorate of Plans, in the office of the deputy Chief of Staff for operations at USAF HQ. Promoted to major general on 5 September 1952, Hansell was the senior Air Force member, Military Studies and Evaluations Division, Weapons Systems Evaluation Group, Office of the Secretary of Defense, in Washington, D.C. Awarded the Distinguished Service Medal, Legion of Merit, Silver Star, Distinguished Flying Cross, and Air Medal, General "Woody" Hansell retired from the USAF in May 1955 and died 14 November 1988.

Richard C. DeAngelis

References

Bowman, Martin W. *USAAF Handbook, 1939–1945.* Mechanicsburg, PA: Stackpole Books, 1997.

Morrison, Wilbur H. *Point of No Return: The Story of the Twentieth Air Force.* New York: N.Y. Times Books, 1979.

Hanson, Robert M. (1920–1944)

First lieutenant in the United States Marine Corp Reserve; World War II Pacific ace with 25 confirmed kills. Hanson flew with VMF-215 and was awarded the Congressional Medal of Honor, Navy Cross, and Distinguished Flying Cross.

Robert M. Hanson was born on 4 February 1920 in Lucknow, India. The child of missionary parents, he was a prewar heavyweight wrestling champion in the United Provinces. He witnessed the Nazi seizure of power in Austria firsthand.

Lieutenant Hanson joined VMF-215—the Fighting Corsairs—flying the F4U Corsair in August 1943 in time to participate in the landings on the Japanese stronghold of Bougainville. He also was involved with the 24 January 1944 New Britain Island operations. Hanson became an ace on 1 November 1943 after downing three Japanese aircraft for a total of five. VMF-215 claimed two other top Marine aces by the end of the war: Captain Donald N. Aldrich (20 kills) and Captain Harold L. Spears (15 kills).

Over Empress Augusta Bay on 1 November 1943, he engaged six Japanese torpedo-bombers, destroying one and forcing all to jettison their explosives before reaching their target. On 24 January 1944, flying high cover alone after being cut off from his division over enemy-held Simpson Harbor, Hanson attacked a large number of Zeros attempting to intercept U.S. bombers, shooting down four that were confirmed and claiming a fifth that was not. Hanson had developed a reputation as an aggressive and skilled aviator who often engaged the enemy in spite of their superior numbers.

On 3 February 1944, while strafing a lighthouse, which served as a flak tower and observation post, on Cape St. George, New Ireland, his aircraft was hit by flak. Hudson was unable to get out of the plane before it crashed into the ocean and disintegrated. He was 23 years old.

Robert Hanson shot down 25 Japanese aircraft between August 1943 and February 1944. He was the third, the youngest, and the last Marine Corsair pilot to earn the Medal of Honor.

Scott R. DiMarco

References

Medal of Honor Citation. 1stLt ROBERT M. HANSON.

Sims, Edward H. *Greatest Fighter Missions of the Top Navy and Marine Aces of World War II.* New York: Ballantine Books, 1962.

Styling, Mark, and Jerry Scutts. *Corsair Aces of World War 2.* Osceola, WI: Motorbooks International, 1995.

Harris, Arthur T. (1892–1984)

Chief of RAF Bomber Command during much of World War II; nicknamed "Bomber" Harris, he became a figure of continuing controversy. He joined the Royal Flying Corps in 1915, becoming a fighter pilot, then served in a variety of interwar line and staff positions. By 1939, he commanded a Bomber Command group and rose to deputy Chief of Air Staff in 1940.

He was named chief of Bomber Command (and was knighted) in 1942. His was the initiative behind nighttime saturation—or, as his critics put it, indiscriminate—bombing. Harris argued that the RAF lacked the strength and technology for effective pinpoint bombing and could not sustain the aircraft and crew losses such attacks caused. He thus adopted urban area-bombing as a means of attacking German morale. He launched the first 1,000-bomber raid in May 1942, with more to follow.

From November 1943 into early 1944, his bombers concentrated on missions to Berlin in an attempt to knock Germany out of the war by strategic air attack alone. But mounting bomber losses, poor weather, and improving German air defenses limited the effort. With his dedication to the saturation campaign, Harris came into increasing conflict with Allied leaders who wanted a more flexible use of airpower, including tactical support of ground forces before and after D-Day.

The RAF bombing of Dresden in February 1945, which killed tens of thousands and destroyed much of that ancient city when the war was nearly won, quickly became infamous and remains controversial. Harris retired in 1946. He was overlooked in the customary end-of-war honors, although he was promoted to Air Marshal and in 1953 was created a baronet.

Christopher H. Sterling

References

Harris, Arthur. *Bomber Offensive.* London: Collins, 1947.

_______. *Despatches on War Operations: 23 February 1942 to 8 May 1945.* London: Frank Cass, 1995.

Saward, Dudley. *"Bomber" Harris: The Story of Marshal of the Royal Air Force, Sir Arthur Harris—The Authorized Biography.* London: Cassell/Buchan and Enright, 1984.

Hartmann, Erich (1922–1993)

The world's most successful fighter pilot. A member of the Luftwaffe's highest-scoring fighter wing, Jagdgeschwader 52 (52nd Fighter Wing), "Bubi" (Baby) Hartmann shot down 352 aircraft, 345 of them Soviet, while flying 825 combat missions. Hartmann was himself shot down 16 times and escaped once from brief Soviet captivity. He was the eighteenth member of the Wehrmacht to receive the Oak Leaves with Swords and Diamonds to the Knight's Cross of the Iron Cross from Hitler.

On 8 May 1945, he surrendered to the U.S. Army, but as a member of an Eastern Front unit he was turned over to the Red Army, which held him until 1955. He was one of the last POWs to be released from Soviet captivity. He joined the Bundesluftwaffe—West Germany's postwar air force—and had a modestly successful peacetime career as a fighter pilot and unit commander until he spoke out against his unit's equipment, the Starfighter. He resigned as a colonel after 14 years of postwar service and became a civilian flight instructor. Hartmann never fully regained his health after his long imprisonment and died in 1993 at the age of 71.

Donald Caldwell

See also

German Air Force (Luftwaffe)

References

Obermeier, E. *Die Ritterkreuzträger der Luftwaffe, 1939–1945, Band I: Jagdflieger* [Recipients of the Knight's Cross]. Mainz: Verlag Dieter Hoffmann, 1989.

Hawker Aircraft

The British firm H. G. Hawker Engineering, Ltd., was registered on 15 November 1920. T. O. M. Sopwith was the guiding spirit behind the new firm, which soon suffered an unexpected tragic loss when test pilot Harry Hawker was killed in a crash.

The company had Fred Sigrist as its works manager and Captain B. Thomson as its chief designer. Sydney Camm joined the firm in 1923, becoming chief designer in 1925 and beginning a series of designs that would prove to be mainstays of the Royal Air Force for the next half-century. Other key members who names would become famous were Fred Raynham and P. W. S. "George" Bulman.

Camm and Sigrist developed a system of metal construction that would prove to be key to a long series of first-rate designs. The most significant of the early developments was the Hart of 1929, which was faster than existing RAF fighters. A delightful aircraft to fly, the Hart was used throughout the British Empire. It inspired a two-place fighter variant, the Demon, whose later models featured a Frazer-Nash turret. More than 17 variants of the basic Hart were built—a total of some 3,020 aircraft, a tremendous production run for a fabric-covered biplane. The variants included the Audax, Demon, Hardy, Hector, Hind, Hoopoe, Nimrod, Osprey, and several others.

The principal fighter variant of the series was the lovely Fury, the first aircraft supplied to the RAF that was capable of more than 200 mph. The aircraft was widely exported, flying for Yugoslavia, Persia, Portugal, Norway, and Spain.

Sydney Camm knew that the biplane formula, however refined, was now obsolete and in 1933 (after the firm had grown to become Hawker Aircraft Ltd.) forwarded proposals for a monoplane fighter replacement. By 1934, the design had been refined to include a Rolls-Royce Merlin engine, retractable landing gear, an enclosed canopy, and a radical

One of the most advanced Hawker-Siddeley designs was developed into the Hawker Harrier, capable of a vertical takeoff. (Walter J. Boyne)

The Hawker Sea Fury served in Korea in the ground attack role. Some surviving examples race at Reno. (Walter J. Boyne)

Often overlooked because of the interest in the Supermarine Spitfire, the Hawker Hurricane was nonetheless the most important RAF fighter in the Battle of Britain. (U.S. Air Force)

new armament package featuring four guns in each wing. This plane was the Hurricane, and it was first flown on 8 November 1935 by Bulman. This was also the year in which the firm expanded, acquiring Gloster to form the Hawker-Siddeley Group. By June 1936, sufficient tests had been passed to earn an order for 600 aircraft, a massive number for the time.

The Hurricane was followed by the Typhoon and Tempest aircraft, much more sophisticated but still plainly showing their Sydney Camm origins.

After the war, Hawker entered the jet age with enthusiasm, producing a long series of designs including the Sea Hawk and the Hunter. The most advanced Hawker-Siddeley design was the Kestrel, a vertical-takeoff fighter that would be developed as the Harrier. The Harrier would be manufactured both by Hawker-Siddeley and McDonnell Douglas. In 1977, under legislation by the British government, a corporation called British Aerospace was created, made up of British Aircraft Corporation, Hawker-Siddeley Aviation, Hawker-Siddeley Dynamics, and Scottish Aviation.

Walter J. Boyne

See also

Camm, Sydney; Gloster Aircraft; Hawker Hunter; Hawker Hurricane; Hawker Typhoon and Tempest; Hawker-Siddeley Aircraft; Sopwith, Thomas O.M.

References

Mason, Francis K. *Hawker Aircraft Since 1920.* Annapolis, MD: Naval Institute Press, 1991.

Hawker Hunter

The British Hawker Hunter first flew in July 1951 and entered service with the RAF in July 1954. The Hunter was regarded as a pilot's airplane—stable, responsive, pleasant to fly—and would exceed the speed of sound with barely a twitch on the Mach meter. It was a highly aerobatic, rugged, and elegant aircraft; its only real fault was a shortage of range, particularly in the earlier versions.

Hunters were involved in several air combats during the Indo-Pakistani wars and in the Middle East. The Hunter was similar to the MiG-19 at medium to low levels in speed and turn rate, although the MiG could roll faster. Compared with the late-model F-86 Sabre, the Hunter had better acceleration, deceleration, and climb but was generally inferior in a turning fight except at high Mach.

Almost 2,000 fighter (F.1–F.6) and trainer (T.7–T.8) versions of the Hunter were produced in the United Kingdom and under license in Holland and Belgium, and many T.7,

T.8, FGA.9, FR.10 and GA.11 aircraft were converted from earlier marks. The Hunter was operated by 19 countries, and some examples were still in service with India and Zimbabwe at the turn of the twenty-first century.

Andy Blackburn

See also
India-Pakistan Airpower

References

Mason, Francis K. *The British Fighter Since 1912.* London: Putnam, 1992.

Hawker Hurricane

The mainstay of RAF Fighter Command during the early years of World War II. The Hurricane saw front-line service in fighter, tactical reconnaissance, and ground attack roles until after the end of hostilities. During World War II, Hurricanes served in every theater and shot down more enemy aircraft than any other Allied type and more than all other British aircraft types combined. Approximately 14,670 Hurricanes and Sea Hurricanes were built between November 1935 and September 1944.

The Hurricane I was a docile but highly maneuverable airplane, a very stable gun platform. It was also extremely strong, being capable of withstanding maneuvers that would pull the wings off many contemporaries. The Hurricane I was 30–40 mph slower than the Spitfire I but had a better turning circle and a superior rate of roll, particularly at high speed, although it tended to lose out above 20,000 feet because of its thicker wing.

The Hurricane II entered RAF service in September 1940 and had an uprated Merlin XX of 1,260 bph; the Mk.IIB was armed with 12 0.303-inch Browning machine guns; later Mk.IICs had four 20mm Hispano cannons. The Hurricane Mk.IID was a specialized antitank version with two 40mm cannons and was mainly used in the Western Desert and Russia; the Mk.IV had additional protective armor and a universal wing that could accept 40mm cannons, rockets, or bombs.

The Sea Hurricane Mk.IB and Mk.IIC were broadly equivalent to the standard Hurricane Mk.I and Mk.II but had slightly lower performance due to the extra equipment fitted (such as catapult spools, arrester hooks). During 1942 and well into 1943, Sea Hurricanes were the Royal Navy's primary air defense asset.

Andy Blackburn

See also
Aircraft Armament; Britain, Battle of; Camm, Sydney; Pattle, Marmaduke Thomas St. John; Supermarine Spitfire

References

Mason, Francis K. *The Hawker Hurricane.* Bourne End, UK: Aston, 1990.
Mason, Francis K. *The British Fighter Since 1912.* London: Putnam, 1992.

Hawker-Siddeley Aircraft

The Hawker-Siddeley Group once comprised Hawker, de Havilland, Gloster, Armstrong Whitworth, Armstrong Siddeley, A.V. Roe, Folland, and Blackburn. This situation remained unchanged until a major reorganization undertaken in 1963 that saw the emergence of Hawker-Siddeley Aircraft (HSA) and Hawker-Siddeley Dynamics (HSD). Eventually, Hawker-Siddeley would be subsumed into a government-organized conglomerate.

The new HSA company carried on manufacturing the products of the original companies, changing only the type prefix to HS. Thus, the Argosy freighter was redesignated from the AW650 to the HS650, the Avro 748 to the HS748. Other aircraft under the company's umbrella were the Hunter and the Buccaneer, as well as the Dominie T.1 navigation trainer. Another trainer and light strike aircraft built under the aegis of HSA was the Gnat T.1, which was also built under license in India as the Ajeet.

Products developed and built by HSA alone included the Hawk trainer, which replaced the Gnat in RAF service. This was followed by the most prestigious of programs: the Harrier jump jet. Developed from the P1127 experimental aircraft via the Kestrel multinational development aircraft, the Harrier continues in development and production to this day.

HSA was also responsible for development of the HS801 Nimrod antisubmarine aircraft. The initial testbeds for the Nimrod were conversions of a pair of unsold Comets. The Nimrod has undergone continued development since introduction, and 22 examples are now being rebuilt to the MRA.4 standard for continued service.

HSD became responsible for developing weaponry for the companies' products. Missiles developed by and supported by HSD included the Firestreak and Red Top missiles for the Lightning. Missiles sponsored by HSD included the U.K. versions of the Martel TV guided missile.

Both companies disappeared in 1977 after the enforced merger with Britain's other U.K. aviation companies to form British Aerospace. The Dynamics division name survived a little longer until the whole conglomerate was renamed BAe Systems in 1999.

Kev Darling

References
Mason, Francis K. *Hawker Aircraft Since 1920.* London: Putnam, 1991.

Hawker Typhoon and Tempest

British World War II fighter-interceptors. The Typhoon entered operational service with the RAF in September 1941. A large and powerful fighter, it was designed as an interceptor, but its high-altitude performance was disappointing because of its thick wing; it had very effective armament and was a good gun platform. It was also the first operational fighter to be fitted with a bubble canopy that gave unrestricted rearward vision.

The Typhoon's introduction into service was rushed, and it gained a reputation for unreliability; the Napier Sabre engine was initially unreliable, there were problems with carbon monoxide seepage, and the aircraft was prone to flutter-induced failure of the entire tail section. All these problems were eventually resolved, and the Typhoon became an effective ground attack fighter, distinguishing itself during the Battle of the Falaise Pocket in 1944. In combat, the Typhoon was not a particularly agile aircraft but could turn slightly tighter than the Focke-Wulf Fw 190A; it was not as good in a climb but slightly better in a dive; its rate of roll was much lower, but it was slightly faster at all heights. More than 3,300 Typhoons were built, all of them serving with the RAF.

The Tempest prototype was converted from a production Typhoon and was initially designated Typhoon II. It had a new, thinner, laminar-flow wing and revised tail surfaces. The major production version (Mark V) was about 20 mph faster than the Typhoon. It was an even better gun platform and had the same bubble canopy; it entered service in February 1944.

In combat, the Tempest was more responsive than the Typhoon and had spring tab ailerons that gave it a particularly good roll rate at high speed (up to 545 mph). A heavy and very clean aircraft, its dive acceleration was outstanding. The Tempest was about 40 mph faster and had much better dive acceleration and zoom-climb capabilities than the Fw 190A. Turning circles were very similar, but the Fw had a much better rate of roll. The Tempest was 40–50 mph faster than the Bf 109G-2, but its climb was not as good. It had slightly better zoom-climb and dive acceleration, it could turn tighter, and it had a better rate of roll above 350 mph.

The Tempest V was very successful in combat; it had sufficient performance to shoot down German jets and was heavily involved in the defense of southern England against V-1 missiles. It was probably the best low- to medium-altitude fighter of World War II. Almst 1,400 Tempests of various marks were built, and some remained in RAF service until June 1951. Both aircraft types were fitted with various versions of the Napier Sabre engine.

Andy Blackburn

See also
Aircraft Armament; Camm, Sydney; Falaise-Argentan pocket; Focke-Wulf Fw 190; Messerschmitt Bf 109; V-1 Missile and V-2 Rocket

References
Mason, Francis K. *The British Fighter Since 1912.* London: Putnam, 1992.

Heinemann, Edward H. (1908–1991)

Aeronautical engineer. Edward H. Heinemann received the Collier Trophy in 1953 for his design of the Douglas F4D "Skyray," the first carrier-based fighter aircraft to reach Mach 1 in level flight. Heinemann's auspicious career resulted in more than 20 fighter, bomber, and rocket aircraft.

After having worked on the Northrop Gamma, Heinemann is known for the Douglas SBD and DB-7, the AD series, D-558 research aircraft, F4D Skyray, A-3 attack bomber, and the sleek A-4D1 Skyhawk. His are remarkable achievements, for he left school at age 17 to work as a draftsman, studying mathematics and engineering on his own.

Hired in 1926 to work for the Douglas Aircraft Company, Heinemann accepted a position at the Northrop Corporation in 1932 and was elevated to chief engineer when it became the El Segundo Division of Douglas Corporation. He designed the Northrop XBT-1, the first all-metal low-wing monoplane built to U.S. Navy specifications. The XBT-1 led to the SBD Dauntless, which joined the U.S. Navy fleet in 1938.

To develop a bomber that would compete favorably in weight, load-carrying capability, and performance, Heinemann designed the versatile AD-1 Skyraider, modifying it at the last moment to utilize the R-3350 power plant. In 1944, he collaborated to design a research aircraft that would take off under its own power and approach the speed of sound. Heinemann designed the D-558-1 Skystreak and the D-558-2 Skyrocket. In 1947, Heinemann started the design that would become, in 1951, the F4D for which he received the Collier Trophy.

Ed Heinemann received the Guggenheim Medal in 1978 and the National Medal of Science in 1983. He was enshrined in the National Aviation Hall of Fame in 1981 and the International Aerospace Hall of Fame in 1982. A unique leader and outstanding engineer, Ed Heinemann retired in

1973 from his position as General Dynamics's corporate vice president of engineering and became an aeronautical consultant. Born in Saginaw, Michigan, on 14 November 1908, Heinemann died on 26 November 1991 at the age of 83.

Charles Cooper and Ann Cooper

References

Francillon, Rene J. *McDonnell Douglas Aircraft Since 1920.* Annapolis, MD: Naval Institute Press, 1988.

Rausa, Rosario. *Ed Heinemann: Combat Aircraft Designer.* Annapolis, MD: Naval Institute Press, 1980.

Heinkel Aircraft

German aircraft manufacturer. Ernst Heinkel (1888–1958) built his first airplane in 1911 but was seriously injured when it eventually crashed. He worked subsequently for Albatros, Hansa-Brandenburg, and Castiglioni, designing seaplanes for the latter. Heinkel formed his own company in 1922 and produced a variety of fighters, trainers, and observation aircraft for export.

Of all the German companies, Heinkel was most devoted to military aircraft by the early 1930s. The company was reorganized in 1935 and moved to larger quarters. The He 51 biplane fighter entered service in 1936 and fought in the Spanish civil war. The He 59 was designed as a torpedo-bomber and for use in reconnaissance. The He 70 fast mailplane was turned to military service. The He 72 Kadett trainer was widely used. The twin-engine He 111 was also initially designed for airline use but became the most widely used (more than 7,000 copies) German bomber. The He 112 lost out to the Bf 109 as the standard German single-engine fighter aircraft.

One of the most notable achievements was the world's first flight of a jet aircraft, the Heinkel He 178, flown by Erich Warstiz on 27 August 1939.

The He 115 was a twin-engine floatplane used for reconnaissance and minelaying as well as torpedo-bombing and first flew in 1938. After production of nearly 140 examples, the aircraft was phased out as obsolescent by late 1940.

The He 162 Salamander became an operational jet fighter—more than 800 were being manufactured at the very end of the war. The sophisticated He 177 Greif (Griffon) first flew in 1939 but never overcame engine overheating problems (with its four engines coupled in two nacelles) to become the successful heavy bomber intended. The He 219 Uhu (Owl) made a successful night-fighter in limited numbers (nearly 300) after 1943. By late 1944, the 27 subsidiary plants and factories employed nearly 50,000 workers. Heinkel was reformed in 1955 and participated in several multination airplane projects. In 1964, it was merged into VFW and disappeared as a separate firm.

Christopher H. Sterling

See also

Heinkel He 111

References

"Heinkel." In William Green, *The Warplanes of the Third Reich.* Garden City, NY: Doubleday, 1970, pp. 258–373.

Griehl, Manfred. *Heinkel Combat Aircraft.* London: Arms and Armour, 1992.

Turner, P. St. John. *Heinkel: An Aircraft Album.* New York: Arco, 1970.

Heinkel He 111 (1934–1945)

German commercial transport and military bomber. The high-speed, low-wing, twin-engine monoplane was state-of-the-art when designed in 1934 but remained in service until 1945, when it was long obsolete.

He 111As were underpowered, and improved engines enabled the Kondor Legion's He 111Bs and He 111Es to achieve great success in Spain. Six He 111Cs served with Lufthansa but proved cramped and uneconomical. Bottlenecks in Daimler Benz engine production prevented large numbers of He 111Ds and He 111Ps from entering service. Turkey purchased 40 He 111Fs with improved wing design. Initially designed as torpedo-bombers, 90 He 111Js served as conventional bombers. Twelve "Siamese twin" He 111Zs were built as monstrous glider tugs. He 111Hs were the most widely used version, known for pleasant handling, good stability, and maneuverability. He 111s had five seats, one cannon, four to five machine guns, and up to 5,512 pounds of bombs. With maximum bombload, maximum speed was 217 mph, range was 1,212 miles, and ceiling was 21,980 feet.

Some 7,300 He 111s were built and served on every front. Defensive armament proved inadequate even in Poland and Norway, and He 111s suffered such heavy attrition against Britain that they flew only night sorties after mid-September 1940. Moreover, range and bombload were insufficient for truly effective strategic bombing. Torpedo-armed He 111s inflicted heavy damage on Allied convoys in the Arctic and Mediterranean in 1941–1942. They performed well enough as tactical bombers against the Soviets but lacked the range to reach industrial targets in the Urals. After 1943, He 111s mainly served as transports, although some launched mines, guided weapons, and V-1 rocket-missiles (including 1,200 V-1s against Britain).

James D. Perry

With uses such as command and control, liaison, reconnaissance, wire laying, rotation of troops in the battle line, plane guards (ready rescue) on aircraft carriers, supply of frontline troops, adjustment of artillery fire, and artillery raids, helicopters have become indispensable to military forces. (Walter J. Boyne)

References

Green, William. *Warplanes of the Third Reich.* New York: Galahad Books, 1986, pp. 287–308.

Helicopter Operations in the U.S. Army

Since it first procured small Bell YR-13 helicopters in 1946, the U.S. Army has found increasing uses for helicopters, including incorporation into the combat arms.

The Korean War provided the Army its first opportunity to use helicopters in combat. In early 1951, the Army's H-13 Sioux assumed the medical-evacuation role from the Air Force, thus enhancing the survivability of wounded soldiers. H-13s and H-23 Ravens were also distributed to combat commands for experimentation. Without doctrine to guide them, Army commanders were soon using them for liaison, command and control, supply, wirelaying, river-crossing, artillery fire adjustment, and reconnaissance. Encouraged by Marine successes with transport helicopters, the Army sent two H-19 Chickasaw companies to Korea to experiment with troop movement and supply of front-line troops. The experiments were successful, convincing the Army that it had made the correct decision to organize 12 transport helicopter battalions.

The Vietnam War has been called the "Helicopter War" with good reason. After U.S. support began in 1961, few operations were begun without helicopter lift of troops. To counter guerrilla ambush tactics against South Vietnamese troops, the Army injected H-21 Shawnee helicopter transport units into Vietnam in 1961. Flying South Vietnamese troops into combat, U.S. officers developed immediate response units called "Eagle Flights" that used various tactics to destroy guerrillas.

Because landing zones came under enemy fire, the Army put machine guns in H-21 doorways for suppressive fire when landing, but this was unsatisfactory. In 1962, the Army sent armed UH-1 Hueys to Vietnam to escort the troop transports. As UH-1s replaced the H-21s for troop-carrying, the armed Hueys proved too slow. Using UH-1 components, Bell Helicopter developed the AH-1 Cobra attack helicopter especially for the escort and attack roles. Some critics thought that all helicopters would be shot down, but the machines proved tough and survivable.

President Lyndon Johnson's decision to send U.S. troops to fight the war in 1965 brought a new phase to helicopter warfare. Trained in airmobile operations, the 1st Air Cavalry Division (Airmobile) demonstrated its ability to fight North Vietnamese regulars in the Ia Drang highlands. Using CH-47s, the division airlifted artillery to firebases prior to airlifting troops to give them adequate fire support. Combined with close air support and armed Hueys, the 1st Air Cavalry Division had great combat power.

As the number of units in Vietnam increased, they had helicopter units attached to them in addition to their own organic aircraft. The 1st Aviation Brigade was organized to control, maintain, and train these attached helicopter units. The brigade adopted a policy of decentralized control of its units, sending them where they were most needed.

The survivability of helicopters in combat was questioned from the beginning of the war, but never as intensely as during Operation LAM SON 719. In February and March 1971, U.S. helicopters flew South Vietnamese troops into Laos to destroy huge enemy supply dumps and to disrupt enemy movements south. The North Vietnamese countered with tanks and a sophisticated air defense. They shot down 107 helicopters, but Army leaders believed that the destruction of supplies justified the helicopter loss, set at one-fourth of 1 percent of sorties flown.

LAM SON 719 and the Easter Offensive of 1972 enabled the Army to use helicopters as antitank weapons. Using mainly antipersonnel munitions in LAM SON 719, AH-1 Cobras destroyed six tanks and immobilized eight. After North Vietnamese armor poured across the demilitarized zone in the Easter Offensive of 1972, helicopters helped stop them. UH-1s armed with TOW missiles destroyed more than 50 tanks and other vehicles, the first major use of helicopters in the antitank role. During this offensive North Vietnamese troops fired SA-7 heat-seeking missiles at helicopters. This necessitated modifying helicopter exhausts to direct them upward into the rotor wash, thus reducing the heat signature. Helicopters were also fitted with decoy flares.

In the 1980s, Army helicopters were used in two major operations. In the invasion of Grenada in 1983, UH-60 Black Hawks carried Delta Force troops to attack Richmond Hill Prison. Of the 14 Black Hawks participating, seven were heavily damaged and one shot down, so the mission was aborted. Four Black Hawks carrying Rangers from Barbados attacked Calvigny compound, resulting in the destruction of three of them when they met heavy fire upon landing.

In the 1989 Panama invasion, the Army made extensive use of helicopters already positioned at its Panamanian installations. When 82d Airborne Division units parachuted at Panama's airport, UH-60s picked them up for air assaults on key Panama Defense Force strongpoints. An AH-1 Cobra supported an air assault by two UH-60s inside a prison holding political prisoners.

The 1991 Gulf War witnessed a most intense and successful use of helicopters. Coalition strategy required a joint force to hold the southern boundary of Kuwait while an amphibious force threatened a landing on the Kuwaiti coast. Thus fixed in place to meet both threats, Iraqi forces would be unable to stop another secretly assembled joint force from swinging shut like a giant door against the Euphrates River. This movement would trap Iraqi forces inside Kuwait and permit the destruction of their equipment.

The giant door, hinged at the southern Iraq–Kuwait border, consisted of the most mobile joint forces, especially the VII Corps, heavy in armor, and the XVIII Airborne Corps, heavy in air assault troops. Both corps had fighting helicopter units that had trained with their divisions.

The main helicopters used included OH-58 Kiowas for scouting and targeting; AH-64 Apaches for antitank and reconnaissance missions; AH-1 Cobras for escort and antitank use; UH-60 Black Hawks for troop transport, command and control, and electronic countermeasures; and CH-47 Chinooks for troop transport, supply, and artillery placement. With their ability to fire 30mm cannons, 70mm rockets, and Hellfire laser-guided missiles, and to see through rain and dark, the Apaches had the greatest combat power.

Before the ground war started, helicopter units had several important duties. First was to screen the assembling VII Corps and XVIII Corps so that the enemy could not detect them. Next was to conduct reconnaissance across the desert to find suitable places for forward refueling and rearming points. An important mission for Apaches was to destroy two Iraqi border radar sites to give the USAF clear airspace toward Baghdad. Flying low after dark to avoid detection, the Apaches attacked at a standoff distance of two kilometers with missiles.

When the ground war began, Apaches and Cobras flew in advance of VII Corps to provide intelligence on enemy positions and to attack armor. Kiowas and Cobras flew flank security to warn against approaching Iraqi forces and to contact friendly units. To avoid VII Corps artillery fire, it became necessary to send helicopters some 12 miles in advance of the battle line. Apaches had a field day killing armor and other vehicles.

The most mobile unit in the XVIII Airborne Corps was the 101st Airborne Division (Air Assault). It formed the edge of the swinging door and had to advance some 200 miles by the second day of battle. This rapid advance was made possible by Chinooks and Black Hawks, which carried troops and supplies, especially ammunition and fuel. Without the advanced ammunition and fuel, Apaches could not have closed the door at the Euphrates. Near the river, Apaches of the 101st Airborne killed hundreds of vehicles that were backed up while trying to flee Kuwait. They also blocked the causeway across the marshes with wrecked vehicles and destroyed a pontoon bridge across the river. Although a cease-fire was in effect on February 28, the Iraqi Hammurabi Division offered combat on March 1, and the Apaches and Cobras destroyed its equipment. Overall, helicopters proved indispensable for waging midintensity warfare against this well-armed foe.

John L. Bell

References

Bolger, Daniel P. *Americans at War, 1975–1986: An Era of Violent Peace.* Novato, CA: Presido Press, 1988.

Dunstan, Simon. *Vietnam Choppers: Helicopters in Battle, 1950–1975.* London: Osprey, 1988.

Helicopters

From their first practical development in the 1930s, helicopters have gradually become indispensable to military forces.

Development and Early Military Use

Anton Flettner of Germany was the first person to develop a helicopter used in military operations. His Fl 282 in 1942 served the liaison role on German warships in the Mediterranean and Baltic Seas. In 1944, Flettner's Fl 285, carrying two depth charges, was the first antisubmarine warfare (ASW) helicopter.

Encouraged by Igor Sikorsky's development of the VS-300 helicopter in 1940, the U.S. military services ordered about 400 Sikorsky helicopters during World War II (models R-4, R-5, and R-6). In 1944, a light rescue airplane was forced down behind Japanese lines in Burma. A U.S. Army R-4 rescued the pilot and three casualties. Thus began the medical-evacuation role. In early 1945, the Army Air Forces used R-5s for search and rescue in Burma and China. In January 1945, two Sikorsky HNS-1s were placed on a British merchant ship for convoy air patrol across the North Atlantic. The rough weather made it impossible for them to fly until 10 days out, so they were considered unsuitable for the ASW mission.

Beginning in early 1945, the U.S. Navy began experimenting with sonar-dipping helicopters for ASW use. These experiments led to the commissioning of the first ASW squadron at Key West in 1951. It used the Piasecki HUP. In 1961, the SH-3A Sea King became the first U. S. helicopter designed for ASW use.

The U.S. Marines experimented with helicopters for amphibious landings after World War II. The Bikini tests showed how a nuclear blast could devastate a fleet assembled for a traditional amphibious landing. The Marines believed that in the future ships must be dispersed lest they become nuclear targets. This would make amphibious landings very difficult. To solve this problem, the Marines formed an experimental helicopter squadron in 1947 to develop tactics and doctrine for helicopter assaults from the sea. Although the helicopters of the time were inadequate, the Marines devised the needed doctrine while waiting for better machines. Conventional landing craft would still be needed after helicopter assaults had secured a beachhead.

Development of Tactics and Doctrine

The U.S. Navy tested helicopters after World War II for mine countermeasures (MCM). The first use of helicopters for MCM occurred in the Korean War when helicopters were used to locate mines in Wonsan Harbor. The Navy commissioned its first MCM squadron, HM-12, in 1971. Receiving CH-53A Sea Stallions at first, the squadron later procured RH-53Ds, designed specifically for MCM. This squadron cleared mines from Haiphong Harbor in 1973 and from the Suez Canal in 1974 and 1975.

In addition to MCM development, the Korean War saw the first combat uses of helicopters in many roles: command and control, liaison, reconnaissance, wirelaying, rotation of troops in the battle line, plane guards (ready rescue) on aircraft carriers, supply of front-line troops, adjustment of artillery fire, and artillery raids.

As communist guerrillas threatened British control of Malaya from 1948 to 1960, the British used helicopters in counterinsurgency operations. The French also fought insurgencies in Vietnam and Algeria in the 1940s and 1950s, but in neither case did helicopters assure victory. Helicopters did provide mobility and firepower in Algeria, where Muslim guerrillas struck at will in the countryside. While landing troops near rebel bands, the French discovered that they needed suppressive fire. This could best be provided by an armed helicopter capable of flying with the troop transports. Various configurations of weapons were hung on helicopters, and a combination of machine guns and rockets worked best. Consequently, the French were the first to develop the technique of an air assault amid an armed enemy.

The French experience caught the attention of the U.S. Army, which was developing tactics and doctrine for waging war on a nuclear battlefield. Generals James Gavin and Hamilton Howze were the leaders in this movement. In 1962, Secretary of Defense Robert McNamara ordered the Army to convene a Tactical Mobility Requirements Board at Fort Bragg to test ideas of air mobility and air assault. Headed by General Howze, this board conducted many tests and concluded that these ideas were feasible. The Army next organized the 11th Air Assault Division (Test) at Fort Benning in 1963 to conduct exercises and develop tactics and doctrine. An aviation brigade was organized to support the division. The 11th Air Assault Division was converted into the 1st Air Cavalry Division (Airmobile) and sent to Vietnam, where it proved the validity of the concepts. A similar division, the 101st Airborne Division (Air Assault), was later organized and proved its worth in the Gulf War.

The Vietnam War provided several innovations in helicopter warfare. Units specially trained in airmobile and air assault tactics were used for the first time. The introduction of the AH-1 Cobra marked the first time that the attack helicopter was used in warfare. Cobras and TOW-armed Hueys were used as antitank weapons. Heavy-lift helicopters gave greater mobility by moving heavy equipment. The CH-54 Tarhe (Sky Crane) and the CH-53 Sea Stallion provided this heavy-lift capability. The U.S. Army also received the first specially designed scout helicopter—the OH-6 Osage.

The Afghanistan War (1979–1989) marked the first extensive use of Soviet helicopters in counterinsurgency warfare. Soviet operations against the mujahideen used mainly the Mi-8 Hip and the Mi-24 Hind. The Mi-8 carried troops, and the Mi-24 was an attack helicopter. Hampered by a lack of air assault doctrine and experience in mountain fighting, the Soviets at first appeared inept. The mujahideen repelled air assaults at first with machine guns, rocket-propelled grenades, and mortars. As the Soviets became more proficient in air assaults, the mujahideen countered with captured SA-7 heat-seeking missiles and U.S. shoulder-fired Stinger missiles. These missiles, employed about 1988, proved devastating to helicopters. Having lost some 800 helicopters and thousands of troops, the Soviets withdrew from the war.

The Falkland Islands War (1982) demonstrated the great utility of helicopters in long-range naval warfare and amphibious operations. Both the British and the Argentines used helicopters, a total of about 200. Naval helicopters provided ASW protection for the British fleet around the clock. When an Exocet missile damaged a British destroyer, helicopters rescued the crew. Although most amphibious landings were made by landing craft, helicopters were essential in supplying the troops and providing suppressive fire as they moved to capture the town of Stanley.

The U.S. Navy commissioned the first Light Airborne Multipurpose System (LAMPS) squadron in 1973. The LAMPS system gave helicopters with various sensors to smaller ships to extend their eyes and ears and to integrate helicopter sensors with the ships' weapons and targeting systems. In 1984, the Navy established the LAMPS Mark III program, using SH-60B helicopters. These aircraft could detect submarines with acoustical devices or by magnetic anomalies. Distant ships, aircraft, or missiles showed up on the helicopters' radar. Sensor data could be transmitted directly to the ship for defensive response. The SH-60Bs, equivalent to the Black Hawks, could carry an array of weapons, including homing torpedoes, depth charges, and air-to-ship missiles.

While the Navy was improving its defensive capabilities, the U.S. Army was developing a new attack helicopter. The result was the AH-64 Apache. This helicopter has the ability to fly and acquire targets in all kinds of weather and attack with an array of weapons. During the Gulf War, Apaches formed the spearpoints of the two maneuver corps. They functioned as aerial main battle tanks, firing laser-guided Hellfire missiles at enemy tanks from a distance of miles. Most times the Iraqis were not aware of the source of the missiles destroying their tanks. In closer combat, the Apache's 70mm rockets and 30mm guns were formidable.

Helicopters have found more and more military applications through the years and have become essential to many types of military operations.

John L. Bell

See also

Gavin, James; Howze, Hamilton Hawkins

References

Brown, David. *The Royal Navy and the Falkland War.* Annapolis, MD: Naval Institute Press, 1987.

Coates, John. *Suppressing Insurgency: An Analysis of the Malayan Emergency, 1948–1954.* Boulder: Westview Press, 1992.

Dunstan, Simon. *Vietnam Choppers: Helicopters in Battle, 1950–1975.* London: Osprey, 1988.

Fails, William R. *Marines and Helicopters, 1962–1973.* Washington, DC: History and Museums Division, Headquarters, United States Marine Corps, 1978.

Grau, Lester W., trans. and ed. *The Bear Went over the Mountain: Soviet Combat Tactics in Afghanistan.* Washington, DC: National Defense University Press, 1996.

Hassig, Lee, ed. *Sky Soldiers.* Alexandria, VA: Time-Life Books, 1991.

Jalali, Ali Ahmad, and Lester W. Grau. *The Other Side of the Mountain: Mujahideen Tactics in the Soviet-Afghan War.* Quantico, VA: United States Marine Corps Studies and Analysis Division, 1995.

Henschel Aircraft

German aircraft manufacturer; originated with the 1848 Henschel und Sohn concern, a major world manufacturer of railway locomotives that subsequently added trucks, buses, and machine tools to its product line. Henschel first considered entering aviation in 1931, when it negotiated to take over troubled Junkers, but in 1932 announced its own aviation subsidiary.

Henschel Flugzeugwerke AG was created in March 1933, based initially at Berlin-Hohannisthal but moving two years later to the larger Berlin-Schönefeld. It planned to manufacture other companies' designs under license and built the Ju 86D and Do 17 and later the important Ju 88. In 1936, Henschel established an aviation engine subsidiary as a Daimler Benz licensee and eventually built multiple factory locations.

Henschel's own designs were less successful, though two reached volume production. Its Hs 123 biplane dive-bomber was ordered in 1936 and tested in Spain in 1937. It became Germany's last operational biplane when used as a ground attack bomber in Poland, France, and Russia in 1939–1941.

The Hs 126 parasol-wing monoplane spotter aircraft was widely used, later as a trainer and for glider-towing; nearly 600 were built. The Hs 129 antitank and close support aircraft, with its triangular fuselage, was the firm's most successful model (860 manufactured). Yet six years of effort (1938–1944) on the Hs 130 high-altitude bomber proved fruitless. The Hs 132 single-engine dive-bomber jet was captured by the Russians prior to its first flight. The firm also manufactured guided air-to-surface missiles.

Henschel was restarted in 1954, again focusing on railway work and based at Kassel. Henschel joined Nordflug in 1955 to build the Noratlas transport. Though it purchased licenses to make Sikorsky helicopters, control of the company was sold to VFW in 1969.

Christopher H. Sterling

References

Gunston, Bill. *World Encyclopedia of Aircraft Manufacturers.* Sparkford, UK: Patrick Stephens, 1993.

"Henschel Flugzeugwerke A.G." In William Green, *Warplanes of the Third Reich.* New York: Doubleday, 1970, pp. @\Alt:374–403.

HERCULES (1942)

German-Italian code name for the invasion of Malta that would have curtailed British interdiction of Axis supply lines from Italy to Libya.

Italian dictator Benito Mussolini long coveted Malta, and invasion planning began in 1935. The Italian navy refused to invade in 1940 or 1941 due to exaggerated views of Malta's defenses and unwillingness to risk ships. Hitler considered the Mediterranean a secondary theater and hesitated to employ airborne forces after the near-disaster on Crete. In 1941, rather than invade, he ordered air attacks to suppress British forces.

Preparation for HERCULES began in early 1942. Luftwaffe units flew 11,500 sorties in March and April, dropping some 7,200 tons of bombs and using carpet-bombing (for the first time ever) and rocket-propelled bombs to penetrate fortifications. The prerequisites for HERCULES were met: British air and naval power on Malta were neutralized, and no British fleet was available in the Mediterranean to respond. Mussolini met Hitler on April 30 and urged immediate invasion. Hitler, however, preferred to preempt British offensive preparations in Cyrenaica before assaulting Malta. HERCULES was postponed until July, and Luftwaffe units in Sicily moved to Africa to assist Afrika Korps commander Erwin Rommel.

In June, Rommel's Tobruk victory created a dilemma: Malta or Egypt? Mussolini argued for Malta. Hitler thought that the Italian Navy might flee, stranding German airborne troops on Malta, and wanted to invade Egypt before British reinforcements arrived. HERCULES was shelved again, and British forces on Malta soon resumed harassing Rommel's supply lines.

HERCULES would have employed one German and two Italian airborne divisions, six Italian infantry divisions arriving by sea, 500 Ju 52 transports, 500 gliders, captured Russian tanks, 200 landing craft, and Italian naval support. More than 100,000 invaders would have confronted 30,000 defenders. German and Italian airborne divisions would have seized the Luqa airfields, where another Italian airborne division would have reinforced. Italian infantry would have taken the Valetta beaches and made a diversionary attack on Marsa Scirocco. Finally, airborne and amphibious forces would have combined to capture Valetta.

Malta's topography favored the defenders. The coast was mainly cliffs, with very few beaches suitable for invasion. The countryside was divided into small fields surrounded by stone walls—perfect obstacles to gliders. Rocky terrain concealed many natural and man-made fortifications. HERCULES would not have been easy but probably would have succeeded. If executed in 1940 or 1941, it might have had a major strategic impact. In 1942, however, HERCULES could only have delayed the inevitable Axis defeat in North Africa that resulted from the Allies' Operation TORCH.

James D. Perry

References

Bekker, Cajus. *The Luftwaffe War Diaries.* New York: Da Capo, 1994.

Bradford, Ernle. *Siege: Malta, 1940–1943.* New York: William Morrow, 1986.

Kesselring, Albrecht. *The Memoirs of Field Marshal Kesselring.* Novato, CA: Presidio Press, 1989.

Herrman, Hajo (1913–)

German airman during World War II. Herrmann was born in Kiel on 1 August 1913. He volunteered for the new German air force (Luftwaffe) in August 1935 and was trained as a pilot of transport planes and bombers. From August 1936 to April 1937, he served with the Kondor Legion in the Spanish civil war, mainly flying transports. He participated in the Polish, Norwegian, and French campaigns in 1939–1940, flying Heinkel He 111s in Kampgeschwader 4.

Herrmann also flew bombing and antishipping missions against England in the fall of 1940, having been transferred to Kampgeschwader 30, which was equipped with the Junkers Ju 88 bomber. On 13 October 1940, while still a first lieutenant, he was awarded the Knight's Cross.

Being one of the brightest and most imaginative pilots, Hermann was always entrusted with the most difficult tasks. As a captain and squadron leader, he continued bombing and antishipping strikes against Malta, Greece, and North Africa in the spring of 1941. After two months of staff work with IX Air Corps, and now commander of a bomber group, he flew antishipping and other missions against Britain, the Allied Arctic convoys, and the Murmansk railroad from July 1941 to July 1942.

He was then transferred to the Technical Group of the Luftwaffe General Staff and later became General of Bombers, where he was responsible for tactical and technical requirements for aircraft and frequently participated in the conferences of the director-general of air armament. New insights into the general air war situation were possible at this level, and his contacts with the intelligence department of the Luftwaffe General Staff convinced him that fighter production should henceforth have priority over the bombers because Germany was on the defensive. This earned Hermann—the bomber pilot—the contempt of his comrades and the distrust of fighter pilots. Nonetheless, he maintained his opinion.

In the meantime, the radar-based German fighter defense system was always oversaturated and nearly invalidated by the bomber streams and by the new electronic countermeasures systems, including Window (chaff). On 27 June 1943, Hermann proposed to the commander in chief of the Luftwaffe, Hermann Goering, that night-fighter defense tactics be modified to a radical new scheme. This was the so-called Wild Boar plan that allowed the concentration of masses of single-engine day-fighters against the bomber streams independent of radar guidance. By using searchlights and flares for illumination and direction-finding, and by exploiting the fact that the bombers could easily be recognized against the clouds over burning cities, the fighters could make contact without radar.

The new tactics required boldness because the German antiaircraft artillery were already firing at the bombers, but it proved very successful as a last resort after German radar was blindfolded by Window as of 25 July 1943. On the basis of this success, Hermann was ordered to establish the "Wild Boar" Fighter Geschwader 300. He later became commander of this unit and of the 1st Fighter Division.

Still a major, he received the Oak Leaves to the Knight's Cross on 2 August 1943 and the Swords to the Oak Leaves on 23 January 1944 as a full colonel.

Hermann was behind the diversion of the pilots of the dwindling bomber force to the fighter arm. The bomber pilots were capable of instrument flying while the fighter pilots, lacking experience in instrument flight, suffered heavy casualties when the weather was poor.

In January 1945, Reichsmarschall Goering wanted Hermann, now famous as a specialist in emergency solutions, to become General of Fighters, replacing Adolf Galland. Strong opposition from the fighter force made Goering drop this plan. Galland and his backers had long supported the idea of the "Big Blow," in which single-engine fighters would be carefully saved until a large enough force could be assembled to do immense damage to inbound Allied bomber formations. Ram attacks became a feature of this idea. Pilots volunteered for what was essentially a suicide mission because they were patriotic and wished to stop the terrible bombing of their country. (Some may have volunteered in order to avoid being transferred to an infantry unit.)

Under Hermann, commander of the 9th Fighter Division, a special ram fighter force (Sonderkommando Elbe) was set up in the late winter of 1944–1945. It carried out its only mass attack on 7 April 1945, with negligible results and heavy losses.

Hermann was credited with 320 combat missions as a bomber pilot and 50 missions as a fighter pilot. As a bomber pilot he sank 12 ships of 65,000 gross register tons, and as a fighter pilot he gained nine victories over four-engine bombers. After the war he spent 10 years in Soviet prisons and POW camps, before being released on 12 October 1955. He later studied law and became a successful attorney in Düsseldorf in 1965. Hermann married, had two sons, and continued to pursue sport flying.

Horst H. Boog

References

Dahl, Walther. *Rammjaeger: Las Letzte Aufgebot.* Heusenstamm: Orion-Heimreiter-Verlag Heusenstamm, 1971.

Herman, Hajo. *Bewegtes Leben, Kampf- und Jagdflieger, 1935–1945.* Stuttgart: Motorbuch-Verlag Stuttgart, 1984.

Hess, Rudolph (1894–1987)

High-ranking Nazi official who in May 1941 undertook a controversial mission seeking peace between Germany and Britain. He had joined the Nazi Party in 1920, soon became Adolf Hitler's personal secretary, and was made deputy party leader when the Nazis reached power in 1933. Apparently distressed by the war against Britain, feeling that the two countries had common cause against the Soviet Union, and seeing his own role declining in Germany, Hess took action. After three prior failed attempts, on 10 May 1941 he piloted an Me 110 twin-engine fighter aircraft from Berlin and bailed out over a field near Glasgow, Scotland. He sought to meet with the 14th Duke of Hamilton (a wing commander in the RAF whom Hess had not met) to offer the British peace terms to end their role in the war before Germany invaded Russia (which took place the next month).

Whether Hitler knew of Hess's plans beforehand is not clear, though it seems unlikely on the available evidence. The British imprisoned Hess for life on two of four counts at the Nuremberg war-crimes trials in 1946. Hess was incarcerated at Spandau in Berlin, where he committed suicide in 1987 at age 92. His 1941 mission and subsequent imprisonment remains shrouded in mystery, and conspiracy theories abound.

Christopher H. Sterling

References

Hamilton, James Douglas. *The Truth about Rudolph Hess.* Edinburgh, UK: Mainstream, 1993.

Leasor, James. *The Uninvited Envoy. The Mysterious Flight of Rudolph Hess.* New York: McGraw-Hill, 1962.

Hiroshima

Site of the first wartime atomic bombing, by the United States on 6 August 1945. Japan's eighth largest city at the time, with a population of more than 350,000. Hiroshima is located at the mouth of the Ota River on southwestern Honshu Island. An important manufacturing center with shipyards, textile plants, and other industries, the city was also headquarters of the Fifty-Ninth Japanese Army.

On the morning of the attack, the city center was teeming with people on their way to work. Among them were more than 8,000 conscripted high school students who were demolishing buildings to create firebreaks as a defense against expected incendiary bombardments. At 7:09 A.M. the city's civil defense administration sounded an air-raid warning. A single B-29 weather aircraft had appeared over the city to measure conditions. It reported temperatures of 26 degrees Celsius and a humidity of 80 percent. At 8:15 A.M. the USAAF B-29 Superfortress *Enola Gay*, under the command of Colonel Paul W. Tibbets, dropped an atomic bomb (codenamed "Little Boy") at an altitude of 9,600 meters.

The bomb was a gun-assembled uranium (U-235) device. Two pieces of U-235 were shot against each other. When they met they formed a critical mass and produced a fission reaction and ultimately a chain reaction. The energy that was produced in this process created heat and radiation.

At 570 meters, 43 seconds after release, the bomb detonated, producing an explosive power equivalent to 14,000 tons of TNT. The epicenter immediately reached a maximum temperature of several million degrees Centigrade. Atmospheric pressure exceeded 300 bars. The busy city center, with its packed trams and buses, was now an inferno. Firestorms, blasts, shockwaves, burning houses, charred corpses, and blinded bodies tried to escape the hellfire. The city was flattened over an area of 13 square kilometers. Some 70,000 of 76,000 buildings were destroyed or seriously damaged. Nine out of 10 people in a radius of 1,000 meters from the epicenter were killed instantaneously.

Although casualty figures became an important battleground in the emotionally charged postwar debate over the legitimacy of the bombings, conservative estimates count approximately 130,000 people dead and the same number wounded. An additional 70,000 people died by 1950 of radiation illness, and 81 percent of the city had been destroyed.

The attack has become embedded in a complex web of memories and interpretations. During the Cold War, Hiroshima became a semimythic symbol for the nuclear menace, a visible reminder of the potentially disastrous consequences of the arms race. In the post–Cold War world, Hiroshima has become a contested memory. The emotional public debate on the plans of the Smithsonian Institution's Air and Space Museum to publicly display the *Enola Gay* in 1995 as part of an exhibit commemorating the fiftieth anniversary of the end of World War II amply demonstrated how national and collective identities in Japan and the United States are still shaped by the bombing of Hiroshima.

Frank Schumacher

References

Herken, Gregg, *The Winning Weapon: The Atomic Bomb and the Cold War, 1945-1950.* New York: Vintage Books, 1982.

Hershey, John. *Hiroshima.* New York: Vintage Books, 1989.

Hogan, Michael J., ed. *Hiroshima in History and Memory.* Cambridge: Cambridge University Press, 1996.

Ho Chi Minh Trail

An elaborate system of mountain and jungle paths and trails used by North Vietnam to infiltrate troops and supplies into South Vietnam, Cambodia, and Laos during the Vietnam War. Using a 30,000-man workforce, construction began in May 1959 to connect a series of old trails leading from the panhandle of North Vietnam southward along the upper slopes of the Annamese Cordillera into eastern Laos and Cambodia and thence to South Vietnam. Starting south of Hanoi in North Vietnam, the main trail veered southwestward to enter Laos, with periodic side branches running east into South Vietnam. The main trail continued southward into eastern Cambodia and then emptied into South Vietnam at points west of Da Lat. Spurs were also constructed off the main trail into base areas, such as the A Shau Valley in I Corps and into War Zone C in III Corps.

The network of trails and volume of traffic significantly expanded in the 1960s, but it still took more than a month to march from North to South Vietnam. U.S. aircraft repeatedly bombed the trail during Operations STEEL TIGER, TIGER HOUND, and COMMANDO HUNT.

Although the flow of men and supplies from North Vietnam was slowed and North Vietnam was forced to divert enormous assets into keeping the route repaired, airpower was never able to close the Ho Chi Minh Trail completely.

The trail was continually improved and by the late 1960s could accommodate heavy trucks and was supplying the needs of several hundred thousand regular North Vietnamese troops active in South Vietnam. By 1974, the trail was a well-marked series of jungle roads (some of them paved) and underground support facilities such as hospitals, fuel-storage tanks, and weapons and supply caches. The Ho Chi Minh Trail was the major supply route for the North Vietnamese forces that successfully invaded and overran South Vietnam in 1975.

James H. Willbanks

See also

ARC LIGHT; Cambodia Bombings; COMMANDO HUNT; ROLLING THUNDER; STEEL TIGER

References

Prados, John. *The Blood Road: The Ho Chi Minh Trail and the Vietnam War.* New York: John Wiley and Sons, 1999.

Staaveren, Jacob Van. *The United States Air Force in Southeast Asia: Interdiction in Southern Laos, 1960–1968.* Washington, DC: Center for Air Force History, 1993.

Stevens, Richard Linn. *The Trail: A History of the Ho Chi Minh Trail and the Role of Nature in the War in Vietnam.* New York: Garland, 1993.

Holloway, Bruce K. (1912–1999)

Remembered as commander in chief of Strategic Air Command from 29 July 1968 through 1 May 1972. Under Holloway's command, SAC faced an increasingly divided role: tactical bombardment and aerial refueling in Southeast Asia versus its primary mission of strategic nuclear warfare as part of the early evolution of détente. Holloway was a strong champion of SAC's nuclear role and worked successfully to minimize the number of SAC aircraft sent to Southeast Asia.

Holloway's early years are less well known but equally illustrious. Beginning in January 1942, he flew Curtiss P-40s as part of the famed Flying Tigers. A year later he replaced Robert L. Scott as commander of the 23d Fighter Group. During his tenure with the Flying Tigers, Holloway shot down 13 Japanese aircraft. He went on to serve in a number of leadership roles throughout his career, including commander of the U.S. Air Forces, Europe, and as USAF vice Chief of Staff. General Holloway retired in 1972.

Robert S. Hopkins

See also

American Volunteer Group; ARC LIGHT; Cold War; Strategic Air Command; Vietnam War

Horikoshi, Jiro (1903–1982)

Creator of the Mitsubishi A6M Zero fighter. Jiro Horikoshi was born in 1903 in Fujioka, Grunma Prefecture, Japan. His interest in aircraft began in grade school while he was reading newspaper accounts of the air war in Europe. During his senior year in high school he was faced with the decision of what to study when he graduated. He decided on aeronautical engineering and in April 1923 began his studies in the newly formed Aeronautics Department at the University of Tokyo.

In 1926, Jiro joined Mitsubishi as an engineer in the airframe design section. Jiro's first major design project was the Prototype 7, a navy monoplane fighter. The project was part of a prototype competition that the Japanese used to select new aircraft. Both Prototype 7 aircraft built for the competition crashed during flight-testing. It was a rather inauspicious start for Jiro—but one that gained him a great deal of experience.

Jiro's next project was the Prototype 9 or Type 96 No. 1 carrier-based fighter. This aircraft, the A5M, was known to the Allies as "Claude," a top performer during its time. It was very fast and had excellent handling characteristics, which pilots particularly favored.

When the specifications for the Prototype 12 aircraft came to Mitsubishi in 1937, Jiro was once again called upon to lead the development. The Prototype 12 would become the Mitsubishi Type Zero carrier-based fighter, Model 11. The Zero would be the backbone of the Imperial Japanese Navy from 1940 to 1945.

While Jiro completed work on the Zero he was also tasked to produce a new aircraft the Prototype 14, the J2M Raiden ("Jack" to the Allies). The Raiden was an interceptor, used with very limited success against U.S. B-29 raids.

Jiro's final design was in progress when the war ended. It was the A7M Reppu ("Sam" to the Allies), in flight-testing when the war came to an end.

David A. Pluth

References

Horikoshi, Jiro. *Eagles of Mitsubishi: The Story of the Zero Fighter.* Trans. Shindo and Wantiez. Seattle: University of Washington Press, 1981.

Horner, Charles A. (1936–)

U.S. Air Force general. Charles A. "Chuck" Horner was born on 19 October 1936. Upon graduating from the University of Iowa, he was commissioned an officer in the United States Air Force and completed pilot training in 1959. During the Vietnam War, he flew more than 110 combat missions in F-105 Thunderchief and Wild Weasel aircraft and went on to command two fighter wings, two air divisions, the Ninth Air Force, and U.S. Space Command.

As commander of U.S. Central Command Air Forces in 1990, he was designated the overall air component commander during the Gulf War. As such, he orchestrated and led the highly successful Coalition air campaign against Iraq from August 1990 to April 1991. Horner was subsequently advanced to four-star rank and given command of all U.S. military space resources. He retired from active duty in September 1994.

Paul G. Gillespie

See also

DESERT SHIELD; DESERT STORM; Gulf War

References

Hallion, Richard P. *Storm Over Iraq: Air Power and the Gulf War.* Washington, DC: Smithsonian Institution Press, 1992.

McFarland, Stephen L. *A Concise History of the United States Air Force.* Washington, DC: Air Force History and Museum Program, 1997.

Horten Flying Wings

Unique German aircraft that used the flying-wing concept. German engineers Walter, Reimar, and Wolfram Horten were designers and builders of flying-wing aircraft, beginning with gliders, from the end of the 1920s to the late 1940s. (Wolfram was killed in combat in 1940, Reimar died in 1993, and Walter died in 1998.) Their first manned glider, the Ho 1, designed in 1931, flew in 1933. A series of gliders were designed and flown to evaluate various configurations and structures, culminating in five models built for powered flight—the Ho V, Ho VII, Ho VIII, Ho IX, and Ho XII.

The Ho V, built in 1937, was powered by two Hirth HM60R 80-shp engines and was the first Horten aircraft to demonstrate commercial or military potential. (However, the first actual military use of Horten aircraft was when several Ho IIs and IIIs were converted to freight-carrying for demonstration of capability to carry materials across the English Channel.) Two Ho Vs flew, both with two seats, one of mainly plastic, using sheet, sandwich, and laminate, the other a plywood-covered steel-tube-center structure and wooden outer wing panels. A crash of the first version demonstrated that the brittleness of the plastic made it an unsuitable material. The second version was rebuilt with a single seat for an upright pilot versus the prone pilot cockpit for the first version and some previous Horten aircraft.

The Ho VII, designed as a trainer for pilots flying all-wing aircraft, was a scale-up of the Ho V, being powered by two Argus AS-10-C 240-shp engines. Three were ordered, but only one was completed; it flew in May 1943. A production contract for 20 Ho Vs was received in 1944, but none had been delivered by war's end.

The Ho VIII was a 1942 conceptual design for a 158-foot-span all-wing transport to be powered by six Argus AS-10-C engines with pusher propellers, a payload of 60 passengers, and a range of 3,700 miles. It began construction in autumn 1944 as an aerodynamic testbed for the planned Horten Ho XVIII "Amerika Bomber."

The Ho IX was conceived as a fighter-bomber, with wooden wings and a welded-steel-tube structure (all plywood-covered) with jet engines. The Hortens had been aware of jet engine development, and the concept of the Ho IX was stimulated by witnessing a flight of the Me 163 in August 1941. Starting in early 1942, concepts were designed around the Bramo/BMW P3302 engine, then the smallest-diameter engine available. Construction started in June 1942. When the Hortens were advised in late 1942 that the P3302 engine had been canceled, they selected the BMW 003 as the next-best. Its larger diameter necessitated redesign of the already-started center structure. In early 1943, an opportunity arose to propose the Ho IX design to meet a requirement for an aircraft to carry a 1,000-kilogram bomb 1,000 kilometers at 1000 kph, which they did, receiving contract coverage in August 1943 for two prototypes (V1 and V2).

About this time, Horten was advised that the BMW 003 was not going to be qualified when expected and that the Jumo 004 would have to be used. It was decided to complete the V1 as a glider with fixed landing gear so as to quickly gain flight experience. The V2 was started shortly after the V1, and its center section was also redesigned for the BMW 003, but the existing structure was not reworked for the Jumo 004, as no change in size was expected. However, Jumo 004 engines were not obtained until March 1944 and were 20 centimeters greater in diameter than anticipated because the accessory section had been changed.

The Hortens were not receiving official communications on engine status because sometime before engine delivery their contract had been canceled by the Reich Air Ministry. From that time, the Ho IX's continuing development was unique in being "bootlegged" from government funds without official sanction. Because of the delay caused by having to switch to the Jumo 004 engine, the V2 did not fly until 18 December 1944, seven months later than it would have had the BMW 003 been available. The V2 crashed on its third flight on 18 February 1945; however, by this time Gotha had been contracted to develop the production version (Go 229) and further redesigned the engine installation. Several Gotha prototypes were nearing completion when the war ended.

The Ho XII was a primary trainer built without contract coverage, designed and built for a six-cylinder DKW engine, that flew without the engine in December 1944. There was no production.

On 12 March 1945, the Hortens received a contract for the Ho XVIII, a four-jet long-range all-wing bomber. After the war, the Ho XVIII design was revised as a piston engine–driven transport, with no success. In 1948, Reimar Horten emigrated to Argentina and there designed the IA.38, about two-thirds the size of the Ho VIII, powered by four 450-shp engines, with a payload of 6 tons.

Douglas G. Culy

References

Dabrowski, H.P. *Flying Wings of the Horten Brothers.* Atglen, PA: Schiffer, 1995.

Horten Ho 9. Atglen, PA: Schiffer, 1999.

Myra, David. *Horten 229—Monogram Close-Up 12.* Boylston, MA: Monogram Aviation, 1983.

Howard, James Howell (1913–1995)

World War II double-ace, Medal of Honor winner, and USAF brigadier general. Born in Canton, China, on 8 April 1913, James Howell Howard died in Bay Pines, Florida, on 18 March 1995. After graduation from Pomona College in 1937, Howard became a naval aviator. He returned to China to join the American Volunteer Group—the Flying Tigers—under Claire Chennault. In the Flying Tigers, Howard flew P-40s against Japanese Zeros, I 97s, and Nakajima Ki 27s. In 56 missions, he destroyed six opponents and became an ace over Burma and China.

After the Flying Tigers disbanded, Howard went to Boxted, England, with the 354th Fighter Group of the Ninth Army Air Force. The 354th flew P-51s that replaced P-38s and P-47s to defend B-17s and B-24s on bombing missions over Germany. German opponents flew Messerschmitt Bf 109s and Bf 110s, Focke-Wulf Fw 190s, and Junkers Ju 88s. During a mission on 11 January 1944, Howard single-handedly defended 30 B-17s against 30 German fighters. He shot down four opponents and scared others away. All 30 B-17s survived. Consequently, Howard received the Congressional Medal of Honor—the only European theater pilot to do so—and eventually became an ace over Europe. Howard retired from the Air Force Reserve in 1966.

Gary Mason Church

See also

American Volunteer Group; Boeing B-17 Flying Fortress; Burma; Chennault, Claire L.; Consolidated B-24 Liberator; Curtiss P-40 Warhawk; Focke-Wulf Fw 190; Germany, and World War II Air Battles; Junkers Ju 52/3m, Ju 87 Stuka, and Ju 88; Lockheed P-38 Lightning; Messerschmitt Bf 109; Nakajima Aircraft; North American P-51 Mustang; Republic P-47 Thunderbolt; United States Army Aviation

References

Howard, James H. *Roar of the Tiger: From Flying Tigers to Mustangs—A Fighter Ace's Memoir.* New York: Orion Books, 1991.

Jordan, Kenneth N. *Yesterday's Heroes: 433 Men of World War II Awarded the Medal of Honor, 1941–1945.* Atglen, PA: Schiffer Military History, 1996.

Howze, Hamilton Hawkins (1908–1998)

U S. general who led the Army to adapt aviation to combat. As an armor commander in North Africa and Italy in World War II, Howze chafed at his troops' lack of mobility in mountainous terrain. After the war he advocated using helicopters in combat to increase Army mobility.

From 1955 to 1958, Howze served as the first director of Army aviation under General James Gavin. In this position Howze did many things. He tried to persuade the Army to use helicopters to solve tactical problems studied in Army schools. Establishing a program for senior officers to become pilots, he sold them on aviation and gained adherents to his views. Howze intervened with the Air Force to save the UH-1 program and the Huey as the Army's future combat helicopter. He also named aircraft after American Indian tribes and publicized the capabilities of helicopters in public demonstrations. The enlargement of pilot training and aviation support facilities were also major concerns.

Howze's leadership resulted in the greater acceptance and experimentation with aviation within the Army, but he went farther. In 1960, he served on the Rogers Board and recommended the creation of air cavalry units mounted in helicopters. His advocacy of air cavalry resulted in his appointment in 1962 as president of the Tactical Mobility Requirements Board at Fort Bragg. The so-called Howze Board tested many air assault concepts and found them feasible. Its work led in 1963 to the creation of the 11th Air Assault Division (Test) that refined many of the Howze Board's concepts. The need for a highly mobile force in Vietnam in 1965 led to the conversion of the 11th Air Assault Division into the 1st Air Cavalry Division, which did excellent service in Vietnam and validated the revolutionary ideas of Howze and his mentor James Gavin.

John L. Bell

See also

Gavin, James; Howze, Hamilton Hawkins

References

Howze, Hamilton Hawkins. *A Cavalryman's Story: Memoirs of a Twentieth-Century General.* Washington, DC: Smithsonian Institution Press, 1996.

Hump Airlift

World War II air route over the Himalayas between India and China. The Hump was first surveyed in November 1940 by the China National Aviation Corporation (CNAC), a Sino-American airline, as a possible air-freight link to China in the event that the Burma Road was severed. Although the hazards of flying over the Santsung Range, where mountain peaks reached to 15,000 feet, were recognized, officials of the airline believed that the route could be operated if the situation became desperate.

In the spring of 1942, the fall of Rangoon and Japanese advances into northern Burma closed the Burma Road. As President Franklin D. Roosevelt declared in May 1942 that routes to China must be kept open, the Army Air Forces had no choice but to attempt the challenging mountainous airlift.

Operations over the Hump began in the late spring of 1942 with Douglas transports from CNAC and the Tenth Air Force flying from Dinjan in Assam Province, India, to Kunming, China, a distance of 500 miles. Progress in developing the route came slowly and painfully, with a limited number of aircraft and crews being pushed to their operational limits.

On 1 December 1942, the Air Transport Command (ATC) took over responsibility for the Hump route from the Tenth Air Force. Colonel Edward H. Alexander brought a new spirit to the enterprise, but operational difficulties and Japanese air action continued to plague the airlift. By July 1943, monthly tonnage from India to China stood at 3,451 tons, less than half the amount that President Roosevelt was demanding. A reorganization is September 1943 saw Brigadier General Earl Hogg assume command of the India-China Wing of the ATC with Colonel Thomas O. Hardin in charge of the airlift.

Tonnage increased under the hard-driving leadership of Hardin, who instituted night-time operations over the route. By December 1943, ATC was carrying 12,000 tons a month to China. The cost, however, proved high. Between June and December 1943, 135 aircraft and 168 airmen fell victim to enemy fighters, bad weather, and treacherous terrain.

Beyond the staggering operational problems, the need to divert Hump tonnage to other tasks frequently meant that materiel destined for the Chinese fell short of expectations. For example, the use of B-29s to bomb Japan from bases in China consumed 30,000 tons of precious cargo during 1944. Nonetheless, thanks to more and better aircraft, especially C-46s, Hump tonnage rose to 23,675 in August 1944.

In September 1944, Brigadier General William H. Tunner replaced Hardin. Destined to become the Air Force's premier airlifter, Tunner soon had the route operating with impressive efficiency. By the end of the year, 30,000 tons a month were being carried to China. Tunner believed that virtually any amount of cargo could be flown over the Hump if he had the requisite facilities and men.

By the end of the war, 650,000 tons of vital supplies had been carried from India to China, with more than half the total being flown during the first nine months of 1945. No doubt, this materiel played a vital role in keeping China in the war and tying up large numbers of Japanese troops. The experience also provided the Air Force with a solid foundation for future airlift operations during the Berlin crisis of 1948–1949 and the Korean War.

William M. Leary

See also

Tunner, William H.

References

Craven, Wesley F., and James L. Cate, eds. *The Army Air Forces in World War II, Volume 7: Services Around the World.* Chicago: University of Chicago Press, 1958.

Leary, William M. *The Dragon's Wings: The China National Aviation Corporation and the Development of Commercial Aviation in China.* Athens: University of Georgia Press, 1976.

Tunner, William H. *Over the Hump.* New York: Duell, Sloan, and Pearce, 1964.

Hunsaker, Jerome Clarke (1886–1984)

U.S. pioneer in aeronautical engineering. Jerome C. Hunsaker was born in Creston, Iowa, on 26 August 1886. He graduated from the U.S. Naval Academy in 1908 and received advanced degrees in naval architecture and mechanical engineering from MIT. In 1913, he translated Gustave Eiffel's *The Resistance of the Air and Aviation* and a year later established one of the nation's first aeronautical engineering programs at MIT. He became a proponent of engineering science, committed to the concept that scientific theories could inform engineering practice.

During and after World War I, he was responsible for the Navy's airplane and airship design and procurement and later served as an assistant naval attaché in London and Paris. After leaving the Navy in 1926, he developed a weather-reporting and airway-navigation system for Bell Labs, and as vice-president of the Goodyear-Zeppelin Corporation he proposed the establishment of commercial airship lines. In 1933, he returned to MIT as head of the Department of Mechanical Engineering and later was in charge of the new Department of Aeronautical Engineering.

In 1941, Hunsaker became chairman of the National Advisory Committee for Aeronautics (NACA). He encouraged NACA to become more active in the development of aircraft power plants, established new laboratories, and moved the organization in the direction of basic research. After the war, Hunsaker was the chief proponent of the civilian-government "unitary" wind-tunnel program. He resigned as chair of NACA in 1956 on the eve of the space age. In retirement, Hunsaker remained active as a technical consultant and was a member of numerous federal aviation committees and investigatory boards. He died in Boston on 10 September 1984 at the age of 98.

William F. Trimble

References

Bird, Alice Hunsaker. *Jerome Clarke Hunsaker: A Life in Aeronautics.* Henley-on-Thames, UK: Privately published, 1982.

Hunsaker, Jerome C. *Aeronautics at the Mid-Century.* New Haven: Yale University Press, 1952.

Trimble, William F. "Jerome C. Hunsaker, Bell Labs, and the West Coast Model Airline." *Journal of the West* 36 (July 1997): 44–52.

HUSKY (1943)

Allied code name for the invasion of Sicily during World War II. Plans drawn up in Cairo on 18 March 1943 called for teaming the Ninth and Twelfth Air Forces in North Africa to make combined attacks on the Italian island. With the fall of Tunisia in early May, heavy bombers turned their attention toward Sicily. Some 4,000 sorties were flown against airfields by aircraft from the North African Air Forces for eight days prior to the invasion. Axis resistance resulted in the loss of 139 of their aircraft.

The invasion was 10 July 1943. A force of 160,000 men, aboard an armada of some 2,000 ships, departed ports in Tunisia, Tripoli, Tobruk, and Egypt and steamed toward Sicily. The seaborne landings began at 2:45 A.M.

During the night of 9–10 July, two airborne assaults were executed—the first Allied parachute assault in the war. Some 1,600 British paratroops from the 1st Airborne Division were brought to battle aboard gliders towed by 133 C-47s from the USAAF's 51st Troop Carrier Wing (51st TCW). Although no tow planes were lost, 12 gliders crashed in the landing zone, 47 ditched in the sea, and the remainder were scattered about the island.

The second airborne assault was made by the U.S. 82d Airborne Division using 226 C-47s. The aircraft, from the 52d TCW, dropped 2,781 paratroops and 891 parapacks. Their objective was to seize enemy airfields. Unfortunately, their landings were scattered, causing them to alter plans and operate against communications targets.

Approximately 4,000 aircraft from the RAF and the Ninth and Twelfth Air Forces flew against targets in Sicily on 9–10 July, rendering Axis airpower virtually helpless.

A major enemy counterattack was mounted against the U.S. forces near Gela. A third airborne assault was launched on the night of 11 July. A force of 2,300 paratroops from the 504th Parachute Regiment were brought to battle aboard C-47s from the 52d TCW. The Army generals advised the ground forces on the island of the airdrop. The Navy assured that it would obtain antiaircraft-free passage for the planes. The approach was flown over the Navy task force that had not been informed of the new airdrop. Hence, the formations of C-47s met with withering antiaircraft fire from the ships. Some of the aircraft had to make two or three passes over the drop zone to get the paratroops in. Of the 154 C-47s on this mission, 23 were shot down. More than half of the returning planes were severely damaged.

On the night of 13 July, the 51st TCW was tasked with bringing in a force of British paratroops to take a bridge near Catinia. Once again, the Navy had not been informed, and 11 of the 124 C-47s were shot down by friendly fire; another 50 were damaged. In the debacle, 27 aircraft returned to base with full or partial loads.

A major investigation was initiated at the behest of General Dwight D. Eisenhower. RAF Air Marshall Arthur Tedder added his comments to the report, stating that antiaircraft fire at night is ineffectual and almost uncontrollable. Lessons learned from Operation HUSKY were taken into account for Operation OVERLORD, the June 1944 cross-Channel invasion of the European continent.

Late in the campaign, the USAAF introduced Rover Joe, an early forward air controller who called in coordinated air strikes in support of ground operations.

Alwyn T. Lloyd

References

Brereton, Lewis H. *The Brereton Diaries—3 October 1941–8 May 1945.* New York: William Morrow, 1946.

Rust, Ken C. *Ninth Air Force Story.* Temple City, CA: Historical Aviation Album, 1982.

______. *Twelfth Air Force Story.* Temple City, CA: Historical Aviation Album, 1975.

Hutton, Carl Irven (1907–1966)

U.S. Army brigadier general. Hutton played a pivotal role in the development of the armed helicopter. Born in Terre Haute, Indiana, he graduated from West Point in 1930 and served in various field artillery and quartermaster assignments during the next decade. A distinguished record in World War II culminated with his command of the 2d Armored Division Artillery during the campaigns in France and Germany. A pilot and light plane owner before the war, he became an enthusiastic supporter of field artillery organic aircraft in combat.

Following the war, Hutton earned his liaison pilot wings and then served as director of the Department of Air Training at the Field Artillery School from 1947 to 1949. Promoted to brigadier general in 1953 while commanding the 24th Infantry Division Artillery in Korea, he became commandant and commander of the recently established Army Aviation School and Center at Fort Rucker, Alabama, in August 1954, a post he held for three years. He initiated and vigorously supported Colonel Jay D. Vanderpool's experiments with armed helicopters even in the face of skepticism by the Army Chief of Staff, General Maxwell D. Taylor. Hutton retired in 1961.

Hutton had a blunt, take-no-prisoners style that hid a discerning intellect and a deep interest in military history. One of several officers in the mid-1950s who recognized the need for an armed helicopter, he was the one with the authority and moral courage to initiate the experiments, take the inevitable criticism, and defend the program. Without him, the development of an airmobile division in the 1960s was simply inconceivable.

Edgar F. Raines Jr.

References

Bergerson, Frederic A. *The Army Gets an Air Force: Tactics of Insurgent Bureaucratic Politics.* Baltimore: Johns Hopkins University Press, 1980.

Bradin, James W. *From Hot Air to Hellfire: The History of Army Attack Aviation.* Novato, CA: Presidio Press, 1994.

Raines, Edgar F. Jr. "Organic Tactical Air Transport, 1952–1965." *Military Review* 80 (January-February 2000): 84–89.

I

Ia Drang Valley, Battle of (1965)

The first major engagement of the war between regular U.S. and North Vietnamese forces. In this action, elements of the 3d Brigade, 1st Cavalry Division (Airmobile), fought a pitched battle with communist main-force units in the Ia Drang Valley of the Central Highlands.

On the morning of 14 November 1965, Lieutenant Colonel Harold G. Moore's 1st Battalion, 7th Cavalry, conducted a heliborne assault into Landing Zone X-Ray near the Chu Pong Hills. The 1st Cavalry troopers soon found themselves in a desperate three-day battle with two North Vietnamese regiments. The fighting was bitter, but tactical air strikes and artillery support took their toll on the enemy, and Moore's soldiers held against repeated communist assaults. Another key factor were the ARC LIGHT B-52 missions that were flown in direct support of U.S. ground troops in contact for the first time.

By the third day of the battle, the Americans, having been reinforced and supported, had gained the upper hand. The battle resulted in 834 North Vietnamese soldiers confirmed killed, and it was believed that another 1,000 communist casualties were likely. In a related action during the same battle, 2d Battalion, 7th Cavalry, was ambushed by North Vietnamese forces as it moved overland to Landing Zone Albany. Of the 500 men in the original column, 150 were killed and only 84 were able to return to immediate duty; Company C suffered 93 percent casualties, half of them deaths. Despite these casualties, senior U.S. officials in Saigon declared the Battle of the Ia Drang Valley a great victory.

The battle was extremely important, because it was the first significant contact between U.S. troops and North Vietnamese forces. The action demonstrated that the North Vietnamese were prepared to stand and fight major battles when they so chose, even though they would take serious casualties. Senior U.S. military leaders concluded that U.S. forces could inflict significant casualties on the communists in such set-piece battles and that this would lead to a war of attrition as U.S. forces tried to wear down the communists in massive search-and-destroy missions. The North Vietnamese also learned a valuable lesson during the battle: They saw that they could counter the effects of superior U.S. firepower through close-in fighting, which became their normal practice for the rest of the war.

James H. Willbanks

See also

ARC LIGHT

References

Moore, Harold G., and Joseph Galloway. *We Were Soldiers Once and Young: Ia Drang—The Battle That Changed the War in Vietnam.* New York: Random House, 1992.

Stanton, Shelby. *The Anatomy of a Division: 1st Cav in Vietnam.* Novato, CA: Presidio Press, 1987.

Ilya Muromets

Russian World War I bomber. Aeronautical engineer Igor Sikorsky designed and built the world's first four-engine bomber by 1914. The aircraft had a wingspan of nearly 100 feet and weighed more than 10,000 pounds. The most advanced model had a range of 5 hours and a ceiling of more than 9,000 feet. It carried a bombload of 1,000–1,500 pounds and was equipped with up to seven machine guns. Four 150 horsepower Sunbeam V-8 engines allowed the bomber to cruise at 75–85 mph. The rear fuselage possessed sleeping compartments for a crew of five, a washroom, a small table, and openings for mechanics to climb out onto the wings to service the engines during flight.

More than 75 Ilya Murometses were deployed against the

Central Powers along the Eastern Front from 1915 to 1918. These aircraft conducted more than 400 bombing raids against targets in Germany and the Baltic nations. During the war, only one bomber was lost to enemy action. In February 1918, many Ilya Murometses were destroyed by the Russians to prevent capture by advancing German forces. A few of the bombers lingered on into the 1920s, flying under the new Soviet banner.

Mark E. Kahn

See also
Sikorsky, Igor I.; World War I Aviation

References

Millbrooke, Anne. *Aviation History.* Englewood, CO: Jeppesen Sanderson, 1999.
Taylor, John W. *Sikorsky.* Gloucestershire, UK: Tempus, 1998.

Ilyushin Aircraft

Influential Russian aircraft designer and manufacturer. Sergei Vladimirovich Ilyushin (1894–1977) became involved in aviation during World War I and began designing aircraft after graduating from the Zhukovsky Military Aviation Engineering Academy in 1926. He spent his early career working to review aircraft designs and develop requirements for the nascent Red Air Force. Ilyushin began actual design work in earnest in the early 1930s in cooperation with other designers and finally as the head of his own bureau in 1936.

Ilyushin's DB-3/Il-4 medium bomber entered service in 1937 and served throughout World War II as a standard bomber and torpedo-bomber for both the air force and the navy. Ilyushin's most famous design, the Il-2 Shturmovik, was built in greater numbers than any other wartime aircraft. The Shturmovik was the bane of German troops and vehicles on Eastern Front battlefields. Ilyushin won the Hero of Social Labor Award for the Il-2 and, in 1945, won the Stalin Prize for the successor aircraft, the Il-10.

The Il-10 served in many Soviet satellite air forces following World War II, including those of the People's Republic of China and the Democratic People's Republic of Korea during the Korean War. Ilyushin's design bureau did not rest on its well-deserved wartime laurels but produced the Soviet Union's first jet bomber, the Il-28, and a series of transport and commercial aircraft. The twin-engine Il-28 first flew in 1948 and soon became a staple in many of the world's air forces. These aircraft were part of the air defense system that the Soviet Union installed in Cuba precipitating the Cuban Missile Crisis in 1962. The People's Liberation Army Air Force is only now clearing its inventories of its license-built version, the Hong-5.

Ilyushin's transport aircraft still provide much of the strategic mobility that the Russian military possess. The Il-62, Il-76, and Il-86 jet airliners have served with the Soviet and then Russian state airline, Aeroflot, since entering service in the 1970s. Although Ilyushin retired from design work in 1970 and died in 1977, his influence on Russian aviation continues.

Mark A. O'Neill

See also
Ilyushin Il-2 Shturmovik

References

Greenwood, John T. "The Designers and Their Aircraft." In Robin Higham, John T. Greenwood, and Von Hardesty, eds., *Russian Aviation and Air Power in the Twentieth Century.* London: Frank Cass, 1998.
Kozlov, M. M., ed. Velikaya Otechestvennaya Voina, 1941–1945 Entsiklopediya [Great Patriotic War, 1941–1945 Encyclopedia]. Moscow: Sovetskaya Entsiklopediya, 1985.

Ilyushin Il-2 Shturmovik

Soviet ground attacker aircraft. Sergei V. Ilyushin's greatest contribution to the success of the Red Army during World War II was the Il-2 Shturmovik. The Il-2, nicknamed "Schwartzer Todt" (Black Death) by the Germans, helped the Soviet military destroy the Wehrmacht during the massive ground battles on the Eastern Front from 1941 to 1945.

In 1937, Ilyushin began work on his self-designated "Flying Tank" without obtaining prior approval from Joseph Stalin. The Il-2 was remarkable because Ilyushin integrated an armored steel, nickel, and molybdenum shell into to the airframe that protected the crew, engine, and fuel system. He submitted his design directly to Stalin in early 1938 and began constructing prototypes in February 1939. Bureaucratic delays postponed production, but Ilyushin continued to test the aircraft at his own facilities. A new liquid-cooled AM-38 engine and cannons were added to increase the Il-2's speed and firepower. Il-2 production began in March 1941 and the aircraft entered service just prior to the 22 June 1941 German invasion of the Soviet Union.

The Shturmovik was one of a number of rude surprises that the Soviets had for the invading Wehrmacht, but the Il-2 was not available in large numbers and was vulnerable to fighter attack from the rear. Eventually, the Il-2 and the modernized Il-10 were produced in greater numbers than any other aircraft in World War II, with 36,000 Il-2s alone built for the air force and naval aviation. Operational ground attack units, such as the 198th Shturmovik Aviation Regiment,

Josef Stalin stated that the Ilyushin Il-2 was as important as bread and air to the Soviet army. It was produced in great numbers and became veritable flying artillery on the Eastern Front. (Jean Cottam)

began adding a rear-facing machine gun and gunner as a field modification by 1942. Factories began delivering the new two-seater Il-2s by the fall of 1942, which substantially reduced the numbers lost to Luftwaffe fighters.

Often operating in division-sized formations in air armies attached directly to Soviet fronts (the rough equivalent of army groups) and comprising as much as 30 percent of the entire Soviet air force inventory, this heavily armored single-engine aircraft extended Soviet firepower throughout the depth of the battlefield. Working with tanks, infantry, and artillery as part of a revolutionary combined arms team, the Il-2 and other ground attack aircraft destroyed enemy tanks, vehicles, and artillery in direct support of the Red Army. In order to accomplish this task, the Shturmovik was equipped with 23mm cannons, aerial rockets, bombs, and special antitank bomblets that burned their way through the thin roof and engine deck armor on German tanks and other vehicles.

The Shturmovik demonstrated its flexibility and utility during the siege of Stalingrad as it helped close the aerial blockade that ensured that the German Sixth Army could not be resupplied. By the Berlin operation of April 1945, the Il-2 was a vital part of the massive 7,500-plane Sixteenth Air Army. Ilyushin's design not only contributed to the Red Army's victory over Nazi Germany but also influenced aircraft design and tactics to the present day. The U.S. Air Force's A-10 Warthog is simply the modern equivalent of Ilyushin's Flying Tank.

Mark A. O'Neill

See also
Ilyushin Aircraft

References

Hardesty, Von. *Red Phoenix: The Rise of Soviet Air Power, 1941–1945.* Washington, DC: Smithsonian Institution Press, 1982.

Stapfer, Hans-Heiri. *Il-2 Stormovik in Action.* Aircraft Number 155. Carrollton, TX: Squadron/Signal, 1995.

Imperial Russian Air Service

The Imperial Russian Air Service had its origin in the observation balloon units that were formed in 1885 and expanded after the Russo-Japanese War. In 1909, the czar's cousin, Grand Prince Mikhail Aleksandrovich Romanov, recognized the military implications of Louis Blériot's historic flight across the English Channel and began to promote aviation in Russia. As a result of his sponsorship, in 1910 both the army and the navy established flying services, with Grand Prince Mikhail himself commanding the Army Air Service. He bought aircraft abroad and promoted the founding of domestic aviation firms such as Dux, Grigorevich, RBVZ, Anatra, Lebedev, and Sikorsky.

During the next few years, flying became fashionable among the younger nobility and included a number of women pilots. One of these early female pilots, Princess Evgeniya Shakhovskaya, joined the air service in 1914 and became the world's first female combat pilot.

In contrast to its general image as backward and unprepared, Russia in August 1914 had the largest air force in the world, with some 250–300 aircraft and 11 airships. Germany, by contrast, had 230–246 aircraft and Austria only 35; France and Britain had 160 and 110 aircraft, respectively. Although historians have pointed out that most of Russia's aircraft were old and almost unflyable, the designs of other countries in 1914 were not much better.

Russia's real problem lay in its industrial infrastructure, which was totally inadequate to keep pace with the design and production of military aircraft, which evolved rapidly during World War I. Instead, Russia was soon reduced to purchasing outdated castoffs from Britain and France and trying to produce licensed copies, generally in inadequate numbers. There were two significant exceptions to this grim scene. The Grigorevich firm produced a series of small and medium flying boats that proved superior to the Germans' in combat over the eastern Baltic and Black Seas, and the Sikorsky factory designed and produced the world's first four-motor heavy bomber, the Ilya Muromets. During the war 93 Ilya Murometses were produced and flew 400 sorties, dropping 65 tons of bombs and proving almost indestructible to German fighters.

There were also difficulties finding adequate numbers of recruits capable of being trained as pilots and observers, as illiterate peasants still constituted more than 90 percent of the population. Still, the Imperial Russian Air Service was able to grow from about 40 detachments in 1914 to 135 detachments by the time Russia left the war.

During the war, 26 Russian pilots became aces, scoring a total of 188 air victories. Among them was leading ace Aleksandr Kozakov, but possibly the most significant was Captain Aleksandr Nikolaevich Prokofiev de Severskii, who scored six air victories as a naval pilot flying over the Baltic in 1916 after his leg had been amputated in 1915. After the Russian Revolution he emigrated to the United States, achieving fame as Alexander de Seversky. While the achievements of Russia's air aces seem paltry next to those of Germany, France, and Britain, we should remember that even over the Western Front aerial combat was a rarity until late 1915. Suitable fighting machines began to appear only in 1916, and almost all the leading Western aces scored the great majority of their victories in 1917 and 1918, by which time the Russians had already left the war. Further, the vast spaces of the Eastern Front and the fewer numbers of German and Austrian aircraft committed meant that contact between enemy aircraft occurred less often.

After the abdication of Nicholas II in February 1917, the army, and the air service in particular, continued fighting, and the air service even continued fighting briefly after the Bolshevik coup in November. However, as the army collapsed and ground crews went over to the communists, operations became impossible. Some of the noble pilots were lynched by revolutionary ground crews, and others either went over themselves or fled to areas controlled by the anti-communist Whites. The Imperial Russian Air Service became ashes, out of which emerged the Air Fleet of the Workers' and Peasants' Red Army.

George M. Mellinger

See also

Kozakov, Aleksandr; Seversky Aircraft; Seversky, Alexander P. de

References

Durkota, Alan, Thomas Darcey, and Viktor Kulikov, *The Imperial Russian Air Service: Famous Pilots and Aircraft of World War I.* Mountain View, CA: Flying Machines Press, 1995, pp. 58–71.

Independent Bombing Force (World War I)

Ostensibly interallied strategic bombing force formed during World War I. Insofar as legal niceties can be preserved during war, the Allies had always been careful to announce that bombing that might hit enemy towns was being done in specific retaliation for some attack already mounted by the Germans. This position kept faith with international treaties entered into prior to the war that prohibited the bombing of cities except in reprisal to a specific attack.

In late 1917, therefore, when the formation of a long-range bombing force came under discussion, this qualification still had to be observed, although there was also concern that the Germans should not be the only civilian population to escape being attacked. The governments, therefore, kept open the possibility of bombing military objectives no matter where they might be located.

In October 1917, Major General Hugh Trenchard, field commander of the Royal Flying Corps, was notified that he would head an Inter-Allied Independent Air Force that would be under the supreme command of French Marshal Ferdinand Foch. This chain of command was thought necessary because should Allied armies break through and press into Germany, aerial units under Trenchard would have to move there as well to stay within range of targets.

As it happened, however, there was no interallied presence in the force that was fielded; only British units were present. In the early months of 1918, the 41st Wing, and then units simply designated as Independent Force, RAF, operated out of Luxeuil, the same airfield near Nancy that No. 3 Wing had operated from in 1916.

Those squadrons utilized de Havilland D.H. 9s/9as and Handley Page O/400 bombers to perform missions against targets in Germany. At least, that is what was intended. In fact, weather and the still-deficient navigation technology combined to scuttle more missions than were completed. Missions begun in anticipation of hitting strategic targets, such as factories in German towns, typically were diverted to tactical targets (generally railroads or airfields) just behind the lines.

World War I came to an end before the technological issues preventing true strategic bombing could be solved. By 1939, that technology was in place and the missions that had to be abandoned in 1918 could be fulfilled.

James Streckfuss

See also

Royal Flying Corps/Royal Naval Air Service/Royal Air Force; World War I Aviation

References

Raleigh, Sir Walter, and H. A. Jones. *The War in the Air: Being the Story of the Part Played in the Great War by the Royal Air Force.* 6 vols. Oxford: Clarendon Press, 1922–1937.

Indian and Pakistani Airpower

India and Pakistan, the two major powers in South Asia, have been locked in mutual hostility ever since the partition of the Indian subcontinent in August 1947. The trauma of partition led to human carnage, bloodshed, and violence on both sides. Further, Pakistan's forcible occupation of one-third of the Kashmir Valley in the 1947–1948 war with India turned into a root cause of their perpetual animosity. Since then, the countries have fought three wars: in September 1965, December 1971, and May 2000 (the Kargil conflict).

The perceptions of mutual threat prompted Islamabad and New Delhi not only to raise their armed forces but also to increase and upgrade airpower as an integral part of military strategy to ensure maximum security and safeguard territorial integrity and sovereignty.

At the time of partition, the nations inherited a split air force that was weak in quantitative and qualitative terms. The assets of the Royal Indian Air Force were divided on a one-third basis, under which Pakistan and India got two and six fighter squadrons, respectively. In view of India's military advantage, Pakistan's leaders heavily banked upon airpower while structuring the Pakistani air force on a tactical-cum-offensive strategy to counter any Indian threat to its security. Its air force got a potential boost from the United States when Pakistan joined U.S.-sponsored military alliances (SEATO in 1954 and CENTO in 1955).

As a result, Pakistan acquired F-104A Starfighters, B-57B Canberras, the highly sophisticated F-16 fighter, and AWACS from the United States. Pakistan received additional support from France (Mirage-series fighters), China (MiG-21, F-6, F-7P), Australia (Mirage III), and Muslim countries of the Middle East.

India looked to the former Soviet Union for military hardware to meet its defense requirements. India acquired MiG-21 fighters from Moscow and Mirage 2000s from Paris in the 1970s and 1980s, in addition to Jaguars from the United Kingdom. The Indian air force added 44 MiG-27 fighters to its inventory during 1992–1993.

In view of these developments, the Pakistani government gave an advance of $600 million to the United States to purchase an additional 40 F-16 aircraft, but they were not delivered when the first Bush administration placed an arms embargo on Pakistan in October 1990 under the Pressler Amendment (1985), which prohibited U.S. military and economic assistance to any country that was engaged in building nuclear weapons. The Clinton administration amended the Pressler Amendment in January 1996, as a one-time waiver that enabled Pakistan to get military assistance and spare parts worth $368 million.

After the May 1998 nuclear tests carried out by India and Pakistan, both countries increased their airpower and replaced old aircraft. India acquired two AWACS A-50s from Russia; no other country in the region possesses such aircraft. India had already acquired Su-30 and MiG-29 from Russia under the defense deal. During Russian President Vladimir Putin's visit to India in 2000, the countries signed defense agreements. Russia will deliver military hardware worth $3 billion including Su-30 fighters, the *Admiral Gorshkov* aircraft carrier, and two squadrons of MiG-29K fighters. Also, India will manufacture 140 Su-30MKI aircraft under license and will upgrade 50 Su-30 planes. India is trying to procure at least one airborne early warning system from Israel. The delivery of 10 Mirage 2000Hs from France at the cost of $328 million is expected to be completed by 2004. This will give India an air edge over Pakistan. India is planning to purchase 350 multirole planes and other gadgets at an estimated cost of $25 billion over 15–20 years.

In response, Pakistan is moving forward to field 150–200 S-7 multirole combat aircraft, replacing its old fleet of F-6s,

Indian and Pakistani Airpower

Aircraft Type	*Combat Radius*	*Inventory*	*Supplier*
India			
Su-30 MK	1200 km	30	Russia
Mirage 2000H/TH	750 km	35	France/U.K.
Jaguar S(I)	550 km	88	France/U.K.
Mig-27	250 km	147	Russia
Pakistan			
Mirage III EP	600 km	16	France
Mirage 5	650 km	52	France
F-16A/B	950 km	25	U.S.

SOURCE: Rodney Jones, Regional Studies (Spring 2000): 13.

A-5s, and F-7s. The S-7s will have look-down-shoot-down targeting, night-combat, and electronic-jamming capability. The S-7 is a multirole, multimission project commenced by Pakistan as far back as 1991. Pakistan is in the process of acquiring the latest F-7MG aircraft from China.

The defense budgets of India and Pakistan for fiscal year 2000/2001 show that India's defense outlay is more than four times greater (R587.87 billion) than that of Pakistan (R133.5 billion). But in terms of gross domestic product, India spends 3.2 percent on defense, whereas Pakistan spends more than 4 percent. The above table illustrates the comparative strength of the nuclear-capable high-performance strike aircraft of India and Pakistan until 1999.

India and Pakistan will continue modernizing their air forces as a counteroffensive strategy and will keep readying their fighter aircraft for the delivery of nuclear weapons, in addition to upgrading various missile systems.

B. M. Jain

Indochina

During the period 1945–1954, France fought to regain control over its possessions in Indochina: Cochinchina, Annam, Tonkin, Cambodia, and Laos. These were occupied by Japan during World War II and then witnessed the rise of an anticolonial movement led by local communists. France's postwar weakness significantly complicated its military efforts—including the use of airpower—in Indochina.

The air war in Indochina formally was one-sided. The only air forces employed were those of France and its allies. Yet local forces paid great attention to the abilities and limits of airpower in strategic planning and operational and tactical decisions. This enabled communist-led peasant guerrillas to challenge French air supremacy asymmetrically and contributed to their victory. Additionally, the French air experience in Indochina emphasized the importance of the principle of economy and distribution of forces and the crucial need to suppress enemy air defenses during ground support operations.

The aerial conflict in Indochina also had a formidable international dimension: Japan, Britain, China, as well as the Soviet Union and the United States were involved, though in different forms and on different stages during the conflict.

In the fall of 1945, British and French forces were airlifted to French Indochina to establish order after the Japanese surrender. This brought the allies into conflict with the communist-led Vietminh movement, which declared the independence of Vietnam (Cochinchina, Annam, Tonkin).

In 1945–1946, the British provided combat air support and allowed some Japanese air transport units (the so-called Gremlin Task Force) for the advancing French troops in Cochinchina, Annam, and Cambodia. During the 1946–1949 campaign in Tonkin and Laos, French airpower supplied ground support as well as delivering troops and cargo in jungle and mountainous terrain. The French expeditionary corps also used parachute-dropping to gain control over Luang Probang and Haiphong and employed combined air/airborne and ground assaults in two large-scale operations: PAPILLON (Hoah Binh, April 1947) and LEA (Viet Back, October 1947).

In April 1947, the French made the first aircraft-carrier strike in its military history. During the war French air forces and naval aviation (one or two French aircraft carriers were constantly off the Indochinese shores) developed close and effective interservice cooperation.

In Indochina the French had an extremely diverse aircraft inventory, including the Supermarine Spitfire IX, North American Mustang, Consolidated PBY-5 Catalina, Douglas C-47, as well as other allied types. There were also German Ju 52 transports and Japanese Nakajima Ki 43 fighters. This wide variety of types created serious maintenance and operational problems.

As continental China fell under communist control and the Korean War began, the international setting of the war in Indochina changed dramatically. The United States sent additional planes to the French. The Vietminh managed to transform its guerrilla bands into a disciplined and highly motivated regular army supplied from China and the Soviet Union.

In 1950–1952, both sides employed the mobile warfare operations. The French escalated airpower involvement in Indochina (more than 10 major air bases and 275 planes at its high) using aircraft in the combined air/airborne-ground operations. These were mostly successful in eliminating about a third of the Vietminh combat force.

The French air force contributed to the victorious campaign by bombing raids (the French used napalm for the first time in December 1950), supporting the airborne assaults (Operation LORRAINE, Na-San, December 1952), as well as providing supplies and transportation for troops (the Lang Son, Ninh Binh, and Hoah Binh battles).

In order to consolidate and explore the 1950–1952 military successes, the French command under General Jean de Lattre de Tassigny introduced some strategic, operational, and tactical innovations. It assembled forces (including air units) into combined mobile strike groups. To compensate for the shortage of bombing power, which the campaign revealed, the French began to use transports as bombers.

Additionally, the French command developed the concept of air-supported and air-supplied combat outposts and fortified supply centers for control over territory and antiguerrilla operations. Despite some initial successes in northern Laos, the idea of airmobile warfare in difficult climate and complex terrain seriously overestimated French capabilities in Indochina.

The Vietminh forces under General Vo Nguyen Giap understood the vital role of airpower in the new French strategy. They decided to challenge by shifting guerrilla operations deep inside Indochina—almost at the limit of the maximum range of most of the French planes flying from their bases in coastal areas and aircraft carriers. Additionally, the Vietminh used terrain to cover its movements, employed massive artillery assaults on enemy airfields, and concentrated antiaircraft fire.

French self-assurance and underestimation of the enemy met revolutionary tactics when the French, under new commander General Henri Navarre, tried to lure the enemy into a decisive battle inside Vietminh-controlled territory. This course, accompanied with growing logistical problems and air-support limits, led to the military disaster at Dien Bien Phu in 1954.

The French were on their own. With the surrender of the French garrison in Dien Bien Phu, the war was virtually over. France lost 59 aircraft (48 shot down, 11 destroyed on the ground), 167 planes damaged, 270 airmen killed, and 380 missing in action; 70 civilian crewmembers were killed as well.

The critical shortage of French strike airpower, which the conflict had revealed, led to the restoration of the separate bombing force within the French air force. The French also assisted in creating the South Vietnamese air force. The war experience had also proved the value of air defense for the communist forces and shaped the buildup of the North Vietnamese military. For China, the Soviet Union, and particularly the United States, the war paved the way for further involvement into conflicts in Indochina.

Peter Rainow

See also

Colonial Wars; Dien Bien Phu, Battle of; French Air Force; French Naval Air Force; Vo Nguyen Giap

References

Armitage, M. J., and R. A. Mason. *Air Power in the Nuclear Age, 1945–1982.* London: Macmillan, 1983.

Flintham, Victor. *Air Wars and Aircraft: A Detailed Record of Air Combat, 1945 to Present.* New York: Facts on File, 1990.

Prados, John. *The Sky Would Fall: Operation Vulture—The U.S. Bombing Mission in Indochina, 1954.* New York: Dial Press, 1983.

Inoue, Shigeyoshi (1889–1975)

Japanese admiral. Inoue graduated from the Naval Academy in 1909. After sea service and a two-year posting to Switzerland, he graduated from the Naval Staff College in 1924. More sea service, important staff billets, and two years as naval attaché in Rome followed before Inoue made rear admiral in 1935. In 1937, Inoue headed the Naval Affairs Department in the Ministry of the Navy and, after promotion to vice admiral in 1939, became the China Area Fleet Chief of Staff.

In 1940, Inoue headed up the Naval Aviation Bureau. He launched a major attack on the navy's shipbuilding program, particularly battleship construction, and strategic planning for a war with the United States. He posited a protracted war rather than the lightning conflict Japanese strategists envisaged and clearly appreciated Japan's weakness relative to America's industrial might and strategically advantageous position. He concluded that success required powerful long-range land-based air forces, numerous effective convoy escorts backed by strong integrated surface, air, and submarine task forces, and well-trained and -prepared amphibious assets. Even then, Japan would fight at long odds.

Inoue's radical views led to his transfer in August 1941 to command of Fourth Fleet. His forces captured Guam and Wake and then moved through the Southwest Pacific archipelagos to Rabaul. Inoue, however, lost his command after the Port Moresby operation failed in the Coral Sea; he became superintendent of the Naval Academy.

Late in the war Inoue regained favor. He was promoted admiral and became simultaneously navy vice minister and chief of both the Navy Technical Bureau and Naval Aviation Bureau.

Paul E. Fontenoy

See also

Coral Sea, Battle of the; Japanese Naval Air Force, Imperial; Netherlands East Indies; Philippines; Rabaul; Yamamoto, Isoroku

References

Dull, Paul S. *A Battle History of the Imperial Japanese Navy, 1941–1945.* Annapolis, MD: Naval Institute Press, 1978.

Evans, David C., ed. *The Japanese Navy in World War II in the Words of Former Japanese Naval Officers.* Annapolis, MD: Naval Institute Press, 1986.

Willmott, H. P. *Empires in the Balance: Japanese and Allied Pacific Strategies to April 1942.* Annapolis, MD: Naval Institute Press, 1982.

INSTANT THUNDER (1990)

Code name for the initial Coalition plan and air campaign in response to the Iraqi invasion of Kuwait on 2 August 1990. A small group of airpower advocates in the Pentagon—the so-called Checkmate office—proposed a conventional strategic air campaign to liberate Kuwait. The group, which was under the direction of Colonel John Ashley Warden III, had one clear purpose in mind: force Iraq's army out of Kuwait by applying airpower in a strategic offensive directly against the sources of Iraqi national power. The concept was praised and condemned; although changes were made, the original concept remained at the heart of what became the strategic air campaign (Phase I) of Operation DESERT STORM.

INSTANT THUNDER, as presented to the U.S. military and political leadership between 9 and 20 August 1990, was bold, imaginative, and innovative but not in accord with then current military doctrine and what was operationally attainable and politically acceptable. The concept's stated objectives were to "isolate Saddam [Hussein]; eliminate Iraq's offensive and defensive capability; incapacitate the national leadership; reduce the threat to friendly nations; and minimize the damage to enhance rebuilding." INSTANT THUNDER provided the U.S. leadership with an offensive option that did not exist at the time, and it gave the overall planning a strategic orientation.

As intelligence and targeting information improved during planning, Brigadier General Buster Glosson and Lieutenant Colonel David A. Deptula developed the concept in accordance with theater requirements. On 17 January 1991, the target list had increased from 84 to 481, and as the war progressed several more targets were attacked. What was solely an airpower concept—focusing predominantly on the Iraqi decisionmaking apparatus in Baghdad—became a comprehensive air campaign, and the effectiveness of this part of the air campaign compared to the larger effort against Iraqi troops in the Kuwait theater of operations remains widely disputed. INSTANT THUNDER, with its focus on strategic bombing, remains a controversial issue within the wider airpower debate, as does its genesis and relationship to the final air campaign plan.

John Andreas Olsen

See also

Deptula, David A.; DESERT STORM; Warden, John A. III

References

Gordon, Michael R., and Bernard E. Trainor. *The General's War: The Inside Story of the Conflict in the Gulf.* Boston: Little, Brown, 1995.

Mann, Edward C. *Thunder and Lightning: Desert Storm and the Airpower Debates.* Maxwell AFB, AL: Air University Press, 1995.

Reynolds, Richard T. *Heart of the Storm: The Genesis of the Air Campaign Against Iraq.* Maxwell AFB, AL: Air University Press, 1995.

Iran Hostages Rescue Operation

Operation EAGLE CLAW, the failed special operation to rescue Americans taken hostage by militant Iranian students who seized the U.S. Embassy in Tehran. In January 1979, the followers of Ayatollah Ruhollah Khomeini, a conservative Muslim clergyman, forced Reza Shah Pahlavi, who had ruled Iran for 37 years, to flee abroad. On 4 November 1979, militant Iranians, who supported the Ayatollah and opposed Western influences, stormed the U.S. Embassy in Tehran, the capital of Iran, taking 66 Americans hostage. Thirteen were soon released, but for the release of the other 53 Iran demanded a U.S. apology for acts committed in support of the shah, his return to face trial (unimportant after his death in July 1980), and the return of billions of dollars that he was said to have hoarded abroad.

Negotiations did not secure their release, so President Jimmy Carter ordered the Department of Defense to draw up plans for a rescue mission. The plan called for a joint task force using helicopters to insert commandos to assault the embassy and extract the hostages. The operation, launched on the evening of 24 April 1980, was plagued by problems from the beginning. It was ultimately aborted with the force at the intermediate staging area in Iran, called Desert One, because mechanical failures left the force without enough helicopters to complete the mission. The operation turned into a disaster when one of the helicopters sliced into a C-130 on the ground, causing a tremendous explosion. Eight Americans were lost in the debacle. The hostages were not released until January 1981, 444 days after they entered captivity.

The most important result of the raid's failure was a reassessment of America's Special Operations Forces (SOF), which ultimately led to the creation of the United States Special Operations Command, a unified joint headquarters with responsibility for all SOF. The ad hoc arrangements faced by the planners and executors of Operation EAGLE CLAW would no longer be necessary.

James H. Willbanks

See also

Helicopters, Military Use; Lockheed Martin C-130 "Hercules"

References

Christopher, Warren, Gary Sick, Harold H. Sauders, and Paul H. Kreisberg, eds. *American Hostages in Iran: The Conduct of a Crisis.* New York: Dane, 1997.

Kyle, James H. *Guts to Try: The Untold Story of the Iran Hostage Rescue Mission by the On-scene Desert Commander.* New York: Renaissance House, 1994.

Stein, Conrad R. *The Iran Hostage Crisis.* New York: Children's Press, 1994.

Iraqi Air Force

In the period of the Iran-Iraq War (1980–1988), the Iraqi Air Force (IQAF) emerged as the sixth-largest air force in the world. With some 30,000 active personnel and such aircraft as the MiG-29 Fulcrum, Su-24 Fencer, and Mirage F l, the IQAF was organized into two bomber squadrons, about 20 fighter ground attack squadrons, about 15 interceptor squadrons, and one reconnaissance squadron. Its formations were disposed in 24 major operating bases with more than 100 airfields and six times as many shelters.

With 10,000 men in the Air Defense Command, Iraq had a land-based air defense system that divided the country into five operational sectors providing a comprehensive cover through an integrated network of radars, antiaircraft guns, and some of the latest French and Soviet surface-to-air missiles. The Iraqi strategy during the 1991 Gulf War was to draw the Coalition into a costly battle of attrition. The strategy depended on high survivability and the effectiveness of Iraq's land-based air defense network, but the Coalition's offensive neutralized the Iraqi system within the first days.

The IQAF did not challenge the Coalition for air superiority, and when hardened aircraft shelters proved vulnerable 148 aircraft were sent to Iran for safety. In the course of the war, the IQAF lost more than half of its combat aircraft (the aircraft sent to Iran were not returned), half its major command, and control centers and large numbers of munitions and antiaircraft guns. The overall estimates of Iraqi losses are uncertain, but the IQAF still consists of some 30,000 men. The command and control system has been largely restored, and some 300 combat aircraft survived the bombing. Although the IQAF retains half its 1990 numbers, its warfighting capability is difficult to assess. It has the advantage of lessons learned, but economic sanctions have made acquisitions of spare parts and new equipment difficult, and the continuous operations in the no-fly zones have weakened training and readiness. At the moment, missiles seem to be the preferred solution; with biological and chemical weapons being prepared, the IQAF sustains a considerable domestic and regional air strike capability.

John Andreas Olsen

Israel Aircraft Industries (IAI)

After the 1948 War of Independence, Israel was determined to have an indigenous armament industry, and an aircraft factory was considered essential. First established in 1953 as Bedek Aviation, the firm changed its name to Israel Aircraft Industries in 1967. Over the years, the firm has produced domestic as well as foreign designs. It excels in modifying designs from other countries for manufacture in Israel.

One of the first indigenous designs was the twin-boom IAI Arava, a twin-engine turboprop transport capable of carrying up to 18 passengers. Of the 90 built, many were sold abroad.

IAI established itself as a leader in the executive aircraft market when it acquired the manufacturing rights for the North American Rockwell Jet Commander, manufacturing and selling it as the Westwind. The Westwind was succeeded by the Astra, a much more advanced aircraft featuring a swept wing.

In the military field, IAI developed the Kfir, based on the Mirage III airframe modified to use a General Electric J79 turbojet. A total of 212 Kfirs were built and served as a first-line fighter for the Israeli Defense Force. A much more ambitious project was the Lavi, an indigenous design that promised great performance but was canceled because of high costs.

Walter J. Boyne

References

Donald, David, gen. ed. *The Complete Encyclopedia of World Aircraft.* New York: Barnes and Noble, 1997.

Gunston, Bill. *World Encyclopedia of Aircraft Manufacturers.* Sparkford, UK: Patrick Stephens, 1993.

Israeli Air Force

Few military organizations have the mystique of the Israeli Air Force (IAF). What began in 1947 as a literal hodgepodge of mercenary pilots flying war-surplus fighters, bombers, and transports had by 1967 become synonymous with air

Israel has done a magnificent job of adapting foreign warplanes to its needs, and never more so than with the IAI Kfir, a highly modified version of the Dassault Mirage 5. (Lon Nordeen)

supremacy. The predecessor to the IAF—the Shen Aleph (Air Service)—was established in November 1947, although flying clubs known as Sherut Avir date from the early 1930s. The air service was reorganized into the Heyl Ha'Avir in May 1948, concurrent with the founding of the state of Israel. It operated whatever airplanes it could buy, ranging from Czech Avia S-199s to Dragon Rapides to B-17s. Pilots were typically from the British Commonwealth, notably Canada and South Africa, or Sabras who had flown previously with the RAF. Among the latter is Ezer Weizman, famous for his all-black Spitfire, who eventually commanded the IAF.

By the mid-1950s, Israel had established a strong relationship with France and bought jet aircraft such as the Ouragan and Mystère to combat Egyptian and Syrian MiG-15s and MiG-17s. Israel was all too willing, therefore, in October 1956 to join with France and Britain in attacking Egypt. The IAF conducted paradrops at key passes in the Sinai, facilitating a rapid Israeli ground advance. By 1967, the IAF faced an imminent Arab assault and undertook one the most decisive operations in the history of air supremacy, destroying most of the Arab air forces on the ground in a preemptive attack.

This fractured the Franco-Israeli weapons link, and the IAF turned to the United States for replacement aircraft. By 1970, these included F-4Es, which were pressed into service during the War of Attrition through late 1973.

The October War demonstrated crucial weaknesses in the IAF, most notably its shortcomings in electronic countermeasures and defense suppression. These were remedied with follow-on purchases of the F-15 and F-16, with the F-16s including locally configured "Wild Weasel" variants. Israel also built a derivative of the Mirage III (the Kfir). These all saw service in 1982's "Peace for Galilee" operations over Lebanon and Syria, where Israeli fighters destroyed some 80 MiGs with no losses. Since then, the IAF has focused on indigenous high-technology weaponry such as the canceled Lavi fighter and the Israeli AWACS, which has even seen export sales. Undoubtedly, the key to success for the IAF has been its ability to achieve air supremacy, its effect on the morale of Israelis and their opponents, and its ability to supply and manage the battlefield.

Robert S. Hopkins

See also

Air Superiority; Egyptian Air Force; Israel Aircraft Industries; Israeli-Arab Conflicts; Osirak Nuclear Reactor; Six Day War; Suez Crisis; Syrian Air Force; Yom Kippur War

References

Dupuy, Trevor N. *Elusive Victory.* New York: Harper and Row, 1978.

Halperin, Merav, and Aharon Lapidot. *G-Suit.* London: Sphere Books, 1990.

Nordeen, Lon. *Fighters over Israel.* New York: Orion Books, 1990.

Israeli-Arab Conflicts

Since the formation of the state of Israel, five major conflicts have occurred in the region (1948–1949, 1956, 1967, 1973–1974, and 1982) between various Arab states and Israel. Each conflict resulted in an Israeli victory due to superior airpower.

After declaring independence in 1948, Israel fought against forces from Egypt, Syria, Transjordan (later Jordan), Lebanon, and Iraq. Prior to the conflict, the Israelis purchased 25 Czechoslovakian Avia S.199 aircraft. The Israeli Air Force (IAF) received four of the planes by May 29. On that day, Israel's first fighter squadron attacked Egyptian forces en route to Tel Aviv, halting their advance at Ad-Halom.

For the duration of the war the IAF fought on all fronts, frustrating Arab attempts to divide the country in half and inflicting numerous kills against Egyptian Dakota aircraft. Mechanical failures with the Avia led the IAF to purchase four North American P-51D Mustangs from the United States. Shipped to Israel in crates labeled as agricultural implements to circumvent the embargo on military equipment to the Middle East, two of the aircraft participated in the last five months of the War of Independence, conducting reconnaissance and strike fighter/interceptor missions. On the last day of fighting, the Mustangs, armed with six 12.7mm machine guns and six 127mm rockets under the wings, shot down three Egyptian Macchi MC-205s.

At the conclusion of hostilities, the Mustangs continued to operate as the front-line force but were gradually phased out in favor of jets. However, when the 1956 Suez Crisis broke out the IAF removed the planes from storage and, with range capabilities reaching 2,080 miles and a maximum speed of 427 mph, used them to bomb enemy bases as far away as North Africa. In an effort to disrupt Egyptian military communications, the IAF attached a weighted cable to the tail of the Mustangs designed to cut telephone lines; several planes lost their cables before arriving in Egypt, but the pilots improvised by cutting lines with their wings. After the United Nations sponsored a truce between Great Britain, France, Israel, and Egypt, the IAF retired its remaining Mustangs.

In 1967, Egyptian forces attacked Israel in the Six Day War. The IAF responded in a coordinated air-land attack that resulted in a quick and decisive victory. The IAF relied on the French Mirage III, with a special version—the Mirage 5—being developed for the IAF. During the war the French government placed an embargo on military sales to the Middle East; following the Israeli raid on the Beirut airport in 1968, the administration canceled Israel's order for 50 Mirage 5s.

Through private acquisition and espionage, the Israelis obtained blueprints and proceeded to construct its own version. In January 1968, U.S. President Lyndon Johnson agreed to sell Phantoms to the IAF (44 F-4Es and six RF-4Es). These aircraft, used during the War of Attrition between Egypt and Israel after the Six Day War, illustrated Israel's air superiority, routinely flying over Cairo. Other operational aircraft during this period included three Dassault models (Ouragans, Mystères, and Super-Mystères) and Vautours from Sud-Ouest. Deployed as the primary defense against Russian-made SAMs, the Phantoms destroyed Egypt's missile sites.

Egypt responded by negotiating the purchase of 80 MiG-21 fighters from the Soviet Union. On 30 July 1970, Israeli Phantoms destroyed five Russian-operated MiG-21s, an act that resulted in an armistice on 7 August 1970.

The Yom Kippur War began at noon on 6 October 1973. Egyptian and Syrian forces attacked Israeli forces on the Suez Canal to the south and the Golan Heights to the north. Responding to attacks on Israeli population centers, the IAF attempted to destroy SAM sites along the Golan Heights, but when that strategy failed the IAF deployed two squadrons of 16 F-4 Phantoms across the Syrian border to destroy the enemy's command center. Flying low to avoid detection and maintaining radio silence, the F-4s reached Damascus undetected, releasing five tons of ammunition each before returning to Israel. The element of surprise worked to their advantage, with Syrian defenses destroying only one IAF plane. For the duration of the war the IAF also operated an Israeli-manufactured aircraft, the Nesher.

In 1978, the Palestine Liberation Organization initiated attacks against Israel from bases in Lebanon. After several years of continued fighting, the IAF attacked Beirut in 1982, forcing Palestinian guerrillas to evacuate the city after a 10-week siege. The Palestinians dispersed throughout the Arab world. Israel continues to maintain a buffer zone between Lebanon and its own territory. The IAF currently responds to all threats against the state of Israel by terrorists and foreign countries.

Cynthia Clark Northrup

See also

Israel Aircraft Industries; Osirak Nuclear Reactor; Six Day War; Suez Crisis; Yom Kippur War

References

Brom, Shlomo, and Yiftah Shapir, eds. *The Middle East Military Balance, 1999–2000.* Cambridge: MIT Press, 2000.

Schulze, Kirsten E. *The Arab-Israeli Conflict.* New York: Longman, 1999.

Italian Air Force (Post–World War II)

In June 1946, a referendum transformed Italy from monarchy to republic. In consequence, the Regia Aeronautica adopted the new name Aeronautica Militare (the Italian Air Force, or ItAF). Together, the limitations imposed by the 1947 peace treaty and the wartime devastations gave reason to doubt the very survival of the ItAF, but the Cold War allowed it to be rebuilt and then expanded as a mainly tactical force.

Initially, the use of surplus British and U.S. aircraft led to accidents caused by aircraft condition as well as different standards. Although still organized under the prewar territorial concept, with combat units assigned to four Air Zones (later three Air Regions), NATO membership introduced the ItAF to modern tactics and doctrine. The jet era arrived in 1950 with the de Havilland Vampire, so simple that its engine was the only real innovation, but British influence was soon ousted by the Mutual Defence Assistance Program. The abundance of U.S. aircraft, mainly various models of F-84 fighter-bombers and F-86E fighters, allowed considerable expansion and improved technology levels. A surface-to-air missile unit was formed in 1959 and deployed in the northeast. A brigade armed with Jupiter missiles and U.S. nuclear warheads in the south was disbanded in the aftermath of the Cuban Missile Crisis.

The key event of the 1960s was the selection of the Lockheed F-104 Starfighter, which would shape units and policies for more than 40 years. From 1982, strike units received the sophisticated Tornado, which in 1991 would equip the Italian contingent in the Gulf War. Although modest in numbers (eight aircraft, 226 sorties, 257 tons of bombs), this was the first ItAF combat campaign after World War II. The experience underlined the need for tankers, precision-guided munitions, and command and control assets.

The 1990s were marked by growing instability in the Balkans, which turned Italy into a massive logistics base for NATO forces; in addition, the ItAF participated in RED FLAG exercises and was employed in Somalia. In 1999, the ItAF introduced a new functional organization that placed all operational assets under the Air Fleet, supported by a Logistics Command and a Training Command. The ItAF served in combat against Serb targets.

Women were admitted to the ItAF in 2000. Future plans revolve around the Eurofighter and Joint Strike Fighter, increasing airlift capability, and reducing personnel to 44,000.

Gregory Alegi

See also

ALLIED FORCE; Cuban Missile Crisis; Eurofighter Typhoon; Gulf War; Joint Strike Fighter; Lockheed F-104 Starfighter; North Atlantic Treaty Organization; Panavia Tornado; Somalia

References

Alegi, Gregory, and Marco Amatimaggio. *The Fighter Interceptor Brigade.* Taranto: Sinapsi, 2000.

Catalanotto, Baldassare, and Hugo Pratt. *Once Upon a Sky: 70 Years of Italian Air Force.* Rome: Lizard, 1993.

Italian Aircraft Development

In 1913, Italy's Army Aviation Battalion launched a competition to select a two-seat general-purpose airplane. Although the entrants failed to meet the stringent requirements, the event achieved its goal of stimulating aircraft manufacture in Italy. Licenses, mainly French, put production on a firm basis but limited innovation.

Gianni Caproni took a different path, selling his fledgling company to the army but continuing to serve as technical director. Army funding allowed the construction of a number of prototypes, including the Ca.3 bomber (1914), which was the first important original Italian design. Its success owed much to the use of proven structural elements; more important, it made possible the aerial bombardment strategy advocated by Giulio Douhet. Like the U.S. DH-4 Liberty Plane program, the plan for 4,000 Ca.5s was crippled by its misunderstood magnitude, and the bomber was undeservedly tainted by the resulting postwar controversy.

The dependency on foreign technology continued throughout World War I, with successive adaptations of the Farman pusher by SIA and of the Aviatik B.I by SAML and Pomilio. Despite the failure of the Ansaldo attempt to break the Nieuport-Macchi fighter monopoly, its SVA was a milestone in Italian aeronautical design and pioneered scientific airframe stressing and wind-tunnel testing. Production considerations were incorporated at an early phase, minimizing the use of high-grade steel and other scarce materials.

Nieuport-Macchi rapidly established itself in the flying boat field, but other Italian aircraft were disappointing. Italy also operated the largest airship fleet after Germany. Douhet recognized airships as costly and cumbersome in 1914, but despite heavy combat losses they were eliminated in only 1928; their chief proponent, Umberto Nobile (1885–1978), eventually accepted an offer to head the Soviet dirigible program.

By November 1918, a significant design capability had been developed, and several important prototypes were on hand; the industry had swollen from 17 to 355 companies, including 27 airframe manufacturers, with more than 12,000 aircraft delivered and at least as many on order. On the minus side, the many failures and production delays had imbued the military with mistrust toward domestic designs. The early post–World War I period was dominated by war-surplus aircraft and engines, depressing innovation. Piaggio and Ansaldo introduced all-metal construction with Dornier and Dewoitine licenses; Romeo acquired steel-tube technology from Fokker, whereas Fiat developed its own. Engines came from France and Britain, with Fiat again representing a significant exception.

To protect industrial resources during the economic slump, three-year planning was introduced in 1930. Prices were determined on a cost-plus basis and orders allotted among companies in fixed proportions, with each type ordered from at least two manufacturers for standardization. Due to funding limitations, types were frequently upgraded and replaced only for measurable progress. Companies were asked to specialize by aircraft categories (e.g., fighters for Fiat and bombers for Caproni). Research was stimulated through design competitions: between 1926 an 1933, the Regia Aeronautica purchased some 160 prototype or experimental aircraft, including those used to establish world records for distance and endurance (SIAI Marchetti S.64, 1928–1931) and speed (Macchi seaplanes for the Schneider Cup, 1926–1931, and the 1934 absolute record).

Although the fascist policy of self-sufficiency restricted imports, Italo Balbo limited its impact on aviation and ensured the acquisition of U.S. technology, including Packard diesel engines and the Travel Air R racer. The Atlantic formation flights gave great impulse to instrumentation, both through licenses (Sperry gyros, Siemens direction finders) and domestic developments (OMI-Biseo blind-flying panel). By 1934, retractable landing gear, flaps, slats, and cantilevered monoplane wings had all been introduced. The SIAI Marchetti S.79 trimotor (1934) and Nardi FN.305 sportplane (1934) incorporated all simultaneously but mated them to traditional steel-tube fuselages and wooden wings that required skilled labor and high-quality wood; Fiat introduced the all-metal G.2 in 1932 but was plagued by unsophisticated aerodynamics and so added stressed-skin structures a decade later.

Throughout this period, Italian aircraft were comparable with those of other European nations; then, the wars in Ethiopia and Spain blocked the path of evolution. Increased budgets went to operations, pilot training, airfield construction in Africa, and greater output of existing types. Combined with the plan to achieve a 3,000 combat aircraft strength by 1939, this consumed the additional resources without producing lasting improvements. Although other European nations rearmed, Italian industry failed to increase factory capacity and to generalize stressed-skin metal structure; similarly, small orders deterred investment in modern production systems. Reggiane, organized along U.S. lines, was a significant but isolated exception. Further records were established, but at the expense of quality. With the exception of the world altitude records set in 1934–1939 by the Caproni Ca.113/161bis family, most were in limited categories or for point-to-point flights. In addition, results often depended more on skilled crews than on generally applicable technology.

Perhaps realizing the looming threat of obsolescence, the ministry launched a massive modernization plan that increased design competitions from the previous average of 2–3 per year to 15 in 1938–1939 yet failed to produce a single type employed operationally in World War II. Indeed, the major Italian combat aircraft were the result of previous competitions (e.g., the Macchi C.200, developed in response to the 1936 interceptor competition), private initiative (Cant Z.1007, Fiat CR.42), or adaptation (S.79).

The inability to produce acceptable engines over 1,000 horsepower was the main cause of this failure, but contributing factors included unrealistic performance goals, duplication of effort, small numbers of graduate engineers and scientists, low investment, and political interference (often at the request of industry, which exploited the regime's full-employment policy). In late 1939, Alfa Romeo acquired the license to the Daimler Benz DB.601 engine, but production began in 1941, and monthly deliveries never exceeded 60; the situation was repeated in 1943 with the Fiat-built DB.605. The failure of the 1,350-hp Alfa Romeo 135 radial doomed a generation of twin-engine designs and explains the Italian predilection for trimotors.

In turn, the lack of adequate engines generated the illusion that better performance would be achieved through innovative airframe design, providing yet more stimulus for new competitions and interference in development. Nowhere was this more evident than with the Fiat G.55 fighter. Launched as a "superfighter" in 1939, it was still not operational in summer 1943 despite orders for 3,600; the "lightweight fighter" propounded by SAI Ambrosini shared the same fate, mainly because no aerodynamic miracle could overcome the limitations of a 750-hp engine. A more realistic approach of continuous improvement, strictly linked to necessary power increases, allowed Macchi to develop its fighter family with minimal disruption to production and adequate performance. Despite this, Macchi types never exceeded 46.6 percent of fighter orders, and in the first half of 1943 Fiat still claimed 40.7 percent of fighter orders against Macchi's 34.7 percent.

When the war showed equipment to be as important as airframe and engines, Italy was handicapped by a lack of modern radios and heavy guns. In addition, manufacturers tended to produce their own accessories (in the case of Fiat, down to ball bearings), with little specialization and progress. Even when the Regia Aeronautica standardized Piaggio propellers for its fighters, Fiat fought to use its own. German requests for industrial coordination foundered because of a widespread fear of subjugation. The workforce rose to 160,000 by 1943, efficiency remained low, and the modest prewar monthly production target of 350 aircraft was never achieved.

Production plans for 1944–1945 revolved around large-scale production of the Fiat G.55 fighter, multiple variants of the Cant Z.1018/Breda Z.303 family, and limited quantities of Macchi and Reggiane types. All were scuttled by the September 1943 armistice, finally bringing Italian industry under German control. A few existing programs were allowed to continue, but efforts were concentrated on repairs, subassemblies, and tooling for German industry. Together with Allied air attacks in March-April 1944, this conspired to keep Italian wartime production at 11,000 aircraft.

Italy emerged from World War II without an aviation industry. Employment shrank to about 6,000 and was largely occupied with nonaeronautical work. Survival depended on overhauls and political connections. The engine business never recovered its modest design capability, and U.S. surplus aircraft limited the prospects for larger aircraft, forcing important companies like Breda, Caproni, and Cant out of the market.

Design activity resumed with light aircraft. Although established companies received military orders for piston trainers, Piaggio correctly viewed the United States as the largest aviation market but achieved only limited sales there. New designers like Stelio Frati (b. 1919) and Luigi Pascale (b. 1923) made their debut. Their most successful designs were the SIAI Marchetti SF.260 (1964) and Partenavia P.68 (1970), still in production together with the F.22 (1989) and P.92 (1993). Meteor, founded by Furio Lauri (b. 1918), went from light planes to remotely piloted vehicles before being acquired by Aeritalia.

Although the air force funded a limited experimental program, including the Aerfer family of light interceptors, the abundant supply of Military Direct Assistance Program aircraft made domestic production of aircraft pointless. The first postwar Italian combat aircraft to enter production was the Fiat G.91 light tactical fighter (1956), designed to a NATO specification drawing heavily upon F-86 experience. Other companies sought success abroad. Piaggio sold its P.149 to Germany, but the real surprises came from the Agusta-Bell helicopters and the Aermacchi MB.326/339 jet trainers.

The F-104G program involved virtually the entire Italian aviation industry, raising its technology levels, production capabilities, and ambitions. A decade later the Tornado was another milestone, but national programs told a different story. Like the industry, research funding was fragmented, and government viewed the sector as an opportunity to create jobs rather than technology. As a result, new products were developed very slowly (the Fiat G.222 was conceived in 1962, flew in 1970, and reached units in 1978; the Agusta A-109 was conceived in 1969, flew in 1971, and was delivered to the army in 1978); frequently, industry launched derivative designs at the expense of sales potential, as with the SF.260 turboprop versions. Other aircraft, like the G.222, were hampered by their high cost.

The so-called 1977 aviation bill funded the CBR-80, a fighter-bomber/reconnaissance successor to the G.91, which eventually became the AMX (1984). The most ambitious Italian aircraft ever built, the AMX was also the most controversial. It suffered from cost overruns (in part caused by production cutbacks) and technical troubles but was successfully used in the Balkans in 1997–1999. A similar fate befell the Agusta A-129 antitank helicopter, handicapped by the philosophy of lightness and unable to achieve export sales despite the good performance demonstrated in Somalia, including shipboard operations.

Weakened by the lack of commercial success and the collapse of military markets that followed the end of the Cold War, industry attempted to revamp older products and accelerated its strategy of partnerships and participation in advanced international programs like the Eurofighter Typhoon. Agusta launched three new helicopters, including the BA609 tilt-rotor with Bell, but by 2001 the Aermacchi M-346 lead-in fighter, based upon the experience of the Russian-Italian Yak-130 program, was the only significant new fixed-wing project under way with Italian leadership.

Gregory Alegi

See also

Aeritalia; Aeronautica Nazionale Repubblicana; Agusta; Alenia; Ansaldo; Balbo, Italo; Breda; Cant Aircraft; Caproni Aircraft (Post–World War I); Ethiopian War; Eurofighter Typhoon; Fiat; Italian Air Force; Lockheed F-104 Starfighter; Macchi Aircraft; Panavia Tornado; Piaggio Aircraft; Regia Aeronautica (Pre–World War II); Regia Aeronautica (World War II); SIAI Marchetti; Spanish Civil War

References

Alegi, Gregory. *L'aile brisée* (The Broken Wing). Paris: Lariviere, 2000.

"L'Aermacchi" and "Il duro dopoguerra della SIAI Marchetti." In *Ali a Varese 3*. Varese: Provincia di Varese/GAE, 1998.

Cattaneo, Gianni. "L'illusione del caccia leggero." *Aerofan* 18, nos. 72–73 (2000).

McMeiken, Frank. *Italian Military Aviation, 1943–1983*. Leicester, UK: Midland Counties, 1984.

Thompson, Jonathan. *Italian Civil and Military Aircraft, 1930–1945*. Fallbrook, CA: Aero, 1963.

Italian Campaign (1943–1945)

Support of the Allies' protracted land campaign in World War II to take the Italian Peninsula. After the fall of Sicily in August 1943, Allied forces invaded mainland Italy in September at Salerno (Operation AVALANCHE) near Naples, Taranto (SLAPSTICK), and across the Straits of Messina in the toe (BAYTOWN). The heaviest air resistance was at Salerno.

Coincident with the landing at Salerno was the surrender of Italy to the Allies. When the Italian fleet attempted to escape from its northern base at La Spezia to Malta, German Dornier Do 217 aircraft based in southern France attacked and sank the battleship *Roma* with newly developed Fritz-X glider bombs, a true guided missile.

After defeating German forces at Salerno, the U.S. Fifth Army and Eighth Army linked up and overran most of southern Italy, including the Foggia complex, which became an important base for the strategic bombers of the Allied Fifteenth Air Force.

German forces stopped the Allies along the Gustav Line, which stretched across Italy through mountainous terrain north of Naples. The campaign through the winter consisted of repeated Allied attacks that made only small gains against this position, which included Monte Cassino.

Allied efforts to break the Gustav Line were finally successful in May 1944 with Operation DIADEM, an attack from the south that took Cassino and linked up with the Anzio beachhead. Rome fell on 5 June. DIADEM was assisted by Operation STRANGLE, a massive interdiction campaign against German communications and logistics. Strangle was succeeded in the fall by Operation MALLORY MAJOR, which continued operations against German communications in northern Italy. But with bad weather approaching, German forces rallied and held the Allies along the line of the northern Appenines.

After the loss of Rome, the Luftwaffe largely abandoned the air war in Italy, leaving only a few Ju 87s for night harassment and loyal Italian fighter aircraft for defense of industrial sites in northern Italy. The remainder of the campaign in Italy consisted of Allied ground support and interdiction missions against negligible opposition and strikes against remaining industrial targets in northern Italy.

Allied air forces in Italy also provided important support to Marshal Tito's partisans in the Balkans. Transport aircraft (C-47s and Italian Z.1007s and SM.82s flying for the Allies) provided essential supplies to Tito, and direct attacks against German forces stopped an antipartisan operation in May 1944. Allied airpower based in Italy eventually severely degraded Axis rail capability in the Balkans.

Frank E. Watson

See also

Anzio; Cassino, Battle of; HUSKY; STRANGLE

Salerno; References

Beale, Nick, Ferdinando D'Amico, and Gabriele Valentini. *Air War Italy, 1944–1945: The Axis Air Forces from the Liberation of Rome to the Surrender.* Shrewsbury, UK: Airlife, 1996.

Craven, Wesley, and James Cate. *The Army Air Forces in World War II, Volume 3: Europe: Argument to V-E Day, January 1944 to May 1945.* Washington DC: U.S. Government Printing Office, 1951.

Italo-Turkish War (1911–1912)

First use of heavier-than-air aircraft in combat. In September 1911, Italy committed an expedition against the Turks in Libya. After Tripoli fell in October, aircraft were unloaded in the port and prepared for use. On 23 October, Captain Carlos Piazza flew the first operational combat sortie in a heavier-than-air aircraft, completing a reconnaissance mission outside of Tripoli in a Blériot 11. Three days later, Captain Ricardo Moizo's Nieuport became the first aircraft to sustain combat damage when it was hit by Turkish rifle fire.

On 1 November, a Lieutenant Govotti, in an Etrich "Taube," became the first pilot to fly a bombing mission, dropping grenades on Turkish troops at Taguira Oasis. Other missions included the dropping of propaganda leaflets inciting insurrection among Libyan tribesmen, but reconnaissance and artillery spotting remained the primary missions. Other firsts in the campaign included the first night missions, night bombing, and the first operational air casualties from both ground fire and accidents.

The Italian feats in Libya were widely reported and had significant influence on the development of all fledgling air forces in the short months before World War I.

Frank E. Watson

References

Mason, Francis K. *War in the Air.* New York: Crescent Books, 1985.

Iwamoto, Tetsuzo (1916–1955)

Imperial Japanese Navy lieutenant (junior grade). Iwamoto was born in 1916 in Hokkaido Prefecture. He attended Masuda Agricultural and Forestry High School. Iwamoto entered the naval barracks at Kure as a seaman in 1934. In 1935, Iwamoto was transferred to maintenance duty. In December 1936, he entered and graduated from the pilot training course and became a fighter pilot.

In early 1938, Iwamoto was assigned to the 12th Air Group, which took part in central China operations. Iwamoto's entry into combat was a very successful one. His first mission was to Nanchang, where he shot down five enemy aircraft. While in China, Iwamoto flew a total of 82 sorties, tallying 14 aircraft shot down and making him the top ace of the so-called China Incident.

During the early stages of World War II, Iwamoto served on the carrier *Zuikaku.* While onboard, Iwamoto participated in the Pearl Harbor attack, Indian Ocean operations, and the Battle of the Coral Sea. From there, Iwamoto's travels brought him to Paramushir Island, Rabaul, Truck Island, and finally back to Japan to participate in the defense of the homeland. Iwamoto's final victory tally is somewhere between 80 (Japanese historians' total) and 202 (Iwamoto's claim). Tetsuzo Iwamoto died in 1955 of complications from a war wound.

David A. Pluth

References
Hata, Ikuhiko, and Yasuho Izawa. *Japanese Naval Aces and Fighter Units in World War II.* Annapolis, MD: Naval Institute Press, 1989.
Sakaida, Henry. *Imperial Japanese Navy Aces, 1937–1945.* London: Osprey, 1998.

Iwo Jima

Sustained air campaign during 1944–1945 to wrest the strategically important island of Iwo Jima away from Japanese control. By mid-1944, two Japanese airfields operated on Iwo Jima, with a third under construction. All served to stage aircraft and support attacks against the U.S. advance toward Japan's home islands.

From August 1944, U.S. forces subjected the island to one of the Pacific War's longest sustained aerial bombardments. Saipan-based Seventh Army Air Force B-24s launched 10 raids in August, 22 in September, and 16 in October. Airfields were their principal targets, but they also attacked shipping.

The B-24s ceased their attacks to support B-29 operations against Japan itself that commenced in November. The Japanese responded by raiding Saipan with aircraft staged through Iwo Jima, causing substantial B-29 ground losses. A major U.S. retaliatory attack followed on 8 December—62 B-29s and 102 B-24s dropped 814 tons of bombs on the airfields. Nevertheless, this attack and subsequent daily B-24 raids until 15 February 1945—bringing total bomb tonnage dropped on the island to 6,800 tons—did not close the airfields for more than a few hours or halt the flow of Japanese reinforcements.

In preparation for landings on Iwo Jima, fast U.S. carriers struck the Japanese mainland on 12–17 February, attacking manufacturing plants, aviation facilities, and shipping. They then joined 12 escort carriers of the support group in the preinvasion bombardment of the island.

After the 19 February landings the fast carriers and support group provided fighter defense, antisubmarine patrol, artillery observation, photoreconnaissance, and direct support strikes for the Marines in their bloody struggle to subdue the island. Japanese torpedo-bombers and kamikazes from Okinawa struck back at the invasion fleet, damaging several vessels. The fast carriers withdrew on 1 March to prepare for the Okinawa operation, but the escort carriers, aided by Saipan-based B-24s, continued their support of the Marines until the island was officially secured on 16 March.

Paul E. Fontenoy

See also
Japan, Air Operations Against; Kamikaze Attacks; Mitscher, Marc Andrew; Okinawa; Spruance, Raymond A.; Task Force 38/58

References
Craven, Wesley F., and James L. Cate, eds. *Army Air Forces in World War II, Volume 5: Pacific: Matterhorn to Nagasaki, June 1944–August 1945.* Washington, DC: Office of Air Force History, 1953.
Frank, Richard B. *Downfall: The End of the Imperial Japanese Empire.* New York: Random House, 1999.
Morison, Samuel E. *Victory in the Pacific, 1945.* Boston: Little, Brown, 1960.

J

Jabara, James (1923–1966)

USAF colonel; the world's first jet ace, and the second-highest scoring U.S. ace of the Korean War with 15 victories. Holder of the Distinguished Service Cross, Distinguished Flying Cross (six Oak Leaf clusters), Silver Star with Oak Leaf cluster, Air Medal (24 Oak Leaf clusters), and the British Distinguished Flying Cross.

James Jabara was born on 10 October 1923 in Oklahoma but raised in Wichita, Kansas. The son of hard-working Lebanese immigrants, he rose in the Boy Scouts to the rank of Eagle Scout while still working in his family's grocery store. Graduating in 1943 from the Army Air Corp's officer flight school, he flew more than 100 missions in the P-51 Mustang with the Ninth Air Force's 363d Fighter Group. In 1944, the wiry Jabara earned his first Distinguished Flying Cross with 1.5 German kills.

Jabara, flying the F-86A Sabre Jet with the 334th Fighter Inceptor Squadron of the 4th Fighter Interceptor Wing, began operating in Korea in December 1950. He got his first kill on 3 April 1951 over MiG Alley and the Yalu River. By the end of that month he was the leading U.S. scorer with four kills. The 334th was rotated to Japan, but it was decided to keep Jabara in Korea to make ace.

On 20 May 1951, during his sixty-third of an eventual 163 missions, Captain James Jabara became the world's first jet-versus-jet ace. Over Sinuiju, 28 Sabre Jets were jumped by 50 MiGs. After a failed attempt to drop one of his auxiliary fuel tanks, he was still able to down two MiGs with gun kills. He was awarded another Distinguished Service Cross and ordered back to the States on a publicity tour.

Jabara volunteered to go back to Korea in early 1953. Between late May and mid-July, he quickly became a triple-ace. By 15 July 1953, he had shot down his fifteenth MiG. He ended the Korean War as the second-leading U.S. ace.

Rising quickly through the ranks of the Air Force, Jabara had all the qualities of the stereotypical U.S. fighter-pilot ace. He was disciplined, heroic, patriotic, a hard-drinking smoker, a dedicated family man, and an exceptional aviator. In 1966, while delivering a plane to Vietnam, he was able to fly a combat mission and get assigned to a 100-mission tour of duty.

James Jabara shot down five-and-a-half aircraft in World War II and destroyed four more on the ground. In Korea, flying F-86s, he became the first American jet ace and went on to become the second-ranking American ace in Korea, with fifteen victories. (U.S. Air Force)

The first African-American four-star general, Daniel "Chappie" James, in a characteristic pose before his Phantom. (U.S. Air Force)

On 17 November 1966, at the age of 43, James Jabara was killed in an automobile accident near Delray Beach, Florida.

Scott R. DiMarco

See also

North American F-86 Sabre; North American P-51 Mustang

References

Dorr, Robert F. *Korean War Aces.* London: Osprey Aircraft of the Aces Series, 1995.

Miner, Craig H. *James Jabara: Hero.* Wichita, KS: Sullivan Lithographics, 1984.

James, Daniel "Chappie" (1920–1978)

First African American U.S. Air Force four-star general. Daniel James was born in Pensacola, Florida, the youngest of 17 children, and was nicknamed Chappie for an older brother. James grew up watching Navy planes. He did not join the Navy, though, because he did not want to be a cook (the armed services at this time were still segregated, and opportunities for blacks were few). In 1939, when a federal law authorized civilian pilot training at universities, he was a student at the Tuskegee Institute. In his senior year James enrolled in the Civilian Pilot Training Program run by the Civil Aeronautic Authority.

His basic flight training was in a Piper Cub, then Stearman PT-17s and PT-19s at Moton Field, home of the 99th Pursuit Squadron, the famous Tuskegee Airmen, commanded by Benjamin O. Davis Jr. Although stationed at Selfridge, Michigan, and Freeman, Indiana, during racial disturbances, James was not involved. In January 1946, he moved to Lockbourne, Ohio, still a segregated base.

After desegregation of the armed services, in 1949 James went to Clark Air Base in the Philippines. During the Korean War, he flew 100 missions in P-51s and F-80s. In 1950, Captain James returned to Clark, then moved to Griffiss Air Force Base, New York, and flew F-86s. Next he went to Otis Air Force Base, Massachusetts, where he became the first African American commander of an integrated fighter squadron in the continental United States.

By 1960, he was a lieutenant colonel at RAF Bentwaters. During the turbulent 1960s, his lack of activism and favoritism to blacks, as well as camaraderie with whites, made him the object of ridicule from radicals. During a tour of Vietnam, he flew under Robin Olds, participating in the famous Operation BOLO.

At Wheelus, Libya, in 1968 he faced down Muammar Qaddafi at the main gate, hand on revolver. He got his first star in 1970 and in 1975 became the first black four-star general. James overcame his youthful reputation as a brawler to serve as a speaker for the Pentagon on patriotism, loyalty, and commitment to the POW/MIA effort. In 1977, he had a heart attack; he retired in 1978 and died shortly thereafter.

John Barnhill

References

McGovern, James R. *Black Eagle: General Daniel "Chappie" James, Jr.* Montgomery: University of Alabama Press, 1985.

Phelps, J. Alfred. *Chappie.* Novato, CA: Presidio Press, 1991.

Japan, Air Operations Against (1942–1945)

Despite widespread awareness about the vulnerability of the Japanese home islands to air attack—reinforced by the results of the Doolittle Raid on Tokyo on 18 April 1942—U.S. plans for an air war against Japan remained vague until well into 1943 because of American limitations in resources and technology.

The development of the Boeing B-29 Superfortress changed this situation. Eventually, more than 1,000 of the long-range aircraft were deployed in the Twentieth Air Force under the direct control of the Army Air Forces commander, General Henry "Hap" Arnold, subdivided into the XX and XXI Bomber Commands. Under pressure to get results from his expensive very-heavy bomber program, he fielded the new aircraft even before testing had been completed.

In June 1944, B-29s from Major General Kenneth Wolfe's XX Bomber Command began bombing Japan from China as part of Operation MATTERHORN. The campaign was plagued by logistical problems that got worse when Japanese troops overran advanced Allied airfields in China. Arnold replaced Wolfe with the USAAF's premier problem-solver, Major General Curtis LeMay. However, even he could not make MATTERHORN a success.

Arnold's greatest hopes for an airpower victory over Japan rested with Brigadier General Haywood "Possum" Hansell's XXI Bomber Command, which began operations from the Mariana Islands in November 1944. Hansell was one of the architects of the precision-bombing doctrine, but his operations also had little success. Poor facilities, faulty training, engine failures, cloud cover, and jet streams at bombing altitudes made precision methods impossible. Hansell seemed unwilling to change his tactics, however, and Arnold feared that he would lose control of the heavy bombers to Allied Pacific theater commanders without better results, so he consolidated both bomber commands in the Marianas under LeMay and relieved Hansell.

LeMay instituted new training and maintenance procedures but still failed to achieve useful results with daylight high-altitude precision attacks. He decided to resort to low-level incendiary raids at night. Although area-firebombing went against dominant Air Forces doctrine, flying at low altitude reduced engine strain, required less fuel, improved bombing concentration, avoided high winds, and took advantage of weaknesses in Japanese defenses. LeMay's systems analysts predicted that he could set large enough fires to leap firebreaks around important industrial objectives. His first application of the new tactics, Operation MEETINGHOUSE, against Tokyo on the night of 9 March 1945, produced spectacular destruction and was the deadliest air raid of the war.

Once enough incendiaries were stockpiled, the fire raids began in earnest. Warning leaflets were also dropped, which terrorized 8 million Japanese civilians into fleeing from cities. When General Carl Spaatz arrived in July to take command of U.S. Army Strategic Air Forces in the Pacific, including the Eighth Air Force redeploying from Europe, and to coordinate strategic air operations supporting the invasion of Japan, he had a directive to shift the air campaign from cities to transportation. But there was too much momentum behind the fire raids, sustained by operational tempo, training programs, and bomb stockage.

By the time Spaatz arrived, naval carrier strikes were also hitting key industrial objectives in Japan. More important, a submarine blockade had crippled the Japanese economy, the Russians were about to attack Manchuria, and Spaatz maintained direct command over the 509th Composite Group of B-29s specially modified to carry atomic bombs. Directed by Washington to deliver these weapons as soon as possible after 3 August, Spaatz ordered the attacks on Hiroshima and Nagasaki. These different elements combined with the incendiary campaign to comprise the series of blows that produced Japanese surrender.

As with the atomic bomb, there is still debate over the effects and morality of the firebombing raids. LeMay's bombers burned out 180 square miles of 67 cities, killed at least 300,000 people, and wounded more than 400,000. His 313th Bomb Wing also sowed 12,000 mines in ports and waterways, sinking almost 1 million tons of shipping in about four months. LeMay remained convinced that his conventional bombing could have achieved victory by itself. LeMay,

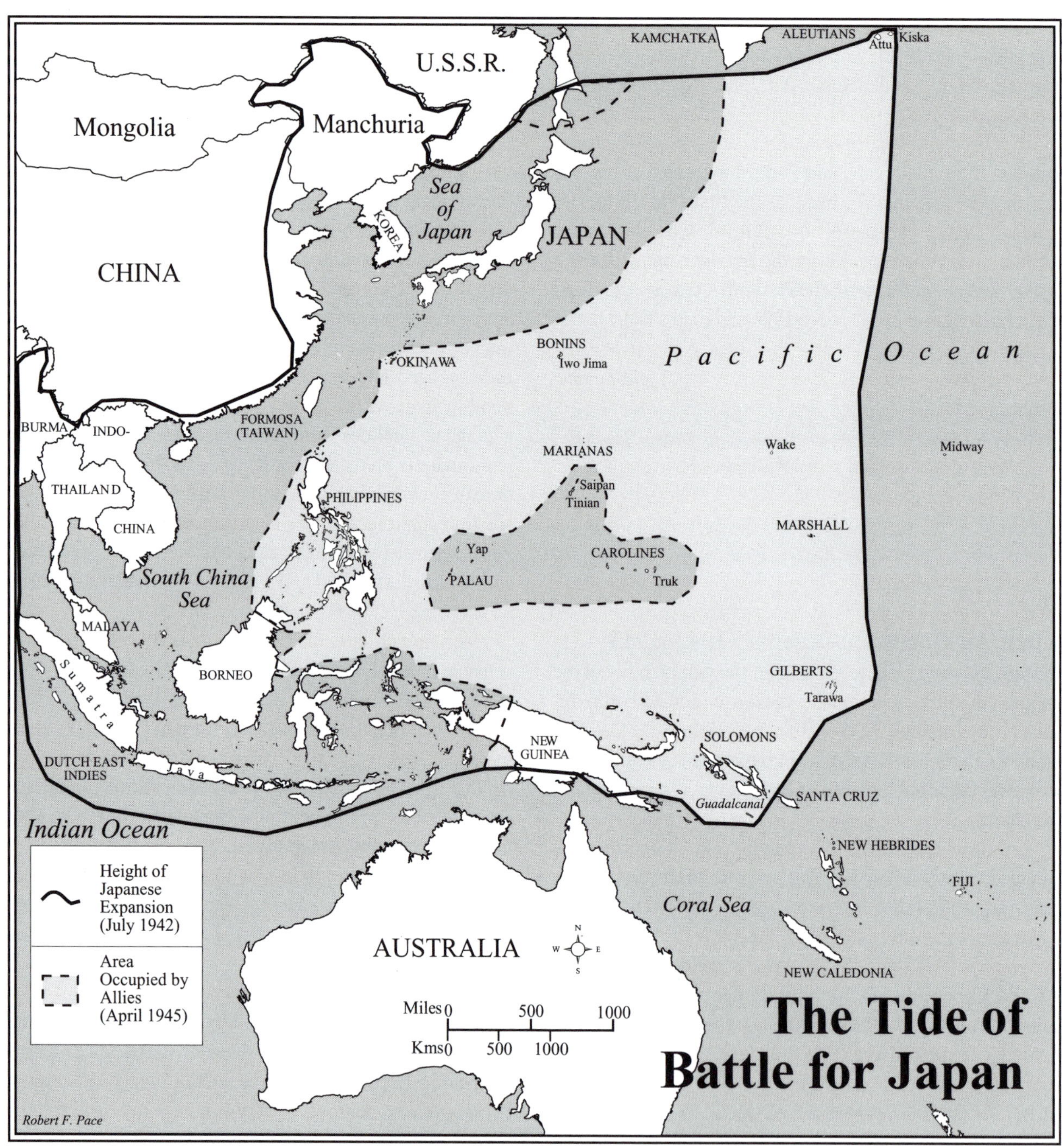

his tactics, and the legacy of the atomic bombs would be a primary influence in the shaping of the new United States Air Force.

Conrad C. Crane

See also

Atomic Bomb; Boeing B-29 Superfortress; Doolittle, James H.; Hiroshima; LeMay, Curtis E.; Nagasaki; Spaatz, Carl Andrew; Tokyo Air Raids

References

Hansell, Haywood S. Jr. *Strategic Air War Against Japan*. Washington, DC: U.S. Government Printing Office, 1980.

Japanese Air Self-Defense Force (JASDF)

The air force component of the post–World War II military forces of Japan, established with the creation of the Japanese Self-Defense Forces (JSDF) in 1954. The founding of the JSDF ended the demilitarization that had been imposed on Japan by the United States and its Allies at the end of World War II. The emphasis on self-defense in the new military force structure was a reflection of the Japanese constitution and internal political attitudes toward the military, which outlawed offensive military capabilities and prevented operations outside Japan until a 1994 law allowed limited peacekeeping operations abroad. Additionally, U.S. deterrence forces and the presence of U.S. military units in Japan provided protection for the homeland.

The Japanese Air Self-Defense Force was molded by close links to the United States Air Force. The bulk of the combat aircraft were of U.S. design (F-86s, F-104s, F-4s, and F-15s), although they were often built by Japanese industry, which also produced Japanese-designed trainers and a ground attack variant. The bulk of the inventory has been interceptors, with a small attack force for support of the Ground Self-Defense Force (GSDF) and the Maritime Self-Defense Force (MSDF). The JASDF also has operated transports (C-130s and domestic C-1s), helicopters (CH-47Js and UH-60s), and airborne early warning and control aircraft (E-2Cs and a modified version of the Boeing 767). Additionally, the JASDF controls the homeland defense surface-to-air missiles (Nike-J and Patriot) while the GSDF controls the tactical SAMs (Hawks).

The missions of the JASDF have been territorial air defense, including surveillance and identification of violators of national airspace; air rescue; airlift operations; air traffic control and weather; and civil relief operations, both domestic and, after 1994, overseas, with major activities in Cambodia and Rwanda. The JASDF also collaborates with the MSDF in protecting the sea lines of communications, and it supports the MSDF and the GSDF in defending against invasions of the Japanese home islands.

Jerome V. Martin

Japanese Army Air Force, Imperial (JAAF)

The air force component of Japan's imperial ground forces during World War II. The Imperial Japanese Army Air Force finds its origins in 1877 with the use of balloons. In 1904, the army used balloons in the Russo-Japanese war, carrying out 14 successful missions.

Officially there were no organizational efforts until July 1909, when the Provisional Military Balloon Research Society was formed. This included members from both the army and the navy as well as staff from Tokyo Imperial University. The society purchased its first aircraft in 1910 and made its first flight on Japanese soil in December.

In December 1915, the army organized its aircraft into the Air Battalion, Army Transport Command. In 1919, Major General Ikutaro Inouye became the first commander of the Army Air Division. In 1925, the Air Corps was established and became an equal part of the army with the infantry, artillery, and cavalry.

The first major conflict that the Army Air Corps was involved in was the so-called Manchurian Incident of September 1931. The army had little trouble establishing air superiority over Chinese forces during the conflict.

From 1932 to 1937, a major modernization of the Air Corps occurred. At this time, the second Sino-Japanese conflict began. The army primarily concentrated aircraft on ground support duties while the navy fought for air superiority and handled long-range bombing operations.

Another concern during this time was the threat of the Red Air Force and the Manchukuo-Siberian border. After a bitter conflict with Soviet forces at Nomonhan, the Japanese began to develop aircraft to fight an eventual battle with the Soviets. These aircraft were designed to fight in the cold of the region, not for long missions over the great expanses of the Pacific.

Early in the Pacific War, the JAAF had many successes. It advanced with little opposition in most areas until July 1942, when it had reached its limit. From late 1942 until October 1944, it suffered increasing losses, particularly in New Guinea, to U.S. forces and in China to Chinese forces. These forces were being resupplied with newer and better aircraft, whereas the JAAF was still equipped with the aircraft it had started the war with.

Finally, in 1944 new fighters and bombers began to arrive. It was simply to late to do anything but slow the advance of the Allies. With the first B-29 missions that bombed mainland Japan, the army's focus shifted to homeland defense. The aircraft assigned to this mission lacked the high-altitude abilities necessary to be effective.

David A. Pluth

See also

Japanese Naval Air Force, Imperial

References

Francillon, Rene J. *Japanese Aircraft of the Pacific War.* Annapolis, MD: Naval Institute Press, 1995.

Japanese Naval Air Force, Imperial (JNAF)

The air force component under the Imperial Japanese Navy during World War II. The birth of Japanese naval aviation occurred in 1912. The navy had been part of the Provisional Military Balloon Research Society, which had been established as a joint effort with the army. The army dominated the society, and the navy decided to withdraw and create its own organization, the Kaigun Kokujutsu Kenkyu Kai (Naval Aeronautical Research Association). This event would be a bone of contention between the army and navy for many years to come.

The naval association sent six officers to France and the United States to acquire seaplanes and learn to fly and maintain them. The operation was a success, and a new naval air station was established on the Oppama Coast near Yokosuka. Within the year, the Imperial Japanese Navy commissioned their first seaplane tender, the *Wakamiya Maru.*

In 1916, the first Navy Air Corps was activated, the Yokosuka Kokutai. In 1917, the first completely Japanese-designed aircraft was built at the Yokosuka naval arsenal.

After World War I, the navy became intrigued with the idea of launching aircraft from ships. In June 1920, a deck was mounted to the *Wakamiya Maru,* and a Sopwith Pup was launched successfully from the deck. Then, in late 1921, the *Hosho*—the world's first true aircraft carrier—was launched. Other ships had been modified to carry aircraft, but the *Hosho* was designed from the ground up to be an aircraft carrier.

It was not until 1932 that a major push was made to develop true carrier aircraft. The navy issued Specification 7-Shi for a carrier-based aircraft to be built. The navy had developed a system where it would submit a specification to a number of manufacturers, which would compete to have their design accepted for service. This specification was thought to be extremely important to the navy in its development of attack aircraft and fighters. However, only one aircraft, the E7K1 Alf, was placed into production in quantity. The failure was primarily due to high expectations and limited technology at the time. Two years later, navy specifications would be met, and the first of the dominant Japanese aircraft would start to appear in the arsenal.

It was about this time that the navy entered the second Sino-Japanese conflict. The results were outstanding. Japanese fighters and bombers forced the Chinese to withdraw their aircraft or lose them. There was also one additional benefit to the war with the Chinese. Beyond the experience gained, it gave the Imperial Japanese Navy a chance to further organize and develop effective air combat tactics. These would become very useful during the Pacific War.

Because of its collection of long-range aircraft and aircraft carriers, the navy would become responsible for all campaigns in the Pacific islands. It would also be responsible for the attack on Pearl Harbor.

In the first six months of the war in the Pacific, the navy was extremely effective. Its experience in China and its organization made it a formidable foe. However, in June 1942 at Midway Island, U.S. carriers dealt the navy a heavy blow, sinking four aircraft carriers. This loss of ships and aircraft stopped the Japanese advance in the Pacific.

At this point of the war, it appeared that the industrial production of the United States and the abundance of pilots available to Allied forces could not be equaled by the Japanese. Japan was quickly running out of trained pilots as well as materials to produce aircraft and ships.

In October 1944, the Imperial Japanese Navy developed a new tactic: kamikaze attacks. A kamikaze would dive his aircraft, loaded with bombs, into Allied ships. The tactic did minimal physical damage given the number of aircraft and pilots that it sacrificed. Hostilities in the Pacific War continued until August 1945, when the order for surrender was given. This spelled the end of the Imperial Japanese Navy until the postwar years.

David A. Pluth

See also

Nakajima Aircraft

References

Francillon, Rene J. *Japanese Aircraft of the Pacific War.* Annapolis, MD: Naval Institute Press, 1995.

Mikesh, Robert C., and Shorzoe Abe. *Japanese Aircraft, 1910–1941.* London: Putnam Aeronautical Books, 1990.

Jeschonnek, Hans (1899–1943)

The longest-serving Luftwaffe Chief of Staff. Jeschonnek became a pilot at the age of 17 and served with Erhard Milch during World War I. He remained in the interwar German army, the Reichswehr, and rose quickly in rank, especially after he and his mentor Milch joined the newly established Luftwaffe.

Jeschonnek became Luftwaffe Chief of Staff in February 1939 and rose to full general, but he fell out with both Milch and Hermann Goering, who blamed him for the operational failings of the Luftwaffe. Jeschonnek was well known for his enthusiastic, unquestioning obedience to Hitler but was unable to hold his own in the cutthroat competition for the Führer's favor. On the morning of 18 August 1943, the day after the USAAF's first raid on Schweinfurt and Regensburg, Jeschonnek received word of the RAF's damaging attack on the German rocket research facility at Peenemunde the previous night and then shot himself. He left the following note: "I can no longer work together with the Reichsmarschall [Goering]. Long live the Führer."

Donald Caldwell

See also

German Air Force (Luftwaffe)

References

Corum, J. *The Luftwaffe: Creating the Operational Air War, 1918–1940.* Lawrence: University Press of Kansas, 1997.

Muller, R. *The German Air War in Russia.* Baltimore: Nautical and Aviation, 1992.

Johnson, Clarence L. "Kelly" (1910–1990)

U.S. aeronautical engineer. As the founder and leader of Lockheed's legendary Skunk Works, Kelly Johnson became famous for building revolutionary aircraft under tight deadlines and maximum security.

Clarence Leonard Johnson was born on 27 February 1910 in Ishpeming, Michigan, the seventh of nine children born to Swedish immigrants. His Irish-sounding nickname was bestowed on him by grade school classmates on account of his fiery temper. From the age of seven or eight, he had access to his father's workshop, and he quickly showed mechanical aptitude.

The Johnsons were bitterly poor, and Kelly learned the lather's trade at age 12 to help support the family. The next year, the Johnson family moved 300 miles to Flint, where opportunities were better. There Kelly finished high school and attended junior college.

He went on to the University of Michigan, where he majored in aeronautical engineering. With a friend, he subcontracted for use of the university's wind tunnel and made enough money to cover school expenses by testing and modifying auto-body designs for Studebaker.

Johnson interviewed with Lockheed upon graduation in 1932, only to be told there were no jobs available. Advised to try again later, he went back to Michigan to earn a master's degree. Going to work for Lockheed in 1933, he worked with chief engineer Hall Hibbard to redesign the Lockheed Electra, adding a twin tail for improved directional control. The redesigned Electra was a technical and commercial success, assuring Lockheed's future.

After leading design teams for the Constellation transport and the P-38 Lightning fighter, Johnson teamed up with Hibbard again to build America's first jet aircraft, the P-80 Shooting Star. The demands of this program led to the creation of Lockheed's fabled Skunk Works, an experimental group under Johnson's direct supervision, where designers and workers could cooperate closely and red tape was eliminated. Here Kelly found his niche, revealing himself to be a brilliant manager as well as engineer. Intense, driven, and totally devoted to the job, he inspired his people to achieve much more than they might have in a more relaxed atmosphere. Johnson's leadership led to the completion of a prototype aircraft in an incredible 143 days from the signing of the initial contract.

Given a free hand at the Skunk Works, Johnson went on to lead the efforts to create the USAF's premier reconnaissance airplanes, the U-2 and the SR-71. Due in part to Johnson's passion for secrecy, both spyplanes flew successfully for several years before the public learned any details about the aircraft or their missions.

Johnson married Althea Young in 1937. She died of cancer in 1969, after encouraging Kelly to remarry. He married Maryellen Meade, his secretary, in May 1971. She died in October 1980 of complications from diabetes, also encouraging

One of the greatest aircraft designers in history, Kelly Johnson stands next to one of his prize productions, the Lockheed U-2. (U.S. Air Force)

Kelly to remarry. Declaring himself too old to waste time for appearance's sake, he married Nancy Horrigan a month later.

In 1986, he broke his hip in a fall. Apart from a trip to the Skunk Works to see an SR-71 take off one last time, he never left the hospital. His final years were heartbreaking, as a general physical decline and advancing senility devastated the proud, robust Johnson. He died on 21 December 1990.

Mark E. Wise

See also

Lockheed Aircraft; Lockheed F-104 Starfighter; Lockheed P/F-80 Shooting Star; Lockheed P-38 Lightning; Lockheed SR-71 Blackbird; Lockheed U-2

References

Boyne, Walter J. *Beyond the Horizons: The Lockheed Story, 1908–1995.* New York: St. Martin's, 1998.

Johnson, Clarence L. "Kelly," with Maggie Smith. *Kelly: More Than My Share of It All.* Washington, DC: Smithsonian Institution Press, 1985.

Rich, Ben R., and Leo Janos. *Skunk Works: A Personal Memoir of My Years at Lockheed.* Boston: Little Brown, 1994.

Johnson, Robert S. (1920–1998)

U.S. World War II fighter ace. Robert S. Johnson was born on 21 February 1920 in Lawton, Oklahoma. He entered Army aviation in November 1941 and trained in Missouri and Texas before being assigned to fly fighters. In July 1942, he traveled to Bridgeport, Connecticut, to join Hub Zemke's Wolfpack, the 56th Fighter Group. After checking out on the new Republic P-47B fighter, he sailed for England on the *Queen Elizabeth* in January 1943.

Johnson scored his first aerial kill on 13 June, when he broke formation to attack a German Focke-Wulf fighter. Renowned for his phenomenal eyesight, superior marksmanship, and aggressive nature, his list of victories quickly grew. In only 91 missions flown from April 1943 through May 1944, he scored an impressive 27 victories, second in the European theater only to Francis Gabreski's 28. In June 1944, Johnson came home to a White House welcome and spent the remainder of the war touring and speaking in the United States. Johnson's decorations include the Distinguished Service Cross, Silver Star, and Distinguished Flying Cross.

After the war, Johnson worked for Republic Aviation and later became an insurance executive. In 1958, he collaborated with Martin Caiden on his autobiography, *Thunderbolt!* Johnson died on 27 December 1998 in Tulsa, Oklahoma.

Daniel Ruffin and Steven A. Ruffin

References

Heaton, Colin D. "Wolfpack Ace Robert S. Johnson." *Military History* (August 1996).

Johnson, Robert S., with Martin Caiden. *Thunderbolt!* New York: Ballantine Books, 1959.

Joint Strike Fighter (JSF)

The Joint Strike Fighter project is developing an aircraft that will serve as the primary attack aircraft for all three U.S. military services and replace the Harrier in British service. It is likely, assuming that the development effort is successful, that the JSF will enjoy widespread export potential to other countries; estimates run as high as 6,000 aircraft being produced, but 3,000 is the more likely number.

Three different variants of the JSF are under development: a conventional aircraft for the U.S. Air Force, a larger-wing variant for the U.S. Navy, and a vertical/short takeoff and landing (V/STOL) version for the U.S. Marines and Britain. The goal of the program is to make these three variants as similar as possible to minimize costs.

Two contractor teams developed JSF prototypes. One team led by Boeing built two X-32 demonstrators; the Lockheed Martin team built two competing X-35 aircraft. Both teams presented their aircraft to the public in early 2000 and flew them later that year. The winner, Lockheed Martin, was announced to great fanfare in October 2001. The contract to build the JSF, valued at some $200 billion, represented the largest defense contract ever awarded.

Dennis R. Jenkins

References

Sweetman, Bill. *Joint Strike Fighter.* Osceola, WI: Motorbooks International, 1999.

Jointness

A U.S. military concept that calls for the separate services (Army, Navy, Air Force, and Marine Corps) working in concert to accomplish assigned missions. Although there has always been cooperation between the services, the passage of the Department of Defense Reorganization Act (more commonly known as the Goldwater-Nichols Act) in 1986 mandated integration of organizations, doctrines, resources, and command. This initiative evolved because of concerns over service parochialism and other issues that often played a major role in several less-than-successful military operations, such as the DESERT ONE debacle (the aborted

Iran hostage rescue mission) and Operation URGENT FURY (Grenada).

Under the concept of jointness, it is anticipated that no single service will operate alone. Rather, the services will work in concert as a unified team. Individual service perspectives, forces, and doctrines are integrated to increase the effectiveness of the entire force.

The Goldwater-Nichols Act strengthened the office of the Chairman of the Joint Chiefs of Staff and clarified the chain of command by stating that operational authority ran from the president to the secretary of defense and then directly to nine joint commanders in chief (who were assigned regional or functional areas of responsibility). The service chiefs and service secretaries were excluded from command responsibilities but were charged with recruitment, training, and equipping their service forces for the commanders in chief to use in carrying out operational missions.

James H. Willbanks

References

Lovelace, Douglas C. Jr., and Thomas Durrell-Young. *U.S. Department of Defense Strategic Planning: The Missing Nexus.* Carlisle Barracks, PA: Strategic Studies Institute, U.S. Army War College, 1995.

Powell, Colin. *My American Journey.* New York: Random House, 1995.

Jones, David C. (1921–)

USAF general; one of the most important U.S. military leaders during the Cold War who figured in critical decisions of the period. Noted for his ability to bring together opposing points of view, Jones was especially valuable in bridging the requirements of different political administrations. Jones was the ninth Chief of Staff of the U.S. Air Force (1974–1978). He was also the ninth Chairman of the Joint Chiefs of Staff (1978–1982).

Commissioned from the aviation cadet program in 1943, Jones did not see combat in World War II, serving as a flying instructor. However, during the Korean War he flew more than 300 hours in B-29s, gaining the combat experience that made him valuable as an aide to Major General Curtis E. LeMay at Strategic Air Command headquarters. LeMay valued the qualities of the native of Aberdeen, South Dakota, and Jones soon found himself on a fast track to the top. His senior positions included commander of Second Air Force/SAC and commander in chief of U.S. Air Forces in Europe.

Jones was the champion of two highly controversial bomber programs, the North American XB-70 and the Rockwell B-1 and, as a result, became a controversial figure. The controversy became more intense when, as Chief of Staff, he reluctantly supported President Jimmy Carter's decision to cancel the B-1. This was at a time when he was pushing force improvements, which involved, among other things, significant reorganization within the USAF. One of his most important contributions was as an ardent advocate of one of the most valuable force multipliers in history, the Airborne Control and Warning System (AWACS).

As two-time chairman of the Joint Chiefs, he served in a number of important roles, including chairman of the SALT discussions and negotiator for the Panama Canal Treaty of 1978.

Jones retired in 1982 and went on to a very successful career in private life, expending much of his effort on improving educational materials.

Walter J. Boyne

See also

Strategic Arms Limitation Treaty

References

Boyne, Walter J. *Beyond the Wild Blue: The History of the United States Air Force, 1947–1997.* New York: St. Martin's, 1997.

Bright, Charles B., ed. *Historical Dictionary of the U.S. Air Force.* New York: Greenwood Press, 1992.

Junkers Aircraft

German aircraft manufacturer. Hugo Junkers (1859–1935) established his first factory in 1889 to make engines and later heating devices. He patented a flying-wing metal airplane design in 1910 and was soon pioneering all-metal construction methods, building an experimental wing in 1915. The first use of corrugated light-alloy skin in an aircraft came with the J 4 of 1917 and marked Junkers products into the early 1930s.

In 1919, the J (later F) 13 appeared, designed to carry six passengers and widely used during the 1920s. It was the first purpose-built all-metal passenger airplane; more than 300 of various models were built. This was expanded into the three-engine G 23 and G 24 airliners of the mid-1920s. The last of the company aircraft before adopting the "Ju" prefix, the G 38 was a giant for 1929—designed to carry up to 30 passengers in the fuselage and wing compartments. Two were built, plus six in Japan under license. Junkers retired in 1932 and lost control of the company in 1934 to the Nazi government.

The separate airframe and engine concerns were combined in 1936. The Ju 160 single-engine airliner of 1934 carried six plus a crew of two. Nearly 50 were built. The Ju 86 was developed as a twin-engine bomber and airliner, first flying

At its peak during the Blitzkrieg period, the Junkers Ju 87 was eventually relegated to occasional ground attacks. (U.S. Air Force)

in 1934. More than 800 of various bomber models were built, compared to perhaps 60 civil airliners. The Ju 90 40-seat airliner first flew in 1937, and the 11 examples were transferred from Lufthansa to Luftwaffe service. About 55 Ju 290 four-engine reconnaissance aircraft were built, one of which flew round-trip from France to just short of New York City to test its long-range bombing capacity. Only two of the giant Ju 390 six-engine transports were built. The Ju 287 was the final Junkers product and the only jet aircraft. Its four Jumo engines were mounted in pairs–two on the forward-swept wing, two on the front fuselage. Only two were built. Some 140,000 workers were employed toward the end of the war.

Christopher H. Sterling

See also

Junkers Ju 52/3m, Ju 87 Stuka, and Ju 88

References

"Junkers." In William Green, *The Warplanes of the Third Reich.* Garden City, NY: Doubleday, 1970, pp. 404–522.

Schmitt, Günter. *Hugo Junkers and His Aircraft.* Berlin: VEB Verlag für Verkehrswesen, 1988.

Junkers Ju 52/3m, Ju 87 Stuka, and Ju 88

First flown in May 1932, the German Junkers Ju 52/3 was a three-engine transport. Pilots favored its BMW trimotor design because it of its reliability. The early version, the Ju 52/3m, carried 15–17 passengers plus a crew of three and was sold around the world as a passenger airliner. When Germany began to rearm, Junkers modified the model and produced a bomber, the Ju 52/3mg3e. When the Spanish civil war broke out, the Kondor Legion and the Nationalist air force were supplied with Ju 52 bombers, troop transports, cargo transports, and air ambulances. The transport version had one 13mm machine gun in an open-air gun turret on the top of the plane near the tail and two 7.92mm machine guns that were manually aimed from the plane's windows; the bomber could carry a payload of 3,307 pounds. Junkers continued to make the transport version, which served the Luftwaffe until the end of the war.

The Junkers Ju 87 Stuka was a low-wing cantilever dive-bomber and ground attack aircraft. First flown in late 1935, the Ju 87A entered production in 1937 powered by the Junkers Jumo engine. The Stuka derived its name from the German for "dive-bomber"—*sturkampfflugzeug.* It was fitted during the blitzkrieg period with screaming whistles would terrify civilians when the aircraft was put into a steep dive. Main armament for this plane from 1939 to 1943 included two 7.92mm machine guns in its wings, one 7.92mm MG 15 machine gun in the rear cockpit (later replaced with an MG 81), and four 110-pound bombs on wing racks. Junkers built many different versions of the aircraft, including transporters and glider tugs, but its most successful ver-

One of the most versatile of the German aircraft, the Junkers Ju 88 was tested extensively at Wright Field during World War II and may today be seen, in its original German markings, in the Air Force Museum in Dayton, Ohio. (Gene Furnish)

sion was the Ju 87G1. This close-support aircraft's armament consisted of two 37mm BK Flak 18 or Flak 36 cannons mounted under the wing. As German air superiority faded, the thinly armored, slow-moving Stuka was relegated to occasional ground attacks.

The twin-engine Junkers Ju 88 first flew in late December 1936 and entered regular service in September 1939. Originally prototyped as a civilian transport, the Ju 88 could carry three to six crewmembers and a variety of armaments. Powered by either Junker Jumo or BMW engines, this highly maneuverable, well-built aircraft was one of the best in the Luftwaffe's arsenal. It filled many roles, including bomber, close support, reconnaissance, torpedo-bomber, trainer, and unguided missile. However, its most famous role was as a night-fighter against Allied bombers. The Ju 88 was still being produced when German factories were overrun in 1945.

Brian B. Carpenter

References

Gunston, Bill. *The Illustrated Encyclopedia of Combat Aircraft of World War II.* London: Salamander Books, 1978.

Vanags-Baginskis, Alex. "Stuka Ju 87." In *The Great Book of World War II Airplanes.* New York: Crescent Books, 1987, pp. 523–571.

K

Kaman Aircraft

U.S. helicopter manufacturer. In 1945, Charles H. Kaman formed Kaman Aircraft Corporation to manufacture helicopters. Having an aeronautical engineering degree from Catholic University, he began work for United Aircraft in 1940 designing propellers in the helicopter division. By 1943, he headed the aerodynamics department and worked to improve helicopter stability. His invention of a servo-flap rotor-control system to reduce vibration was not well received at United, so he formed his own company. His first helicopter, the K-125, was homemade. His second, the K-190, featured contrarotating and intermeshing dual rotors but no tailrotor, a design that gave great stability and lift.

In 1952, Kaman began manufacturing helicopters for the military. The U.S. Navy procured helicopters similar to the K-190 for training, utility, and medical evacuation. The Navy designated this helicopter HTK-1 and later TH-43E. In 1958, the Navy, Marines, and Air Force procured the K-600, an enlarged HTK-1. These services designated their models, respectively, the HUK, HOK, and H-43A Huskie. The Air Force acquired 193 Huskies and used them for rescue and firefighting. These helicopters were later converted from piston to turboshaft engines. Production ceased in 1965. In 1962, the Navy began receiving from Kaman 190 HU2K Seasprites for rescue and utility operations between ships. In the 1970s, the Navy converted 105 of these to antisubmarine warfare and designated them the SH-2 to serve in the Light Airborne Multipurpose System I (LAMPS I). LAMPS gave the Navy its first manned antisubmarine warfare helicopter capable of operating from ships other than aircraft carriers. In 1981, Kaman reopened helicopter production to provide the Navy with more SH2F Seasprites because some ships could not accommodate the SH-60B LAMPS III helicopter.

In the 1970s, Kaman Corporation diversified to lessen dependence on defense contracts. It developed a large aerospace distribution business in addition to aircraft production. Kaman's contributions to helicopter development included several firsts: a servo-controlled rotor, a gas-turbine engine, twin-turbine engines, composite rotor blades, and a remote-controlled helicopter.

John L. Bell

References

Grant, Tina, ed. *International Directory of Company Histories.* Vol. 12. Chicago: St. James Press, 1988.

Polmar, Norman, and Floyd D. Kennedy Jr. *Military Helicopters of the World.* Annapolis, MD: Naval Institute Press, 1981.

Kamikaze Attacks

Desperate suicide attacks undertaken by Japanese pilots during World War II to deliberately ram Allied naval vessels. Kamikaze attacks often caused more damage than conventional bombs or torpedoes. The Japanese term *kamikaze*—"divine wind"—refers to a storm that destroyed a Mongol invasion fleet off Japan in 1281. It was the most common term used to describe these attacks in Japan, and the only term used by the Allies.

Kamikaze pilots did not consider their actions to be suicide attacks in a Western sense but rather the opposition of Japanese moral and spiritual conviction against Western scientific and material advantages. Many kamikaze pilots died with the utmost faith that their sacrifices would reverse the course of the Pacific War, and many wished to continue fighting—and dying—after the Japanese capitulation, though the final consensus was to respect the order to surrender.

By October 1944, Japan had lost the technological edge it had enjoyed in aircraft performance at the start of the Pacific War. In addition, attrition had left Japan with few expe-

A dreaded sight, and one of the most dangerous of the war: the end of a kamikaze's journey. (U.S. Navy)

rienced pilots. These factors combined to make successful conventional attacks on Allied ships rare. Although individual Japanese had crashed their planes into enemy ships and aircraft prior to this date (as had pilots from other nations, including the United States), it was the suggestion of Vice Admiral Onishi Takijino that such attacks become policy. Kamikazes were first operational in the Philippines campaign of 1944, sinking the U.S. escort carrier *St. Lô.* Kamikazes struck again at Iwo Jima, and at Okinawa kamikazes came in massed waves called *kikusui* (floating chrysanthemums). These attacks represented the high point of kamikaze operations. Additional aircraft were set aside to use in kamikaze attacks against the Allied fleet during the invasion of Japan but were never used.

Initial kamikaze attacks used existing types of aircraft. Later, modifications were made to allow heavier bombloads. Japan even went so far as to develop a rocket-driven, human-piloted bomb known as the "Okha" (Cherry Blossom) or "Jinrai" (Thunderbolt) to the Japanese and the "Baka" (Idiot) to Allied forces. The kamikaze concept expanded beyond aircraft to include manned torpedoes, explosive-laden motorboats, midget submarines, and finally the great battleship *Yamato,* which steamed from port with enough fuel to reach the Allied fleet but not—according to some accounts—with enough to return.

Although the kamikazes did cause considerable damage to the Allied fleet, sinking or damaging several hundred ships, the kamikazes were unable to reverse the course of the war. Most of the inexperienced pilots were shot down by veteran Allied fighter pilots well short of their targets or perished in a hail of antiaircraft fire. The rocket bombs made more difficult targets for Allied defenders but had to be carried into battle by slow, unmaneuverable bombers, which were often shot down short of their release point. Most of the seaborne kamikazes failed, and U.S. carrier aircraft sunk *Yamato* long before it neared any Allied surface vessel. It might even be said that the fanatical resistance exemplified by the kamikaze convinced U.S. leaders that nothing short of the atomic bomb could persuade Japan to give up the fight. Thus, the kamikaze may well have brought a new order of destruction to the Japanese people in their efforts to defend the homeland.

Grant Weller

See also

Atomic Bomb; Iwo Jima; Japanese Army Air Force, Imperial; Japanese Naval Air Force, Imperial; Okinawa; Philippines

References

Inoguchi, Rikihei, and Tadashi Nakajima. *The Divine Wind.* Washington, DC: Naval Institute Press, 1958.

Munson, Kenneth. *Fighters and Bombers of World War II 1939–1945.* London: Peerage Books, 1969.

Nagatsuka, Ryuji. *I Was a Kamikaze.* London: Abelard-Schuman, 1972.

Kammhuber, Josef (1896–1986)

Luftwaffe general best known for establishing Germany's nighttime air defenses. Kammhuber was an infantryman in World War I. He was selected to join the interwar army, the Reichswehr, attended the school for General Staff officers, and in 1935 transferred to the Luftwaffe. He commanded a bomber wing in the early campaigns of World War II and was chosen in mid-1940 to set up the German defenses against nighttime Allied bombing.

The Kammhuber Line that he devised required the close control of each night-fighter by a ground operator and was successful until RAF Bomber Command decreased the spacing within its bomber streams and then blinded enemy radars with Window (chaff, or air-dropped aluminum strips). Kammhuber was slow to adapt his defenses to the new tactics and was relieved of his position on 15 September 1943. He was given no important command for the rest of the war. However, when the postwar Bundesluftwaffe (West German air force) was established in 1956, Kammhuber was named as its first commander in chief, with the rank of major general. He established the organization of the new service and integrated it into the defenses of Western Europe.

Donald Caldwell

See also

German Air Force (Luftwaffe)

References

Obermeier, E. *Die Ritterkreuztraeger der Luftwaffe, 1939–1945, Band 1: Jagdflieger* [Recipients of the Knight's Cross]. Mainz: Verlag Dieter Hoffmann, 1989.

Kamov Helicopters

One of two Soviet design bureaus specializing exclusively in helicopters. Nikolai Ilich Kamov was born in 1902, in Siberia like his colleague Mikhail Mil. After completing technical school, Kamov first became a locomotive engineer, but in 1926 he became a pilot and soon turned to design work. In 1929, he was part of the design collective that created the first Soviet autogyro, and until 1945 he worked for a series of other design bureaus, sometimes with Mil as his assistant. In 1945, Kamov founded his own design bureau, the first in Russia dedicated exclusively to helicopters, and in 1947 he designed Russia's first practical helicopter, the Ka-8. The Ka-8, of which three were built, was intended for shipboard use. In 1954, 16 examples of the similar Ka-10 entered experimental naval service.

From the beginning, Kamov and Mil took different paths. Whereas Mil's designs were conventional and intended primarily for the army, Kamov designed exclusively for the navy and with only a couple of exceptions invariably used a coaxial contrarotating twin-rotor system. Kamov's first real success was the Ka-15, of which 354 were built from 1955 to 1959, used for shipboard reconnaissance, liaison, and training. From 1959 to 1961, 111 of the similar but slightly larger Ka-18s were built. The classic Kamov Ka-25 "Hormone" entered production in 1964. By 1972, when production ceased, 267 had been built, primarily as dedicated shipboard antisubmarine warfare (ASW) helicopters but also for aerial mining countermeasures, search and rescue, and midcourse flight correction and guidance for early naval cruise missiles. The Ka-25's success was in part the result of the commissioning of the Soviet navy's two helicopter carriers, the *Moskva* and *Leningrad,* and the development of new classes of cruisers and destroyers designed to utilize the Ka-25's capabilities.

From 1976, the Ka-25 was replaced by a new family of helicopters (code-named "Helix" by NATO). The basic version was the Ka-27, built in both antisubmarine-warfare and search-and-rescue variants, and the Ka-28, which was merely a version for export. The Ka-29TB was a heavily modified variant with nose armament and rocket pylons intended as an assault troop transport for Soviet naval infantry. By the late 1990s, almost 400 examples of these versions had been built, together with almost 150 of a dedicated civilian version, the Ka-32. In the mid-1990s, the Ka-31 (also called Ka-29RLD) was developed as a shipboard airnborne early warning helicopter, with a rotating dish beneath the fuselage.

In addition to building military helicopters, Kamov also built about 1,000 examples of the Ka-26 and its later developments, the Ka-126 and Ka-226, civilian helicopters for use as a crane, crop sprayer, and other uses.

In 1982, Kamov began development of a new single-seat attack helicopter, the Ka-50, in direct competition to Mil's Mi-28. Kamov has proven adept at public relations, naming the Ka-50 the "Black Shark" and sending it to air shows around the world in a dramatic black finish, where it performed aerial maneuvers, including true loops, previously considered impossible for helicopters. The Russian army decided to break with tradition and selected the Ka-50 in preference to the Mi-28 as its next-generation attack helicopter. This helicopter has also been marketed to the world, including NATO countries and even the United States. Kamov has developed a side-by-side two-seat version, the Ka-52 Alligator, which will function as both a combat trainer and (with advanced avionics) as an all-weather attack helicopter. The

Ka-60 is intended to be the army's next tactical troop transport and has forsaken the coaxial contrarotating rotor for a single main rotor and a tail unit much like the French Dauphin.

Nikolai Kamov died on 24 November 1973 and was succeeded by Sergei Mihkeev.

George M. Mellinger

See also

Mil Aircraft

References

Everett-Heath, John. *Soviet Helicopters: Design, Development, and Tactics.* London: Jane's Information Group, 1983.

Gunston, Bill. *The Encyclopedia of Russian Aircraft, 1975–1995.* Osceola, WI: Motorbooks International, 1995.

Kármán, Theodore von (1881–1963)

Mathematical prodigy from Budapest, Hungary, who became a U.S. physicist. He graduated in 1902 from Budapest University, working from 1903 to 1906 at the Technical University of Budapest. Von Kármán left Budapest to study at Göttingen and then in Paris, where he watched some pioneering aviation flights. Such flights piqued his interest to apply mathematics to aeronautics. In 1911, von Kármán made an analysis of the alternating double row of vortices behind a flat body in a fluid flow, a phenomenon now known as Kármán's Vortex Street.

The following year von Kármán accepted a position as director of the Aeronautical Institute at Aachen, Germany. Von Kármán visited the United States in 1926 and four years later accepted a post as director of the Aeronautical Laboratory at the California Institute of Technology. In 1933, von Kármán founded the U.S. Institute of Aeronautical Sciences, where he continued his research on fluid mechanics, turbulence theory, and supersonic flight. In addition, von Kármán studied applications of mathematics to engineering, aircraft structures, and soil erosion.

Albert Atkins

References

Goldstein, S. *Theodore von Kármán, 1881–1963.* London: Biographical Memoirs of Fellows of the Royal Society of London 12 (1966).

Kartveli, Alexander (1896–1974)

One of the most important and innovative aircraft designers in U.S. history. Alexander de Seversky had founded the Seversky Aircraft Corporation in Farmingdale, New York. After Kartveli emigrated to the United States, Seversky almost immediately hired his fellow immigrant as chief engineer, and they proceeded to design a number of very advanced aircraft, including the SEV-1XP, which outperformed the Curtiss P-36 Hawk during a 1936 Army Air Corps competition. Known by the military designation P-35, it was the first modern U.S. Army fighter, incorporating a metal fuselage, low-set wings, retractable landing gear, and a radial engine.

In 1939, Seversky was removed as head of his company, and the Republic Aircraft Corporation was born. The first major aircraft to emerge from the new company was the P-47 Thunderbolt, using an innovative wing from the fertile mind of Kartveli. At the end of the war he designed a sleek flying photolab called the XF-12A, initially planned as a four-engine postwar transport; American Airlines canceled its orders, and only two prototypes were built for the Air Force. Postwar, Kartveli designed the F-84 Thunderjet/Thunderstreak, then led the team that developed the F-105 Thunderchief. He was also heavily involved with a 1960s-era Air Force project called Aerospaceplane—to design and build an orbital logistics vehicle—a decade before NASA attempted a similar concept (the Space Shuttle). The radical turboramjet-powered XF-103 was another stillborn Kartveli design, a victim of the propulsion community not being able to produce a suitable engine to power the Mach 3 interceptor.

Kartveli was never as well known as Kelly Johnson, his equal at Lockheed. But for the half-decade that Seversky and Republic manufactured aircraft on Long Island, Kartveli contributed significantly to the science of flight and the readiness of the U.S. military. Alexander Kartveli died in 1974.

Dennis R. Jenkins

See also

Republic Aircraft; Republic F-105 Thunderchief; Republic F-84 Thunderjet/Thunderstreak; Republic P-47 Thunderbolt; Seversky Aircraft

References

Wagner, Ray. *American Combat Planes.* 3rd ed. Garden City, NY, Doubleday, 1982.

Kawanishi Aircraft

Japanese airframe manufacturer. Kawanishi Kokuki K.K. was formed in 1928 after taking over the assets of Kawanishi Engineering Works. During World War II, Kawanishi was the sixth largest producer of combat aircraft in Japan. Kawanishi produced only airframes, with engines being provided by outside sources.

The Kawanishi George was a major step forward for Japan, as it was capable of meeting the U.S. Hellcat and Corsair on equal terms. Like all Japanese aircraft later in the war, however, it was handicapped by quality control problems. (U.S. Air Force)

Kawanishi had a total of four plants. Three—Himeji northwest of Kobe, Naruo near Osaka, and Konsan between Osaka and Kobe—produced airframes. The fourth plant (Takarazuka, located north of the Naruo plant) was a component plant that supplied parts to the others.

During World War II, Kawanishi produced three primary aircraft. The N1K Kyofu (Allied code name "Rex") was the first Japanese floatplane fighter specifically designed for that purpose.

The N1K1/2-J Shiden (Allied code name "George") was a land-based design developed from the Rex. From December 1942 to early 1945, some 1,000 aircraft of this type were produced. The highly maneuverable George was one of the few fighters at the end of the war that was a good match for the Allied F6F Hellcats and F4U Corsairs.

The H8K (Allied code name "Emily") was probably the best flying boat of the war serving any nation. The Emily was the largest of all naval aircraft and the fastest and most maneuverable flying boat in the Imperial Japanese Navy. The Emily carried out a variety of missions: reconnaissance, torpedo attacks, bombing, patrol, and transport. Approximately 160 Emilys were produced by the end of the war.

David A. Pluth

References

Francillon, Rene J. *Japanese Aircraft of the Pacific War.* London: Putnam Aeronautical Books, 1970.

Staff of Airview. *General View of Japanese Military Aircraft in the Pacific War.* Katosha, 1956.

Kawasaki Aircraft

One of the major Japanese industrial groups in the twentieth century. Kawasaki manufactured aircraft—including what many consider to be the best Japanese fighter of the war—before and during World War II and again after 1954.

Kawasaki Heavy Industries was formed in 1878 as Japan's first shipbuilder and in 1918 established an aircraft department—perhaps the first in the country. Initially, the company made substantial use of foreign personnel and designs at its Kobe headquarters. By 1920, it had built a factory and airfield. Its first government contract was for 300 copies of a license-built version of a Salmson reconnaissance aircraft for the army.

By 1923, Kawasaki had hired Richard Vogt (later with Blohm and Voss) as chief designer; he stayed for a decade and trained many others. Among his designs were the Type 88 biplane reconnaissance bomber (1927), of which more than 1,000 were manufactured; the Type 92 biplane fighter (1930), with nearly 400 made in two versions; and the Ki 3, the country's last biplane bomber (1933), some 240 being made.

After Vogt's departure the Ki 10, the last Japanese biplane fighter (1935), appeared (600 manufactured, some by Nakajima). The Ki 32 monoplane single-engine light bomber (1937) was also made in large numbers (850) and later became a trainer. In 1937, the aircraft branch was spun off into a separate firm; aircraft engines followed in 1939.

Kawasaki's wartime total production of 8,250 aircraft made it third among Japanese firms. The key aircraft included the 1939 Ki 45 twin-engine ground attack plane ("Nick" to the Allies) later used as an excellent night-fighter. About 1,700 were built, and four became the first kamikaze aircraft used in May 1944. The Ki 61 Hein (Swallow; "Tony" to the Allies) liquid-cooled fighter of 1941 was in service by 1943; some 2,600 were made.

Disaster can lead to unexpected innovation. One of the best Japanese fighters of World War II, the Ki 100, was the product of such an emergency. The manufacturer had 275 completed Ki 61 airframes when its engine factory was destroyed by Allied bombing. In desperate need of fighter aircraft, those airframes were modified to take a Mitsubishi radial engine rather than the intended Kawasaki inline motor. First flown in February 1945, the result startled its creators as one of the fastest and most maneuverable aircraft ever built. With a top speed of more than 365 mph, performance surpassed the Ki 61. The new models were in service by May. In June, manufacture began of the Ki 100–1b, with a cut-down rear fuselage and bubble canopy. Nearly 100 had been made by the end of the war. Three prototypes of an improved version were built just before the surrender.

The company was revived in 1954 to overhaul U.S. aircraft and develop its own new models. The latter included the C-1 high-wing twin-jet cargo plane (first flight 1970) and the T-4 jet trainer (first flight 1985).

Christopher H. Sterling

References

Collier, Basil. *Japanese Aircraft of World War II.* London: Sedgwick and Jackson, 1979.

Francillon, Rene J. *Japanese Aircraft of the Pacific War.* Rev ed. London: Putnam, 1987.

Kearby, Neel (1911–1944)

United States Army Air Corps lieutenant colonel. Kearby was born on 5 June 1911 in Wichita Falls, Texas. He graduated in 1936 from the University of Texas and took flight training at Randolph and Kelly Air Force Bases.

In October 1942, Kearby was chosen as group commander of the 348th Fighter Group. He was disappointed to find out that there was little equipment and few pilots actually assigned to the 348th. After more than six months of preparations and training, Kearby and the 348th sailed for New Guinea and the air war against Japan.

There was some skepticism upon arrival that the P-47 Thunderbolt was not the proper aircraft for the job in the South Pacific. Through a series of mock dogfights with the P-38 Lightning, Kearby proved the P-47 to be a fighter that could hold its own and even dominate the best aircraft of its time.

Kearby scored his first two victories on 4 September 1943 by shooting down a Japanese fighter and a bomber. Kearby was awarded the Medal of Honor for his actions of 11 October 1943. Kearby shot down six Japanese aircraft while leading a flight of four aircraft over Wewak.

Kearby was killed in action on 5 March 1944. While on a sweep of the Wewak area, he and his flight shot down three bombers when one of the escort fighters, a Nakajima Ki 43 "Oscar," opened fire at short range and shot down Kearby. He had achieved the status as one of the top U.S. aces, with 22 victories in a six-month period.

David A. Pluth

References

Stafford, Gene B. *Aces of the Southwest Pacific.* Carrollton, TX: Squadron/Signal, 1977.

Stanaway, John C. *Kearby's Thunderbolts.* Atglen, PA: Schiffer Military History, 1997.

Kenney, George (1889–1977)

United States Army Air Corps/Air Force general. George Churchill Kenney was born in Yarmouth, Nova Scotia, on 6 August 1889. From 1907 to 1911, he attended the Massachusetts Institute of Technology. In June 1917, he enlisted in the Signal Corps Aviation Section, and by December 1917 he was commissioned as a first lieutenant. In 1919, Kenney was promoted to captain and became the commanding officer of the 91st Aero Squadron. From 1926 until 1935, Kenney served in a variety of assignments; in March 1935 he was promoted to lieutenant colonel.

Kenney was next assigned to Wright Field, Ohio, as chief of production. In 1940, he was promoted to colonel and sent to France as the assistant air attaché. Kenney was promoted to brigadier general in January 1941 and to major general in February.

In March 1942, Kenney was assigned to be commanding general of the Fifth Air Force. Kenny became General Douglas MacArthur's top air aide and commander of the Fifth Air Force in July 1942. In October 1942, Kenney was promoted to lieutenant general. Kenney led the air war against Japan in the Southwest Pacific through the end of the war. Kenney was promoted to full general in March 1945.

Postwar, Kenney was assigned to the Military Staff Committee of the Joint Chiefs of Staff and continued in that position until March 1946. In April 1946, Kenney was named commanding general of Strategic Air Command and served in that capacity until 1948, when he was named commandant of Air University. Kenney retired in August 1951. He passed away on 9 August 1977.

David A. Pluth

References

Griffith, Thomas E. *MacArthur's Airmen.* Lawrence: University Press of Kansas, 1998.

"Biography of General George C. Kenney." Available online at the U.S. Air Force website, www.af.mil.

Kesselring, Albert (1885–1960)

Luftwaffe commander best known for leading the tenacious Axis ground defense of Italy. Kesselring spent World War I as an artillery officer and on divisional and corps staffs. He was retained in the Reichswehr, the interwar army, where he gained a reputation for his administrative skills.

He transferred to the Luftwaffe in 1933, two years before its existence was openly acknowledged, and was named its Chief of Staff after the death of his predecessor. In 1937, he left Berlin for his first operational posting as an airman and spent the first years of World War II in command of Luftflotte 1 (First Air Force) and Luftflotte 2. He was promoted to field marshal in 1940 during the Battle of Britain.

When Luftflotte 2 transferred from the Eastern Front to the Mediterranean in December 1941, Kesselring gained an additional responsibility—that of *Oberbefehlshaber Sued* (commander in chief, Southern Front). His diplomatic skills were tested fully in dealing with Erwin Rommel, his field commander, and with his allies, the Italians. He succeeded Rommel as field commander in early 1943, retaining his higher command, and conducted a skillful fighting retreat up the Italian Peninsula from September 1943 to March 1945, when he replaced Karl von Rundstedt as *Oberbefehlshaber West* in Germany. The Western Front was already in the process of collapsing, and Kesselring surrendered his forces on 7 May.

Kesselring was condemned to death in 1947 as a war criminal, but his sentence was commuted to life imprisonment, and he was released from prison in 1952. His career was the most varied of any World War II air force general, and his record in Italy ranks him among the top defensive ground commanders of the war.

Donald Caldwell

See also

German Air Force (Luftwaffe)

References

Corum, J. *The Luftwaffe: Creating the Operational Air War, 1918–1940.* Lawrence: University Press of Kansas, 1997.

Kesselring, Albrecht. *The Memoirs of Field-Marshal Kesselring.* London: William Kimber, 1953.

Khalkin Gol Air Battles (1939)

Also known as Nomonhan, the eastern tip of Mongolia saw a clash between the Soviet Union and Japan beginning on 10 May 1939 as a minor border disagreement and escalating to involve multidivision forces on both sides before ending on September 16. Although the Soviet ground forces decisively defeated the Japanese army, the Imperial Japanese Army Air Force managed to dominate the Red Air Force.

Initially, the Soviets had only 82 aircraft in Mongolia; the Japanese had about 500 aircraft available, but they committed only 32 at the start. Both sides rushed in reinforcements, leading to the largest air battles since 1918, often involving more than 100 aircraft on each side. The Soviets found they were suffering a 3:1 loss ratio and dispatched their most successful veterans of Spain. During the fighting the Soviets introduced the I 153 biplane, the cannon-armed version of the I 16, and made the first ever use of the RS-82 rocket in an air-to-air role.

Throughout the battle both sides exaggerated their claims. The Soviets claimed 645 victories for 207 losses, and the Japanese claimed 1,260 victories 162 losses.

George M. Mellinger

See also

Japanese Army Air Force, Imperial; Nakajima Aircraft; Polikarpov, Nikolai N.; Smushkevich, Yakov "General Douglas"; Tupolev Aircraft

References

Coox, Alvin D. *Nomonhan: Japan Against Russia.* Stanford: Stanford University Press, 1990.

Khe Sanh

North Vietnamese attack against U.S. Marine Corps outpost. As the Vietcong attacked in South Vietnam during January 1968, North Vietnamese Army (NVA) regulars conducted a campaign of their own just south of the demilitarized zone (DMZ). General Vo Nguyen Giap organized an attack against the Marine outpost at Khe Sanh. Giap was attempting to recreate the conditions and success of Dien Bien Phu (the victory against the French in 1953), and for this purpose he employed two NVA divisions with a third in reserve. In this confrontation, the Marine garrison and the devastating array of U.S. Air Force munitions defeated the NVA.

The Khe Sanh base, located in northwestern South Vietnam 6 miles from the Laotian border and 14 miles south of the DMZ, posed a threat to the Ho Chi Minh Trail that linked North Vietnamese supply depots with communist forces deployed in South Vietnam. The place was difficult to defend: A chain of hills overlooked the plateau from the north and northwest, and drinking water came from a river that passed through enemy-controlled territory. Early in the year fog shrouded the base on most mornings, complicating air operations and limiting visibility from defensive positions.

In anticipation of a siege that would last for more than 70 days, the Marines quickly buoyed their forces at Khe Sanh to 6,000. Over the ensuing weeks the enemy steadfastly shelled the base and attempted to overrun it. One of the largest attacks was launched on 29 February. Previously planted electronic sensors first alerted defenders. In the ensuing encounter the Marines and their allies called upon mortars, artillery, tactical aircraft, and B-52 heavy bombers to create a barrier of high explosives at various approaches. The attack faltered before the enemy reached the berm line, and within two weeks U.S. intelligence reported that the NVA troops were withdrawing from the area. On 1 April Operation PEGASUS, the land advance to Khe Sanh, commenced and Khe Sanh was soon relieved.

Khe Sanh would not become Dien Bien Phu. Indeed, compared to the ill-fated French base, Khe Sanh was generously supported by artillery and air. More than 150,000 artillery and mortar shells were fired in defense of the Marine base and during Operation NIAGARA (the supporting the battle with both tactical air and B-52s), and a variety of aircraft dropped some 100,000 tons of bombs during round-the-clock attacks in all sorts of weather. The B-52s would perform 2,548 sorties and drop 53,162 tons of bombs. In addition, U.S. transport aircraft effectively sustained the garrison with more than 12,430 tons of supplies.

Compared to U.S. casualties (199 killed and 1,600 wounded) at Khe Sanh between 20 January and 31 March 1968, hostile forces suffered some 10,000 casualties (dead and wounded). President Lyndon B. Johnson claimed Khe Sanh as a victory. When awarding the Presidential Unit Citation to the 26th Marines, the president paid tribute to the "most overwhelming, intelligent, and effective use of airpower in the history of warfare." He further saluted the "endurance—and the artillery—of the Marines at Khe Sanh." But perhaps General William C. Westmoreland's assessment is much more apropos: He concluded that the "key to our success at Khe Sanh was firepower, principally aerial firepower." As he would tell the Third Air Division personnel at Andersen Air Force Base on 13 June 1968, "The thing that broke their backs was basically the B-52s."

George M. Watson Jr.

References

Bonds, Ray, ed. *The Vietnam War: The Illustrated History of the Conflict in Southeast Asia.* London: Salamander, 1979.

Nalty, Bernard C. *Air Power and the Fight for Khe Sanh.* Washington, DC: Office of Air Force History, 1986.

Shulimson, Jack. *U.S. Marines in Vietnam: The Defining Year, 1968.* Washington, DC: Headquarters U.S. Marine Corps, History and Museums Division, 1997.

Khomyakova, Valeriya (1914–1942)

Russian female military aviator in World War II. Valeriya Khomyakova was one of the women who volunteered to fly in the Soviet Women's Air Regiments in 1941 and was assigned to the 586th Fighter Aviation Regiment, where she

Valeriya Khomyakova was the first woman to shoot down an aircraft at night. Given the marvelous service of Soviet women in aviation, it is amazing that it took the rest of the world (include the postwar Soviet Union) so long to begin using women pilots. (Jean Cottam)

was appointed deputy squadron commander. On the night of 25 September 1942, she intercepted and shot down a German bomber over Stalingrad. This was the first victory achieved by a woman pilot at night (Klavdiya Nechaeva and Lidya Litvyak both had scored day victories). She was killed in a flying accident on the night of 5–6 October 1942.

George M. Mellinger

References

Cottam, Kazimiera J. *Women in Air War: The Eastern Front of World War II.* Nepean, Canada: New Military, 1997.
Noggle, Anne. *A Dance with Death: Soviet Airwomen in World War II.* College Station: Texas A&M University Press, 1994.

Khryukin, Timofei T. (1910–1953)

Soviet air force general in World War II. Timofei Timofeevich Khryukin was born on 21 June 1910 in Eisk, Russia. He joined the army in 1932 and completed flight school the next year. In 1937 and 1938, he flew the Tupolev SB as a volunteer in Spain and then China. He received the Hero of the Soviet Union award on 22 February 1939. At the start of the German invasion in World war II, he commanded the air units of the Twelfth Army in the Kiev Military District. In June 1942, he became the first commander of the Eighth Air Army, fighting on the Southwest Front and later the Stalingrad Front, where he proved an unusually effective commander. In May 1944, he was promoted to colonel general. From June 1944, he was commander of the First Air Army on the Belorussian Front. On 19 April 1945, he received a second Hero award. After the war he served as deputy commander in chief of the air forces. He died on 19 July 1953.

George M. Mellinger

See also

Soviet Volunteer Pilots; Stalingrad, Battle of

References

Fetzer, Leland, trans., and Ray Wagner, ed. *The Soviet Air Force in World War II: The Official History.* Garden City, NY: Doubleday, 1973.

Kindelberger, James H. "Dutch" (1895–1962)

U.S. aircraft designer and airpower advocate; general manager and chief executive officer of North American Aviation who championed the initial design and development of what became the P-51 Mustang fighter of World War II.

Born on 8 May 1895 in Wheeling, West Virginia, Kindelberger attended the Carnegie Institute of Technology but left to become an Army pilot upon U.S. entry into World War I. He became an instructor pilot based at Park Field in Memphis, Tennessee. Following the war, Kindelberger joined the Martin Aircraft Company as chief draftsman and assistant chief engineer. In 1925, he joined Douglas Aircraft in California as chief engineer, aiding in the development of the DC-1 and DC-2.

In 1934, Kindelberger became president and general manager of General Aviation, later renamed North American Aviation, Inc. At first the company concentrated on modification work to other manufacturers' products, but it offered its first original design, the NA-16 trainer, to the government and won that contract. Following that success, the company produced a string of aviation classics.

North American's most famous design, however, was the P-51 Mustang fighter. Originally offered to the British by Kindelberger as an alternative to the Curtiss P-40, the P-51 was designed and produced in less than 120 days. When eventually paired with the Rolls-Royce Merlin engine, the P-51 became one of the best fighters of World War II.

James Kindelberger served as chief executive officer of North American until 1960. During that time, the company transformed from an aircraft manufacturer to a prime contractor for the space program. He remained chairman of the board until his death on 27 July 1962.

Braxton Eisel

References

Boeing Corporation, Historical Services. *Biographies—James Howard "Dutch" Kindelberger.* Seattle: Boeing, 2000.
Delve, Ken. *The Mustang Story.* London. Arms and Armour. 1999.

King, Ernest Joseph (1878–1956)

U.S. Chief of Naval Operations during World War II. Born in Lorain, Ohio, on 23 November 1878, King attended the U.S. Naval Academy, saw service as a midshipman aboard the USS *San Francisco* during the Spanish-American War, and graduated with his commission in 1901. Up through World War I, he served on cruisers and battleships, commanded the destroyers *Terry* and *Cassin,* and was Chief of Staff to the Atlantic Fleet's commander.

In 1922, King underwent submarine training. He subsequently commanded Submarine Division 3 and the submarine base in New London, Connecticut. In 1926, he made another major career change, becoming a naval aviator at the advanced age of 48. King's aviation career included command of the carrier *Lexington.* He was chief of the Bureau of

Aeronautics and the Patrol Force, U.S. Fleet. He was promoted to rear admiral in 1933.

In February 1941, King was promoted to full admiral and assigned as commander in chief, Atlantic Fleet. In that position he oversaw initial convoy and antisubmarine efforts prior to the declaration of war with Germany. Following actual war in December 1941, King was named commander of the entire U.S. Fleet, as well as Chief of Naval Operations. He served in these roles throughout the war, the only person to hold both posts simultaneously.

King's position on both the U.S. Joint Chiefs and the Allied Combined Chiefs of Staff placed him at the critical juncture of U.S.-Allied policy and strategy. Despite the approved Allied strategy (Germany First), King remained a powerful advocate for increased naval emphasis on the war against Japan. He was equally determined to limit the impact of Allied desires on U.S. strategy, which made him very unpopular with his British counterparts. Nevertheless, King heavily contributed to virtually all of the major Allied conferences. If nothing else, King's repeated insistence that the U.S. Navy stay on the offensive against Japan made Admiral Chester Nimitz's successful operations possible. Moreover, King provided his subordinate in the Pacific with superb strategic guidance and, when possible, also diverted invaluable combat and amphibious forces in that direction.

King's unwillingness to cooperate with the British in the Battle of the Atlantic was perhaps his only serious strategic misstep. The Navy's tenfold growth during this period, however, while simultaneously winning a two-ocean war, was ample evidence of King's overall brilliance as a strategist and logistician. King was promoted to five-star rank in late 1944. Nimitz, his former subordinate, replaced him as Chief of Naval Operations in December 1945. King subsequently served as a naval adviser to the president and the secretary of the Navy until his death in Portsmouth, New Hampshire, on 25 June 1956.

Michael S. Casey

See also

Atlantic, Battle of the; Leahy, William D.; Nimitz, Chester William

References

Buell, Thomas B. *Master of Sea Power: A Biography of Fleet Admiral Ernest J. King.* Annapolis, MD: Naval Institute Press, 1995.

Hall, George M. *The Fifth Star.* New York: Praeger, 1994.

Kites

The use of kites can be traced back to imperial China. One account claims that a Chinese general, Han Xin, flew a kite over enemy position round 200 B.C.E. to measure the distance between his position and the enemy's walls. He then had a tunnel dug slightly longer than the length of rope used, reaching under the walls to enter the city.

Elsewhere in Asia, kites were used in religious rituals in Korea and among the Maori. The appearance of the kite in Europe is subject to conjecture. Some records suggest that the Roman armies of Trajan used a windsock contraption that hissed as it burned, instilling fear in enemy troops.

The modern kite seems to have been inspired from the Chinese design. The kite wasn't used in Europe until the sixteenth century, and then only for entertainment. By the nineteenth century, in parallel to ballooning experiments and recreational kites (a kite club existed in Philadelphia in the 1830s), several pioneers took to developing a science of kite-flying. Sir George Cayley was the first to study the aerodynamics of kites when he designed glider models. Alexander Graham Bell investigated the possibility of a radial-shaped kite.

The most successful pioneers were Lawrence Hargrave, who in 1894 succeeded in rising while suspended to a "kite train" in 1896 and 1898; and Louis Baden-Powell, who completed a similar experiment, reportedly rising above 200 feet. In addition, Captain William Cody used the principle of large kites to carry an entire camera operated by a timing device.

Several experiments were carried out to test the feasibility of using manned observation kites for military purposes. The U.S. Navy sent several officers to Hempstead, Long Island, to learn of the advantages of manned kites from Samuel F. Perkins.

In France the military saw little use for kiting, preferring instead to focus on the potential of ballooning. Soon however, reports that the Cody type could carry a camera prompted similar experiments on the continent. Indeed, aerial photography from a balloon was extremely expensive and time-consuming, so attaching a timing device to a camera was attractive.

In 1910, the French war ministry went one step farther and asked Captain Jacques Saconney to design a kite train capable of lifting an observer up to 1,800 feet. Despite successful tests, the war interrupted these experiments in favor of tethered balloons and blimps, considered more stable.

During World War II, kites were used as aerial targets by U.S. forces, the idea arising from Paul Garber, who would become famous as a curator at the Smithsonian Institution.

Guillaume de Syon

References

Baden-Powell, B.F.L. "Man-Lifting War Kites." *Aeronautics* 4, 39 (May 1911): 53–54.

Hart, Clive. *The Prehistory of Flight.* Berkeley: University of California Press, 1985.

Kittinger, Joseph W., Jr. (1928–)

One of the first Americans to experience the harsh environment of space; in 1957 he piloted a balloon to 70,000 feet in the USAF's Project Manhigh. His objective was to test life-support equipment for use in high-altitude programs. Kittinger had been working with Dr. John Paul Stapp when selected to test-pilot the Manhigh balloon.

Manhigh proved that, given proper protection, man could survive in space. Kittinger's second balloon project was Excelsior. The purpose was to test the new Beaupre parachute for high-altitude uses such as the U-2 spyplane.

The Beaupre incorporated a small stabilization chute that would open 16 seconds after ejection. This would prevent a flat spin and allow Kittinger to return safely to earth. Two test jumps were made from above 70,000 feet. Excelsior III took Kittinger to 102,800 feet, at which point he exited the gondola from "the highest step in the world." The chute worked, and Kittinger fell safely to earth, having fallen at speeds in excess of 700 mph, becoming the only human being to break the sound barrier without a vehicle.

Kittinger has gone on to many other aviation accomplishments. During 11 months as a North Vietnamese POW after being shot down, he formulated plans for what in 1984 became the first solo transatlantic balloon crossing. Still very active in the aviation community, Kittinger was inducted into National Aviation Hall of Fame in 1997.

Erich Streckfuss

References

Ryan, Craig. *The Pre-Astronauts.* Annapolis, MD: Naval Institute Press, 1995.

Koldunov, Aleksandr (1923–1992)

Soviet World War II fighter ace and later commander of the PVO (Antiaircraft Defense Forces). Aleksandr Ivanovich Koldunov was born on 20 September 1923 in Moshchinovo, Russia. He completed flight school and joined the 866 IAP (Fighter Air Regiment) flying Yak fighters on the Southwestern Front in May 1943. During the war he flew over Ukraine, the Balkans, and finally Hungary. He was recognized as a Hero of the Soviet Union on 2 August 1944. By the end of the war Captain Koldunov flew 412 sorties and fought 96 air combats, scoring 46 individual victories and one group victory. He was awarded a second Hero honor on 23 February 1948. On 7 November 1944, he was involved in an incident when USAF P-38s of the 82d Fighter Group mistakenly attacked a Soviet armored column northwest of Belgrade and fought an air combat with the protecting Yaks. During this combat Koldunov shot down three P-38s before ending the combat.

After the war Koldunov was assigned to the PVO and held a number of sensitive posts. In 1978, he was promoted to marshal of aviation and appointed commander of the PVO and a deputy minister of defense. Koldunov's term was marked by a number of incidents, including the destruction of Korean Air Lines Flight 007 over the Sea of Japan on 1 September 1983 with the loss of 269 lives. The final blow to the marshal came on 28 May 1987, when Mathias Rust flew his Cessna from Helsinki at low level to land in Red Square. Koldunov resigned two days later. He died on 7 June 1992.

George M. Mellinger

References

Bodrikhin, Nikolai. *Sovetskie Asy, ocherki o Sovetskikh letchikakh* (Soviet Aces: Sketches of Soviet Pilots). Moscow: TAMP, 1998.

Seidl, Hans D. *Stalin's Eagles: An Illustrated Study of the Soviet Aces of World War II and Korea.* Atglen, PA: Schiffer, 1998.

Koller, Karl (1898–1951)

The Luftwaffe's last Chief of Staff. Koller volunteered for service in the Bavarian army at the start of World War I and served as a pilot on the Western Front after learning to fly. Koller joined the Bavarian state police in 1920 and did not reenter the armed forces until 1936, when he joined the Luftwaffe as a major. His entire Luftwaffe career was spent as a staff officer. He was promoted from Luftwaffe director of operations to Chief of Staff when Werner Kreipe was sacked by Hitler in November 1944.

Like his predecessor, Koller was disgusted with his superior, Hermann Goering, but he managed to keep his now meaningless post until war's end. His last rank was lieutenant general; his last official duty was to fly to Berchtesgaden to notify Goering of Hitler's decision to die in Berlin. Goering's carefully worded message to Hitler—inquiring whether this meant that Goering was to take over the government—was apparently suggested by Koller but resulted in Goering's house arrest and the loss of all his titles.

Donald Caldwell

See also

German Air Force (Luftwaffe)

References

Muller, R. *The German Air War in Russia.* Baltimore: Nautical and Aviation, 1992.

Smith, J., ed. *The Koller War Diary.* Sturbridge, MA: Monogram Aviation, 1990.

Korean War

The Korean War began on 25 June 1950 and lasted until 1953. The North Korean People's Army, equipped with Soviet weapons, crossed the 38th Parallel to take over South Korea. The U.S. military presence in the Far East was undermanned, and its equipment was outdated with the exception of the Air Force, which had a mixture of World War II piston-engine aircraft and a reasonable number of Lockheed F-80 jet fighters. The North Koreans and their Soviet advisers were under the impression that President Harry Truman and the United States did not consider South Korea to be within the U.S. sphere of influence.

The United States used airpower to slow down, then stop, the invaders. On 26 and 27 June, the top priority was to evacuate U.S. citizens and t-p ranking South Korean officials out of Seoul. A Norwegian freighter happened to be in Inchon Harbor, getting most of the people out on the first day. The remainder of personnel were flown out by C-54 transports on 27 June. On that day the North Korean air force made an aggressive move to interrupt the air traffic in and out of Kimpo Air Base (Seoul).

The only air cover available was from several flights of F-80s and a flight of North American F-82 Twin Mustangs, one of which scored the first victory of the Korean air war. U.S. jet aircraft lacked the necessary range for combat over Korea. After a flight from Japan, they had only a few minutes over the target area. As a stopgap, the tiptanks were increased in size to give the F-80s additional flying time.

The momentum of the North Korean forces allowed them to compress the UN forces into a narrow perimeter around Pusan. The perimeter defenders were sustained by aircraft of the Far East Air Force, which provided close air support and interdiction of supplies. On 15 September, General Douglas MacArthur used the newly arrived 1st Marine Division to make a daring amphibious landing at Inchon. This caught the North Korean military completely off-guard, and a lightning-fast thrust to the east by the Marines cut off enemy supply lines. The result was a mass retreat by the North Koreans and breakout from the Pusan perimeter.

Three weeks after the Inchon landing, the U.S. Eighth Army was crossing the 38th Parallel with orders to keep going. During late September, the B-29 Superfortresses began the systematic destruction of North Korea's industrial assets. On 19 October, ground forces entered the North Korean capital of Pyongyang. By this time, the UN air armada was destroying everything that moved, with only a very limited amount of equipment escaping into Manchuria.

The Korean War took a different course when, after many warnings that it would intervene, the Chinese People's Army crossed the frozen Yalu River in vast numbers. On 3 November, General Walton H. Walker ordered his Eighth Army to begin withdrawing to the south. The Soviet-built swept-wing MiG-15 appeared in significant numbers during November, and for the first time communist forces threatened to gain air superiority. The 4th Fighter Wing was rushed in, with their new North American F-86 Sabres, to counter this threat. This began the long series of F-86–versus–MiG-15 battles in the notorious MiG Alley near the Yalu River.

By Christmas Day 1950, more than 500,000 Chinese troops had pushed UN forces out of North Korea, crossing the 38th Parallel. On 14 January 1951, the Chinese were halted right after they captured Wonju, and this became the farthest point into South Korea that they would achieve. U.S. aircraft were working around the clock to halt the flow of supplies out of Manchuria, and by early February the results were beginning to show as some areas along the front lines began to sag and the Chinese began to fall back.

By late spring 1951, the lines had stabilized and a battle of position began that would last another 27 months. By now the opposing ground forces were well dug in, and neither side could gain much ground and hold it. The Chinese held the edge in manpower, and the UN forces held the edge in firepower. This situation could change only if the enemy were able to accumulate enough supplies to initiate a substantial offensive. With this in mind, UN airpower continued to destroy anything that moved southward. The spectacular aerial duels between the F-86 and MiG-15 continued, for it was essential for UN forces to maintain air superiority, allowing their bombers and fighter-bombers to operate almost with impunity. The Chinese knew they had no chance to gain ground if they couldn't move enough supplies to sustain a major offensive, so all movement had to be carried out at night. This was countered by USAF Douglas B-26 and Marine night-fighter aircraft interdicting trains and truck convoys.

Although airpower could not win the Korean War for the United Nations, it did neutralize the communist forces and force the communist leadership to enter an armistice. On 10 July 1951, truce negotiations began at Kaesong. They were moved over to Panmunjom on 12 November 1951, where they would remain until the war ended. For the first few months there were high hopes that the war would end soon, but these meetings would continue on and off for the next two years, with the Korean War officially ending on 27 July 1953.

Warren E. Thompson

References

Futrell, Robert F. *The United States Air Force in Korea, 1950–1953.* Rev. ed. Washington, DC: Office of Air Force History, 1983.

Stewart, James T. *Air Power: The Decisive Force in Korea.* Princeton, NJ: D. Van Nostrand, 1957.

U.S. Marine Corps HQ. *U.S. Marines in Korea, 1950–1953.* Vols. 1, 3–5. Washington, DC: Historical Branch USMC, 1962.

After the introduction of the MiG-15 fighters by the Soviets, the North American F-86 Sabres were brought in to combat them, spawning a long series of furious battles. (Smithsonian Institution)

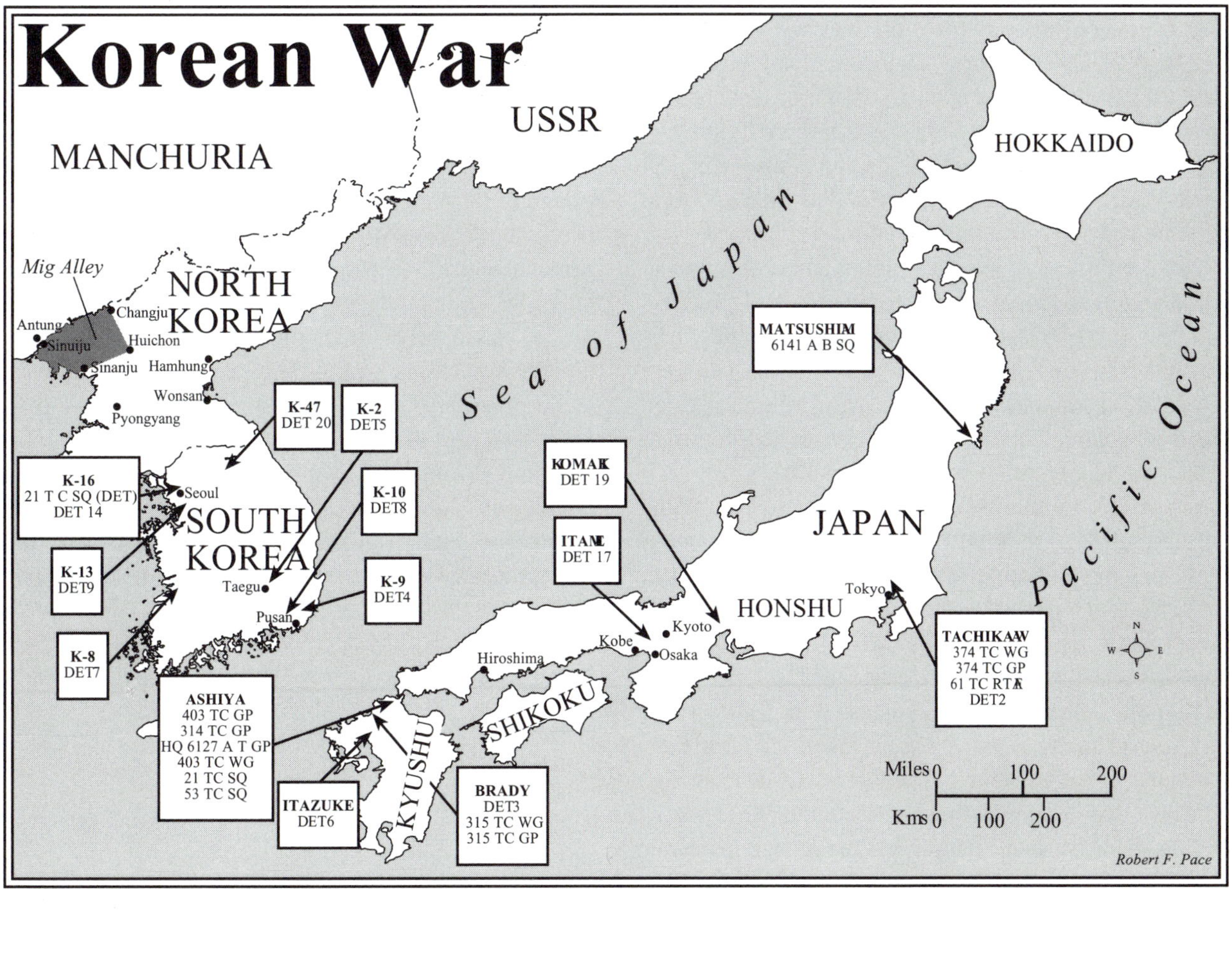

Korean War

USSR
MANCHURIA
HOKKAIDO
Sea of Japan
Pacific Ocean
Mig Alley
NORTH KOREA
Antung
Sinuiju
Changju
Huichon
Sinanju
Hamhung
Wonsan
Pyongyang
K-47 DET 20
K-2 DET5
K-16 21 T C SQ (DET) DET 14
Seoul
SOUTH KOREA
K-10 DET8
K-13 DET9
Taegu
K-9 DET4
Pusan
K-8 DET7
MATSUSHIM 6141 A B SQ
KOMAKI DET 19
ITAMI DET 17
JAPAN
HONSHU
Tokyo
Kyoto
Kobe
Osaka
Hiroshima
TACHIKAWA 374 TC WG 374 TC GP 61 TC RTK DET2
ASHIYA 403 TC GP 314 TC GP HQ 6127 A T GP 403 TC WG 21 TC SQ 53 TC SQ
SHIKOKU
KYUSHU
ITAZUKE DET6
BRADY DET3 315 TC WG 315 TC GP
Miles 0 100 200
Kms 0 100 200
N W E S
Robert F. Pace

Korolyov, Sergei (1907–1966)

Ukrainian-born aeronautical designer. Sergei Korolyov became interested in aeronautics when he witnessed a flight demonstration over Kiev in 1913. He studied in vocational school, graduating in 1924, and enrolled at the Kiev Polytechnic Institute to study aeronautics before transferring to Moscow Higher Technical School two years later.

By 1929, Korolyov had distinguished himself in glider design, and Andrei Tupolev served as his thesis adviser. Over the following two years he developed an interest in space travel and worked with Friedrickh Tsander, a pioneer of rocket-motor design.

In 1933, he became deputy engineer to the Reaction Propulsion Institute; although it included many space enthusiasts among its members, it was geared toward devising military applications for rockets. In 1934, Korolyov conceived the design of a winged rocket and began studying the problem of automatic stabilization. However, in 1938, during the Stalinist purges, Korolyov was arrested and sentenced to 10 years on trumped-up charges. Incarcerated in Siberia, he was moved around and continued to work in rocket design until his release in 1944. A year later, commissioned a colonel in the Red Army, he flew to Germany to evaluate the V-2 rocket.

Over the following five years, Korolyov extrapolated German technology and improved on the knowledge gained from a small team of German engineers. After indigenously producing the R-1, a copy of the V-2, Korolyov then focused on ballistic missile design. His R-2 model was a 20-ton missile that could fly over 300 miles. The R-3 design failed, but the R-5 (identified in NATO publications as the SS-3 "Shyster") reached well over 700 miles.

Korolyov, who now headed an important design bureau (OKB-1), also had to oversee an enormous staff of engineers and deal with political imperatives at the same time. This meant that he often needed to check for problems in designs himself, as many collaborators, fascinated with their chief, dared not point out shortcomings in tests. He was ordered to focus on a long-range intercontinental ballistic missile. Korolyov and his team came up with what would become the one-and-a-half stage ICBM R-7 Semyorka. Propelling a test warhead some 4,000 miles in August 1957, it became known as the SS-6 Sapwood and would be used in modified form to propel Soviet space vehicles into orbit. This included Yuri Gagarin's Vostok mission, as well as Voskhod.

Korolyov's great passion since he began designing space vehicles had always been to reach the moon and Mars. Consequently, he began planning the three-stage R-7 but also oversaw other designs intended to send unmanned spacecraft to Venus. By then, Korolyov was the dean of spacecraft design in the Soviet Union; as such, he had to face challenges to his supremacy based on politics, finances, competing programs, and jealousy. One such case was the dual development of a moon rocket for the transport of two or three cosmonauts.

Although he oversaw the initial design, Korolyov's untimely death from cancer prevented him from overseeing testing of the behemoth N-1 rocket. It is unclear whether his presence would have helped prevent the failure of the project, but it is certain that his absence contributed to the Soviet lunar program's demise. Korolyov was a household name in Soviet military and aerospace circles, but his identity remained classified for years. No pictures of him alone appeared until his death. The Nobel Committee, intent on honoring the scientist who had made Gagarin's flight possible, inquired in 1963 about his name and status, only to be told that the inventor of the booster was the Soviet people.

Guillaume de Syon

See also

Gagarin, Yuri; KOSMOS; Sputnik; Voskhod; Vostok

References

Harford, James. *Korolev.* New York: Wiley, 1997.

McDougall, Walter. *The Heavens and the Earth: A Political History of the U.S. Space Program.* Baltimore: Johns Hopkins University Press, 1997 [1985].

Korten, Guenther (1898–1944)

Luftwaffe Chief of Staff. Korten served as an engineering officer in World War I. He remained in the service, trained as a pilot, and was an early transferee to the Luftwaffe, where he served in a variety of positions and rose rapidly through the ranks. He left Berlin to take command of Luftflotte 1 (First Air Force) and was named to succeed Hans Jeschonnek after the latter's suicide in August 1943.

He proved to have a more forceful personality than Jeschonnek and took strong positions on Luftwaffe operations and equipment. This aroused the wrath of Hermann Goering, and Korten was apparently to be forced to resign his position, but his career was cut short by the 20 July 1944 attempt to assassinate Hitler by means of a briefcase bomb. The blast fatally injured Korten, who died two days after his promotion to full general.

Donald Caldwell

See also

German Air Force (Luftwaffe)

References

Corum, J. *The Luftwaffe: Creating the Operational Air War, 1918–1940.* Lawrence: University Press of Kansas, 1997.

Muller, R. *The German Air War in Russia.* Baltimore: Nautical and Aviation, 1992.

References

Harvey, Brian. *Race into Space: The Soviet Space Programme.* Chichester, UK: Ellis Horwood, 1988.
Peebles, Curtiss. *Guardians: Strategic Reconnaissance Satellites.* Novato, CA: Presidio Press, 1987.

KOSMOS

Kosmos is the Russian word for "space" and has been used to refer to any Soviet or Russian spacecraft whose purpose (scientific, military, or otherwise) does not fit into the parameters of established programs, such as Vostok, Voskhod, or Soyuz. In addition, one type of satellite launcher constructed in Ukraine and based on the R4 IRBM launcher also bore the Kosmos name. Consequently, for years the term caused confusion in Western circles.

There have been well over 2,000 unmanned KOSMOS missions, ranging widely in their goals. The first Soviet reconnaissance satellite successfully launched was *Kosmos 4* in 1962. Kosmos names were also assigned to trial missions and to hardware prototypes, such as *Kosmos 47 and 57,* which tested empty Voskhod capsules. *Kosmos 110* (22 February–16 March 1966), a biosatellite mission that carried two dogs, may have served as a test for both later biomissions and for Voskhod 3, which never flew. *Kosmos 434,* launched in August 1971, remained aloft for 10 years and, before it fell back to earth, was announced to have been a test for a Soviet lunar module.

Paralleling its manned space program, the Soviet Union also developed a space-based electronic intelligence network, launching the first such machine, *Kosmos 103,* in December 1965. Other functions carried out included early warning, with the first successful operational system going up as *Kosmos 903, 917,* and *931* in 1977.

The Soviet Union began using nuclear-powered satellites in the 1970s, and the general public became aware of the matter when an ocean-surveillance satellite, *Kosmos 954,* fell in Canada and dispersed its radioactive cargo.

Besides prototype spacecraft and test missions, the Kosmos designation has also been applied to Soviet shuttle development flights. Thus, on 3 June 1982 and on 15 March 1983, *Kosmos 1374* and *1443* were launched and recovered. In both cases, an Australian plane was able to photograph the recovered vehicle, which turned out to be a spaceplane, reportedly nicknamed "Kosmolyot."

The Kosmos designation remains in use, but with the fall of the Soviet Union and drastically reduced funding for Russian space activities, the term tends to apply mostly to military satellites.

Guillaume de Syon

Kozakov, Aleksandr (1889–1919)

Leading Russian fighter ace of World War I. Aleksandr Aleksandrovich Kozakov was born on 15 January 1889 near Kherson, Russia, to a family of minor nobility. Kozakov was educated in military schools and commissioned a *kornet* (junior lieutenant) in a cavalry regiment. In early 1914, he was admitted to the flying school at Kacha. Graduating in October 1914, he was promoted to *poruchik* (lieutenant) and sent to the IV Corps Aviation Detachment, where he flew the Morane G two-seat monoplane. Since his aircraft could not carry a machine gun, in March 1915 he experimented with using a grappling hook and cable to attack enemy aircraft. In his first combat encounter the device failed, but Kozakov brought the enemy down by ramming its upper wing with his landing gear, the second ramming attack in history. He was able to land his own damaged Morane.

In September 1915, he was promoted to *stabsrotmistr* (captain) and transferred to the IXX Corp Aviation Detachment, where he was able to fly a Nieuport 10 armed with an obliquely mounted Maxim machine gun. Though this device was difficult to aim, he was finally able to shoot down an enemy aircraft on 17 June 1916, followed by several more successes. At the end of August, Kozahov commanded the 1st Battle Aviation Group, which was formed from several Russian flying detachments that were to be Russia's first specialized fighter units. The units received the Nieuport 11 and Nieuport 17 Scouts to fly. On 2 December 1916, Kozakov scored his fifth air victory, becoming an ace. Kozakov scored his seventeenth confirmed (plus three more unconfirmed) air victory on 26 November 1917.

The Bolshevik Revolution caused Kozakov to leave the military in early 1918. Strongly conservative in sentiment, when the civil war broke out he resisted the repeated attempts of the Bolsheviks to pressure him into joining the Red Army and instead rallied to the anticommunist Whites, joining the British intervention forces at Murmansk in June 1918. The British promoted him to major and appointed him commander of the Slavo-British air squadron. During July he flew numerous air support sorties in the Sopwith Snipe against the Red forces and was awarded the British Distinguished Flying Cross, in addition to the numerous czarist medals he had been awarded. However, the anticommunist movement in northern Russia was a lost cause. On 1 August 1919, just after taking off from his airfield, Kozakov stalled and crashed in what witnesses agreed appeared to be a suicide.

George M. Mellinger

See also
Imperial Russian Air Service; Taran

References
Durkota, Alan, Thomas Darcey, and Viktor Kulikov. *The Imperial Russian Air Service: Famous Pilots and Aircraft of World War I.* Mountain View, CA: Flying Machines Press, 1995, pp. 58–71.

Kozhedub, Ivan (1920–1991)

Soviet fighter pilot and top-scoring Allied ace of World War II. Ivan Nikitovich Kozhedub was born in the Sumy region, Ukraine, on 8 June 1920. After learning to fly in an aeroclub, he joined the army in 1940 and completed military flight school in February 1941. Kozhedub was fortunate to be retained as an instructor and missed the slaughter of the first two years of war, entering combat only in March 1943 with the 240 IAP (Fighter Air Regiment), flying the La-5. Thus, for his entire career Kozhedub was able to fly aircraft the equal of his enemies. He received his first Hero of the Soviet Union (HSU) honor for 26 victories on 4 February 1944 and his second HSU on 19 August 1944. By the end of the war, Kozhedub had flown 330 sorties and scored 62 official individual victories. He claimed that he actually shot down more than 100 enemy aircraft, but many were unconfirmed because they were destroyed deep in enemy territory; he never bothered to count his group kills. Among his victories was an Me 262, shot down in February 1945, one of six jets claimed by Soviet pilots. He was awarded his third HSU on 18 August 1945, an award equaled only Marshal Georgy Zhukov and Aleksandr Pokryshkin. There were two more unofficial victories, which Kozhedub regretted. In April 1945 over Berlin, he was attacked by four unfamiliar fighters and shot down two before noticing the white stars. One surviving Mustang pilot reported that he had been shot down by a red-nosed Fw 190, which is how he misidentified Kozhedub. From March 1951 to February 1952, Kozhedub commanded the 324 IAP in combat over North Korea, although he did not fly combat missions on Stalin's personal order. Kozhedub continued flying fighters until 1970. In 1978, he retired from active duty with the rank of marshal. He died on 8 August 1991.

George M. Mellinger

See also
Fighter Air Corps, 64th; Kursk, Battle of

References
Bodrikhin, Nikolai. *Sovetskie Asy, ocherki o Sovetskikh letchikakh* (Soviet Aces: Sketches of Soviet Pilots). Moscow: TAMP, 1998.
Seidl, Hans D. *Stalin's Eagles: An Illustrated Study of the Soviet Aces of World War II and Korea.* Atglen, PA: Schiffer, 1998.

Kreipe, Werner (1905–1967)

Luftwaffe Chief of Staff with the shortest term in the office. Kreipe enlisted in an artillery regiment after World War I and joined the Nazi Party in time to take part in the 1923 Muenchen Beer Hall Putsch. He was commissioned in the Reichswehr (the interwar army), trained as a pilot, and was soon accepted into the Luftwaffe, where he quickly rose in rank while serving in a variety of staff and command positions.

He became Luftwaffe Chief of Staff after the death of Guenther Korten but argued vocally with Hitler over the employment of the Me 262 and was relieved after only four months in the position. Kreipe ended the war as a lieutenant general in command of the Air War Academy. Postwar, he became a civil servant in the West German government.

Donald Caldwell

See also
German Air Force (Luftwaffe)

References
Cooper, M. *The German Air Force, 1933–1945: An Anatomy of Failure.* London: Jane's Information Group, 1981.
Corum, J. *The Luftwaffe: Creating the Operational Air War, 1918–1940.* Lawrence: University Press of Kansas, 1997.

Kuban Air Battles

Major air campaign that marked the shift from German to Soviet air superiority on the Eastern Front during World War II. During April and May 1943, as the Germans struggled for their last North Caucasus foothold, Luftflotte 4 (Fourth Air Force) clashed with the Soviet 4 and 5 Air Armies, the Black Sea Fleet Aviation, and Long Range Aviation. Air activity was intense, often seeing as many as 100 air combats a day.

German forces began with about 900 aircraft, including the latest models of the Bf 109G and the Hs 129, and featured some of their top units, including Jagdgeschwader 52 with Erich Hartmann. The Soviets began with about 600 aircraft, swelling to 1,150 in May. The Soviets also committed their newest aircraft, including the first use in the south of the Douglas A-20, as well as the Bell P-39D, flown by Aleksandr Pokryshkin's air division.

The Soviets showed a new aggressiveness in flying offensive fighter sweeps, and they introduced new tactics, including German-style four-plane formations and Pokryshkin's Kuban Ladder, a stacked formation. Also playing a distinguished role was the Soviet women's night-bomber regiment. The campaign ended suddenly on 7 June, at which point the Soviets had claimed 1,100 German aircraft destroyed; the Germans claimed 2,280 victories, but the tide of the air war had turned against them.

George M. Mellinger

See also
Hartmann, Erich; Night Witches; Pokryshkin, Aleksandr

References

Hardesty, Von. *Red Phoenix: The Rise of Soviet Air Power, 1941–1945.* Washington, DC: Smithsonian Institution Press, 1982.

Kursk, Battle of (1943)

Celebrated tank battle of World War II during which air operations played an important role. Both sides employed air divisions in support of the operation. As for the German Luftwaffe, 1st Division, consisting of two *luftflottes* (air forces) with a total of 2,050 aircraft, was made available. Because Operation CITADEL called for a two-prong attack against the Russian stronghold at Kursk, Army Group Center was supported by Luftflotte 6 commanded by General Ritter von Greim; Army Group South was supported by General Otto Desslach's Luftflotte 4.

On the Russian side, three air armies were made available to defend the Russian salient. The Sixteenth Air Army under Marshal S. I. Rudenko supported the Central Front, the Steppe Front was supported by Fifth Air Army under Colonel General Goryunov, and the Voronezh Front was supported by Air Marshal S. A. Krasovski's Second Air Army.

Air operations began the first day when long-range radar alerted the Germans to a preemptive attack by the Second Air Army on airfields around Kharkov. The Germans, preparing for preemptive strike of their own, were able to get all serviceable aircraft airborne. The Russian force of 450 airplanes, expecting to catch the Germans by surprise, took heavy losses when it ran into waiting German fighters, giving the Germans air superiority in that sector.

The Battle of Kursk saw Germans using aircraft to make up for losses suffered at Stalingrad and in Africa. Specialized Junkers Ju 87G Stukas and Henschel Hs 129Bs were used as flying artillery to compensate for weak ground artillery. Their formations were responsible for killing hundreds of Russian tanks. On the Russian side, Ilyushin Il-2M3 Shturmoviks armed with 37mm cannons were used with devastating effect against German armor.

In addition to the flying antitank weapons, the Germans armed their Focke-Wulf Fw 190As with SD-1 and SD-2 antipersonnel containers that rained down fragmentation bomblets on infantry and artillery positions. The Russians concentrated on antitank operations and getting as many aircraft as possible into the fighting. In the end, quantity overshadowed quality. The Luftwaffe, unlike the Russians, did not have a steady supply of replacements for men and materiel. In order to bring the 1st Division to its preinvasion strength, all other air units on the Eastern Front had to be stripped of every available aircraft.

By 9 July, with the German attack faltering on the northern prong of the offensive, 50 percent of Luftflotte 6's forces were shifted southward to support a possible breakthrough. In the end, Operation CITADEL fell short of its goals, and the offensive was suspended with the U.S. invasion of Italy. The combat initiative passed into Soviet hands and was never relinquished.

Brian B. Carpenter

See also
Ilyushin Il-2 Shturmovik; Stalingrad, Battle of

References

Cross, Robin. *Citadel: The Battle of Kursk.* New York: Sarpedon, 1993.
Dunn, Walter S. *Kursk: Hitler's Gamble, 1943.* Westport, CT: Praeger, 1997.

Kutakhov, Pavel (1914–1984)

Soviet World War II fighter ace, later commander of the Red Air Force. Pavel Stepanovich Kutakhov was born on 16 August 1914 in Malokirsanovka, Russia. He completed flight school in 1938 and flew during the Russo-Finnish war in 1939–1940. He began World War II as a captain assigned to the 145 IAP (Fighter Air Regiment), later designated the 19 GIAP (Guards Fighter Air Regiment), based near Murmansk, where he spent the entire war. In May 1944, he was promoted to colonel and appointed regiment commander. For most of the war he flew the U.S. P-39 Airacobra, in which he scored all but one of his victories. By the end of the war he flew 367 sorties and fought 79 air battles, scoring 13 personal and 28 shared kills.

After the war he was one of the first Soviet officers to train in jets and later held a series of important assignments. In March 1969 he became commander in chief of Soviet air forces and deputy minister of defense. In 1972, he was promoted to chief marshal of aviation. During his tenure as commander, Kutakhov did much to modernize the Red Air Force, paying particular attention to lessons of the Vietnam War and the defeats of the Soviets' Arab allies by the Israelis. He reequipped the Red Air Force with modern aircraft, introduced new weapons systems such as laser-targeting, and sponsored improved tactics and operating procedures. It was also on his watch that the Soviets greatly expanded their MiG diplomacy, spreading modern Soviet aircraft across the world in unprecedented numbers. In 1984, he received his second honor as Hero of the Soviet Union on his birthday. He died in service on 3 December 1984.

George M. Mellinger

References

Bodrikhin, Nikolai. *Sovetskie Asy, ocherki o Sovetskikh letchikakh* (Soviet Aces: Sketches of Soviet Pilots). Moscow: TAMP, 1998.

Seidl, Hans D. *Stalin's Eagles: An Illustrated Study of the Soviet Aces of World War II and Korea.* Atglen, PA: Schiffer, 1998.

L

Lafayette Escadrille/Flying Corps

Anxious not to miss the war in which their country had declared neutrality, many Americans left the United States to enlist in other nations' militaries. During 1915, a small group including Norman Prince and William Thaw, among others, began lobbying the French government for the formation of an all-American squadron. In May 1916 their efforts were realized with the formation at Luxeuil-les-Bains of Escadrille N (Nieuport) 124—the Escadrille Américaine. Original members included Prince, Thaw, Kiffin Rockwell, Elliot Cowdin, Bert Hall, James McConnell, and Victor Chapman. The unit was commanded by a French officer, Capitaine Georges Thénault.

Over several months, the novelty and political problems inherent in a squadron of volunteers from a neutral country flying over the front generated a flood of publicity and diplomatic problems between Washington and Berlin. Campaigning for reelection with an antiwar slogan ("He kept us out of war"), President Woodrow Wilson was not happy with the situation and made a request to the French for a name-change. After brief consideration of the rather colorless Escadrille des Voluntaires, Dr. Edmund Gros—an American doctor practicing in Paris who had been involved in helping form the unit and had since been its Paris representative and unofficial recruiter—suggested the name Escadrille Lafayette.

The Lafayette quickly attracted more than enough recruits to fill one unit, the overflow going to other French escadrilles, giving rise to the term "Lafayette Flying Corps" in reference to any American serving with French aviation. Ironically, the Flying Corps outlived the Escadrille, as the latter ceased to exist on 18 February 1918 when it was transferred to the U.S. Air Service as the 103d Aero Squadron, whereas members of the former continued on with the French right up to the Armistice.

Originally valued by the French as a propaganda tool, the Escadrille and Flying Corps rendered distinguished service, earning unique places in American and French aviation history.

James Streckfuss

See also

Lufbery, Gervais Raoul

References

Gordon, Dennis. *Lafayette Escadrille Pilot Biographies.* Missoula, MT: Doughboy Historical Society, 1991.

Hall, James Norman, and Charles B. Nordhoff. *The Lafayette Flying Corps.* Port Washington, NY: Kennikat Press, 1964.

Mason, Herbert Molloy Jr. *The Lafayette Escadrille.* New York: Konecky and Konecky, 1964.

Parsons, Edmund C. *I Flew with the Lafayette Escadrille.* Indianapolis: E. C. Seale, 1963.

Langley, USS

First U.S. aircraft carrier. The *Langley* began its career as the USS *Jupiter,* a collier. The keel for the *Jupiter* was laid down on 18 October 1911, it was launched on 24 August 1912, and it was completed on 7 April 1913. It was the first Navy vessel to be powered by a turbo-electric system and served during World War I, most notably when *Jupiter* and the collier USS *Neptune* transported the Navy's 1st Aeronautic Detachment to France in June 1917.

Following the end of the war, as a result of the British success with the HMS *Argus,* the U.S. Navy felt a need to investigate the concept of the aircraft carrier. On 15 April 1919, the Navy Board voted to convert *Jupiter* to an experimental aircraft carrier. *Jupiter* was decommissioned at the Norfolk Navy Yard on 24 March 1920, and the conversion began under the designation CV 1. It was commissioned as a carrier on 20 March 1922, renamed after aeronautical pioneer Samuel Pierpont Langley. *Langley* displaced 13,989 tons and measured 542 feet by 65 feet; the wooden flight deck measured 523 feet by 65 feet; lift was 36 feet by 46 feet. It also had two catapults (originally), two seaplane cranes, an interior gantry crane, and stowage for 251,000 gallons of aviation fuel. The original flight-deck arresting gear was similar to that used on the *Argus,* but this was later replaced by a totally athwartship system. The *Langley* began aircraft dock trials in October 1922, and the first takeoff was made on 17 October 1922. The first catapult takeoff occurred on 18 November 1922. In December 1922, the *Langley* began to receive its first air component—Squadron VF-1.

By the mid-1930s, the experimental value of the *Langley* had come to an end, and it was decommissioned on 25 October 1936 at the Mare Island Naval Shipyard for conversion to a seaplane tender. It reemerged on 25 February 1937 with the designation AV 3. Japanese aircraft sank the *Langley* on 27 February 1942 while en route to Tjilatjap, Java, with a cargo of U.S. Army Curtiss P-40 aircraft.

Noel C. Shirley

References

Layman, R. D. *Before the Aircraft Carrier.* Annapolis, MD: Naval Institute Press, 1989.

Shirley, N. C. *U.S. Naval Aviation, 1910–1918.* Atglen, PA: Schiffer, 2000.

Laos

The U.S. involvement in Vietnam came through Laos, a sparsely populated, neutralist kingdom consisting mostly of rugged mountains, tropical jungles, and dense rain forests. From 1964 through 1972, the United States flew well over 1 million combat sorties to drop almost 3 million tons of bombs. Much of the war was secret, with the primary focus of the bombing aimed at the Ho Chi Minh Trail.

For the purposes of bombing, Laos was divided into three parts. In Operation BARREL ROLL, conventional air strikes carried out mostly by Air Force planes operating from Thailand and unconventional operations based in Laos and Thailand supported Hmoung guerrillas in their fight against North Vietnamese regulars and the indigenous communist Pathet Lao. In the South, Operation COMMANDO HUNT ranged over the STEEL TIGER and TIGER HOUND areas of the Ho Chi Minh Trail, with the latter being the focus of the bombing in areas of the trail in the border areas contiguous to South Vietnam.

Operation BARREL ROLL began on 14 December 1964 and at first consisted of only eight sorties per week. As the war escalated, USAF F-105s and F-4s poured into bases in Thailand, and the Air Force's 56th Special Operations Wing at Udorn Royal Thai Air Force Base joined the more conventional attacks with their unmarked T-28s flown by Air Force commandos, Thai mercenaries, and Laotian pilots trained by the United States. As the war developed, a special unit of U.S. forward air controllers known as Ravens and Air Force officers who lived in Laos as civilian officials with the U.S. Agency for International Development. They directed strikes, usually with great accuracy, in support of the Hmoung from Cessna 0–1 "Birddog" aircraft. Their operations were under the control of the U.S. Embassy in Vientiane and supported logistically by Headquarters Seventh/Thirteenth Air Force at Udorn.

In southern Laos, where 98 percent of the bombs fell, the air war focused on the Ho Chi Minh Trail. From February 1965, the bombing started in earnest with Operation STEEL TIGER directed at bombing troop encampments, supply depots, and truck parks. The distinction between STEEL TIGER and TIGER HOUND had to do with who controlled the targeting, with targets in the latter being chosen by Seventh Air Force in Saigon while STEEL TIGER came under the control of Thirteenth Air Force in Thailand. Operation COMMANDO HUNT subsumed both campaigns in November 1968, and distinctions between the two operating areas became academic with the ultimate authority for all air strikes in Laos remaining firmly in control of the ambassador in Vientiane.

Targets in Operation COMMANDO HUNT included roadways, pathways, and waterways as well as storage areas and staging bases. The trail's defenses, consisting of an estimated 1,200 antiaircraft guns, were also attacked by fighter-bombers using napalm and cluster bombs and, after 1969, laser-guided bombs. The centerpiece of Operation COMMANDO HUNT became the attack on truck traffic. Although Air Force estimates of the number of trucks destroyed (more than 12,000 in one six-month period in 1970) proved overly optimistic, but subsequent Vietnamese documentation has attested to the tremendous struggle involved in moving troops and supplies southward.

Air America, the CIA-run airline, added a final ingredient into what was sometimes dubbed the "Alice in Wonderland War," and the role played by Air America, along with other contract airlines, was vital in moving supplies and Laotian soldiers from one unimproved airstrip to another. Air America crews, many of whom lived with their families in Vientiane or in Udorn, a Thai provincial capital 50 miles south of the Laotian border, also provided important intelligence information based on their long experience in the theater and their intimate knowledge of the land. Air America crews flew World War II–vintage C-46 Commandos, C-47s, and newer C-123s along with Pilatus Porter aircraft capable of landing on small, unimproved dirt strips. Additionally, their unmarked gray Huey helicopters and larger Sikorsky H-34s played a key role in rescuing downed aircrews as well as moving guerrilla teams into and out of secluded landing zones.

Earl H. Tilford Jr.

References

Ballard, Jack S. *Development and Employment of Fixed-Wing Gunships, 1962–1972.* Washington, DC: Office of Air Force History, 1982.

Littauer, Raphael, and Norman Uphoff, eds. *The Air War in Indochina.* Rev. ed. Air War Study Group, Cornell University. Boston: Boston Publishing Company, 1971.

Robbins, Christopher. *Air America.* New York: Putnam, 1979.

______. *The Ravens: The Men Who Flew in America's Secret War in Laos.* New York: Crown, 1987.

Van Staaveren, Jacob. *Interdiction in Southern Laos, 1960–1968.* Washington, DC: Center for Air Force History, 1993.

Lavochkin Aircraft

One of the most important Soviet fighter design bureaus during World War II. Semyon Alekseevich Lavochkin was born on 11 September 1900 in Smolensk. After serving with the Red Army, he studied engineering during the 1920s and worked with the Tupolev and other design and manufacturing bureaus. During the 1930s, he became involved with the development of plastic-impregnated plywood as a construction material as well as *delta-drevsiny,* a plastic-impregnated birch laminate.

In 1938, he joined with Vladimir P. Gorbunov and Mikhail I. Gudkov to found a design bureau specifically to use this material in fighter design. Their first design used an improved material—*shpon.* The I-301 had numerous problems needing correction, and before completion of the first batch the type was modified as the LaGG-3. This single-engine fighter, capable of about 310 mph, entered production at the beginning of 1941, and by the time of the German invasion 322 examples had been delivered, though few reached active units.

Unfortunately, this aircraft's modern appearance belied its inadequate performance, which quickly gave the LaGG an evil reputation. As production quality in the factories declined under the stress of war, production aircraft became even worse. Pilots grimly said its initials stood for *lakirovannyi garantirovannyi grob* (lacquered guaranteed coffin). Still, many of the leading Soviet aces scored a considerable portion of their victories flying the type, and it remained in production until 1944, with 6,528 aircraft produced.

During 1942, a shortage of the M-105 inline motor forced Lavochkin to experiment with marrying an M-82 radial motor to the LaGG's fuselage. The serendipitous result was the transformation of a relative failure into one of the greatest fighters of World War II, the La-5, with a speed of almost 400 mph. During late 1944, an even more powerful derivative, the La-7, entered service. The top-scoring Allied ace, Ivan Kozhedub, scored all his victories flying these aircraft. Production of the La-5 and La-7 eventually totaled 16,504. Further developments of the basic design were the La-9, which flew in 1946, and the La-11 of 1948. About 1,200–1,400 of each type were produced, and some were given to the Chinese and North Korean air forces. Some Soviet La-11s saw limited combat over Korea as night-fighters.

Lavochkin produced a number of jet fighters, of which only the La-15 entered production. This aircraft had better flight performance than the MiG-15, but its delicate landing gear and complicated systems made it unsuitable for wide use. During the 1950s, Lavochkin's bureau increasingly was redirected to the design of surface-to-air missiles, and after Lavochkin's death in June 1960 the design bureau was dispersed.

George M. Mellinger

See also

Fighter Air Corps, 64th; Kozhedub, Ivan

References

Gordon, Yefim, and Dmitrii Khazanov. *Soviet Combat Aircraft if the Second World War.* Vol. 1. Leicester, UK: Midland Counties, 1998.

Gunston, Bill. *The Encyclopedia of Russian Aircraft, 1875–1995.* Osceola, WI: Motorbooks International, 1995.

Leahy, William D. (1875–1959)

Chairman of the Joint Chiefs of Staff throughout World War II. Leahy was born in Hampton, Iowa, on 6 May 1875 and attended the U.S. Naval Academy, graduating in 1897. He saw combat in the Spanish-American War, the Philippine Insurrection, and the Boxer Rebellion. During World War I, his vessels performed escort and patrol duties in the Caribbean and the Atlantic. Subsequent tours included command of the cruiser *St. Louis* and the battleship *New Mexico.*

In 1927, he was promoted to rear admiral. Staff assignments included chief of the bureaus of ordnance and navigation. He went on to command Battleships Battle Force and Battleships Force before assignment as Chief of Naval Operations from 1937 to 1939. Throughout these years, Leahy was one of the most influential of those naval officers who considered the battleship as the centerpiece of the U.S. fleet.

Leahy retired at the mandatory age in mid-1939 but was named governor of Puerto Rico by President Franklin Roosevelt. Two years later, Leahy was appointed ambassador to

Vichy, France, a critical diplomatic post. In mid-1942, Leahy was recalled to active duty, becoming Roosevelt's Chief of Staff.

He subsequently assumed duties as Chairman of the Joint Chiefs of Staff. In his new position, Leahy played a pivotal role in the U.S. and Allied war efforts. He helped translate policy into effective military strategy. Leahy did his best to reconcile the strategy of Germany First with a two-front naval war. Like Admiral Ernest King, the Chief of Naval Operations, Leahy himself would have preferred a greater naval effort in the Pacific, but he made the balanced approach effective nonetheless. Leahy was promoted to five-star rank in 1944.

Upon Roosevelt's death, he continued to serve President Harry Truman, but with less effectiveness. Opposed to the use of atomic weapons on both moral and practical grounds, Leahy was unable to influence the decision to drop the bomb on Japan. Following the war, he oversaw the reorganization of the military services and tendered valuable advice on Cold War strategy.

In 1949, he retired for a second time, somewhat disillusioned after presiding over massive demobilization, deep defense cuts, and ineffective geostrategic handling of the Soviet Union. He died in Bethesda, Maryland, on 20 July 1959.

Michael S. Casey

See also

Arnold, Henry H. "Hap"; Hiroshima; King, Ernest J.

References

Adams, Henry H. *Witness to Power: The Life of Fleet Admiral William D. Leahy.* Annapolis, MD: Naval Institute Press, 1985.

Hall, George M. *The Fifth Star.* New York: Praeger, 1994.

Heaton, Dean R. *Four Stars: The Super Stars of United States Military History.* Baltimore: Gateway, 1995.

Leigh-Mallory, Trafford (1892–1944)

RAF air chief marshal. The son of a clergyman, Leigh-Mallory (known by his contemporaries as "LM") joined the infantry at the beginning of World War I but soon transferred to the Royal Flying Corps. He returned to France as a pilot and eventually commanded an observation squadron.

After the Armistice, LM held various assignments at home and in the empire, including a stint as an instructor at the Army Staff College. The outbreak of World War II found him as commander of the 12th Fighter Group during the Battle of Britain, where he became embroiled in a major controversy over air strategy with his superior, Air Chief Marshal Hugh Dowding. LM won, and Dowding was pushed into retirement.

In early 1944, LM was named commander in chief of the Allied Expeditionary Air Force for Operation OVERLORD under Supreme Allied Commander General Dwight Eisenhower. Initially, this position involved only the control of tactical aircraft—LM's background. However, Eisenhower believed more air assets were needed to ensure the success of the invasion, so he demanded, and received, control of the strategic bombers. Airmen in Britain and the United States greatly objected to this extension of LM's authority. As a consequence, the Allied commanders conspired behind his back to deny LM any real influence. He was aware of what was happening but was powerless to prevent it.

In November 1944, the air chief marshal and his wife were killed in a plane crash en route to a new command in Ceylon.

Phillip S. Meilinger

See also

Britain, Battle of; Dowding, Hugh C.T.

References

Dunn, Bill Newton. *Big Wing: The Biography of Air Chief Marshal Sir Trafford Leigh-Mallory.* Shrewsbury, UK: Airlife, 1992.

Richards, Denis, and Hilary St. George Saunders. *The Royal Air Force, 1939–1945.* 3 vols. London: HMSO, 1974.

LeMay, Curtis Emerson (1906–1990)

Early aviator and airpower advocate; U.S. general. Born in Columbus, Ohio, on 14 November 1906, LeMay, after graduating from high school, was unable to attain an appointment to West Point. He went on to earn a degree in civil engineering from The Ohio State University and a commission through the ROTC in 1927. Although he was an honors graduate, he became a Reserve lieutenant but was unable to attend flight school. LeMay took his case to the commander of the Ohio Air National Guard and was rapidly processed through for aviation cadets, earning his wings on 27 October 1929.

LeMay served as a pursuit pilot, then attended navigation school at Rockwell Field, California. His next assignment was with the 2d Bombardment Group, where he taught navigation and served as group navigator on the Goodwill missions to Latin America and for the interception of the Italian liner SS *Rex*.

Next came command of the 305th Bombardment Group, equipped with B-17s. He took the group to England during September 1942. As a brigadier general he commanded the 3d Bombardment Division within the Eighth Air Force in England. The division was equipped with both B-17s and B-24s. Recognizing the performance differences between the aircraft, LeMay opted for an all–B-17 division. On 17 October 1943, he led the 3d Bombardment Division on a mission to Regensburg, Germany, and recovered in North Africa. (It was on this date that the 1st Bombardment Division was held on the ground due to weather and made a late departure to bomb Schweinfurt. The 1st Bombardment Division lost 60 aircraft that day.)

Promoted to major general in March 1944, he was assigned to the China-Burma-India Theater, where he commanded the XX Bomber Command, equipped with B-29s. He moved to Guam, where he commanded the XXI Bomber Command, then the Twentieth Air Force through the end of World War II. General LeMay was in charge of all very heavy bombardment operations in the Pacific, using B-29s to strike the Japanese home islands.

After World War II, General LeMay orchestrated and participated in a series of B-29 long-range record-setting flights from the Pacific to bases within the United States.

In 1947, General LeMay became the first USAF deputy Chief of Air Staff for research and development. Next he commanded U.S. Air Forces in Europe. When the Soviets closed off the city of Berlin, General LeMay instituted the Berlin Airlift and placed Major General William H. Tunner, who had organized and directed the aerial resupply of China over the Hump (Himalayan Mountains), in charge of Operation VITTLES—the Berlin Airlift.

On 20 October 1947, LeMay was promoted to lieutenant general. He became the second commander of the recently formed Strategic Air Command (SAC). Considered the father of SAC, he took a floundering command and made it into the world's foremost air arm. General LeMay was a severe taskmaster when it came to performance of duty.

Observing the deplorable state of the command in the performance of its primary mission—strategic bombardment—General LeMay intensified training. He instituted a program in which key bomber crewmembers were cross-trained in each other's jobs. Next he established a bombing competition, wherein he pitted each bomb group against the others within SAC. He rewarded hard work by instituting the Spot Promotion Program whereby entire crews were raised one rank for superlative performance during the bombing competitions and for superior airmanship under adverse conditions.

General LeMay kept a list of his so-called select crews beneath the glass top on his desk. They were the best of the best in the command, the individuals he knew he could trust when the chips were down.

He worked hard and expected the same from everyone in his command. He also looked out for those in his command and their families. Shortly after SAC moved from Andrews AFB, Maryland, to Offutt AFB, Nebraska, he worked with members of Congress to obtain decent housing for SAC's single airmen in what was known as Wherry Housing. He sought support from the community and established the SAC Consultation Committee, composed of senior civic leaders. It was through this committee that he worked community issues and in return sought local and national support for his command.

General LeMay paved the way for aerial refueling first for SAC then for the entire USAF, followed by all U.S. forces and their allies. He moved SAC from a piston-powered force to an all-jet force through development of the B-47, B-52, and KC-135.

General LeMay considered the stewardship of nuclear weapons to be a very grave undertaking. He led by precept and example and expected the same from all of his officers and non-commissioned officers.

During his tenure at SAC be was designated Commanding General of Strategic Air Command, commander, then Commander in Chief. The latter was the result of SAC being designated a specified command reporting directly to the Joint Chiefs of Staff.

Throughout his career, Curtis E. LeMay was a visionary for airpower. He continually worked within the level of his command to develop, plan, staff, and execute innovative concepts.

In July 1957, General LeMay became vice Chief of Staff. He was elevated to USAF Chief of Staff on 1 July 1961, where he served until his retirement on 1 February 1965.

Alwyn T. Lloyd

See also

Boeing B-17 Flying Fortress; Boeing B-47 Stratojet; Boeing B-52 Stratfortress; Boeing KC-135; Consolidated B-24 Liberator

References

LeMay, General Curtis E., and MacKinlay Kantor. *Mission with LeMay—My Story.* New York: Doubleday, 1965.

Lloyd, Alwyn T. *A Cold War Legacy: A Tribute to Strategic Air Command, 1946–1992.* Missoula, MT: Pictorial Histories, 2000.

Lend-Lease Aircraft

Lend-Lease was the U.S. aid program transferring, among other items, U.S. aircraft to Allied nations before and during World War II.

Lend-Lease was designed to assist Great Britain, which was fighting Germany and Italy. The English had run out of financial resources to buy military hardware. Lend-Lease bridged the gap between British needs and funds. By the formal end of hostilities (2 September 1945, when Japan officially surrendered aboard the USS *Missouri* in Tokyo Bay), the United States had supplied its 40 wartime Allies with more than $48 billion in goods.

By volume, the two most significant beneficiaries of Lend-Lease aircraft were Great Britain and the Soviet Union. England and its Commonwealth received more than 38,800 U.S. airplanes of 75 different types. Because Great Britain manufactured a variety of military aircraft, Lend-Lease aircraft merely augmented most of its inventories. Exceptions were the Dakota and Hudson, which filled a need for air transports and coastal reconnaissance. Great Britain, in turn, extended Lend-Lease by exporting some 2,000 Hurricanes and 1,300 Spitfires to the Soviet Union.

The Soviet Union received more than 18,000 aircraft from the combined arsenals of Great Britain (4,570) and the United States (14,018). Similar to the British, the Soviets manufactured a large number (115,596) of aircraft in multiple types. Unlike Great Britain, however, the Soviet Union had long-term lapses in warplane production due to Luftwaffe bombing and German troops. Germany's successes forced the Soviet Union to transfer approximately 100 aircraft factories eastward to, and beyond, the Ural Mountains. Although the Soviets employed heroic measures to reconstruct their aircraft industry, the move, coupled with a shortage of skilled workers, disrupted production in some cases for a year. The Reconstruction Finance Corporation opened a $100 million line of credit for Moscow. Other funds were advanced by the U.S. Treasury based upon future receipt of Soviet gold. President Franklin Roosevelt did not officially name the Soviet Union eligible for Lend-Lease until 7 November 1941.

U.S. aircraft sent to Soviet Russia followed three routes: by sea to Murmansk and Archangel, by sea and air to Iran, and by air from Alaska to Siberia. German submarines and aircraft made the northern sea route to the Soviet Union extremely hazardous; the route to Iran was safer but expensive in time and fuel. Alaska-to-Siberia proved to be the best route, but only after months of discussion between Americans and Russians and only after the United States agreed with Stalin that Russians would fly Lend-Lease planes from U.S. territory, avoiding any U.S. presence in Siberia. Regardless, more than half (7,926) of all Lend-Lease aircraft reached Soviet Russia via this route. Lend-Lease aircraft were not decisive in the Soviet victory on the Eastern Front of the European Theater, but they were significant.

James K. Libbey

References

Pearcy, Arthur. *Lend-Lease Aircraft in World War II.* Osceola, WI: Motorbooks International, 1996.

Lewandowska (Dowbór-Muśnicki), Janina (1908–1940)

Second lieutenant in the Polish air force; the only Polish woman incarcerated in the Soviet Kozelsk POW camp. She was born in Kharkiv, Ukraine, the elder of two daughters of Colonel-General Józef Dowbór-Muśnicki. Extremely independent and determined, she devoted herself entirely to a flying career. In 1937, she was sent to Lviv to take a military course in radiotelegraphy. Shortly before the outbreak of the war, she married instructor-pilot Mieczysław Lewandowski. After the wedding she returned home to Poznań to put her own affairs in order. Sadly, the young couple were never reunited.

After mobilization was ordered in August 1939, she was drafted for service in the 3d Regiment, stationed near Poznań at No. 3 Air Base. On 1 September, she was dispatched eastward by train with remnants of base personnel. After many adventures, was taken prisoner on 22 September.

There is no doubt, as confirmed by eyewitnesses, that Lewandowska was imprisoned at Kozelsk. However, her name is missing from the German Katyn list of exhumed identified bodies. Perhaps, in an attempt to hide her true identity (her father was especially hated by the Bolsheviks), she destroyed her documents and memorabilia prior to her death. It is also possible that she was killed in Kozelsk or elsewhere.

Kazimiera J. Cottam

See also

Polish Auxiliary Women's Air Force Service; Sosnowska-Karpik, Irena

References

Bauer, Piotr. "The Wartime Fate of Janina Lewandowska" (in Polish). *Skrzydlata Polska,* no. 31 (30 July 1989): 7.

Muszyński, Adam, comp. *The Katyn List* (in Polish). 4th ed. London: Gryf, 1982. Reprinted by the Omnipress Agency, Journalists' Employment Co-op, and Polish Historical Society, Warsaw, 1989.

Leyte Gulf, Battle of (1944)

The largest naval battle of World War II—actually a series of battles—sparked by the Allied invasion of the Philippines. The campaign for the Philippines began with massive carrier air raids by Admiral W. F. Halsey's Task Force 38 on Formosa and Luzon in early October 1944. These attacks crippled land-based Japanese air forces for the upcoming battle.

The invasion of the island of Leyte began on 17 October. Allied land-based B-24 bombers supported the operation from newly opened bases at Morotai and Biak, but U.S. carrier task forces provided the primary means of air cover.

On 23 October, the remaining Japanese land-based air force, some 160 strong, attacked the U.S. carriers, sinking USS *Princeton.* In a notable single accomplishment, U.S. Navy Commander David McCampbell shot down nine Japanese aircraft within one hour. Although these Japanese attacks caused concerned, they were premature, and the heavy losses they took eliminated the last significant Japanese land-based air strength before the main battle was joined the next day.

The Imperial Japanese Navy reacted to the Leyte landings with its long-planned Operation SHO-1. Three Japanese task forces converged on the Philippines from Singapore, Borneo, and Japan. Northern Force, under Admiral Ozawa Jizaburo, was a carrier group approaching from Japan, virtually empty of aircraft and serving only as a decoy to distract the U.S. carrier force. Center Force, under Admiral Kurita Takeo, was a battleship fleet including the giant *Yamato* and *Musashi.* Southern Force, under Admiral Nishimura Shojo, consisted of cruisers and older battleships approaching from Borneo.

On 24 October, approximately 260 U.S. carrier aircraft attacked the Japanese Center Force in the Battle of the Sibuyan Sea. After 19 torpedo hits and 10 bomb hits, the massive battleship *Musashi* sank. Kurita ordered the force to turn about and withdraw. Unknown to the Americans, this course reversal was only temporary.

The Japanese Southern Force was defeated by a U.S. surface battle fleet at the Battle of Surigao Strait in the last battleship-versus-battleship action of the war during the night of 24 October. With Kurita's force withdrawing and the fighting at Surigao Strait turning in favor of the Americans, Halsey's Task Force 38 moved north to engage the Japanese carrier force. This it did in the Battle of Cape Engano, which effectively took the U.S. heavy carriers out of the rest of the coming battle.

Unobserved by the Americans, Kurita's Center Force had again reversed direction and at dawn on 25 October was entering Leyte Gulf as it steamed toward the largely unprotected U.S. transport fleet lying off Leyte. Between the transports and the Japanese surface fleet was a small group of slow escort carriers, identified as Taffy-3, under Vice Admiral Thomas L. Sprague. The Japanese opened fire on the Americans, beginning the engagement often known as the Battle off Samar. Surprised and vulnerable, these escort carriers bravely turned into the wind, toward the Japanese, and flew off their complement of Avenger bombers. These aircraft (along with aircraft of Taffy-2, farther south), inexperienced in attacks on naval targets, pressed home their attacks on the Japanese ships. They were joined by several destroyer escorts conducting torpedo attacks and aided by intermittent rain squalls and smokescreens. These forces attempted to harass and distract the Japanese as the escort carriers attempted to flee to the south. The escort carriers *Gambier Bay* and three destroyers escorts were sunk by gunfire, but the planes of Taffy-3 sank the cruisers *Chikuma* and *Chokai.*

In spite of his success, with the remaining escort carriers even more vulnerable and the U.S. transports still lying virtually defenseless to the south, Kurita had second thoughts. Worried about his vulnerability to further air attack, Kurita recalled his advanced units and again withdrew to the north, and the U.S. invasion fleet was saved. It was a vital mistake and cost the Japanese any chance of victory in the battle. Kurita's fears, however, were well-founded; the heavy cruiser *Suzuya,* light cruisers *Nashiro* and *Kinu,* and several destroyers were sunk by U.S. aircraft as they withdrew through San Bernadino Strait.

Leyte Gulf was also the first introduction of kamikaze attacks, which damaged several U.S. ships and sank the escort carrier *St. Lô.*

Leyte Gulf is significant in that it was only one of three major daylight surface naval actions during the entire Pacific War (with Java Sea and Komandorski Islands). Airpower generally prevented daylight operations of surface fleets in close proximity with the enemy. The battle is notable in that the mere threat of airpower saved the U.S. transport fleet from possible destruction, showing clearly that surface battle fleets held only a shadow of their former power.

Frank E. Watson

See also

Cape Engano, Battle of; Kamikaze Attacks; McCampbell, David S.

References

Cutler, Thomas. *Battle of Leyte Gulf, 23–26 October 1944.* New York: HarperCollins, 1994.

Woodward, C. Vann. *The Battle for Leyte Gulf.* New York: Macmillan, 1947.

Liberty Engine

The Liberty, originally named and trademarked as the USA Standardized Engine, was conceived to be a standardized engine of low risk. It was to have interchangeable parts wherever possible, incorporating the best that had already been demonstrated by U.S. and European industry.

On 29 May 1917, E. J. Hall, chief engineer of Hall-Scott, and J. G. Vincent, chief engineer of Packard, were brought together by E. A. Deeds of the Aircraft Production Board, and they assembled the conceptual design of the engine family with the help of three draftsmen, completing four layout views of the V-8 by 6 June 1917.

On 8 June, a team of 150 men started detail design with initial priority on the V-8. Within a few weeks, priority was shifted to the V-12, but the V-8 was first to run, on 3 July 1917, with the V-12 running on 13 August 1917. The L-8 first flew on 21 August 1917. The L-12 completed its first 50-hour test on 25 August, but real qualification testing was not completed until 6 February 1918. By this time the production process had started. Although directed to be a joint venture, development was conducted by Packard, which built the first 11 engines (six V-8s and five V-12s) with some fabrication assistance from the automobile companies; however, Hall-Scott played a significant, although not well-documented, role.

Production contracts were signed in August and September 1917 for 56,000 L-12s and 6,000 L-8s with six companies (Packard, Lincoln, Ford, General Motors [Cadillac and Buick], Nordyke and Marmon, and Trego). The Trego contract was canceled before production commenced. The first production engine was run in December. Since development and production were concurrent, production was slowed by a great number of changes—1,398 documented changes by 25 June 1918.

Certain government agencies chose to sue several of the producers for excess profits and other illegalities. Most cases were without merit. Packard and Lincoln received short shrift for their major contributions to the program, although Lincoln-built engines were supposed to be the most durable and reliable. Some 20,348 L-12s were built.

During World War I, the Liberty engine was installed in 3,431 de Havilland DH-4 and 107 Handley Page 0-400 (U.S.-version) aircraft, as well as a number of experimental installations. After World War I, Libertys (some remained in service until 1942) were specified for a great many U.S. aircraft because of the oversupply manufactured. This discouraged aircraft-engine development for at least five years and was responsible for U.S. tardiness in readying high-powered engines for World War II.

Douglas G. Culy

References

Dickey, Philip S. III. Smithsonian Annals of Flight Number 3. *The Liberty Engine, 1918–1942.* Washington, DC: National Air and Space Museum, 1968.

Liberty, USS

Notorious military incident in which Israeli aircraft and naval vessels attacked a U.S. ship in 1967. The *Liberty,* an electronic intelligence gathering vessel, was off the Egyptian coast on 8 June 1967 during the height of the Six Day War. In the early afternoon, Israeli Super Mystere B2s and *Ayah*-class torpedo boats attacked the *Liberty* in a series of sustained and well-orchestrated waves. Two hours later, 34 Americans were dead, with more than 170 wounded; the *Liberty* was still afloat but badly crippled. The crew acted with considerable courage in the face of the attack, and Captain William McGonagle was awarded the Medal of Honor for his personal heroism. Israel claimed the attack was an accident and that the *Liberty* was mistaken for an Egyptian vessel. The United States quickly accepted this explanation and hushed up the event. Over time, however, *Liberty* crewmembers and others raised legitimate questions—and corroborating evidence—about the attack, showing that Israel knowingly tried to sink the *Liberty* and lied about Israeli intentions and that U.S. commanders willingly accepted these lies. Motives for these duplicitous behaviors remain enshadowed in diplomatic secrecy and claims of national security, especially by Israel.

Robert S. Hopkins

See also

Ferrets; Six Day War; *Pueblo,* USS

References

Borne, John E. *The U.S.S.* Liberty: *Dissenting History vs. Official History.* New York: Reconsideration Press, 1995.

Ennes, James M. *Assault on the* Liberty. New York: Random House, 1979.

Pearson, Anthony. *Conspiracy of Silence.* London: Quartet, 1978.

LINEBACKER (1972)

U.S. code name for bombing campaign in response to the North Vietnamese Easter Offensive. When the North Vietnamese launched a massive three-pronged invasion of South Vietnam in late March 1972, U.S. President Richard Nixon ordered Operation LINEBACKER, a resumption of the strategic bombing of North Vietnam, which had been discontinued since the cancellation of Operation ROLLING THUNDER.

The purpose of the operation, which lasted from 31 March to 23 October, was to halt the invasion. It had three objectives: destroy military supplies inside North Vietnam; isolate North Vietnam from outside sources of supply; and interdict the flow of supplies and troops to the battlefields of South Vietnam. The operation saw a number of technological innovations, including laser-guided bombs, electro-optical–guided bombs, and the long-range electronic navigation (LORAN) bombing system.

U.S. Air Force and Marine aircraft from bases in South Vietnam and Thailand and Navy aircraft from carriers in the South China Sea flew some 41,000 sorties over North Vietnam during the operation, dropping a total of 155,548 tons of bombs. In addition, aircraft mined North Vietnamese harbors, closing them to ocean traffic.

U.S. bombing destroyed 10 MiG bases, six major power plants, and all large oil storage facilities in North Vietnam. Some 75 aircraft were lost in this operation.

In October 1972, in response to progress in the peace negotiations then under way in Paris, LINEBACKER was scaled back and limited to the area south of the 20th Parallel. LINEBACKER achieved all of its objectives and played a major role in halting the North Vietnamese invasion.

James H. Willbanks

See also

ARC LIGHT; Boeing B-52 Stratofortress; LINEBACKER II; ROLLING THUNDER

References

Berger, Carl, ed. *The United States Air Force in Southeast Asia.* Washington, DC: U.S. Government Printing Office, 1977.

Momyer, William. *Airpower in Three Wars: World War II, Korea, and Vietnam.* Washington, DC: U.S. Government Printing Office, 1978.

LINEBACKER II (1972)

Code name for the operation that came to be known as the so-called Christmas bombings—intense bombing campaign against North Vietnam in late 1972 to coerce the North Vietnamese back to the negotiating table. When North Vietnamese negotiators walked away from the Paris peace talks in December 1972, U.S. President Richard Nixon issued an ultimatum for them to return to the talks "or else." The North Vietnamese rejected Nixon's demand, and the president ordered an all-out air campaign against the Hanoi-Haiphong area to force an agreement on a cease-fire. This operation involved the concentrated use of B-52 strategic bombers supported by Air Force fighter-bombers flying from bases in Thailand and Navy fighter-bombers flying from carriers in the South China Sea.

During the intensive air campaign, 700 B-52 and 1,000 fighter-bomber sorties were flown against targets near Hanoi and Haiphong, dropping 20,000 tons of ordnance on airfields, petroleum storage facilities, warehouse complexes, and railroad marshalling yards. During the LINEBACKER II raids, the North Vietnamese fired more than 1,000 surface-to-air missiles (SAMs) at the attacking aircraft and deployed MiG fighter-interceptor squadrons. Eight MiGs were shot down, two by B-52 tailgunners. U.S. losses were 26 aircraft shot down, including 15 B-52s. Three aircraft were downed by MiGs; the rest, including the B-52s, were downed by SAMs. Nine were shot down during the first three days of the operation, causing a change in tactics that had more favorable results.

U.S. antiwar activists labeled the LINEBACKER II raids the "Christmas bombings," and the charge was made that it involved carpet-bombing—the deliberate targeting of civilian areas with widespread bombing designed to completely cover a city with bombs. However, the bombing was targeted against military targets; 1,318 died in Hanoi and 305 in Haiphong.

By 26 December, the Christmas bombing had inflicted heavy damage on all assigned targets. With its air defenses in shambles and most military targets destroyed, Hanoi was virtually defenseless, and on 26 December the North Vietnamese agreed to resume negotiations. LINEBACKER II ended on 29 December. The Paris Peace Accords were signed less than a month later on 23 January 1973.

Some airpower advocates point to LINEBACKER II as evidence that the war could have been won by airpower alone, but this argument neglects the fact that Nixon's policy aims in 1972 were much more modest compared to Lyndon Johnson's in 1965–1968.

James H. Willbanks

See also

ARC LIGHT; Boeing B-52 Stratofortress; LINEBACKER; ROLLING THUNDER

References

Allison, George B. *LINEBACKER II: A View from the Rock.* USAF Southeast Asia Monograph Series, Volume 6. Washington, DC: U.S. Government Printing Office, 1979.

Morrocco, John. *The Vietnam Experience: Thunder from Above: The Air War, 1941–1968.* Boston: Boston Publishing Company, 1984.

______. *The Vietnam Experience: Rain of Fire.* Boston: Boston Publishing Company, 1985.

Link Trainer

The Link Model C-3 trainer was the brain child of Edwin A. Link Jr., who began his career performing engineering work for his father's firm, the Link Piano and Organ Company in Binghampton, New York. In the early days of aviation, the most difficult aspects were bad weather and nighttime flights. In the 1920s, this meant that when pilots could not see outside their cockpits they had to depend on their instruments, or what is known as Instrument Flight Rules (IFR). Learning to do this was dangerous. For new pilots the only way to learn was by trial-and-error, and an error often resulted in a crash or even death.

In late 1927 and early 1928, Edwin Link, an avid pilot himself, began developing an IFR ground trainer in the basement of his father's piano factory. In mid-1928, he left his father's employ to spend all of his time building the Model C-3 trainer. He received his first patent for the trainer on 14 April 1929 and his final patents in 1931. Initially used as an amusement ride, the Link Trainer eventually became the first ground-based flight trainer that could generally simulate the behavior and control responses of an aircraft in flight. It consisted of a system of electrical motors and bellows that reacted to a manual stick and rudder controls that simulated the motion of flight.

Over the next five years, most Link Trainers were sold to amusement parks. Even though United States Army Air Corps officials recognized a need for the "Pilot Maker," as Link dubbed the stubby blue box, they lacked funds to purchase the trainer. In February 1934, USAAC pilots, badly lacking IFR experience, began flying airmail across the United States. Within days bad weather and nighttime flights had cost five pilots their lives.

Army officials began a search for solutions. They invited Link to visit the Newark Airport in New Jersey to demonstrate his toy. As fate would have it, on the day of the presentation the weather turned bad. The fact that Link landed his plane so easily using his instruments—skills developed using his own invention—provided Army leaders with an object lesson. USAAC officials were also impressed by the formal demonstration, and in March 1934 they bought six trainers that soon proved well worth the price.

The trainer looked like a small, box-shaped airplane, with a fuselage, wings, and a tail. It rested on a fixed platform and had the ability to take various positions, like a plane in flight. The hooded cockpit had a joystick, a rudder, flight instruments, earphones, and a microphone, with the last items used to communicate with the instructor. The Link Trainer was designed to be unstable, thus requiring the pilot to be in control throughout the exercise. Once a pilot was inside, it soon became clear who the experts and novices were. Eventually, USAAC leadership installed one or more Link Trainers at each of its principal flying fields.

The Link Trainer received its greatest use during World War II and the Korean War. The instructor could simulate various weather, air and mechanical conditions, and changes at a moment's notice. In this way the Link Trainer was as close to flying as trainees could get without actually leaving the ground. In addition, it allowed pilots to face crisis situations without risking their lives. It was even used to train pilots to bail out of stricken aircraft.

Indeed, virtually every U.S. pilot in World War II trained on the Link. During the war, Link built 6,721 C-3s for the Army and 1,045 for the Navy. During World War II and Korea, nearly 9,000 Link Trainers significantly reduced flight-training time for almost 500,000 pilots. It also cut costs. In 1945, an AT-6 training aircraft cost $10 per hour to operate, whereas the Link cost four cents per hour.

Following the success of its original Trainer, the Link Corporation went on to build many other simulators and ground trainers for air and spaceflight training. The C-3s also proved very durable; many are still displayed in several aviation museums throughout the world.

For his contribution to aviation and national defense, Edwin A. Link Jr. was inducted into the National Aviation Hall of Fame in Dayton, Ohio, in 1976. Most experts agree that Link's original Trainer pointed the way to today's sophisticated trainers and simulators that are still training pilots, cutting costs, and reducing accidents and injuries.

William Head and Diane Truluck

References

Air Materiel Command Monograph. *Case History of the Link Trainer.* Patterson Field, OH: 1945.

Link, Edwin A. Jr. "The Link Trainer." *Aeronautics* (2 October 1940): 271–286.

Maurer, Maurer. *Aviation in the U.S. Army, 1919–1939.* Washington, DC: Office of Air Force History, 1987.

Lippisch, Alexander Martin (1894–1976)

German aircraft designer of the Messerschmitt Me 163 Komet. Alexander Martin Lippisch born in Munich in 1894. Educated in Berlin and Jena before joining the German armed forces in World War I, he later designed delta-wing aircraft and was technical department chief at the German Research Institute for Soaring Flight.

In 1939, Lippisch designed the experimental DFS-194, a delta-wing craft powered by a rocket engine with only a vertical tailfin. Successfully tested at Peenemünde, 70 of the newly designated Me 163 Komets were ordered by the Luftwaffe. Lippisch oversaw production of more than 300 at Messerschmitt.

Although severely limited in range, the Komet interceptor hit speeds above 600 mph and climbed over 15,000 feet per minute. The Me 163 was the world's only operational rocket-engine fighter.

Lippisch came to the United States after the war and was employed at Collins Radio in Cedar Rapids, Iowa. There he worked on his delta wing, receiving numerous patents for wing-in-ground-effect craft. He died on 11 February 1976.

Jerry D. Snead

References

Ethell, Jeffery L. *Komet: The Messerschmitt 163,* New York: Sky Books Press, 1978.

Lippisch, Alexander M. *Alexander M. Lippisch Papers.* Special Collections Department, Iowa State University Library, Ames, Iowa, MS-243.

Ziegler, Mano. *Messerschmitt Me 163 Komet.* Vol. 1. Atglen, PA: Schiffer, 1976.

Litvyak, Lidya (1921–1943)

World War II Soviet fighter ace and the most successful female fighter pilot. Lidya Vladimirovna Litvyak (known as

Lidya Litvyak was the highest-scoring Soviet woman ace, with eleven air-to-air victories. She was killed on 1 August 1943 and later posthumously awarded the honor of Hero of the Soviet Union. (Jean Cottam)

Lilya) was born in Moscow on 18 August 1921. She learned to fly prewar and worked as a flying instructor. In October 1941, she volunteered for the Women's Aviation Regiments organized by Marina Raskova, being selected for the 586 IAP (Fighter Air Regiment). In September 1942, she was one of a flight of four women pilots transferred to a male-pilot IAP. Initially greeted with skepticism, she was transferred out of several units before finding a home in the 73 GIAP (Guards Fighter Air Regiment), where she earned the respect of the other pilots. She flew 168 missions and scored 11 personal and three group victories, plus one balloon, and was herself shot down twice and wounded twice. Western reports that Captain Olga Yamshikova scored 17 victories are due entirely to mistaken translation. Litvyak was shot down on 1 August 1943, but because her death could not be confirmed she was denied the honor of Hero of the Soviet Union (HSU). After her body was found in 1989, she was awarded a posthumous HSU on 5 May 1990.

George M. Mellinger

References

Cottam, K. J. *Soviet Airwomen in Combat in World War II.* Manhattan, KS: MA/AH, 1983.

Cottam, K. J., ed and trans. *In the Sky Above the Front: A Collection of Memoirs of Soviet Airwomen Participants in the Great Patriotic War.* Manhattan, KS: MA/AH, 1984.

Myles, Bruce. *Night Witches: The Amazing Story of Russia's Women Pilots in World War Two.* Novato, CA: Presido Press, 1983.

Noggle, Anne. *A Dance with Death: Soviet Airwomen in World War II.* College Station: Texas A&M University Press, 1994.

Locarno Conference

The October 1925 conference held in Locarno, Switzerland, that provided further structural maintenance of the postwar peace in Europe. Crucial to the so-called Locarno Pact was the guarantee of borders between Germany and its neighbors and a resolution not to attack another signatory nation without a mandate from the League of Nations. In addition, signatories pledged mutual support in the event of an unprovoked attack by a third power. So important was this pact that its three negotiators were awarded the Nobel Prize. Missing from the accords, however, were specific pledges by Germany not to attack Poland or Czechoslovakia; neither were Great Britain and France obliged to protect these states' frontiers. The 1928 Kellogg-Briand Pact reinforced the ideas of Locarno, especially the commitment of France, Britain, and the United States to renounce war as a means of resolving conflict. Ultimately, Germany felt little restraint in annexing portions of Czechoslovakia and invading Poland, contributing to the start of World War II.

See also

Versailles Treaty

References

Churchill, Winston S. *The Second World War, Volume 1: The Gathering Storm.* Boston: Houghton Mifflin, 1948.

Weinberg, Gerhard L. *The Foreign Policy of Hitler's Germany.* Cambridge: Cambridge University Press, 1970;

Lockheed Aircraft

Lockheed was responsible for some of the most interesting aircraft ever developed, including the Model 14 Hudson, P-38 Lightning, C-69 Constellation, P-80 Shooting Star, T-33 Training Star, F-104 Starfighter, U-2 Dragon Lady, SR-71 Blackbird, F-117 Nighthawk, C-130 Hercules, C-141 Starlifter, and C-5 Galaxy.

Founded by three brothers—Malcolm, Allan, and Victor Loughead—Lockheed can trace its history to the Alco Hydro-Aeroplane Company of 1912. Alco failed in 1913, but during 1916 Allan and Malcolm teamed up again to form the Loughead Aircraft Manufacturing Company. It failed in 1921. During 1926, Allan convinced a group of bankers to let him try again and, tired of the constant mispronunciations, changed the company's spelling to the phonetic "Lockheed." With the assistance of the visionary engineer John K. "Jack" Northrop, Allan Loughead built a solid reputation for the new Lockheed Aircraft Company and, by 1928, had 50 employees at his Burbank, California, factory.

In mid-1929, a buyout offer was presented to the Lockheed board of directors. Much to the chagrin of Allan Loug-

The interception of bomber aircraft under all weather conditions was a very difficult proposition, and the Lockheed F-94 was derived from the basic T-33 as an interim measure. (Walter J. Boyne)

head, the board accepted, and Lockheed became a subsidiary of the Detroit Aircraft Corporation. Allan Loughead left, never to return to the company he had founded.

Gerald Vultee was hired to replace Northrop, who had left to form his own firm, and construction of the Vega, Air Express, Sirius, Orion, and Altair series of aircraft continued to be profitable but proved insufficient to offset the losses of the parent corporation. On 27 October 1931, Detroit declared bankruptcy; Lockheed soldiered on for a while and finally discontinued operations on 16 June 1932.

Robert Gross bought the assets of the Lockheed subsidiary from bankruptcy, maintaining the company name. Gross hired Lloyd Stearman as general manager and set about designing a modern twin-engine all-metal monoplane transport—the Model 10 Electra.

During World War II, Lockheed built its own aircraft, including the P-38 and variants of the Model 14, and manufactured the Boeing-designed B-17 Flying Fortress under license. Between 1 July 1940 and 31 August 1945, Lockheed built 19,077 aircraft and was counted as the fifth-largest aircraft manufacturer in the United States.

After the war, Lockheed's Kelly Johnson became a legend by developing such aircraft as the U-2 and SR-71. The main production programs were not the fighters and spyplanes built in Burbank and Palmdale but featured the large military transports built in Marietta, Georgia. The Lockheed Missiles and Space subsidiary developed all of the U.S. submarine-launched ballistic missiles (Polaris, Poseidon, and Trident), as well as most of the spy satellites between 1960 and 1999. Other subsidiaries produced electronic warfare equipment, managed the processing and launching of the Space Shuttle, and supported the Department of Energy. Lockheed merged with Martin Marietta in 1995, creating the Lockheed Martin Corporation. In October 2001, Lockheed Martin was awarded the largest U.S. defense contract in history—worth some $200 billion—to manufacture the Joint Strike Fighter.

Dennis R. Jenkins

See also
Lockheed Martin Aircraft

References

Boyne, Walter J. *Beyond the Horizons: The Lockheed Story, 1908–1995.* New York: St. Martin's, 1998.

Lockheed F-104 Starfighter

Single-seat Mach 2 interceptor. Conceived by Kelly Johnson as a lightweight cannon-armed fighter, it saw limited use with the USAF but enjoyed success with 14 other air forces, largely in multirole all-weather variants. Officially known as Starfighter, its sleek fuselage and small wings earned it the nickname "missile with the man inside." Despite an early reputation for being dangerous to fly, its actual safety record is similar to other single-engine jet fighters.

Proposed to the USAF in November 1952, the J65-powered prototype took to the air on 4 March 1954 with Tony

LeVier at the controls. With a General Electric J79, stretched fuselage, and new air intakes, the Starfighter achieved twice the speed of sound; other improvements included boundary-layer control, combat flaps, and AIM-9 Sidewinder heat-seeking missiles. The F-104A entered operational service in January 1958 and established sensational speed, altitude, and climb records. Some F-104C fighter bombers served with Tactical Air Command in Vietnam, but changing requirements led to canceled orders and hasty transfer to Air National Guard units, those in Puerto Rico serving until 1975.

The Starfighter began a new career in October 1958 when it was selected by the Bundesluftwaffe in the nuclear-capable G (Germany) variant. Seven European countries followed, bringing F-104G production to 1,536 (including two-seaters) of the 2,578 Starfighters built. Their manufacture was then the largest international aviation program and paved the way for European collaboration.

A final F-104S variant, with a greater-thrust engine, improved radar, and semiactive AIM-7 Sparrow missiles, was designed for Italy. Manufactured by Aeritalia until 1979, these were the last Starfighters built and, twice updated, were still in front-line service as interceptors in 2001.

Gregory Alegi

See also

Italian Air Force; Italian Aircraft Development; Lockheed Aircraft

References

Donald, David, and Jon Lake, eds. *Encyclopedia of World Military Aircraft.* London: Aerospace, 1996.

Francillon, René J. *Lockheed Aircraft Since 1913.* 2nd ed. London: Putnam, 1987.

Lockheed Hudson

The Lockheed Hudson was a direct outgrowth of the company's commercial Model 14 Electra. The Hudson was originally designed to meet a British requirement for a coastal reconnaissance bomber. An initial contract for 250 was issued, and the first of the type flew on 10 December 1938. A total of 1,338 Hudsons were purchased directly for the RAF and

The export versions of the Lockheed F-104 did very well, and none better than the F-104S, manufactured by Aeritalia. (Gregory Alegi)

RAAF before the aircraft became part of the Lend-Lease program. The latter aircraft carried the USAAF designation A-28. The USAAF procured 52 A-28s for the RAF, followed by 450 A-28As configured as troop transports. With more powerful engines, another 416 were built as A-29s for the Lend-Lease program, as were another 384 A-29As configured for troop transport. More than 20 RAF squadrons operated the Hudsons.

A number of Hudsons returned for USAAF service in the antisubmarine role. One of these A-29s was credited with the first successful attack on a German U-boat during World War II. Another 24 repossessed A-29Bs became photographic reconnaissance aircraft for the USAAF. The USAAF procured an additional 300 Hudsons as AT-18s and AT-18As for use as gunnery and navigational trainers, respectively. The U.S. Navy procured 20 Hudsons with the designation PBO-1. They were flown by VP-82 at Argentia, Newfoundland, and were responsible for the Navy's first two U-boat sinkings in World War II.

Alwyn T. Lloyd

References

Pearcy, Arthur. *Lend-Lease Aircraft in World War II.* Osceola, WI: Motorbooks International, 1996.

Swanbrough, Gordon, and Peter M. Bowers. *United States Military Aircraft Since 1909.* Various eds. London: Putnam, 1963, 1981, and 1989.

Swanbrough, Gordon, and Peter M. Bowers. *United States Navy Aircraft Since 1911.* London: Putnam, 1968 and 1976.

Lockheed Martin Aircraft

Major U.S. defense contractor. The end of the Cold War and the projected decline in military spending forced a consolidation in the U.S. aviation industry. One of the earliest mergers, perhaps one of the most natural and complementary, was that of Lockheed Martin in 1995.

The Lockheed Corporation and Martin-Marietta each counted some 60 percent of their business in the defense market. Each filled a need not met by the other in products and services, a situation that boded well for the new company, which was officially formed on 16 March 1995. The new entity was organized into four major sectors, within which there were almost 50 major operating companies. In addition, Lockheed Martin had major investments in five large subsidiary firms.

Once merged, Lockheed Martin made additional investments, acquiring important elements of the Loral Corporation. A proposed further consolidation, with Northrop Grumman Corporation, was not consummated because of antitrust concerns.

The new corporation emerged with strong product lines in the fields of aeronautics and aerospace and has become the sole major competitor to the other giant of U.S. aerospace, the Boeing Company, which acquired McDonnell Douglas in 1997. An unusual situation has resulted in the aviation industry in which the two firms are partners in some ventures (e.g., the Lockheed Martin F-22) and rivals in others (e.g., the Joint Strike Fighter.) In October 2001, Lockheed Martin bested its rival and was awarded the largest U.S. defense contract in history—worth some $200 billion—to manufacture the Joint Strike Fighter.

Walter J. Boyne

See also

Lockheed Martin F-22 Raptor

References

Boyne, Walter J. *Beyond the Horizons: The Lockheed Story, 1908–1995.* New York: St. Martin's, 1998.

Lockheed Martin C-130 Hercules

A four-engine turboprop transport that has become the standard for military STOL transports. Besides its role as a troop and paratroop transport, it has been the platform for many different missions: the AC-130 Spectre gunship; EC-130 jamming aircraft; HC-130 aerial recovery aircraft; MC-130 aircraft for special operations, including airdropping and psychological warfare; DC-130 drone control aircraft; the JC-130 for the recovery of space capsules. The EC-130V is an airborne early warning and maritime surveillance aircraft. It also serves as an airborne and ground refueling aircraft.

In peacetime, C-130s provide emergency evacuation and humanitarian relief. Many of the earliest C-130s are still active today.

The first C-130 was delivered to the USAF in 1955, and production continues. More than 2,100 C-130s have been built, flown by more than 60 nations worldwide.

Henry M. Holden

References

Bowman, Martin. *Lockheed C-130 Hercules.* Ramsbury, UK: Crowood, 1999.

Lockheed Martin C-5 Galaxy

A four-engine transport, the largest in the U.S. Air Force inventory. It can carry 261,000 pounds of cargo for 3,500 miles or fly indefinitely with aerial refueling. The Galaxy is a

LAPES stands for Low Altitude Parachute Extraction System, shown here in combat. (U.S. Air Force)

"drive-through" airplane for both nose and tail loading. The C-5 is 243 feet long with a 223-foot wingspan.

The C-5 has three major compartments. The forward upper deck seats a crew of four: pilot, copilot, and two flight engineers. Behind the wing on the upper deck is the second compartment, with seats for 75 people. The third is the cargo compartment. The floor is 121 feet long and can hold six Greyhound transcontinental buses, seven UH-1 Huey helicopters, or 270 passengers.

Henry M. Holden

References

Veronico, Nicholas A., and Jim Dunn. *Giant Cargo Planes.* Osceola, WI: MBI, 1999.

Lockheed Martin F-117 Nighthawk

The USAF's premier stealth strike aircraft. The strange shape of the F-117 was dictated by the requirement to design an aircraft with very low radar reflectivity. When Lockheed and Northrop were asked by the Defense Advanced Research Projects Agency (DARPA) in 1974 to design a stealth demonstrator that would be invisible to radar, Lockheed was confronted with a dilemma. Its engineers had a formula that could predict the radar reflectivity of any given shape, but the computers of the era were simply not up to the task. The answer was to use a series of flat surfaces, which the computer could model, instead of continuously curving surfaces. The theory was that the flat surfaces could be angled in such a way as to reflect the microwave energy away from the radar site, thus allowing the aircraft to go undetected.

The approach worked, and Lockheed manufactured two demonstrator aircraft under the code name "Have Blue." Although both aircraft crashed during the test program, DARPA and the Air Force were sufficiently impressed to order production aircraft under the code name "Senior Trend" in 1977. Eventually, 59 aircraft were manufactured by Lockheed's famed Skunk Works. The F-117 is unable to exceed the sound barrier and relies on its advanced fly-by-wire control system to provide artificial stability.

Despite losing several aircraft during testing and train-

Looking more like a spacecraft from a Stephen Spielberg movie than a fighter, the Lockheed Martin F-117A stealth fighter revolutionized warfare. (U.S. Air Force)

ing, the F-117 program remained firmly under wraps at the test facility (Groom Lake, Nevada) and, later, at a new secret base (Tonopah, California). Finally, on 10 November 1988 the Air Force publicly announced that it was operating a stealth fighter. The first operational use of the F-117 was during Operation JUST CAUSE on 19–20 December 1989 to capture Panamanian strongman Manuel Noriega. Just over a year later, F-117s struck the first blow during Operation DESERT STORM to liberate Kuwait. The first combat loss of an F-117 was on 28 March 1999, about 30 miles northeast of Belgrade during the NATO bombing of Yugoslavia. The F-117 continues to be upgraded and is expected to serve for the foreseeable future.

Dennis R. Jenkins

See also

DESERT STORM

References

Aronstein, David C. and Albert C. Piccirillo. *Have Blue and the F-117: Evolution of the "Stealth Fighter."* Reston, VA: AIAA, 1997.

Jenkins, Dennis R. *Lockheed Martin F-117 Nighthawk.* WarbirdTech Series Volume 25. North Branch, MN: Specialty Press, 1999.

Lockheed Martin F-16 Fighting Falcon

USAF fighter. Conceived as the low component of a high/low force (the McDonnell Douglas F-15 Eagle was the high component), the F-16 has gone on to be one of the most produced jet fighters in history. The YF-16 made its first flight on 4 February 1974 and won a flyoff against the Northrop YF-17 on 13 January 1975. The original program for 650 aircraft expanded to 1,388 for the U.S. Air Force alone. Foreign sales began in June 1975 when a four-nation European consortium (Belgium, Denmark, the Netherlands, and Norway) announced plans to manufacture 348 aircraft under license. Israel and Iran quickly followed, although the Iranian contract was canceled after the fall of the shah before any aircraft were completed.

The original single-seat F-16A and two-seat F-16B were followed by improved F-16C/D models in 1984. The first F-16 capable of using either Pratt and Whitney or General Electric engines was delivered in 1986, the first version capable of night attack in 1988, and a more powerful Block 50 version in 1991. The first production F-16 was delivered in 1978; the one-thousandth was delivered in 1983, the two-thousandth in early 1988, and the three-thousandth in late 1991. The worldwide F-16 fleet surpassed 1 million flight hours in 1986, 2 million in 1988, 3 million in 1990, 4 million in 1992, 5 million in 1994, and 8 million in 1998.

The F-16 program has grown into the largest multinational coproduction effort in history. Assembly lines have operated in Fort Worth, Belgium, the Netherlands, Turkey, and South Korea. Thirteen countries have participated in coproduction of the F-16, and major components of the aircraft have been produced in several other countries. Almost

One of the most important competitions of all time pitted the Lockheed Martin YF-22 against the Northrop Grumman YF-23. The YF-22 emerged the winner by a narrow margin, but the knowledge and experience Northrop Grumman gained may be seen in future unmanned combat aerial vehicles. (U.S. Air Force)

4,000 F-16s have been delivered to 19 air forces around the world. In addition, an improved variant of the F-16 is now in production in Japan as the Mitsubishi F-2 (FS-X).

Dennis R. Jenkins

References

Peacock, Lindsay. *On Falcon Wings: The F-16 Story.* RAF Fairford, UK: RAF Benevolent Fund Enterprises, 1997.

Wagner, Ray. *American Combat Planes.* 3rd ed. Garden City, NY: Doubleday, 1982.

Lockheed Martin F-22 Raptor

The ultimate development of the Lockheed/Boeing/General Dynamics YF-22 Lightning II, which was one of the two contenders in the Advanced Tactical Fighter (ATF) competition that also spawned the Northrop/McDonnell Douglas YF-23. Each consortium produced two ATF prototypes powered by different propulsion systems (two Pratt and Whitney YF119 or YF120 engines). At the end of the ATF competition, the USAF selected the YF-22 airframe/YF119 power plant combination as the winner.

The F-22 is classified as an air-dominance fighter and is being optimized to supplement and then fully replace the Boeing F-15 Eagle air superiority fighter by the year 2025. The F-22, built in partnership with Boeing, is a dedicated low-observable (stealth) air vehicle that was designed for a first-look/first-shoot/first-kill combat scenario. In other words, operational F-22s will detect their opponents before they themselves are detected, launch their missiles, and destroy their adversaries before being discovered.

The Raptor is powered by two augmented 35,000-pound/thrust Pratt and Whitney F119-PW-100 turbofan engines. The engines feature a vectored thrust system for extraordinary agility and maneuverability and enable the F-22 to fly supersonically without use of afterburners.

A dedicated weapons system, the F-22 is armed with a single M-61A2 Vulcan 20mm cannon, two AIM-9 Sidewinder heat-seeking missiles, and up to six AIM-120 Slammer radar-guided missiles. These weapons are carried internally to aid the F-22's stealthy characteristics.

At this writing, the F-22 was scheduled to begin entering service with the 1st Fighter Wing at Langley AFB, Virginia, in late 2003–early 2004. It was to meet its initial operational capability in late 2005–early 2006.

Steve Pace

References

Pace, Steve. *F-22 Raptor: America's Next Lethal War Machine.* Walter J. Boyne Military Aircraft Series. New York: McGraw-Hill, 1999.

Aesthetically one of the most attractive fighters of all time, the Lockheed P-38 was a star in Pacific operations, where two engines were life insurance for pilots in combat. (U.S. Air Force)

Lockheed P-38 Lightning

The first twin-engine single-pilot fighter to be mass-produced and the first with tricycle landing gear. Development began with a 1937 Air Corps specification for a high-performance fighter (360-mph top speed and a 6-minute climb to 20,000 feet). The resulting Lockheed XP-38 twin-engine twin-tail fighter first flew on 27 January 1939 but was lost due to pilot error landing after a dramatic 7-hour transcontinental flight. The YP-38 and production aircraft orders followed, entering service in late 1941. More than 10,000 were built by the end of the war, and the type saw service in every theater.

The USAAF top ace, Richard Bong, scored all of his 40 kills with a P-38. Several P-38s, operating at extreme range, jumped and shot down the plane transporting Japanese Admiral Isoroku Yamamoto in April 1943. The D model was the first to be called Lightning, a name bestowed by the British. The F model added wing racks for external arms; J and L versions were the most heavily produced; and M was a black-painted night-fighter. Some 500 unarmed F-4 and F-5 versions were used in reconnaissance and photointelligence missions. Maximum speed of most models exceeded 400 mph. Few remained in USAF service for long after the war, though some served in the air forces of other countries.

Christopher H. Sterling

See also

Bong, Richard I.; Johnson, Clarence L. "Kelly"; Lockheed Aircraft

References

Bodie, Warren M. *The Lockheed P-38 Lightning: "It Goes Like Hell"* Hiawassee, GA: Widewing, 1991.

Grantham. A. Kevin. *P-Screamers: The History of the Surviving Lockheed P-38 Lightnings.* Missoula, MT: Pictorial Histories, 1994.

Johnsen, Frederick A. *Lockheed P-38 Lightning.* WarbirdTech Series Volume 2. North Branch, MN: Specialty Press, 1997.

Lockheed P/F-80 Shooting Star

The first mass-produced U.S. jet fighter. Shortly after the British had flown the Whittle-powered Gloster Meteor, Lockheed legend Kelly Johnson, in one week, laid out the basic design for the P-80, using Britain's newly developed de Havilland Halford H-1 turbojet. Although the USAAF contract called for a prototype in 180 days, the first arrived at Muroc Dry Lake in 139 days and flew only four days later on 8 January 1944.

The USAF procured 525 P-80As. At production model No. 346, the Allison J33–17 engine was introduced, and subsequent production F-80s were powered by these engines.

The first product of Lockheed's soon-to-be-famous Skunk Works, the XP-80 is being flown here by the famous test and racing pilot Tony LeVier. (U.S. Air Force)

Because of the difficulty pilots were having adjusting to the single-seat P-80 (seen here), Lockheed developed a two-seated version and renamed it the T-33. (Walter J. Boyne)

On 19 June 1951, a P-80A bested the British Gloster Meteor IV 616-mph speed record by 7.73 mph.

Another 240 of these aircraft were procured as P-80Bs and featured an ejection seat, cockpit cooling, canopy anti-icing, underwing rocket launchers, and an improved J33–21 engine. The Air Force accepted 670 F-80Cs with increased engine thrust and improved armament.

With tricycle gear, the aircraft mounted six .50-caliber machine guns in the nose; the F-80C could also carry either two 1,000-pound bombs or 16 x 5-inch rockets externally.

Although it did not arrive in time to serve in World War II, the F-80 saw combat in the Korean War. With two 165-gallon external tanks, the F-80C's radius of action was increased from 100 miles to 225 miles (with a full rocket load). Field-developed Misawa tanks increased the radius of action to 350 miles. Although a pair of these 265-gallon tanks offered an additional hour of flight time, there were concerns about overstressing the wing tips.

In what was believed to be the first jet-to-jet dogfight, an F-80C downed a MiG-15 on 8 November 1950. Production of the F-80 had ended when the Korean War started. The strain of combat flying took its toll on the airframes—they deteriorated faster than they could be repaired. By the spring of 1952, an average of 7,500 maintenance man-hours per aircraft would have to be expended after just four months of operational flying.

The RF-80A had an extended and deepened nose to accommodate photographic equipment. A number of these aircraft were deployed to Korea, where they provided valuable service. The last of the 152 RF-80As produced was retired from service in 1957.

Alwyn T. Lloyd

References

Knaack, Marcelle Size. *Encyclopedia of U.S. Air Force Aircraft and Missile Systems, Volume 1: Post–World War II Fighters.* Washington, DC: Office of Air Force History, 1978.

Swanbrough, Gordon, and Peter M. Bowers. *United States Military Aircraft Since 1909.* Various eds. London: Putnam, 1963, 1981, and 1989.

Lockheed SR-71 Blackbird

Supersonic spyplane capable of legendary performance. On 26 April 1962, Lockheed test pilot Lou Schalk took the first flight in this aircraft at the classified test facility in the desert of Groom Lake, Nevada. The aircraft was far more advanced than anything in the sky; when made public several years later, it would capture the world's fascination as few other aircraft ever have.

Three distinct variants were manufactured; surprisingly, none of them ever had an official name. Unofficially, they have all been referred to as Blackbirds and Habu—good nicknames for the fastest, highest-flying air-breathing aircraft in the world. The Lockheed model number of the first variant was A-12, but by a sort of inspired perversity it came to be called Oxcart, a code name also applied to the CIA program under which it was developed. The other two variants carried the Air Force designations YF-12 and SR-71.

The Blackbird was the first aircraft capable of sustained operations at Mach 3 (2,000 mph) and could attain altitudes in excess of 90,000 feet. The CIA's single-seat A-12 version was the first to become operational, and a total of 13 aircraft were built, including a single two-seat trainer. Due mainly to political considerations, only 29 operational missions were flown over Vietnam and Korea before the A-12 was retired in 1968. The three Air Force YF-12 interceptors were never seriously considered for production but proved very useful to both the Air Force and NASA in various test programs.

The definitive SR-71 version, code-named "Senior Crown" by the Air Force, made its first flight on 22 December 1964. The flight lasted just over an hour and attained a maximum speed of just over 1,000 mph. All 31 of the original SR-71s were delivered by the end of 1967. One additional aircraft, a trainer, was built up from parts of a YF-12A that had crashed at Edwards AFB and used the forward fuselage from the structural test article. The two-seat SR-71 was equipped with a much wider variety of cameras and sensors than the earlier A-12, including a sophisticated signals/electronic intelligence–gathering system.

The SR-71 operated for 25 years from special facilities at Beale AFB, California, Kadena AB, Okinawa, and RAF Mildenhall, England. As far as is known, SR-71s never made overflights of the Soviet Union, but they overflew almost every other troublespot in the world, providing valuable intelligence that could not be obtained from satellites of the era. The Air Force first tried to retire the aircraft in 1990, but Congress ordered its reactivation in 1995. A lack of mission and funding finally forced its permanent retirement in 1997.

Dennis R. Jenkins

References

Crickmore, Paul F. *Lockheed SR-71: The Secret Missions Exposed.* Oxford, UK: Osprey, 1993.

Jenkins, Dennis R. *Lockheed SR-71/YF-12 Blackbirds.* WarbirdTech Series Volume 10. North Branch, MN: Specialty Press, 1997.

Lockheed T-33

USAF jet trainer. By 1947 it was obvious that the typical Air Force combat pilot was having difficulty adjusting to the

Introduced as the fastest, highest-flying air-breathing aircraft in the world, the Lockheed SR-71 captured the world's fascination as few other aircraft ever have. (Walter J. Boyne)

new jet fighters. Although each pilot was given extensive ground-schooling, his first flight experience in a jet was always solo—no two-seat jet fighters yet existed. In early 1947, Lockheed committed $1 million to design, manufacture, and test a two-seat variant of the P-80.

An uncompleted P-80C was taken off the production line and modified into a two-seat trainer. Tony LeVier took the first TP-80C on its maiden flight on 22 March 1948, and it was discovered that this longer aircraft performed better than its single-seat counterpart.

Two weeks later, the Air Force ordered 20 production TP-80Cs, although the designation was officially changed to T-33A on 11 June 1948. The Navy was sufficiently impressed to order 26 similar TO-2s. Eventually, Lockheed manufactured 5,691 T-33s of various models; an additional 656 were built by Canadair in Canada, and 210 were manufactured by Kawasaki in Japan. The aircraft would serve with more than two dozen air forces around the world, and some are still operating today.

Dennis R. Jenkins

References

Miller, Jay. *Skunk Works: The First Fifty Years.* Leicester, UK: Aerofax/Midland Counties, 1993.

Lockheed U-2 Dragon Lady

U.S. spyplane. Clarence L. "Kelly" Johnson was a legendary aircraft designer who headed the famous Lockheed Skunk Works where the U-2 spy aircraft was manufactured. The initial contract for 20 aircraft contained the condition that the first one fly less than a year later. Johnson made that milestone and returned $2 million from the original $54

Yet another triumph of Lockheed's Skunk Works, the Lockheed U-2 was redesignated TR-1 in a later production version but retained the classic slender lines of the original. (U.S. Air Force)

million contract, one of the rare instances of a cost underrun in modern aerospace history.

The U-2 was ordered back into production twice, a rare occurrence. The second production run of a much different variant (the U-2R) occurred 10 years after the original. The third run was 12 years after the second, although this time the aircraft were virtually identical to the second batch.

Much of the U-2's history and current operations remains classified. The first operational mission was over communist Central Europe on 20 June 1956. Overflights of the Soviet Union ended on 1 May 1960, when Francis Gary Powers was shot down in a U-2C over Sverdlovsk. Later, overflights would be made of communist China and most troublespots around the world.

The aircraft continues to provide remarkable service even though its demise was predicted 30 years ago when spy satellites became the intelligence community's technology of choice. Interestingly, the Dragon Lady has long outlived its heir-apparent, the Mach 3 SR-71 Blackbird, another Kelly Johnson design. There are currently no plans to phase out the U-2 from service, and efforts to replace it with unmanned aerial vehicles are running into considerable development delays.

Dennis R. Jenkins

See also
Powers, Francis Gary

References

Jenkins, Dennis R. *Lockheed U-2 Dragon Lady.* WarbirdTech Series Volume 16. North Branch, MN: Specialty Press, 1998.

Miller, Jay. *Skunk Works: The Official History.* Leicester, UK: Aerofax/Midland Counties, 1991.

Pocock, Chris. *Dragon Lady: The History of the U-2 Spyplane.* Shrewsbury, UK: Airlife, 1989.

Loehr, Alexander (1885–1947)

Luftwaffe general; executed after World War II for ordering mass killings in the Balkans. Loehr began his military service in 1906 in a Hungarian infantry regiment. In World War I, he was a staff officer in the Austro-Hungarian army. He joined the Austrian air force after the war, became its commander in 1936, and moved into the German Luftwaffe when Germany absorbed Austria in 1938.

He commanded Luftflotte 4 (Fourth Air Force) in the Polish, Balkan, and early Russian campaigns and was promoted to full general in May 1941. After 1942 he held ground commands in the Balkans. He was convicted of war crimes by a Yugoslavian court and was hanged in 1947.

Donald Caldwell

See also
German Air Force (Luftwaffe)

References

Corum, J. *The Luftwaffe: Creating the Operational Air War, 1918–1940.* Lawrence: University Press of Kansas, 1997.

Logistics

Broadly: matériel acquisition, transportation, maintenance, construction, and operation of facilities required to support military activity. During World War I, the fledgling U.S. aircraft industry, under the wartime control of the Bureau of Aircraft Production, was unable to develop and produce the quantity of combat aircraft necessary to equip the Army Air Service.

As a result, the Army Air Service relied primarily on French manufacturers for aircraft, engines, and spares. During the war, the Supply Section oversaw the acquisition of air materiel in Europe and operated a system of depots in France for distributing supplies and assembling aircraft. The bulk of munitions and fuel, though, was transported to the expeditionary forces from the United States by ship, an arrangement that has remained constant to the present day.

During the interwar years, the Army Air Corps established the basic logistics organizational structure that still exists. In 1926, the Army Air Corps created the Materiel Division, which managed the acquisition of aircraft, spares, and supplies and operated a series of depots in the United States and overseas that served as central supply points and as aircraft and equipment overhaul centers. Supply and maintenance organizations served down to the base, group, and even squadron level. During World War II, U.S. industry produced all air-war materiel required by the United States, as well as much of the materiel consumed by the Allies.

As part of the overall mobilization, the Army Air Forces dramatically expanded its support activities and organizations to achieve "logistics mass"—the national ability to produce and ship to the combat theaters an uninterrupted flow of equipment and supplies required for continuous combat operations. For most of World War II, Air Service Command and Air Materiel Command served as the primary logistics support organizations. Because its forces were dispersed throughout the globe, the AAF created in-theater logistics organizations and depots to provide theater support.

The Korean War marked several milestones in air logistics support. The introduction of jet aircraft shifted the focus away from supporting large numbers of simple aircraft to supporting smaller numbers of complex aircraft equipped with components that had to be shipped back to a depot for repair and reuse. The return flow of the logistics pipeline thus grew in proportion to the complexity of aircraft and equipment. For the first time, a theater logistics support organization, the Far East Air Materiel Command, maintained daily electronic communications with its primary center of support, HQ Air Materiel Command. The Air Force possessed long-range heavy transports capable of carrying substantial quantities of materiel, dramatically cutting transportation time of critical items. Soon after the Korean War ended, the USAF began using electronic computers to track supply inventories and forecast consumption, greatly reducing the amount of materiel required to be stockpiled.

During the Vietnam War, the vast U.S. industrial base, improved communications and jet transportation, allowed the USAF to support its combat forces at an unprecedented level. As had been the case in Korea, the greatest logistics problem facing the USAF was the need to build the air bases, port facilities, and ground transportation infrastructure necessary to support the air war.

Operation DESERT STORM proved to be a logistics triumph. Utilizing prepositioned materiel and air-transportable bare-base assets, spares kits, and munitions packages, combat-ready USAF air units moved into numerous Persian Gulf bases in a matter of weeks. Satellite communications and portable computers linked in-theater supply and maintenance personnel with their points of support in the United States and Europe. Operation ALLIED FORCE carried these advances one step farther with the use of fast transportation provided by commercial air transportation carriers, which helped cut to a few days the time between when a spare part was requisitioned and when it arrived at a deployed unit.

The U.S. air strikes and related actions in Afghanistan in 2001 pushed logistics to new limits.

William Head

See also

DESERT STORM

References

Carlin, H. P., et al. *Logistics: An Illustrated History of AFLC and Its Antecedents, 1921–1981.* Wright-Patterson AFB, OH: Air Force Logistics Command, Office of the Command Historian, 1981.

Rutenberg, David C., and Jane S. Allen, eds. *The Logistics of Waging War, Volume 1: American Logistics, 1774–1985—Emphasizing the Development of Airpower.* Gunter Air Force Station, AL: Air Force Logistics Management Center, 1985.

Snyder, Thomas J., et al. *The Logistics of Waging War, Volume 2: U.S. Military Logistics, 1982-1993—The End of "Brute Force" Logistics.* Maxwell AFB, AL: Air Force Logistics Management Center, 1993.

London Naval Agreement (1930)

The 1930 agreement resulting from a conference hosted by Great Britain and attended by representatives of the United States, France, Italy, and Japan for the purpose of regulating the use of submarines for military purposes and placing a moratorium on the construction of capital ships. Meeting in London from 21 January–22 April 1930, the parties agreed to extend the limitation on aircraft carriers under the Washington Five-Power Treaty (1922). Although France and Italy refused to sign the new treaty, the United States, Great Britain, and Japan agreed to limit battleship tonnage to a 10:10:7 ratio, respectively. The term of the treaty extended to 1936, with another scheduled conference to be held in December 1935, at which time Japan withdrew from the agreement.

Cynthia Clark Northrup

See also

Washington Naval Conference

References

Fanning, Richard W. *Peace and Disarmament: Naval Rivalry and Arms Control, 1922–1933.* Lexington: University Press of Kentucky, 1995.

LOOKING GLASS

Mission of Strategic Command's 7th Airborne Command Control Squadron aircraft to ensure command, control, and communications with U.S. nuclear forces even if the enemy destroys ground-based command centers. LOOKING GLASS aircraft were aloft continuously from 3 February 1961 until 24 July 1990, after which they remained on constant ground or airborne alert. Strategic Air Command controlled LOOKING GLASS until replaced by Strategic Command on 1 June 1992.

LOOKING GLASS aircraft were originally USAF EC-135s based at Offut AFB but were replaced on 1 October 1998 with Navy E-6Bs based at Tinker AFB. EC-135s and E-6Bs can determine the status of missiles in silos, launch them, or change their targets. The E-6B also carries a very low frequency system to communicate with ballistic missile submarines. LOOKING GLASS aircraft fly random patterns from their operating base and can remain aloft 72 hours with refueling. Aircrews consist of five officers, nine enlisted aircrew, plus the airborne battle staff commanded by an Air Force general or Navy admiral.

Seven operational teams from all the armed services form the airborne battle staffs. Each team has a chief, a communications officer, an airborne launch control officer, a single integrated operational plan adviser to advise the commander on war plans, an intelligence officer, and a logistics officer to find safe bases for returning bombers and tankers. Each team also has an emergency actions NCO, who knows the formats, contents, and wording of messages used to execute war plans, and a force status NCO, who tracks every strategic weapon in the inventory.

James D. Perry

References

United States Navy. "Fact File: E-6 Mercury." Available online at http://www.chinfo.navy.mil/navpalib/factfile/aircraft/air-e6a.html.

United States Strategic Command. "Fact Sheet: EC-135 Looking Glass." Available online at http://www.stratcom.mil/factssheets/ec135.html.

Lovett, Robert A. (1895–1986)

During World War II, served as assistant secretary of war for air and was the civilian focal point for the most powerful air force in the world. A graduate of Yale University, Lovett served in the Naval Air Service in World War I. Following the war from 1919 to 1921, he studied both law and business administration at Harvard University. He became a partner in the investment firm of Brown Brothers Harriman and Company. He also toured U.S. factories and maintained his business friendships with the leading industrialists of the time. He discovered an alarming lack of direction and coordination from Washington regarding aircraft production, which induced him to conclude that America was not up to the task that full-scale warfare might entail.

Lovett's report on his aviation ideas gained the attention of Secretary of War Henry L. Stimson, who offered him the position of special assistant for air matters and, subsequently, the office of the assistant secretary of war for air. From April 1940 until the end of World War II, Lovett was vitally concerned that nothing threaten industry's adherence to realistic aircraft production schedules. He attempted to settle labor disputes, at times intervening when the Office of Production Management and, subsequently, the War Production Board were at odds with the USAAF's contractors, subcontractors, and suppliers. Lovett tried to strengthen the management of inefficient aircraft manufacturing companies. During the war, Lovett acted as a sounding board for industry's complaints and requests. Stimson's clearer conception of Lovett's role led him to pronounce, "Whatever authority the Secretary of War has, you have."

He participated in the USAAF reorganization of March 1942, and his ideas influenced the character of the postwar United States Air Force. The manner in which Lovett and USAAF Chief General Henry H. "Hap" Arnold divided authority and responsibility established the pattern for civilian and military interactions at the top echelon of the USAAF and throughout the War Department.

Lovett so impressed Army Chief of Staff George C. Marshall that when the latter became secretary of state after the war he recruited Lovett as his undersecretary. Lovett would also become Marshall's deputy and successor when the general agreed to become secretary of defense in 1950.

George M. Watson Jr.

References

Fanton, Jonathan A. "Robert A. Lovett: The War Years." Ph.D. diss., Yale University, 1978.

Pogue, Forrest, *George C. Marshall: Statesman, 1945–1959.* New York: Viking, 1987.

Truman, Harry S. *Memoirs, Volume 2: Years of Trial and Hope.* New York: Doubleday, 1956.

Ludendorff, Erich (1865–1937)

German general during World War I and commander of Germany's air force. Aside from praising Manfred von Richthofen, whom Ludendorff thought was worth "three divisions," little direct evidence is available on his attitude toward aviation. However, his actions imply he thought it worth a great deal.

Upon America's entry into World War I, Ludendorff went to the German High Command with an argument for expanding aviation based on the new threat. Even though it would come at the expense of other essentials, Paul von Hindenberg and Ludendorff endorsed the so-called *Amerika Programme,* which doubled the pursuit force, created 17 new artillery aviation units, and increased aviation by 24,000 men.

James Streckfuss

See also

World War I Aviation

References

Hoeppner, Ernst von. *Germany's War in the Air.* Nashville, TN: Battery Press, 1994.

Luetzow, Guenther (1912–1945)

Outstanding Luftwaffe fighter pilot and combat commander who was considered an upright, model officer by his peers and subordinates. Guenther "Franzl" Luetzow joined the Reichswehr (Germany's interwar army) in 1931, received his pilot training at the secret German base in the Soviet Union, and in 1934 joined the still-unacknowledged Luftwaffe. He led a fighter squadron in the Kondor Legion in Spain, was successful in the French campaign, and was promoted to command Jagdgeschwader 3 (JG 3; 3d Fighter Wing) during the Battle of Britain. He led JG 3 with great success in the early part of the Russian campaign. After air victory number 92 he became the fourth recipient of the Oak Leaves with Swords to the Knight's Cross of the Iron Cross. He was grounded in October 1941, after his 101st victory, and spent three years as a colonel in fighter command and staff positions. In January 1945, he led the so-called Fighter Pilots' Revolt, a frank denunciation of Hermann Goering and the Luftwaffe leadership, and narrowly escaped arrest. He was instead named fighter commander for northern Italy, a region that had no German fighters, but was recalled to join Galland's Jagdverband 44—the "Jet Unit of the Aces"—in March 1945. He began flying missions before he had regained his fighter pilot's touch or mastered his new aircraft, the Me 262, and failed to return from a mission in late April, probably the victim of a USAAF P-51. Luetzow's body has never been found.

Donald Caldwell

See also
German Air Force (Luftwaffe)

References
Obermeier, E. *Die Ritterkreuztraeger der Luftwaffe, 1939–1945, Band 1: Jagdflieger* [Recipients of the Knight's Cross]. Mainz: Verlag Dieter Hoffmann, 1989.

Lufbery, Gervais Raoul (1885–1918)

Lafayette Escadrille ace. Raoul Lufbery came into the world just like the Lafayette Escadrille itself, the product of one American parent and one French. Raised by his mother's family, Lufbery by World War I had spent nearly half his life wandering the world doing odd jobs. The last few peacetime years he spent as mechanic for the pioneer aviator Marc Pourpe.

When war erupted they enlisted together, but Pourpe was killed in late 1914; Lufbery sought pilot training as vengeance. His original assignment was to bombers, but upon formation of the U.S. volunteer unit—N (Nieuport) 124, which became the Lafayette Escadrille—Lufbery was transferred and soon proved his worth as a fighter pilot, becoming the Lafayette's top scorer and the first American ace of aces.

When the Lafayette Escadrille transferred en masse to the U.S. Air Service, Lufbery left the unit (which had become the 103d Aero Squadron) and was assigned first to the 95th and later to the 94th Aero to mentor the new U.S. pilots. As a major with the 94th Aero, he fell or jumped from his burning aircraft on 19 May 1918 while pursuing a German two-seater.

James Streckfuss

See also
Lafayette Escadrille/Flying Corps

References
Franks, Norman L.R., and Frank W. Bailey. *Over the Front.* London: Grub Street, 1992.
Gordon, Dennis. *Lafayette Escadrille Pilot Biographies.* Missoula, MT: Doughboy Historical Society, 1991.
Hall, James Norman, and Charles B. Nordhoff. *The Lafayette Flying Corps.* Port Washington, NY: Kennikat Press, 1964.

Luke, Frank, Jr. (1897–1918)

The Arizona balloon-buster. Considering that official policy at the time made it difficult for one without college to enlist in the Air Service, how Frank Luke was accepted is unknown. But despite his background, which included work as a cowboy and gold miner, Luke managed to get into flight training at the new service's facility at San Diego.

Once abroad, Luke's debut was delayed by assignment as a ferry pilot, a common frustration for those anxious for combat. He finally arrived at the 27th Aero Squadron in the summer of 1918. His first patrol resulted in a claim that was confirmed but not believed by most in the squadron. As a result, Luke was shunned by most with the exception of Lieutenant Joe Wehner, another outcast. On the opening day of the Saint Mihiel Offensive, however, Luke proved his mettle by downing a German observation balloon, the first of 14 that would fall to him over a 17-day period. He made history 6 days later by becoming the first U.S. pilot to down five enemy aircraft (two balloons and three aircraft) in one patrol. Tragically, Wehner was lost on the same mission. A few days later, Luke lost another wingman, Ivan Roberts.

The night before his last outing, Luke had gone AWOL and was being considered for court-martial when he left, against orders, on his fatal patrol. During that mission, on the early evening of 29 September 1918, he downed three balloons before being hit by ground fire and forced to land behind German lines. Wounded, Luke was crawling toward a stream when he died either futilely exchanging gunfire with an approaching group of Germans or perhaps firing his gun to signal for medical help. Instead of being tried on charges, he posthumously became the first aviation Medal of Honor recipient. Luke Air Force Base in Arizona is named in his honor.

James Streckfuss

See also
Balloons; SPAD XIII

References
Franks, Norman, and Frank W. Bailey. *Over the Front.* London: Grub Street, 1992.
Hall, Norman S. *The Arizona Balloon Buster.* Garden City, NY: Doubleday Doran, 1928.
Kosek, John. "The Search for Frank Luke." In *Over the Front* 13, 4. League of World War I Aviation Historians, 1998.